CONTENTS

ACKNOWLEDGEMENTS

This is the third edition of a book that was conceived more than ten years ago. It would not have stood that test of time had it not been for the team that helped produce the early editions: Nigel Redman, Mike Unwin, Marianne Taylor, Sylvia Sullivan and Julie Bailey. Nigel and Julie have again been instrumental in the production of this edition, and Marianne has again been a wonder at producing distribution maps. All three editions have benefited from the skill and patience of D & N Publishing.

We have been privileged to be able to use some of the best artwork available. The artists Hilary Burn, Martin Elliot, Alan Harris, Peter Hayman, Stephen Message, Laurel Tucker and Dan Zetterström have produced outstanding illustrations that compliment our text, although Laurel sadly did not live to see her work in print.

Much of the data in this book comes from an army of volunteer fieldworkers whose observations and counts have been made public through publications and websites of the British Trust for Ornithology, the RSPB and Birdlife International. We hope this book will inspire even more people to offer their services for this type of fieldwork in future.

Finally, we would like to thank the RSPB for, once again, endorsing our work and helping it to reach an ever-growing audience of readers who love our countryside and want to discover more about the birds that inhabit it – and are concerned about their future.

Peter Holden and Tim Cleeves

RSPB HANDBOOK OF
BRITISH
BIRDS

THIRD EDITION

PETER HOLDEN
and TIM CLEEVES

Illustrations by
Hilary Burn, Martin Elliott, Alan Harris, Peter Hayman,
Laurel Tucker and Dan Zetterström

First published 2002 by Christopher Helm, an imprint of A & C Black
Publishers Ltd., 36 Soho Square, London W1D 3QY
Second edition published 2006
Third edition published 2010

www.acblack.com

ISBN 978 1 4081 2735 3

A CIP catalogue record for this book is available from the British
Library

Typeset and designed by D & N Publishing, Baydon, Wiltshire

Printed in China by C & C Offset Printing Co., Ltd

10 9 8 7 6 5 4 3 2 1

Previous page: Goldcrest (Laurel Tucker)
Page 4: Buzzards (Dan Zetterström)

Front cover and spine: Great Spotted Woodpecker (Stephen Message)
Back cover above: Common Tern (Hilary Burn)
Back cover below: Waxwing (Laurel Tucker)
Front flap: Grey Heron (Hilary Burn)

PHOTOGRAPHIC CREDITS
p7 top, world map, Melissa Dockstader (Shutterstock); p7 bottom,
Robin singing, Graham De'ath (Shutterstock); p8 top, Manx
Shearwaters, Chris Gomersall (rspb-images.com); p8 bottom, Pied
Flycatcher, Mark Sisson (rspb-images.com); p9 top, Wryneck, Florian
Andronache (Shutterstock); p9 bottom, Puffins, Rick Price (www.
photolibrary.com); p10 top, seabird colony, Jerome Whittingham
(Shutterstock); p10 bottom, Avocet, Juniors Bildarchiv (www.
photolibrary.com); p11 Knots, Gerhard Schulz (www.photolibrary.
com); p12 top, Goldfinch, Sally Wallis (Shutterstock); p12 bottom,
Long-tailed Ducks, Jens Bruun; p15 top, Corncrake, Ainars Aunins
(Shutterstock); p15 middle, Redshank, Herbert Kratky (Shutterstock);
p15 bottom, Wren, Sue Robinson (Shutterstock).

FOREWORD

Birds and the RSPB have taken over my life! It's been a fantastic journey: from early years as a junior RSPB member discovering the excitement of the North Kent Marshes, then going on to lead the RSPB's team in south-east England, and helping to save those same marshes I had grown to love. Now I have the privilege of leading the whole RSPB in its conservation mission – protecting those birds that I had grown up with, and others that, as pictures in books, inspired my childhood imagination.

Many of those species benefited from RSPB conservation. Red Kites fly again in many parts of the UK – having been driven to the brink of extinction in Wales a hundred years ago. Bitterns still boom in England – in reedbeds enlarged and made wetter by the RSPB – and Corncrakes are gradually returning to some of their original haunts thanks to painstaking conservation work.

While the RSPB celebrates many successes, there are huge issues facing wild birds and the countryside. Birds I remember as common are now declining: the Cuckoo is heard less often and the Turtle Dove, surely so evocative of the English countryside, is becoming a rarity. We must ensure they do not become just a picture in a book and they flourish once again in our woods and fields.

Conservation of birds and nature is serious. It is the responsibility of government, working with voluntary organisations, to produce national policies that will make a difference. The RSPB is fortunate to have dedicated staff and over a million members – all people committed to ensuring we have a country fit for birds and wildlife, both now and into the future. However, we should not forget the pure joy of being out in the natural world and experiencing wildlife where it happens – in our gardens, in the wider countryside and, of course, on RSPB reserves.

Books on birds inspired me in my formative years, and I treasured the one that held the key to understanding what I saw around me. Now we have a huge range of books on identification, biology and on conservation, but not many bring all that information into one volume as the authors have done here. I sincerely hope this handbook will be your key to discovering more about the birds around you, and it will lead you to a host of enjoyable experiences – and that you will treasure this book and the insight it will help to unlock.

Mike Clarke
RSPB Chief Executive
June 2010

THE RSPB

Founded in 1889 to fight the trade in feathers from wild birds, the RSPB has become one of the world's largest and most influential conservation charities. It is a leading member of BirdLife International and represents that federation in the UK. It has over a million members, including over 170,000 young people. Over a million people, both members and general public, visit its reserves each year.

With its origins in campaigning, the RSPB still campaigns today on issues that threaten wild bird populations. The issues may be as diverse as the location of wind farms or the reintroduction of once extinct species such as White-tailed Eagles.

LAND RESERVED FOR BIRDS AND ALL NATURE

The RSPB owns or manages over 200 nature reserves. Among these are some of the most important places for birds and nature in the UK. All major habitats are included: from Forsinard in the Flow Country of Sutherland to the heathland of Arne in Dorset and from the dramatic sea cliffs of South Stack on Anglesey to the newly created fenland landscape of Fenstanton in Cambridgeshire.

CAMPAIGNING FOR ALL NATURE

The RSPB believes that birds are true indicators of the quality of life. If bird populations are healthy, like the miner's canary, then the health of our environment is also good. Conversely, if there are potentially damaging influences on the environment, then the RSPB is quick to express views based on scientific analysis of the issues and advocate change. The RSPB speaks not only for birds, but also for all nature – as it is impossible to consider birds in isolation from the rest of the natural environment. This work promotes the concept of sustainability and involves the RSPB in debates on contemporary issues such as the future of agriculture, 'green energy' and climate change.

ACTIVE MEMBERS

To succeed in its work the RSPB needs supporters. Its large membership of over a million people helps influence national environmental policies. Supporters not only provide much of the funding that enables the RSPB to carry out its work, but they also provide practical help. Each year over 13,000 members and other supporters volunteer to take action for birds and wildlife by working for the RSPB in a variety of ways. In addition, many thousands help with simple research projects such as the annual Big Garden Birdwatch, which enables people in their homes to contribute their observations and to help monitor the health of local bird populations.

TODAY AND FOR THE FUTURE

This book is part of the RSPB's commitment to lifelong learning. The Society believes that a greater understanding of birds and nature is fundamental to its conservation mission. The authors believe that from knowledge of birds, both common and less familiar, will grow a desire to want to protect these wonderful creatures to enrich our lives, not only in our lifetimes but for future generations.

Further information
The Royal Society for the Protection of Birds
The Lodge, Sandy, Bedfordshire, SG19 2DL
Tel: 01767 680551
www.rspb.org.uk

A LAND OF BIRDS

The British Isles are a stepping stone in the Atlantic for birds flying to and from the Arctic.

It is no accident that the British Isles are important for wild birds. Here, on the edge of the Atlantic Ocean, our rocky islands rise out of food-rich seas and are warmed by the Gulf Stream. Positioned conveniently off the landmass of Europe, they form a large 'stepping stone' in the sea from which birds can travel on to Iceland and Greenland, and even to the Arctic wildernesses of northern Canada or Siberia. The British Isles are at a geographical crossroads for the world's greatest travellers – birds.

The seas are not as rich as they once were, the climate is changing, and human influence on the land is enormous, yet there is still a fascinating array of wild birds inhabiting or visiting these islands. Politically divided between the UK and the Irish Republic, and further subdivided into Northern Ireland, England, Scotland and Wales, birds recognise none of these boundaries, and together these islands provide a treasure trove of experiences for anyone willing to go and look – and for which this book is a key.

SPRING

Many of our small birds remain close to their summer homes. Local Robins, Wrens and Dunnocks will set up their territories early in the year in preparation for nesting. But for a great many species the onset of the breeding season is a trigger for movement, often over vast distances.

In Africa, small birds like Wheatears and Redstarts start building up their energy for long-distance flights to the British Isles. Some species will fly through the night and make non-stop flights taking a day or two to reach our shores. Swallows, on the other hand, will leave their South African winter grounds in March to arrive back here a month or so later – but they are unusually slow migrants, flying and feeding by day and roosting in flocks at night.

Out at sea, birds are also on the move. Auks such as Puffins and Guillemots, Manx Shearwaters and Fulmars have mostly spent the winter out of sight of land, but now they are setting out to return to their breeding colonies, drawn to the same colonies and often the same mates as the previous year.

Robins in Britain and Ireland hold territories in winter.

Manx Shearwaters will have spent the winter at sea.

Further south, in the Southern Ocean, another species will be flying northwards: Arctic Terns that see almost 24 hours of daylight during the Antarctic summer will now fly north. Many fly over and beyond the Arctic Circle to breed, and thus experience a second summer with 24-hour daylight! Other terns will not have to travel quite so far. Off the coast of West Africa many will have spent the winter feeding in the warm shallow seas, and will return to the British Isles to nest. Even the Ospreys from Scotland, which abandoned their cold northern waters for a time, will

Pied Flycatchers will have spent the winter in Africa.

now be leaving their West African coastal wintering grounds to fly north again – arriving back here in late March.

Some birds returning to the landmass of western Europe may be blown off course or take avoiding action to miss bad weather. At such times they may inadvertently cross the English Channel or the North Sea, and arrive exhausted on our shores. These are vagrants, which, after a stop to refuel, will usually try to resume their journey.

The approach of spring is our opportunity to observe some of these remarkable journeys at first hand. Swallows perched on a wire may be the first clue that the migrants have returned. A visit to woodland in southern England, such the RSPB reserves of Tudeley or Garstone, will find Willow Warblers and Chiffchaffs that have also newly returned, and further west at Nagshead the Pied Flycatchers, freshly returned from Africa, will use nest boxes near the public nature trails.

Near the coast, sites like Dungeness, Lodmoor, Minsmere or Saltholme will be places that many migrants make their first landfall. Some are familiar and predictable, like Wheatears and Yellow Wagtails, but others might be rarer vagrants like Hoopoes or Wrynecks.

To find returning seabirds one needs to visit their breeding colonies. Common Terns nest on reserves such as Havergate Island, Marshside and Belfast Harbour, or inland at Rye Meads. But for birds like

Guillemots and Puffins, places like South Stack, Bempton Cliffs, Fowlseugh or the dramatic colonies of Orkney and Shetland are the places to go when the birds return. It is humbling to see great rafts of Puffins riding the waves off somewhere like Coquet Island and knowing they are about to experience land for the first time since leaving it the previous August.

SUMMER

Spring slips imperceptibly into summer, and the breeding season for birds reaches a crescendo with its early morning dawn chorus. Birds will sing at any time of day, but it is early morning they are most keen to re-establish their territories. Some, of course, will sing at night as well. For nocturnal species such as owls and Nightjar the reason is obvious, but for a diurnal species like the Nightingale the reason why it should sing all through the night is more mysterious. Their song-season is understandably short and is best heard in southern woodlands, like those at Blean or the wooded areas of Minsmere in May and early June.

While many birds make their presence known through their songs, their nesting behaviour is usually harder to observe. There is a good reason for keeping a nest site secret, with so many potential predators around – both avian and mammalian. Whether a species nests in a tree or on the ground, you can be certain that other creatures will be on lookout for it – often as food for their own young.

Some species, however, allow us an insight into their private lives at breeding times, and it is worth finding these

Wrynecks are now mainly passage migrants to our shores.

exciting places. Guillemots make no nests and lay their eggs, and rear their young, on bare rock ledges. A safe viewpoint at South Stack, Rathlin, Bempton Cliffs or any of the Scottish seabird colonies allows you to witness the daily routine of bringing up offspring in this hostile environment. Alongside the Guillemots are usually Razorbills, Fulmars, Kittiwakes and Shags. There are often Eiders down below, in the sea. The sight of so many individuals of different species, all struggling to rear their young at the same time, is an experience not to be missed. These seabird cities have more than a passing resemblance to our own cities; they are noisy and often smelly, and we can watch tender family life played out alongside commuting, high-rise living and the occasional mugging!

Away from the cliffs, many breeding bird colonies are on coastal marshes such as those at Minsmere, Leighton Moss and Titchwell. From the shelter of purpose-built hides visitors can watch elegant Avocets marshalling their errant families

Rafts of Puffins form new breeding colonies as birds return from their winter at sea.

A seabird colony resembles a busy city with activity at all levels.

of cute downy young and then fiercely attacking any intruder that dares to approach too close – even if it happens to be as large as a Shelduck or even a heron. Shelducks have their own, very different approach to family life – the parents frequently abandon their young, and allow crèches of mixed ages to form. Most adults leave the marshes and estuaries and go off to sea to moult. This is an aspect of family life that we can observe if we take time to stop and watch.

One species that engages in highly visible drama in summer is the Marsh Harrier.

Avocets with young are quick to attack an intruder.

It is not for nothing that the scientific family name is *Circus*. Its courtship and territorial display is a combination of swooping and diving at quite a height, but the drama increases as the male passes food to the female. He will do this by circling the nest-site until the female is flying below him, and then dropping the food that she will expertly catch in mid-air. This public spectacle can often be seen at Minsmere, Leighton Moss, Titchwell and Blacktoft Sands.

AUTUMN

It is hard to identify the beginning of autumn. For many birds autumn starts long before the leaves on the trees change colour. For some, autumn migration starts around Midsummer's Day. Many waders, for example, leave their breeding areas and start to move to their wintering locations during June. Small parties of Lapwings flying overhead in mid-June are often the first sign of autumn, or a Greenshank visiting a coastal pool for a few days before it sets off again to spend the winter in Africa.

By August, autumn (or more accurately, post-breeding) migration is well under way. Many of the waders that nested in the high Arctic are on their way south. Knot from Greenland cross to Iceland and on to the British Isles, others come to us from Siberia. Here on our estuaries they will moult from the brick-red summer plumage into the grey winter plumage before most will head on south, down the East Atlantic Flyway, which takes them down the west coast of Europe and Africa. While on British and Irish estuaries they regain lost energy by feeding at low tide on invertebrates in the mud. As the tide turns and rises, the birds are driven into ever larger wheeling flocks, which is one of the most rewarding wildlife spectacles to be seen in our countryside.

Finding migrating waders means visiting some of the more remote parts of our shoreline. Some of the last true wildernesses to be found in the British Isles: Snettisham, the Ribble Estuary, Morecambe Bay, Culin Sands and Nigg Bay, are just some of the places to see this spectacle – if the tide is right.

After the waders come the wildfowl: ducks, geese and swans. Again these ground-nesters such as Pink-footed Geese and Pintail have bred in the far north, where food is plentiful, predators scarce and where there are long hours of daylight to rear their young. But the Arctic nesting season is short, and by September and October vast numbers are heading south, while others such as Pochards, which nested in Central Europe, move out to the coasts to escape any snow and ice. All these reach the British Isles in their millions. Some ducks will join our local birds on park ponds, gravel pits and reservoirs, while others will use our coastal marshes.

Whooper and Bewick's Swans gather in large numbers on the Ouse Washes. Whoopers are also on northern lakes and lochs, such as Loch Winnoch, Vane Farm, Lough Foyle and Lower Lough Erne. Pink-footed Geese mass at Snettisham and Vane Farm, Barnacle Geese at Mersehead and on Islay. Everywhere there are ducks; from the urban reserves of Rye Meads and Sandwell Valley to the rural fields of Otmoor or at Pulborough Brooks – the latter tucked in under the Sussex Downs.

WINTER

Instead of having to go to look for birds, in winter many come to find us – especially if we put food out in our gardens. While kitchen scraps have always been acceptable, these days there is a good selection of commercial bird food available as

Knots 'refuel' by feeding on some of our large estuaries. At high tide they may gather in thousands.

well. A wide range of different foods is likely to encourage a variety of species. The familiar residents of Blue and Great Tits, Chaffinches and Greenfinches will visit most gardens, but they may be joined by Coal Tits, Great Spotted Woodpeckers and, in some places, Siskins. Recently Goldfinches and Long-tailed Tits have discovered the delights of garden feeders and are now regular visitors to many gardens.

Feeding birds was once carried out for our own enjoyment, but with the decline in the populations of many wild birds, and increasing food shortages in the countryside, garden bird feeding now has a more serious consequence, and is regarded as an important activity in the conservation of many of our smaller species.

Beyond our gardens winter birdwatching has its special attractions. Braving the cold, our estuaries and seashores are well worth a visit. Many waders will remain all winter and the great flocks of geese commute from fields where they have been feeding back to the coast at dusk. On the sea ducks gather: Eiders inshore, perhaps with Red-breasted Mergansers. Further out there may be Red-throated Divers, which may have nested in the north of Scotland, and the Great Northern Diver, which will probably have nested in Iceland. Then there are the 'sea ducks', which seldom venture inland. Flocks of Common Scoters gather along some sheltered coasts, and also in the firths and estuaries of Scotland and Ireland, and may be joined by wonderful Long-tailed Ducks, which are only winter visitors to

The number of Goldfinches visiting bird feeders has increased in recent years.

our shores from Iceland, Scandinavia and Northern Russia.

December may be mid-winter, but for birds the passing of the shortest day usually triggers the first indication that spring will soon return. Robins adopt a more cheerful 'spring' song around Christmas and on mild days in January, and Blackbirds and Great Tits may be heard singing loudly. Some species nest early, with Grey Herons at Northwood Hill and West Sedgemoor often on eggs by the end of February – a good time to observe them, before there are any leaves on the trees.

And with herons nesting and the first of the summer migrants returning by March it is a reminder that four seasons have passed, and the ornithological calendar is about to restart.

Flocks of Long-tailed Ducks visit British and Irish coastal waters in winter.

USING THIS BOOK

This book aims to help as many people as possible develop a greater understanding of the birds that share our towns, our countryside and all the other habitats that make up the rich mosaic of the British Isles.

The content of the book describes 285 species that breed in Britain and Ireland or are seen here regularly; and we have included a further 24 rare migrants or vagrants that occur less frequently, but might be encountered by the lucky observer.

The birds are mostly arranged in the normal scientific order, with related species appearing close together. However, we have changed the order slightly in a few places to ensure similar-looking species appear on facing pages. Each account begins with the usual English name followed by the accepted scientific name. Where the 'international name' differs, this is given on the line below. The international names, devised to avoid confusion where there are other closely related species, have been taken from The Status of Birds in Britain and Ireland, and are the names adopted by the British Ornithologists' Union.

IDENTIFICATION
This book is not principally intended to be a field guide. Identification is only a beginning, not an end in itself. It is a key to discovering much more about the life of each species and how it is faring in our modern world.

All the most common plumages are described – adult, summer, winter, immature or juvenile – as are flight actions and other key aids to identification. There are also a few words about the annual cycle of moult as this may influence what a species looks like and how it behaves.

At the end of Identification the SEE ALSO notes cross-refer to other species that appear similar. These may be closely related, as in the case of Chiffchaff and Willow Warbler, or appear superficially similar as with Red-throated Diver and Cormorant.

HABITS
This describes special characteristics that may aid identification, but also tell the observer more about bird behaviour.

VOICE
The section on sounds is also intended to aid identification. Descriptions of song and calls are highly personal and we advise the reader also to take advantage of the many excellent CDs and other recordings that are on the market and will help to bring our descriptions to life.

HABITAT
It is important to know where a species normally lives. We have looked beyond the breeding habitat and included the places where the bird may be found at other seasons. Readers should note, however, that many species will often be seen away from their usual habitats – this is one of the joys, challenges and frustrations of birdwatching!

FOOD
We have attempted to be quite specific by giving the common name of the most usual food items (for example we have given 'bullhead, loach, minnow, sticklebacks and small chub' as the food of Kingfisher, rather than the rather bland statement that the bird eats fish).

BREEDING
This summary for each species includes a description of the nest site, the number of eggs laid, the respective roles of male and female, the length of incubation, the time taken for the young to fledge and the age at which they become independent. Readers should note that the times given can sometimes vary by a few days, depending on local environmental conditions. We also state when there is more than one brood in the year; where this number is not given it is implicit that only one brood is reared.

MOVEMENTS AND MIGRATIONS
The movements and migrations of birds are among the natural wonders of the

world and we cover this topic for each species. We have also included here the maximum recorded age. It must be emphasised that this is not the 'average' age, but the oldest that is known. As this information is based on a relatively small sample of ringed birds, it is very likely that many individuals exceed this age.

POPULATION

We have reproduced the latest estimations of the numbers of birds, or breeding pairs. All bird numbers fluctuate from season to season and from year to year; but where we know about long-term trends we have included this information.

CONSERVATION

Following naturally from the current population we include a section on topical conservation issues. Here we summarise some of the influences on bird populations and some measures conservationists are taking to reverse declines.

DISTRIBUTION

A map indicates the approximate distribution of a species in the British Isles and is colour coded to show the status: resident, summer visitor, winter visitor or passage migrant. The words alongside attempt to indicate the world distribution.

RED ALERT

For many years wild bird conservation effort was directed at preserving our rarest species: those on the brink of extinction or which had arrived in the UK and nested in small numbers. The work to protect the last of our native Red Kites in Wales in the early part of the 20th century, and the guarding of the Ospreys after their return to Scotland and their more recent arrival in England and Wales, are examples of this important work.

But today, with unprecedented use of natural resources by humans, the pressure on our wildlife in general and birds in particular is immense. As we have learnt more about the distribution and abundance of wild bird populations we have begun to realise that many species we regard as common are also potentially endangered. The familiar Song Thrush was the first to start to disappear from our gardens and was soon followed by House Sparrow and Starling. Although not in danger of imminent extinction, these declines represented an enormous loss of biodiversity and raise concerns about the future of these species.

Since 1990 scientists have been closely monitoring all British and Irish bird populations, and periodically publishing a list of species most at risk.

KEY TO MAPS

The maps in this book give an approximate indication of the distribution of each species at different seasons of the year.

Green: resident, areas where species may be seen throughout the year and where they breed

Yellow: summer visitor, areas where the species may be seen in summer and usually breed

Blue: winter visitor, areas where species spend the winter, but do not breed

Pink: passage migrant, areas that species visit at times of migration – generally spring and autumn

For distribution at sea, colours are restricted to areas where birds will be visible to observers and therefore only inshore waters have been mapped.

This red, amber and green categorisation, which currently includes 52 red-listed species and 126 amber-listed, is basic information for the UK's Biodiversity Action Plans. These plans help to steer the work of both Government's nature conservation agencies and non-governmental organisations, and there is a similar scheme covering Ireland.

The authors have adopted a similar 'traffic light' system for colour-coding pages (there are a few rarities or introduced species without a code). Indications of population change for each species and the specific threats are described in more detail in each of the Population and Conservation sections – essential information for the reader who wants to understand how and why our wild bird populations are changing. Population figures are seldom precise, and are generally estimates based on the most recent surveys.

The 'RED LIST' of endangered or vulnerable species includes those that are globally threatened, those that have declined over the past 200 years, those whose breeding populations have fallen by more than 50% in 25 years, those whose breeding range is contracting and those that breed elsewhere and whose non-breeding population in the UK has fallen by 50% or more.

Corncrake, a species in long-term decline.

The 'AMBER LIST' includes species where falling populations or contracting ranges are more moderate and also some that are recovering, having previously been included on the red list.

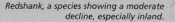

Redshank, a species showing a moderate decline, especially inland.

The 'GREEN LIST' is those for which there are no current concerns – although these species' populations often show modest rises or falls from year to year and are monitored by annual surveys, mostly carried out by volunteers.

Wren, a species with a mostly stable population.

BIRD TOPOGRAPHY

HOUSE SPARROW

ear — nape — crown — forehead
neck side — ear coverts
hindneck
mantle
scapulars
back — upper mandible
tertials — bill
secondaries — lower mandible
rump — chin
uppertail coverts — throat
tail — (upper) breast (chest)
lesser coverts
breast side
median coverts
(lower) breast
alula (bastard wing)
greater coverts
primary coverts
undertail coverts
primaries
vent
flank
belly
claw
toe

LITTLE STINT

brace — mantle
upper scapulars
lower scapulars
tertials
lesser coverts
greater coverts
median coverts
tibia
tarsus
hind toe

BLACK-HEADED GULL

terminal band
secondaries
trailing edge
leading edge
primaries

worn adult male (spring)

Some passerines change their appearance radically through feather wear rather than moult.

fresh adult male (autumn)

REDSTART

Mute Swan *Cygnus olor*

IDENTIFICATION

125–155 cm. One of our largest birds with rounded head and long, graceful, S-shaped neck and pointed tail. Adult is white with orange bill with a black base. A black knob at the base of the bill is largest on the male. Head is sometimes stained rusty orange. Juvenile brown/grey, becoming whiter by its first autumn. Immatures have washed-out orange bill. Large black feet sometimes rest on the bird's back. Unlike Whooper and Bewick's Swans the tail is pointed when up-ending. Female moults before the male. Moults between June and November and becomes flightless for 6–8 weeks.

SEE ALSO: Bewick's Swan p18, Whooper Swan p19.

HABITS

Waddling walk. Takes off from water by running along the surface before becoming airborne. Flies with neck extended and regular, slow wingbeats. Flocks fly in diagonal lines. Aggressive posture has arched wings, neck drawn back and rapid jerky advance across the water. Courtship takes place in late winter with synchronised head dipping and necks and breasts pressed together. Normally strictly territorial, but there are a few traditional nesting colonies. Feeds mainly during the day, but continues after dark.

VOICE

Mostly silent, but makes a loud hiss when angry and other snorting sounds. Loud throbbing 'waou, waou' noise made by wings in flight. Young birds make a high-pitched whistle.

HABITAT

Breeds close to lakes with shallow feeding areas, slow-flowing rivers, canals and occasionally beside salt and brackish water. Visits arable fields, areas of short grass and, more rarely, sheltered coastal waters.

FOOD

Feeds by dipping its head into water and sometimes up-ending. Also picks up grit from river bottoms. Eats aquatic plants and other vegetation. Plant food includes stonewort, starwort, hornwort, water crowfoot, various pondweeds, soft grasses and algae. Also eats small animals including insects and snails. Grazes on short grass. Takes bread and other food from humans.

BREEDING

Pairs first breed at 3 or 4 years. Once paired, 'divorce' is rare. The nest is built of reeds, rushes and other vegetation near water – on a bank, an island or in a reedbed. The nest may be 4 m wide and built by both sexes, male passing material to female. 5–7 eggs are incubated by female and guarded by male. Eggs hatch after 36 days. Young feed themselves. When small the young may be carried on their parents' back, which helps to keep them warm and protect them from pike. Young fly after 120–150 days and usually leave their parents' territory during their first autumn.

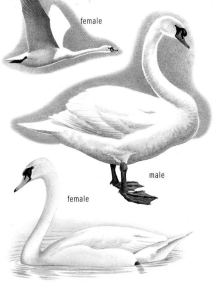

female
male
female

juvenile

MOVEMENTS AND MIGRATIONS

Some stay on territory all year, others move short distances and form winter flocks. Juveniles join winter flocks and non-breeders remain in these flocks in summer. Some travel to traditional areas to moult. In cold weather some from Europe arrive in eastern England. Oldest bird over 28 years.

POPULATION

Once prized as a food for banquets, these swans were introduced to many parts of Europe, so that the present population is a mixture of wild and semi-feral flocks. There may be 25,000 pairs in the UK and 10,000 in Ireland.

CONSERVATION

It was specifically protected by laws of 1387. A recent population increase may be due to better protection in most of Europe. The problem of lead poisoning on lowland rivers has been largely solved by a 1987 ban on the sale of lead fishing weights. A similar ban on the use of lead in shotgun cartridges would also help the Mute Swan. Vandalism, however, continues to be a significant cause of nest failure in some urban areas.

DISTRIBUTION

This swan breeds wild in northern and eastern Europe and also in parts of Asia. It has been introduced into North America, South Africa, Australia and New Zealand.

Bewick's Swan *Cygnus columbianus*

INTERNATIONAL NAME | TUNDRA SWAN

IDENTIFICATION

115–117 cm. Smaller than Mute Swan. Our smallest swan. Rather goose-like, with a rounded head, smaller bill and shorter and proportionally thicker neck than Whooper Swan. Adult white with black-and-yellow bill. Yellow pattern at base of bill is highly variable, but generally rounder or squarer than the pointed wedge pattern on a Whooper's bill. Neck and underparts may become stained rusty orange. Juvenile is uniformly grey with flesh-coloured bill that darkens and becomes partly yellow during the first winter. Immatures have some grey feathers on their head and neck until their second winter. When up-ending has a blunt-ended tail.
SEE ALSO: Mute Swan p17, Whooper Swan p19.

HABITS

In flight, the neck and body are shorter, and wings beat faster than Whooper Swan. In winter it feeds and roosts in flocks. Generally, it feeds in water less than 1 m deep, and also on saltmarshes and arable fields. It roosts on water, where it may continue feeding after dark, or it may visit arable fields at night.

VOICE

Call is a soft, mellow, yelping 'oop, oop', or 'hoo, hoo'.

HABITAT

Visits low-lying wet pastures, flooded grasslands, saltmarshes, lakes and reservoirs in winter. Sometimes feeds on arable fields close to wetland roosts. Breeds on the Russian tundra where there are low, swampy, grassy areas with pools, lakes and rivers.

FOOD

Leaves, shoots and roots of pondweeds, milfoil, floating sweet grass, marsh foxtail, marsh yellow-cress and other aquatic plants, and rye grass and clover. Visits farmland to feed on waste potatoes, carrots and winter wheat.

BREEDING

Does not breed in Britain or Ireland. Nests further north than any other swan and the breeding cycle needs to be completed in 100–110 days before the Arctic weather deteriorates. Pairs stay loyal and 'divorce' is rare. When one bird dies over half will find a new mate within a year. Young form pairs during their second or third year. Breeding usually starts between 4 and 6 years old. Family groups stay together for the winter and travel back to their breeding grounds as a group. Some young associate with their parents for several years until paired.

MOVEMENTS AND MIGRATIONS

Bewick's Swans leave Siberia in the first half of September and arrive in Britain in mid-October. The Netherlands and Germany are the other main European wintering areas. Some migrants also reach France and other European countries. Most British and Irish birds start their return migration before the end of March. The oldest wild bird was 20 years old.

POPULATION

Around 8,000 individuals winter in the UK and a further 1,000 in Ireland, together making almost half of the European population. This number has increased in recent years while winter populations elsewhere have remained stable.

CONSERVATION

Specially protected. Many deaths are inflicted directly or indirectly by man: flying into overhead cables being the most common. Lead poisoning from shotgun cartridges and illegal shooting on migration are other problems. The loss of traditional wetlands has resulted in 90% of the European winter population being concentrated on just 10 sites. These critical sites require protection to ensure enough vegetation to sustain winter swans and good water quality. The relationship with farmers close to wintering sites will need careful management. In future the effects of climate change and the growth in oil, gas and mineral exploration in Siberia may affect this species.

DISTRIBUTION

Breeds in northern Russia and in North America. Migrants fly to a small number of traditional wintering areas. The Russian population reaches western Europe, especially the Netherlands, Britain and Ireland. There are only a small number of sites where the majority of birds congregate.

juvenile

Whooper Swan *Cygnus cygnus*

IDENTIFICATION

145–160 cm. Slightly smaller than Mute Swan with long bill giving 'Roman-nosed' appearance. Neck is usually straight, but sometimes forms a graceful curve. Neck appears long and thin – often with an obvious kink at the base. Adult white with a black-and-yellow bill. Yellow on bill extends beyond the nostril and ends in a point. Some have rust-coloured staining that is lost during the winter moult. Immature has grey body that becomes whiter during the winter. Some grey feathers remain until its second winter. Its bill is reddish grey until the black and yellow appears. Larger than Bewick's Swan with longer body, longer wings, angular head, longer neck and triangular, not rounded, yellow patch on its bill. When up-ending it has a square-ended tail. Adults moult their flight feathers after breeding and are flightless for several weeks. Female moults when young are small, but male waits until female is almost ready to fly.

SEE ALSO: Bewick's Swan p18, Mute Swan p17.

HABITS

In flight, it looks heavier than Bewick's, with larger head, slower wingbeats and longer neck and body. In winter it is often seen in flocks, but is not colonial when nesting. Winter flocks consist of family units and non-breeders. Often feeds by up-ending.

VOICE

Loud whooping or trumpeting call.

HABITAT

In winter, visits lowland farmland near the coast, flooded fields or inland lakes. It may be seen in sheltered coastal bays. Feeds in shallow water or on land during the day, and roosts on open water at night. Main breeding grounds are boggy areas with pools and upland lakes, often with reeds or other

juvenile

vegetation. Some Icelandic feeding areas are rich in iron compounds, which stain the birds' feathers.

FOOD

Leaves, stems and roots of aquatic plants: pondweed, stonewort, marsh yellow-cress and horsetail. Also water snails. On farmland it eats potatoes, grain from stubble fields, grass, oilseed rape and winter cereals.

BREEDING

It does not nest until 4–5 years old. Courtship begins in winter and most pairs probably stay together until one dies. The nest is close to water, often on a small island, and is a large mound of reeds and sedges that is built by both sexes. 3–5 eggs are laid as soon as the ice melts and are incubated by the female for 35 days. Both parents tend the young, which feed themselves and are brooded at night. They fly after about 87 days, and remain with their parents for the first autumn and winter and the start of the return migration.

MOVEMENTS AND MIGRATIONS

Migrants from Iceland arrive in Britain and Ireland in October and leave before mid-April. Generally found further north in Britain than Bewick's. Scandinavian and Siberian populations winter in eastern Europe and the Black Sea. Oldest ringed bird was 26 years.

POPULATION

Winter population of Britain and Ireland is around 25,000 birds. The Irish population has grown in the last 30 years. A small number of wild birds remain in northern Britain and a few breed most years. There are a few feral birds that occasionally breed wild.

CONSERVATION

Specially protected. Main threats are from collisions with overhead power lines, disturbance of the few nesting pairs and poisoning from lead from shotgun cartridges. The estuaries and wetlands visited during migration and for winter roosts need special protection.

DISTRIBUTION

Breeds on the tundra in Iceland and Scandinavia. Also nests in northern Russia and northern Asia. Winters as far south as the Mediterranean. Most Icelandic birds migrate to Britain and Ireland while those from Scandinavia winter in Europe, and a few arrive in eastern England.

Bean Goose *Anser fabalis*

IDENTIFICATION

66–84 cm. Slightly smaller and less bulky than a Grey-lag Goose. This is a tall goose with a long, wedge-shaped bill, a slender, almost swan-like neck, orange legs and a yellow and black bill with a variable pattern. The male is generally a little larger than the female. The adult is brown, with a very dark sooty brown head and upper neck, uniform brown upperparts with pale barring and white under the tail. The brown breast has fine, pale barring and there is a white line at the edge of its folded wings. The juvenile is similar to adult but duller and sometimes paler. Some birds have white feathers around the base of the bill, but not enough to be confused with a White-fronted Goose. In flight, the upperwing is uniformly dark. It moults all its flight feathers simultaneously and is flightless for about a month before its autumn migration.
SEE ALSO: Greylag Goose p23, Pink-footed Goose p21, White-fronted Goose p22.

taiga race

juvenile
tundra race

HABITS

It swims well but less often than most other geese. The dark brown upperwing and rather long, slender neck are obvious in flight. It is usually sociable, except when nesting, although the flocks tend to be smaller than those of other geese. In autumn, the flocks are first made up of families that are then joined by non-breeders. Flocks fly to their roosts at dusk and leave again at dawn. When airborne they generally fly in 'V' formation or in lines.

VOICE

Not as noisy as other geese – gives an 'ung-ank' or an 'ow, ow, ow, ow' call.

HABITAT

In Britain it spends the winter in open country. The winter roosts are on lakes or flooded fields close to the feeding grounds. The northern breeding grounds are either within pine (taiga) forests or birch scrub, or in open areas of low wet tundra, on small offshore islands or near pools or streams.

FOOD

It feeds by grazing grasses, clover, cereals, potatoes and other crops.

BREEDING

This species does not breed wild in Britain or Ireland. Both parents tend the young and in autumn families migrate together, and stay together until the following breeding season.

MOVEMENTS AND MIGRATIONS

Family parties from Scandinavia arrive in Britain during late September and early October and leave in March. On their breeding grounds some of the forest birds move north to the tundra after breeding and before migrating for the winter. Sometimes a small number of Bean Geese accompany White-fronted Geese from Russia and arrive in Britain. Oldest 25 years.

POPULATION

Usually 500 individuals winter in Britain, most of them in Norfolk and central Scotland.

CONSERVATION

Like other members of this family, Bean Geese can be unpopular with farmers as they spend time on agricultural land during the winter and graze grass and growing cereals. Research, however, has shown that this winter grazing does no economic damage to the crops. There are now fewer breeding in Sweden and Norway than there were 20 years ago and this may have been caused by increased human disturbance, changes in agriculture and some direct persecution.

DISTRIBUTION

Southern Scotland and Norfolk are the only places that these birds are regularly seen in Britain in winter. Small numbers are occasionally seen elsewhere, usually in the company of other geese. There are several races of Bean Goose. The Western race breeds in northern Scandinavia and north Russia. Other races breed in northern Russia and north Asia. Most of the Western race of Bean Goose winter in southern Sweden, Germany and the Netherlands, and a few of these visit Britain in winter.

Pink-footed Goose *Anser brachyrhynchus*

IDENTIFICATION

60–75 cm. Smaller than Greylag Goose. Pinkish-grey with dark head and neck, and short, pink bill with variable dark marks. At a distance it appears compact and daintier than other geese. It has a shorter neck, a darker, rounder head and a greyer body. Legs and feet are pink. The pale edges to the back feathers give a barred effect and its underparts are closely barred. White line on body below its wings. In flight, blue-grey forewing that is not as pale as that of Greylag. Juvenile is darker with dull, yellowish legs, less distinct barring on back and mottled underparts. Adults moult their flight feathers simultaneously and are flightless for about 25 days before autumn migration.

SEE ALSO: Bean Goose p20, White-fronted Goose p22, Greylag Goose p23.

HABITS

A sociable goose except when nesting. Winter flocks contain up to 40,000 birds that mainly consist of family groups. Flocks move from their night-time roosts to their feeding areas at dawn and return at dusk. Feeding flocks travel up to 30 km and both roosts and feeding areas are used year after year. It also has 'rest stations' on grasslands or marshland pools. When landing it frequently slide-slips and tumbles as it loses height.

VOICE

Call is higher pitched and less harsh than other geese – often an incessant and rather musical 'wink, wink'.

HABITAT

Roosts on estuaries, mudflats, freshwater lakes, moorland pools and floodwater, and visits nearby farmland to feed. Winters in hilly areas, moors and mosses as well as lowland marshes. Prefers large fields, especially stubble fields in autumn, winter cereals, potatoes and suger beet and other arable crops.

FOOD

Feeds on vegetable matter including grain, winter cereals and root crops, including sugar beet, and also on grass. In summer, it eats leaves and shoots, roots and fruits, especially bistort, horsetails and cotton grass.

BREEDING

This species does not breed in Britain or Ireland. The pair bond generally lasts for life. In Iceland it nests in inaccessible river gorges where it is safe from ground predators. In Spitsbergen, where there are fewer predators, it nests in flatter habitats. Both parents tend their young and the families remain together in the first winter and only break up at the start of the next nesting season.

MOVEMENTS AND MIGRATIONS

When the young are 10–20 days old, family groups come together to moult and form large, flightless flocks. Some of the moulting flocks travel considerable distances on foot. There is also a massive moult migration of mainly non-breeding birds from Iceland to Greenland in June. Once their new feathers are grown Greenland birds fly first to Iceland and then the majority move on to Scotland or England. Migrants arrive in Britain during October and return north in April. The oldest surviving bird was over 38 years.

juvenile

POPULATION

In winter there are over 241,000 individuals in the UK (80–90% of the European population) and fewer than 50 in Ireland. Numbers in England have recently increased, especially in East Anglia, around the Wash.

CONSERVATION

Protected in the close season. The recent increase is probably due to more favourable conditions – larger fields, easily found food on farmland in winter, and better protection at winter roosts. The main threats are in its breeding areas in Iceland where numbers are affected by hunting and by the creation of hydro-electricity schemes.

DISTRIBUTION

There are two European populations: one in Spitsbergen and another in Iceland and Greenland. Greenland and Iceland birds winter in Scotland and England. Spitsbergen birds winter in western Europe, especially Denmark and the Netherlands.

White-fronted Goose *Anser albifrons*

INTERNATIONAL NAME   GREATER WHITE-FRONTED GOOSE

IDENTIFICATION

65–78 cm. Smaller than Greylag Goose. Appears larger and longer necked than Pink-footed Goose, with deeper chest and rather grey-brown head and white forehead. Body and neck are also grey-brown with variable black, blotchy bars on underparts. Back is brown and crossed with pale lines. Legs are orange and the bill of the Eurasian race is pink. Greenland race is generally larger and darker, with a longer, heavier, orange bill. Juvenile lacks the white forehead and black breast bars. The white forehead is gained during first winter but it is the second autumn before black bars appear on the belly. Flight feathers are moulted simultaneously and it becomes flightless for 25 days after nesting.

SEE ALSO: Bean Goose p20, Pink-footed Goose p21, Greylag Goose p23.

year, and even then the previous year's young may associate with their family group. On their breeding grounds, after the young have hatched, families join together. A few feral birds are free-flying in Britain and at least one pair has nested successfully.

MOVEMENTS AND MIGRATIONS

The race that breeds in Greenland almost exclusively winters in Scotland and Ireland. It crosses the Atlantic via Iceland and arrives in October. The race that breeds in northern Europe and Russia visits southern England. Both races leave their wintering grounds in March or April. Oldest bird 25 years.

Eurasian race

juvenile

juvenile

Greenland race

HABITS

Rather agile, and can rise almost vertically from the ground. In flight, wings appear longer and narrower than those of other geese. Flocks that roost together comprise many family groups. Large flocks cross the sky in lines, 'V's and chevrons, especially at dawn and dusk. These big flocks break up into smaller feeding groups during the day.

VOICE

Cackling calls that are higher pitched than Greylag and with a laughing sound to them.

HABITAT

Winters on low-lying, wet grassland close to coastal marshes, saltings, lakes and river valleys, including wet pastures and flood meadows. Feeds on agricultural land, including grass and cereal crops. In Ireland visits raised blanket bogs. Breeds on the Arctic tundra, close to lakes, rivers and pools.

FOOD

Vegetarian. Eats leaves, stems, roots and seeds of a variety of plants. In winter, feeds on grain, potatoes, sugar beet, horsetails, rhizomes of couch grass and roots of cotton grass. Feeds during the day, and sometimes at night.

BREEDING

Wild birds do not breed in Britain or Ireland. Pairs form after 2 years, but do not normally breed until 3 years old. Once formed, pairs generally stay together for life. Both parents tend young and the family stays together until the adults start breeding the following

POPULATION

18,000 winter in Scotland with smaller numbers in England and Wales and 10,000 in Ireland, including 50% of the world population of globally threatened Greenland White-fronts.

CONSERVATION

Protected in Scotland. Chief threat to the Greenland race has been from hunting in Iceland and the expansion of the Canada Goose into its breeding grounds. In Ireland, the drainage of bogs has forced the species onto agricultural land where it has been doing well. However, disturbance at feeding and roosting sites, and the construction of wind farms in remote areas, are a cause of concern.

DISTRIBUTION

There are two races that visit the British Isles. One comes from the west coast of Greenland and mostly winters in and around Wexford in Ireland and on Islay in the Inner Hebrides. The other race comes from northern Russia and winters at 11 sites in southern England, especially around the Severn and Swale estuaries. More Russian birds arrive if winter weather is severe elsewhere in Europe.

Greylag Goose *Anser anser*

IDENTIFICATION
75–90 cm. Large goose, but usually smaller than most Canada Geese. Grey-brown with a thick neck and large head. Neck has four or five dark lines down the side formed by ridges of feathers. Back has a barred appearance and the pale grey breast and belly are slightly mottled with darker marks. Forewing and underwing are noticeably pale. Feathers under the tail are white. The large bill is orange with a white tip and the legs and feet are flesh-pink. Juveniles have darker bills and legs and less noticeable pale barring on the back. Flight feathers are moulted simultaneously so birds are flightless for about 4 weeks between May and August. Non-breeding birds moult before breeding pairs.
SEE ALSO: White-fronted Goose p22, Pink-footed Goose p21, Bean Goose p20.

HABITS
Flocks fly in lines or 'V's, but are less organised over short distances. In the air it looks powerful and flies fast on broad wings. It runs further than other geese when taking off.

VOICE
Loud cackling and honking calls – can sound rather like sheep at a distance.

FOOD
Eats roots, tubers, leaves, stems, flowers and seeds of plants such as grasses, sedges and rushes. Grazes on land or takes floating vegetation such as pondweed and duckweed. On farms it eats spilt grain, grass and root crops.

BREEDING
Breeds near fresh water and some nest close together in colonies. The nest is often under a tree or bush and comprises a mound of vegetation with sticks and lined with grass and feathers. In Scotland the nest may be amongst heather. Egg laying starts in late March and the female incubates the clutch of 5–7 eggs while the male guards a small territory around the nest. The eggs hatch after about 28 days. Young and adults flock together with other families after a few weeks. Young fly after 50 or 60 days. Families stay together for their first year.

MOVEMENTS AND MIGRATIONS
Icelandic Greylags migrate to Britain in September and October and return to their breeding grounds by April or May. Scandinavian birds travel through the Netherlands and France to winter in Spain. Others fly through eastern Europe to Turkey and North Africa. Oldest wild bird 23 years.

POPULATION
The Scottish breeding population is 3,200 pairs and increasing. The feral population in the UK is around 32,000 pairs and growing. In Ireland there are about 1,000 feral birds in summer. In Britain and Ireland in winter, with migrants and feral birds, there may be more than 120,000 individuals.

CONSERVATION
May be hunted in the wildfowling season. This species has reduced its European range because of drainage of its nest-sites. The organised introductions of the 1930s and 1960s have successfully established new breeding populations in England. Traditional wintering sites for migrant populations continue to require protection although conflicts with agricultural interests may need addressing in future.

HABITAT
In Britain breeds near freshwater lakes, often on islands, and visits local farms and meadows to feed. Elsewhere in Europe nests in marshes, reedbeds and tundra. Winter flocks roost on estuaries, marshes, river islands, freshwater lakes and reservoirs. During the day feeds on farmland. Feral populations often inhabit urban areas, including parks.

DISTRIBUTION
Most domestic geese are descended from the Greylag. Native wild population in northern Scotland and the Western Isles. Farther south there is a growing population that originated from introductions during the 20th century. Migrant Greylags winter in northern England and Scotland. Once it was widespread in Europe, but breeding sites are now scattered in north and east. These birds winter as far south as the Mediterranean or North Africa.

Canada Goose *Branta canadensis*

male (gander), until the young have left the nest. The nest is built on the ground by the female. She gathers twigs, leaves, reeds and grasses and lines the nest with down feathers from her body. Nests are usually near water and under the shelter of a bush or at the base of a tree – often on islands. The female generally starts laying in late March and incubates the 5–7 eggs while the gander stands by. The eggs hatch after 28–30 days, goslings leave the nest soon after hatching and are tended by both parents – the female brooding them at night while they are small. Young can fly after 40–48 days. Young birds stay with their parents until the following breeding season and breed when 3 years old.

MOVEMENTS AND MIGRATIONS
In its native homeland of North America different races of Canada Geese vary from being long-distance migrants to being totally sedentary. In Britain a regular moult migration has gradually developed with young birds from the Midlands and Yorkshire flying to northern Scotland to moult. They leave their breeding areas in late May and return in early September. Cold winter weather means that some birds from Britain cross the English Channel and visit France. The Scandinavian population migrates south for the winter. The oldest known wild bird survived 27 years.

POPULATION
There may be 82,500 Canada Geese in the UK and over 1,000 in Ireland.

CONSERVATION
May be hunted in the wildfowling season and is protected at other times, but may be considered a nuisance in some public parks.

IDENTIFICATION
56–110 cm. There is a wide variety of sizes of Canada Goose, depending on which race a bird belongs to, although most birds in Britain are among the largest at 90–100 cm. Male larger and heavier than female. Large brown goose with black neck and head and broad white band from back of face joining under chin, pale brown breast and flanks and white under the tail. Bill and feet are black. Juvenile similar to adult. Flight feathers are moulted simultaneously and the bird is flightless for 3–4 weeks in June–July.
SEE ALSO: Barnacle Goose p25, Brent Goose p26.

HABITS
Gregarious outside breeding season. Swims frequently and up-ends to reach food in deeper water. Also grazes on land. Flies with powerful wingbeats, often in rather ragged flocks, but will form lines of 'V's on longer flights. Roosts in large flocks on water or mud banks. Flocks either walk or fly to these roosts at dusk.

VOICE
Deep, resonant, trumpet-like calls.

HABITAT
Lives near lowland lakes, often in urban and city parks and also around flooded sand and gravel pits and reservoirs. Tolerates lakes surrounded by trees, but these geese also need short open grass areas for feeding. A number of Yorkshire birds nest on moorland in heather and rushes well away from open water.

FOOD
Feeds on roots, tubers, stems, grass, leaves, fruits and seeds. Other plants include winter wheat and other cereals, grain, beans, clover, rushes and pondweeds. Also eats the leaves of crack willow and strips leaves from the common reed.

BREEDING
Often nests in loose colonies in which there are separate territories that are defended, especially by the

DISTRIBUTION

A native of North America; breeding in the north and wintering in the south. Introduced to Britain in the 17th century and into northern Europe where it has flourished. Widespread in England, southern Scotland and parts of Ireland. Apparently wild birds of the smaller northerly races sometimes arrive with Barnacle or White-fronted Geese.

Barnacle Goose *Branta leucopsis*

IDENTIFICATION
58–70 cm. Smaller than Canada Goose. Black, white and grey goose with creamy white face, dusky marks between eye and bill. Back of head, neck and breast are all black. Back blue-grey crossed with black-and-white bars. Flanks pale grey and lower belly gleaming white. Black legs are proportionally longer than most other geese. Black bill is small and rather delicate. Pale face of juvenile is more mottled and back is greyer with less distinct bars. Flanks are less clearly barred than on adults. Moults flight feathers simultaneously and becomes flightless for 3–4 weeks before its autumn migration.
SEE ALSO: Canada Goose p24, Brent Goose p26.

juvenile

HABITS
Wings appear rather pointed in flight. The black-and-white head, and black neck and breast help to identify this goose, even at a distance. Usually seen in noisy flocks that contain family groups as well as single birds and pairs without young. It flies in 'V's and lines like other geese.

VOICE
Call is a single bark that is higher pitched than most other geese. Can resemble yapping of dogs, especially when heard from a distance.

HABITAT
Visits coastal lowlands in winter, sometimes feeding on estuaries or bogs, but more often on nearby farmland, with clover, grass and cereal crops and in fields with some shallow water nearby. In the Arctic it nests on steep, dramatic cliffs either near the sea or overlooking fjords with rich feeding areas close by.

FOOD
Grazes vegetation, especially leaves, stems and seeds. Also uses bill to pull up roots and crush harder matter. In winter, eats plants such as rushes, grasses, clover, plantains, thrift, samphire, buttercup, woodrush and daisies.

BREEDING
On their Arctic breeding grounds some colonies nest on islands but many are on tall, inaccessible cliffs.

The goslings jump from their nests soon after hatching. Although many perish, the fact that cliff-nesting continues must mean it is far safer than losing eggs or small young to foxes and other predators on flatter, more accessible ground. After breeding the young geese stay with their parents until the following breeding season. Pairs stay together for life.

MOVEMENTS AND MIGRATIONS
Three separate populations from the Arctic start to arrive in Britain and Ireland in October and stay until late March or early April. Greenland birds fly first to Iceland before migrating to Ireland and the Western Isles of Scotland. Spitsbergen birds migrate via the Norwegian coast to winter on the Solway Firth. Those from Siberia that breed on Novaya Zemlya winter in western Europe. In cold winters, a few of these cross the North Sea to reach eastern Britain. The oldest known wild Barnacle Goose survived for 26 years.

POPULATION
Over 80,000 winter in the UK (over 20% of the world population) and 9,000 in Ireland. Numbers have increased at all sites over the last 50 years. There are also over 1,000 feral birds, which appear to be increasing.

CONSERVATION
Protected at all times. Where the birds are most numerous there have been conflicts with farmers. The enrichment of pasture has created an ideal habitat and birds are now competing with the needs of livestock. A combination of bird scaring, the provision of conservation refuges and government payments to farmers have helped to solve this problem in the short term.

DISTRIBUTION
Breeds in Greenland, Spitsbergen and Arctic Russia. Greenland and Spitsbergen birds winter in Scotland and Ireland and Russian birds winter in Europe. The largest numbers are in Ireland, the Hebrides in western Scotland (especially Islay) and the Solway Firth. Smaller numbers may visit eastern Britain.

Brent Goose *Branta bernicla*

dark-bellied juvenile

dark-bellied

pale-bellied

IDENTIFICATION

56–61 cm. Similar in size to a Mallard but more upright and with a longer neck. Plump with rather short black legs and small black bill. Head, neck and upperparts of the body are dark, apart from a small white neck patch. Underparts variable, but under the tail always white. Three races visit Britain and Ireland: dark-bellied birds from Siberia and Russia, and two races of pale-bellied birds from Greenland and Spitsbergen. Dark-bellied race has breast and belly almost as dark as its back with some mottling. Pale-bellied races are similar except that the breast and belly are paler grey-brown. Juveniles are similar to their adults but lack the white collar and have pale edges to the folded wing-coverts. Flight feathers are moulted simultaneously and the geese become flightless for about 3 weeks in July and August, before migrating in autumn.
SEE ALSO: Barnacle Goose p25, Canada Goose p24.

HABITS

Swims frequently and rides high in the water. Often up-ends to reach food. In flight, wings look pointed and rather duck-like. Flies in lines that undulate, but less often in 'V's than other geese. Generally in flocks, but birds may spread out across their feeding grounds. Flocks contain family groups, pairs without young and individual birds.

VOICE

The single 'waruk' calls mix together in flocks to form a dog-like yelping or babbling that carries a long way, and the clamour grows louder as flocks take to the air.

HABITAT

Winter feeding grounds are along seacoasts and estuaries where there are mudflats and intertidal zones with sufficient plant food. In recent years has frequently moved on to adjacent farmland. Breeds on the Arctic tundra, close to shallow pools or the sea.

FOOD

Grazes vegetation on land or finds food in water. Traditional food is eelgrass that grows in some estuaries. Also eats algae, and saltmarsh plants such as glasswort, sea aster and various grasses. Birds that visit agricultural land graze the shoots of winter cereals, grass and oilseed rape.

BREEDING

Does not breed in Britain or Ireland. With only about 100 Arctic days in which to rear a family, bad weather or the early onset of winter significantly affects breeding success. Families migrate together and remain together until the following breeding season.

MOVEMENTS AND MIGRATIONS

Breeding birds leave the Arctic by early September and start to arrive at their wintering sites in October. They return in March or April. Greenland birds stop for a time in Iceland and Russian migrants feed around the Baltic. Some of these geese survive for 28 years or more.

POPULATION

All three populations have increased in recent years. There are around 100,000 in the UK and 21,000 in Ireland, which together represent nearly half the world population.

CONSERVATION

Following a shortage of eelgrass in the 1930s, the wintering population dropped sharply. Conservation of the wintering areas, restrictions on hunting and their move onto agricultural land has helped numbers recover. Concerns remain: loss of sites to sea-level rise, disturbance by human recreation, conflicts with farming interests and a lobby to allow the species to be shot again are all factors that will need careful management.

DISTRIBUTION

Breeds farther north than any other goose. Dark-bellied race that breeds in Siberia and in northern Russia winters mainly in England and France. Pale-bellied race from Canada and Greenland winters in Ireland. Other pale-bellied birds breed in small numbers in Spitsbergen and winter in Denmark and north-east England – especially on the Northumberland coast.

Egyptian Goose *Alopochen aegyptiaca*

IDENTIFICATION

63–73 cm. Larger than Shelduck. It is a long-legged, sturdy-looking goose that stands erect when not feeding. When extended, the neck looks long and curved. It is buff-coloured with a reddish-brown back, pale grey underparts and a dark mark on breast. The neck and head are paler, mottled and with a brown patch around the eye and a narrow neck-band. Wings are dark with a green speculum and a conspicuous white wing-patch. The bill is small and pink. The legs and feet are also pink. Juveniles are paler and lack the eye and breast-patches. It moults in winter and summer and may become flightless for a short time after breeding.

grey variant

juvenile

FOOD

The food requirements in Britain are not well known. It is mainly vegetarian, feeding on seeds and leaves of grasses and other aquatic plants. In South Africa, it visits farmland to feed.

BREEDING

The nest-site may be in a variety of locations: under a bush, in a hole in a bank, or in a hole in a tree. In Africa it sometimes uses buildings or the old tree nests of large birds such as herons. A clutch of 8 or 9 eggs is laid in late winter. Incubation is by the female and the eggs hatch after about 28 days. The young feed themselves and are looked after by both parents. They are slow to grow adult feathers and it is about 70 days before they can fly. The family then stays together for weeks, and sometimes months before young birds become independent. These young birds probably first breed when they are 2 years old.

MOVEMENTS AND MIGRATIONS

In Britain the population appears to be mainly resident. In Africa movements are complex and appear to be linked to summer rains. In South Africa some undertake movements of 1,100 km.

POPULATION

Estimated to be over 1,000 individuals, and the population appears to be growing rapidly in some places.

CONSERVATION

The first introductions were probably from South Africa in the late 1700s. By the 1960s there was a small population established in Norfolk and since then there has been considerable growth in the population and expansion into new areas. In South Africa the farming community sometimes considers it to be a pest.

HABITS

It swims with its tail held higher than its shoulders and it may dive to avoid predators. In flight, the large white wing-patches are distinctive. Usually it feeds in family groups or in larger loosely formed flocks.

VOICE

Generally it is silent, but the male and female have different distinctive calls. The call of the male is a husky wheezing call, and the female makes a high-pitched 'hur, hur, hur, hur'.

HABITAT

This goose breeds around lowland lakes, especially ornamental lakes. Also on reservoirs and flooded gravel workings. In its native Africa it is found in a wide variety of wetland habitats.

DISTRIBUTION

A feral population breeds in scattered locations in England and Wales, but is most common in Norfolk and it is currently colonising the East Midlands of England. There is another feral population in Germany. In Africa it is widespread south of the Sahara Desert and also on the upper Nile in Egypt.

DABBLING DUCKS IN FLIGHT

male

SHELDUCK p30
Heavy and slow flight, usually individuals in pairs together.

SHOVELER p31
Appears 'front heavy' with fast flight.

male

female

male

female

WIGEON p32
Narrow wings with head and neck moving up and down. Often in flocks.

female

male

PINTAIL p33
Long neck and tail, and small head obvious in flight.

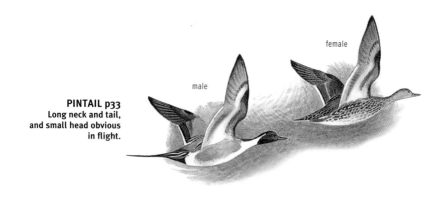

male
female

GADWALL p34
Fairly large with white underwing and obvious white speculum.

MALLARD p35
Large and heavy duck with broad but pointed wings and rounded tail.

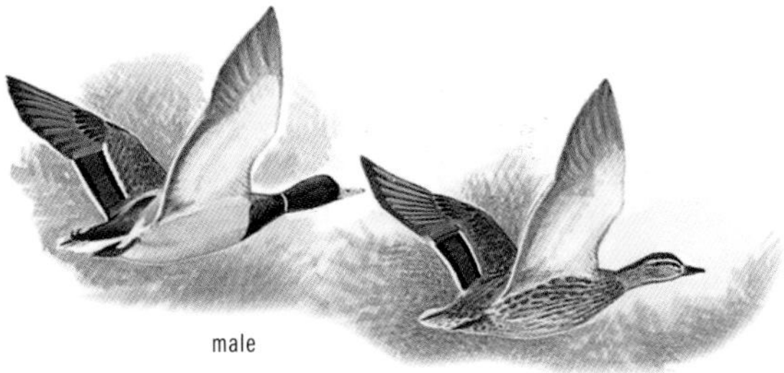
male
female

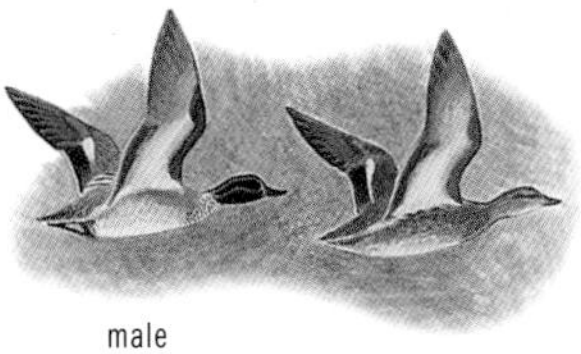
male
female

TEAL p36
Pointed wings and rapid agile flight – often twisting and turning.

GARGANEY p37
Heavier and longer-necked than Teal.

male
female

Shelduck *Tadorna tadorna*

INTERNATIONAL NAME COMMON SHELDUCK

IDENTIFICATION

58–67 cm. Larger than a Mallard. Large white duck with bottle-green head and neck, chestnut breast-band and black 'shoulders'. The broad bill is blood-red and the legs are pink. Male larger and brighter than female with pronounced knob at the base of his bill in spring. The black-and-white wing, black-tipped tail and a dark streak down centre of the belly show in flight. Juvenile less well marked with grey-brown back and head and whitish face and throat. During moult the adults look whiter and less well marked. Flight feathers are moulted simultaneously and adults are flightless for 25–31 days between July and October. SEE ALSO: Shoveler p31.

juvenile

female

male

juvenile

HABITS

Swims high in the water and up-ends to reach submerged food. Also wades, sweeping bill from side to side to sift food out of mud. In flight, looks heavy, with slow wingbeats. Outside the breeding season forms loose flocks.

VOICE

Male usually silent or makes sweet-sounding whistles. The voice of the female is lower, giving a growling 'ark-ark-ark' call.

HABITAT

Most numerous on sheltered coasts and estuaries where there are sandbars and mudflats. In recent years has adopted some inland sites, including gravel workings and reservoirs. Visits farmland near the coast. In western Europe favours coastal habitats, but in central Asia lives around salt lakes and marshes, often in steppe and semi-desert many kilometres from the sea.

FOOD

Feeds on invertebrates, including shellfish, crabs, shrimps, worms, sandhoppers and larvae of flies and other insects. The chief food on many estuaries is a tiny snail called *Hydrobia*. Small fish and some plant material are also eaten.

BREEDING

Nests amongst dense vegetation, in a hole, often an old rabbit burrow, or in other crevices or gaps under buildings. Occasionally off the ground in a tree or building. Nests comprise straw, grass and down feathers from the female's breast. 8–10 eggs are laid in April or May. Incubation is by the female and lasts for about 30 days. Young feed themselves within hours of hatching. Female leads her young to a food-rich area where they often mix with other young Shelducks. A few non-breeding adults ('aunties') often tend the crèches of young while the parents migrate to their moulting areas. Young fly after 45 days.

MOVEMENTS AND MIGRATIONS

After breeding most migrate to traditional moulting areas. Thousands gather in the Heligoland Bight off the German coast. Other moulting areas have recently been discovered on some British estuaries. Shelducks return slowly and territories may not be reoccupied until spring. Additional birds from western Europe arrive in Britain in winter. Oldest bird 24 years.

POPULATION

In summer there are up to 11,000 pairs in the UK and 1,000 in Ireland. Numbers have increased recently and inland colonisation may have resulted from coastal breeding sites becoming overpopulated. After breeding, there may be over 80,000 Shelducks in Britain.

CONSERVATION

Estuaries and coastal dunes have long been regarded as ripe for development and many feeding areas were destroyed in the 20th century. Port and marina developments, new harbours, increases in invasive plants such as *Spartina*, and recreational pressures all threaten the habitat on which the Shelduck depends. Sea-level rise is likely to reduce the intertidal zone on which Shelducks feed.

DISTRIBUTION

Breeds around coasts of Britain and Ireland and also a few inland places in England, southern Scotland and Wales. In Europe restricted to the north-west coast, from France to Norway and a few scattered breeding sites along the northern Mediterranean. Also lives around the northern shores of the Black Sea and across central Asia to China.

Shoveler *Anas clypeata*

INTERNATIONAL NAME **NORTHERN SHOVELER**

IDENTIFICATION

44–52 cm. Smaller than Mallard with heavy-looking body, flatter head and much longer, broader bill. Male has white neck and breast, dark green head, orange flanks and belly and white patch before black under-tail. Dark back has long black, blue and white feathers. Female similar to female Mallard, but with white underwings and dark belly. In flight, both sexes show powder-blue on wings, male's being brighter than female's. Juvenile resembles female, with young males only gradually acquiring adult plumage. Moult takes place between June and September with males beginning first. Simultaneous moult of flight feathers results in birds being flightless for about 4 weeks. Male in eclipse resembles female, but with darker upperparts and redder underparts.
SEE ALSO: Shelduck p30, Garganey p37, Mallard p35.

male

female

HABITS

Swims with breast low in the water and the huge bill nearly touching the surface. When up-ending, the long wings cross over at the tips, unlike Mallard's. Sometimes a group swims in a line or a circle, filtering the water disturbed by the bird in front. Shovelers are agile and their pointed wings appear set far back, due to the thin neck and big bill. Outside the breeding season usually in small groups but sometimes in bigger flocks.

VOICE

Generally rather quiet. Male has a quiet 'took, took' call as rival males chase each other. Female makes a soft quacking sound.

HABITAT

Breeds in marshes or lowland wet grassland that is close to shallow, open water. In winter, found on inland marshes, small lakes and pools, and around the fringes of reservoirs and other larger water bodies. Small numbers visit coastal marshes.

FOOD

Up-ends and occasionally dives for food, but usually filters surface water through serrations along edges of the bill. Feeds on tiny creatures, including crustaceans, small water snails, insects and their larvae. Also eats seeds and leaves of water plants.

BREEDING

Shovelers establish a small territory that they defend vigorously in the early stages of nesting. Nest is on ground, close to water, in a hollow lined with grasses and down and where 9–11 eggs are laid from April onwards. Incubation is by the female for 22 days. The male abandons his mate during incubation. The female tends the ducklings until they become independent after 40–45 days.

MOVEMENTS AND MIGRATIONS

Shovelers are migratory. Most British and Irish breeding birds leave by October and fly to western Europe; some reach North Africa. Others from Iceland, northern Europe and Russia winter in western Europe and Britain. Between February and May breeding birds gradually return to their territories. The oldest ringed bird survived over 20 years.

POPULATION

1,000–1,500 pairs breed in the UK and fewer than 100 in Ireland. During the November peak migration there may be over 15,000 in the UK and 2,500 in Ireland. Recently the numbers breeding and overwintering here have fallen.

male eclipse

CONSERVATION

Protected during the breeding season. Lowland wet grassland has been under pressure from drainage and changes in agricultural practice for many years. Many breeding sites are subject to flooding in spring due to changes in flood plain management. Most of the best sites are protected and managed, and expansion seems likely to come only from the creation of new wetlands.

male

female

DISTRIBUTION

Breeds in eastern England, with smaller numbers in south-west England, Wales, Scotland and Ireland. More widespread in winter, frequenting any suitable habitat in lowland Britain or Ireland. Breeds in Europe from the Baltic almost to the Mediterranean and eastwards across Asia to Mongolia. Also found in North America. European birds winter as far south as tropical Africa.

Wigeon *Anas penelope*

INTERNATIONAL NAME EURASIAN WIGEON

IDENTIFICATION
45–51 cm. Smaller than Mallard. Medium-sized duck with round head and small bill. Head and neck of male are chestnut, forehead is yellow, breast pink and body grey with a white stripe on the wing. Tail is black and pointed. In flight, male shows white wing-patches. Female is a similar shape to the male, but is mottled reddish or grey-brown, with pale pinkish flanks. Both sexes have a dull green speculum and a white belly in flight. Juveniles resemble females. Immature males resemble adult male, but lack white wing-patches. Complete moult between June and September and birds are flightless for several weeks. The eclipse male is a rich mottled chestnut.
SEE ALSO: Pochard p41.

male

HABITS
In flight, neck appears short, wings narrow, and tail longer and more pointed than in many other ducks. Birds migrating often move their necks up and down in a conspicuous way. For most of the year Wigeon are found in large flocks, but are generally solitary when nesting.

VOICE
Call of male is a far-carrying, musical, two-syllable whistle, 'wee-ooo'. Call of female is a rather harsh growl.

HABITAT
Breeds near shallow, freshwater lakes, pools and rivers where there is cover nearby for nesting. In northern Europe, breeds close to the tundra, but also nests in wooded areas, although not dense forests. Traditional wintering grounds were estuaries and coastal marshes, but in recent years many have moved inland and winter around lowland lakes, including reservoirs and gravel pits.

rufous female

grey female

FOOD
Grazes on land or finds food in the water. Sometimes follows other species such as Coots and swans and benefits from their waste food. Eats mainly vegetation, especially stems, leaves and roots of plants such as grasses, buttercups, algae, pondweeds, and especially eelgrass (*Zostera*), which grows on estuaries.

BREEDING
Nesting begins in April or May. Nest is a hollow amongst thick cover. It is lined with grasses and leaves and the female adds her own down feathers. Clutch is 8 or 9 eggs. Only the female incubates and the male generally leaves during incubation. The eggs hatch after about 24 days. The young are able to feed themselves straight away, but are brooded by the female while they are small. They fly after 40 days and become fully independent at this time.

MOVEMENTS AND MIGRATIONS
Northerly populations are migratory. In Britain and Ireland the largest numbers arrive in October. They return the following spring, eventually arriving back on their breeding grounds by May. At least one wild Wigeon survived more than 34 years.

POPULATION
There are over 300 breeding pairs in Britain. In the UK in winter there are over 400,000 birds, and 82,000 in Ireland. The population may be increasing.

female   male

CONSERVATION
Wigeon are protected in the breeding season. Largest numbers congregate on saltmarshes and coastal marshes, where drainage and habitat loss have concentrated Wigeon at a number of important sites, some of which are nature reserves. The birds will seek out areas free from disturbance and wildfowling. Increased recreational use of coastal sites and the loss of wet grassland and saltmarshes remain the main threats.

DISTRIBUTION
Wigeon nest in central and northern Scotland and also in northern England. There are individuals that spend the summer farther south, but these do not usually breed. Other Wigeon breed in Iceland, Scandinavia and northern Russia. Most of these winter around the ice-free coasts of Europe, especially in Britain and Ireland. Other European Wigeon reach the Mediterranean and the coast of North Africa.

Pintail *Anas acuta*

INTERNATIONAL NAME NORTHERN PINTAIL

IDENTIFICATION

51–66 cm. Slightly larger than Mallard. An elegant duck with a long, thin neck, long tail, rounded head, long delicate grey and black bill and dark green speculum, edged with white at the rear. Male has chocolate-brown head with broad white stripe running down neck. Body finely barred grey with black line along side often covered by the long cream and black, drooping back feathers. Tail black and white, with two greatly elongated black feathers. Female has a shorter tail and is mottled brown, but paler and greyer than other female ducks, with slender grey bill, pale brown head and neat scalloped brown and buff flanks. Juvenile similar to the female, but with darker back and is more heavily streaked and spotted. Pintails moult between July and September. In eclipse, males resemble females, but are greyer and more uniformly marked. Both sexes are flightless for about 4 weeks. SEE ALSO: Mallard p35, Shoveler p31.

HABITS

In flight, the long neck, small head, curved back, pointed wings and tapering tail distinguish it from other ducks. Seen mainly in small flocks that sometimes fly high, in a 'V' formation. Sexes form separate flocks in late summer.

VOICE

Generally less noisy than other ducks. Variety of calls similar to Mallard, but quieter. Male has a drawn-out 'greee' and female has a series of deep quacks.

female

male

BREEDING

Nests on ground amongst grasses or other cover within 200 m of water. A hollow is lined with leaves and grass and always with down feathers from female's breast. Female incubates 7–9 eggs for 22–24 days. During incubation, male generally leaves female. Young can swim and feed themselves soon after hatching and are able to fly after 40 days.

MOVEMENTS AND MIGRATIONS

Male Pintails leave breeding sites in May or June and many fly to traditional moulting areas. Females also migrate to moulting sites after breeding. By September the southward migration is under way. Pintails from Iceland, Scandinavia, the Baltic States and Russia winter in Britain and Ireland. British breeding Pintails stay here. Oldest known bird was over 27 years.

POPULATION

Fewer than 30 pairs breed in the UK and Ireland. Always a rare breeding duck, numbers have fallen in recent years. In Russia and Finland there have been large declines. Over 28,000 individuals winter in the UK and 7,000 in Ireland (40–50% of the European population).

CONSERVATION

Protected during the breeding season. The reason for the recent decline is unclear, but protection and careful management of its breeding sites are essential. In some places American mink may limit breeding success. Reduced pressure from hunting in Europe and Russia would help its long-term future. Protection of sanctuary sites on estuaries will boost winter survival.

juvenile

female

male

male eclipse

HABITAT

Breeds in wetlands with shallow water, close to grassland and open habitats. In winter, moves to sheltered coasts and estuaries, and some Pintails visit large inland wetlands such as flooded grassland and reservoirs with shallow edges.

FOOD

Feeds on a variety of plant and animal material taken from the water – often by up-ending and using its long neck to reach into deeper water. Plants include pondweeds, docks, sedges and grasses. Animal matter includes water beetles, fly larvae, snails, leeches and, in salt water, shrimps and marine snails.

DISTRIBUTION

Breeds in scattering of suitable sites in Britain and, rarely, in Ireland. Winters on coastal marshes, large estuaries and large inland wetlands and moves from site to site. Elsewhere breeds in northern and eastern Europe, Russia and North America. Many Pintails from western Europe reach the African tropics for the winter.

Gadwall *Anas strepera*

male

IDENTIFICATION
46–56 cm. Smaller than Mallard.
A rather undistinguished duck with a bold white speculum. Seen at close quarters, male has finely barred or freckled plumage that appears grey at a distance. Rear part of the body and tail are black. White speculum frequently shows clearly as a patch on sides of a swimming bird and is obvious in flight. Bill is grey. Female resembles a slim female Mallard, but with greyer plumage, a whiter belly, white speculum and orange sides to bill. During their summer moult, Gadwalls become flightless for about 4 weeks and it is then that the male resembles the female, but is greyer with plainer upperparts.
SEE ALSO: Mallard p35.

HABITS
Appears buoyant on the water. Wings are rather pointed. Often follows other feeding waterbirds such as Coots and Mute Swans and forms small, loose flocks in winter. Gadwalls do not nest in colonies, but several females may sometimes nest within 5 m of each other.

VOICE
Usually rather silent. Male has a deep, rasping croak, often given in flight. Call of female more like a higher-pitched version of a Mallard's 'quack'.

HABITAT
Breeds on lowland lakes or slow-flowing rivers with vegetated edges and islands. Recently in Britain it has colonised old gravel workings and the shallow edges of reservoirs. In winter it uses other, larger areas of water, including estuaries.

FOOD
Mainly vegetarian, feeding on plant material in water, either on the surface or by up-ending. The most common food includes stems, leaves and seeds of pondweeds, sedges, rushes, grasses and stonewort. Insects, water snails and small amphibians may also be eaten, probably accidentally.

male eclipse

BREEDING
Nests on the ground, often on small islands. The nest is usually among dense vegetation and quite close to water. In some places nests in more open locations close to terns or gulls, which help the Gadwall by chasing away predators. The 9–11 eggs are laid into a hollow lined with grass and the duck's own down. The female alone incubates, and the male usually deserts her during the 24-day incubation period. The young are able to feed themselves after hatching and continue to be brooded by the female while small. They fly after 45 days and become independent of their mother at about the same time.

MOVEMENTS AND MIGRATIONS
Present in all seasons, but more widespread in winter, with additional arrivals from Iceland and northern and eastern Europe. Some British and Irish birds appear to be sedentary while others move into Europe in autumn. Oldest bird 21 years.

POPULATION
700–1,500 pairs nest in the UK and fewer than 100 pairs in Ireland. Over 17,000 individuals winter in Britain and Ireland and numbers continue to increase.

CONSERVATION
Protected during the breeding season. Wild birds may have colonised some Scottish sites in the early 1900s, but other populations were artificially introduced in the 1800s, especially in East Anglia. Recently the East Anglian population appears to have spread west and north. It is important their wintering areas are left undisturbed. In Russia, where most European birds breed, there has been a recent decline.

female

male

female

DISTRIBUTION
Most numerous in the south and east of England, but has colonised many other places in Britain and Ireland in recent years. It is also found in widely scattered locations in central and southern Europe and also in Asia and North America. In winter it is more widespread and migrants are found around the Mediterranean.

Mallard *Anas platyrhynchos*

IDENTIFICATION
50–65 cm. Our most familiar duck. Large and heavy-looking, with long body and long and broad bill. Speculum is iridescent purple/blue edged with white. Male has dark green head, yellow bill, white neck-ring, purple-brown breast, mainly grey body and black curly upper tail feathers. Female brown with darker mottling, dark crown, dark eye-stripe, pale breast, orange bill and orange legs. Juveniles resemble females but have more finely streaked flanks. Mallards have been domesticated for centuries and various plumages have evolved: from almost black to pure white. Mallards moult after breeding and are flightless for 4–5 weeks. Males resemble females during moult, but have blacker crown and yellowish bill. SEE ALSO: Teal p36, Gadwall p34.

HABITS
Usually seen in small flocks. Can rise vertically out of water if disturbed. Mallards are often tame where they live close to humans, but are more timid in remote locations. Pairs sometimes form in autumn and stay together until spring. Some males are bigamous, and promiscuity and rape are not uncommon. Ducklings can dive to avoid danger and adults also dive occasionally.

VOICE
Calls of female are varied and include the familiar 'quack' that is often repeated many times in quick succession. Call of male is a quieter, low, rasping 'crrrib'.

HABITAT
Lives on large and small lakes and slow-flowing rivers that are fairly sheltered, and with shallow margins for feeding, including park lakes, reservoirs, small pools and coastal marshes. In winter, flocks visit larger water bodies and may also be seen on the sea. Breeds in a variety of wetlands, from the Arctic tundra to the sub-tropics.

FOOD
Feeds day or night, on land or in water. Food is picked off the surface, found by submerging head and neck, or gathered from deeper water by up-ending. Plants include leaves, shoots and seeds of water plants, and cereals. Also insects and their larvae, bread and other foods from humans and, rarely, small fish, mammals and birds.

BREEDING
Nesting starts in February if the weather is mild. Nest is a shallow depression ringed with grasses or small twigs, and lined with down. Usually hidden amongst vegetation such as nettles or brambles in a hedge bottom, or sometimes in woodland, in the crown of a tree. Female incubates 11–14 eggs. During incubation, male generally deserts female and plays no part in tending the young. Eggs hatch after 27 days. Young are able to swim, dive and feed themselves soon after hatching. They are independent after 50 days. Usually one brood, but female may re-lay if clutch is destroyed.

MOVEMENTS AND MIGRATIONS
Mallards in Britain may be resident or migrant. Many that breed in Iceland and northern Europe spend the winter in Britain and Ireland. Other populations from eastern Europe and Russia migrate in autumn and swell the numbers remaining in western Europe. There is a record of a Mallard surviving for over 23 years.

POPULATION
Up to 127,000 pairs breed in the UK and 10,000 in Ireland. Peak winter numbers are around 370,000 individuals in the UK and 20,000–50,000 in Ireland. The population has declined by over 30% in recent years.

male
male eclipse
female
male
juvenile male
female
juvenile female

CONSERVATION
Protected in the breeding season. British and Irish population has been supplemented by birds released for sport. Hunting pressure and habitat destruction may be a problem in future.

DISTRIBUTION
Widespread in Britain and Ireland in summer and winter, wherever there are suitable wetland habitats, although scarce in upland areas. The most widespread duck in the world, breeding in Europe, Asia and North America and it has also been introduced to Australia and New Zealand.

Teal *Anas crecca*

INTERNATIONAL NAME EURASIAN TEAL

IDENTIFICATION
34–38 cm. Smaller than Mallard. Small, compact duck with short neck. Male has chestnut head, dark green eye-patch that extends to back of head, grey body with white lateral stripe and spotted breast. Also has a yellow patch on the side of its black tail. Female like small, delicate, boldly marked female Mallard with small bill, dark crown and dark green speculum that is bordered by white stripes that show in flight. Wings are pointed and flight is very rapid. Moults during summer. Male in eclipse resembles female, but with darker upperparts and grey bill. Flight feathers are moulted simultaneously and birds are flightless for about 4 weeks.
SEE ALSO: Mallard p35, Wigeon p32.

male

HABITS
Usually in small flocks except when nesting. An agile duck that can rise vertically from the water if disturbed. Teals in flight will twist and turn and their rapid wingbeats and pointed wings can make them appear more like waders than wildfowl. Often inactive during the day and feeds mainly at night.

VOICE
Call of male is a piping, far-carrying whistle, 'prip-prip'. Female's call is a rapid, high-pitched quacking.

HABITAT
Breeds mainly on wet moorland, bogs and marshes in upland areas. Some nest in lowland marshes or near the coast. Some breeding sites may be in, or close to, woodland. In autumn and winter, visits lakes, ponds, gravel pits, reservoirs and coastal lagoons. In Europe and Asia ranges from the edge of Arctic tundra to the fringes of arid deserts.

FOOD
Eats a variety of food that it finds in mostly shallow water, by pecking from the surface, filtering water through its bill, or up-ending. Chief food is seeds of rushes, grasses and other plants such as pondweed, dock, birch and buttercup. In summer it eats animals such as water snails, fly larvae, water beetles and worms.

BREEDING
Pairs form during winter before moving to their breeding sites. Nesting begins in mid-April. Teal nest closer to the water's edge than any other duck species, which helps deter predators. A hollow is lined with leaves and grass, and down from the duck's breast. The female incubates 8–11 eggs and the male often leaves as incubation begins. Young hatch after about 21 days and can feed themselves soon after hatching. They become independent at about 30 days. They are able to breed at 1 year old.

MOVEMENTS AND MIGRATIONS
Most Teal are migratory, with birds from Iceland, northern Europe and Russia reaching Britain and Ireland during October and November and leaving again in March. In cold winters additional Teal from the Netherlands may cross the North Sea or fly to France or Spain. In Europe many undertake a summer moult-migration after breeding. Oldest ringed bird was over 21 years old.

male   female

POPULATION
Fewer than 2,800 pairs nest in the UK and 1,000 pairs in Ireland. The population has fallen by at least a third since 1970. In winter, almost 200,000 birds, or 30–40% of the European population, may winter in the UK and a further 30,000–50,000 in Ireland.

CONSERVATION
Protected during breeding season. Planting commercial forests in the Teal's traditional upland breeding areas may have caused some declines. Safeguarding remaining breeding areas and lowland wintering sites is essential.

female

juvenile

Garganey *Anas querquedula*

juvenile

IDENTIFICATION

37–41 cm. Smaller than Mallard but longer than a Teal. Slightly oblong head shape, with flat crown and straight grey bill. Male has broad white stripes over the eyes that curve down and meet at back of neck. Breast mottled brown, flanks finely barred with grey, belly white and back has black-and-white drooping feathers. In flight, shows blue-grey forewing. Female similar to female Teal but paler with whiter throat, pale patch at base of grey bill, darker eye-stripe that contrasts with pale stripe over eye, diffuse dark line across face and darker crown. In flight, forewing of female is grey. Juvenile like female with stripy head and lacks Teals' pale line under tail. Moults between May and August, with the male starting first. Flight feathers are lost simultaneously and adults are flightless for 3–4 weeks. Male in eclipse resembles the female, but with the sides of the head heavily streaked.

SEE ALSO: Teal p36.

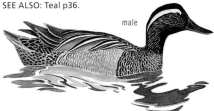

male

HABITS

In flight, it looks a little heavier and longer necked than a Teal. Outside the breeding season, it is usually seen in pairs or small groups.

VOICE

Calls of male include a dry rattle and a burping sound used in display. Female has a quiet 'quack' like a Teal.

HABITAT

It breeds in water meadows, flooded grasslands and in reedy and marshy pools or ditches where there is plenty of cover from grasses, rushes and other vegetation. It searches out similar habitats outside the breeding season.

female

FOOD

Mostly feeds while swimming, either from the surface or by up-ending. It eats insects and their larvae, including water beetles, flies and midges. It also feeds on water snails, freshwater shrimps, worms and the spawn and young of frogs. Plants are also eaten, especially the stems, leaves or seeds of water weeds, reeds, sedges, grasses, rushes, docks and duckweed.

BREEDING

Pairs form in winter and arrive together on their breeding grounds where a small territory is established. Nesting begins in April and a depression is lined with leaves, grasses and down. Female incubates the 8 or 9 eggs for about 22 days. During incubation the male generally leaves the area. Young can feed themselves soon after hatching and fly after 35–40 days.

MOVEMENTS AND MIGRATIONS

This is our only summer migrant duck that arrives in Europe in March and returns to its African winter quarters between July and October. Where Garganeys are numerous, large gatherings often form while the birds moult before migration. Western European Garganeys have two distinct autumn migration routes, one through Spain and the other through Italy. In spring, however, most birds return via Italy. One ringed bird survived for 14 years.

POPULATION

Fewer than 75 pairs breed in Britain. This small population has increased slightly in recent years. Elsewhere in Europe the population has declined sharply.

female

male

CONSERVATION

Protected in Britain by special penalties at all times. Wetland drainage and poor management of its breeding sites is responsible for the decline in Europe. Good management of wetlands in Europe and Africa is essential for the future of this species. Protection in its winter quarters and reduced pressure from hunting on migration would also help.

DISTRIBUTION

The Garganey breeds in scattered locations in England and a few sites in Scotland, but it is much scarcer in Wales and Ireland. Small numbers of non-breeding birds visit British wetlands in spring and autumn. Garganeys also breed in France, northern and eastern Europe, Russia and in central and eastern Asia. Most spend the winter in tropical Africa although a few winter around the Mediterranean.

DIVING DUCKS IN FLIGHT

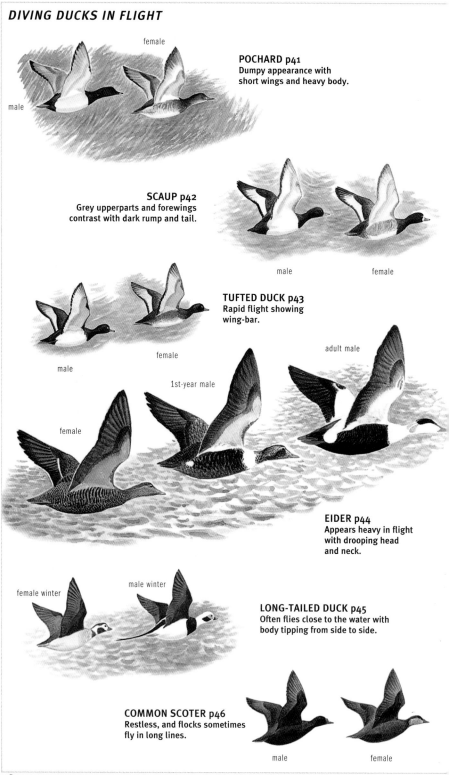

female

POCHARD p41
Dumpy appearance with
short wings and heavy body.

male

SCAUP p42
Grey upperparts and forewings
contrast with dark rump and tail.

male

female

TUFTED DUCK p43
Rapid flight showing
wing-bar.

female

adult male

male

1st-year male

female

EIDER p44
Appears heavy in flight
with drooping head
and neck.

female winter

male winter

LONG-TAILED DUCK p45
Often flies close to the water with
body tipping from side to side.

COMMON SCOTER p46
Restless, and flocks sometimes
fly in long lines.

male

female

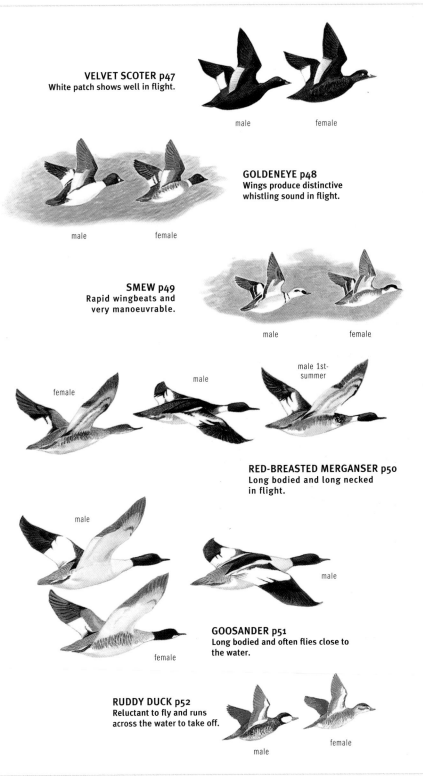

VELVET SCOTER p47
White patch shows well in flight.

male

female

GOLDENEYE p48
Wings produce distinctive
whistling sound in flight.

male

female

SMEW p49
Rapid wingbeats and
very manoeuvrable.

male

female

female

male

male 1st-
summer

RED-BREASTED MERGANSER p50
Long bodied and long necked
in flight.

male

male

GOOSANDER p51
Long bodied and often flies close to
the water.

female

RUDDY DUCK p52
Reluctant to fly and runs
across the water to take off.

male

female

Mandarin *Aix galericulata*

IDENTIFICATION
41–49 cm. Smaller than Mallard. Plump duck with a thick neck, a large head and a small bill. For most of the year male is striking, with green and purple crest, chestnut-orange ruff, broad pale stripe from eye to nape, white eye-ring, purple breast, orange-brown flanks and dark back. The uniquely shaped inner wing feathers form 'sails' on the back. Bill is red. Female grey-brown with spotted flanks, a spectacle-like mark around and behind the eye and tiny grey bill. In flight, shows dark wings with a white trailing edge and a pale belly. Moults between May and August and is flightless for about a month during that period. Male in 'eclipse' plumage resembles female but with less obvious face marks, a redder bill and glossier plumage.

male eclipse

male

HABITS
Swims with body high in the water, seldom up-ending. Frequently perches on fallen tree trunks and on tree branches overhanging the water. Takes off easily from water or land and flies rapidly, even among trees.

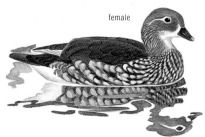

female

VOICE
Usually rather silent. Displaying males have a variety of calls including a soft whistle. Female has a soft croak, often given in flight.

HABITAT
Breeds around lowland lakes and rivers where there are trees and bushes, and branches overhanging the water. Lakes surrounded by rhododendron appear to be especially attractive. Also common in wildfowl collections and as an 'ornamental duck' in public and private parks.

FOOD
Omnivorous. Feeds on aquatic insects in spring and summer and mainly vegetarian at other times, eating seeds and nuts, especially acorns in autumn. Also eats snails.

BREEDING
In Britain, Mandarins begin breeding in mid-April. Usual nest-site is in a hole in a tree, usually an oak, sometimes at ground level but more often off the ground – up to a height of 10 m and sometimes more. Little nest material is used, but the clutch of 9–12 eggs is laid into a cup of down feathers. The eggs are incubated by the female for about 28 days. Young leave the nest quickly and feed themselves. The female continues to care for them and the male sometimes roosts close by. Young fly after 40 days and can breed when 1 year old.

MOVEMENTS AND MIGRATIONS
The British population appears to be sedentary although individual birds will travel considerable distances. Mandarins in Asia are migratory with northern and western populations migrating while the population in Japan is mostly sedentary.

POPULATION
There may be as many as 7,000 Mandarins in Britain.

CONSERVATION
The species was present in Britain before 1745, but most of the current population is descended from birds that escaped or were released during the 20th century. Over the last 25 years the population has grown and new areas have been colonised. This increase is in contrast to the Asian population, which appears to be declining for reasons that are unclear. There are now probably as many Mandarins in Britain as there are in Japan. The chief limit to further expansion may be competition with Jackdaws and squirrels for holes in trees.

male

female

DISTRIBUTION

Mostly found in southern and central England, but populations are also established north into Scotland and west into Wales with a small number in Northern Ireland. Elsewhere feral populations have become established in California, Germany and the Netherlands. The species originated in the Far East where it is native to eastern Siberia, China, Korea and Japan.

Pochard *Aythya ferina*

INTERNATIONAL NAME COMMON POCHARD

IDENTIFICATION
42–49 cm. Smaller than Mallard. This diving duck has a short neck and a round head. Male pale grey with rusty red head and neck and black breast and tail. Female yellowish brown with a dark crown and rather blotchy cheeks. Juvenile like female but is grey-brown with pale cheeks and neck. In flight, both sexes show pale grey stripe on wing. Moult takes place between June and October with male beginning first. Flight feathers are moulted simultaneously and birds are flightless for 3–4 weeks. In eclipse plumage male resembles female, but with more uniform brown head and greyer back.

male

SEE ALSO: Tufted Duck p43.

male eclipse

HABITS
Appears to spend a lot of time asleep as it mostly feeds at night. Usually seen in small groups, or larger flocks outside the breeding season. In many flocks in the UK there is frequently a higher proportion of males to females. Swims rather low with the tail flat on the water and patters along the surface to take off. In flight, short wings and heavy body give dumpy appearance and rapid wingbeats make whistling sound.

VOICE
Usually silent except during courtship when male makes a soft, wheezing 'wiwwierr'.

female winter

female summer

HABITAT
Breeds on lowland lakes, flooded gravel pits and reservoirs where there is plenty of vegetation growing in the water. Winters in similar habitats, but also on larger lakes and reservoirs. Visits estuaries, but rarely seen on open sea.

FOOD
Usually it dives to feed. Dives are often preceded by an obvious jump. Females tend to dive in shallower areas. Plant food includes leaves, stems and seeds of a variety of water plants including stonewort, pondweed, milfoil, sedges and grasses. Also eats water snails, small fish, tadpoles and insects and their larvae.

BREEDING
Pairs form in late winter while in flocks or at breeding sites. Nesting begins in April when female constructs a shallow cup of reed stems and other material close to water or amongst reeds. Nest is lined with down. Male generally leaves female during incubation. Female incubates 8–10 eggs for 25 days. Young feed themselves soon after hatching and become independent before they can fly at 50 days. Sometimes young from several families group together.

male

female

MOVEMENTS AND MIGRATIONS
Most are migratory. Moulting flocks form in late summer. Autumn migration takes place in September and October, with the males moving before the females. Many of the birds that winter in Britain migrate here from northern and eastern Europe and central Russia. Additional birds from the Netherlands arrive in cold winters. Oldest survived for 22 years.

POPULATION
About 500 pairs nest in the UK and fewer than 50 pairs in Ireland. Breeding population has increased in recent years. In winter in Britain and Ireland the number of Pochards may reach over 95,000 individuals although numbers have fallen recently by up to 40%.

CONSERVATION
Protected during the breeding season. It first nested in Britain in about 1800 and gradually colonised new sites, helped by the creation of gravel pits and reservoirs. Breeding birds are susceptible to disturbance and need water bodies that are unpolluted.

DISTRIBUTION
Most breed in eastern England and lowland Scotland, and only small numbers in Ireland. In winter, widespread on lowland waters throughout Britain and Ireland. Breeds around the Mediterranean, but the largest populations are in northern and eastern Europe and eastwards across Asia. In Europe, winters as far south as the Mediterranean and a few reach tropical Africa.

Scaup *Aythya marila*

INTERNATIONAL NAME / GREATER SCAUP

IDENTIFICATION

42–51 cm. Diving duck with broad body, round head and large, wide bill with tiny black 'nail' at tip. Male has black head and neck with greenish sheen. Sides of body and belly are white, back is finely barred dark grey and white and tail black. Female dark brown with a variable white patch at the base of the bill and a pale buff crescent on the edge of cheeks. Juvenile resembles a female, but with a narrower patch around the bill. In flight, it has a broad white stripe running the length of the wings. It moults between September and November and is flightless for 3–4 weeks. In eclipse the male remains distinctive, but much duller than in breeding plumage. SEE ALSO: Tufted Duck p43.

male   female

male

HABITS

Seen in flocks for most of the year. Ratio of males to females in these flocks varies, from a preponderance of males in the north to a majority of females in the south. Some flocks can number hundreds or thousands of birds. Generally swims rather low in water and dives frequently. Rarely seen on land.

VOICE

Generally silent. Male has a soft, dove-like call during courtship and female has a low growl.

HABITAT

Usually seen on the sea in winter. Visits sheltered coasts and bays, and may visit freshwater lakes near the sea. It occurs in much smaller numbers on reservoirs and freshwater lakes away from the coast. Elsewhere it is a species that breeds on or close to the Arctic tundra, or in open northern forests.

FOOD

Chief food is shellfish, especially the blue mussel, which is obtained by diving. Other shellfish include cockles, periwinkles and the tiny marine snail called *Hydrobia*. Insects, crustaceans and plant material are also eaten.

BREEDING

Pairs form while in their winter flocks or on their breeding grounds. Nests singly or in colonies, and sometimes among colonies of gulls or terns. Nest is on ground near to water and usually well concealed by low vegetation. The female incubates 8–11 eggs for more than 26 days. Male usually leaves the female during incubation. Young sometimes join with other families and fly after about 40 days. They remain with the female until they can fly, sometimes longer.

MOVEMENTS AND MIGRATIONS

Moult generally takes place on breeding grounds and the birds move south in August. A few males delay their moult until they reach their winter quarters. Moves to the coast for the winter and most undertake long-distance migrations. The largest numbers reach Britain and Ireland in late October and remain until February or March. Some immatures remain in their winter areas during the following summer. Oldest 14 years.

POPULATION

Some stay all summer in suitable habitats and sometimes a pair will nest. The last estimate in winter was 13,000 birds in Britain and Ireland, but numbers are falling, perhaps by over 50% in the last 25 years.

CONSERVATION

Specially protected at all times. The majority of Europe's Scaup population is concentrated in relatively few areas in winter. This makes it vulnerable to pollution and disturbance by recreation, and there is a need for international cooperation to ensure important sites are specially protected. Some large winter flocks have deserted traditional sites as coastal waters become cleaner and less rich in food.

female summer

male 1st-winter

female winter

Tufted Duck *Aythya fuligula*

IDENTIFICATION
40–47 cm. Smaller than Mallard. Diving duck with short neck, rounded head and relatively large, broad bill with broad black tip. Male glossy black with white flanks, white belly and drooping crest from back of head. Bill blue-grey and eyes golden. Female brown with darker upperparts, paler, yellowish flanks and white belly. Some females show whitish patch at base of bill and pale feathering under the tail. In flight, obvious white stripe runs length of wing. Annual moult takes place between June and October. Males moult first and both sexes are flightless for 3–4 weeks. In eclipse, male resembles female, but has darker upperparts and loses its crest.
SEE ALSO: Pochard p41, Scaup p42.

HABITS
Looks buoyant on water and frequently dives with a distinct jump. Often forms large flocks outside breeding season. In parks and places where it lives close to people it sometimes becomes very tame. Winter flocks frequently contain more males than females.

VOICE
Male generally silent, except for a low whistle during courtship. Female makes a harsh 'karr', especially in flight.

male

female

male eclipse

female (pale base to bill variant)

female (white-vented variant)

HABITAT
Breeds around inland lakes, flooded gravel pits, reservoirs and slow-flowing rivers. Often lives close to built-up areas. Avoids deep water, unless there are also shallow bays and margins. In winter, gathers on larger water bodies and occasionally on the sea.

FOOD
Sometimes up-ends, but usually dives to collect food from the bottom of a lake or river. It eats freshwater mussels (especially the zebra mussel), also freshwater shrimps, crustaceans and insects and their larvae, such as caddis fly. Plants include pondweed and sedges.

BREEDING
Pairs form in late winter or spring. Nesting begins in May when female builds a nest of grasses, rushes and reeds that she lines with down. Solitary nests are not uncommon, but Tufted Ducks often nest colonially, generally amongst cover and close to water. Female incubates 8–11 eggs for 25 days and during this time the male may leave the area. Young feed and fend for themselves soon after hatching and can fly after 45 days. The female often leaves them before this time.

MOVEMENTS AND MIGRATIONS
Many of the Tufted Ducks that breed in southern Britain are resident, but others are migratory. Some British breeding birds reach Portugal, especially during cold weather. Most of those that nest in Iceland fly to Britain and Ireland during September and October. Others from northern Europe migrate south or west to winter in western Europe, including Britain. The winter migrants start to return to their breeding grounds in February. The oldest ringed bird was 22 years old.

female

male

POPULATION
Over 10,000 pairs breed in the UK and up to 2,500 pairs in Ireland. In winter, there may be 120,000 individuals in the UK and 36,000 in Ireland, although numbers fluctuate. During the 20th century the numbers both breeding and wintering increased.

CONSERVATION
Protected only during the breeding season. Freedom from disturbance, especially from water sports during spring, is important to ensure breeding success. The construction of reservoirs and the increase in flooded gravel pits, together with the arrival of the zebra mussel, which has become an important food for this species, have contributed to its success (although this may be limited by rats and mink).

DISTRIBUTION
Widely distributed in lowland England, Scotland and Ireland, but rather more scarce in Wales. In winter it is a little more widespread. Tufted Ducks breed in Iceland, parts of France, northern Europe and across Asia as far as Japan.

Eider *Somateria mollissima*

INTERNATIONAL NAME COMMON EIDER

male

female

male eclipse

male 1st-summer

female

male

periwinkles, crabs, starfish and sea urchins. Fish are sometimes eaten when they can be easily caught. Incubating females will sometimes eat plant material, including berries.

BREEDING
Courtship starts in winter, when males are seen throwing their heads back and 'cooing'. Breeding begins in late April. Eider nests are often within colonies of Arctic Terns. Nest is in a hollow near the sea, sheltered by rocks or vegetation, but may be in the open. It is lined with down from female's breast. Female incubates 4–6 eggs for 25–28 days and seldom feeds during this period. Male protects female prior to egg laying but generally leaves during incubation. Young swim and dive soon after hatching and broods often join together in crèches tended by a few females. Young are independent after 55 days and fly at 65 days.

MOVEMENTS AND MIGRATIONS
British and Irish birds do not generally move far from their breeding grounds and there are several traditional gathering places for moulting birds. In autumn, migrants from the Baltic and the Netherlands arrive on the east coast of Britain. Oldest was 35 years.

POPULATION
About 31,000 pairs breed in the UK and 1,000 in Ireland. It expanded its range during the 19th century and gradual expansion may be continuing. However, the UK winter population of about 80,000 individuals has fallen by 28%.

CONSERVATION
Winter flocks are vulnerable to accidental and deliberate discharges of oil. Control of shipping in sensitive waters and rapid response in the case of accidents will safeguard this and other seabirds. Loss of feeding sites owing to commercial development of estuaries is also a concern, as is predation of breeding birds by animals such as foxes.

IDENTIFICATION
50–71 cm. Slightly larger than Mallard. Sea duck with fat body, short neck, large head and long wedge-shaped bill. Male white with black crown, flanks, belly and tail. Breast tinged pink and the sides of the head are lime green. Female brown with darker barring and mottling, distinctive long forehead. Juvenile resembles female, but young males take 4 years to acquire adult plumage; until then they have a variety of black-and-white patchy plumages. In flight, male shows large white wing-patches and female has a dark speculum bordered with thin white bars. Eiders moult between June and August and are flightless for a few weeks from July to August. In eclipse the male is blackish with white on the wing.
SEE ALSO: Shelduck p30, Long-tailed Duck p45.

HABITS
Sociable, often seen in groups in summer and forms much larger flocks in winter. Looks heavy in flight, with drooping head and neck. Flocks frequently fly in lines low over the water. Dives with its wings half open.

VOICE
Silent for most of the year but male has a dove-like cooing call, 'ar-oooo', when displaying.

HABITAT
A marine species that lives around rocky coasts. In spring it requires suitable islands or low-lying land close to the sea for nesting. After breeding, birds often move to estuaries and other sheltered coasts rich in food.

FOOD
Eiders dive to search for food on the seabed. Chief prey is the blue mussel and other shellfish. It also eats

DISTRIBUTION

Breeds in Scotland, parts of northern England and the north of Ireland. In winter it spreads south as far as the south coast of England, and is most numerous on the east coast. The species is found all round the Arctic Circle with the nearest populations being in Iceland and Scandinavia. It winters as far south as northern France. Some young birds remain in their wintering sites for their first spring and summer.

Long-tailed Duck *Clangula hyemalis*

IDENTIFICATION

40–47 cm. Smaller than Mallard, but the tail of the male may add 13 cm. Small neat sea duck with small round head, steep forehead, all-dark wings in flight and white belly. In winter, male is mainly white with brown 'Y' mark on its back in flight, brown breast-band and a large dark cheek patch. In summer has a streaked brown back, dark head and neck and a pale greyish-white cheek patch. Adult male has very long central tail feathers. Female in winter shows a white collar, white face with dark lower cheeks and dark crown. She has a warmer brown breast-band. In summer, female has a darker face than in winter. Females have short tails. Juvenile is like female in summer, but with a less contrasting face pattern. Flight feathers are moulted between July and September, during part of this time the birds are flightless for a few weeks. It has a unique moult as some back feathers are moulted four times a year and some head and neck feathers three times.

SEE ALSO: Pintail p33,
Eider p44.

female winter

HABITS

The Long-tailed Duck swims high in the water and dives easily with a small jump and wings partly open. Usually seen in flocks, except in the breeding season. Sometimes winter flocks are large, comprising several hundred birds. Birds chase each other in small parties and splash-land after a short flight. The species is often in very rough water. Flies more readily than many other sea ducks and often travels close to the water, tipping its body from side to side, like Puffin or Little Auk.

VOICE

Compared with other sea ducks the Long-tailed is quite noisy, with the yodelling calls of the males being made throughout the year and at any time of day or night. Female makes a low quacking.

male 1st-autumn

HABITAT

Winters on the sea, some distance from the shore and only occasionally visits inland lakes and reservoirs. Breeds on freshwater pools, lakes and rivers mainly within the Arctic Circle.

FOOD

Dives to search mainly for crustaceans and molluscs, especially blue mussels, cockles, clams and crabs. Also eats sandhoppers, small fish such as gobies and some plant material.

BREEDING

Long-tailed Ducks display in their winter flocks and some pairs form at this time. The species does not, however, breed in Britain or Ireland. In spring, the birds wait along northern coasts of Scandinavia until there is a thaw and they can move to their nesting areas in the tundra. Nesting colonies often spread out over a large area. Females lay 6–8 eggs that are incubated for up to 29 days. Males desert females during incubation. Young mature quickly; they can fly after 35 days and are quickly independent.

male winter

MOVEMENTS AND MIGRATIONS

In parts of its range males travel up to 1,000 km to moult. Elsewhere it moults closer to its breeding areas. After moulting, some move south while others remain in ice-free waters close to their breeding grounds. Oldest bird 22 years.

POPULATION

The UK winter population is around 16,000 individuals, mainly in Scotland, and a few hundred in Ireland.

CONSERVATION

Protection of the major wintering sites is a conservation priority as large concentrations of these ducks are vulnerable to oil pollution at sea. Routing oil tankers away from sensitive sites and rich feeding grounds will help this and other species that winter at sea.

female winter   male winter

DISTRIBUTION

Mostly a winter visitor to British and Irish coasts, especially northern Scotland, Shetland and Orkney. A few non-breeding individuals remain in British waters for the summer. Breeds in northern Europe, Asia and North America, mostly north of the Arctic Circle.

Common Scoter *Melanitta nigra*

IDENTIFICATION

44–54 cm. Smaller than Mallard. Deep-bellied sea duck with a pointed tail. Male all black with narrow yellow patch on top of the bill. Female dark brown with darker crown and pale patch on cheeks and upper neck. Juvenile similar to female. In flight, wings are plain with no obvious marks, only flight feathers look a little paler. Moults between July and October with males beginning first and females later. Flightless for 3–4 weeks. In eclipse plumage male becomes a little duller with browner underparts.
SEE ALSO: Velvet Scoter p47.

male

HABITS

Large flocks of moulting birds gather in late summer, autumn and winter, and some smaller flocks of non-breeding birds remain in their winter quarters during summer. Swims buoyantly, often with tail slightly cocked, and dives with a small forward jump. Flocks appear restless with birds often standing on their tails and exercising their wings. Flies frequently and often forms long straggling lines low over the water, sometimes higher.

VOICE

Limited range of calls can be heard while birds are in flocks, especially during courtship, the most frequent being whistling and piping.

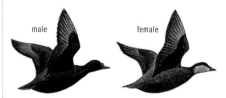
male   female

HABITAT

In Britain and Ireland seen in inshore waters. Breeds near small moorland lochs, or on wooded islands in larger lochs. Rarely seen inland on reservoirs and lakes outside the breeding season.

FOOD

Chief food is molluscs, especially the blue mussel, which it finds by diving. Also eats cockles, clams and other shellfish, crabs, insects, small fish and plant material.

BREEDING

Pairs start to form in the winter flocks. They move to their breeding grounds where male defends female until incubation and then he deserts her. Nest is in a hollow lined with grass, moss and down. The preferred site is close to water, on an island or on the margin of a lake and concealed in vegetation. Female

incubates 6–8 eggs for over 30 days. Young can swim and feed themselves soon after hatching and some broods merge together. Young can fly after 45 days.

MOVEMENTS AND MIGRATIONS

A few Common Scoters overwinter in ice-free waters near where they breed. Others migrate. The first movement is away from the breeding grounds to traditional sites where flocks congregate to moult. There are a number of places around the British and Irish coasts where flocks gather, and larger concentrations of northern European birds are found off the coast of Denmark. Some remain in the moulting area all winter while other populations migrate further south or west. Oldest known bird was 16 years.

POPULATION

There has been a rapid decline and there are now only about 50 pairs in the UK and up to 100 in Ireland. In winter, the population in UK coastal waters is over 50,000 individuals and over 23,000 in Ireland.

male 1st-winter

female

CONSERVATION

The UK population is in a precarious state and is specially protected at all times. Like other marine species that winter in flocks, there is a real possibility of large numbers being wiped out by an oil spillage unless shipping lanes avoid specially identified sites. Disturbance at winter feeding grounds by boat traffic is a problem, often linked to offshore wind farm maintenance. As the species is one of our rarest breeders the nesting areas and feeding sites need to be monitored and the best conditions maintained.

DISTRIBUTION

Small numbers breed in Ireland and northern Scotland. Larger numbers winter around British and Irish coasts, especially in Wales and the north-east coast of Scotland. The Common Scoter also breeds in northern Europe and northern Russia. It winters along the west coast of Europe and North Africa.

Velvet Scoter *Melanitta fusca*

male

IDENTIFICATION

51–58 cm. Similar in size to Mallard and larger than Common Scoter. A sea duck, with a long bill rather like an Eider's, a thick neck and a pointed tail. Males have a small knob at the base of their bills. Both sexes have a white patch on the rear of the wing that shows well in flight or when wing-flapping, but is often hidden when swimming. The male is velvety black with a small white patch under the eye. The female is brown with two pale patches on the side of its head. The Velvet Scoter moults during the summer, with the male beginning before the female, and both sexes become flightless for 3–4 weeks. While moulting, the male is much duller.
SEE ALSO: Common Scoter p46, Eider p44.

HABITS

The Velvet Scoter may be seen in small groups and birds often cock their tails. Often they are loosely associated with flocks of Common Scoters. They sometimes feed in the rougher water close to rocks and islands and dive without jumping and with wings partly opened.

VOICE

Generally rather quiet, but sometimes croaking or growling calls can be heard from flocks in winter.

female

female (well-marked)

HABITAT

In Britain and Ireland it is found in marine habitats, either in rough seas on exposed coasts or more sheltered bays and inlets where there is a supply of food. It is very rarely found on inland waters. In the breeding season it inhabits northern lakes, pools and rivers, often in wooded areas and sometimes near the coast.

FOOD

Dives to feed on shellfish, especially blue mussels, cockles and dog whelks. It also eats crabs, sea urchins, small fish, insect larvae and some plant material.

BREEDING

Although some birds sometimes summer in British waters they have never been proved to breed in Britain or Ireland. Courtship takes place in the flocks during the winter. The female tends the young and the male leaves the nest-site during incubation. Some females look after young from a number of broods. The young can fly after about 50 days.

MOVEMENTS AND MIGRATIONS

There are some large gatherings of moulting birds in Russia and also off the Danish coast in September and October. Large numbers pass through the Baltic Sea in October and November, but the return migration is late, often peaking in Sweden in mid-May. Most birds are present around British coasts between mid-September and May. The oldest survived for more than 12 years.

POPULATION

It is thought that up to 3,000 individuals winter in Britain, with most being in eastern Britain.

male   female

male 1st-winter

CONSERVATION

The Velvet Scoter is specially protected. Although the European population is currently stable there are concerns for the long-term future of this species. The large concentrations of moulting birds in late July/August and in winter make the birds susceptible to oil pollution incidents. In addition there is hunting pressure both in Scandinavia and on their breeding grounds. There is a need for the important moulting areas and winter feeding sites to be protected from damaging pollution and intensive fishing.

DISTRIBUTION

In Britain mainly a winter visitor to the east coast – especially Scotland, Norfolk and north-east England. Smaller numbers are seen on migration on the south coast. Largest numbers concentrate in a few relatively small areas, especially off the Danish coast. In spring, most return to their breeding grounds in northern Europe or northern Russia. A very small number still breed in Turkey. Also found in North America and in northern Asia. All populations move to coastal areas farther south for the winter.

Goldeneye *Bucephala clangula*

INTERNATIONAL NAME   COMMON GOLDENEYE

IDENTIFICATION
42–50 cm. Smaller than Mallard. Medium-sized diving duck with rather large, domed head and small bill. Male appears black and white, with greenish-black head, and circular white patch in front of yellow eye. Back and tail are black and breast, underparts and flanks are white. White stripes along the sides of the back. In flight, male shows black wing-tips and large area of white on the inner wing. The smaller female is mottled grey, with chocolate-brown head, square white wing-patch and white collar. Immature female resembles adult but lacks a white collar. Young males develop their dark head during their first winter. Moults between July and September and is flightless for 3–4 weeks. Male moults 3 weeks before female. For a time he resembles female, but has a darker head. SEE ALSO: Smew p49, Goosander p51.

HABITS
Usually in small groups and sometimes forms larger flocks in winter. Adult males may be in a minority in these flocks. Frequently dives. In flight, wingbeats produce a loud, distinctive whistling sound. Courtship displays are frequent in winter as males throw their heads back and display their white breasts.

VOICE
Usually silent unless displaying. Loud 'zeee-ZEEE' and quieter 'rrrrrrrr' usually accompany displays of male.

BREEDING
Pairs start to form in the winter flocks and nesting starts in mid-April. Nest is in a hole in a tree several metres off the ground. There is little nesting material except for down from female's breast. At first male is territorial, but he deserts female during incubation. Female incubates 8–11 eggs for 29 days. At a day old the young jump from their nest and female takes them to a rearing area, often some way from the nest-site, where they swim and dive and feed themselves. They are independent at about 50 days and fly after 57 days.

MOVEMENTS AND MIGRATIONS
Males move away from their breeding sites while the females remain with eggs or young. In autumn additional birds arrive from Scandinavia and northern Europe and breeding birds move to the coast or lowland waters, returning to breeding sites in February or March. Oldest bird 16 years.

POPULATION
About 200 females usually nest. In winter the number of individuals increases to over 25,000 in the UK and 9,600 in Ireland.

CONSERVATION
First nested in Scotland in 1970. Since then birds have been attracted to specially designed nest boxes erected close to lakes and rivers. It appears there are limited nest-sites (holes) in Scottish forests, perhaps because of the lack of mature trees, or the lack of the Black Woodpecker nest-holes that are used by Goldeneyes elsewhere in Europe. More nest boxes could help this species.

female

male

male 1st-winter

female 1st-winter

female

male

HABITAT
Breeds close to lakes and rivers in forests. Outside breeding season it visits inland lakes and reservoirs and also the sea, especially in sheltered bays and estuaries.

FOOD
Feeds on a variety of food, some of which it finds by turning over stones under water, including freshwater mussels, insect larvae such as stonefly, caddis fly and mayfly, small fish and plant material such as pondweed. In marine habitats it feeds on shrimps, small crabs, blue mussels, cockles, periwinkles, small fish and plants.

DISTRIBUTION
Breeds in the highlands of Scotland and a few non-breeding birds summer farther south in England, Wales and Ireland. In Winter, it visits lakes, large rivers and sheltered coasts, and is most numerous in the north and west of Britain. Goldeneyes breed in northern Europe, across Asia and North America. All move south of their breeding areas for the winter.

Smew *Mergus albellus*

IDENTIFICATION

38–44 cm. A little larger than Teal. Small compact diving duck with a steep forehead and a delicate toothed bill (sawbill). Male is white with a black mask, black back, fine black lines on the sides of the breast and faintly barred grey flanks. Crest on the crown that is raised during display. Female is smaller, mottled grey, with a striking reddish-brown head and sharply contrasting white cheeks and throat. Both sexes have black-and-white wings, with male showing more white than female. Juvenile resembles female, but with less obvious white wing-patches.
SEE ALSO: Goldeneye p48, Goosander p51.

female

HABITS

Where common it is sociable and may be seen in small, and occasionally large, flocks. In Britain and Ireland generally arrives singly or in very small groups. Swims buoyantly and dives frequently and quickly. Tends to be rather shy and takes off easily from water, manoeuvring in limited space. In the air it has rapid wingbeats. Does not generally mix with other ducks except sometimes Goldeneyes, although fishing Smews often attract a following of gulls, eager to snatch a quick meal. Has hybridised with Goldeneye.

male

MOVEMENTS AND MIGRATIONS

Autumn migration begins in September when Smews start to leave their breeding grounds. They pass through the Baltic countries during October and November and the main arrival in the North Sea countries does not take place until December or January, following cold weather further east. Some will continue across the North Sea to Britain to escape freezing weather. Females and juveniles travel further south-west than the males, many of which remain in northern Germany. Return migration gets under way in March and it reaches its breeding grounds in May or early June.

POPULATION

The wintering population in Britain and Ireland is around 250 individuals.

CONSERVATION

The number of Smews wintering in Britain fell during the second half of the 20th century for no obvious reason. Little is known about this attractive duck on its breeding grounds and its pattern of migration has been little studied. Whatever the cause of the possible decline any conservation effort will need to focus on the breeding sites and protection during migration as well as at the major wintering areas.

male   female

VOICE

Generally silent. The only calls are those associated with courtship or when alarmed. The most frequent calls have been variously described as creaking, grunting and rattling.

HABITAT

In winter in Britain and Ireland it is found on inland lakes and reservoirs, and sometimes on quite small areas of water. It will also visit shallow, sheltered coastal waters and estuaries. Its breeding grounds are in northern wet forests.

FOOD

In winter, the chief food is fish, especially small salmon, trout, gudgeon, minnows, plaice and sand eels. In summer, it mainly feeds on insects and their larvae.

BREEDING

Does not breed in Britain or Ireland. Birds sometimes display in winter, before the pairs return north to nest. Nests in holes in trees, especially in the nest-holes made by Black Woodpeckers. Like most other male ducks, Smews abandon their mates during incubation.

DISTRIBUTION

In winter, small numbers of Smews visit Britain and Ireland, mostly on large lakes, reservoirs and estuaries in East Anglia and south-east England. Smews breed in small numbers in Norway and Sweden but most are in northern and eastern Siberia. In Europe a few spend the winter as far south as the Mediterranean. The largest winter concentrations are along the coast and large rivers of the Netherlands, Denmark and Germany.

Red-breasted Merganser *Mergus serrator*

IDENTIFICATION

52–58 cm. Size of Mallard. Long-bodied diving duck belonging to a group known as sawbills. Smaller and thinner necked than Goosander with wispy crest and long, very thin, red bill. Male has dark green head, white collar, grey and white body and spotted chestnut breast. Female grey with reddish-brown head that merges with pale throat and grey neck. Juvenile resembles dark female, but with shorter crest. In flight, male shows white patches on his wings while female has smaller wing-patches. Females have one dark bar across the wing-patches, adult males have two. Mergansers moult between mid-July and September, with male moulting a month earlier than female. During moult both sexes are flightless for a month. In eclipse, male resembles female, but retains much more white on wings.

SEE ALSO: Goosander p51, Great Crested Grebe p66, Smew p49.

HABITS

Swims low in the water and regularly dips its head below the surface when searching for food. Dives frequently. Often seen in small, single-sex groups, but larger flocks form in winter. In flight, looks long-bodied and long-necked.

VOICE

Usually silent, but makes rough croaking or rasping sounds, especially when displaying and nesting. Usually silent at other times.

HABITAT

Breeds near lakes, slow-flowing rivers and sheltered bays and inlets on the coast. Favours areas with woods or some other cover. Usually seen on the sea in winter, but occasionally on inland lakes and rivers.

FOOD

Feeds mainly on fish such as young salmon and trout, perch, grayling, herring, cod, plaice and sand eel. It also eats small crabs, shrimps, prawns and aquatic insects. Newly hatched ducklings feed mainly on insects.

BREEDING

In winter, makes bowing and stretching courtship displays as pairs begin to form. Nests are on ground close to water, usually among tree roots or bushes, or in a crevice in a bank, or between rocks. Nest is a depression with some local material and lined with down. Male deserts female during incubation and female alone incubates the 8–10 eggs for 31 days. The young are covered with down and leave the nest soon after hatching. They feed themselves and are cared for by female, but some broods join together. Female frequently leaves before young are full-grown and a single female, or 'auntie', often cares for a crèche of young. They are independent after 60–65 days and then leave the area, often feeding in shallow tidal waters.

MOVEMENTS AND MIGRATIONS

British breeding birds are mainly resident. Some Red-breasted Mergansers from further north migrate and reach Britain and Ireland in late autumn and remain until March, and some immature birds remain for longer. Lives 21 years or more.

POPULATION

More than 2,500 pairs breed in Britain and Ireland. Wintering individuals may total 10,000 in the UK and over 3,000 in Ireland. Breeding increased in Scotland between 1885 and 1930. In the 1950s it started colonising northern England, and first nested in Wales in 1953. Fewer pairs have nested inland in Scotland and Ireland in recent years, while in England and Wales the population, generally, has remained constant.

CONSERVATION

Its diet of fish has brought the species into conflict with angling and sport fishing. Many birds are killed, both legally and illegally, to protect fish stocks, although there is no evidence that it has seriously reduced fish populations. It is also vulnerable to oil pollution and to the siting of wind farms in shallow coastal waters.

male 1st-summer

male

female

male

female

female

DISTRIBUTION

Breeds in Scotland, especially western and central Scotland and the islands and the Highlands, north-west England, north-west Wales and the west of Ireland. It also breeds in northern Europe, Asia and North America.

Goosander *Mergus merganser*

IDENTIFICATION
58–66 cm. Larger than Mallard. Large-headed, long-bodied, thick-necked diving duck with slender, long, hook-tipped red sawbill. Male has white body, flushed pink in winter, black back and dark green head. Female has grey body, reddish-brown head (darker than female Red-breasted Merganser) with bulbous, drooping crest, an obvious white throat, brown neck and grey breast. Juvenile resembles dull female. In flight, male looks black and white with black-and-white wings, while female has smaller squarer white wing-patches. Moult takes place between July and September and both sexes are flightless for about a month. In eclipse, male resembles female, but with larger white wing-patches.
SEE ALSO: Red-breasted Merganser p50, Great Crested Grebe p66, Smew p49.

buildings. Nest is mainly made with duck down. Female alone incubates the 8–11 eggs for 30–32 days. Young leave the nest after a day or two and those in trees jump to the ground. Newly hatched ducklings are covered in down and feed themselves. Some ducklings will ride on their mother's back. Sometimes several families will join together. Juveniles are independent after 65 days and leave their nesting area.

MOVEMENTS AND MIGRATIONS
Apart from the moult migration to Norway by some males, British breeding Goosanders live year-round in Britain. Others from north-east Europe and Russia migrate and some reach Britain in November or December and remain for the winter. They return northwards in March. Goosanders can live to 14 years or more.

POPULATION
There are 2,600 pairs breeding in the UK and up to 50 in Ireland. This increases to over 16,000 in winter. First nested in Scotland in 1871 and by 1941 had spread to England. It has since continued its southward colonisation.

male

female

male 1st-summer

male

female

HABITS
Swims low in the water. When searching for food repeatedly dips its head under water as it swims and dives frequently. Outside the breeding season often in small groups; larger flocks form in winter. In flight, it looks very long-bodied and frequently flies close to the water. Sometimes a pair or group of Goosanders fish cooperatively by swimming in a line as they drive fish forward.

VOICE
Mostly silent. Some soft calls during courtship and occasional 'growls' when disturbed.

HABITAT
Breeds in upland and hilly areas with lakes and slower-flowing rivers, usually close to woods or forests. Outside the breeding season mostly seen on freshwater lakes, old gravel workings, reservoirs and, less frequently, estuaries and sheltered sea inlets.

FOOD
Feeds on a wide range of fish, including young salmon, young trout and eels. Also eats small mammals and insects. When small, Goosander ducklings feed mainly on insects.

BREEDING
Courtship starts in winter when males can sometimes be seen bowing and stretching. Nests in holes in trees, broken-off tree stumps and also in suitable nest boxes. Will also nest on ground, in rock crevices or under

CONSERVATION
Its diet of fish and its recent increase has brought it into conflict with angling and sport fishing interests. The numbers of licences allowing the killing of Goosanders to protect fish stocks have increased, although there is no evidence that the species has seriously reduced fish populations.

DISTRIBUTION
Breeds in Scotland, northern England, Wales and a few farther south. In winter, found on large inland lakes and reservoirs and some lowland rivers in Britain especially in the north. Rare in Ireland. The species breeds around the Arctic Circle – in Europe, Asia and North America – and some winter as far south as the Black and Adriatic Seas.

Ruddy Duck *Oxyura jamaicensis*

IDENTIFICATION

35–43 cm. Smaller than Mallard. Small, dumpy, thick-necked diving duck with large, broad bill and a stiff tail. Male has a bright blue bill, blackish head and neck, brilliant white cheeks, chestnut body and white under the tail. He also has two small 'tufts' on his crown, which are erected during display. From August and through the winter he becomes browner, with black speckles on the white cheeks and a grey bill. Female is dull brown with a blue-grey bill, dark brown cap, and paler cheeks that are crossed with a brown band. Juvenile is like female but paler with less obvious cheek-mark. Male starts to moult July–August, and female a month later. Both sexes are flightless for several weeks. During moult, male assumes his winter plumage.

HABITS

Its stiff tail often lies flat on the water or cocked up above its back. Swims buoyantly and dives quickly; sometimes it just sinks below the water without diving. Reluctant to fly, it takes off by running across the water. Remarkable courtship display includes one performance where the male traps air under his dense breast feathers and in a special air sac, then beats this protrusion rapidly with his bill. This has the effect of creating a hollow drumming sound and producing a series of bubbles.

male
male summer
female

female
juvenile

VOICE

Generally silent but during display there are non-vocal sounds associated with 'breast-beating' as well as various rattles, ticking noises and burps.

HABITAT

Breeds around shallow lowland lakes with abundant fringing water plants, and will occasionally visit coastal waters, especially in North America. In winter it often moves to larger water bodies.

FOOD

Feeds during the day on a wide variety of food, including insects and their larvae, water snails, worms and seeds of water plants.

BREEDING

Female builds a platform of reeds, rushes and leaves around vegetation growing in the water. She incubates 6–10 eggs for 25–26 days alone, although the male, and sometimes a second male, remains in the vicinity of the nest and the young family. Occasionally a female 'dumps' a clutch of eggs into the nest of another Ruddy Duck. The young swim and dive soon after hatching. Some females abandon their ducklings after about 3 weeks and rear a second brood. The young fly after 50–55 days.

MOVEMENTS AND MIGRATIONS

In North America the species is migratory. A large proportion of the British population gather on favoured reservoirs in south-west England to winter and most northern breeding sites are vacated. A few British breeding birds make long-distance movements into Europe, and have been seen in Spain, Morocco and as far north as Iceland and Norway.

POPULATION

The population is in rapid decline due to a government-backed eradication programme; it may soon cease to nest in Britain.

CONSERVATION

Became established in Britain after escaping from wildfowl collections. Its subsequent spread to the Continent, and especially to Spain, was a problem. In Spain there is a small, endangered population of the closely related White-headed Duck. Hybrids of these two species produce fertile young. Because of the attraction of the Ruddy Duck to the White-headed Duck, and because the Ruddy Duck is a dominating species, it was feared that it would exterminate White-headed Ducks in western Europe unless its expansion was curbed.

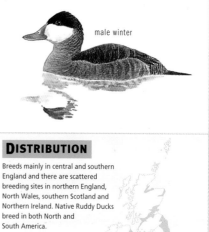
male winter

DISTRIBUTION

Breeds mainly in central and southern England and there are scattered breeding sites in northern England, North Wales, southern Scotland and Northern Ireland. Native Ruddy Ducks breed in both North and South America.

Quail *Coturnix coturnix*

INTERNATIONAL NAME   COMMON QUAIL

IDENTIFICATION

16–18 cm. Smaller than Grey Partridge. Tiny game bird with yellowish-brown streaked upperparts, paler underparts and yellow stripe through dark crown. Male has plain reddish-brown breast and variable head marks that consist of dark bands round throat and through eye. Female has a spotted breast and less distinctive head marks. Juvenile resembles female. It has a different wing shape from a young Grey Partridge: wings are broader at base but distinctly narrow at tip – like a snipe. Quails moult between June and September, but they sometimes suspend their moult and migrate with old and worn flight feathers and then resume their moult in their winter quarters. SEE ALSO: Grey Partridge p59.

HABITS

A very secretive bird that is reluctant to leave cover and is more easily heard than seen, even where numerous. If disturbed it often drops back into cover after a short, direct flight. On longer flights its action is freer and more like a Starling.

VOICE

'Whip, whip-whip' (said to sound like 'Wet my lips') is the most commonly heard call. It is repeated up to eight times at a burst. The call may be heard at any time of day or night in spring, but especially around dawn and dusk. Males also have a curious little growling noise – like a cat.

HABITAT

Lives in open country where there are few trees and bushes, especially grassland and large cereal fields where the vegetation is dense and usually dry, such as chalk downland. On migration appears in almost any habitat, but on wintering grounds lives in grasslands and other low vegetation.

male

FOOD

Seeds of plants, such as poppy, fat hen, hemp-nettle and dock, and also insects and their larvae including beetles, ants and grasshoppers.

BREEDING

In Britain begins breeding in May. Males arrive first and call to attract females. Nest is on the ground in dense cover. Female incubates 8–13 eggs for 17–21 days. Young feed themselves soon after hatching and are cared for by female. Males may mate with more than one female and generally do not stay with their families. Young flutter off the ground at about 11 days, but are not fully capable of flight until 19 days. They stay together for 30–50 days before becoming independent and can breed at 3 months old.

MOVEMENTS AND MIGRATIONS

The Quail is the only member of this family that is a migrant to Britain and Ireland. Arrives in late April and May and returns in late summer to central Africa, south of the Sahara Desert. Migrations are complex and not fully understood. In some years a second 'wave' appears later in the summer and breeds in

male

juvenile

August and September. The oldest known wild Quail survived for at least 8 years.

POPULATION

In recent years an average of 450 calling males has been heard in the UK, with fewer than 20 in Ireland.

CONSERVATION

The Quail is specially protected at all times. It is declining over most of Europe owing to agricultural intensification in its breeding areas, hunting during its migration and drought in its wintering grounds. Sympathetic farming in its major breeding areas is needed as is a reduction of hunting around the Mediterranean and in North Africa.

DISTRIBUTION

The birds can be heard from the south coast to Shetland. The highest numbers are usually in Dorset and Wiltshire, but also in East Anglia, the Welsh Marches and south-east Scotland. In some years can be found in scattered locations across England, Wales and southern Scotland – with a few reaching Ireland. In other years the species is found mainly in southern England. Also breeds in Europe, Asia and Africa.

Red Grouse *Lagopus lagopus*

INTERNATIONAL NAME WILLOW PTARMIGAN

IDENTIFICATION

37–42 cm. Larger than Grey Partridge. Plump with small head, slightly hook-tipped bill and short black tail. Often appears hunched up, but neck is extended when the bird is alert. Adult has reddish-brown, mottled plumage with white stripe on underwing. Male has a red wattle above its eye and redder plumage than female, although it becomes paler in summer. The legs and feet are covered in off-white feathers. Moult begins in June with the primary flight feathers. Most of the other feathers are moulted between August and November.

SEE ALSO: Black Grouse p56, Ptarmigan p55.

HABITS

Alternates between fast whirring wingbeats and glides on bowed, square-ended wings. Territorial when nesting, but forms family parties from July, and families may join together in 'packs' in autumn.

male

VOICE

Crowing call is a loud, gruff 'go-back, back, back'. When disturbed will often make a sharp 'kwok, kok-ok, ok'.

female

male

HABITAT

Requires extensive heather moorland away from trees, but also inhabits areas of upland bog, rough grazing and even some coastal heaths. In parts of Europe lives among dwarf willow and other low-growing plants.

FOOD

Feeds mainly on the ground, but also in trees in winter. Food is mostly vegetable matter, especially heather shoots but also eats invertebrates such as crane flies. Small young feed on insects, including click beetles, crane flies, sawfly larvae and other small flies as well as heather and other moorland plants.

BREEDING

Male displays by calling, puffing out his feathers, drooping his wings, holding his tail stiffly above his back and moving with a stiff walk. He also rises almost vertically and then, calling, drifts down on deeply curved wings. In late April or May 6–9 eggs are laid in a hollow that is scraped by the female amongst thick heather or soft rush. Female incubates, but male is never far away. Young are active soon after hatching and feed themselves. Flight feathers grow quickly and

they are capable of flight at 11–12 days, although they are not fully grown until 30–35 days and remain with their family for 6–8 weeks.

MOVEMENTS AND MIGRATIONS

Resident in Britain and Ireland. Males may travel no further than 1.5 km and females up to 8 km in their lifetime. Snowy weather can force it from the hills and down to nearby farmland to feed. In Russia it is partly migratory. The oldest wild bird survived over 7 years.

POPULATION

There are 155,000 breeding pairs in the UK with a further 1,000–2,500 in Ireland. During the 20th century the population fell, and there may be only half the number of Red Grouse there was in 1920.

CONSERVATION

Protected under the Game Acts, Red Grouse may be shot outside the close season. In some areas populations fluctuate in cycles caused by a parasitic worm, and by competition as densities increase, which is then followed by a movement away to areas with poorer feeding. Much of the heather moorland on which the Red Grouse is dependent has been lost through overgrazing and afforestation. Moorland management is labour-intensive and the highest densities of Red Grouse are found where gamekeeping occurs.

DISTRIBUTION

In Britain lives in the uplands of the north and west, with a smaller fragmented population in Ireland. Willow Grouse occurs across northern Europe, Asia and North America.

Ptarmigan *Lagopus mutus*

INTERNATIONAL NAME   ROCK PTARMIGAN

female summer

male summer

female autumn

male autumn

IDENTIFICATION

34–36 cm. A little smaller than Red Grouse but similar in shape. Beautifully camouflaged and rather dove-like on the ground. In summer, male is closely barred grey, brown and black with a white belly and wings. In autumn, dark parts become grey and in winter it becomes totally white except for tail and eye-patch, which remain black throughout the year. A red wattle above the eye is enlarged when breeding. Female has similar plumage to male, but generally browner in summer, darker in autumn and lacks a black eye-patch in winter. Juvenile has grey-brown tail and brown wings.
SEE ALSO: Red Grouse p54.

male summer

male winter

HABITS

More likely to be heard than seen, but often very tame. When disturbed, more inclined to crouch and rely on camouflage than to fly. During the breeding season usually seen in pairs. Family parties form in the summer and it then lives in flocks until March when territories are established with a songflight. Chooses hollows in snow for roosting at night, even in summer.

VOICE

Call of female is a high-pitched cooing. Male has series of loud and rapid clicks. Call is a harsh croak and rasping noises, and its alarm is a grating sound.

HABITAT

Found only in the Scottish Highlands, the Ptarmigan lives in the highest mountains, rarely below 1,000 m, where there is little vegetation, scattered boulders and bare rock pavements, and where the snow lies longest in summer. Often to be found among the boulders and scree that break up this barren landscape. Outside Scotland it is associated with Arctic or Alpine conditions, and in the far north it lives at lower altitudes, even at sea level.

FOOD

Plant shoots, berries, leaves and seeds, including heather, bilberry and crowberry. Uses its feathered feet to dig in the snow to find food. Young Ptarmigan eat insects.

BREEDING

Breeding starts in late April and May. Both birds make several shallow scrapes before one is lined with a small amount of vegetation. A bush or boulder usually shelters the nest. The female incubates 5–8 eggs for 21 days. The newly hatched young leave the nest quickly and are able to feed themselves. They are tended by both adults and brooded by female. Flight feathers grow quickly, young can take to the air at as early as 10 days and are independent after 10–12 weeks.

MOVEMENTS AND MIGRATIONS

The Ptarmigan is resident and seldom moves far from its breeding sites. Severe winter weather sometimes forces the birds down from the highest ground to the edge of forests, but it will also move to higher ridges where the wind blows the snow away.

POPULATION

There are around 10,000 pairs in Scotland, although an accurate estimate is difficult, owing to the inaccessible nature of the habitat. In the last hundred years the Ptarmigan has disappeared from hills in southern Scotland and the Western Isles, but the numbers breeding in the remaining areas appear stable.

CONSERVATION

Sheep have grazed out areas of bilberry and heather leaving the Ptarmigan with less food. Crow numbers have increased around tourist attractions and there is increased mortality from birds hitting wires associated with ski developments. Also, with global warming, the relatively few areas of montane habitat in Britain are predicted to become smaller.

DISTRIBUTION

In Britain found only in the highest mountains in the Highlands of Scotland. Found in Arctic regions of Europe, Asia and North America and also in the Alps and Pyrenees.

female winter

male winter

Black Grouse *Tetrao tetrix*

female

male

Identification

40–55 cm. Larger than Red Grouse. Male glossy black with a red wattle over the eye, white wing-bar and a black, lyre-shaped tail with white undertail feathers used in display. Female smaller, grey-brown with darker freckles and bars, pale wing-bar and a slightly forked tail. Male and female show white under the wings in flight. Females show a thin, pale wing-bar on the upperwing. Juvenile looks like a small and pale female. Black Grouse moult in late summer when males become duller for a short time.
SEE ALSO: Red Grouse p54, Capercaillie p57.

Habits

Feeds mainly on the ground. Communal displays at dawn and dusk at traditional sites known as 'leks' that are used throughout the year, but especially in spring and also autumn mornings. In a lek, males strut and posture to each other, trying to establish dominance, all the time making a far-carrying bubbling song and harsh, scolding sounds. Leks attract females and mating takes place nearby. In winter gathers in flocks during the day and roosts in groups at night, often in long heather. In some areas may roost in trees.

Voice

Mostly silent except around the lek. Male has loud pigeon-like 'cook-roo'. Female has loud cackle or 'kok, kok' flight call.

Habitat

Its home is the uplands, around the edges of moors and hill farms. In some areas found in young forestry plantations. Also found around the edges of ancient pine forests.

Food

Mainly vegetarian, feeding on bilberry, heather shoots, cotton grass buds, annual meadow plants, birch catkins and buds and juniper berries. Females eat flowering tips of cotton grass prior to egg laying. Will also feed on spilt oat grains and search for seeds in hay fields. In winter, often feeds in trees and shrubs, eating berries, leaves and shoots. Chicks eat insects for the first 2 weeks, especially sawfly larvae and caterpillars.

Breeding

Nesting begins in April. After displaying and mating, male has nothing to do with the family. Female makes shallow scrape on the ground that she lines with grass and moss. The 6–11 eggs are incubated for 25 days. Newly hatched young are mostly able to feed themselves while being tended by the female. If danger threatens, young can fly from about 10 days, but they are not fully independent for about 3 months.

Movements and migrations

In Britain highly resident, with birds spending entire lifetimes in just 1 or 2 square kilometres. Elsewhere, some Black Grouse move considerable distances. This appears to be triggered by population increases rather than cold weather. Oldest 12 years.

male
displaying

Population

Estimated to be about 5,000 displaying males each spring. There has been a huge decline in the number of Black Grouse over the last 100 years.

Conservation

Black Grouse have declined throughout Europe, due to ploughing or draining traditional meadows, over-grazing by sheep and deer and loss of arable farming. Wire fences, erected to keep deer out of plantations, have caused casualties and increasing numbers of crows and foxes may be adding to the decline. Removing or marking fences, reducing numbers of deer and sheep, improving forest management and more sympathetic farm practices may help them to recover.

female

male

DISTRIBUTION

Lives in the uplands of the north and west: in Wales, the north Pennines and in Scotland. The species is also found from the Arctic to the Alps and east across Asia.

Capercaillie *Tetrao urogallus*

INTERNATIONAL NAME WESTERN CAPERCAILLIE

IDENTIFICATION

60–87 cm. A huge grouse with broad wings and tail. Male is turkey-like, glossy black with dark brown wings, white marks on the belly and under the tail and bold white shoulder-patches. Red wattle over the eye and pale bill. Long, broad tail raised and fanned when bird is displaying to intruders, including humans. Female is smaller, brown, heavily barred black, with a reddish patch on the breast and paler underparts. Juvenile resembles female.
SEE ALSO: Black Grouse p56.

HABITS

Seen singly and in groups. Despite its size this can be an elusive species, often sitting quietly in pine trees or on the forest floor. Males gather at dawn in spring and 'lek' to attract females. They are aggressive towards rival males and fighting is fairly common. Many females may be attracted to a lek at which larger males are generally dominant and mate with the most females. Flight is like that of other game birds, a succession of rapid flaps followed by a glide on downcurved wings. The long neck is stretched outwards in flight.

VOICE

At the lek the males have an amazing song that is a series of double 'clicks' and ends in a loud 'pop', likened to a champagne cork coming out of the bottle!

HABITAT

Found in the remaining tracts of ancient Caledonian pine forest and a few other Scottish forests that are well managed, where there are mature trees and open clearings resulting in the pine regenerating naturally and a rich and varied ground cover. In other parts of Europe it sometimes lives in deciduous woodland.

FOOD

Mainly vegetarian. Usually feeds on the ground, but also flies into trees to find food, especially in winter. Eats needles, buds and small cones from the Scots pine, other conifers and from juniper. Also eats berries from plants such as bilberry. Chicks feed on a large number of insects when small.

BREEDING

Makes a shallow scrape on the ground, lined with grass and pine needles, usually amongst dense cover and often at the foot of a tree. Mating takes place at the 'lek' and males have nothing further to do with the family. Female incubates 7–11 eggs for 25 days. The young quickly leave the nest and are able to feed themselves. They are capable of flight to escape danger from 2–3 weeks, although they are not fully grown for 2–3 months, when they also become independent of their mother.

MOVEMENTS AND MIGRATIONS

Not a migrant in Britain, although some young birds may wander from their breeding sites. The oldest known wild bird lived for more than 9 years.

POPULATION

The population has declined by 80% in 25 years and is now around 2,000 birds, although that decline may have halted due to better forestry management.

CONSERVATION

Extinct in Britain and Ireland by 1785, the Capercaillie was reintroduced into Scotland in the 19th century. For a time it was fairly widespread, but since 1970 its range has contracted. It now survives only in well-managed woodlands where there is reduced grazing from deer and a mixture of old and young Scots pine. It suffers from collisions with deer fences and predation by foxes and crows that may be increasing on traditional shooting estates. Protected under the Game Acts, and disturbing birds at their leks is also illegal.

female

male

male

female

Hilary Burn

DISTRIBUTION

In Britain found only in the Highlands of Scotland, particularly in the eastern Highlands. In Europe breeds in northern and eastern forests and in mountain ranges farther south. Also found in Russia.

Red-legged Partridge *Alectoris rufa*

IDENTIFICATION
32–34 cm. Slightly larger than Grey Partridge and smaller than Pheasant. This attractive game bird has plain grey-brown upperparts, boldly striped black, white and chestnut flanks and a white chin and throat bordered with black, with black spotting spreading like a necklace on the bluish breast. Feet and bill are red. Female is smaller than male. Juvenile lacks bold head markings of the adult but has more stripes on face and spots on neck than the Grey Partridge. It flies with a whirr of wings followed by a glide on downcurved wings, when the red tail is usually obvious.
SEE ALSO: Quail p53, Grey Partridge p59.

HABITS
Often more obvious than the Grey Partridge. More active during the day and tends to walk away or scatter when disturbed. Males will frequently perch on vantage points in their territories, such as straw bales, posts or even a barn roof. Like the Grey Partridge, generally seen in groups or 'coveys'. Some of these coveys can be quite large – up to 40 or more – where the species is common.

juvenile

VOICE
Can be quite noisy, with the adults giving a loud chuffing 'chuck-chukka-chuff'.

HABITAT
The Red-legged Partridge does well on large modern open fields, especially on sandy or light soils in eastern Britain and may sometimes be found in open woodland near to fields, or on newly dug sand and gravel workings.

FOOD
It feeds on seeds, leaves and roots of a wide variety of plants that grow in and around agricultural land, and also larger seeds such as beech mast. A few insects are also eaten, especially by chicks.

BREEDING
The male makes several shallow scrapes on the ground. In late April or May, the female chooses one and lays 10–16 eggs. Many pairs produce a second clutch that is incubated simultaneously by the male. Incubation lasts for about 23 days. Young are able to fly from danger after 10 days, but are not fully grown until 50–60 days. If one clutch is laid both parents tend the family and if there are two clutches each parent leads their own brood, although eventually families will join together to form coveys. The young stay with their family throughout their first winter.

MOVEMENTS AND MIGRATIONS
The British population is resident. Most individuals seldom move more than a few kilometres from where they hatched. The oldest known wild bird survived for more than 6 years.

POPULATION
There are estimated to be 72,000–200,000 occupied territories in the UK and a few birds in Ireland. But the picture is confused by the large number that are reared and released before each shooting season; at this time there may be 1.5 million individuals.

CONSERVATION
Deliberately introduced into Britain as a game bird in 1673 and the species is still commonly reared in captivity and released for shooting. Since the 1930s it has increased as the Grey Partridge has declined, although there is no evidence that the Red-leg has driven out the Grey. Indeed, where both species are numerous, it is the Grey that is dominant. The Red-legged Partridge is protected under the Game Acts, and may be shot outside the close season.

DISTRIBUTION
It is mainly found in eastern England but also breeds farther west, with small numbers in Scotland, Wales and a very few in Ireland. Its traditional home is southern France, the Iberian Peninsula, northern Italy and some Mediterranean islands.

Grey Partridge *Perdix perdix*

IDENTIFICATION

29–31 cm. Smaller than Pheasant. Plump with small head and short legs. Well camouflaged, with brown and grey streaked plumage, chestnut bars on its flanks and grey breast. Face is orange and it has dark brown horseshoe mark on its belly. Female smaller with less obvious horseshoe mark. In flight, shows a reddish tail. Juvenile lacks the marks of the adult and is streaked like a young Pheasant. Moults between June and October, with the female beginning when the eggs hatch. Second, partial moult before breeding.

SEE ALSO: Red-legged Partridge p58, Quail p53, Pheasant p60.

HABITS

For most of the year 6–15 individuals form flocks called 'coveys' and pairs form in late winter. Most active at dawn and dusk. When feeding or resting appears hunched up. If disturbed it is reluctant to fly and will often crouch and rely on camouflage for protection. In flight the wingbeats are rapid, followed by a glide on bowed wings, but it seldom flies far.

The young leave the nest quickly and mostly feed themselves. After about 15 days they can fly to escape danger, but they are not fully grown until about 100 days. Juveniles stay with their parents for their first winter.

MOVEMENTS AND MIGRATIONS

Resident, seldom moves more than a few kilometres from where it hatched. In parts of eastern Europe some are migratory. Oldest survived for over 5 years.

POPULATION

During the last 25 years the population has fallen by over 80% and the species is also declining in other parts of Europe. There are now 70,000–75,000 pairs in the UK and fewer than 20 in Ireland.

CONSERVATION

Protected under the Game Acts, and may be shot outside the close season. Once it was widespread in Britain, but the decline during the 20th century has been remarkable. The cause is linked to changes in farm management. Loss of wide field margins and

male

female

male

juvenile

VOICE

Grating 'kerr-ick' given during day and night and especially around dawn and dusk. 'Kip-ip-ip' flight call if disturbed.

HABITAT

A bird of open grassland that has adapted to live on farmland. Prefers open areas of low grass with dense cover for nesting and dry areas for dust bathing. Most numerous where there is both pasture and cereal fields with thick hedges. Benefits from uncultivated areas, wide (unsprayed) field margins and stubble fields in winter. Mostly in lowland areas but also on hill farms in the Pennines and Scotland.

FOOD

Mainly leaves and seeds of plants such as knotgrass, and chickweed. Also insects, especially caterpillars and other larvae. Young Grey Partridges feed on a range of invertebrates including aphids, sawflies, ant larvae, weevils and beetles.

BREEDING

Nest is on ground, under cover of a thick hedge or among dense vegetation. Female makes shallow depression lined with grass and leaves. Occasionally two females use the same nest. An individual will lay 13–16 (sometimes up to 29) eggs in late April or May. Incubation is by female and lasts for about 24 days.

sheltering hedgerows giving cover for nests, autumn cereal sowing that eliminates winter stubble, insecticides that reduce food and herbicides that control weeds are all affecting its survival. The increase in ground predators such as foxes probably exacerbates the problem. Possible solutions include support for farmers who make special efforts to retain partridges, including leaving wider field margins unsprayed and improving hedgerow management.

DISTRIBUTION

Breeds in lowland Britain and at only a few sites in Ireland. Most numerous in central and eastern England and south-east Scotland. Also found in central and southern Europe, parts of Russia and has been introduced into North America.

Pheasant *Phasianus colchicus*

INTERNATIONAL NAME COMMON PHEASANT

IDENTIFICATION
53–89 cm. This large game bird has a rather long neck, small head and long tail. Male is brilliantly coloured, with an iridescent, copper-coloured body marked with dark scallops on the breast and flanks, metallic green head and neck, red face and small ear-tufts. The very long ginger tail is crossed with dark bars. Interbreeding of different races has produced a variety of plumage colours. Some have an obvious white neck-ring, others are dark bottle green. Smaller female is brownish-yellow with dark flecks on upperparts and flanks and long tail. Juvenile similar to female with a less regular patterned plumage and a shorter tail. Pheasants start their annual moult in June and males appear rather scruffy for about 3 months.
SEE ALSO: Golden Pheasant p61.

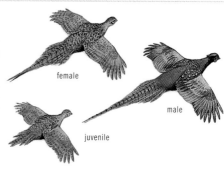

female

male

juvenile

female

male

HABITS
At home on the ground, but often roosts in trees or bushes at night. If disturbed either runs from danger or sits tight before suddenly bursting out of cover and rising steeply with a whirr of wings. In flight, beats its wings rapidly and then glides with wings bowed. In places where it is not hunted may become rather tame, but elsewhere skulking and secretive. Pheasants spend much of year in flocks or small groups.

VOICE
Most usual crowing call is a far-carrying, resonant 'kor-ork, -ok- ok' often accompanied by energetic and noisy flapping of wings. This call is often heard at dusk and in response to sudden loud noises such as gunshots or thunder.

HABITAT
Found in woodland edges, copses, close to thick hedges and also in more open country where there are reed-filled ditches.

FOOD
Takes a wide variety of foods including grain and other seeds such as acorns, and also berries and fruits of blackberry, hawthorn and many other shrubs. Eats leaves and roots of daisies and other related plants, and insects in summer, especially ants and beetles.

BREEDING
A cock Pheasant often has a harem of two or more females. Usual site for a nest is on the ground amongst vegetation, but some are off the ground on, for example, a straw bale. The 10–14 eggs are laid between March and June and incubated by the female. Male has little to do with the young, which hatch after 23–28 days. Chicks are brooded by the female and can feed themselves. By 12 days they can lift off the ground if danger threatens, but they are not fully independent until 70–80 days old.

MOVEMENTS AND MIGRATIONS
Resident in Britain and Ireland and non-migratory throughout its range. Wild Pheasants may live for more than 7 years.

POPULATION
Difficult to estimate the total population owing to the large number released each year for shooting.

There may be 1.8–1.9 million breeding females in the UK and up to 100,000 in Ireland.

CONSERVATION
Protected under the Game Acts, and may be shot outside the close season. Birds are reared by keepers and released for shooting. Grain put out for pheasants often benefits wild birds, and the retention of woodland for pheasant shooting also benefits other species. Not a native species to western Europe, it was introduced to Britain by the Normans, and was introduced into Scotland and Ireland in the 16th century.

DISTRIBUTION

Found in suitable habitat throughout Britain and Ireland, except the north-west of Scotland. Truly wild Pheasants breed in south-east Russia and Asia. They have been introduced to Europe, North America and New Zealand.

Golden Pheasant *Chrysolophus pictus*

male

female

IDENTIFICATION
60–115 cm. Smaller than a Pheasant but with a much longer tail. The exotic-looking male has orange-red underparts, golden-yellow head, dark green upperparts and yellow and black barred feathers on the back of the neck that can be fanned out in display. The female is only a little smaller than the male, but with a much shorter tail. She is yellow-brown with fine black barring. The juvenile is similar to the female, but the barring is less regular. The attractive body feathers are moulted between May and September.
SEE ALSO: Pheasant p60.

HABITS
This is a very secretive species that is hard to observe in the wild. It is generally reluctant to fly, and even when avoiding a predator it is likely to run swiftly through the dense vegetation. When not nesting this pheasant is usually seen singly or in groups of two or three. Males are solitary for most of the year, but come together to call and display to each other and set up new territories during February. Rival males sometimes fight fiercely. At night it roosts in trees.

VOICE
This species is seldom heard except for a crowing call during the breeding season that is a loud and metallic 'chak' or 'cha-chak'.

HABITAT
In Britain it lives all the year in dense, dark woodland with bare ground, especially young forestry plantations over about 10 years old.

FOOD
Very little is known about its food requirements. In its native China it has been reported feeding on leaves, buds, insects and spiders.

BREEDING
The nest is a shallow depression on the ground. The clutch of 5–12 eggs is laid in April or May and incubated by only the female for about 23 days, apparently without leaving the nest. The young are able to feed themselves and are tended by the female. The chicks can flutter off the ground at about 12–14 days but it is not known when they become fully independent.

MOVEMENTS AND MIGRATIONS
The small British population makes no local movements or migrations.

POPULATION
This is a difficult species to survey. It is thought that there are about 100 pairs in Britain, but there are recent reports of local declines, and the number may now be smaller.

CONSERVATION
This exotic species was introduced to parts of England and Scotland from China more than 100 years ago and is still commonly kept in collections. The recent decline in feral populations may be due to increasing ground predators such as foxes. The law prohibits further introductions of this species into the wild.

DISTRIBUTION
In Britain it is found in a few widely dispersed locations in lowland areas, including the Brecklands of East Anglia. The natural home of this species is the mountains of central China.

Black-throated Diver *Gavia arctica*

IDENTIFICATION

58–73 cm. Larger than Mallard. Larger, with thicker neck than Red-throated Diver, and heavier, straighter bill. Head appears rounded, or with steep forehead. In summer, body is dark with a block of white marks on the back. The head is grey with a black throat, black-and-white stripes on side of the neck and a small single white 'chin strap' mark. On the water in winter it has contrasting dark and white plumage, prominent white thigh patches and less white on the sides of neck and cheeks than the Red-throated. The dark cap comes down to level of eye and the bill looks pale. First-winter birds are less clearly marked. Breeding plumage is moulted in September or December and flight feathers are moulted in spring.
SEE ALSO: Red-throated Diver p64, Great Northern Diver p63, Cormorant p76.

HABITS

Swims low in the water. Bill usually held horizontal but may sometimes point slightly upwards, resembling Red-throated. Can look slim and elegant or chunky, depending on how the neck is held. Like other divers it frequently rolls on its side to preen its belly feathers. In flight, looks black and white and heavier than Red-throated, with the neck held straighter and wings more central on the body. More solitary than Red-throated but small flocks form outside the breeding season and groups often gather at fishing sites in the early morning.

VOICE

Mostly silent except on breeding grounds where it has a loud, drawn-out wail.

HABITAT

Mostly breeds on large inland lakes with small islands and will fly to other lakes where food is plentiful. After breeding, it moves to sheltered bays and coastal waters, occasionally visiting inland lakes and reservoirs in winter.

FOOD

Dives to chase prey under water. Feeds mainly on fish, such as Arctic charr, small brown trout, herring, sprats, sand eels, minnows and also insects and crustaceans.

BREEDING

Pairs usually remain faithful for life. Male builds the nest of moss and water weed with help from the female, in shallow water close to the shore, often on a small island. Female incubates the usual clutch of 2 eggs for 28–30 days with help from the male. Young leave the nest within 24 hours and are fed by their parents. Chicks are often left alone by parents and are aggressive to each other. They fly after about 60 days.

MOVEMENTS AND MIGRATIONS

Most birds move to the coast after breeding. Other Black-throated Divers from northern Europe are thought to arrive around British and Irish coasts in autumn and winter. Larger numbers appear if the Baltic wintering areas start to freeze over. These divers can live for 27 years.

POPULATION

About 200 pairs breed in Scotland, a slight increase since the 1980s. In winter, the number increases to around 700 individuals around the coasts of the UK.

CONSERVATION

Specially protected. Breeding birds are affected by changes in water level, introductions of predatory fish like pike which compete for food, development of fish farms and disturbance at nest-sites. At sea it is threatened by pollution, and changing fish populations. Some use artificial floating islands specially developed to help nesting birds overcome the problem of changing water levels. In future the siting of fish farms and hydroelectric schemes away from sensitive conservation areas, effective fisheries conservation and more care by birdwatchers, anglers and tourists will all help the small breeding population.

summer

winter

summer

winter

juvenile

DISTRIBUTION

In Britain, this species breeds only in north-west Scotland. It also breeds on the Arctic tundra in Europe, Russia and North America. Northern populations move south in autumn, with some birds reaching the Mediterranean.

Great Northern Diver *Gavia immer*

INTERNATIONAL NAME COMMON LOON (N. AMERICA)

IDENTIFICATION

70–90 cm. Substantially larger than a Mallard. Large, heavy-looking diver with a dagger-like bill, a large head, a thick neck and a steep forehead. In summer, it is black and white with chequered back, black head and neck that can appear iridescent green, and a white, barred collar. In winter, it is dark grey and white. Dark crown descends below the eye and is broken by a pale eye-ring. Head and neck generally darker than the back, with a suggestion of a dark half-collar at the base of the neck. Black and white areas are less clear-cut than on Black-throated. First-winter birds have brown backs barred with paler feather edges. This diver moults its black-and-white feathers after breeding and has a full moult in late winter when it becomes flightless.
SEE ALSO: Red-throated Diver p64, Black-throated Diver p62, Cormorant p76.

HABITS

Swims low in the water and dives smoothly and powerfully. Often searches for food with head partially submerged. If alarmed, will swim with only its head and neck above water. Frequently preens underparts while rolling on its side.

Needs large areas of water to launch into the air. In flight, it is heavy-looking with slower, more shallow wingbeats than other divers and large feet that project behind tail. Usually solitary in winter, but small groups may form, especially in the north. Dives regularly for a minute or more.

VOICE

It makes a variety of eerie yodelling calls in the breeding areas, but is mostly silent at other times.

HABITAT

In winter, many Great Northerns visit coastal waters and only a few arrive on large inland lakes and reservoirs. On the sea this species tends to feed further from the shore than Red- and Black-throated Divers. Breeding areas (not in Britain or Ireland) are around medium or large lakes, where there are plenty of fish.

FOOD

Mainly fish, especially haddock, herring and sand eel. Also insects and their larvae, and crustaceans, including crabs and shellfish.

BREEDING

Usually lays 2 eggs in a nest made of vegetation and built close to water's edge. The young frequently ride on the parents' backs when small. They are able to breed after 2 years.

MOVEMENTS AND MIGRATIONS

Some young migrate with their parents. Migrants start to arrive on the Scottish coast in August and more follow during autumn and a few winter as far south as the Mediterranean. Most leave Britain and Ireland by early May and return to their northern breeding grounds.

POPULATION

Despite frequent sightings in summer in western Scotland, and suspicion that some may have nested, this species is known only to have nested here successfully on one occasion – in 1970 when two adults were seen with two young. The following year a single bird paired with a Black-throated Diver and produced one hybrid young. In summer small numbers remain around the coasts of Scotland and Ireland. Winter numbers increase to almost 3,000 individuals in the UK (mostly in Scotland) and 1,400 in Ireland.

summer

1st winter

winter

CONSERVATION

Specially protected. The main threats are from oil pollution in winter, declining fish stocks and fishing nets that trap and kill feeding birds. Tight controls and enforcement of measures to reduce oil pollution, both deliberate and accidental, and the sympathetic management of inshore fisheries will help protect this species.

DISTRIBUTION

Most Great Northern Divers seen in Britain and Ireland in winter come from Iceland, but some are from Greenland or Arctic Canada.
A few non-breeding birds spend the summer around the coast of north-west Scotland and on a few large lakes in Scotland and Ireland.

summer   winter

Red-throated Diver *Gavia stellata*

INTERNATIONAL NAME RED-THROATED LOON (N. AMERICA)

IDENTIFICATION

53–69 cm. Size of Mallard. More rounded head and slimmer neck than other divers and rather delicate, up-swept bill. In summer, adult has grey body, velvety grey head, delicate streaks on hindneck and a dull red throat patch that appears dark in poor light. In winter, it is grey-brown and white, with fine white spots on its back. Neck is white at the front and sides and dark at the back. The white on the face extends around the dark eye. Immatures look browner and less well marked. Adult plumage is moulted after breeding, when it becomes flightless. Between February and April it moults into breeding plumage.
SEE ALSO: Black-throated Diver p62, Great Northern Diver p63, Cormorant p76.

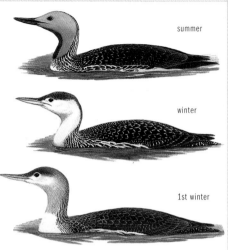

summer

winter

1st winter

HABITS

Swims low in the water with bill pointing slightly upwards. Often remains partly submerged when alarmed. Frequently rolls on its side in the water as it preens its white belly. In flight, looks thin-necked and hump-backed, and head and neck move up and down. Wingbeats rapid, with wings lifted higher above back than other divers. Small flocks, sometimes of 100 or more, gather on the sea in winter. Flies high when commuting between breeding pools and feeding areas. Takes off easily and, when landing, planes down and strikes the water with considerable force. It performs noisy displays in the air during the breeding season.

VOICE

Usually silent. At breeding sites it can be noisy, giving excited crescendo of calls like a high-pitched, wailing 'ya-roo, ya-roo, ya-roo'.

HABITAT

Breeds around shallow pools (lochans) on moors and bogs. Occasionally nests around larger lakes (lochs) and flies to coastal waters or larger water bodies to feed. Outside the breeding season it is found around the coast, especially in shallow, sandy bays, and is only rarely seen on inland waters.

FOOD

It feeds mainly on marine fish such as cod, herring, sand eel and sprat but also takes some freshwater fish including small salmon, trout and roach. Also eats some crustaceans and insects.

BREEDING

The nest is a heap of moss or aquatic vegetation built close to water's edge or in water among vegetation. The 1 or 2 eggs are spotted with dark marks and incubated mostly by female for 26–29 days. The young leave the nest within 24 hours and are fed by their parents. They fly after about 50 days. They first breed at 2–3 years.

MOVEMENTS AND MIGRATIONS

Breeding birds move to the coast in autumn. Some travel to the French coast, and may reach the Mediterranean in cold winters. Migrants from Europe and Iceland winter around British and Irish coasts, and there are noticeable movements in spring and autumn. At least one survived for 23 years.

POPULATION

About 1,250 pairs breed in the UK and fewer than 10 in Ireland. Recent aerial surveys show the winter population to be over 17,000 individuals. The species increased after persecution ceased during the 19th century, with the largest expansion taking place on Shetland, which now has more than 30% of the UK population

CONSERVATION

Threatened by oil spills, being caught in fishing nets, changes in fish populations, drainage of moorland breeding sites, and disturbance when breeding. Some young are eaten by otters. Re-routing tankers away from sensitive wintering areas, avoiding tree planting close to lochans, fisheries conservation and more care by birdwatchers and tourists will all help. Floating islands created to help breeding Black-throated Divers have also benefited Red-throats.

DISTRIBUTION

In Britain, breeds only in north-west Scotland, especially in Orkney and Shetland, with a few in Ireland. It winters all round the coast. Also found in northern Europe, Russia and North America.

summer

winter

Little Grebe *Tachybaptus ruficollis*

IDENTIFICATION
25–29 cm. Smaller than a Moorhen. It is a small, dumpy bird, with a pale 'powder-puff' below its tail. Head is rounded, and the neck shorter than other grebes. The small bill has pale patches at its base that become yellow in summer. Breeding plumage is dark brown with chestnut neck and cheeks. Winter plumage is brown with darker crown and paler cheeks and neck. Juvenile resembles adult in winter, but has two short dark stripes behind eye, and first-winter birds are paler and sandier than an adult. In flight the wings look plain. Complete moult after the breeding season. Flight feathers are moulted simultaneously, resulting in a flightless period of 3–4 weeks.
SEE ALSO: Black-necked Grebe p69, Slavonian Grebe p68.

HABITS
Very secretive and more likely to dive than to fly. Sometimes scuttles across the water. Dives frequently and hunts food under water. If disturbed it will dive and emerge out of sight among waterside vegetation. If seriously alarmed, remains submerged with only its head above water. Frequently swims with undertail feathers fluffed up. Usually solitary outside breeding season, but small groups may form in sheltered waters and sometimes roost together. A small territory is defended fiercely. These territories may be occupied all year, but some only for the breeding season and others only in winter.

summer

VOICE
The most common call is a loud trilling, or whinny, that is used during courtship or territorial disputes. Sometimes given by a pair of birds as a duet

HABITAT
Breeds on lakes or slow-flowing rivers and canals. Some of the lakes are small and may be either in open or in wooded areas. On large lakes it prefers sheltered bays. In autumn and winter, many move to larger lakes and sheltered coasts.

FOOD
Mainly feeds on insects and their larvae, water snails and small fish such as minnows and young carp.

BREEDING
Male and female build a floating nest of water weed among plants growing in shallow water, or attach it to branches that are touching the water. The 4–6 eggs are white when laid, but become brown through staining. Both sexes incubate and the eggs hatch after 20 days. The young are covered with down and quickly leave the nest. They may ride on the adults' back or, more often, return to the nest platform to rest safely. Both parents feed them. They are also given feathers to eat that might help in the formation of pellets. They become independent at 30–40 days and fly at about 45 days. 2–3 broods each year

MOVEMENTS AND MIGRATIONS
Mainly resident, but in winter often leaves smaller lakes and congregates on larger waters. Birds breeding in the north of Britain and Ireland tend to move south in autumn – a few may reach France. Little Grebes from Europe migrate south-west and some arrive in Britain. The oldest known individual survived for 13 years.

POPULATION
6,000–12,000 pairs breed in the UK and 1,000–2,500 in Ireland. In winter, numbers usually increase, and more arrive in cold weather. The population appears stable. Although it has disappeared from some rivers and canals, it has also spread into new areas.

CONSERVATION
Little Grebes breed more successfully on lakes than on rivers because the changes of water level are less acute. Sympathetic management of lowland rivers, monitoring and safeguarding water quality, reducing the feral mink population, and preventing disturbance by anglers and powerboats would help this species.

winter

juvenile

DISTRIBUTION
Found in most parts of Britain and Ireland. It is also widespread in Europe, parts of the Middle East, Asia and central and southern Africa.

Great Crested Grebe *Podiceps cristatus*

IDENTIFICATION

46–51 cm. Smaller than Mallard. Long white neck and dagger-like bill. In summer, chestnut and black frill around head. Blackish head plumes raised during courtship. In winter, it is grey and white with a dark back and black crown, and a black line from the bill to the eye. Small young are striped black and white like 'humbugs'. Juveniles have dark stripes across their faces. A complete moult follows the breeding season. Flight feathers are moulted simultaneously and birds become flightless for 3–4 weeks.
SEE ALSO: Red-necked Grebe p67, Red-throated Diver p64.

juvenile riding on parent

HABITS

In flight, long neck is extended, feet trail and large white patches on front and back of wings are visible. If disturbed, will usually dive rather than fly. Often swims with head and neck resting on back, revealing very obvious white breast. Dives frequently to hunt for food. Elaborate courtship displays involve a pair facing each other and head shaking. Courting pairs also make synchronised dives followed by the pair emerging holding water weed and engaging in a short 'weed-dance' as they rise out of the water. Small young regularly ride on their parents' backs to protect them from predators such as pike. The young of first broods sometimes help to rear small young of second broods.

BREEDING

Pairs often form in winter. The nest is built among vegetation or branches growing in the water, or sometimes out in the open. The nest is often a floating heap of water weed and other plants. Both adults build the nest and take turns to incubate the 2–6 eggs. Eggs are covered when the adults leave the nest as a defence against crows and other predators. Incubation takes 28 days and begins with the first egg, so that the young hatch over a period of several days. Both adults feed the young. The diet includes feathers that may help in the formation of pellets. The brood is split between the parents and the two groups live largely independently. After about 8 weeks the young are able to feed themselves, but the parents may continue to feed them for a further 15–23 weeks. They fly at about 10–11 weeks. Often two broods in the south.

MOVEMENTS AND MIGRATIONS

Many move to large lakes, reservoirs and the sea in autumn. Northern populations are migratory and British birds are joined by migrants from north-west Europe for the winter. Oldest 19 years.

POPULATION

Around 9,400 adults in the UK and up to 2,500 in Ireland. Almost exterminated in the British Isles in the 19th century, it made a remarkable recovery during the 20th century and the population is now considered stable.

CONSERVATION

Once hunted for 'grebe-fur', the fine breast feathers used in the Victorian fashion industry. Helped by the construction of reservoirs and flooded gravel pits. The main threats are now fluctuating water levels and disturbance by water sports.

winter

summer

winter

juvenile

VOICE

Occasional growling 'gorr, gorr', especially during courtship and when nesting.

HABITAT

Breeds on large, shallow inland lakes with vegetation around the margins. Sometimes nests on slow-flowing rivers. In winter, many move to large lakes and reservoirs; also seen on the sea. Readily adopts flooded gravel workings and ornamental lakes in urban areas.

FOOD

Feeds mainly on fish, including roach, rudd, minnows and eels. Also takes aquatic insect larvae and small amphibians.

DISTRIBUTION

Found in lowland Britain and Ireland. Also breeds in Europe, the Middle East and Asia. There are other populations in Africa and Australia.

Red-necked Grebe *Podiceps grisegena*

IDENTIFICATION
40–50 cm. Smaller than Mallard. This grebe has a thick neck and a stout, dark bill with a yellow base. It is not as elegant as a Great Crested Grebe, with a wedge-shaped, sometimes rounded head, making it look more front-heavy. In summer, it has whitish cheeks and reddish-brown neck and breast. Its crown is black and its body dark brown. Juveniles have dark marks across their pale faces and paler chestnut on the neck. In winter, it is duller with dusky sides to the face and neck, a white collar and a white breast. The black cap comes down to the level of the eye. Sides of body can look whiter than Great Crested Grebe's body. It moults from its breeding plumage between July and September.

SEE ALSO: Great Crested Grebe p66, Black-necked Grebe p69, Slavonian Grebe p68.

HABITS
It flies strongly with rapid wingbeats. Two white wing-patches show in flight, but a much smaller area of white on the forewing than on Great Crested. When swimming it looks rather buoyant – more like the smaller grebes – and it jump-dives very energetically. Usually seen singly or in pairs. Catches fish under water. Most dives last less than 30 seconds.

winter

BREEDING
It sometimes associates with gulls when breeding. The nest-site is usually among reeds or other plants growing in the water. The nest is a floating heap of aquatic vegetation built by both male and female. The 4 or 5 eggs are incubated for 20–23 days. The brood is split between the adults and the young fly at about 72 days.

MOVEMENTS AND MIGRATIONS
Leaves its breeding sites after nesting and moves to coastal waters or to large inland lakes. Birds from north-east Europe move south or west in late summer. Many arrive in the North Sea and some winter along British coasts between October and March. More arrive in Britain if their northern European wintering areas become iced over.

POPULATION
Fewer than 20 individuals spend the summer in Britain each year. A pair nested successfully for the first time in Scotland in 2001. In winter, the population grows to around 200 individuals, with more in cold winters.

CONSERVATION
Potential breeding sites are kept secret and some birds that were thought to be nesting have been given special protection. In winter there is some danger from fishing nets and inappropriately sited wind farms. Both breeding and wintering sites may be affected by human recreational activity.

summer

winter

VOICE
Mostly silent. Surprisingly loud hooting or wailing song given in courtship and territorial encounters during the breeding season.

HABITAT
In Britain and Ireland it is mostly seen in winter, either on the open sea or in sheltered estuaries. Some individuals occasionally visit large inland lakes. In summer a few birds live on inland lakes were there is usually cover from reeds and other plants.

FOOD
In winter, it feeds mainly on fish, such as herring, gobies and sand eels, and also shrimps and prawns. In summer, feeds on insects and their larvae and also fish such as sticklebacks.

DISTRIBUTION
Mostly seen around the east coast of Britain in winter. Summering birds mainly in the south and east of England, but nesting has taken place at a secret location in Scotland. Found in Europe, parts of Russia and North America, close to the Arctic Circle. Most populations migrate for the winter.

Slavonian Grebe *Podiceps auritus*

INTERNATIONAL NAME   HORNED GREBE (N. AMERICA)

IDENTIFICATION

31–38 cm. Similar size to Moorhen. Long neck, stubby bill and flat crown. In summer, has large yellow tufts (horns) on the sides of head, black cheek feathers, chestnut neck and flanks, and dark back. Black and white in winter, flat crown, almost wedge-shaped head and white cheeks that almost meet on the back of the head. Breast and front of neck are pure white and the well-defined black cap comes down to eye level, but often with a pale patch between eye and bill. Juvenile dusky, less well marked and with traces of dark stripes across cheeks. Male moults August–September, female probably starts a month later.
SEE ALSO: Little Grebe p65, Black-necked Grebe p69, Red-necked Grebe p67, Great Crested Grebe p66.

summer

HABITS

Usually seen singly or in small numbers on the sea in winter, but small groups form at times of migration. In flight, shows one and sometimes two white patches on wings. When nesting, has courtship displays that include pairs rearing up and facing each other in a 'penguin-like' position and head-shaking. There is also a 'weed-rush', where the birds dive, surface with water weed, meet face to face, turn and rush side by side for 5–10 m across the water. In summer, snaps insects from the air or off plant leaves or catches them by skimming the water surface with bill or by diving. Dives last less than 30 seconds, but it can stay under water for a minute or more.

VOICE

Mostly silent. It has a hard, guttural trill during courtship. It also has various threat and contact calls while breeding.

HABITAT

Breeds on large or small inland lakes that usually have vegetation such as sedges or horsetails growing out into the water. In winter, found on larger lakes, estuaries and sheltered coastal areas.

FOOD

Mainly insects in summer, including stoneflies, other flies and their larvae, and beetles. Fish include sticklebacks, trout and eels. Both adults and young eat a lot of feathers.

BREEDING

Pairs form in winter or on migration. Nest is built from water weed by both adults, and anchored to water vegetation. Lays 4–5 eggs that are incubated by both birds for around 24 days. Young are covered with down and swim soon after hatching. They regularly ride on their parents' backs when small. They are fed by the adults and become independent at 45 days and fly after 55 days.

MOVEMENTS AND MIGRATIONS

Most birds leave their breeding lakes in late summer and fly to coastal waters or larger inland lakes. Scottish, Icelandic and Scandinavian birds winter around North Sea coasts, as far south as the Bay of Biscay. Scottish birds return to their breeding lochs in March or early April.

POPULATION

First nested in Scotland in 1909 and increased to around 70 pairs in the 1990s, but has since fallen to around 20 pairs. In winter, there are probably less than 800 individuals around British and Irish coasts, with internationally important numbers gathering in Orkney, east coast firths and on some inland waters.

CONSERVATION

Specially protected. Wave action and flooding is a natural threat. Many breeding sites are secret to protect the birds from egg collectors, and disturbance by birdwatchers. Stocking of lochs with rainbow trout can change the ecology and potentially affect breeding success. The wintering populations are internationally important and threatened by any changes to fish stocks and oil pollution.

winter

winter

juvenile

DISTRIBUTION

The most northerly and most coastal of the grebes. Breeds at a few sites in the Scottish Highlands; also in Iceland, Scandinavia, Russia and North America. Found in coastal waters south of its breeding areas in winter.

Black-necked Grebe *Podiceps nigricollis*

IDENTIFICATION
28–34 cm. Smaller than a Moorhen. Small head and steep forehead, peaked crown and delicate up-swept bill. Often shows fluffy white feathers under its tail. In summer, has an untidy tuft of yellow feathers behind eye; rest of head and neck is black. Reddish-brown on sides sometimes extends onto neck. In winter, black and white with a black cap to below the level of the eye, dusky cheeks and a pale vertical crescent to the rear of the cheeks. The breast generally looks very white. A dark band on the nape is thicker than Slavonian's when viewed from behind. Flight is strong with rapid wingbeats and shows a white triangle on the rear of wing (Slavonian shows white on front and rear of the wing).
SEE ALSO: Red-necked Grebe p67, Slavonian Grebe p68, Great Crested Grebe p66.

HABITS
This is the most social of the small grebes, with pairs nesting in colonies and small flocks forming outside the breeding season. It dives to find food and is often reluctant to fly. Dives last around 30 seconds, but it can stay under water for a minute or more. Displays involve head shaking, a pair rising out of the water with their breasts pressed together, and then rushing across the water side by side.
Nesting birds are secretive.

summer

winter

juvenile

winter

VOICE
A chittering trill and a plaintive 'wheeooo wheeooo' are heard at breeding sites. It is mostly silent at other times.

HABITAT
This grebe breeds on shallow inland lakes fringed with water plants and with plenty of insects and small fish. The species will take advantage of newly flooded areas. In winter it visits larger inland lakes, sheltered estuaries and is sometimes seen in shallow coastal waters.

FOOD
Mostly eats insects such as water beetles, dragonfly larvae, caddis flies and mayflies. It also eats small fish and water snails.

BREEDING
It often gains protection by breeding among colonies of Black-headed Gulls. Both sexes work together to build a floating nest of water weed among emergent vegetation. Several nests may be built before one is selected and a clutch of 3 or 4 eggs is laid. Incubation is by both adults for about 21 days. Young are covered in down and quickly leave the nest. They frequently ride on their parents' backs when small.

MOVEMENTS AND MIGRATIONS
In August, it starts to leave its breeding areas. Birds from central and northern Europe move south-east or south-west, and some reach Britain by November. Return migration starts during March when small groups may arrive on inland lakes. Occasionally there have been unexpected colonisations of new areas.

POPULATION
The first breeding record for Britain or Ireland was in Wales in 1904 and in 1930 the first Scottish breeding pair was located. Since then a few pairs, usually fewer than 40, have nested successfully. Winter numbers increase to around 120 individuals around British coasts, with higher numbers during autumn migration.

CONSERVATION
Specially protected. Disturbance from boats and water sports can threaten some nests. Predation from pike, rats and escaped mink and terrapins may be a problem. There are relatively few suitable breeding sites with emergent vegetation, and so loss of habitat and drainage of temporary shallow lakes reduces the opportunities for colonisation.

DISTRIBUTION
Breeds in Scotland and at sites in northern and north-west England and the East Midlands, with a few pairs occasionally nesting elsewhere. The species is found from Denmark eastwards into eastern Europe, Russia, South-east Asia and in North America.

Sooty Shearwater *Puffinus griseus*

IDENTIFICATION

40–51 cm. Smaller than Herring Gull. This is a large, dark shearwater with a dark brown, cigar-shaped body and long, narrow wings. The bill is slender and dark and the all-dark plumage is broken by the silvery underwing-coverts that appear, from a distance, to form a white stripe. The total moult takes place between May and August while the species is in the North Atlantic.

SEE ALSO: Great Shearwater p304, Manx Shearwater p72, Cory's Shearwater p71, Fulmar p78.

HABITS

In flight its wings appear to be set relatively far back on the body and also often look swept back. Usually it flies close to the waves with several strong wingbeats followed by a long glide. Sometimes it will bank steeply before gliding down and resuming its direct line of flight. When swimming it sits high in the water, looking quite buoyant. It often associates with feeding whales and it scavenges around fishing vessels.

VOICE

Mostly silent while at sea, but raucous calls and screams have been reported.

HABITAT

It lives on the open ocean and is seldom close to land while in the North Atlantic. Breeds on remote islands in the southern oceans.

FOOD

It eats fish such as caplins and sand eels, also squid, crustaceans and offal from fishing vessels. It scavenges around whales, taking damaged and disoriented fish, and probably also feeds on whale faeces.

BREEDING

Does not breed in Britain or Ireland.

MOVEMENTS AND MIGRATIONS

After breeding, during the southern summer, it starts to move northwards through the Pacific and Atlantic Oceans in April and May. Atlantic birds follow the east coast of South and then North America and then gather in considerable numbers off the coast of New England and Newfoundland. In July many cross the North Atlantic and pass through British and Irish coastal waters between August and October en route back to their southern breeding grounds – a journey that has taken them clockwise around the Atlantic Ocean.

POPULATION

Numbers vary considerably from year to year and sometimes hundreds are seen off headlands. Worldwide this is one of the most numerous seabirds.

CONSERVATION

Sustainable fisheries and protection of inland nesting colonies from introduced ground predators and habitat destruction are needed to conserve this species. Global warming may already be having an impact on its food supplies as its numbers are dropping, especially off the Californian coast.

DISTRIBUTION

It is usually seen in small numbers from British and Irish coasts. It breeds on islands close to Antarctica and spends the northern summer in the North Atlantic. This shearwater also roams the Southern Ocean and the Pacific.

Cory's Shearwater *Calonectris diomedea*

IDENTIFICATION
45 cm. Smaller than Herring Gull. A large, heavily built shearwater, with a large head, pale bill and long wings. It has mid-brown upperparts, with pale-edged feathers giving a scaly effect. The underwing is very white with a neat dark rim around the edge and tip. At close range the pale yellow bill with dark tip is visible. The brown head merges with the brown of the neck and there is no suggestion of a dark cap or a pale collar. Some individuals have a darker tail with a faint white crescent at the base, but this is not as obvious as with Great Shearwater.
SEE ALSO: Great Shearwater p304, Manx Shearwater p72, Sooty Shearwater p70, Fulmar p78, juvenile Gannet p79.

HABITS
Its flight can appear lazy, with relaxed, rather loose downward wingbeats followed by a long, low glide on bowed wings. The wings look more angled than other similar species. In calm conditions its flapping is more gull-like, but in rougher, windier conditions it may bank and tower. It frequently follows ships and may often be seen in small flocks. Most of its feeding takes place after dark. It takes food from the surface, but also plunge-dives to slightly greater depths. Feeding birds often associate with whales, dolphins and sometimes other large seabirds such as Gannets.

VOICE
It is mostly silent away from its breeding colonies.

HABITAT
A bird of the open oceans, travelling great distances out of sight of land. Breeds among rocks and scree on islands.

FOOD
It feeds on fish such as herring and other sea creatures such as squid and crab, and also offal discharged from fishing vessels.

BREEDING
This shearwater does not breed in Britain or Ireland. It nests in colonies on the ground, in tunnels or small caves among rocks and boulders and it lays only one egg. The chick is tended by both parents, but is eventually deserted and then makes its own way to the sea.

MOVEMENTS AND MIGRATIONS
It is present around its breeding colonies from February to October. Non-breeders and breeding birds outside the breeding season range across the North Atlantic and follow the coast of Africa as far south as South Africa. Some birds travel north after breeding and reach the Bay of Biscay and the south-west coast of Britain and Ireland. Smaller numbers are seen off the east coast of England between April and early October. These birds presumably enter the North Sea via the English Channel. Relatively few reach Scottish coasts.

POPULATION
Up to 1,500 sightings annually around Britain and Ireland, but numbers vary from year to year.

CONSERVATION
The main threat to this species comes from predation of young birds by rats and cats in their island colonies.

DISTRIBUTION
The species breeds on Mediterranean Islands and on Atlantic islands such as the Azores and Madeira. Migrant Cory's Shearwaters reach the coasts of south-west England and southern Ireland in late summer. Outside the breeding season it visits both the northern and southern Atlantic.

Manx Shearwater *Puffinus puffinus*

IDENTIFICATION
31–36 cm. Smaller than Herring Gull. It has long, straight, slim wings and a slim bill, with blackish upperparts, white underparts and black cap extending below the eye. The white underwing has a dark border.
SEE ALSO: Cory's Shearwater p71, Great Shearwater p304, Sooty Shearwater p70, Balearic Shearwater p73.

HABITS
This is the most common shearwater around the coasts of Britain and Ireland. It flies with a series of rapid, stiff wingbeats followed by a long glide as it banks and turns low over the waves or, in strong winds, rises and falls. Often several will fly in a line, rising and falling as they ride the air currents – they can look alternately black and white as they change the angle of their bodies. Food is taken from the surface of the water or by plunge-diving and flocks gather where food is plentiful. It is colonial when nesting, and some colonies have hundreds or thousands of pairs close together. It swims 'duck-like', and rafts of hundreds of swimming birds will form on the sea close to colonies as dusk approaches, but it only approaches land after dark.

VOICE
At sea it is generally silent. At the nest it has a variety of weird calls, including crowing, cooing, howls and screams.

HABITAT
A bird of the open ocean except when nesting. Nests on offshore islands with soft soil.

FOOD
Fish, especially herring, sardines and sprats. Also feeds on other sea creatures such as squid.

BREEDING
Nests in burrows on flat or sloping land close to the sea. Burrows are excavated in soft soil by both sexes, and old rabbit burrows may also be used. One egg is incubated for about 50 days. The pair takes turns to incubate, with each turn averaging almost 6 days. The young are fed only at night, on regurgitated fish. Parents may miss one, two or even three nights owing to bright moonlight, bad weather or difficulty in finding food. Parents desert young at about 60 days old. The chick then leaves the nest-burrow 8–9 days later and heads for the open ocean.

MOVEMENTS AND MIGRATIONS
A long-distance migrant that returns to its breeding areas in late February, March or early April. Migration south begins in July as it heads for its winter quarters off the coast of South America. It is possible that it returns by a different route, by crossing the Atlantic and returning northwards along the coast of Africa. It does not breed until 5 or 6 years old and may live for over 50 years.

POPULATION
There are around 300,000 pairs breeding in the UK and 33,000 in Ireland. The UK has responsibility for 80–90% of the European breeding population.

Although the population of the largest colonies appear stable, smaller colonies may be declining.

CONSERVATION
The largest threat to this species comes from alien mammals, especially rats and cats, introduced to islands where there are shearwater colonies. Eradication of rats from some islands, such as Lundy in the Bristol Channel, has resulted in some birds returning.

DISTRIBUTION
The Manx Shearwater breeds on a few islands off the west coast of Britain and Ireland. It also nests on a few other islands off the coast of Europe and Africa. Outside the breeding season it ranges widely in the north-west Atlantic.

Balearic Shearwater *Puffinus mauretanicus*

IDENTIFICATION

34–39 cm. A little larger than the closely related Manx Shearwater, but it is not crisply black and white. Instead the western Mediterranean Balearic Shearwater is definitely brown above and dull below. The underwing is dark round the edges and brownish-white in the centre. The belly is brownish-white. It can be mistaken for a Sooty Shearwater but is clearly shorter winged and lacks the shining white line in the centre of the wings shown by that species. It may appear 'pot-bellied' compared to the sleeker Manx. Moults between June and October, off French and Spanish coasts.

SEE ALSO: Manx Shearwater p72.

HABITS

It flies strongly with rapid, shallow wingbeats, and wings are held stiffly like those of the Manx Shearwater. In strong winds it frequently glides side on to waves. It will settle on the water to rest and often plunge-dives for food.

MOVEMENTS AND MIGRATIONS

The Balearic Shearwater starts to leave the Mediterranean in May and many go north towards the Bay of Biscay, although some birds stay around the Balearic Islands all year. In Britain and south-west Ireland small numbers are seen from headlands and boats mainly between May and September. Unlike the Manx Shearwater this species mostly stays in European inshore waters, off Spain and France, for the winter.

POPULATION

Up to 2,000 individuals are seen annually in Britain, mostly off Cornish coasts, and along the English south coast; more have been seen in the North Sea in recent years.

CONSERVATION

Critically endangered with a world population of some 1,700 pairs. They are now required to migrate 20% further afield in search of food due to changing distribution of fish stocks. Breeding birds require sustainable fisheries and islands free of domestic and feral cats, common genets and rats.

paler variant

darker variant

VOICE

Migrants are either silent or out of hearing range.

HABITAT

Breeds on offshore islands in the western Mediterranean, coming ashore only at night. Nests in rocky crevices on cliffs or on cave ledges. The rest of the time it lives at sea, but it tends to feed closer inshore than the Manx Shearwater.

FOOD

It eats small fish such as anchovies, sardines, sprats, and also squid and small shrimps.

BREEDING

Nests earlier than the Manx Shearwater. A single egg is laid between end of February and April in a rock crevice or on a cave ledge. Young birds fledge by July.

DISTRIBUTION

This shearwater is regularly seen off the coast of south-west Ireland, west Wales and in the North Sea. Breeds on the Balearic Islands and off the south coast of France.

Storm Petrel *Hydrobates pelagicus*

INTERNATIONAL NAME   EUROPEAN STORM-PETREL

IDENTIFICATION
14–18 cm. Slightly larger than a sparrow. Sooty-black plumage with a vivid white band above the tail and spreading round the sides. Underwing has a thick white stripe down the middle. Compared with other petrels the wings are rather short. Tail short and square-ended. Juvenile similar to adult. Moult starts while the adults have young and continues into the autumn.
SEE ALSO: Leach's Petrel p75, House Martin p205.

HABITS
The fluttering flight and short glides close to the water are rather 'bat-like'. Feeds with wings raised in V-shape and feet pattering on water surface. May feed in large flocks and sometimes follows ships or keeps company with other feeding seabirds. Swims duck-like, sitting high in the water and normally only approaches land after dark. Sometimes solitary, but often in loose flocks and sometimes in larger numbers.

VOICE
Usually silent except at breeding colonies where males make a far-carrying, purring 'a-rrrrrrr' call from their burrows.

HABITAT
A bird of the open ocean, except when nesting. Rarely seen close to the coast, except when approaching nests or in late summer when strong winds may drive migrating birds closer to the shore. Breeding sites are on islands with rocky outcrops, boulders, walls or ruined buildings with crevices for nesting and usually close to deep water.

FOOD
Mainly small fish, such as sprats and herring, plankton, jellyfish and small crustaceans and squid. It also feeds on offal and other waste from ships at sea.

BREEDING
Nests in crevices between boulders, in stone walls, in rabbit burrows and will sometimes share a burrow with a Manx Shearwater. One egg is incubated by both adults, which take equal turns lasting about 3 days each. Eggs hatch after about 40 days. Young are brooded continuously for a week and then left as their parents forage for food at sea during the day, returning at night to feed the chick on regurgitated food. The young leave their burrow at about 62 days. They are independent almost at once and quickly disperse into the open ocean. They return to their original colony after 2 or 3 years, but will not breed until at least 4 years old.

MOVEMENTS AND MIGRATIONS
Most British and Irish breeding birds leave coastal waters in September and October. Migrants arrive at the wintering grounds off South Africa from mid-November and leave again in March. Breeding birds are present at breeding colonies from early May. Storm Petrels live to 31 years or more.

POPULATION
Largest numbers breed in the Faroe Islands, but British and Irish colonies are also very large, with 99,000 pairs nesting in Britain and Ireland. While the population as a whole is stable, there has been a decline on some islands owing to predation by cats and rats.

CONSERVATION
Protection of internationally important breeding colonies is essential to safeguard this species for the future. The elimination of feral cats and rats from their breeding islands is a sound first step.

DISTRIBUTION
In Britain and Ireland it mainly breeds on the west coast, on islands facing the Atlantic. Feeds on the edge, and beyond the edge, of the Continental Shelf, where the water may be 100 m deep or more. Also breeds in Iceland, the Faroes and Norway, with smaller colonies on islands in the Mediterranean, Atlantic islands such as Madeira and the Canary Islands, and Morocco. Winters in the western Atlantic as far south as South Africa.

Leach's Petrel *Oceanodroma leucorhoa*

INTERNATIONAL NAME | LEACH'S STORM-PETREL

IDENTIFICATION

19–22 cm. Size of Starling. Plumage brownish-black with narrow white, horseshoe-shaped rump. A dark line running through centre of the white rump is often very difficult to see. Tail forked. Wings are longer, narrower and more pointed than a Storm Petrel's and have prominent pale diagonal bar on upper surface. Underwing is dark. Body appears long and more slender owing to longer tail. Moults in its winter quarters during November to February.
SEE ALSO: Storm Petrel p74, Black Tern p173, House Martin p205.

HABITS

Oceanic; normally approaches land only to breed, and then only at night, or when forced into coastal waters by severe weather. Generally seen alone or in small groups. Flight light and buoyant, rather like a tern, as it banks and turns. Wings are angled strongly at the carpal joint and, head on, they look kinked. When feeding it will frequently patter the surface with its feet, as if walking on the water, especially when the wind is strong, but it seldom alights on the water. Leach's Petrels often approach ships at sea after dark.

VOICE

Usually silent at sea. Loud calls at breeding colonies variously described as 'musical', 'crooning', 'churring' and 'purring' or a crowing 'her-kitti-werke'.

HABITAT

Lives on the open ocean for most of the year. Breeds on remote offshore islands among rocks and boulders, and sometimes in stone walls or ruined buildings. Occasionally after rough weather, it becomes stranded on reservoirs or lakes well away from the sea.

FOOD

It takes food from the water surface by feeding on microscopic sea creatures such as tiny shrimps, crustaceans known as copepods and plankton. It will also follow feeding whales and seals and take offal and other waste material.

BREEDING

Pairs remain faithful from year to year. Nests in huge colonies and approaches land only after dark. Uses its feet to dig nesting tunnels in soft soil, but also nests in crevices in rocks and other holes. Sometimes several will use side tunnels off a single main entrance. The male may build a small nest of grass stems. Both birds take equal turns of several days to incubate the one egg. Eggs hatch after about 40 days. Young are brooded by an adult for about 5 days and then left during the day while adults forage far out to sea, returning to feed the chick only after dark. Young desert their burrows at around 65 days and quickly leave their breeding colonies. They reach breeding maturity at about 4 years.

MOVEMENTS AND MIGRATIONS

Birds return to their breeding colonies from late April and leave again in September or October. In autumn, gales sometimes force them close to land, particularly in north-west England. After breeding, British and Irish birds move into the Atlantic and most migrate southwards to winter in the tropics. Some individuals reach South Africa and the Southern Ocean. A few may remain in the North Atlantic for the winter.

POPULATION

This is an extremely difficult species to census. There are thought to be 48,000 pairs in the UK (20–30% of the European population) and up to 300 in Ireland.

CONSERVATION

Protecting the few colonies from mammalian predators, especially rats and cats, is a priority. The species is specially protected.

DISTRIBUTION

One of the most numerous seabirds. Only a small number of colonies have been found in Britain and Ireland, and all of these are on remote offshore islands. These petrels feed far out to sea, usually beyond the edge of the Continental Shelf of Europe. Other colonies are on both the east and west coasts of North America and on some North Pacific Islands.

Cormorant *Phalacrocorax carbo*

INTERNATIONAL NAME | GREAT CORMORANT

IDENTIFICATION

80–100 cm. Size of a large goose. Large body, long, thick neck, long powerful bill and long sloping forehead and crown. Adult black with white on its face and thighs in spring. Juvenile dark brown, usually with pale, almost white, underparts. Some immatures also have white underparts, while others resemble adults, but without white thighs or faces. Some birds of the race *'sinensis'* from Europe now breed in eastern Britain. Wing and body feathers moulted between June and December. Head and neck feathers moulted before breeding.
SEE ALSO: Great Northern Diver p63, Red-throated Diver p64, Shag p77.

HABITS

Frequently stands with wings extended or swims like a large duck, with bill raised upwards. It dives with a little leap upwards before submerging under water. Often it is seen singly, but larger numbers gather at roosts and at feeding sites. Nests in colonies, sometimes numbering 100 nests or more. Flies with neck outstretched, rather like a goose, and sometimes soars over land. Groups may fly in lines or in a V-shape. Perches on the ground, on posts, on tree branches and on power lines and pylons.

winter   juvenile

VOICE

Noisy at breeding sites and in roosts. Loud guttural 'agock-agock-agock' call made by adults, but mostly silent at other times.

HABITAT

Traditionally associated with rocky coasts and estuaries, but increasingly common on lakes and rivers many kilometres from the sea, especially in winter. Coastal breeding sites are on cliffs, stacks and rocky islets. Inland breeding colonies are in trees close to food-rich lakes and rivers.

FOOD

Feeds on fish, especially flatfish such as plaice and flounder, but it also catches cod, sprats and blennies. On inland waters it catches a wide variety of fish, including trout.

BREEDING

The male builds the nest with some help from the female. Materials include twigs, reeds and, at the coast, seaweed. Both adults incubate their 3 or 4 eggs for about 30 days. Young are brooded when small and fed by both parents. They fly after about 50 days but continue to return to the nest to be fed for a further 40–50 days before becoming fully independent. They first breed when 3 years old.

MOVEMENTS AND MIGRATIONS

Resident. Birds move away from breeding colonies after the young fledge. Some reach France, Spain or Portugal, and some from northern Europe arrive in south-east England in winter. Oldest bird 23 years.

POPULATION

Over 8,000 pairs in the UK and 4,550 in Ireland. Some coastal colonies declining but inland colonies are increasing. More than 36,000 individuals winter in Britain and Ireland.

summer

juvenile

CONSERVATION

The chief threat to the Cormorant comes from human persecution. Conflict – both real and perceived – with angling interests continues, and Cormorants can now be legally shot under licence. Such laws are hard to monitor and it is likely that many more are killed illegally. Depletion of local fish stocks and marine pollution are also a threat.

DISTRIBUTION

In spring and summer, breeding colonies are found along rocky coasts and islands in the south, west and north of Britain and around Irish coasts, as well as at a few inland lakes. Found all around the coast in winter and also on inland lakes and rivers. Immature and other non-breeding birds continue to frequent winter feeding sites throughout the year. Outside Britain and Ireland Cormorants breed across Scandinavia, Europe, Russia, China, India and parts of Africa, New Zealand and Australia, as well as Iceland and small numbers in North America.

winter

Shag *Phalacrocorax aristotelis*

INTERNATIONAL NAME   EUROPEAN SHAG

Identification

65–80 cm. Larger than Mallard. Smaller and slimmer than Cormorant with smaller head and thinner bill. Head shape different from Cormorant, with steeper forehead and peak to the crown above the eyes. Breeding adult is oily greenish-black with yellow at base of the dark bill and curly crest on the front of the head. At close range it has a scaly-looking back and a purplish sheen. Non-breeding adults are browner with a pale throat and lack the crest. Juveniles are brown, and lack the whitish under-parts of a juvenile Cormorant. Immatures are also brown with less blotchy underparts than Cormorant and with pale edges to the wing feathers, creating a scaly pale panel. Complex moult whereby flight feathers are moulted gradually from July to November then delayed until February when moult resumes until all have been replaced and the process begins again.
SEE ALSO: Red-throated Diver p64, Cormorant p76.

winter

summer

juvenile

Habits

Frequently stands with wings partly outstretched. Usually makes a distinctive forward jump before diving and these dives may last for 40 seconds. Often flies close to water surface. Wings are shorter and tips more rounded than Cormorant's, and flight is more rapid, with wings raised higher above the back.

Voice

Mostly silent. At nest it makes a series of grunts and clicks.

winter

Habitat

More at home on rough seas than Cormorant. Found in inshore waters close to rocky coasts and islands. Rare on fresh water.

Food

Mostly feeds on fish, especially sand eels, herring, cod and many other fish found in inshore waters. Feeds singly or in flocks where there is an abundance of fish.

Breeding

Nests in colonies. May keep the same mate from year to year, but some change mates and some males may be bigamous. A small territory is defended around a nest built on cliff ledges, either just above high water mark, or much higher above the sea. The male selects a site for the nest that is built by both sexes from seaweed, vegetation and material found floating on the sea. A clutch of usually 3 eggs is incubated by both birds for about 30 days. The chicks are fed by both parents on regurgitated food. The young fly after 48 days, but continue to be fed by their parents for several more weeks before becoming independent. The young breed after 3–4 years.

Movements and migrations

Present throughout the year. Outside the breeding season seldom moves far from breeding areas, although there appears to be a southern movement by some individuals. After severe storms there may be 'wrecks' that result in shags being seen at a variety of wetland sites, sometimes far from the sea. Maximum age 30 years.

Population

There are over 27,000 pairs in the UK and over 3,000 in Ireland. The population has declined by 45% in recent years, and there are occasional fluctuations at some colonies that are not fully understood, but probably linked to food availability (especially the lack of young herring or sand eels).

Conservation

Predators such as cats, feral cats and mink can decimate colonies. Like all fish-eating seabirds its future depends on a sustainable supply of fish. Sea temperature changes and the loss of sand eels present the biggest current threat. The species also suffers from oil discharged into the sea. Legislation preventing pollution and stricter controls over shipping routes will help.

DISTRIBUTION

Breeds around the rocky coasts of northern and western Britain and along the south coast to the Isle of Wight. In Ireland the largest colonies are in the north. Also found around the Atlantic coast of Scandinavia, Iceland, the Faroe Islands, France, Spain, Portugal, North Africa and parts of the Mediterranean.

winter

juvenile

Fulmar *Fulmarus glacialis*

INTERNATIONAL NAME   NORTHERN FULMAR

IDENTIFICATION
45–50 cm. Smaller than Herring Gull. Gull-like but has a thick neck and a strong stubby bill with pronounced nostrils. Body usually white with a greyish back and tail; grey wings with a pale patch at base of primaries. The white head has dark 'smudge' in front of the eye. Those from the Arctic are darker, with duskier bodies and more uniform dark grey upperwings. Adult Fulmars have a complete body moult while at sea between August and October. Primary feathers regrow rapidly.
SEE ALSO: Herring Gull p158, Kittiwake p165, Gannet p79.

dark morph

HABITS
Flight is distinctive with a series of rapid, shallow wingbeats followed by a glide on stiff, straight wings. Often glides low over the sea with wing-tips almost touching the water or riding the air currents along cliff edges, flapping its wings only when losing height. Gathers in flocks on the sea or around a source of food. Pairs perform a noisy greeting ceremony when both adults meet at their nest. Feeds by picking food from the water's surface or sometimes making a clumsy dive.

VOICE
Pairs cackle to each other on their nests and feeding flocks cackle raucously – otherwise silent.

HABITAT
A true seabird that is often seen many kilometres from land. Breeds all around British and Irish coasts where there are suitable cliffs. Also nests on buildings close to the sea.

FOOD
Crustaceans, sand eels and other fish and waste from fishing trawlers. Also eats carrion.

BREEDING
Fulmars keep the same mate for life, unless one dies. Colonies vary from a few nests to several hundred and the same birds will use the same site year after year. A single egg is laid on a narrow ledge with no nest material, or sometimes on soft soil. Incubation takes 52 days. The female incubates first and then disappears for about 7 days before returning to share the incubation with her mate. Both parents feed the young, with one or other adult staying on the nest to protect it for the first 2 weeks. Young fly after 46 days and are immediately independent. For the first 4 years they live at sea, often hundreds of kilometres from land.

MOVEMENTS AND MIGRATIONS
After breeding most fly out to sea, but colonies are seldom completely deserted. The young fledge in September and by October many adults are back on their breeding ledges. By January all the breeding sites are usually occupied. Many juveniles find their way to the coast of Newfoundland. They may return to their breeding colony after 4 or 5 years, but will not breed until 9 years old. Fulmars may live for 40 years.

POPULATION
Fulmars started breeding in Shetland in 1878. They went on to colonise cliffs around British and Irish coasts. Current annual breeding population is estimated at over half a million pairs. After a long increase, numbers in Britain have declined by 25% in the last 25 years.

CONSERVATION
After a long period of expansion it appears the population is falling. This decline may be caused by food shortages due to changes in the fishing industry or climate change. Other problems come from predators such as mink, rats or crows, and from waste material floating on the sea, which the birds ingest. Thousands are also killed by long-line fishing in the North Atlantic.

DISTRIBUTION
Most numerous in the north and west, but breeds all round British and Irish coasts where there are suitable cliffs. In winter, lives in the North Atlantic. Also breeds in Greenland and North America. There is another race of Fulmar in the North Pacific.

Gannet *Morus bassanus*

INTERNATIONAL NAME   NORTHERN GANNET

IDENTIFICATION

87–100 cm. Larger and longer necked than any gull, with a long body, long pointed wings, pointed tail and dagger-like bill. Adult pure white with black wing-tips and yellowish-orange head in spring that becomes paler in winter. Juvenile grey-brown with white flecks. Immatures have a white belly and various intermediate plumages with increasing amounts of white before growing the adult plumage after 4 years. Gradual moult generally starts after the breeding season and continues into the autumn.

SEE ALSO: Herring Gull p158, Fulmar p78, Cory's Shearwater p71.

HABITS

Flies with powerful wingbeats followed by an effortless glide. When feeding it will fly up, steady itself and then drop, folding the wings and dive, bill first, into or under the sea. Often large numbers congregate where food is plentiful. Nests are in huge colonies.

VOICE

Dry, cackling calls from feeding groups. Noisy at colonies with growls, especially when greeting mates at the nest.

HABITAT

Lives on the open ocean, far from land, for most of the year, and most feeding takes place in cold waters over the continental shelves. Colonies are on exposed islands or remote, precipitous sea cliffs.

FOOD

Fish, chiefly herring and mackerel in the breeding season, but also caplin, sprat, sand eel and many other species. An individual will sometimes steal fish from other Gannets and, occasionally, other species.

BREEDING

Nest is a substantial pile of seaweed and other material found floating on the sea and sometimes mixed with earth and grass pulled from nearby. This mixture is stuck together with the bird's own droppings and added to year after year, mostly by the male. The Gannet has no brood patch and parents take it in turns to incubate the single egg under their webbed feet. The egg hatches after 44 days. At first the chick is brooded between the parent's webs and both adults feed it. At about 90 days, after being left to starve for about 10 days, it leaves the nest and enters the sea, where it swims on the surface for 2 to 3 weeks before starting to fish for itself.

MOVEMENTS AND MIGRATIONS

Many are present in British and Irish waters throughout the year. Young leave their colonies in August and September and head for the African coast. Some adults also migrate to West Africa but most winter further north. Breeding birds start to return to their colonies in January. Gannets live an average of 16 years, but the oldest survived over 37 years.

POPULATION

220,000 pairs nest in the UK and 36,000 in Ireland, which is over 60% of the world population.

CONSERVATION

Although the population appears stable or slightly increasing, it is significant that humans have inflicted most known causes of death. Gannets are caught in fishing nets, snagged by polyethylene cord brought to the nest and killed by oil or other pollution. Sustainable fishing is essential, although Gannets also benefit from the unwanted 'by-catch' of the fishing industry.

juvenile

adult   immature

DISTRIBUTION

Most Gannet colonies are in the north and west of Britain and Ireland. It also breeds in northern France, Norway, Iceland, the Faroe Islands and on the north-east coast of North America. It is widespread in the North Atlantic for most of the year. Many young move south to African waters and both adults and young feed along the European and North African coasts outside the breeding season.

Little Egret *Egretta garzetta*

winter

IDENTIFICATION
55–65 cm. Much smaller than a Grey Heron. An elegant white heron with a long, slender neck, fine black bill, black legs and greenish-yellow feet. In spring, it has fine plumes on its breast and back and two very long plumes on its hindneck. Immatures lack the plumes and yellow feet. Bare skin at the base of the bill varies in colour, but is usually grey.
SEE ALSO: Grey Heron p83, Great White Egret p306.

HABITS
Feeds singly and breeds in colonies. Stands motionless or sometimes feeds energetically by dashing after prey. It can feed in deep water and sometimes waves its wings to keep its balance. It will stir up water and mud with its feet to disturb its prey. Flight is leisurely with occasional glides. Legs trail and the head is drawn back into the body. Wings are rounded and look bowed. It generally roosts in groups in trees and bushes where it is an agile climber. The fine plumes are used in display at the nest.

VOICE
Usually silent except at breeding colonies when it makes a variety of croaking and quacking calls.

HABITAT
Marshes with shallow water, river banks, estuaries and tidal inlets. In Britain the breeding sites are in trees close to nesting Grey Herons.

FOOD
Feeds on small fish, especially sticklebacks, loaches, tench and small carp, and also amphibians and aquatic insects. Coastal birds take crustaceans including shrimps.

BREEDING
It breeds in trees, bushes and (elsewhere in Europe) on the ground in reedbeds. Nests may be within a few metres of each other. Both adults build a platform of sticks or reeds. The 4–5 eggs are incubated by both sexes. The young hatch after 21 days and are fed by both parents on regurgitated food. The young leave the nest after about 30 days and clamber around the branches of nearby trees until they fly 10–15 days later.

MOVEMENTS AND MIGRATIONS
In autumn European birds migrate south-west to reach their wintering areas in central Africa. Juveniles disperse widely, many moving north before also migrating southwards. Some overwinter around the Mediterranean. In recent years increasing numbers have spent the winter in Britain and Ireland, and these have formed the nucleus of a growing resident breeding population.

POPULATION
Decimated for the plumage trade in the 19th century, the species gradually recovered during the 20th century and expanded its range northwards. It was an infrequent visitor to Britain until 1989 when there was an influx in autumn. That pattern has continued. There are now more than 1,600 individuals in Britain and Ireland in autumn. The first pair nested in Britain in 1996 and in Ireland in 1997. Numbers have increased to over 450 pairs and are still growing rapidly, and spreading to new areas.

CONSERVATION
British and Irish breeding populations of Little Egrets are the most northerly in the world. They require protection from disturbance, especially during the breeding season. It appears to be set to continue its colonisation of Britain and Ireland, although this expansion could be affected by any severe winter weather.

winter

summer

juvenile

DISTRIBUTION

Resident in southern Britain and Ireland. The species is found in Europe, Africa, Asia and Australasia. Most breeding populations move south for the winter.

Cattle Egret *Bubulcus ibis*

IDENTIFICATION
48–53 cm. Much smaller than a Grey Heron, a compact white heron with much shorter bill, neck and legs than Little Egret. Legs are greyish-yellow. In breeding plumage has top of head, lower back and breast orange buff. The bill is yellow and the feathers under it are longer than those above, giving a distinctive 'jowl'. Walks strongly and often sways as it moves. In flight legs do not project as far as Little Egret's, and it lacks the bright yellow feet of that species.
SEE ALSO: Little Egret p80.

winter

summer

winter

HABITS
Spends much more time away from water than other egrets and herons, often following cattle and other livestock. Eats insects that are disturbed by grazing animals and will perch on the backs of cattle. It is a sociable bird often found in small groups. Roosts communally, usually in trees or high scrub. It will follow tractors ploughing and, in Africa, will treat wild game animals – like rhinoceros – in the same way it interacts with cattle.

VOICE
Away from breeding colonies and roosts it is often silent. Adult make a harsh croaking 'rick-rack' call and a short harsh 'raa' call when defending nesting areas from predators and rivals.

HABITAT
Where common in Europe it can be seen in a wide range of habitats, including pasture fields, ploughed land, rubbish tips, golf courses, airfields, rice fields, marshes and river banks. It follows a range of grazing animals in tropical grasslands. In Britain it favours grasslands grazed by cattle and sheep.

FOOD
A wide range of insects – especially grasshoppers, crickets, flies and butterfly and moth larvae. Other food includes earthworms, frogs, toads and their tadpoles, lizards and fish.

BREEDING
First bred in Britain in 2008 in Somerset. This followed an influx of over 100 birds into south-west England and Ireland in the winter of 2007/2008, including a group of 18 together in Cornwall. The egrets make a stick nest, sometimes lined with grass, in a tree or bush above or close to water. A clutch of 4–5 eggs is laid. Both sexes incubate for 24 days. Young are fed on regurgitated food and are ready to leave the nest when 20 days old, but they stay on nearby branches until ready to fly at 30 days old.

MOVEMENTS AND MIGRATIONS
European-bred birds disperse randomly after breeding and also wander during the autumn and winter. Some reach Egypt and Morocco. Some birds breeding further south in Africa colonised South America in the late 1800s and spread to the USA. The fact that birds arrive in Britain and Ireland in winter, often after strong west winds, led to one theory that these latest Cattle Egrets are from North America rather than Europe. However, the European population is getting larger and our Cattle Egrets may have come from France or Spain.

POPULATION
Over 400 have been seen in Britain in the last 60 years and numbers in Ireland have been increasing too. As the numbers of birds in Europe and Africa continue to increase there is no reason why this highly adaptable species should not colonise Britain and Ireland in the next few years.

CONSERVATION
Continuing pastoral farming in lowland river valleys will help this species. If signs of nesting are seen, such as stick carrying in spring, it is important to ensure that suitable small woodlands and tall thorn thickets are left undisturbed until any young can fend for themselves.

DISTRIBUTION
Arrives in both spring and autumn/winter, especially in south-west England and south-west Ireland. Still scarce away from these areas and southern England.

Night Heron *Nycticorax nycticorax*

INTERNATIONAL NAME   BLACK-CROWNED NIGHT HERON

juvenile

VOICE
The call is a hoarse croak, often given in flight. Otherwise usually silent except at breeding colonies.

HABITAT
It favours areas of fresh water for feeding, and dense trees and bushes for roosting. It feeds in shallow water at the edge of reedbeds, alongside rivers, canals and ditches. Elsewhere in the world where the species is common it may feed in brackish or salt water.

FOOD
It feeds on fish, including carp and eels. It also takes frogs, small mammals and birds.

IDENTIFICATION
58–65 cm. Smaller than Grey Heron with a short, thick neck, large head and a stout, crow-like bill. The head and body appear to merge when resting. The adult is striking, with black back and crown, grey wings and body and three long white head plumes. The juvenile is brown with large white spots on its back and wings and pale grey underparts with large brown streaks. A first-summer bird has a brown crown, grey-brown back, less streaking on the underparts and spotted wings. A second-summer immature has dull uniform upperparts, pale underparts and a blackish crown. SEE ALSO: Grey Heron p83, Bittern p85.

HABITS
It is most active at dawn and dusk and roosts during the day in thick cover, usually high up in trees and large bushes. It flies from its daytime roosts to favourite feeding areas at dusk and continues feeding after dark. It is sociable when breeding and at its roosts, but usually seen singly in Britain and Ireland. It perches freely in trees and clambers easily among branches. It stalks prey and sometimes hovers, swims or dives to catch fish.

BREEDING
This species has not successfully nested wild in Britain or Ireland. There was a long-established colony of free-flying Night Herons of the North American race that breed in Edinburgh Zoo. One pair of apparently wild birds established a territory in Somerset in 1997.

MOVEMENTS AND MIGRATIONS
After breeding, Night Herons disperse from their colonies and travel in all directions. By September and October most start to head south and cross the Mediterranean and the Sahara Desert to winter in Africa. A few overwinter in Europe. In Britain, Night Herons have been seen in every month of the year, and especially in spring and early autumn.

POPULATION
A small number, usually fewer than 20, arrive in Britain and Ireland most years.

CONSERVATION
Moderate decline in Europe. Tired migrants should not be disturbed, and adults arriving in spring require privacy in case they attempt to breed.

juvenile

DISTRIBUTION
Individuals that arrive in Britain in spring are generally seen in central and southern England. Autumn migrants are most often observed along the east coast. This species is found in Europe and Africa, and it winters in central and southern Africa. Others are found in North and South America, and Asia.

Grey Heron *Ardea cinerea*

IDENTIFICATION
90–98 cm. Very large, with a long neck, long legs and a dagger-like bill. Adult grey, black and white. Head white with white centre to the black crown that ends in a long, black wispy crest. Whitish neck has rows of black marks. Back is blue-grey and the large flight feathers are dull black. Adult's bill changes from yellow to partly reddish in breeding season. Juvenile appears sleeker and greyer than adult and lacks the long plumes. Adults start to moult after the breeding season and complete this by November.
SEE ALSO: Night Heron p82, Bittern p85.

HABITS
Usually solitary, but also seen in groups. Often stands hunched up with head resting between shoulders. When hunting the neck is elongated. In flight, head is drawn back, neck bulges and legs and feet extend well beyond tail. When hunting, walks with great stealth and stands motionless for long periods with neck curved ready to strike. Sometimes wades in deep water. Crown feathers raised in display.

MOVEMENTS AND MIGRATIONS
Do not usually migrate. A few from Britain reach Ireland and others reach the Netherlands, France and even Spain. Some Grey Herons from northern Europe arrive in eastern Britain for the winter. Elsewhere they are long-distance migrants; some European birds are known to cross the Sahara Desert. At least one individual survived for more than 35 years.

POPULATION
Has been persecuted in the past. Following a series of mild winters, by 2007 the population was 13,316 pairs in the UK and up to 10,000 in Ireland.

CONSERVATION
Herons require unpolluted water with a good, sustainable supply of food and safe places to nest. Heronries should not be visited during the breeding season for fear of disturbance.

juvenile

VOICE
Usually silent, apart from loud 'frank' or 'kaark' call, often given in flight. At nesting colony there are a variety of croaking calls.

HABITAT
Usually seen on the ground, near shallow edges of lakes, slow-flowing rivers, marshes or estuaries, but also stands in fields away from water or perches in trees. Generally it nests in tall trees, but sometimes on the ground in reedbeds or on a cliff ledge.

FOOD
Feeds mainly on fish. From fresh waters the species include roach, perch, sticklebacks and also goldfish from garden ponds. In coastal areas catches eels, flounders, wrasse and crabs. Small mammals, birds, amphibians and insect larvae are also eaten occasionally.

BREEDING
Breeds in colonies (called heronries) although single nests are not uncommon. The large nest of sticks is usually at the top of a deciduous or coniferous tree, 25–40 m off the ground and generally in the same tree as several other nests. Nests built by both adults; males bring the materials and females undertake construction. 3 or 4 eggs are incubated by both sexes and hatch after 25–27 days. Young brooded for about 18 days and for the next week or so an adult remains at the nest. At around 20–30 days the young leave and start to clamber around the branches. They eventually fly when about 50 days old, but may continue to return to their nests for a further 10–20 days and then begin to disperse from their colonies.

DISTRIBUTION
Found throughout Britain and Ireland except in mountainous areas. Most numerous in lowland areas where there are lakes or rivers. Also breeds in central and northern Europe with a few scattered locations farther south. Some northern European birds winter around the Mediterranean. Also found in Africa and Asia.

Purple Heron *Ardea purpurea*

juvenile

IDENTIFICATION
78–90 cm. Smaller and darker than a Grey Heron with very long thin neck, narrow head and long, pointed bill giving the head and neck a snake-like appearance. The body is slender and legs are long with noticeably long toes. The adult has ginger head and neck with black crown, bold black lines running across the face and down the neck and long black plumes. The breast and flanks are chestnut with long plumes hanging down the lower breast. The back is grey and may appear purplish at close range. Juveniles are browner with head, neck and back warm brown and upper-wings mottled brown. First-summer birds are like adults but keep the brown wing-coverts.
SEE ALSO: Grey Heron p83, Bittern p85.

HABITS
Noticeably active around dusk and dawn. Sometimes wades in deep water. Skulks among waterside vegetation and fishes with neck either coiled or outstretched at an angle of about 60 degrees over the water. Usually solitary. In flight, it has shorter wings and a greater neck bulge than the Grey Heron, and its feet look very large as they project beyond the tail.

VOICE
Usually silent but does have a hoarse croak, rather like Grey Heron.

HABITAT
Feeds in marshes, reedbeds and other wetlands. Migrants visit reedbeds, river banks, estuaries and sometimes the seashore.

FOOD
Feeds on fish, including carp, perch, sticklebacks and eels. Also takes insects and their larvae, including water beetles and dragonflies. Will catch and kill small mammals, such as shrews and water voles, and eats amphibians including frogs and newts.

BREEDING
It does not breed in Britain or Ireland. Continental breeding colonies are either on the ground in reed-beds or in trees.

MOVEMENTS AND MIGRATIONS
Adults that occur in Britain are mostly seen in April and May. After fledging, juveniles disperse in all directions. The few that reach Britain are nomadic for the rest of the summer. The majority of the European population of adults and juveniles migrates south-east or south-west in autumn and crosses the Sahara Desert to winter in central and southern Africa. A few remain around the Mediterranean for the winter. Breeding birds return to their colonies between March and May.

POPULATION
Fewer than 20 individuals arrive in Britain each year.

CONSERVATION
As an occasional visitor there is little that can be done for this species in Britain. If a pair were to show signs of breeding then the site would need to be safeguarded.

DISTRIBUTION

A rare visitor to Britain and Ireland, most often seen in south, south-west and eastern England, but rarely occurs elsewhere. It breeds in suitable areas in central, southern and eastern Europe. The species is also found in southern and eastern Asia and in Africa.

Bittern *Botaurus stellaris*

INTERNATIONAL NAME   EURASIAN BITTERN

IDENTIFICATION
70–80 cm. Smaller than a Grey Heron. This is a small, heavy-looking heron with a dagger-like bill and longish legs. The golden-brown feathers are mottled with black and it has a black crown and 'moustache'. Feathers are moulted after breeding and moulting completed by November or December.
SEE ALSO: juvenile Night Heron p82, Grey Heron p83.

HABITS
Very secretive and hard to observe. Beautifully camouflaged when among reeds. Moves slowly and stealthily through reedbeds by grasping reed stems in its long toes. May appear tall, thin and upright, especially when nervous, elongated as it stalks food, or hunched up. Flies on broad rounded wings, with head drawn back and legs trailing. Neck may be extended during short flights. Flight usually slow, low and leisurely, appearing rather owl-like, but it may also soar at considerable heights.

VOICE
The 'boom' of the male is heard from January to April, especially at dawn and dusk. The sound is rather like the noise that comes from blowing across the top of a glass bottle! It is resonant, and travels up to 5 km. It also gives a harsh 'aark, aark'.

HABITAT
The Bittern lives in freshwater swamps and marshes and spends most of the time among thick vegetation, particularly the common reed or *Phragmites*. Seldom seen far from cover. In winter, visits smaller reedbeds and marshes.

FOOD
Mainly feeds on fish, especially rudd and eels, but also frogs and other amphibians, insects, mammals such as water voles, and small birds. It feeds by day and is particularly active at dawn and dusk.

BREEDING
The male defends a large territory from other males during late winter and spring. He booms from a regularly used 'calling place' within the territory and attracts one or more females with which he mates, but thereafter has very little to do with rearing the young. The nest is a platform of reeds and other water plants with a lining of finer material. 4–6 eggs are incubated by the female. The young hatch after 25 days and are fed by the female for the next 7 weeks or so. Males that have only one female may help by bringing some food to the nest. Soon after the young are able to fly they leave their home territory and move to other reedbeds for the autumn.

MOVEMENTS AND MIGRATIONS
Bitterns disperse from their breeding grounds in late summer. They may visit small reedbeds, old gravel workings and riverside marshes. By midwinter they are joined by others from northern and eastern Europe. The survivors return to their traditional reedbeds in late winter and may be able to breed at 1 year old. They live to 11 years or more.

POPULATION
The Bittern became extinct as a breeding species in Britain and Ireland by 1900, but recolonised and reached a peak of 80 males in the 1950s; it then declined rapidly and only recently has there been more than 80 booming males again. Numbers increase to 50–150 individuals during winter.

CONSERVATION
The Bittern is specially protected. It is particularly vulnerable to cold winters. The small breeding population depends on a few large and specially managed reedbeds, most of which are nature reserves. Improved management of existing reedbeds and the creation of extensive new reedbeds will improve the chances of its survival in Britain, but sea-level rise threatens some of its traditional coastal sites.

juvenile

Now restricted in summer mainly to nature reserves in East Anglia and Lancashire. More widespread in winter, especially in south-east England. This species is found in suitable habitats in Europe, North Africa and central and eastern Asia.

White Stork *Ciconia ciconia*

IDENTIFICATION
100–115 cm. Larger than a Grey Heron. It is a huge bird with long neck, long red legs and red pointed bill. It is white with black flight feathers although on some individuals the white plumage may become soiled and discoloured. The juvenile resembles the adult, but with a dull bill and the black on the wings appears browner.
SEE ALSO: Little Egret p80, Grey Heron p83, Great White Egret p306.

HABITS
It flies with extended neck and legs that project far beyond its tail. Wingbeats are slow and deliberate and it frequently glides, especially in thermals when it will rise to a great height before peeling off and slowly descending again on rigid wings. On migration thousands will travel together – using thermals to gain height – and converge at sea-crossings. On the ground it walks sedately or chases prey on foot, with some wing-waving. Perches on trees and buildings.

VOICE
Generally it is silent. Breeding birds make a loud bill-clattering display while at their nesting platforms.

HABITAT
It feeds in open wetlands or damp meadows or pastures. Also found beside pools, ditches and slow-flowing streams.

FOOD
It eats a wide variety of small animals, catching insects, such as crickets and grasshoppers, and small mammals when the weather is dry, and aquatic insects and frogs in wet conditions. Other food includes lizards, earthworms and other animals including small mice, birds and carrion. In eastern Europe will occasionally eat small tortoises. It follows the locust swarms in Africa.

BREEDING
The White Stork does not nest in Britain or Ireland. In Europe the nests are in tall trees, and also on the tops of buildings, towers and pylons.

MOVEMENTS AND MIGRATIONS
A few White Storks remain in southern Europe over winter, but most migrate to tropical Africa. They leave their breeding grounds in August, and European birds head either south-west or south-east. Those in the west migrate into Africa via the Straits of Gibraltar, while those in the east migrate around the eastern end of the Mediterranean. Large migrating flocks form at the major sea-crossings. Migrants return to their breeding sites between February and April when a few appear to overshoot their European breeding grounds and arrive in Britain.

POPULATION
It declined in western Europe during the 20th century. A small number, usually about 20, arrive in Britain each year during April and May but also in August or September. A number of zoos and collections of waterfowl keep White Storks and some of these birds may be escapees.

juvenile

CONSERVATION
Declined in western Europe due to habitat loss and intensive farming. Protection of remaining feeding sites and the re-creation of traditional feeding areas would help. Insecticide use in Africa to control locusts has removed food, and droughts have also affected food supplies. Prevention of habitat destruction in eastern Europe is a priority. There have been reintroduction programmes in parts of Europe.

DISTRIBUTION

This is a rare visitor to Britain each year. The species breeds in Europe, from the Baltic to the Mediterranean. It also breeds in north-west Africa and eastern Asia. It winters in tropical Africa as far south as South Africa.

Spoonbill *Platalea leucorodia*

INTERNATIONAL NAME EURASIAN SPOONBILL

sociable, with touching nests. Nests are built on the ground – usually a large pile of reeds, twigs and grasses. Members of a colony will band together to drive away intruders. For many birds in the colony egg laying is synchronised so both the laying and hatching dates are similar, and most of the young in the colony are of a similar age. The 3 or 4 young are also very sociable and move from nest to nest. They are cared for by both their parents and fly after 45 days. They continue to be fed by parents for up to 10 weeks.

MOVEMENTS AND MIGRATIONS

Most spoonbills arrive in Britain in April and May. More arrive in July and August, as juveniles from mainland Europe disperse from their breeding colonies. Migration starts in August as birds begin to head south. Some spend the winter in western Europe, including a few in Britain. Others remain around the Mediterranean or winter in West Africa and the northern tropics. In Spain, egg laying may start as early as January. Dutch birds arrive back at their colonies during February.

POPULATION

As many as 70 birds a year are seen in Britain and up to 4 pairs have attempted to nest. In eastern Europe there has been a marked decline in numbers. In western Europe there has been an increase, especially in the Netherlands.

CONSERVATION

Specially protected. Breeding colonies and feeding areas require strict protection during spring and summer. In addition, some of the wetlands they use on migration and the wintering grounds in Africa need to be conserved. Drainage of wetlands for agriculture and tourist developments, pollution of waterways and loss of reedbeds all affect Spoonbills.

IDENTIFICATION

80–90 cm. Smaller than Grey Heron, but larger than Little Egret. Large, white and heron-like with long black legs and long black spoon-shaped bill with yellow tip. In spring and summer adult has yellow breastband and shaggy crest. Juvenile has black tips to its wings and a pale yellow bill.
SEE ALSO: Grey Heron p83, Little Egret p80, Great White Egret p306.

HABITS

Usually seen on the ground, but will also perch in trees and bushes. Nests in colonies and feeds in small groups or singly, but seldom mixes with other species. In flight, neck is extended and long legs project beyond the tail. Tends to fly low down or sometimes soars at a greater height. Often it feeds after dark and roosts during the day. Its feeding technique is to wade and sweep its bill from side to side.

VOICE

Generally silent; even in a nesting colony the main sounds are an occasional deep grunting and bill snapping.

HABITAT

Breeds in coastal marshes and river valleys where there is open water with reeds and other vegetation. Sometimes breeds on islands. Outside the breeding season, frequently visits estuaries and coastal inlets.

FOOD

Mainly insects and their larvae, especially water beetles, dragonflies and caddis flies. Also eats small fish, small amphibians, aquatic snails and some vegetation.

BREEDING

Spoonbills have not bred regularly in Britain since the 17th century. In recent years, visiting pairs have been seen building nests, and in 1999 a pair reared two young. In other places their colonies are very

juvenile

DISTRIBUTION

It is an annual visitor to the south and east coasts of England, and less common elsewhere. These vagrants roam widely, but recently nest building has been observed in Cheshire, Norfolk, and Dumfries and Galloway. This species is also found in central and southern Europe, and other races breed in Africa and Asia.

BIRDS OF PREY IN FLIGHT

GOSHAWK p100   male

RED KITE p97

juvenile

BUZZARD p92

juvenile

SPARROWHAWK p101   female

HONEY-BUZZARD p91   dark juvenile

HEN HARRIER p94   female

female

MARSH HARRIER p96   female

MONTAGU'S HARRIER p95   female

ROUGH-LEGGED BUZZARD p93

GOLDEN EAGLE
p99

adult

juvenile

WHITE-TAILED
EAGLE p98

juvenile

HOBBY p104

PEREGRINE
p105

adult

KESTREL
p102

female

MERLIN p103

female

OSPREY p90

adult

Osprey *Pandion haliaetus*

IDENTIFICATION

55–58 cm. Slightly longer in the body than Buzzard but has much longer wings, looking almost gull-like at times. Light brown breast-band, clean white underparts and wing-linings and a dark patch at bend of wings. Tail is short, dark above and barred below. Adult has uniform brown upperparts and a white head with a thick black stripe through and behind its yellow eye. Juveniles have buff tips to their brown feathers, giving a scaly appearance. Annual moult begins in June, but is 'suspended' for annual migration and then continued in Africa.

SEE ALSO: Buzzard p92.

HABITS

Generally seen singly except at nest. Often perches near feeding areas, favouring dead branches or a post in the water. In flight, long wings often appear kinked at the joint. When hunting for fish it half folds up the wings and hurtles into the water, stretching its legs out in front to grasp the prey. It can also grab fish quickly from the water's surface. It carries its prey head first to limit air resistance.

VOICE

Usually silent but near the nest a shrill 'pieu-pieu-pieu'.

HABITAT

Lives near inland lakes, large rivers, coastal lagoons and estuaries. In Britain associated with places that have both lakes for feeding and mature trees for nesting. In winter also inhabits coastal areas of Africa.

FOOD

Although a few small mammals, reptiles and amphibians are taken, the vast majority of food is fish including perch, carp, pike, trout and salmon.

BREEDING

Male generally returns to the nest-site first. When female returns he performs an aerial switch-backing display. In Britain the nest of sticks is usually built in a tree, but in other parts of its range it will nest on cliffs and man-made structures such as pylons. The 2 or 3 eggs are laid in April. Female incubates the eggs, with male taking occasional turns. Incubation begins with the first egg. Young hatch after about 37 days and are fed by both adults. They fly at about 50 days, but depend on their parents for a further month or two before beginning their migration.

MOVEMENTS AND MIGRATIONS

They leave their breeding grounds in mid-August and head south on a broad front. They will stop at good feeding areas, but some cross the Sahara Desert before reaching their African winter quarters in late September. Adults return the following March; young may remain in Africa or follow more slowly. The oldest known Osprey was 26 years old.

juvenile

POPULATION

Almost 200 pairs nest in Britain. The species has recently spread into England and Wales, a remarkable increase in 50 years.

CONSERVATION

Specially protected in the UK and Ireland. Once relatively common, it was exterminated in Britain by 1916. It returned and, despite robbery by egg thieves, it eventually re-established itself on Speyside, thanks to round-the-clock protection by the RSPB. Secret sites, helpful landowners, artificial nests and hard work by volunteers and professional conservationists all contributed to the re-colonisation, not only of Scotland, but now also England and Wales.

DISTRIBUTION

Migrating Ospreys stop and feed at suitable habitats almost anywhere in Britain, especially at reservoirs and large lakes. They breed in central and northern Scotland and a few now breed in England and Wales. The species breeds from Scandinavia south to the Mediterranean, across Asia, in Australia and in North and Central America. European birds winter in tropical Africa.

Honey-buzzard *Pernis apivorus*

INTERNATIONAL NAME   EUROPEAN HONEY-BUZZARD

IDENTIFICATION

52–60 cm. A little longer-tailed than Buzzard with slender, pigeon-like head. Birds vary from pale to dark. Tail has dark band at tip and two bands near base. Along hind edge of wing has dark band that is 'S' shaped, curving into the body. Paler birds show dark patch on bend of wing. Male has grey head, grey-brown upperparts and variable plumage. Female is darker, browner and more obviously barred on body. Juvenile is also variable, with darker brown plumage, often a white forehead, almost black tips to wings and dark secondary feathers. Tail is crossed by several indistinct bars. Juveniles with pale heads often have a dark eye-patch. Adults start their moult whilst breeding but finish it in Africa. Juveniles start a protracted moult in their second year.

SEE ALSO: Buzzard p92, Rough-legged Buzzard p93, Goshawk p100.

juvenile

female

HABITS

Different flight profile from Buzzard; wings held either flat or drooped slightly downwards, deep and lazy, 'elastic' wingbeats; wings held straight and flat and tail fanned when soaring. When displaying or advertising its territory, male will carry out an undulating sky-dance where the wings are raised high above body. Spends more time feeding on ground than other birds of prey. Shy and usually seen singly except when large flocks are concentrated at narrow sea-crossings on migration.

VOICE

Generally silent, but make a piping 'pi-aa' in the breeding season.

HABITAT

Breeds in lowland deciduous or mixed woods, forests and copses and in upland conifer and mixed woodlands. In Britain conifers are preferred for nesting. It especially favours woodland with rides and glades. Winters in equatorial and other African forests.

FOOD

Uniquely adapted to feeding on the larvae of insects, especially wasps and bees that it digs up with its rather blunt claws and from which it is protected by the scaly head feathers. Also eats lizards, frogs, some mammals and birds.

BREEDING

Nesting begins in late May. Both sexes build nest on a branch of a large tree and often use the old nest of a large species such as a crow as a foundation. Nest is made of twigs and branches with some live, green material. Both birds share the incubation of the 2 eggs, which hatch after 30–35 days. At first, young are mainly brooded by female. Male provides most of the food for female and chicks for about 18 days, after which both parents share the hunting. The young fly at about 42 days, but are not independent until 75–100 days.

MOVEMENTS AND MIGRATIONS

Breeding birds arrive in Europe in May and leave again in mid-August and September. Large numbers converge at major sea-crossings such as Falsterbo at the southern tip of Sweden, Gibraltar, Messina in southern Italy and Istanbul in Turkey.

POPULATION

Up to 69 pairs have nested in Britain in recent years. Around 100 other migrant Honey-buzzards are normally seen in Britain each year, but in September/October 2000 over 2,000 were seen.

CONSERVATION

Specially protected. British breeding birds are usually at secret locations to protect them from egg thieves. Numbers have increased in recent years, perhaps as a result of occupation of maturing upland conifer forests. Increases in wasp grubs owing to climate change may have contributed to the increase.

male

male
(pale)

DISTRIBUTION

Seen as a passage migrant in eastern Britain in late spring and autumn, it also nests in southern and eastern England, Wales, northern England and northern Scotland. The species also breeds in most of Europe and Russia. It winters in tropical and southern Africa.

Buzzard *Buteo buteo*

INTERNATIONAL NAME COMMON BUZZARD

IDENTIFICATION

51–57 cm. Large thickset bird of prey with wide rounded head, short neck, broad rounded wings with 'fingered' ends and a rather short, broad tail. Female larger than male. Colour is very variable, but never has the dark bands in the wings or tail of Honey-buzzard. Common plumage medium-brown with a pale crescent on breast, browner wing-linings and paler flight feathers. Upperwing is darker, more uniform brown. Buzzards hold their wings in a shallow 'V' when soaring and gliding. Juveniles are usually dark and streaky. Moult takes place between March and November. Female starts to lose flight feathers during incubation. Moulting Buzzards show obvious gaps in their wings.

SEE ALSO: Honey-buzzard p91, Rough-legged Buzzard p93, Golden Eagle p99.

HABITS

Buzzards soar and glide with head hardly extending in front of the wings. Will frequently hang in the air almost motionless looking for prey, and will also hover, with slower wingbeats than Kestrel. Also spends a lot of time perched in trees, on posts or on poles from where it can easily swoop down on prey. Hunts for worms on the ground. Usually seen singly or in pairs, although migrating birds in Europe may gather in larger numbers.

juveniles

juvenile

VOICE

Call a mewing 'peee-uu', which may be heard at any time of year.

HABITAT

Breeds where there are trees or crags for nesting. Small farms with trees and hedges in hilly areas with some moorland is still the stronghold, but a recent expansion into eastern Britain has brought it into arable lowland areas. Also lives where there are extensive forests and along rocky coasts.

FOOD

Small mammals, especially voles and rabbits, birds such as young pigeons and crows, and also insects, reptiles, earthworms and carrion.

BREEDING

Nest made of sticks and lined with bracken, moss and other softer materials. Often the same nest is added to year after year. Breeding begins in April or May.

Both adults incubate the clutch of 2 or 3 eggs, but the female has the longest shifts, while the male provides most of the food. Eggs hatch after about 34 days. Incubation starts with the first egg, thus hatching is spread over about a week. As the young are of slightly different ages the smallest may not survive. Young fly at about 50 days and remain dependent on their parents for a further 40 days or more.

MOVEMENTS AND MIGRATIONS

British and Irish Buzzards seldom move more than 50 km from the nests. In the north and east the species is a migrant. Some from Europe reach eastern Britain in autumn, and winter here. Migration of the eastern race, known as Steppe Buzzards, through the Middle East is spectacular, with thousands gathering at narrow sea-crossings as they migrate into Africa and return again in spring. Maximum recorded age 28 years.

POPULATION

About 40,000 pairs breed in the UK and 200 in Ireland, making it the most numerous raptor in Britain. These numbers are still increasing, especially in the east of England.

CONSERVATION

Buzzards were once widespread in Britain, but were exterminated in much of eastern Britain. Myxomatosis, which reduced the rabbit population, toxic chemicals and unlawful persecution reduced Buzzard numbers during the 20th century. More recently young birds from the west have started to recolonise eastern counties. However, persecution, especially by poisoning, continues to kill many birds each year.

DISTRIBUTION

Most Buzzards breed in the north and west of Britain and in Ireland. Recently there has been a re-colonisation of central England and eastern counties. Buzzards breed from the Arctic Circle south to the Mediterranean and across Asia. Some eastern races winter in Africa.

Rough-legged Buzzard *Buteo lagopus*

IDENTIFICATION
50–60 cm. Slightly larger than a Buzzard but more harrier-like with longer wings and tail and less variable plumage. The female is slightly larger than the male. The upperparts are greyish-brown and the tail is white with a black band at the end. The head is quite pale. Juveniles and adult females show whiter underparts with a dark belly, dark patches at the bend of the wings and dark tips to the wings. The juvenile has a thicker dark terminal band to the tail and paler bases to the primary feathers. Adult males show duller underparts without the dark belly patch and at least two narrower dark bands at the tail tip. It can be difficult to separate this species from pale forms of the Buzzard although general shape and tail pattern are often distinctive.
SEE ALSO: Buzzard p92, juvenile Golden Eagle p99.

HABITS
The Rough-legged Buzzard frequently hovers with wings flapping energetically, or hangs almost motionless as it searches for its prey. It also watches for prey from a perch, which may be a post or a branch of a tree. Like the Buzzard it soars with wings held in a shallow 'V', but in level flight the action is freer and more fluid. When gliding the wings appear to have a slight kink.

MOVEMENTS AND MIGRATIONS
Rough-legged Buzzards leave their northern breeding grounds and migrate south for the winter. Southern migration begins in August and they start their return migration in February. Oldest bird 18 years.

POPULATION
Usually fewer than 50 birds a year are seen in Britain. Very occasionally there have been larger influxes, with over 250 seen in a single winter. In Ireland it is much rarer.

CONSERVATION
The natural population fluctuations of this species are linked to the availability of the small mammals that form a substantial proportion of its diet. However, birds have been found with lethal amounts of agricultural pesticides in them.

juvenile

juvenile

male

juvenile

juvenile

juvenile

VOICE
The most frequent call is a far-carrying and rather mournful 'peeeeooo'.

HABITAT
In Britain it mostly visits open coastal sites, but also needs a small wood or plantation as an evening roost. In summer, this is a species of the treeless uplands of northern Europe, but when the population is expanding will also breed in more wooded areas.

FOOD
The Rough-legged Buzzard feeds mainly on mammals such as rabbits and voles. In Scandinavia in summer voles and lemmings are the main prey items, but it also feeds on small birds, fish, some insects and carrion.

BREEDING
Does not breed in Britain or Ireland. It makes a stick nest on a rock ledge or sometimes in a tree, and lays 3 or 4 eggs. Larger clutches are laid in years when food is abundant. Both adults feed the young, which fly after 40 days and become independent 30 days later.

DISTRIBUTION
This species is a vagrant to eastern England and Scotland. It breeds in Scandinavia, and other races are found in northern Asia and North America. In winter, Scandinavian and Russian birds are found in the low countries and in eastern Europe.

Hen Harrier *Circus cyaneus*

INTERNATIONAL NAME   NORTHERN HARRIER (N. AMERICA)

IDENTIFICATION

44–52 cm. Smaller than Buzzard. It has a long tail and long wings with 'fingered' tips. Male has silver-grey upperparts, white underparts, white rump, black wing-tips and slight blackish trailing edge to wings that sometimes shows in flight, especially on under-wing. Larger female is dark brown with buff marks on wing, grey-brown tail with darker bands and obvious white rump. Disc of stiffer feathers gives an 'owl-like' appearance to face. Underparts are paler and breast is heavily streaked. Juvenile is similar to female but with wing-linings and breast more bright ginger brown. Moult takes place between April and October. Female starts first and gaps can sometimes be seen in the wing.

SEE ALSO: Marsh Harrier p96, Montagu's Harrier p95, Buzzard p92.

HABITS

Seen singly during the day but often gathers in com-munal winter roosts. Buoyant flight when hunting low over ground, with wings forming a shallow 'V' when gliding. In spring, male has a spectacular switchback sky-dance. He also makes food passes to the female by calling to her and either passing food in the air or dropping it for her to catch.

VOICE

Silent except when nesting when it makes rapid 'yikkering' call during sky-dance display and various other scolding calls.

HABITAT

In Britain, a bird of upland heather moors, but it also nests in young conifer plantations. More widespread in winter, visiting lowland farms, fens, southern heaths, river valleys and coastal marshes.

FOOD

Feeds on small birds such as Meadow Pipits, also voles and mice. May also take larger prey, such as rabbits, hares, young waders and game birds.

BREEDING

Nesting begins in April. Nests are usually spaced out, but where a male is mated to more than one female, several nests may be in relatively close proximity. Nest is a pile of local vegetation, generally heather, built among low, dense vegetation at a site that may be damp or dry. Female incubates 4 or 5 eggs for about 34 days. Eggs are laid at 1–3 day intervals and, as incubation begins with the first egg, there is a notice-able age difference between the young. For the first 10–15 days the female tends the chicks and the male provides food. Later the female helps with hunting. Young fly at 37–42 days (males before the females) and they remain with the female for several more weeks.

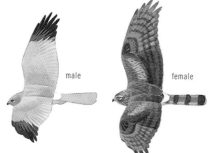

male   female

MOVEMENTS AND MIGRATIONS

In parts of its range this bird may be resident, but in Britain it is a partial migrant, with some birds moving south into Europe, and additional birds from northern Europe arriving for the winter. Males tend to be more likely to leave Britain than females. Oldest bird sur-vived over 17 years.

POPULATION

There are about 400 territories in the UK, almost 50 on the Isle of Man, and over 100 in Ireland.

CONSERVATION

Specially protected at all times. As a result of perse-cution in the 19th century almost exterminated from Britain, but remained in Orkney and some other remote Scottish sites, and also in Ireland. Has since made a gradual comeback, but still faces illegal per-secution on land where there is game shooting. In most European countries Hen Harrier populations are declining owing to habitat loss and persecution.

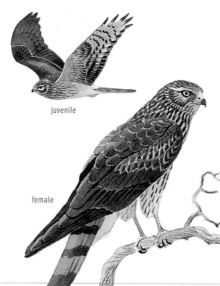

juvenile

female

DISTRIBUTION

Present all year. Breeds in upland areas of Scotland, parts of northern England, Isle of Man, North Wales and Ireland. In winter, it is more widespread. It also breeds from Scandinavia south to Portugal and across much of Asia. There is another race of Hen Harrier in North America.

Montagu's Harrier *Circus pygargus*

female

juvenile

Identification
43–47 cm. Smaller than Buzzard. Montagu's has long wings and tail, but a slimmer body and narrower and more pointed wings than the Hen Harrier. At rest wing-tips reach tail tip. Male is grey above with a grey rump. Grey of head and breast looks rather 'dirty' compared with Hen Harrier. Belly is white with some rusty streaks. In flight, underwing has two black bars, some rufous flecking, upperwing has a distinct black bar and black wing-tips. Female only very slightly larger. She is streaky brown with dark crescent mark on her cheeks and narrower and more U-shaped white rump than a Hen Harrier's and underwing often shows two distinct black bars. Juvenile has rufous, unstreaked underparts, dark brown upperparts that have a scaly look and a narrow white rump.
SEE ALSO: Hen Harrier p94, Marsh Harrier p96, Buzzard p92.

Habits
Soars and glides with wings held in a shallow 'V'. Flight light and buoyant. Generally seen singly or in pairs although in places in Europe where it is common many congregate and hunt together. Like Hen Harrier, has a sky-dance as a courtship display and male uses aerial food passes as part of courtship as well as to provision female during incubation.

Voice
Generally silent, except when nesting. At nest it has a chattering 'yick-yick-yick' call that is higher-pitched than that of a Hen Harrier.

Habitat
Traditionally nested in fens, wet fields, heaths, moors and dunes. In recent years has started to nest in agricultural fields, especially in winter wheat, barley and oilseed rape. Ranges widely outside the breeding season and visits dry grasslands and inland marshes in its African winter quarters.

Food
It is light and agile and suited to catching faster-moving prey. Pounces on small birds such as larks and pipits, and mammals, including voles, shrews and rabbits. It also eats the eggs of other birds, as well as lizards and insects.

Breeding
Breeding begins in May and female builds a nest of reeds, grasses, heather or other local material on the ground. Female incubates 4 or 5 eggs for 28–29 days. Eggs are laid at 2–3 day intervals. As incubation begins with the first egg they hatch at different times, resulting in an age difference between the young. Young fly after 35–40 days and remain with the female for a further 10–14 days.

Movements and Migrations
Summer visitor to southern Britain with a few more appearing on passage in spring and autumn. After nesting, young birds head off in random directions before finally migrating south. A few winter in Europe, but the majority migrate to Africa between July and September and return late March and April. The oldest ringed bird survived for over 16 years.

Population
About 13 females have attempted to nest in Britain in recent years. It declined from about 50 territories in the 1950s to none in 1974. Since then has made a faltering return, but status as regular breeding species remains precarious.

Conservation
Specially protected at all times. The number breeding in Britain is so small that almost every pair requires special protection. The recent nesting switch from marshes to farmland has been fortunate, as productivity of farmland nests has been higher than at traditional sites – provided there is cooperation from the farmer. As a ground-nester it suffers during prolonged periods of wet weather when eggs can become chilled or chicks sodden.

male

juvenile

female

Distribution
The few Montagu's Harriers that breed in Britain are mainly in the south and east of the country. The species nests from southern Sweden to North Africa and east into Russia. It winters in tropical and southern Africa.

Marsh Harrier *Circus aeruginosus*

INTERNATIONAL NAME WESTERN MARSH HARRIER

IDENTIFICATION

48–56 cm. Size of Buzzard but less bulky. Largest European harrier with long, rather broad wings and long tail. Has slim body and long legs. Male has pale head streaked finely with dark brown, tricoloured wings – brown with large grey patches and black wing-tips – and grey tail. Larger female is chocolate-brown with straw-coloured head and similar coloured leading edges to the wings. Juvenile resembles female but often lacks pale marks on wings and sometimes lacks pale head. Moult takes place between April and October. Flight feathers moulted gradually with female beginning before male.
SEE ALSO: Red Kite p97, Hen Harrier p94, Montagu's Harrier p95, Buzzard p92.

HABITS

Whether hunting over a reedbed, or soaring and gliding at a greater height, wings are usually V-shaped. Heavier-looking than other harriers. Before breeding, a pair will undertake aerial displays including a sky-dance comprising deep undulations, with male making mock attacks on female. Aerial food passes take place as male drops prey to the female that she catches in mid-air.

male

female

3rd-year

juvenile

female   male

VOICE

Mostly silent, but during courtship displays the adults have wailing 'kweooo' call.

HABITAT

Traditional breeding sites are in large reedbeds, but in recent years it has colonised smaller reedbeds and arable fields, especially winter-sown wheat and oilseed rape close to feeding areas. Some migrants visit tropical marshes and swamps in winter, but on migration it may be seen in drier areas.

FOOD

Feeds mainly on animals that live in or near marshes and other wetlands. Drops onto its prey from the air. Chief food is small birds, ducklings, game bird chicks and mammals, especially rabbits.

BREEDING

Nesting begins in April. Female builds a nest from grass, reeds and small sticks, on the ground among thick marshy vegetation or in a crop, while male, which may be bigamous, constructs one or more 'false nests' or platforms nearby. Eggs are laid at 2–3 day intervals. Female incubates clutch of 4 or 5 eggs and male brings her food. Incubation starts with the first egg, and as each egg takes 31–38 days to hatch the brood comprises young of varying ages. Male continues to provide food until the young have grown and scattered into surrounding vegetation. Young fly at

35–40 days and female stays with them for a further 15–25 days.

MOVEMENTS AND MIGRATIONS

After breeding most birds head south or south-west towards North and West Africa. The migrants that travel to Africa return again by April. Southern European breeding populations tend to make only local movements and some remain in the UK all winter.

POPULATION

Up to 400 female Marsh Harriers breed in the UK. The small wintering population in Britain is gradually increasing and these are almost all females.

CONSERVATION

Specially protected at all times. Drainage of wetlands and persecution reduced the number and range of this species in the past and it was down to one pair in 1971. Since then the protection of wetland sites has helped a recovery and also the birds started adopting arable fields as nest-sites. With the cooperation of farmers, these nests have been generally safe and many young have fledged successfully.

DISTRIBUTION

Most breed in eastern Britain, especially in East Anglia and Kent, but it also breeds in small numbers in parts of lowland Scotland, Lancashire, Yorkshire and Somerset. A few are seen in Britain in winter. It also breeds in Europe, from the Baltic south to Portugal and east into Russia and Asia. Many of the migrants from Europe winter in central and southern Africa.

Red Kite *Milvus milvus*

juvenile

IDENTIFICATION
60–66 cm. Larger than Buzzard. Elegant and graceful bird of prey with long wings and long forked tail. Reddish-brown body with dark streaks, an orange-red tail and a pale streaked head. In flight, underwing is distinctive with pale patch near the wing-end, dark mark at the bend of the wing and black, fingered tips. Female is larger than male. Juvenile has less distinct streaking on the body, pale brown undertail-coverts (reddish in adults) and a thin white line along upper-wing. Red Kites moult between May and the autumn, and at this time they may have some flight feathers that are noticeably shorter than others.
SEE ALSO: Buzzard p92, Marsh Harrier p96.

HABITS
Soars with an easy, buoyant flight, constantly changing the angle of its tail to steer, while hardly moving its wings. Often the long wings look angled, but are generally flat when gliding. Often seen singly or in pairs but larger gatherings occur at food supplies and communal roosts outside the nesting season.

VOICE
The call is a shrill, mewing 'peeee-ooow'.

juvenile

BREEDING
Nesting begins in late March. The nest of large twigs is usually in the fork of a deciduous tree and is some-times 'decorated' with rags and plastic bags (even underwear!). Sometimes the old nest of another spe-cies, such as Buzzard or Raven, is used. Nest may be used for several successive years. Female incubates 2 eggs, with male taking short shifts. Young hatch after 31 days and are cared for by both adults. They leave the nest after 45 days and sit in nearby trees, but it may be another 25 days before they fly properly, and their parents feed them for a further 15 days.

MOVEMENTS AND MIGRATIONS
Northern and eastern European populations are migratory while those in Britain and southern Europe are mainly resident. Some European migrants reach Britain. Oldest 25 years.

POPULATION
600–1,000 pairs breed in Britain. Both the native Welsh population and birds from reintroduction schemes have nested remarkably successfully in recent years and the breeding population is increasing.

CONSERVATION
Specially protected. Red Kites were once common and even scavenged on London's streets, but persecution drove them almost to extinction in Britain, with only a few remaining in Wales at the beginning of the 20th century. Protection has helped the species recov-er. Since 1989 young birds from Europe have been introduced into several locations in England and Scotland and its numbers are increasing. Productivity of the birds in England and Scotland is higher than in Wales. However, illegal poisoning remains the main 'unnatural' cause of death. There is some concern for the European population, which has recently declined in some places.

HABITAT
Breeds in mature but open woodland, usually in deciduous woods but sometimes in pine. Hunts farm-land, moorland and other open areas, and may scav-enge roadside verges. Roosts communally in woods in winter. Elsewhere in Europe it frequents fringes of marshes, and visits rubbish dumps.

FOOD
Mainly eats carrion, including dead sheep, and scav-enges on rubbish tips. Also catches live prey by diving from the air or dropping from a post feet first and catching its prey. Hunts invertebrates, including earth-worms, mammals such as rats, mice, voles and small rabbits, a variety of birds including young crows, pigeons and, in southern Europe, reptiles.

DISTRIBUTION
Breeds in central Wales, central England and northern Scotland. Also breeds in Europe, from southern Sweden to Mediterranean coast and east to the Ukraine. It is a little more widespread in southern Europe in winter.

White-tailed Eagle *Haliaeetus albicilla*

juvenile

IDENTIFICATION

70–90 cm. Heavier and more bulky than Golden Eagle. Wings are broad, rectangular-looking (like planks!) with obvious 'fingered' tips. Tail short and wedge-shaped. Neck long and strong, with large head and huge powerful bill that is usually obvious, even in flight. Adults are dark with pale heads and white tails. Males are smaller, lighter and with smaller bills than females. Young birds lack pale head and the white tail. Juvenile is dark with streaked underparts and darker head and tail. Second-year birds have paler bellies and third-year birds are darker. It has four or five body moults before reaching adult plumage. Only a proportion of the flight feathers are moulted each year. Moults more or less continuously, although it may pause in winter if food is in short supply.

SEE ALSO: Golden Eagle p99, Osprey p90.

HABITS

Flight is similar to a Heron, with shallow flaps and glides at low levels; at higher levels it soars with wings held flat. It is usually seen singly or in pairs and spends a lot of time perched, standing on the ground, or even standing in shallow water. In late winter and early spring pairs may be seen in display: 'sky-dancing', with gentle undulations, rolling and sometimes touching talons in flight.

juvenile

adult

3rd/4th-cal-year

VOICE

It makes dog-like yapping, high-pitched woodpecker-like 'kew, kew, kew, kew' and a quieter 'ko-ko ko'. Most calls are made near the nest or during courtship.

HABITAT

Lives around rocky sea coasts and islands but also visits large lakes. Immatures may sometimes appear in other habitats, such as farmland in winter.

FOOD

Hunts singly or in pairs and often robs other birds of their prey. Will grab food from the surface of the water and sometimes dives in. Eats cod, herring, trout and eels. Also kills other birds, especially gulls, ducks and auks, and takes rabbits, hares and other mammals. These eagles also eat carrion, and will take advantage of food supplies from abattoirs and discarded fish from fishing boats.

BREEDING

A pair selects one of several traditional nest-sites within a home range. Breeds in trees, on cliff ledges or sometimes on the ground. Nests are built from large sticks and driftwood, and lined with grass, seaweed and sometimes wool. Some nests are used for many years and reach a huge size as material is added year after year. 1–3 (usually 2) eggs are laid in late March or April and most incubation is by female. Young hatch after 40 days and are fed by both parents. They fly after 70 days. Once independent, the immatures roam widely and may join other youngsters at good feeding areas.

MOVEMENTS AND MIGRATIONS

Mainly resident in Britain. Northern European birds winter in central Europe, with a few ranging wider and occasionally arriving in eastern Britain. Oldest 28 years.

POPULATION

There has been a massive decline in White-tailed Eagle populations owing to persecution during 19th and early 20th centuries, although there have been some local recoveries. Recent reintroduction to west coast of Scotland has been successful and the population has increased to over 30 pairs.

CONSERVATION

Specially protected. In Scotland, most sites are secret for fear of attracting egg thieves or disturbance by birdwatchers. Poison baits have accidentally or deliberately killed some of these birds. In Europe a build-up of organochlorine chemicals has affected breeding success. Further reintroduction programmes are planned for Scotland and England.

DISTRIBUTION

A small number now breed on the west coast of Scotland. The species also breeds in northern Europe and Asia. In Europe the largest population is in Norway.

Golden Eagle *Aquila chrysaetos*

IDENTIFICATION
75–88 cm. Much larger than Buzzard, with powerful bill. Adult uniform dark brown with golden-yellow feathers on back of head. Sexes look similar, but female is larger. In flight, wings are long and broad, and trailing edges bulge out. Tail looks longer than that of a Buzzard and head protrudes prominently in front of the wings. Juvenile is darker with white base to the tail, black terminal band and white wing-patches. Immature shows whitish tail with dark band and varying amounts of white at base of flight feathers. Golden Eagles moult slowly and some feathers are retained for 2 years. Outer flight feathers are replaced more frequently than inner flight feathers. It takes 7 years to attain full adult plumage.
SEE ALSO: Buzzard p92, White-tailed Eagle p98.

HABITS
Usually seen singly or in pairs. The huge 2 m wingspan is almost twice that of the Buzzard. On take-off, when carrying prey and in display, flight is slow and laboured with deep wingbeats. Mostly it soars and glides effortlessly using air currents. At these times wings form a shallow 'V' and 'fingered' wing-tips are obvious. Displaying birds circle high up – almost touching – and will fold wings and plunge dramatically before repeating this in a series of loops.

VOICE
Generally silent, but sometimes makes a 'yelping' call.

HABITAT
In Britain lives in wild, open countryside, high moorlands, rugged mountains and remote islands. Outside Britain it breeds in mountain ranges, except those covered with dense forests, and also in flatter habitats where there are trees for nesting.

FOOD
Includes birds such as grouse, crows, seabirds and wildfowl, and also mammals varying in size from voles to young otters and foxes. Deer and sheep are also eaten, although generally as carrion.

BREEDING
Nest, or eyrie, is built of sticks and small branches on a cliff ledge or in a mature tree. Old nests are reused and new material added each year. Clutch of 1–3 eggs is laid in late March or early April. Incubation mostly by female and generally starts with the first egg, leading to a noticeable size difference between chicks. The eggs hatch after 43–45 days. While 2 chicks frequently hatch, it is not uncommon for the older and larger to kill the younger. Both adults provide food and the young fly from about 65 days, but they depend on their parents for a further 90 days or more.

MOVEMENTS AND MIGRATIONS
Young eagles leaving their nest-sites range more widely than adults and there is a tendency for most to head east. Adult Golden Eagles in Britain seldom move far from their territories, but other more northerly populations leave their breeding grounds in autumn and return the following spring. The oldest ringed Golden Eagle survived for over 32 years.

POPULATION
There are 440 pairs of Golden Eagles breeding in Britain and the population is currently stable.

CONSERVATION
Specially protected. Historically it was more widespread, breeding in England, Wales and Ireland. The decline was caused largely by persecution. Current problems include lack of food due to overgrazing by sheep and deer, and afforestation of its upland hunting grounds. Birds in the west generally produce fewer young. It also suffers from attacks by egg thieves, poisoning and illegal killing. Wind farms pose a new risk.

juvenile

DISTRIBUTION
In Britain the Golden Eagle breeds mainly in the Scottish Highlands and Islands. In Europe it breeds from Scandinavia to the Pyrenees and other races are found in southern Europe, North Africa, Asia and North America.

Goshawk *Accipiter gentilis*

INTERNATIONAL NAME NORTHERN GOSHAWK

IDENTIFICATION

48–62 cm. Female almost the size of Buzzard; male is smaller. Looks like huge Sparrowhawk, having rounded wings, but tail is relatively shorter and rounded at edges, not cut square across tip. Adult is grey-brown above with dark patch behind eye giving hooded appearance. Close to, yellow eyes and white 'eyebrow' create fierce expression. Underparts pale and closely barred, and tail also barred. Female is browner than male. Juvenile has a buff, streaked breast. Moults between April and September, with female starting first.
SEE ALSO: Sparrowhawk p101, Buzzard p92, Hen Harrier p94.

juvenile

female

juvenile female

male

HABITS

In flight, appears deep-chested and powerful, with proportionally short wings. Except when nesting, it is generally solitary. An elusive species, but can be seen soaring over its nest-site in early spring. When soaring, the wings are held flat with three or four feathers visible at the wing-tip. Secondary flight feathers are long and bulge, giving an 'S' curve to the rear wing. It can point its wing-tips and look remarkably Peregrine-like. Displaying birds have a sky-dance that involves spreading the white undertail feathers, flapping very slowly on straight wings and, eventually, rising and falling dramatically. Female does the majority of sky-dancing. When hunting, it is remarkably agile and weaves through stands of trees.

VOICE

Most calls are heard close to the nest or when displaying. The most frequent is 'gek-gek-gek', which is also given when birds are alarmed.

HABITAT

Lives and nests in large mature woods and forests. Inhabits both coniferous and deciduous woodland, but also hunts in open countryside.

FOOD

The Goshawk will use cover to surprise its prey. It makes a rapid chase over a short distance and grasps its quarry in its talons. Will also stoop like a Peregrine to gain speed before attacking. It feeds on birds such as Jays, Woodpigeons, Pheasants, Starlings, crows and thrushes. It also kills mammals such as rabbits.

BREEDING

Nesting begins in March or April. A nest of twigs and branches, lined with bark and pine needles, is built in the fork of a large tree, although nests from previous years are often reused. Female incubates the 3 or 4 eggs for 35–38 days and broods the young for their first 8–10 days. She will fiercely attack any potential predators – including humans and even male Goshawks. Young stay in the nest for about 35 days before moving onto nearby branches for a further 10 days, by which time they are able to fly.

MOVEMENTS AND MIGRATIONS

Most British Goshawks do not move far from their breeding sites. Young birds disperse in all directions in late summer. Some northern populations move south in autumn. The oldest ringed bird survived 18 years.

POPULATION

The current population is over 400 pairs. There has been a significant increase in recent years.

CONSERVATION

Specially protected at all times. As a result of persecution and reduction of forests the Goshawk became extinct as a breeding species in Britain at the end of the 1800s. The current breeding population originates from birds that escaped from captivity or that were deliberately released. The colonisation has been hampered by the theft of eggs and young and by other illegal persecution, but the establishment of coniferous forests and their subsequent management by the Forestry Commission has helped this species enormously.

DISTRIBUTION

In Britain the Goshawk is widely though thinly distributed through suitable woods and forests, especially in Wales and southern Scotland. It also breeds in Europe and Russia, and there are other races, including one in North America.

Sparrowhawk *Accipiter nisus*

INTERNATIONAL NAME | EURASIAN SPARROWHAWK

IDENTIFICATION

28–38 cm. Male is smaller than a Kestrel. Sparrowhawks are small, fast-flying birds of prey with long, square-ended tails and broad, rounded wings. Male has a slate-grey back and reddish, barred underparts that can appear orange at a distance. Grey tail crossed with 4–5 dark bars. Female may be 25% larger, heavier-looking, with brown upperparts, paler barred underparts, white stripe over eye and a fierce expression. Juvenile has reddish-brown upperparts and ragged bars on breast. Moult is between May and October, but may be suspended while young are being fed. SEE ALSO: Goshawk p100, Kestrel p102.

HABITS

Secretive and usually solitary. Sometimes seen displaying over its nest-site as it soars on broad, outstretched wings. When displaying in spring, birds often flap their wings slowly and deliberately as they undulate across the sky. They also close their tail feathers and stick out their pale undertail-coverts. These soaring displays may culminate in a spectacular dive with closed wings. In level flight it alternates rapid, flappy wingbeats with a long glide. Takes its prey by surprise, by watching, waiting and attacking swiftly, grasping prey with its foot. Often uses the same flight path when hunting and sometimes dashes along a hedgerow, silently slipping over the top, to startle a flock of small birds on the other side.

female
male

juvenile
male

VOICE

Silent for most of the year. When nesting, most common call is a shrill 'ke-ke-ke-ke'.

HABITAT

A woodland hunter living mainly, but not exclusively, in lowland areas. Also found in urban areas. Nests in conifer, mixed and deciduous woodland where it hunts along woodland edges, rides and clearings. It often visits nearby farmland and gardens to hunt.

FOOD

Mainly birds. Male specialises in taking smaller species such as Chaffinch, Yellowhammer and Great Tit. Female takes larger species such as Blackbird and Starling. Birds up to the size of Woodpigeon may be caught and killed.

BREEDING

New nests of twigs and sticks are built each year in the fork of a deciduous tree or near the trunk of a conifer. Egg laying begins in late April or May and incubation of the 4 or 5 eggs is carried out by the female for 32–36 days. During incubation male supplies female with food. As young grow female also helps supply them with food. At about 28 days they leave the nest and sit in nearby branches until they fly a few days later. They depend on their parents for a further 20 days until they can hunt and feed themselves.

MOVEMENTS AND MIGRATIONS

In Britain largely resident. Although young birds will leave their native woods they do not generally travel more than 16 km. In northern and eastern Europe the species is a migrant and moves into central and southern Europe, and some of these migrants reach eastern Britain. Oldest ringed bird survived for more than 20 years.

male

female

juvenile
male

POPULATION

Over 40,000 pairs in the UK and up to 10,000 in Ireland. Following a sharp decline during the 20th century, the population made a dramatic recovery, although that recovery has slowed and it may now be declining in some areas.

CONSERVATION

Once common throughout Britain and Ireland, it was severely affected by agricultural chemicals, and numbers declined rapidly, especially in southern and eastern England. Legal and voluntary bans on the most toxic chemicals have helped the species to recover. In recent years the Sparrowhawk has also moved into cities, towns and suburbs where there is an abundance of prey and nesting is relatively safe.

DISTRIBUTION

Throughout Britain and Ireland, except in the most mountainous areas or on the most intensive farmland. Also breeds in Europe, from the Mediterranean to the far north of Scandinavia, and also in Asia.

Kestrel *Falco tinnunculus*

INTERNATIONAL NAME   COMMON KESTREL

male

female

IDENTIFICATION

32–35 cm. Small bird of prey with short neck, long wings and long tail. Habitually hovers when hunting. Male has spotted reddish-brown back, grey head and tail and buff underparts with dark spots. It has a black band at the end of its tail. Female slightly larger and browner with variable pattern of black bars on upper-parts and pale breast with dark streaks. Juvenile resembles female, but more boldly streaked below and with broader dark bars on back. Moult lasts almost all year. Main flight feathers are lost gradually between May and September. Feathers are moulted in a sequence, but the most noticeable gaps appear in August and September.

SEE ALSO: Sparrowhawk p101, Hobby p104, Merlin p103.

HABITS

Usually seen singly. Hunts during daylight and also during and after dusk. When hunting it will either hover effortlessly, with tail fanned and wings beating rapidly, or hang motionless, supported by the wind. Also hunts from a prominent perch such as a telegraph pole, or sometimes chases small birds. When soaring, wings appear more rounded at the tips and tail is fanned.

female soaring

male

male hovering

VOICE

Usually silent. Most common call is a shrill 'kee-kee-kee' that is most usually heard near the nest.

HABITAT

Survives in a variety of habitats including towns and cities, but most numerous in areas of rough grassland. Has exploited the food found in grassland within young conifer forests, beside busy roads and on rail-way embankments.

FOOD

Mainly small mammals, especially short-tailed voles. Other mammals include shrews, mice and occasionally larger prey such as moles and rabbits. Larks, pipits and Starling are commonly caught and larger birds such as Blackbird and Collared Dove are also hunted. Kes-trels regularly eat beetles, other insects and worms.

BREEDING

Does not build a nest, but scrapes a depression for its eggs. Uses cliff ledges or buildings, holes in trees and disused nests of large birds. Breeding begins in February with aerial, territorial displays. Female incu-bates 4 or 5 eggs, the male sometimes taking a turn. Young hatch after 28–29 days. For the first 10–14 days they are brooded by the female and then both parents feed them. The young fly after 32–37 days, but rely on their parents for a further month.

MOVEMENTS AND MIGRATIONS

Once independent, young kestrels often travel up to 150 km in no particular direction. In northern Europe and Scandinavia Kestrels that breed in areas covered by snow in winter are migratory and may reach central Africa in winter. Some from upland areas of Britain are partial migrants to lower ground. Migrants from the Low Countries and further east can be found in the winter in south-east England. Kestrels in central and southern Britain are largely resident. Oldest known wild Kestrel lived for 15 years.

POPULATION

There are over 50,000 pairs in Britain and up to 10,000 in Ireland. Recent surveys have detected a decline in the UK and other European strongholds.

CONSERVATION

The decline of the Kestrel has been linked to similar declines of other species that depend on agricultural land. Although the causes are not fully understood, the more intensive management of grassland, with fewer areas supporting voles, more widespread use of insecticides and the loss of wide field margins mean that small mammal populations have reduced. Schemes aimed at restoring hay meadows, providing beetle banks and restoring field margins may be helping.

DISTRIBUTION

Found throughout most of Britain and Ireland although scarce in north-west Scotland and less numerous in Ireland. Also found in most of Europe, Africa and Asia.

Merlin *Falco columbarius*

IDENTIFICATION
25–30 cm. Smaller than Kestrel. Our smallest falcon with short, broad-based, pointed wings and shorter tail than Kestrel. When perched, wing-tips reach about three-quarters along the tail length. Male has blue-grey back, rusty breast with dark streaks and very dark primary flight feathers. Cheeks and nape are rufous. Female larger and browner with pale buff breast streaked heavily with brown and barred tail. Juvenile resembles dark female and has white flecks on nape. Moults between June and September. Female moults earlier than male.
SEE ALSO: Kestrel p102.

the male provides the food. At about 18 days the young leave the ground nests and crouch in the surrounding heather. They can fly after about 32 days and depend on their parents for food for a further month.

MOVEMENTS AND MIGRATIONS
This species is mainly a short-distance migrant but some birds remain on their breeding grounds for most of the year. Migrants from Iceland have been recorded in winter in Ireland and north-west Britain. Some British Merlins have been found in western France in winter. Most Merlins leave their breeding grounds between August and October. Return migration takes place during April and May. The oldest ringed bird lived for more than 12 years.

male

female

male

female

HABITS
Usually a solitary species although occasionally two birds will hunt in unison. Small and compact-looking predator, male not much bigger than a Mistle Thrush, but with direct and dashing flight. Rapid wingbeats are followed by short glides, often low to ground. Chases small birds with agile twists and turns. Regularly perches on posts, walls and boulders. Occasionally has been seen to surprise its prey by approaching on foot.

VOICE
Usually silent, but near a nest the shrill 'kek-kek-kek-kek' call may be heard when the bird is excited or is chasing off intruders such as crows.

HABITAT
Breeds mainly on ground on heather moorland in uplands and in some coastal areas. Increasingly nests in the fringes of maturing conifer plantations. In winter, moves to lowland areas, particularly coastal salt-marshes and farmland.

FOOD
Mainly small birds such as Meadow Pipit, Skylark, Chaffinch and Wheatear. Also takes larger birds such as Mistle Thrush. Other food includes voles, bats, moths and beetles.

BREEDING
Traditionally Merlins in Britain nested on the ground among heather, but in recent years increasing numbers of tree nests have been found, usually in old crow's nests on the edge of conifer plantations. The clutch of 3–5 eggs is incubated by male and female for 28–32 days. At first the female tends young and

POPULATION
About 1,300 pairs nest in the UK and up to 130 in Ireland. It appears that the population is increasing slightly.

CONSERVATION
Specially protected at all times. There has been a historical decline in its population, largely caused by human persecution. The population is now stable or increasing due to reduced persecution and fewer environmental pollutants used in agriculture. However, many of its former breeding sites are now planted with commercial forests and much heather moorland is lost. Quality of moorland is affected by overgrazing by sheep. Some pairs have adapted to nest in trees, in old crow's nests, or artificial nests provided by ornithologists.

DISTRIBUTION
The Merlin breeds in the uplands in the north and west of Britain, and also parts of Ireland. In winter it has a wider distribution and regularly visits lowland farms and coastal marshes. The species also breeds in northern Europe, Asia and North America. In Europe it winters in central and southern Europe and North Africa.

Hobby *Falco subbuteo*

INTERNATIONAL NAME   EURASIAN HOBBY

IDENTIFICATION

30–36 cm. Size of Kestrel but more rakish with long pointed wings and rather short tail. At rest long wing-tips reach to, or even beyond, the tail tip. Adults have slate-grey upperparts, a conspicuous white half-collar, white cheeks with a black 'moustache' and pale under-parts with lines of black streaking. Undertail and thighs are red. Sexes look similar but female is margin-ally larger. Juvenile has brown upperparts with pale edges to the feathers, buff underparts with dark streaks and lacks the red 'trousers' of adult. First-summer immatures resemble 'washed-out' juveniles. Moult, including some flight feathers, begins in August and is completed in its winter quarters.
SEE ALSO: Kestrel p102, Peregrine p105, Merlin p103.

HABITS

Looks like giant Swift in flight, as the wings appear crescent-shaped and the tail is shorter than that of Kestrel. Deep wingbeats, and attitude in flight is one of power and speed. When hunting, capable of rapid bursts of speed and breathtaking turns. Catches drag-onflies and other insects in its talons and eats them as it flies. It can sometimes appear stationary as it flies into the wind.

juvenile

juvenile

VOICE

Usually silent except for shrill 'kyew, kew, kew, kew, kew' calls made in the vicinity of a nest.

HABITAT

Breeds in mature trees on heathlands of southern Brit-ain and also on farmland, in woodland edges, small copses and isolated trees. It hunts over open country-side and also over water. In its African winter quarters it inhabits open landscapes with scattered trees, damp woodlands and wetlands.

FOOD

Catches most of its prey in the air. Young Swallows, martins and Meadow Pipits are frequently caught, but the list includes fast-flying species such as Swift, unlikely species such as Little Owl, and large birds such as Woodpigeon. Insect food includes dragonflies,

grasshoppers and crickets, moths and beetles. Swarms of summer chafers occasionally attract groups of hunting Hobbies. Bats are also caught. The Hobby will rob other predators, such as Kestrel, to obtain prey.

BREEDING

Courtship takes place in May and June, with dramatic aerobatics that involve soaring and diving over breed-ing territory. Nests in trees. The clutch of 2 or 3 eggs is laid in June in the old nest of a large bird such as a crow. Incubation lasts 28–32 days and is mainly by female, with male relieving her for short periods. Male provides most of the food. Young fly after about 30 days but continue to be fed by their parents for at least a month.

MOVEMENTS AND MIGRATIONS

A summer migrant to Europe, arriving in late April and early May and returning between August and Octo-ber. The oldest Hobby to survive in the wild lived for more than 15 years.

POPULATION

2,200 pairs breed in Britain. Population increase and range extended north and west in the last 20 years.

CONSERVATION

Specially protected but still a target for egg thieves. Persecution in past has caused some local extinctions. Shooting and trapping around the Mediterranean remains a problem for migrating Hobbies. In Britain it is thought that the greater availability of crow's nests and the increase in insects (especially dragonflies) owing to climate change has helped this species.

DISTRIBUTION

In Britain it is mainly found in the lowlands of the south and east but it is spreading north into Co. Durham and Northumberland and has recently been recorded breeding in Scotland. In Europe it breeds from the Arctic Circle to the Mediterranean and east into Russia and Asia. European Hobbies winter in southern Africa.

Peregrine *Falco peregrinus*

INTERNATIONAL NAME PEREGRINE FALCON

IDENTIFICATION
36–48 cm. Large and powerful falcon with long, broad-based, bluntly pointed wings and relatively short tail. Adult has blue-grey upperparts and dark blue wings and head. The crown is blackish and it has a conspicuous black 'moustache' contrasting with white face, giving it a hooded look. Pale breast finely spotted and underwing barred. Female is noticeably larger. Juvenile has dark brown upperparts with pale tips to feathers, streaks on underparts and broad buff tip to tail. Moult takes place between April and November, but may be suspended while adults are feeding young.
SEE ALSO: Hobby p104.

juvenile

HABITS
Away from nest it is usually solitary. Swift and agile in flight with fast wingbeats and long glides. Chases prey and attacks it from below or will spot prey a long way off, rise very high and fly fast towards it, dropping with wings folded to increase momentum. Often soars with wing-tips slightly splayed.

VOICE
Usually silent, but may be noisy at nest. If female is disturbed she produces a grating, 'scraa, scraa, scraa', often building to a crescendo. Male's call is higher.

HABITAT
Mostly a bird of open country. Nests on crags or other rock faces, sea cliffs, offshore islands, quarries and, increasingly, on buildings in towns. Hunts over marshes, estuaries and agricultural land outside the breeding season.

FOOD
Feeds mainly on birds captured in flight, either by out-flying them, or stooping on them. Feral Pigeon, Wood-pigeon, Lapwing, Skylark, Black-headed Gull, Blackbird and Starling are among the common prey, but mammals, such as rabbits, are occasionally taken and carrion is eaten during extreme weather conditions.

BREEDING
Some nest-sites have been used for hundreds of years. In Britain they are usually on ledges of cliffs, although old crow's nests in trees may be used. Pairs return in February and perform breathtaking aerobatics as they plunge, dive, roll and stoop. Male supplies female with food, sometimes dropping prey that she catches in flight. The 3 or 4 eggs are laid in March or April. Incubation is mostly by female and lasts 28–33 days. At

first young are tended by female while male provides food; as they grow both adults hunt. Young fly after 39 days and gradually become independent.

MOVEMENTS AND MIGRATIONS
In Britain and Ireland present all year, although some, especially females and juveniles, move away from uplands in autumn. More northerly populations are migratory and some from Europe winter in Africa. The oldest known wild Peregrine survived for 17 years.

POPULATION
Following a population crash during the 20th century, there has been a partial recovery so that now there are 1,500 pairs breeding in the UK and up to 350 in Ireland. Additional birds arrive from Scandinavia for the winter.

CONSERVATION
Historically, the Peregrine was prized for falconry, but has also been persecuted by gamekeepers and landowners and became a target for egg thieves. It was killed during World War II to protect homing pigeons and suffered disastrously from the effects of agricultural insecticides. Control of chemicals and legal protection have helped it to partially recover, but the species remains at risk across much of Europe. There remains the threat of continuing illegal persecution on some sporting estates and from racing pigeon interests.

juvenile

DISTRIBUTION
The Peregrine's stronghold in Britain is the uplands of the north and west and rocky seacoasts. Recently the English south coast has been re-occupied in places. Peregrines now breed on buildings in some towns and cities. In winter it visits many lowland areas although still most frequent in the west. Elsewhere, other races are found in rocky or coastal areas in Europe, Africa, Asia, America and Australia.

Water Rail *Rallus aquaticus*

IDENTIFICATION
23–28 cm. Smaller than Moorhen. Upperparts streaky brown, underparts blue-grey, with grey and white barring on the flanks and white under the tail. Bill is long and red. Long legs and toes trail in flight. Juvenile has a browner face with a pale stripe over the eye, paler, more mottled underparts with no blue-grey, a pale throat and dark bill. After nesting, adults undergo their annual moult. Flight feathers are lost simultaneously and they are flightless for about 3 weeks.
SEE ALSO: Moorhen p108, Spotted Crake p107.

juvenile

HABITS
Usually shy and skulking, and more often heard than seen, but sometimes in winter, or where it becomes used to people, it can be surprisingly confiding. Usually solitary outside the breeding season and defends a winter territory. Its slim body allows it to slip through dense waterside vegetation. Walks cautiously, flicking its tail. When alarmed will run, head down, for cover. Frequently swims over short distances. Flight appears weak and fluttering on rather long wings.

VOICE
Makes a variety of grunts and squeals during the day and night. Most obvious call is a drawn-out, squealing shriek rather like a piglet.

downy young

HABITAT
Breeds in dense reedbeds and marshes with thick, low cover and some open muddy areas. Also alongside rivers, around lakes and ponds and, in winter, in ditches and other wet places. Usually associated with fresh water, but visits brackish lagoons and saltmarshes.

FOOD
Feeds in the water and on land. Catches small fish, freshwater shrimps, frogs, small snails, insects and their larvae. Eats berries and other fruit, and shoots and roots of plants such as watercress. Will catch and eat small birds and it also eats carrion.

BREEDING
Nest is on ground amongst dense vegetation close to water. The 6–11 eggs are laid between March and June. Incubation is for 19–22 days by both parents, although the female takes the largest share. Young are brooded in the nest for a few days and fed by both parents. Once out of the nest they soon feed themselves. They fly at 20–30 days and become independent after about 55 days. A second brood is normal, with breeding often continuing into August.

MOVEMENTS AND MIGRATIONS
British and Irish Water Rails are mainly resident, but northern populations are migratory and in October and November Britain receives birds from northern and eastern Europe. These birds return in March and April. The oldest ringed bird lived for over 8 years.

POPULATION
This is a difficult species to census, but there are thought to be over 1,280 territories in Britain and a further 1,000–2,500 in Ireland. There is some evidence that the breeding population is falling in several parts of its range, including the UK.

CONSERVATION
Once common, but drainage of marshes and fens and loss of vegetation along waterways has reduced its numbers. It is adversely affected by severe winters that freeze shallow water, and dry summers may also present problems. Conversely, changing water levels during wet summers destroy active nests. Recent initiatives by the RSPB and other conservation bodies to recreate large reedbeds should help this species.

DISTRIBUTION
Thinly scattered over much of lowland Britain with larger concentrations in East Anglia. Ireland has higher densities of Water Rails than Britain. Winter distribution is similar, but with rather more individuals being seen in southern England. Breeds in Europe from the Mediterranean to Scandinavia and east into Russia. Also found in Asia and North Africa.

Spotted Crake *Porzana porzana*

IDENTIFICATION
22–24 cm. Similar size to a Starling. This small marsh bird has a green-brown back with dark streaks and white flecks and spots, and blue-grey on the face and throat. The olive-brown breast is covered in pearl-like white spots. The flanks are barred black and white, it has orange feathers under the tail, fine white lines near the tips of the folded wings and the leading edge of the outer flight feather is white. The bill is dull yellow with a red spot at the base. The female resembles the male, but is slightly smaller. The juvenile has a pale stripe over the eye, lacks any blue-grey, has a pale throat and browner breast. Adults moult completely after breeding, and lose all flight feathers. Juveniles start by moulting the head and body, but can suspend this moult while they migrate.
SEE ALSO: Moorhen p108, Water Rail p106.

HABITS
This secretive species skulks in dense vegetation, but some birds can be confiding, especially juveniles in autumn. It is most active at dawn and dusk. If surprised in the open it will run for cover or spring up and fly with dangling legs and fluttering flight before dropping into cover. Usually seen singly. It walks with legs bent, body close to the ground and tail flicking nervously. It swims with an action rather like a Moorhen.

in the nest until all the eggs have hatched. After a few days they leave the nest and feed themselves. They fly after 25 days. There may be two broods in a year.

MOVEMENTS AND MIGRATIONS
Most Spotted Crakes are summer migrants to western Europe, arriving from March to May and returning in September and October. The majority seen in Britain are juveniles, arriving from August to October. A few overwinter in Europe, especially around the Mediterranean. Many European birds cross the Sahara and winter in East Africa. The oldest known individual survived over 7 years.

POPULATION
Up to 26 males have been heard in the UK in recent years and fewer than 5 in Ireland. Historically, it was probably more numerous, but for most of the 20th century it only nested sporadically. During the last 20 years nesting has increased. 50–60 migrant Spotted Crakes are seen each year.

CONSERVATION
The Spotted Crake is specially protected. Most of the marshes that it breeds on are nature reserves and the plans by the RSPB and other conservation bodies to recreate large reedbeds may help this species in future.

female

male

juvenile

male

VOICE
Usually silent during the day, but adults call at dusk and throughout the night in spring. The call is a rapid 'whit, whit', repeated at approximately 1 second intervals and likened to a whip cutting through the air.

HABITAT
Breeds in large freshwater marshes and other wetlands with shallow water and dense vegetation. On migration and in winter it visits similar habitats where it may be found feeding along muddy wetland margins.

FOOD
Among the wide variety of small prey items are insects such as caddis flies, beetles (including water beetles) and moth larvae. It also eats small water snails, fish and worms. Plant material such as seeds, shoots and roots of rushes are also eaten.

BREEDING
The nest is on the ground near water. Both adults incubate the 10–12 eggs for 18–19 days. Young remain

DISTRIBUTION
In Britain it nests in a few widely scattered locations, with most regularly used sites being in East Anglia and northern Scotland. Migrants are scattered widely in autumn, but mostly in eastern England. It breeds from northern Europe to the Mediterranean and also in parts of Africa and Asia. European migrants winter in central and eastern Africa.

Moorhen *Gallinula chloropus*

INTERNATIONAL NAME   COMMON MOORHEN

IDENTIFICATION

32–35 cm. Smaller than Coot. From a distance appears black with a ragged white line along its body, but the back is olive-brown and the head and underparts are blue-grey. Bill is red with a yellow tip and a red 'shield' on the forehead. Long legs and toes are yellowish-green. Under its tail it has white feathers divided by a black line. Juvenile is dark brown with a pale throat and chin and a less obvious line along its body. The body feathers are moulted between May and November. Flight feathers are lost simultaneously and birds are flightless for a short time between June and August.

SEE ALSO: Coot p109, Water Rail p106, Corncrake p110.

HABITS

Constantly flicks its tail as it walks or swims, revealing white undertail feathers. When taking off it runs across the water, trailing its legs as it takes to the air. Once airborne, the legs protrude beyond the tail. It uses its long toes to clamber around in vegetation and it often roosts in trees and bushes. Swims with a distinctive pumping motion and sometimes dives to escape danger. Seen singly or in family groups in summer, but larger groups sometimes form in winter.

VOICE

Wide range of calls, the most familiar being a loud, abrupt 'kurr-uk' that seems to echo across the water. It makes other harsh, croaking calls.

HABITAT

Breeds around freshwater lakes, rivers, ditches and small ponds. Also found in parks in towns and sometimes feeds on farmland adjacent to wetlands.

FOOD

Eats both plant and animal material, feeding on land and in water. Plant food includes duckweed, pondweed, seeds from sedges, docks and buttercup and also berries from blackberry, rose and elder. Animal food includes worms, snails, spiders, insects, small fish and eggs of other birds.

BREEDING

Breeds from March until early autumn. Both parents build the nest among aquatic plants in or near water. It consists of dead reeds and other vegetation. Occasionally it nests in bushes. Both birds incubate the 5–7 eggs for about 21 days. It is not uncommon for two, sometimes three or four, females to lay in one nest. Young are fed by the parents and also by young of earlier broods. By 25 days they can feed themselves, but continue to be fed by their parents until they fly at about 45 days. They become independent between 52 and 99 days. There are two or three broods.

MOVEMENTS AND MIGRATIONS

Birds from Britain and Ireland are mostly resident. Those from northern and eastern Europe migrate south-west. Some reach Britain in autumn and stay until spring. The oldest wild bird survived for over 18 years.

1st-winter

juvenile

POPULATION

There are 270,000 pairs in the UK and up to 100,000 in Ireland. After a small decline in 20th century, the population appears to have stabilised again.

CONSERVATION

Threats come from the methods of managing waterways that often remove bankside vegetation. Maintenance of channels and banks needs to be on a rotation, where some vegetated areas are left uncut, to allow Moorhens and other wildlife feeding and nesting sites. Feral mink may also be a threat to local populations.

DISTRIBUTION

In Britain found in lowland areas, especially in central and eastern England. Scarce in northern Scotland, and the uplands of Wales and northern England. Elsewhere widely distributed, being found in most of Europe, except the far north, and also Asia, Africa and North and South America.

Coot *Fulica atra*

INTERNATIONAL NAME | EURASIAN COOT

IDENTIFICATION
36–38 cm. Larger than Moorhen. Dumpy waterbird, swims strongly with nodding head motion. Adult is slate-black with a white bill and forehead. In flight, shows a pale bar along the trailing edge of the inner wings. Legs are grey with long toes that are partly webbed. In flight, feet stick out well beyond the tail. Juvenile is grey-brown with pale face and throat. Adults begin to moult in May. The flight feathers are moulted simultaneously and birds are flightless for a short time between June and September. Juveniles start to moult their body feathers after fledging and finish by late October.
SEE ALSO: Moorhen p108.

young on the nest for the first 3–4 days and male feeds them. The parents divide the brood between them and continue to feed the young for about 30 days. The young fly at about 55 days. Sometimes two or even three broods are reared in a single summer.

MOVEMENTS AND MIGRATIONS
Many present in Britain and Ireland throughout the year. Birds move to larger lakes in autumn and some leave the country. In Europe Coots in the north and east are migrants and many of these reach Britain and increase local populations, especially in southern and eastern Britain. The oldest survived for over 20 years.

juvenile

1st-winter

HABITS
Frequently seen in flocks and often accompanies swans and other waterbirds, picking up food disturbed or discarded by the larger species. Spends most of its day on water and dives frequently when feeding. Also grazes on short grass where it walks rather awkwardly, and runs with wings flapping. It makes a long, pattering run across the water as it takes off. It can be noisy and quarrelsome and engages in territorial fights during the breeding season.

VOICE
The most usual call is a loud single note, 'kowk', that may be heard during the day and at night.

HABITAT
Generally found on larger waters than Moorhen. Breeds on lakes, reservoirs, flooded gravel pits and large, slow-flowing rivers. Also breeds on park lakes in towns and cities. In winter it congregates on larger bodies of water and, sometimes, on the sea in cold weather.

FOOD
Eats both plant and animal material. Plants include algae, pondweeds, duckweed, bulrush, hornwort and young grasses. Animals include freshwater mussels, water snails, larvae of flies, moths and beetles.

BREEDING
Most nests are built among reeds and other aquatic vegetation and close to other Coot's nests. Some nests are out in the open with little surrounding cover. The large nest is made of plant leaves and stems and lined with smaller material. Nesting begins at the end of April. Incubation of the 5–7 eggs is by both parents and lasts for 21–24 days. Female broods newly hatched

POPULATION
22,000–29,000 pairs breed in the UK and up to 10,000 in Ireland. In winter there may be 200,000 birds in Britain and Ireland. The population appears to be stable although there has been a recent decline in eastern Europe.

CONSERVATION
This species has been helped by the creation of flooded gravel workings in southern and central England and the construction of large reservoirs. These have provided new breeding sites and places where large flocks can gather and feed in winter.

DISTRIBUTION
The Coot is widely distributed in Britain and Ireland, with the largest numbers in the English lowlands. The winter distribution is similar, but with more birds concentrated on the larger water bodies. The species breeds throughout Europe as far north as Finland. It is also found in Asia and parts of North Africa with another race in Australia.

Corncrake *Crex crex*

INTERNATIONAL NAME CORN CRAKE

IDENTIFICATION

27–30 cm. Smaller than Moorhen, and rather chicken-like, with a short, pointed bill and thick neck. Mainly yellow-brown with dark streaks on its upperparts, reddish-brown underparts, with pale barring on its flanks and grey face and breast. The rusty-red wing feathers show at rest and in flight. Wings are quite rounded at the tips, but in full flight look longer and sleeker. Adults moult in July and August. Flight feathers are lost simultaneously and it becomes flightless for a short time.

SEE ALSO: Quail p53, Grey Partridge p59, Spotted Crake p107.

HABITS

Generally solitary except when nesting. Very secretive and more likely to be heard than seen. On the ground walks with high steps and runs swiftly. Able to thread its way through dense vegetation. Usual flight is fluttering, with legs dangling, but over longer distances the flight is more direct and the legs are drawn up under the body.

VOICE

The distinctive song, 'crex-crex', is mostly heard at dusk and during the night. It has been likened to drawing a comb across a matchbox and is the origin of the Corncrake's scientific name.

HABITAT

Prefers thick low vegetation such as grasslands, including meadows, rough pastures and the dry fringes of marshes and fens, but generally avoids wet places. Grasslands cropped for hay are ideal unless they are cut too early. In Europe and Russia breeds in wide river flood plains amongst grasslands, iris beds and drier reedbeds. In winter in Africa inhabits dry grasslands and savanna, and grassy areas close to rivers and marshes.

FOOD

Feeds on insects, including beetles, flies, grasshoppers and ants. It also eats spiders, snails and worms as well as seeds, leaves and stems of plants.

BREEDING

The nest is a shallow cup lined with leaves and built on the ground among dense vegetation, sometimes with longer stems pulled over the top to make a loose canopy. Lays 8–12 eggs, which are incubated by the female for 16–19 days. Young are fed by the female for the first few days after hatching until they feed themselves. They can fly after about 34 days. There may be two broods.

MOVEMENTS AND MIGRATIONS

A summer visitor to Europe arriving in mid-April and leaving again in August or September. Capable of sustained long-distance flights, for example across the Sahara Desert.

POPULATION

There have been over 1,100 males calling in Britain in recent years and a further 150 in Ireland, which is a good indication of the number of breeding pairs. Following 150 years of serious decline the numbers have recently stabilised and are slowly increasing again.

juvenile

CONSERVATION

Specially protected. Once common in much of Britain and Ireland, the decline started as hay fields were first mown mechanically. Earlier grass cutting and the even earlier cutting for silage destroyed nests, adults and young. Suitable habitats were lost to drainage and agricultural intensification. By the end of the 20th century it was virtually extinct in England and Wales and declines were noted across Europe. Conservationists are working with farmers who have Corncrakes on their land to ensure that overgrown field corners are available in spring, and grass fields are mown from the centre out after 1st August. There are recent attempts to reintroduce the species into eastern Britain.

DISTRIBUTION

In Britain breeds mainly in the north-west of Scotland, especially in the Western Isles. In Ireland it is more widespread, but most numerous in the north-west. The species is also found across Europe, from the Pyrenees to the Arctic and east into Asia. Winters in south-east Africa.

Crane *Grus grus*

INTERNATIONAL NAME COMMON CRANE

IDENTIFICATION

110–120 cm. Larger than Grey Heron. Graceful bird with long legs, long neck, sloping body with obvious 'bustle-like' drooping, curved feathers at rear and pointed bill. Mainly grey with black flight feathers, black-and-white head and neck and a red band at the back of the crown. Juvenile has a paler, reddish-brown head and neck. Moults in summer. Flight feathers are lost rapidly in May or June and birds are flightless for about 5 weeks. The flight feathers are not moulted every year. It takes 3 years for young to acquire full adult plumage, through a series of partial moults. SEE ALSO: Grey Heron p83.

HABITS

On the ground it walks gracefully with its neck only slightly curved. Flies with its neck straight (unlike a heron) and long legs protruding well beyond tail. Wings are straight and broad with 'fingered' ends. On migration, and in winter, forms large flocks that fly in 'V' formation, but is seen in pairs or small non-breeding flocks during the spring and summer. A shy bird – especially on its breeding grounds – but has elaborate dancing displays. Family parties remain together for autumn and winter.

juvenile

VOICE

A loud clanging, trumpeting note is given in flight and on the ground.

HABITAT

Requires a site that is safe from predators. Traditional sites are clearings in forests, in fens or other wetlands. In recent times some have adapted to live on cultivated land and breed near ponds in fields and meadows. In winter, lives in open country that is often arable or grassland with scattered trees.

FOOD

Feeds on a variety of plant material such as the shoots of grass, seeds such as acorns and berries. Also eats the leaves of growing crops, including potatoes, wheat, oats and barley. Animal food includes insects such as flies, beetles and caterpillars of butterflies and moths. Snails, worms, small mammals and birds are sometimes eaten.

BREEDING

Nesting begins in April. Nest is on ground, sometimes on a small hill or ridge in a wetland. It is a large pile of vegetation, added to throughout the breeding season, on which usually 2 eggs are laid. Incubation is shared by both parents and lasts 30 days. Young hatch 48 hours apart, are fed by both parents and fly at 65–70 days.

MOVEMENTS AND MIGRATIONS

Cranes leave their northern breeding grounds in autumn to winter in a few traditional sites. Many European Cranes winter in southern Europe, especially France and Spain, and a few in North Africa.

POPULATION

A few migrants are seen annually, mainly in eastern Britain. In England 6–10 pairs have attempted to nest in recent years, and a few young have been successfully reared. Fewer than 40 individuals usually overwinter.

CONSERVATION

The Crane became extinct as a breeding species in Britain in the 17th century. It was a surprise when a few re-established themselves in 1981. Large, undisturbed breeding areas are essential and there are plans for a reintroduction in Somerset. Elsewhere in Europe it has been declining owing to disturbance, shooting and drainage of breeding sites. To prevent further decline the wetland breeding sites, migration stopover sites and wintering areas all need protection.

juvenile

DISTRIBUTION

Most Cranes in Britain are migrating birds that pass through in spring or autumn. On average over 100 birds have been seen in recent years, mainly in late April/early May. They may turn up almost anywhere, but chiefly in the south and east. There is also a tiny breeding population in eastern England. The species' main breeding grounds are in Scandinavia, north-east Europe, Russia and parts of Asia.

LARGE WADERS IN FLIGHT

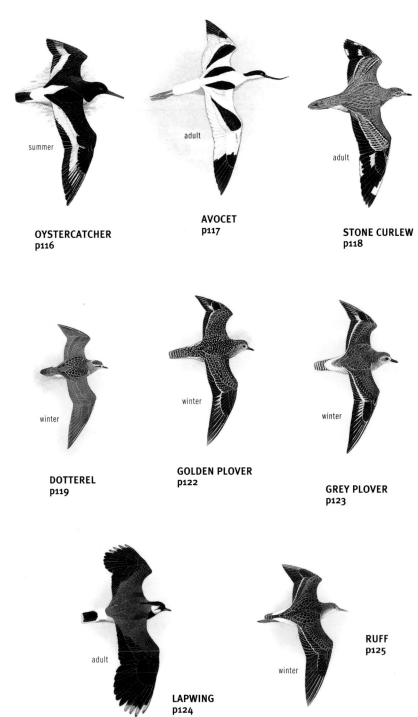

OYSTERCATCHER
p116

summer

AVOCET
p117

adult

STONE CURLEW
p118

adult

DOTTEREL
p119

winter

GOLDEN PLOVER
p122

winter

GREY PLOVER
p123

winter

LAPWING
p124

adult

RUFF
p125

winter

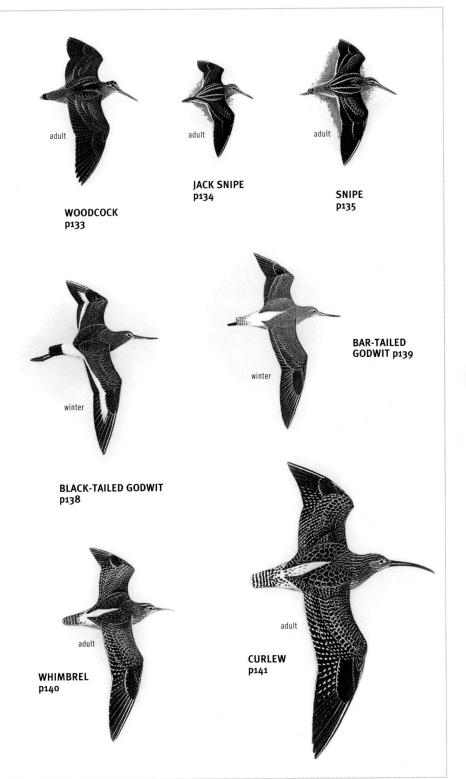

WOODCOCK
p133

JACK SNIPE
p134

SNIPE
p135

adult

adult

adult

BLACK-TAILED GODWIT
p138

winter

BAR-TAILED GODWIT p139

winter

WHIMBREL
p140

adult

CURLEW
p141

adult

SMALL WADERS IN FLIGHT

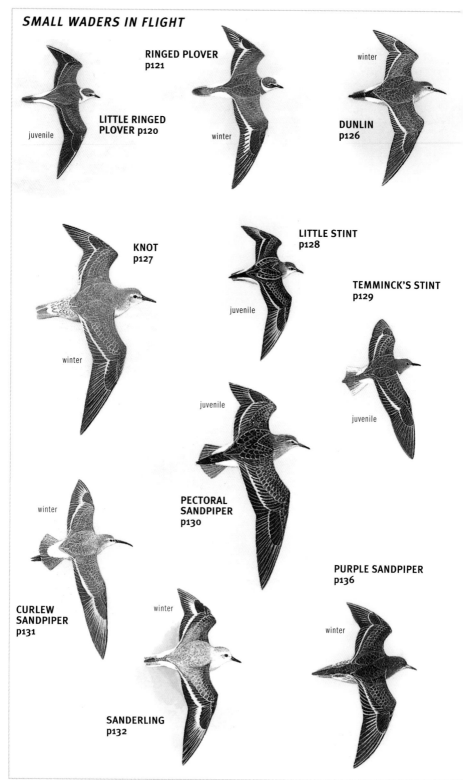

RINGED PLOVER
p121

winter

LITTLE RINGED
PLOVER p120

juvenile

winter

DUNLIN
p126

KNOT
p127

winter

LITTLE STINT
p128

juvenile

TEMMINCK'S STINT
p129

juvenile

juvenile

PECTORAL
SANDPIPER
p130

winter

CURLEW
SANDPIPER
p131

winter

PURPLE SANDPIPER
p136

winter

SANDERLING
p132

TURNSTONE
p137

winter

SPOTTED REDSHANK
p142

winter

winter

REDSHANK
p143

GREENSHANK
p144

winter

WOOD SANDPIPER
p145

juvenile

COMMON
SANDPIPER
p146

summer

GREY
PHALAROPE
p149

1st-winter

winter

GREEN SANDPIPER
p147

juvenile

RED-NECKED
PHALAROPE
p148

Oystercatcher *Haematopus ostralegus*

INTERNATIONAL NAME EURASIAN OYSTERCATCHER

summer

summer

winter

juvenile

summer

IDENTIFICATION

40–45 cm. Large, stocky, black-and-white wader, with long, orange-red bill and reddish-pink legs. Head, breast and back are black and underparts white. In flight, has wide, white wing-bar, black tail and white rump that extends as a 'V' between wings. In winter, many have wide white chinstrap. Juvenile has brown fringes to feathers on its back and grey legs. Adults moult in July, after breeding. Flight feathers are moulted symmetrically and never more than two at a time. Juveniles have partial moult between August and December.
SEE ALSO: Avocet p117, Black-winged Stilt p307.

HABITS

Noisy and excitable, both in winter flocks and on breeding territory. Piping displays are important when establishing a territory, and sometimes 5–30 will come together in 'piping parties' as they run side by side calling loudly. Also in spring it has an advertising display flight and flies with shallow wingbeats, calling above its territory. Outside breeding season gathers in flocks. Sometimes thousands roost together, when forced off feeding grounds by high tides.

VOICE

Usual call is a loud, shrill, piping 'kleep, kleep'.

HABITAT

Breeds on shingle and rocky beaches, dunes, salt-marshes and on the grassy tops of small islands. Inland it nests on shingle banks of rivers, the shores of lakes and on agricultural land in river valleys. Recently some have colonised heathland and gravel pits. In winter Oystercatchers gather on coasts, especially in estuaries.

FOOD

In coastal areas chief food is shellfish such as mussels and cockles. Inland the main food is worms. Also eats crabs and lugworms.

BREEDING

Nests on ground, in the open or among low vegetation. Occasionally a nest is off the ground on a tree stump or the flat roof of a building. There are usually 2 or 3 eggs. Incubation is by both sexes and lasts 24–27 days. Unusually for waders, the young don't feed themselves, but depend on their parents until they fly after 43 days and may not be fully independent until 26 weeks old.

MOVEMENTS AND MIGRATIONS

Some are resident, but others migrate. Most British birds leave inland breeding sites between July and September. Adults generally winter around our shores while juveniles may reach France, Spain and Portugal. Scottish and Icelandic birds winter in western Britain and Ireland, Norwegian birds winter on the British east coast and others from Estonia and Russia visit the Wash. Breeding birds return to their territories between March and May. Oldest was 43 years.

POPULATION

There are over 100,000 pairs breeding in Britain and up to 10,000 in Ireland. Over 330,000 individuals winter in Britain and Ireland. Smaller numbers now winter on the east coast of England.

CONSERVATION

Oystercatchers were once culled in South Wales to protect the commercial cockle industry. Conservationists stopped the killing but the bird is vulnerable if cockle beds are overexploited. During last 50 years species has been colonising inland sites and population has been growing, although recently a small decline in Scotland has been recorded. Coastal breeding is now largely restricted to nature reserves and other protected areas free of recreational disturbance.

DISTRIBUTION

In Britain and Ireland breeds on almost all coasts except the Irish south-east coast. Inland most numerous in Scotland and the north of England, but has spread to areas in the East Midlands and inland Wales and East Anglia. In winter, present around coasts of Britain and Ireland, but largest numbers gather on major estuaries, especially Morecambe Bay and the Solway. Also breeds in Iceland, Europe, Scandinavia, Estonia and Russia. Others breed farther east in Siberia and parts of Asia. Some European birds reach West Africa in winter.

Avocet *Recurvirostra avosetta*

INTERNATIONAL NAME PIED AVOCET

juvenile

IDENTIFICATION

42–45 cm. Medium-sized, elegant back and white wader with long black upcurved bill, long blue-grey legs and webbed feet. Body white with black crown and back of neck and white oval patches on folded wings. In flight, shows black wing-tips, black bar across the wings and a thick black line down either side of the back. The pattern of the juvenile is less clear-cut and browner. Adults moult between June and October with a second moult of body feathers in late winter, prior to breeding.
SEE ALSO: Black-winged Stilt p307.

HABITS

A social species, usually breeding in loose colonies and forming flocks outside the breeding season. On land walks briskly, but also swims and up-ends like a duck. Agile in flight and long legs protrude beyond tail. When feeding sweeps its bill from side to side in shallow water. Quite bold and will attempt to chase away larger species. Will fly above a human intruder and call loudly.

VOICE

Usually silent away from nest. Most common call is pleasant 'clute, clute', which becomes more urgent and strident if the bird is seriously alarmed.

HABITAT

In England most nest near shallow, brackish coastal lagoons with small islands and very little vegetation. In recent years a few pairs have started nesting inland and some inland colonies are becoming established.

FOOD

Feeds on insects, crustaceans and worms. The most common food includes shrimps, ragworms, sandhoppers, the larvae of midges and other flies and beetles.

BREEDING

Nest of roots and leaves of aquatic plants is built in or close to shallow water. Nests in water may be built up to 13 cm high and more material added if water level rises. The 3 or 4 eggs are laid during May. Incubation is by both sexes and lasts 23–25 days. Newly hatched young leave their nest and accompany their parents. Chicks feed themselves and are brooded by their parents while still small. Young fly at 35–42 days but remain with their family for a time.

MOVEMENTS AND MIGRATIONS

British birds move away from nest-sites after breeding and moult on nearby estuaries or cross to the Netherlands and join flocks there. After moulting many move to south and south-west England for the winter, but some may fly on to Spain, Portugal or even Morocco. British breeding birds generally return to their colonies during March. Maximum age 27 years.

POPULATION

Over 1,500 pairs have been breeding in recent years. This is a remarkable increase since the Avocet returned as a breeding species during World War II. Over 3,400 birds can be present in winter.

CONSERVATION

Once nested from the Humber to Sussex, but by about 1840 became extinct as a breeding species. Flooding of the East Anglian coastal marshes during World War II provided perfect breeding habitat. Early protection by the RSPB at Havergate Island and Minsmere, both in Suffolk, helped numbers increase, and eventually it colonised other sites. The species is specially protected and its feeding and nesting requirements are sufficiently scarce that most of the current breeding population is on nature reserves and other protected sites. Sea-level rise – as a result of global warming – may represent the largest threat to breeding, and possibly to wintering, Avocets.

DISTRIBUTION

In Britain, breeding Avocets are largely restricted to the coasts of East Anglia, south-east England nd the Humber, although the species is gradually colonising new sites. Some Avocets winter in East Anglia, but most winter in south-west Britain, particularly on the Exe and Tamar estuaries. In Europe it breeds from southern Scandinavia to the Mediterranean. Also found in Africa and Asia.

Stone-curlew *Burhinus oedicnemus*

INTERNATIONAL NAME **EURASIAN STONE-CURLEW**

IDENTIFICATION

40–44 cm. A large wader with long yellow legs, large head, large yellow staring eye with black pupil, and short yellow bill with black tip. The upperparts, head and breast are sandy brown and heavily streaked. Has pale stripes above and below eye and pale bar across the folded wings, which is bordered above and below with blackish-brown. Wing pattern of male has more contrast than that of female. In flight, wings are boldly marked with white bars. Moult takes places slowly from May until November.
SEE ALSO: Golden Plover p122.

HABITS

Groups will sometimes gather to feed at dusk in the breeding season and flocks are frequent on its wintering grounds. Most active at night. During the day, whether standing or sitting, it can be difficult to see as its camouflaged plumage blends with its surroundings. It often stands upright, but when suspicious, or walking or running, it appears 'hunch-backed' as it holds its head level with its wings.

VOICE

Wailing 'coo-leee' call is reminiscent of a rather shrill Curlew. Vocal at night, especially dusk.

HABITAT

Breeds on bare stony ground, especially in areas with chalk underlying the soil. It requires short (less than 2 cm high) semi-natural grassland areas but may breed on arable farmland, especially if it is cultivated in spring and is sparsely covered and has some bare ground. Also found on some heathland and even on old airfields. In Europe the habitat includes poor stony pastures, sand dunes and margins of deserts. In winter, tends to live in rather similar habitats.

FOOD

Mainly feeds at night, but also during the day when rearing young. Eats a wide variety of small creatures that it picks off the ground, including earthworms, beetles, earwigs, spiders and woodlice.

BREEDING

In Britain nesting begins in April. The birds scrape a hollow on the ground that they line with small stones, rabbit droppings, shells and a little vegetation. The clutch is usually 2

eggs. Incubation is by both sexes and takes 24–26 days. Newly hatched young are covered in down and able to leave the nest, but they are fed by their parents until they are at least half-grown. They fly at 36–42 days.

MOVEMENTS AND MIGRATIONS

Migration begins in August and continues through the early autumn. Birds return to their breeding grounds in late March and April. British Stone-curlews winter in southern Spain, south-west France and north-west Africa. The oldest ringed bird survived for over 17 years.

POPULATION

There has been a long-term decline in Britain: from 1,000 pairs in southern England in the 1930s, there were just 160 by 1985. However, there has been a partial recovery and over 300 pairs currently breed.

CONSERVATION

Specially protected. It has suffered a widespread decline throughout Europe owing to habitat loss to agriculture, forestry and changing farming practices. Predation by foxes is also a problem, as is the theft of eggs by humans. The recent change of fortune in England is due to the RSPB working with farmers, the Ministry of Defence and the Forestry Commission to protect local populations. This includes providing bare ground, pointing out vulnerable nests and safeguarding eggs and chicks during agricultural operations. Some migrants and wintering birds continue to be shot outside Britain.

juvenile

DISTRIBUTION

The British population is mainly confined to the Breckland of Norfolk and Suffolk and around Salisbury Plain in Wiltshire. Breeds in central and southern Europe, south to the Mediterranean, and also in southern Asia and North Africa. It winters in southern Europe and North Africa.

Dotterel *Charadrius morinellus*

IDENTIFICATION
20–22 cm. Medium-sized wader with, unusually, female more colourful and more clearly marked than male. Adult has pale face, dark crown and broad white stripes above eyes that meet at back of head. Upperparts grey-brown and belly black. Chestnut underparts are separated from grey breast by distinctive white band. Throat is white. In autumn and winter less colourful, with scaly-looking brown upperparts, and less obvious eye-stripe and breast-band. In flight, apart from a white streak on the leading flight feather, the wings are plain. Juvenile is like a small Golden Plover, with well marked upperparts, an indistinct breast-band, a finely striped buff breast, dark crown and long creamy stripe over eye.
SEE ALSO: Golden Plover p122.

female summer

winter

male summer

summer

juvenile

HABITS
Many Dotterels are confiding and ignore humans on the breeding grounds. One of only 22 species worldwide where male does almost all the incubating. Female leads in display and has a butterfly-like display flight. She generally leaves male to rear young. After breeding, some adults leave their territories in Scotland and fly on to other hills, or even to Norway where they may rear a second brood.

VOICE
Not generally a noisy species, but if disturbed it makes a 'wet-e-wee' call. Migrants make contact calls which carry a long way, 'pilk, pilk, pilk' or a soft 'kwip'.

HABITAT
Breeds in the Arctic tundra and on mountains. In Britain inhabits high, wide plateaux on largely barren mountain tops, with scattered areas of moss, short grass, sedges, bilberry, heather and lichens below the snow line. In Austria and Russia breeds at over 2,000 m but in northern Europe it may be only 100 m above sea level. On migration, visits low-lying arable farmland, hills and areas of short grass such as golf courses. In the Netherlands has bred on arable sites reclaimed from the sea.

FOOD
Eats spiders, worms, beetles, weevils, sawflies and craneflies, including their larvae (leatherjackets).

BREEDING
Nesting begins in mid-May. Both sexes make a shallow scrape lined with moss, lichens or leaves on bare ground or amongst short vegetation. Male incubates the 2 or 3 eggs for 24–28 days. Female may share the incubation of a later clutch. Young are covered in down and feed themselves. They are tended mainly by the male. They fly after 25–30 days and quickly become independent.

MOVEMENTS AND MIGRATIONS
Small flocks known as 'trips' regularly pause their migration at traditional stopover sites in the Low Countries, the fenlands of East Anglia and a few other sites further north and west during April and May. Breeding birds arrive back on territory as the snow thaws and leave in July or early August.

POPULATION
In good years there are about 630 breeding males in Britain.

CONSERVATION
Specially protected. In 1860 there were some 50–75 breeding males in England, but numbers declined rapidly so that today very few exist. There are threats to the Scottish population: climate change may lead to increase in summer temperatures and loss of montane breeding habitat. Also, disturbance from hill walkers, birdwatchers, tourists and ski developments pose problems.

DISTRIBUTION
Stronghold in Britain is the Scottish Highlands, but it is also found on a few hills farther south. In Europe strongholds are in Scandinavia and northern Russia. Breeds across northern Asia and in a few mountain ranges farther south. British Dotterels winter in Morocco, European birds mostly winter in Spain or North Africa.

Little Ringed Plover *Charadrius dubius*

IDENTIFICATION

14–15 cm. Small wader with round head, short dark bill and rather short slender flesh-coloured legs. Adult has brown back and crown, white collar and black breast-band. A slimmer wader than Ringed Plover and has a distinct yellow eye-ring, white forehead bordered above with black and a thin white stripe above the back band. In flight, wings are plain with no wing-bar unlike Ringed Plover. Juvenile has an incomplete brown breast-band and lacks black markings of adult and pale stripe over its eye. Adults moult between July and November, some starting before their migration and completing it on the winter grounds. Juveniles start to moult body feathers and some tail and wing feathers in autumn.
SEE ALSO: Ringed Plover p121, Kentish Plover p306.

HABITS

Not generally seen in flocks or groups except sometimes in Europe during migration. Feeding action more rapid than that of Ringed Plover. Often noisy and very aggressive towards rivals at start of breeding season, but can be very secretive once it has eggs or young. When displaying has a stiff-winged 'butterfly-like' flight at a low level over its territory.

VOICE

Most usual call heard from breeding birds is a loud 'pee-u' that is often given in flight. It also makes a rapidly repeated 'pip-pip-pip' and a repeated 'gree-a' call during its songflight.

chosen by female. Both birds share the incubation of, usually, 4 eggs. Young hatch after 24 days and feed themselves, although they continue to be brooded by their parents while small and during wet and cold weather. They fly at 25–27 days, but remain dependent on their parents for a further 8–25 days. Some pairs rear two broods in a season.

MOVEMENTS AND MIGRATIONS

Most Little Ringed Plovers leave their breeding grounds in late June and early July with young birds dispersing in all directions. Between July and September most start their southern migration. Birds begin to leave their winter quarters in February and the first generally arrive back in Britain in March. Oldest ringed bird survived for over 9 years.

POPULATION

Population appears to be slowly expanding and there are now over 1,000 pairs nesting each year.

CONSERVATION

There has been a gradual colonisation of England since the species first nested in 1938. The Little Ringed Plover has been gradually spreading north and west, finding suitable man-made habitats in which to rear its young.

juvenile

summer

summer

HABITAT

In Britain most Little Ringed Plovers breed in man-made habitats, usually close to fresh water. Sand and gravel quarries, mining areas, reservoirs and sewage treatment works are all regular breeding sites. In Wales and in Europe it also nests on natural sand and gravel banks that border lakes and rivers. Many of these habitats are transient and it frequently deserts old sites in favour of new ones. Unlike Ringed Plover, it rarely breeds near the sea. In winter, in Africa, it is found on muddy or sandy shores of lakes and rivers, flooded ground and short grassy areas near fresh water.

FOOD

Feeds chiefly on insects, spiders and other small creatures found in or close to shallow water. Includes beetles, flies, larvae of mayflies and dragonflies, freshwater shrimps, worms, small water snails, and also some seeds.

BREEDING

Nest is on bare ground or among low vegetation. The simple scrape is one of several made by male and

DISTRIBUTION

Found mainly in England, especially in northern, central and south-east England, with smaller numbers in Wales and very few in Scotland. Also breeds from the Arctic Circle to North Africa and east to Japan. European birds spend the winter in Central Africa.

Ringed Plover *Charadrius hiaticula*

INTERNATIONAL NAME COMMON RINGED PLOVER

IDENTIFICATION

18–20 cm. Similar to Little Ringed Plover but larger and bigger chested. Adults in summer have white foreheads with black band above, black mask through the eyes, white collar and complete black breast-band. Upperparts are brown, underparts white. Bill is orange with black tip and legs are orange. In flight, there is an obvious white wing-bar and tail has a brown centre and white sides. Juvenile lacks bold black-and-white head pattern, has a smaller, browner breast-band (often broken in the middle) and back and crown have a scaly appearance. Bill and legs are dark. Adults moult between July and November, and some of the flight feathers may be moulted before migration. Juveniles start moulting their tails, body and some wing feathers between August and January.
SEE ALSO: Little Ringed Plover p120, Kentish Plover p306.

HABITS

Feeding actions are typical of plovers: a short run before suddenly pausing and quickly tilting the whole body forward as it picks prey from the ground. When suspicious it will bob its head. May be seen singly, but also forms small flocks and will associate with other small waders. Flight rapid, generally low; in spring it has a 'butterfly-like' flight display on stiff wings.

FOOD

Feeds on a variety of small insects, worms, crustaceans and other creatures, including shrimps, marine snails, beetles, spiders and small fish.

BREEDING

Nesting begins in April. Male prepares nest-scrape in the open or sometimes sheltered by short vegetation. The 3 or 4 beautifully camouflaged eggs are incubated by both sexes for 23–25 days. Young are covered in down and can feed themselves. They fly after about 24 days and soon become independent. There are two or three broods a year.

MOVEMENTS AND MIGRATIONS

Most Ringed Plovers are long-distance migrants, but many of the British and Irish populations are resident or move only comparatively short distances. Canadian and Greenland birds cross the North Atlantic, pass through the British Isles and winter in West Africa. In May there is a strong movement of birds from West Africa through Britain to Greenland, Iceland and Canada, especially on western coasts. Birds from Iceland winter in southern Europe or North Africa, while many from Scandinavia winter in Britain or travel to the Mediterranean or North Africa. The oldest ringed bird survived for 19 years.

summer

summer

juvenile

winter

POPULATION

There are around 5,500 pairs breeding in the UK and 1,000–2,500 in Ireland. 35,000 winter in the UK. In Ireland winter numbers are around 11,500.

CONSERVATION

Threats come from disturbance to nest-sites by holidaymakers, dog walkers and other recreational activities, and also from sea-level rise. In south-east England 70% are now restricted to nature reserves or other protected sites for nesting.

VOICE

Call a distinctive low whistle, 'toolip'. Song during its display flight is yodelling 't'lew, t'lew, t'lew'.

HABITAT

Traditional habitat is sandy or shingle beaches, but it has colonised a variety of inland sites, including sand and gravel pits and former industrial sites. Outside Britain and Ireland is found in similar habitats but also on Arctic tundra. Those that reach Africa feed on beaches, on mud close to lakes and rivers and on areas of short grass.

DISTRIBUTION

Found on suitable beaches around coasts of Britain and Ireland, and is scarce in the south-west of England. Breeds inland in England, Scotland and the west of Ireland. Winters on most coasts, but is scarce inland. Breeds from northern France north to Scandinavia and on the Arctic tundra of Asia. Also breeds in Iceland, Greenland and Arctic Canada.

Golden Plover *Pluvialis apricaria*

INTERNATIONAL NAME   EUROPEAN GOLDEN PLOVER

summer
(northern)

juvenile

summer (northern)

winter

summer (southern)

IDENTIFICATION

26–29 cm.
Medium-sized,
upright wader with small rounded head,
plump body, medium-long legs and short
bill. In summer, brown and gold spangled back
is separated from black face, neck and belly by
white line that gets wider towards belly. Males are
generally blacker below than females. Northern populations are even blacker on face and belly, but similar
birds are found at some British breeding sites. In winter, yellow is duller, breast lined with buff streaks
and belly white. In flight, has a white line in the centre of wings and white underwing. Adults start to moult
while nesting and complete this in autumn. Breeding
plumage is acquired between March and May.
SEE ALSO: Grey Plover p123, Dotterel p119.

HABITS

Typical plover that runs, stops and tilts forward to pick
food. Often feeds at night. Flight usually rapid, but has
butterfly-like display flight. Forms flocks throughout
the year and, in autumn and winter, thousands gather
at traditional sites, often with Lapwings. Some individuals on their breeding grounds are accompanied
by a Dunlin that benefits from the early warning of
danger given by alarm-calling Golden Plover.

VOICE

Most usual call is lonely-sounding 'pu-we'. Songflight
has a longer, far-carrying 'per-we-oo-, per-wee-oo'.

HABITAT

Breeds on short vegetation or bare areas on upland
heaths, blanket bogs, extensive fells and tundra in
northern Scandinavia and Russia. In Britain breeds on
blanket bog, heather moorland and limestone grassland, and feeds on surrounding pastures. In winter,
gathers at traditional inland sites on lowland grassland or arable fields and often roosts on ploughed
fields, coastal marshes and estuaries.

FOOD

Eats a variety of small creatures, especially beetles
and earthworms. Also caterpillars of moths, larvae of
craneflies (leatherjackets), ants, earwigs, spiders,
snails and plant material including berries, leaves and
seeds.

BREEDING

Females sometimes take a second mate, even leaving
the first male with eggs and moving to a new territory
and a new partner. Both male and female prepare a

shallow scrape in mid-April or later. Incubation of the
2–4 eggs is by both adults, although sometimes the
male spends most time on the nest. Young hatch
after 28–31 days and are cared for by both parents.
They fly after 25–33 days and soon become fully
independent.

MOVEMENTS AND MIGRATIONS

Most British breeding birds remain in Britain, moving
to lowland agricultural land or the coast after nesting. In very cold conditions they will move south or
west, and may leave the country. A few British birds
reach Portugal and Spain. The majority that winter in
Ireland and western Britain are from Iceland, others
from northern Europe also visit Britain. Oldest was
12 years.

POPULATION

There are over 23,000 pairs breeding in the UK and
over 200 in Ireland. In winter there may be more than
400,000 individuals in the UK. There has been a recent
decline in breeding pairs.

CONSERVATION

Protected in the close season. Decline may be a result
of a combination of factors. Planting upland forests
destroys moorland, and these waders seldom nest
within 400 m of plantations, which further reduces
the area available to them. Much moorland has been
drained and many peatlands lost. Drainage and
ploughing up of old pastures reduce food supplies
both in summer and in winter.

DISTRIBUTION

It breeds in the uplands of Scotland, northern
England, Dartmoor, Wales and the
west of Ireland. In winter, it avoids
land over about 200 m. It also
breeds in the Faroes, in Iceland,
across northern Europe and into Siberia.
In winter, some northern birds
reach the Mediterranean
and North Africa.

Grey Plover *Pluvialis squatarola*

summer   winter   winter

IDENTIFICATION
27–30 cm. Medium-large wader that appears larger and stouter than Golden Plover and with larger head and heavier bill. Legs are dark grey. In spring, has silver and black spotted upperparts, black face, neck and belly and broad white line running from forehead and down the sides of breast. In winter, loses the black feathers and has a more uniform grey-brown back than Golden Plover. Juvenile has neatly spotted yellow-brown upperparts that are retained through first winter. In all plumages shows a white wing-bar in flight, white rump and has an obvious black patch under the wing, where the wing joins the body. Moult takes place between July and December. Birds starting in July may suspend their moult during their migration and continue on their wintering grounds. SEE ALSO: Golden Plover p122.

HABITS
Feeding birds tend to be solitary and individuals defend their own area of shore. Flocks sometimes form when birds are driven off their feeding grounds by high tides, but generally it is seen in much smaller numbers than Golden Plovers. Feeding action similar to other plovers, and also feeds at night.

VOICE
Most usual call is a lonely-sounding and far-carrying 'plu-oo-wee', often given in flight.

HABITAT
Breeds in low tundra and has not nested in Britain or Ireland. Here it is found mainly in coastal areas, especially estuaries and sandy beaches. Sometimes roosting flocks form on adjacent farmland.

FOOD
Feeds on cockles, other small shellfish, marine snails, lugworms, ragworms and bristle worms.

BREEDING
Does not breed in Britain or Ireland. On its northern breeding grounds nests on ground in a nest-scrape made by both adults. Female normally leaves the family when young are about 12 days old, and probably begins her migration. Young take 35–45 days to fledge and male then migrates.

MOVEMENTS AND MIGRATIONS
This is an impressive migrant with the adults leaving their Arctic breeding grounds in July and August. The first migrant adults arrive in Britain in July and juveniles following a month or so later. There are favourite stopping places such as the German Waddensee and the Wash in England, and in these areas birds start their protracted moult. Males tend to winter further north than females and a high proportion of those wintering in Britain and Ireland may be males. These birds are capable of non-stop flights of 6,500 km and arrive back on their breeding grounds in May. At least one bird lived more than 23 years.

POPULATION
Winter population has been increasing and there may now be over 53,000 individuals in the UK and a further 6,000 in Ireland. Greater numbers are seen during migration.

CONSERVATION
The main threat to Grey Plovers is the loss of habitat along their staging grounds on both the European and North American coasts.

summer

winter

juvenile

DISTRIBUTION
May be found almost all round the coast of Britain and Ireland. The largest numbers arrive in autumn and depart in spring, but a few non-breeding birds may be seen in summer. This species breeds in Arctic Russia, Siberia and North America and it winters on the coasts of Europe, Africa, southern Asia, North and South America and Australia.

Lapwing *Vanellus vanellus*

INTERNATIONAL NAME NORTHERN LAPWING

male summer

female winter

IDENTIFICATION

28–31 cm. Medium-large wader with broad, rounded, black-and-white wings. Dark green back, black breast, white face and underparts, and orange under the tail. Adults have long upsweeping black crest on back of head, the male's being the longest. Males have whiter faces and blacker breasts. In winter, neat buff edges to back feathers give scaly pattern. Juvenile has shorter crest, more scaly back and face is less well marked. Adults moult between June and October and then moult head and some body feathers in February to May. Adult's wings look narrower when moulting.

HABITS

Forms large flocks in autumn and winter that are highly mobile. Flight appears lazy with relaxed wingbeats, and flocks flicker black and white. In courtship, tumbles in aerobatic display during which the stiff flight feathers make a humming sound. Has a 'stop-start' feeding action typical of plovers.

VOICE

Call, from which it gets its alternative name of Peewit, is a rather wheezy, drawn-out 'pee-wit'. The song that accompanies its display is 'pee-wit, wit, wit-eeze wit'.

HABITAT

Breeds mainly on farmland, especially amongst crops cultivated in spring where there is bare soil and low cover. Also on pastures, wet grassland, fens, bogs, marshes and occasionally industrial sites where there is bare ground and damp areas for chicks to feed.

FOOD

Eats a variety of invertebrates living on or in the ground, including earthworms, leatherjackets, beetles, flies, moth caterpillars and ants. Also spiders, small frogs, snails, and some plant material.

BREEDING

Nesting begins in March. Male makes several scrapes on bare ground from which female chooses one. Scrape is lined with grass or leaves. Incubation of the 4 eggs takes around 28 days and is mostly by female. Young are covered with down. They feed themselves soon after hatching and are cared for by both adults. They fly after 35–40 days and become independent soon afterwards.

MOVEMENTS AND MIGRATIONS

Lapwings are seen in Britain and Ireland throughout the year. Some move only 100 km or so. Some go west from Britain to Ireland in autumn while others fly south to France or Spain. Lapwings from Russia and eastern areas arrive in Britain from June to November. Winter flocks react to cold weather by undertaking additional southward movements. The oldest ringed bird lived 23 years.

POPULATION

The UK population is around 156,000 pairs, with fewer than 10,000 in Ireland. In winter there may be over 2 million individuals. The breeding population has been declining, with a fall of over 50% in the last 25 years.

CONSERVATION

The recent decline has been linked to agricultural changes, especially the move from spring to autumn sowing of cereals, which has resulted in the crops being too tall to suit breeding Lapwings in spring. There has also been a reduction in mixed farming and a loss of unimproved damp grasslands, both of which have reduced the feeding areas for chicks.

juvenile

summer

summer

DISTRIBUTION

Widespread breeding species across Britain and Ireland. In winter, may be seen on lowland farmland, and during cold weather more flocks visit coasts. Breeds from Arctic Scandinavia south to Mediterranean and also in parts of Asia and northern Russia. Winters in western Europe and some reach North Africa.

Ruff *Philomachus pugnax*

IDENTIFICATION

Male 26–30 cm, female 20–24 cm. Male size of Red-shank; female (reeve) considerably smaller. Long-necked, with small head, rather short, slightly droopy bill and medium-long legs that are reddish, orange or yellow-green. Male in spring is unmistakable, with an exotic ruff and ear-tufts. The ruff can be black, white or orange, but the marks and colours vary. Females in spring are also variable, some appearing very dark. At other times both are grey-brown, with male sometimes retaining white patch on the neck and pale face. Juvenile is buff with dark feathers on upperparts bordered bright buff and giving a scaly look. In flight, shows narrow white wing-bar and oval patches on either side of the rump. After breeding, birds moult completely, often over a long period. Juveniles moult their body feathers and some wing feathers between August and December.
SEE ALSO: Redshank p143.

male summer

male summer

HABITS

May look 'hunch-backed' but when alert stands very erect. Feeds singly or in small groups. Picks delicately for food at surface of mud. In flight, looks lazy, with relaxed wingbeats and quite long wings. On breeding grounds in spring it has a ritualised display known as lekking. Males dance and display as females choose which to mate with.

VOICE

Generally very silent, even when lekking, but it can make a low 'tu-wit' especially when disturbed.

HABITAT

The main breeding habitat is lowland wet meadows that are grazed in summer and flooded in winter. At other times visits muddy fringes of pools and lakes, and brackish coastal lagoons. Avoids large open estuaries.

or April and males leave in late June. Females and juveniles leave in July. Females tend to winter further south than males. In late summer many juveniles from Scandinavia visit Britain, and many of these migrate on into Africa. Ruff may live 13 years.

POPULATION

Two or three leks are seen most years, mostly in Scotland, but few if any young are raised. Around 700 winter in Britain, with more seen during autumn migration.

CONSERVATION

Specially protected. It became extinct as a breeding bird in Britain in about 1850. There were breeding attempts after this, and in 1963 it re-established itself for a time at the Ouse Washes in East Anglia, which has since become an RSPB reserve. Correct management of grazing animals is essential to prevent overgrazing and trampling of breeding sites.

female summer

female juvenile

male winter

male winter

FOOD

Insects and their larvae, especially midges, craneflies and caddis flies. On migration and in winter they take other flies, beetles, plant material, small fish, shellfish and worms.

BREEDING

The first leks become active in April and nesting begins in late April or May. Female makes a shallow scrape on ground. Clutch of 4 eggs incubated by female alone for 20–23 days. Newly hatched young are covered in down. They leave the nest quickly and are fed by female for first few days, thereafter they feed themselves and fledge after 25 days.

MOVEMENTS AND MIGRATIONS

This is a migrant, but in Britain some are present all year. Birds arrive on their breeding grounds in March

DISTRIBUTION

In Britain it breeds at a few lowland sites, and is more widely distributed during its autumn migration. Some overwinter, generally but not always, near the coast. Britain is at the edge of the Ruff's breeding range. The species nests from Scandinavia south to the Netherlands and east into Siberia. It winters as far south as South Africa.

Dunlin *Calidris alpina*

summer

IDENTIFICATION

16–20 cm. Smallest common wader with medium-length black legs and gently downcurved black bill. Adult in summer has reddish-brown back, white underparts with black patch on belly. In winter, has grey-brown back, grey breast and white underparts. In flight, has white wing-bar and white sides to dark rump. Juvenile in autumn has dark spotting on lower breast and flanks and neat buff edges to back feathers. Different races moult at different times. Adults moult between July and September, and have a partial moult into summer plumage between March and June.

SEE ALSO: Sanderling p132, Curlew Sandpiper p131, Little Stint p128.

winter

HABITS

Gathers in flocks outside breeding season. Some flocks number thousands of birds at important feeding sites where they fly in compact formation, showing alternately white and grey as they bank and turn. When feeding they spread out, but at high tides they form tight roosts on the shore or on nearby fields. Feeds intently, hunched up with head down. On breeding grounds may associate with a Golden Plover, which helps to give warning of danger. Breeding male has an aerial display over his territory. Climbing steeply, he hovers against the wind and then switchbacks, alternately fluttering and gliding until drifting down and settling with wings held above his back in a 'V'.

VOICE

Usual flight call is rough 'treep'. Display song on breeding grounds is a piping trill.

HABITAT

Breeds on wet upland moors but also in saltmarshes and among pools in the wet grassland (machair) in the Western Isles. At other times visits estuaries, mud-flats, coastal pools and shallow water inland.

FOOD

Food is taken from the surface, by probing mud or wading in water. Eats insects such as beetles and fly larvae; also molluscs, microscopic crustaceans and worms.

BREEDING

Nests on ground, on a tussock or under low vegetation. The 4 eggs are laid in May and usually incubated by male during the day and female at night. Some females lay a second clutch and leave male to incubate

juvenile

the first. Young hatch after 22 days and run about and feed themselves. They fly and become independent at about 20 days, but may be abandoned by the female before this. After nesting, adults and young quickly move to the coast.

MOVEMENTS AND MIGRATIONS

It is a migrant although some are present throughout the year. British breeding birds migrate south for the winter. Dunlins from Greenland pass through on migration. Others from Iceland, northern Europe and Russia arrive in autumn to spend the winter on British and Irish estuaries. Dunlins may live for 28 years.

POPULATION

There are over 18,000 pairs breeding in the UK and fewer than 200 in Ireland. About 550,000 individuals may winter in the UK and 100,000 in Ireland. Breeding numbers have declined by over 50% in recent years.

CONSERVATION

The decline in the breeding population is due to increased forestry and changing agricultural practices in the uplands. The species depends on the preservation of wet upland moors and the machair in the Western Isles for nesting. Conservation of estuaries is essential for wintering populations and also for passage migrants. Recreational activities on the coast can disturb roosts, especially in winter.

winter

juvenile

summer

summer

DISTRIBUTION

Breeds in Scotland and the uplands of England and Wales including a few on Dartmoor. It also breeds in the west of Ireland. There are six races world-wide and one breeds in Britain and Ireland while two others migrate here. It also nests in North America, northern Europe and northern Asia. It winters as far south as West Africa.

Knot *Calidris canutus*

INTERNATIONAL NAME RED KNOT

summer

summer (worn)

winter

winter

juvenile

IDENTIFICATION

23–25 cm. Medium-sized stocky wader, larger than Dunlin with relatively short grey-green legs and short straight bill. Breeding plumage brick-red with mottled orange, black and grey back. For the rest of the year, when it is most numerous in Britain and Ireland, it is grey with grey marks on breast and flanks, short pale stripe over eye and white belly. In flight, shows pale rump and dull white wing-bar. Juvenile a little browner than non-breeding adult; back and wings grey with each feather neatly edged black and off-white giving a scaly look. There is an obvious pale stripe over its eye. Adults moult completely between July and November; the flight feathers are moulted over a long period of 90–100 days.
SEE ALSO: Dunlin p126, Sanderling p132.

HABITS

In Britain and Ireland Knots are generally seen in large flocks, sometimes of 10,000 or more. They fly in close formation and perform breathtaking aerial manoeuvres over their feeding grounds as they twist and turn in unison, looking alternately grey and white. At high tide they roost in tight, but fidgety, packs close to the water's edge, on saltmarshes, rocky islands, shingle banks or in a nearby field. When feeding, they spread out to search, head down, for food.

VOICE

Most frequent call is a low-pitched 'knut' and a higher-pitched 'quick-ick', usually given when it takes flight.

HABITAT

In western Europe this is a bird of the seashore, especially estuaries and mudflats, and some feed on rocky headlands. It is rare inland, although single birds, often juveniles, will appear on the fringes of large lakes and reservoirs. Its breeding grounds are on peninsulas, islands and barren plateaux in the Arctic.

FOOD

It probes in the mud for a small shellfish called the Baltic tellin, and also for small cockles, mussels and a snail called *Hydrobia ulvae*. In summer in the Arctic it feeds on a wide range of flies, beetles, worms and plant material including seeds, shoots, buds, leaves and flower heads.

BREEDING

The Knot does not breed in Britain or Ireland. It needs to breed fast during the short Arctic summer. It lays 3 or 4 eggs. Incubation is by both parents and takes only 21–22 days. The young fly after 18–20 days and are quickly independent. The female leaves the family before the young can fly.

MOVEMENTS AND MIGRATIONS

Long-distance migrant. Most leave their breeding grounds in August. Females depart first, followed by males and then the young. All make long non-stop flights and visit traditional sites, usually estuaries, to moult and feed before the next leg of their journey. Most of those that visit British and Irish estuaries breed in Arctic Canada and rest in Iceland before flying to western Europe. They arrive from August and stay to May. A small number of non-breeding birds remain for the summer. Oldest ringed Knot survived over 27 years.

POPULATION

Over 290,000 winter in the UK and 17,000–27,000 in Ireland. Numbers have fallen over the last 15 years.

CONSERVATION

A large proportion of the Knots depend on a few European estuaries to feed and moult. They are, therefore, vulnerable to any changes to these sites, such as barrages, sea-level rise and human disturbance.

DISTRIBUTION

In Britain and Ireland the Knot is found on most major estuaries although it is scarcer in the south-west of England. It breeds in Alaska, Canada and Greenland and in northern Siberia. Different populations winter in South America, Australia and New Zealand.

Little Stint *Calidris minuta*

IDENTIFICATION

12–14 cm. Tiny wader that is smaller than House Sparrow and much smaller than Dunlin. Has short straight bill and rather short black legs. Adult in spring has reddish head and upper breast, finely streaked dark brown back with some delicate mottling and the suggestion of a yellow backward-facing 'V' along its back. The bright spring plumage becomes worn and duller during summer. After moult adult becomes plainer and greyer with a paler face. Juvenile, which is commonly seen in Britain and Ireland, is brown like adult in late summer, but has prominent white 'V' on its back and white stripe below this. Has a pale stripe over the eye that splits to form a second, shorter stripe. In flight, has a white wing-bar, dark centre to its rump and grey outer tail feathers. Adults moult completely between August and March, and have a partial moult in spring.
SEE ALSO: Dunlin p126, Sanderling p132.

the male while she incubates a second clutch. Breeding is quick, with incubation taking only about 20 days. Young fly at about 17 days old. Single-brooded, but can have two clutches and parents look after a brood each.

MOVEMENTS AND MIGRATIONS

Long-distance migrant, leaving the Arctic in August. Juveniles migrate along the Atlantic seaboard, while adults take a more easterly route to Africa via the Mediterranean basin. As so few are seen in Britain in spring it is possible that the birds use a different route for their return migration and arrive back in the Arctic in May or June. Oldest was 12 years old.

POPULATION

It is thought that around 500–700 individuals pass through Britain each autumn.

CONSERVATION

There are no specific conservation measures for this wide-ranging species although carefully managed and protected wetlands help the survival of this and other waders as they migrate through western Europe after the breeding season.

summer

juvenile

summer (worn)

juvenile

HABITS

Feeds very rapidly with a shuffling movement, pecking quickly at the surface of the mud and hardly ever, apparently, looking up. After a good breeding season in the Arctic larger numbers are seen – often flocks of over 50, in poor years flocks of 10 are more usual. Feeding birds are often well spaced as individuals appear to defend a small feeding territory.

VOICE

When disturbed it will give a 'chit' or 'tit' call that is repeated about three times.

HABITAT

In Britain and Ireland may visit the edges of lakes and reservoirs, sheltered estuaries and brackish pools near the coast. Its Arctic breeding grounds are tundra and large islands, or in areas of shallow freshwater pools, lakes and river deltas.

FOOD

Feeds by picking food from the surface or from water, but rarely probes in mud. Eats insects, especially flies and beetles, small worms, tiny shellfish, shrimps and plant material including seeds.

BREEDING

Does not breed in Britain or Ireland. In the Arctic it nests on the ground, making a shallow nest cup lined with leaves and grass. Lays 4 eggs in late June. Some females lay one clutch of eggs and leave their care to

DISTRIBUTION

Passes through Britain and Ireland en route to breeding grounds in spring and return in late summer. The largest numbers are juveniles that are seen in August and September, mainly on east or west coasts of Britain, with just a few seen inland. Some overwinter in Britain. It breeds in northern Norway and across Arctic Siberia. Winters in Africa, India and the Arabian peninsula.

Temminck's Stint *Calidris temminckii*

summer

juvenile

IDENTIFICATION

13–15 cm. Tiny wader, often keeping a horizontal stance, creeping close to the ground. Only marginally longer-winged than Little Stint, with rather short greenish or dull yellow legs. Looks a little like a miniature Common Sandpiper. Head, breast and back of adults in spring are grey-brown (less rusty than Little Stint) with scattering of dark marks on back. Non-breeding plumage is duller and more uniform, with an indistinct head pattern and grey breast. Juvenile also grey above with delicate, scaly pattern. In flight, has white wing-bar and white outer tail feathers. Adults have a partial moult between July and September, which is then suspended until completion between February and April. Juveniles moult between August and the following April or May.

SEE ALSO: Little Stint p128, Dunlin p126, Common Sandpiper p145.

HABITS

If disturbed it is likely to rise steeply and fly erratically like a Snipe, and unlike the Little Stint, which flies lower. On the ground it has a flat back profile and tends to move more slowly than Little Stint and peck more deliberately, rather like Dunlin. Generally seen singly or in very small parties.

VOICE

When disturbed, takes off with a loud, dry trilling 'tirr-tirrr-tirr'.

HABITAT

In Britain and Ireland most likely to be seen around the edges of freshwater lakes, pools and marshes, often close to vegetation. Sometimes visits creeks and brackish lagoons near the sea. Breeds mainly in the Arctic, on flat ground with short grass and crowberry. Most sites are near fjords, deltas, rivers or streams, and sometimes on higher land.

FOOD

Feeds mainly on insects, including beetles, flies, midges, and some plant material.

BREEDING

Nest is on ground amongst vegetation. Some females visit the territories of several males and lay from one to three clutches of 4 eggs. If a female has only one mate, the pair share the incubation, but if she has two or more mates then the males incubate the first and second clutches and the female incubates the last. Young hatch after 21 days and can feed themselves; they are tended by whichever parent incubated the eggs. The young fly at between 15 and 18 days and the parents migrate ahead of their young, even before the young are able to fully fly.

MOVEMENTS AND MIGRATIONS

Many waders migrate by following sea coasts, but Temminck's Stint migrates on a broad front that crosses most of Europe to reach its winter quarters. Adults leave the Arctic in July while juveniles remain until the first half of August. Most are seen in Europe between July and October. They begin to return in March, with most being seen in Britain during May.

POPULATION

First nested in Scotland in 1934. In recent years nesting has been confirmed at a few Scottish locations. Around 100 individuals are seen on migration each year.

CONSERVATION

Specially protected species that only has a toe-hold in Scotland. The original 1934 nesting site, Loch Morlich, is now popular for water sports and with tourists, and the loch edge has become much more vegetated. Nesting has taken place at a few sites that may be used for a number of years and then abandoned. Sites are protected and kept secret to allow the birds every opportunity to breed successfully.

DISTRIBUTION

In Britain and Ireland seen mainly in eastern England. The only current breeding site in Scotland is kept secret. Temminck's Stints breed in northern Scandinavia and Siberia and some winter around the Mediterranean, but most fly on to winter as far south as central Africa. Others from the east winter in southern Asia.

Pectoral Sandpiper *Calidris melanotos*

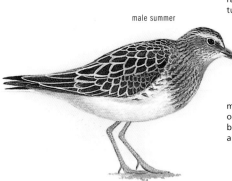
male summer

rarely visits saltwater sites. It breeds on the Arctic tundra.

FOOD
It feeds chiefly on flies, beetles, sandhoppers, worms and some plant material.

BREEDING
The Pectoral Sandpiper does not breed in Britain or Ireland. On its Arctic breeding grounds it nests in June and July. Males often mate with several females, while females may visit other males. Most males leave their breeding areas before the eggs hatch. The female incubates the eggs and tends the young.

IDENTIFICATION
19–23 cm. A medium-sized wader, a little larger than a Dunlin, with yellowish legs, a small head and long wings. It has a prominent pale stripe over the eye. The medium-short, tapering bill is very gently down-curved. Most birds seen in Britain and Ireland are juveniles with dark brown upperparts and pale buff feather-edges forming two lines down either side of the back – rather like a Snipe. The neatly streaked breast ends abruptly in a line across the breast, contrasting with the white belly. The male is larger than the female. Adults have more worn plumage and less noticeable pale stripes on the back. In flight, it has a black line down the centre of the rump with white ovals on both sides and long wings with a faint wing-bar.
SEE ALSO: Dunlin p126, Ruff p125.

HABITS
The feeding action is more leisurely, like a Ruff, rather than the rapid feeding of the smaller waders. Can extend neck when alarmed, giving the appearance of a small Ruff.

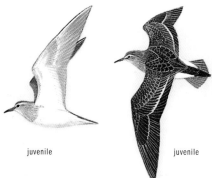
juvenile   juvenile

MOVEMENTS AND MIGRATIONS
Breeding birds leave their breeding grounds between July and September, with the males departing before the females. The Siberian population mostly crosses into North America via Alaska and migrates down to South America between August and November. Northward migration begins in late February and many birds fly over the Caribbean, through the USA and on to the Arctic. Those that arrive in Britain are mostly juveniles in August and September and are probably Canadian birds caught in fast-moving Atlantic depressions as they migrate down the western Atlantic. As many of the adults seen in Britain are on the east coast it is possible that some may have come east from Siberia and go on to winter in Africa.

POPULATION
Average occurrence is over 90 individuals a year in Britain.

CONSERVATION
There are no special conservation measures in place for this species, except that many of the best wetland habitats it visits in Britain are specially protected sites managed for the benefit of birds and other wildlife.

juvenile

VOICE
The normal flight call is a dry, grating 'kreet'.

HABITAT
May be found feeding in shallow freshwater pools, around the edges of lakes, reservoirs and creeks, on old sewage filter beds and other marshy places. It

DISTRIBUTION
Migrant Pectoral Sandpipers may occur in almost any suitable habitat, but the south-west of Ireland, the English south-west peninsula (especially Cornwall) and East Anglia are always favoured. The species breeds in the Arctic: North America and north-east Siberia. The majority winter in South America.

Curlew Sandpiper *Calidris ferruginea*

IDENTIFICATION

18–19 cm. Similar in size to Dunlin, but with a longer neck, longer black legs and a longer, finer and slightly more downcurved bill. In all plumages the white rump is distinctive, although this shows best in flight. In spring, it resembles a small Knot with brick-red underparts and mottled back, although underparts of the female appear scaly. In autumn and winter, it is dusky-grey above and white below, similar to a Dunlin in winter, but cleaner, whiter, with a long white stripe over its eye and fine grey streaking on its breast. The juvenile is paler and cleaner-looking than a Dunlin, with a stripe over the eye and the breast and belly are unspotted, often with a pink flush. In flight it shows a thin wing-bar as well as the white rump. Adults begin the moult of their small body feathers on their breeding grounds in July. Their moult is suspended while migrating and completed on their wintering grounds when the larger flight feathers are also moulted. It has a further partial moult into breeding plumage between January and March, and this is sometimes suspended and completed after migration.
SEE ALSO: Dunlin p126, Knot p127.

summer

HABITS

Can resemble a Dunlin, but more often wades in water when feeding. It will often associate with other feeding waders, especially Dunlin, and is seen singly or in small groups.

VOICE

The most common flight call is a rippling, dry 'chirrup'.

HABITAT

On migration Curlew Sandpipers are found in similar places to Dunlins, including saltmarshes, brackish pools and the fringes of freshwater lakes and pools, often near the coast. It breeds in the coastal lowlands of the high Arctic where there are bogs and pools.

FOOD

Probes in mud or wades in water to find prey such as flies, beetles, shrimps, small marine snails called *Hydrobia* and worms.

BREEDING

Does not breed in Britain or Ireland. It nests on the ground in the Arctic on south-facing slopes that are free of snow. Both parents share the incubation of the eggs. The chicks fledge quickly, but adults migrate ahead of the young; the males leave 21–35 days before the females.

MOVEMENTS AND MIGRATIONS

Curlew Sandpipers that cross Europe follow three routes: around the west coast and on to West Africa, through eastern Europe to the Mediterranean and on into West Africa, and via the Black and Caspian Seas to the Middle East and on to East Africa. Britain and Ireland are on the edge of the western migration route and varying numbers are seen each year. Migrating adults arrive mainly on the east coast from mid-July to August. Juveniles arrive between mid-August and October and are spread more widely across Britain and Ireland. The oldest ringed bird survived 19 years.

POPULATION

500–1,000 migrate through Britain each year and a further 150 may be seen in Ireland. There are some years when large influxes occur.

CONSERVATION

Long-distance migrants require safe, food-rich places to 'refuel' after their long migratory flights. Many wetland sites have been drained for agriculture or are disturbed by recreational pursuits. Many of the best sites for these birds are now specially protected sites such as nature reserves.

juvenile

winter

winter

DISTRIBUTION

In Britain most are seen on the coasts bordering the North Sea, although they do appear farther west, including regular sightings in Ireland. The birds breed in Arctic Siberia and winter from Africa, around the Indian Ocean, to Australia and New Zealand.

Sanderling *Calidris alba*

IDENTIFICATION
20–21 cm. Small, plump, energetic wader slightly larger than Dunlin with short straight black bill and medium-long black legs. For most of year has pale grey upperparts; underparts and most of head are white and there is a black mark at shoulder of folded wing. Breeding plumage reddish-brown above with mottled back, rather like Knot. Juvenile grey, sometimes with buff head and breast and scaly-looking back. In flight it has a prominent white wing-bar and white on either side of a dark rump. Adults have partial moult between March and May, and then start moulting completely between July and November.
SEE ALSO: Knot p127, Dunlin p126.

HABITS
Runs with head hunched in. An extremely active and restless wader that often runs like a 'clockwork toy', following retreating waves in its search for food. It feeds in scattered groups and sometimes forms small flocks. Larger flocks form at high-tide roosts and when migrating.

VOICE
Call given in flight or when flushed is a liquid 'twick, twick'.

HABITAT
In Britain and Ireland usually a coastal species, especially liking sandy shores and estuaries. Infrequently on migration it may visit the edges of large lakes and reservoirs away from the coast. It breeds on the high Arctic tundra near freshwater lakes where there are usually some low-growing Arctic plants such as saxifrage.

FOOD
Takes food from the surface or probes in mud. Eats small crabs, shrimps, shellfish, sandhoppers and marine worms that live in mud and sand or are washed in by the tide. On its Arctic breeding grounds eats insects and some plant material, including buds, seeds and shoots.

BREEDING
Does not breed in Britain or Ireland. On breeding grounds female makes nest scrape. Once a clutch of 4 eggs is complete some females make a second nest and produce a second clutch that they incubate themselves while leaving the male to incubate the first clutch and look after the first family. Incubation takes 23–27 days and the young fly after about 17 days and quickly become independent.

MOVEMENTS AND MIGRATIONS
Long-distance migrant. Adults leave their breeding grounds by mid-August and by September young have also left. Body weight increases by up to 60% to provide energy to fly non-stop for up to 5,000 km. Breeding birds return to their territories in May or June, but a few non-breeding birds remain on British and Irish beaches in summer. Oldest ringed bird survived for 17 years.

POPULATION
Peak numbers of Sanderlings occur in Britain in May or August. Irish numbers peak in winter. The wintering population in the UK has recently been more than 20,000 individuals and an estimated 6,000 in Ireland. Numbers fluctuate from year to year, but overall trend remains constant.

CONSERVATION
Like other waders, Sanderlings need to feed undisturbed to obtain enough food to sustain their long flights and survive the winter. Disturbing feeding birds in winter should therefore be avoided. Development and 'hard' engineering works along coasts is a threat, as is the mechanical cleaning of sandy beaches where seaweed is removed. In future climate change may cause a problem through sea-level rise and changes to Arctic breeding sites.

summer

summer

winter

winter

juvenile

DISTRIBUTION
In Britain and Ireland found where there are long sandy beaches. Scarce in south-west England and along the rocky coasts of mainland Scotland. A few pairs breed in the high Arctic of Spitsbergen, but the majority breed high in the Arctic – on the closest land to North Pole – in Siberia, or in Arctic North America and in Greenland. Winters in South America, South Africa and Australia.

Woodcock *Scolopax rusticola*

INTERNATIONAL NAME EURASIAN WOODCOCK

IDENTIFICATION
33–35 cm. Larger than Snipe. Large bulky wader with short legs, very long straight, tapering bill and large eyes. Reddish-brown upperparts have delicate mottling and underparts are buff with dark barring. Broad blackish crown is crossed with several paler brown lines, not striped like Snipe. Tail has a silver tip that is most obvious from below. In flight, wings appear broad and rounded, and lack any prominent marks. Adults moult between June and November and also have a second moult before the nesting season begins again.
SEE ALSO: Snipe p135, Jack Snipe p134.

HABITS
The beautifully camouflaged plumage, nocturnal habits and secretive behaviour make this species difficult to observe. It is generally solitary and most active at dawn and dusk. In spring, males have an aerial display as they fly over the best breeding habitats with slow, flickering wingbeats, and calling – this is known as 'roding'. The most dominant males rode longest and mate with most females. At other times it flies strongly or, if disturbed, zigzags between trees with agility before dropping into cover. When probing for food, it has a rocking action.

VOICE
When roding it has two to four frog-like croaks, followed by a thin but far-carrying 'tsiwick, tsiwick'.

HABITAT
Nests in deciduous or mixed woodland, young conifer plantations and sometimes on heather moors. Remains in woodland in the winter, although in cold weather may feed in open places such as wet ditches or even gardens. Rare on the coast except when migrating.

FOOD
Probes the moist soil and feels its prey with the sensitive nerve endings at the tip of its bill. Feeds on a range of invertebrates such as worms, beetles and their larvae, spiders, caterpillars, fly larvae and small snails.

BREEDING
The silver tips to the tail are displayed during courtship. Males may mate with up to four females in a season. Female builds a nest on the ground among bracken, dead leaves or brambles, often close to a tree trunk or a dead branch on the woodland floor. In mid to late April the female lays 4 eggs. Incubation is by female and lasts 17–24 days. Young are covered in down and leave nest quickly. They remain associated with female, often within 250 m of the nest, and fly at 20 days old. Usually single-brooded but sometimes two broods.

MOVEMENTS AND MIGRATIONS
Most British and Irish Woodcock are resident but a small proportion is migratory, with a few British birds moving to Ireland for the winter and others moving to France. Over 800,000 Woodcock from Russia, Latvia and Finland arrive in Britain in October and November. Many move south-west, remaining until mid-April. At least one wild bird survived for over 15 years.

POPULATION
There may be 78,000 males in summer in the UK and a further 2,500–10,000 in Ireland. The breeding population appears to have been falling in recent years.

CONSERVATION
Protected during the close season, but may be hunted at other times. Over-hunting, especially in Europe, may be contributing to its decline. Deer browsing has reduced the shrub layer and therefore increased predation. Also drainage and climate change is drying out some wet woodland.

DISTRIBUTION
Found in suitable habitat in summer throughout Britain and Ireland except in the south-west of England. Widespread in lowland Britain and Ireland in winter. The Woodcock breeds from northern Scandinavia south to the Azores and east across Asia to Japan. In winter may reach the Mediterranean area.

Jack Snipe *Lymnocryptes minimus*

IDENTIFICATION
17–19 cm. Smaller and more compact than Snipe, and with a much shorter bill. It also has a more metallic green and purple back, and a dark crown with bold buff stripes above the eye and down the centre of the crown. The dark back has four bright straw-coloured stripes running down it. It moults between July and October, before it migrates, and has a second, partial moult starting in January.
SEE ALSO: Snipe p135.

HABITS
A very secretive wader that is most active at dawn and dusk and is more likely to crouch and freeze than fly if disturbed during the day. When it does fly it often takes off from very close to an observer, lacks the zig-zag flight of the Snipe and generally lands again close by. When feeding or resting it has a characteristic bobbing movement so that the body looks as if it is on a spring as it bounces slowly up and down. It does not form flocks, although several birds will sometimes feed close together.

VOICE
Usually silent outside the breeding season. At nesting time it produces a range of display-flight calls including some sounding like a cantering horse – 'kollarap, kollarap, kollarap…'.

HABITAT
In Britain and Ireland in winter the Jack Snipe feeds in shallow wet and muddy areas, often where there is dense low vegetation such as freshwater marshes, reedbeds, old fens, flooded grassland and the banks of rivers and streams. In summer, it breeds in wet, open areas within taiga and birch forests of the sub-Arctic.

FOOD
Feeds on adults and larvae of a variety of insects such as beetles and flies, and also small snails, worms and some plant material, especially seeds.

BREEDING
It does not breed in Britain or Ireland. Information on its breeding habits is limited but a nest cup is constructed on the ground, often on a small ridge close to water. 4 eggs are laid in early May and the female incubates for up to 24 days. It possibly has two broods.

MOVEMENTS AND MIGRATIONS
Little is known about the migrations and movements of this secretive wader. It leaves its northern breeding grounds in August and European birds appear to move on a broad front south-west across Europe between September and November. They start to return in February, although their northern nesting sites are not reoccupied until either April or May. Oldest ringed bird was over 12 years old.

POPULATION
This species is almost impossible to census. Most recent estimates put the number wintering in the UK as 10,000–100,000 individuals, and the figure may be in the lower part of this range. The large Russian population has declined during the 20th century and so have the numbers wintering in Britain and Ireland.

CONSERVATION
The species is hunted in the UK in winter, and large numbers are shot on the Continent. Conservation of existing large wetlands, the creation of new ones, and the proper management and protection of those identified as being of special importance is a priority for wintering Jack Snipe and other waders. Many smaller wetlands remain vulnerable to drainage, development and loss to encroaching trees and scrub. The breeding grounds especially need to be protected from drainage or other damaging activities.

DISTRIBUTION
It winters in scattered locations in England, southern Scotland, Wales and Ireland and generally avoids upland areas in winter. Migrants may turn up on coastal islands and headlands. It is occasionally recorded in Britain in summer. It breeds in northern Scandinavia and Russia and winters in western Europe and North Africa. The European breeding population winters from west Europe to the Mediterranean and east to south-east Europe.

Snipe *Gallinago gallinago*

INTERNATIONAL NAME COMMON SNIPE

IDENTIFICATION

25–27 cm. Medium-sized stocky wader with extremely long straight bill and rather short legs. Back is dark brown and delicately barred and streaked with paler brown and four straw-coloured stripes (but these are less obvious than on a Jack Snipe). Crown is blackish with a thin buff line down centre, and it has a long buff stripe over eye and across cheeks. Breast is buff with darker arrow marks; belly is white. In flight, has a white trailing edge to pointed wings and a rather short tail. Adults moult between June and October, but there is no obvious change in appearance.
SEE ALSO: Jack Snipe p134, Woodcock p133.

HABITS

Secretive. If disturbed, flies with a zigzag flight, but often crouches and relies on its cryptic camouflage for protection. Does not form large flocks like other waders, but will feed close together in groups and fly in loose flocks called 'wisps'. In spring, it has an undulating display flight over its breeding territory, and on the downward path it makes a bleating sound (called drumming) as air is forced through its stiff outer tail feathers.

juvenile

VOICE

In addition to drumming, it has a rapid 'chip-er, chip-er' alarm call in spring, used in flight and when perched. It also makes a loud rasping 'scaap' when disturbed.

HABITAT

Breeds on moorland bogs and wet pastures in upland areas and in fenland and marshes in low-lying places. In winter, it is more widespread and feeds in almost any lowland marshy place, both around the coast and inland.

FOOD

Probes into wet ground to find food and sometimes feeds in shallow water. Eats worms, insects such as beetles, flies and ants. Also takes larvae and adults of craneflies, caddis flies and damselflies.

BREEDING

Nesting begins in April, but some breed as late as August. Male builds a nest on the ground, usually concealed by vegetation. The female incubates the 4 eggs for 18–20 days. Young are fed by their parents. Once out of the nest the brood is split between the pair, with the male usually taking charge of the first chicks to hatch. Young fly after 19–20 days and become independent at about the same time.

MOVEMENTS AND MIGRATIONS

British and Irish breeding birds tend to move south or west in autumn with many of those from northern England and Scotland reaching Ireland, and some from southern England and Wales reaching France or Spain. Winter migrants from Iceland, the Faroes and other parts of northern Europe over-winter in Britain and Ireland, arriving between September and November and leaving between March and May. Oldest survived 16 years.

POPULATION

48,000 pairs breed in Britain and up to 19,000 in Ireland. During recent years the number breeding in British lowlands has fallen.

CONSERVATION

The breeding habitat for Snipe has been reduced over centuries as wet grasslands, fens and bogs have been drained and rivers deepened. The recent decline in parts of Britain has been linked to changes in agriculture such as improved drainage and the ploughing of traditional grasslands. Also newly planted upland forests have reduced the areas available for nesting. A high proportion of Snipe now breed on nature reserves. There are opportunities to help by financially rewarding farmers for re-wetting sites and introducing cattle grazing at low densities in summer.

DISTRIBUTION

Breeds throughout Britain and Ireland, but densest populations are in the uplands of northern England and in Ireland. There are two races world-wide: one in Iceland and the Faroes, Orkney and Shetland, one found across the rest of Britain and Ireland and across central and northern Europe, Asia, and Africa.

Purple Sandpiper *Calidris maritima*

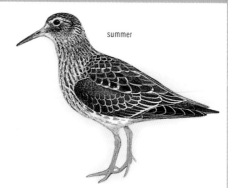

summer

IDENTIFICATION

20–22 cm. Medium-sized wader that is larger, stockier and darker than Dunlin. Bill is downcurved and short legs are bright orange or yellow. In spring, head, back and sides of breast are dark purplish-brown with white streaks around head and neck, and back scaly with white and rusty marks. In winter, it is darker with more uniform upperparts and yellowish base to bill. It has dark streaks along its flanks. Female is larger with slightly longer bill. Juvenile is greyer with pale edges to feathers on its back and some chestnut on the crown. In flight, shows a dark tail with white sides and pale, narrow wing-bar. Adults moult completely between July and September, while they are still close to their breeding grounds, and have a partial moult in spring.
SEE ALSO: Dunlin p126, Turnstone p137.

juvenile

HABITS

In flight, the appearance is of a very dark, rather small wader. Small groups fly swiftly, low over the sea, and often land with a flutter on rocks close to the water where they actively search for food among the rocks and seaweed and avoid the breaking waves by jumping, fluttering and sometimes swimming. Frequently associates with Turnstones. Can be quite tame.

VOICE

Although usually silent, flocks sometimes make a Swallow-like twittering 'wee-wit' as they take off.

HABITAT

Outside the breeding season this is a coastal species that feeds on rocky beaches and islets, around piers and groynes, and also stony beaches or on mussel beds at low tide. Breeds on tundra and, in Scotland, on Arctic-Alpine heath where there are sedges, mosses and lichens interspersed with rocks, scree and gravel.

FOOD

Picks up food left stranded by the tide or pecks amongst mussels or seaweed. In winter, eats small winkles, mussels, dog-whelks, shrimps, small crabs, insects and other tiny creatures washed up by the tide or living among the seaweed. In summer, feeds on insects and spiders and plant material such as seeds.

BREEDING

Nesting starts in June or July. Male makes several scrapes on the ground and female chooses one in which she lays 3 or 4 eggs. Male mostly incubates. Female helps, but sometimes leaves before the eggs hatch. Incubation takes 21–22 days. Young feed themselves and are tended by the male for 3–4 weeks.

MOVEMENTS AND MIGRATIONS

Some birds from Canada, Greenland and Norway winter in Britain. Females leave first, from late June, and males follow with juveniles even later. Adults then stop to moult. The first to reach Britain and Ireland are juveniles, followed by adults in September or October. Return migration is between February and May. Oldest 19 years.

POPULATION

Between one and five pairs have nested in Scotland in recent years. In winter there are about 17,500 individuals in the UK and over 3,000 in Ireland. Winter numbers have decreased recently although the reasons are not understood.

CONSERVATION

Specially protected. First discovered nesting in Scotland in 1978. Breeding areas are secret to protect it from egg thieves and disturbance. There is no other conservation measure as the habitat it requires is widespread in northern Scotland.

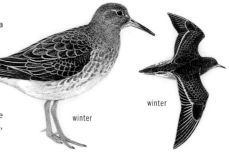

winter

winter

DISTRIBUTION

Winter visitor to almost any rocky coast in Britain or Ireland, but most are found in Orkney, Shetland and along the east coast of Scotland and the north-east coast of England – scarce south of Yorkshire. In Ireland the north and west coasts are favoured, with few nest in the east. A few nest in Scotland. Elsewhere breeds from Canada, Greenland and Iceland to Scandinavia and Siberia. Winters as far south as northern Spain.

Turnstone *Arenaria interpres*

INTERNATIONAL NAME RUDDY TURNSTONE

summer

IDENTIFICATION
22–24 cm. Chunky-looking wader that is smaller than Redshank with large head, short bill and short orange legs. In spring, adult has black-and-white head, black breast and bright orange and brown mottled pattern on back. In winter, all the upperparts, including the head, become mottled grey-brown. Underparts are white. In flight, looks black and white with white wing-bars, white back and shoulder stripes and black-and-white tail. Adults start to moult between July and November; partial moult back into breeding plumage between March and May.
SEE ALSO: Oystercatcher p116, Redshank p143, Ringed Plover p121.

HABITS
Generally seen in small groups that can be rather tame. When feeding busily searches shoreline, dodging waves, and often flicking aside seaweed and small pebbles to reach food. Seldom still, running over rocks, but frequently perches on posts and other objects in water. Often flies close to water and can also swim.

VOICE
Usual call in flight is a rather metallic, twittering 'kit-it-it'. It also has rippling song on breeding grounds that ends in rattling 'quitta, quitta, quitta'.

HABITAT
May visit almost all types of coast, especially where rocks are covered with seaweed, but also feeds on softer sandy and muddy shores, often close to mussel beds. Breeds on small islands and near the sea on bare ground. Also breeds on Arctic tundra in dwarf willows or on barren, rocky ground.

FOOD
Feeds on mussels, barnacles, sandhoppers, periwinkles, crabs and insects. An opportunist feeder: a wide variety of food has been recorded, from household scraps to a human corpse washed up on a beach.

BREEDING
Does not normally breed in Britain or Ireland. Birds arrive back on their breeding grounds already in pairs. Nests are a scrape on bare ground or among low-growing vegetation. The clutch of usually 4 eggs is incubated by both sexes for about 23 days. Female leaves before the young become independent at 19–21 days.

MOVEMENTS AND MIGRATIONS
Turnstones that are seen in Britain breed in northern Europe, Greenland and north-east Canada. Northern European birds pass through Britain in July and August en route to winter in Africa. Those from Canada and Greenland arrive along the coast of western Europe, including Britain and Ireland between August and October. These moult and remain until May: some returning birds stop to feed in Iceland, but others probably fly direct to eastern Greenland. A few first-year birds remain in their winter quarters the following summer. Oldest bird was 22 years.

winter

POPULATION
There is just one possible breeding record, in Scotland in 1976. There are over 52,000 on British shorelines in winter and around 8,500 in Ireland. Comprehensive counts are difficult to undertake given that many birds exist on remote offshore islands, at the foot of cliffs and on long stretches of rocky coasts, but it appears that numbers have declined in some areas in the last 10 years.

CONSERVATION
There are no special conservation measures to protect this species. Changes in distribution of shellfish and other food because of cleaning up of sewage outfalls may affect numbers. Should a small regular breeding population establish itself, then these sites may need special protection.

DISTRIBUTION
Seen around the coasts of Britain and Ireland at all seasons and nested at least once in Scotland. Breeds right round the Arctic Circle, from northern Canada, Greenland, Spitsbergen, Scandinavia, northern Russia, Siberia and Alaska. Winters as far south as Chile, South Africa and Australia, with some birds from North America wintering in western Europe.

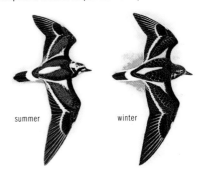

summer   winter

Black-tailed Godwit *Limosa limosa*

male summer

female summer

winter

winter

IDENTIFICATION
40–44 cm. Smaller than Curlew. Large wader with long straight bill, long black legs and long neck. In flight, has broad white wing-bar and white tail terminating in broad black band. In spring, head, neck and breast are chestnut-red (birds of the Icelandic race being the brightest), belly white with dark bars and back mottled grey-brown. After breeding it becomes pale grey-brown above and paler below. There is always a noticeable amount of leg showing above the bend in the leg, unlike Bar-tailed Godwit. Juvenile similar to winter adult, but with warm reddish tinge to neck and breast and coarsely spotted back. Adults moult between June and October. SEE ALSO: Bar-tailed Godwit p139.

HABITS
A graceful wader that often feeds in deep water. On breeding grounds will sometimes perch on posts or trees. Usually in small groups and sometimes forms larger flocks of several hundred in winter. In spring, performs aerial displays over its territory in which it rises and tumbles several times in rapid succession.

VOICE
Most common call is loud clear 'weeka-weeka-weeka'.

HABITAT
Breeds in marshes, damp meadows and bogs near lakes. The few pairs that breed in Britain mainly use lowland wet grassland that is prone to flooding. Outside breeding season main concentrations are on the muddy estuaries and coastal grasslands of the north-west, south and south-east coasts of England, with important numbers on the Wash and in Northern Ireland.

FOOD
In spring and summer feeds on insects, especially the adults and larvae of beetles and flies. Also feeds on worms and small snails.

BREEDING
Nesting begins in early April. Male makes several scrapes on the ground and female chooses one or helps to construct another nest. Nest is well hidden in a tussock. Incubation of the 4 eggs lasts for 22–24 days and is by both sexes. Young feed themselves.

They are cared for by both adults and are brooded during the day while small. They fly after 25–30 days and become independent at about the same time.

MOVEMENTS AND MIGRATIONS
This summer migrant leaves its breeding areas as soon as the young can fly, usually in July. Icelandic birds gradually arrive in western Europe between June and September. Most European breeding birds move south, crossing the Sahara Desert during September. They arrive back on their territories between March and May. Oldest ringed bird lived for over 23 years.

POPULATION
Up to 70 pairs nest in the UK. The less colourful nominate race nests in England and the Icelandic race in Scotland. Scottish birds have increased in number in recent years. Over 15,000 winter in the UK and over 10,000 in Ireland. There are larger numbers during August and September.

CONSERVATION
Specially protected. By 1855 it had stopped breeding in Britain, but in 1952 it nested on the Ouse Washes of East Anglia and later some of the Icelandic race began nesting in Scotland. Benefiting from RSPB protection, other small breeding colonies became established, mostly on nature reserves as most of the lowland wet grassland that it needs for nesting has been lost to agriculture. Overgrazing, trampling of nests by animals and sudden summer floods can be a problem. In Europe breeding populations are declining owing to wetland drainage.

DISTRIBUTION

Seen in summer at several sites in Britain and Ireland, but breeds regularly at only a few of them, mainly in East Anglia. There are three races world-wide, one in eastern Asia, and two races which occur in Britain and Ireland. Icelandic race winters here; European race breeds here and migrates through Britain, but winters in West Africa.

Bar-tailed Godwit *Limosa lapponica*

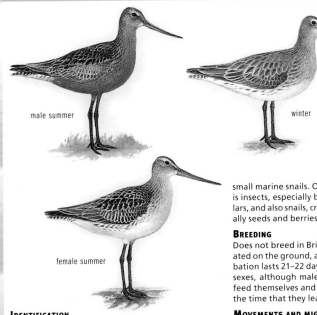

male summer

winter

winter

female summer

IDENTIFICATION
37–39 cm. Larger than Redshank and smaller than Curlew. This large wader has a long, tapering, slightly upturned bill and long legs. Unlike the Black-tailed Godwit, often little leg shows above bend in the leg and it lacks the white wing-bar. Its back is more Curlew-like, with a pale 'V' between wings, white rump and brown barred tail. Short pale stripe above the eye, but this is less obvious than on Black-tailed Godwit. In spring male has brick-red face, neck and underparts and mottled grey-brown back. Female is larger than male with a longer bill and is less colourful in spring. After moult, adult loses bright colours, but has boldly streaked back. Juveniles resemble non-breeding adults with scattered streaks on their buff breasts. Adults moult from the breeding plumage between August and November. Juveniles have a partial moult between September and January.
SEE ALSO: Black-tailed Godwit p138.

HABITS
This species has shorter legs and is more robust than the Black-tailed Godwit, and often wades in deep water. It flies with its neck withdrawn, making it appear smaller and more compact. It forms large flocks outside the breeding season and sometimes performs spectacular aerial manoeuvres.

VOICE
Flight note in flocks is a low, nasal 'kirruc, kirruc'.

HABITAT
In Britain and Ireland this is a coastal species spending most of its time feeding in the intertidal zone or in a high-tide roost close to the coast. Favours sandy or muddy shores, estuaries and sheltered bays. Breeds mainly in sub-Arctic on peat-mosses, swamps and the low tundra near the coast.

FOOD
Feeds mainly on shellfish, lugworms, ragworms and other worms found in coastal sand; also shrimps and small marine snails. On breeding grounds chief food is insects, especially beetles, flies and moth caterpillars, and also snails, crustaceans, worms and occasionally seeds and berries.

BREEDING
Does not breed in Britain or Ireland. The nest is situated on the ground, and 4 eggs are usually laid. Incubation lasts 21–22 days, and is thought to be by both sexes, although male may take major share. Young feed themselves and become independent at about the time that they learn to fly.

MOVEMENTS AND MIGRATIONS
The Bar-tailed Godwit is a migrant that leaves its Arctic breeding grounds after nesting and migrates through Europe between July and October. Some adults moult on British estuaries and then fly south, others stay for the winter. Some juveniles stay only to feed before flying on to Africa. Most wintering birds leave Britain and Ireland in March and April. Oldest ringed bird lived for 34 years.

POPULATION
Peak winter numbers may reach 65,000 in the UK and over 10,000 in Ireland.

CONSERVATION
These long-distance migrants depend heavily on a few coastal wetlands whilst they are migrating and for their winter quarters. While some of these sites are protected others are damaged by land-claim, construction of marinas and barrages, commercial exploitation of shellfish stocks and tourism. Many of the sites in France, Portugal and North Africa are unprotected.

DISTRIBUTION
In winter found all round the coast of Britain and Ireland, but less numerous along the south coast. A few non-breeding birds remain in Britain for the summer. It breeds from northern Scandinavia to Siberia and winters around the North Sea and on the Atlantic coasts of Europe and North Africa. Another race breeds from eastern Siberia into western Alaska.

Whimbrel *Numenius phaeopus*

INTERNATIONAL NAME EURASIAN WHIMBREL

IDENTIFICATION

40–42 cm. Large wader, but smaller than Curlew by about a third, with slightly shorter legs and shorter, straighter bill that curves steeply nearer the tip. It has a dark-centred back, each feather neatly edged buff, with barred flight feathers and finely lined underparts. Unlike Curlew its crown has two broad dark bands separated by a narrow pale stripe. Face pattern is also different to a Curlew, with a more obvious buff stripe over the eye, a dark line through the eye and paler cheeks and throat. Flight is lighter than Curlew and it has a noticeably darker chest, but like Curlew it also has a white rump that extends up between the wings in a 'V' shape. Adults moult their body feathers after nesting, but delay the moult of their flight feathers until they reach their wintering areas.
SEE ALSO: Curlew p141.

HABITS

Often picks food from the surface as well as probing like the larger Curlew. It is usually seen in small groups, often flying in 'V' formation. Larger congregations form at migration stopping places where they feed and rest.

VOICE

The commonly heard call is a rippling whistle 'pe,pe, pe,pe,pe,pe,pe'. Sometimes known as the 'Seven Whistler' on account of the usual number of notes. On its breeding grounds it has a bubbling call, rather like a Curlew.

nest is probably built mainly by the female and is a shallow scrape lined with plant material. Incubation of the 4 eggs is by both sexes and lasts about 27 days. The young feed themselves and are cared for by both adults. They can fly after 35 days and quickly become independent.

MOVEMENTS AND MIGRATIONS

In July Whimbrels begin to leave their northern breeding grounds and move rapidly through western Europe, mainly following coastal routes but many crossing large areas of land, including the western Sahara. First migrants may arrive in South Africa during September but most will winter on the coast of West Africa. The return passage through Europe is mid-April and early May. Oldest 16 years.

POPULATION

Breeds in Scotland. The population peaked at about 530 pairs, mainly in Shetland, but has since declined to fewer than 300. During peak migrations over 3,800 may be seen but numbers vary considerably from year to year.

CONSERVATION

The Whimbrel is specially protected at all times. Climate change bringing colder, wetter springs may have caused Icelandic or Scandinavian Whimbrels to stop over and breed. The cause of the rapid decline of about 50% is unclear.

juvenile

HABITAT

Chiefly occurs on or near the coast, especially estuaries, coastal grasslands and saltmarshes. There have been some notable numbers at regular inland reservoir sites in the Pennines. Breeding grounds are on blanket bogs, old peat cuttings, and short heather and grassland on northern moors.

FOOD

On the coast it eats periwinkles, dog whelks, crabs, sandhoppers and shrimps. Inland it feeds on small snails, slugs, worms, spiders and insects such as beetles and flies.

BREEDING

The Whimbrel nests on the ground, in the open, among short vegetation. Many birds are found breeding near small colonies of Arctic Skua and benefit from the skuas chasing away predators such as gulls. The

In Britain and Ireland the Whimbrel breeds only in the north of Scotland, mostly in Shetland. It visits areas farther south during its spring and autumn migrations. The four races of Whimbrels breed in Alaska and Canada, Iceland and western Russia, eastern Siberia and south-east of the Ural Mountains. The North American race has an all dark rump – it has been seen in Britain. European breeding birds winter mainly in West Africa but some winter as far south as South Africa.

Curlew *Numenius arquata*

INTERNATIONAL NAME EURASIAN CURLEW

female summer

male summer

IDENTIFICATION
50–60 cm. Our largest breeding wader with very long, deeply downcurved bill and long legs. It is grey-brown with long fine dark lines down neck and breast, arrow-shaped barring on flanks and brown barred back. Head is rather plain, lacking the bold stripes on the crown of Whimbrel. In flight, outer flight feathers are darker than the rest of the wing and white rump extends up the back in a shallow 'V'. Female has a longer bill than male. Adults moult completely between June and November.
SEE ALSO: Whimbrel p140, Bar-tailed Godwit p139.

HABITS
Feeding birds at the coast will usually spread out, but congregate in flocks at high tide, and often roost or feed on nearby fields. They may wade in deep water and sometimes swim over short distances. It is a shy bird. Its flight is fast and rather gull-like. On its breeding grounds it sometimes perches on trees and bushes. Male marks its territory with an undulating display flight with shimmering wings and a parachute glide.

VOICE
Common call is a distinctive 'cour-eee' from which it gets its common name. In spring, songflight is accompanied with lonely-sounding, bubbling trill.

HABITAT
Breeds in the uplands on boggy, grassy and heather moorland, hill pastures, hay meadows and also coastal marshes. Some nest on agricultural land in lowland areas. In Europe and Russia nests in river valleys and steppe. In winter, found mainly around coasts, especially estuaries. There are some traditional inland wetland wintering sites.

FOOD
In winter, it probes into soft mud for crabs, lugworms, ragworms, small shellfish, cockles, marine snails and shrimps, and in pastures for earthworms. In summer, it eats insects, especially the larvae of beetles and flies, spiders and worms.

BREEDING
Nests on the ground. Male makes several scrapes and one is selected and lined by female. Site usually in the open on a mound or tussock, but sometimes protected by vegetation. The 2–5 eggs are laid in April or May and incubated for 27–29 days by both adults. Young are covered with down and feed themselves. They are cared for by both parents at first, but female often leaves before they fly at 32–38 days.

MOVEMENTS AND MIGRATIONS
Some Irish birds may be resident, but most British Curlews migrate south-west, with some reaching France and Spain. However adults from Scandinavia and western Europe arrive in Britain and Ireland from late June and juveniles follow in September. Some from Russia also winter in Britain. Scottish birds mostly move to western Britain and Ireland. Oldest was 31 years.

POPULATION
Around 100,000 pairs breed in the UK and over 2,500 in Ireland, although the numbers nesting on grassland and lowland farms have fallen by 25% in recent years. Over 160,000 winter in the UK and over 40,000 in Ireland.

CONSERVATION
Appears to be declining in Europe. Loss of breeding habitat to forestry and the switch to improved grasslands from hay meadows resulting in multiple cutting of grass for silage are two likely causes. Farmers adopting stewardship schemes will help conserve breeding and feeding sites.

DISTRIBUTION
Breeds in the uplands of England, Scotland and Wales and is widespread in Ireland. Common on Orkney, Shetland and the Hebrides. Also breeds in some parts of lowland England. Winters around the coast and a few visit inland sites. Breeds in central and northern Europe and Russia and winters around European and African coasts as far south as South Africa.

Spotted Redshank *Tringa erythropus*

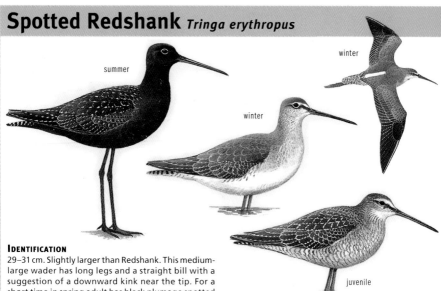

summer

winter

winter

juvenile

IDENTIFICATION

29–31 cm. Slightly larger than Redshank. This medium-large wader has long legs and a straight bill with a suggestion of a downward kink near the tip. For a short time in spring adult has black plumage spotted with white on the back. At other times it resembles Redshank but with longer bill and longer legs. The back is pale grey with some spotting and the pale head has a black line through the eye with white above. Underparts are white. The legs are red and the lower part of the bill is red at the base. In flight, it has a white lozenge-shape on its back and no wing-bar. Juvenile brown above with dusky belly and barring on flanks. Immature in first summer may become darker with heavily barred underparts. Adults moult completely between July and October. In spring, the body plumage is moulted between March and May. Juveniles have a partial moult between August and February. SEE ALSO: Redshank p143, Ruff p125.

HABITS

An elegant wader. In flight, it often looks long and slim with legs trailing. An energetic feeder that frequently wades in deep water, submerging its whole head in its search for food or delicately skimming the surface water. Swims readily. Often solitary or in small groups.

VOICE

Usual flight call is a loud and distinctive 'chu-it'.

HABITAT

Breeds in the Arctic tundra on bogs and marshes surrounded by woodland. Outside the breeding season it visits freshwater sites – shallow pools, floodwaters, reservoir margins and inland lakes but it also can be seen on coastal marshes, in sheltered estuaries and on brackish lagoons. It especially favours creeks and channels.

FOOD

Searches in mud or in water and sometimes chases after prey. Eats adults and larvae of water beetles and flies. Also takes moth caterpillars, shrimps, shellfish, worms and small fish.

BREEDING

Does not breed in Britain or Ireland. It makes a shallow scrape and lines it with leaves and stems. The eggs, usually 4, are incubated mostly by the male. Female may leave the breeding site before the eggs hatch or when the chicks are young. Male looks after young.

MOVEMENTS AND MIGRATIONS

Females form flocks and leave their breeding grounds before the males. Migration starts in mid-June and juveniles follow in July and August with peak migration through Britain and Ireland during September. Return migration is during April and May, therefore females are only on their breeding grounds for 4–5 weeks. A few non-breeding birds remain around the British coasts in summer. Oldest known individual survived for over 8 years.

POPULATION

400–500 birds may be around British and Irish coasts during migrations. Over 100 stay for the winter.

CONSERVATION

Western Europe sees relatively few of the large number of Spotted Redshanks that move to and from the Arctic each year. The conservation of the estuaries and lowland freshwater wetlands they use to stop over and feed at is as important as the management of the brackish lagoons found near the coast, which are usually specially protected sites and nature reserves.

DISTRIBUTION

Breeds in northern Scandinavia and east across northern Russia and Siberia. Winters in small numbers in Britain and Holland, around the coast of western Europe, around the Mediterranean and in West Africa. Most of the population however winter in a very wide range of countries from West Africa eastwards across India and South-east Asia to Vietnam. Much of the migration takes place overland on a broad front. In Britain and Ireland it is widely distributed on migration but wintering birds are mainly found in the south.

Redshank *Tringa totanus*

INTERNATIONAL NAME COMMON REDSHANK

winter

summer

juvenile

winter

IDENTIFICATION

27–29 cm. Medium-sized wader with an orange-red base to its medium-length bill and longish red legs. In spring, adult has a dark brown back with irregular dark markings, heavily lined breast and streaked flanks. In winter, becomes grey-brown with a more uniform appearance, plain grey-brown breast and mottled flanks. Juvenile brown like the summer adult but has neat buff edges to all back and wing feathers and legs are more orange-red. In flight, has very obvious white rear edges to wings and white 'V' up the back. Breeding plumage moulted between June and November; partial moult into breeding plumage between January and May. SEE ALSO: Spotted Redshank p142, Ruff p125.

HABITS

Walks and runs when feeding and also wades and swims. May be seen singly, but not uncommonly forms flocks. Flight sometimes appears a little erratic and it often glides. In spring, has a noisy display as it undulates over territory, calling loudly and gliding to the ground where it pauses with wings raised, displaying the white feathers under its wings. When nesting, frequently perches on fences or posts.

VOICE

Noisy and nervous wader that alerts other birds to approaching danger with ringing 'tew, tew' call. In spring, has a yodelling 'tu-udle, tu-udle' that accompanies display flight.

HABITAT

Half of Britain's breeding Redshanks nest on salt-marshes. Others nest in freshwater marshes, wet grasslands, upland pastures and low moorland areas, often far away from the coast. After nesting, most winter in coastal areas, often feeding on saltmarshes.

FOOD

In coastal areas feeds on shrimps, small fish, shellfish such as cockles, marine snails, small crabs, ragworms and other marine worms. Inland, feeds on earthworms, cranefly larvae, beetles, flies and spiders.

BREEDING

Most eggs are laid in May in a nest made by female in a scrape within rushes or other vegetation. There are usually 4 eggs. Incubation is by both sexes and lasts for 24 days. Young are self-feeding and at first both parents care for the family, but often female leaves before the young fly at 25–35 days.

MOVEMENTS AND MIGRATIONS

Northern breeding birds tend to migrate, while southerly populations are more sedentary. Young Redshanks travel further than older birds, some reaching France and Spain. As many as half of those wintering in Britain may be from Iceland. Some from Scandinavia reach Britain, but most go to southern Europe and North Africa. Oldest ringed bird lived for 26 years.

POPULATION

Over 38,000 pairs breed in the UK and up to 5,000 in Ireland. Breeding population has fallen by 45%, with inland sites the worst affected. Wintering population may exceed 125,000 individuals.

CONSERVATION

Cold winters increase mortality as do dry summers when young find it difficult to feed. Drainage of agricultural land has resulted in the Redshank disappearing from many inland sites. Overgrazing coastal marshes has also removed breeding habitat. Breeding birds are increasingly dependent on nature reserves and other protected sites. Future threats come from inland breeding sites becoming too dry and coastal marshes disappearing through sea-level rise. Grazing agreements on coastal sites and the creation of new marshes will help, as will grants to encourage the re-wetting of farmland and the right stock management.

DISTRIBUTION

The greatest concentrations of breeding Redshanks occur in parts of Scotland and north-west England. In Ireland the largest concentrations are found in the west. Others are on the coastal marshes of eastern and southern England. It winters on coasts where there is suitable feeding habitat. Breeds in Iceland, in Europe from Scandinavia to Spain and east into Asia.

Greenshank *Tringa nebularia*

INTERNATIONAL NAME   COMMON GREENSHANK

IDENTIFICATION

30–33 cm. Medium-large wader with long slightly upturned bill and long greenish legs. Taller and greyer than Redshank. Grey above and white below, with head, neck and sides of breast pale grey. In flight, wings are uniform grey; long white 'V' up the back and pale tail are conspicuous. In spring, back is darker with irregular black spots and streaks and dark 'arrowhead' marks on neck and breast. Juveniles have darker backs with every feather on the upperparts thinly edged with buff. Adults start to moult in June and July, although some suspend this moult during migration. Partial moult between January and May to acquire breeding plumage. Juveniles have a partial moult between August and March.

SEE ALSO: Redshank p143, Spotted Redshank p142, Green Sandpiper p147.

female leaves and begins her migration ahead of the family. Young fly between 25 and 31 days and male often accompanies them on migration.

MOVEMENTS AND MIGRATIONS

One parent, usually the female, migrates in June or July and the young follow with the remaining adult before the end of August. Most Scottish birds winter in south-west Britain and Ireland, but some go on to the Mediterranean or North Africa. Others from northern Europe may winter in Britain but most winter in central and southern Africa. The oldest known bird survived for 24 years.

winter

summer

winter

HABITS

When feeding, probes into wet mud, pecks delicately from the surface or sweeps bill from side to side. Generally seen singly, but may travel in small flocks. Flight rapid and it sometimes twists erratically. On breeding territories may perch on a post or small tree. Male proclaims territory with a songflight of deep undulations, sometimes reaching a great height, before 'tumbling' back to the ground.

VOICE

Loud, ringing 'tew, tew, tew' call is often given in flight. Also has a rich 'ru-tu, ru-tu, ru-tu' song in spring.

HABITAT

In most of its breeding range inhabits open forest or partially tree-grown areas in the sub-Arctic. In Scotland found on lower moors that may be either dry or boggy, but are usually near small pools or peat bogs. Outside the breeding season visits the margins of lakes, rivers and reservoirs and also estuaries and coastal marshes.

FOOD

In summer it feeds on beetles, worms, snails, dragonfly nymphs and small fish. It also eats amphibians such as newts and some plant material. At the coast it eats shrimps, crabs, ragworms and small fish.

BREEDING

Nesting begins in late April. The male makes several nest-scrapes on the ground, in the open, from which the female chooses one. There are usually 4 eggs. Incubation is by both adults and lasts 25–27 days. Young are covered with down and feed themselves. At first both adults tend the chicks, but often the

POPULATION

There are 700–1,500 territories in Scotland. In recent years the range has contracted and the species has left some of its more southerly breeding sites. In winter there are around 700 individuals in the UK and 1,000 in Ireland. Numbers increase to 1,000 or more birds in autumn.

CONSERVATION

Planting of forests on the flow country of Caithness and Sutherland, the drying out of traditional marsh sites and disturbance by leisure activities have all contributed to rob the Greenshank of some its former breeding sites. Climate changes may also be driving birds further north. Current restoration of flow country by the RSPB may help to restore some breeding sites.

DISTRIBUTION

In Britain it breeds in the north of Scotland. It occurs widely both inland and on the coast during migration, and some overwinter particularly around Irish coasts. It breeds across northern Europe, north Russia and northern Asia and winters south to South Africa and Australasia.

Wood Sandpiper *Tringa glareola*

IDENTIFICATION
19–21 cm. Smaller than Redshank with straight bill and conspicuous long creamy white stripe from the bill, over the eye to back of neck. Adults have a 'chequered' brown and white back. Slender neck and fine bill give it an elegant look. Legs are yellowish. In flight, has no wing-bars but lacks the black-and-white appearance of Green Sandpiper. Has square white rump, barred tail, pale greyish-brown underwing and feet that project beyond the tail. In autumn and winter, back is more uniform grey-brown. Juvenile resembles adult in summer but with dense, buff-coloured spots on back and mottled breast. Adult's moult begins on the breeding grounds in July and is usually suspended and completed on migration or on wintering grounds. Has a second partial moult between January and May into breeding plumage. Juveniles have partial moult between August and January.
SEE ALSO: Green Sandpiper p147, Redshank p143.

HABITS
Similar to Green Sandpiper, but less shy and can be noisy when migrating. Bobs its body when curious. Agile in flight and climbs steeply. Has an undulating display flight high over its breeding grounds in spring. Often seen singly, but small groups of three or four can be found.

VOICE
Most common call is a rather dry 'chiff-iff-iff', usually given in flight.

HABITAT
Breeds around marshes and swamps in lightly wooded country in the far north, often on the fringes of forests or in flooded birch woods. Outside the breeding season visits the edges of lakes, reservoirs, flooded grasslands and some brackish pools near the coast, but it is essentially a freshwater wader.

FOOD
Feeds on beetles, flies and the larvae of dragonflies, caddis flies, mayflies and moths. Also takes worms, spiders, shellfish and small fish.

BREEDING
Nest is usually on the ground among dense vegetation, but sometimes in a tree – in an old nest of another bird such as a thrush. It lays 4 eggs. Incubation lasts 22–23 days and is by both sexes. Young feed themselves and fly at about 30 days. Both adults care for them at first, but female generally leaves a few days after hatching.

MOVEMENTS AND MIGRATIONS
Adults start to leave breeding territories in June and move south or south-west on a broad front across Europe, with peak number of adults passing through Britain and Ireland in August and juveniles in September. Congregations form at traditional sites, such as the Camargue in the south of France where birds moult and feed ready for the trans-Mediterranean/Saharan crossing. It leaves Africa in March and makes only brief stops before arriving back on its breeding grounds in late April and May. The oldest ringed bird was 11 years old.

POPULATION
18–21 pairs nest in Scotland.

CONSERVATION
The Wood Sandpiper is specially protected. It nested in England in the 19th century, but it was not until 1959 that it was proved to have nested again in Scotland. Since then it has bred at up to nine sites. Forestry developments have damaged some sites, but there has been a small increase in the number of pairs in recent years. This species is on the edge of its world range in Scotland, but the re-wetting of some traditional marshes may help this wader in future.

winter

summer

juvenile

DISTRIBUTION
A few pairs breed in the Scottish Highlands. On migration visits many freshwater and brackish habitats in Britain and Ireland. Breeds from Scandinavia eastwards across Russia and Siberia to the Pacific Ocean. Winters in West, central and southern Africa, India and South-east Asia.

Common Sandpiper *Actitis hypoleucos*

IDENTIFICATION

19–21 cm. Much smaller than Redshank, this medium-sized wader has a horizontal posture and constantly wags its rear end up and down. Grey-brown above with neat division between a grey-brown breast and pure white underparts. White from underparts extends up towards neck. Rather small head, short neck, short greenish legs, medium-length straight bill and quite a long tail that extends beyond its folded wings. Adults in summer have short blackish marks across back feathers. Wings have a white bar and rump has white sides and a dark centre. Juvenile has paler buff tips to the wing feathers giving a pattern of scaly bands across the shoulders. Adults begin their moult in August and September and continue until March.

SEE ALSO: Green Sandpiper p147, Wood Sandpiper p145.

summer

HABITS

Flight very distinctive, usually close to the water, on stiff, bowed wings that never seem to rise above the level of the bird's body and alternate between a flickering flight and a glide. Has a rather crouching feeding action and habitually bobs, especially when feeding, after landing or when curious. Usually seen singly outside the breeding season but flocks of a thousand or more sometimes gather on their African wintering grounds. Both adults and young will occasionally dive to escape danger.

VOICE

Call is a shrill 'tee wee wee', usually given in flight as an alarm call. Song is a twittering version of the flight call.

winter

HABITAT

Breeds close to fast-flowing hill streams and rivers and also around upland lakes, lochs and reservoirs. On migration and in winter visits freshwater sites in lowland areas such as gravel pits, sewage treatment works, the banks of lakes and rivers and small sheltered estuaries.

FOOD

Usually picks food from the surface rather than probing into sand or mud. Feeds on insects, especially flies and their larvae, beetles, earwigs and grasshoppers. Also eats spiders, worms, freshwater shrimps and small fish.

BREEDING

Nests on ground, usually concealed in vegetation and often close to water. Both sexes make suitable scrapes for the nest and female selects and lines one of them. Both adults share incubation of the 3–5 eggs for about 21 days. Young are covered with down and tended by their parents until they fly at about 27 days.

MOVEMENTS AND MIGRATIONS

Most breeding birds move south-south-west after they finish breeding. Most adults pass through Britain and Ireland during July and August and by September most passage birds are juveniles. They begin to return in March and British breeding grounds are reoccupied in the second half of April. Oldest ringed bird had survived over 14 years.

POPULATION

24,000 pairs breed in the UK and 1,000–2,500 in Ireland. Breeding population has fallen 28% in recent years. Around 100 birds winter in Britain and Ireland.

CONSERVATION

Once bred commonly in lowland Britain and Ireland, but gradually it has retreated into upland areas and is still declining, perhaps owing to the acidification of streams and rivers, which reduces the food available. New footpaths close to rivers, and disturbance from anglers, walkers and others may affect breeding in some popular upland areas. Numbers in Europe have also declined in the last 20 years.

juvenile

DISTRIBUTION

In Britain and Ireland breeds mainly in the north and west. Many more visit other wetland sites on migration and a few overwinter, mostly in south-west England and south-east Ireland. Breeds from Arctic Europe to Spain and east to Japan. A few winter in western Europe, but most winter in central and southern Africa, and other populations travel as far south-east as Australia.

Green Sandpiper *Tringa ochropus*

summer

winter

winter

juvenile

IDENTIFICATION
21–24 cm. Smaller than a Redshank.
This wader is shorter-legged than Wood Sandpiper and has dumpier looking body, making it less elegant. Has straight bill, longer than Wood Sandpiper's. Back and head are dark green-brown. Has a prominent dark streaked breast contrasting abruptly with white underparts. It has white above and in front of its eye but, unlike Wood Sandpiper, this does not extend behind the eye. In summer, has fine white speckling on its dark back. In flight, the upperwing and underwing are dark, which contrasts with the white rump and makes it look somewhat like a House Martin. Juvenile is neatly speckled and spotted with off-white marks on the back and wings. Adults moult from late July and may not complete it until November or December. Some individuals suspend their moult during their migration.
SEE ALSO: Wood Sandpiper p145, Common Sandpiper p146.

HABITS
Rather shy, nervous and secretive wader that frequently bobs when on the ground, wagging its rear end. When disturbed will take off rapidly with a zig-zag flight that resembles Snipe. Can be seen singly or in small groups.

VOICE
When disturbed it frequently makes a distinctive 'tweet, weet, weet' call in flight – the last two notes being higher-pitched.

HABITAT
Outside breeding season visits marshes and muddy fringes of lakes, reservoirs, flood waters, freshwater marshes and rivers, sometimes at the coast, but more often inland. Regular visitor to gravel pit complexes. Over-wintering birds are found in ditches on lowland farmland, near streams, freshwater marshes, sewage works and at watercress beds. Breeds in wet woods and open forests.

FOOD
In winter, feeds on insects and their larvae, including mayflies, stoneflies, caddis flies and other flies and beetles. Also takes freshwater shrimps, worms, small snails and small fish.

BREEDING
Does not usually breed in Britain or Ireland. Unusually for a wader it nests in trees, in the old nests of other species including Woodpigeon and thrushes. Both adults incubate the 3 or 4 eggs. Incubation lasts for 20–23 days and is by both adults, but mainly female. Both parents tend the young at first, but female may leave before they fly at about 28 days.

MOVEMENTS AND MIGRATIONS
Migration begins in June with females moving south before the males and juveniles. Migration takes place across a broad front and many not only cross Europe, but also cross North Africa, including the Sahara Desert. They start to return from March and are back on the breeding grounds by mid-May. Oldest ringed bird was over 11 years.

POPULATION
Most are seen on migration, and 1,000 may over-winter in Britain and Ireland. Small numbers regularly summer in Scotland, and up to 5 pairs attempt to nest in some years.

CONSERVATION
This is such a secretive bird on its breeding grounds that organised protection is almost impossible, and probably unnecessary. It is important that the mixed-age forests and wet woodlands in the Scottish highlands are conserved for this and other specialised breeding birds.

DISTRIBUTION
The species is widespread while on migration and a small population overwinters in Britain and Ireland, mostly in south-east and central England but also north to Cumbria and Northumberland, and some in Wales and southern Ireland. It breeds in Europe from the Arctic Circle south to Denmark and also east across Russia, to Siberia and China. Some winter in western Europe, but most winter from central Africa east to Asia Minor, India, China and South-east Asia.

Red-necked Phalarope *Phalaropus lobatus*

IDENTIFICATION

18–19 cm. Delicate Dunlin-sized wader that is more likely to be seen swimming than wading. Small head, slender neck and fine straight bill. In spring, female has grey head and upperparts, white throat and underparts, an orange patch on the sides of neck and buff lines on its dark back. Male duller with more buff streaking on upperparts. Juvenile has dark crown and obvious buff lines on back and shows a pale oval near the shoulder. First-winter birds start to show grey lines along the back but retain the neat dark flight feathers, edged buff. In flight, shows white wing-bar on dark wings.

SEE ALSO: Grey Phalarope p149, Sanderling p132.

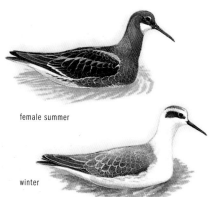

female summer

winter

HABITS

A remarkably tame wader usually seen in Britain on migration, but occurs in small groups on its breeding grounds. In winter, large flocks gather on the open sea. Swims and floats buoyantly with neck held straight as it spins and turns on the water, or bobs its head like a Moorhen when swimming.

VOICE

Most common call is a sharp 'twit', or 'whit' given in flight or on the water.

HABITAT

In Britain breeds near small freshwater marshy pools where there is open water and emergent vegetation, such as in flooded peat cuttings, but also in small pools in hay fields and rough pasture. Sometimes visits freshwater and brackish pools on migration. Winters on the open sea.

FOOD

Feeds while swimming, wading or walking. Chief food is insects, especially flies and their larvae. Also eats springtails, beetles, butterflies, moths, spiders and small worms.

BREEDING

Nests on the ground, close to water, usually in a grassy tussock with grass pulled over the top of the nest. Both sexes make nest-scrapes and female selects one in which to lay her 4 eggs. Eggs are laid in late May or early June. Incubation is by male and lasts 17–21 days. Young quickly move to emergent vegetation where they feed themselves and remain well hidden. They are cared for by male until independent at about 14 days and are able to fly at about 20 days. Once fledged, young leave their breeding site within about 5 days.

MOVEMENTS AND MIGRATIONS

Starts to leave its northern breeding grounds from the end of June. Females leave first followed by males in July and juveniles in August. Migration is still little understood, but northern European birds tend to migrate south-east across Europe and gather in large concentrations on the Arabian Sea by late October. There they remain in their winter quarters until the following April and arrive back on their breeding grounds during May. Oldest 12 years.

POPULATION

The population has suffered a large decline in Britain and is now reduced to a few regular breeding sites in Scotland and in Ireland. The small population fluctuates from year to year, and usually there are 15–30 males holding territory. Migrants in Britain total about 30 birds a year, mostly juveniles in August and September.

CONSERVATION

Specially protected. It has been a target for egg thieves and suffered from the drainage of suitable pools. The current breeding sites require protection and careful management to ensure a succession of pools for feeding and nesting. It is important that grazing animals are restricted in the breeding areas in spring, but are allowed to graze down rank vegetation later on. Climate change may also be affecting British breeders.

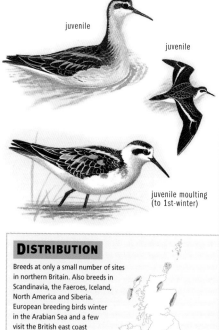

juvenile

juvenile

juvenile moulting (to 1st-winter)

DISTRIBUTION

Breeds at only a small number of sites in northern Britain. Also breeds in Scandinavia, the Faeroes, Iceland, North America and Siberia. European breeding birds winter in the Arabian Sea and a few visit the British east coast in autumn.

Grey Phalarope *Phalaropus fulicarius*

INTERNATIONAL NAME RED PHALAROPE (N. AMERICA)

IDENTIFICATION

20–22 cm. Dunlin-sized wader that is larger and chunkier than Red-necked Phalarope with shorter thicker bill and longer broader wings. Adults in breeding plumage are rare in Britain and Ireland. Most of the year it is pale grey above and white below, with a dark mark behind eye and an almost plain grey back. In breeding plumage has dark brown back streaked brightly with buff, white face patch, yellow bill with dark tip, and varying amount of red on underparts. Male duller than female in summer. Most common plumages in Britain and Ireland are juvenile and first winter – these birds are brown above with all back feathers neatly edged buff, with varying amounts of grey moulting through. Juvenile has thin buff stripes on dark back and pale buff wash to breast. Adults moult between July and November. Partial moult back into breeding plumage during March–May. Juveniles moult their body plumage and some wing feathers in autumn.

SEE ALSO: Red-necked Phalarope p148, Knot p127, Sanderling p132.

female summer

juvenile

HABITS

Very tame wader, commonly swimming and spinning as it feeds. Frequently 'bobs' its head like a Moorhen. The pale non-breeding plumage and buoyant swimming action are reminiscent of a small gull. Will also feed on land near water. Generally seen singly, but larger groups may gather while migrating.

VOICE

Common call is a low 'wit'. Also a 'zhit' call given when a bird is disturbed.

HABITAT

Breeds near the coast in the Arctic, close to brackish lagoons, pools, and boggy meadows on marshy tundra. Winters at sea in the Atlantic Ocean. May visit inland or coastal marshes and pools while migrating.

FOOD

Feeds on land, or while swimming. Eats mainly invertebrates and some plant material. Food includes flies and their larvae, beetles, bugs, springtails, shrimps, worms and spiders. In winter, feeds on marine plankton.

BREEDING

Does not breed in Britain or Ireland. This is a sociable species with birds nesting close together in some places. It nests on the ground, near water. A pair makes a scrape and the female selects one that is then lined by the male. Male incubates the 4 eggs for 18–20 days while female goes off to mate with another male if an excess of males is present. Young feed themselves and are cared for by the male alone until they fly at about 16–18 days.

MOVEMENTS AND MIGRATIONS

There is a staggered departure from the breeding grounds with non-breeding birds leaving in June, females in July and then males with, or followed by, the young. Outside the breeding season those seen on or near land are birds that are off course, usually owing to bad weather conditions. 'Storm-wrecked' birds are most likely to be seen in Europe between September and November but small numbers may be seen through to January. Winters out at sea, off the coasts of South Africa and South America. Most arrive in their winter quarters by November and leave again during March.

POPULATION

Numbers vary, but usually fewer than 200 sightings a year, usually juveniles.

CONSERVATION

Too few occur in Britain and Ireland for any special protection to be necessary, but birds like Grey Phalaropes that winter in discrete areas of the oceans need plankton-rich seas to feed on and they are potentially at risk from pollution.

juvenile

juvenile moulting
(to 1st-winter)

DISTRIBUTION

Very small numbers of migrating birds may occur almost anywhere in Britain or Ireland, but especially in Cornwall. Breeds in Iceland, Spitsbergen, Siberia, North America and Greenland. European breeding birds winter out to sea, in the Atlantic Ocean, off the coast of Africa or the coast of southern USA or South America.

Arctic Skua *Stercorarius parasiticus*

INTERNATIONAL NAME PARASITIC JAEGER (N. AMERICA)

IDENTIFICATION
41–46 cm. Smaller than Herring Gull. Resembles dark gull but with long pointed central tail feathers and long pointed and rather narrow wings with white flashes. There are dark and pale colour morphs, but many adults are intermediate. Dark morph is uniform dark brown below. Intermediate birds are warmer, more golden-brown below, with paler yellow-brown on side of face and neck. Pale morph has a dark cap, white neck, cheeks and underparts and, sometimes, a pale grey-brown breast-band. Juveniles have buff edges to all feathers on their upperparts and central tail feathers have small points. Intermediate juveniles are warm, gingery brown. No juveniles are cold, grey-brown like Long-tailed juveniles and at rest they show pale marks on dark folded primaries, unlike the other two species. Adults moult completely after breeding. Juveniles have protracted moult with flight feathers still moulting the following June.
SEE ALSO: Pomarine Skua p152, Long-tailed Skua p151, Great Skua p153.

juvenile
(intermediate)

juvenile
(dark)

juvenile
(pale)

HABITS
Flight is fast and falcon-like when chasing other sea-birds. Twists and turns and harasses them until they either drop their catch or disgorge their food. On its breeding territory it is very aggressive, attacking intruders, including cattle and humans. Breeds in loose colonies and migrates either singly or in small groups. Swims like a gull.

VOICE
Generally silent. When breeding, most common call is mewing 'ka-aaow'.

HABITAT
In Britain breeds on coastal moorland and islands. Elsewhere breeds on coastal tundra where there is moss, grass or other vegetation. There are usually freshwater pools nearby where the birds bathe. Outside the breeding season spends most of the time at sea, in warm coastal waters.

FOOD
Eats mainly fish, especially sand eels and sprats, which it obtains by harassing other seabirds. Also scavenges on dead mammals and birds. Will take eggs and kill and eat young birds and small mammals such as voles and lemmings. Also feeds on insects and berries.

BREEDING
In Scotland first eggs are laid in May in a nest on the ground in the open. There are almost always 2 eggs and both sexes incubate for 25–28 days. Incubation starts with the first egg, which hatches ahead of the

second. Young are cared for and fed by both parents. Young fly after 25–30 days and are independent after 2–5 weeks. They do not breed until at least 3 years old.

MOVEMENTS AND MIGRATIONS
Migration begins in July when birds that failed to breed and immatures start moving south. Breeding birds leave in August and juveniles in September. Migration around the coasts of Britain and Ireland peaks in September. Some cross the Atlantic, but most follow the coast of Europe and Africa to their wintering area. The oldest ringed bird survived 31 years.

POPULATION
Population has increased over the last 100 years to around 2,100 pairs, although more recently there has been a decline of around 50%.

CONSERVATION
Its conservation is linked to the health of the local sea-bird population, which in turn depends on fish stocks. Decline in sand eels has had a disastrous effect on local seabirds, including the Arctic Skua, and in some years virtually no young were reared in Scotland. The spread of the Great Skua has also impacted on the Arctic Skua, as it predates its young when nesting in close proximity.

summer
(dark morph)

summer
(pale morph)

DISTRIBUTION
In Britain this species is at the southern limit of its range. Breeds in northern Scotland, especially Shetland. Also breeds in Iceland and around the northern coast of Scandinavia, Greenland, North America and Siberia. European population mainly winters off the coast of South Africa.

Long-tailed Skua *Stercorarius longicaudus*

INTERNATIONAL NAME LONG-TAILED JAEGER (N. AMERICA)

IDENTIFICATION

48–53 cm (35–41 cm excluding tail-streamers). Small slim skua the size of Black-headed Gull with long wings. The adult resembles a small pale Arctic Skua with slimmer wings and very long delicate tail-streamers. It is usually very dusky below with only the upper breast pale. Lacks white on the underside of the wings, and has only one or two pale feather shafts on its upperwing. Upperparts are grey with contrasting dark hind edge to the wing and dark flight feathers. There is only one adult phase – pale. Juveniles are very grey-looking birds. They are barred below and have all feathers of their upperparts tipped pale greyish-white. Folded primaries are solid dark, unlike Arctic Skua. In flight, blunt projecting central tail feathers are only just visible. Some juveniles are very dark chocolate-brown but still have barring under the tail and pale edges to their back feathers. Some pale juveniles have almost white heads.

SEE ALSO: Arctic Skua p150, Pomarine Skua p152.

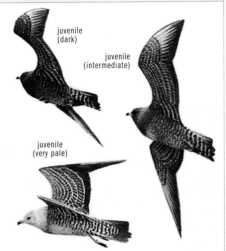

juvenile (dark)

juvenile (intermediate)

juvenile (very pale)

summer

summer

juvenile (intermediate)

HABITS

An elegant seabird that has buoyant, graceful, almost tern-like flight. It chases terns and Kittiwakes but also, on migration, swims a lot and picks for food on the sea's surface.

VOICE

Generally silent when not nesting.

HABITAT

A marine species that sometimes passes through British and Irish inshore waters on migration. It breeds in the far north on Arctic tundra and on fells above the treeline, and it winters at sea. In Scotland second-year and adult Long-tailed Skuas are sometimes present at colonies of Arctic Skuas in summer.

FOOD

On its breeding grounds its main food is small mammals, especially lemmings and some voles. It also eats eggs of other birds, insects, worms and berries. At sea it feeds on small fish, offal and carrion.

BREEDING

The Long-tailed Skua has not been proved to breed in Britain or Ireland. Elsewhere it nests on the ground in loose colonies. Both adults take turns to incubate the 2 eggs for about 24 days and the young fly at about 25 days.

MOVEMENTS AND MIGRATIONS

Migration starts in July and is earlier in years when lemmings are scarce, when fewer birds breed successfully. Migration is rapid and most birds go out into the Atlantic well to the north and then west of Scotland, although some pass along the east coast of Britain. Winter quarters are not properly known, but there are good numbers off the coasts of West Africa, Brazil and Argentina from September until May. Migrating birds are sometimes observed off the west coasts of Ireland and the Outer Hebrides in late May as birds return northwards.

POPULATION

A few birds sometimes summer in northern Scotland and breeding was suspected in 1980. In some years more are seen around British and Irish coasts than in others; for example in 1991 an unprecedented influx produced over 5,300 reports, mostly off the east coast of England and Scotland during September. When onshore winds occur in May there are sometimes reports of 1,000 birds or more off the Outer Hebrides.

CONSERVATION

There are currently no specific conservation measures for this seabird, although it would help to know more about its winter quarters. Like other seabirds this skua would be threatened by unsustainable fishing methods in its winter quarters and in time its northern breeding grounds could be influenced by changes to the climate.

DISTRIBUTION

This species nests in northern Scandinavia, Arctic Russia, Siberia across to Asia, the north of North America and parts of Greenland, with the largest numbers in Russia, Alaska and Canada. It spends the winter in the Pacific, Atlantic and Indian Oceans.

Pomarine Skua *Stercorarius pomarinus*

INTERNATIONAL NAME   POMARINE JAEGER

IDENTIFICATION

46–51 cm. Approaching the size of Herring Gull. Larger and heavier than Arctic and Long-tailed Skuas, with a deeper chest, bulkier body, and a longer, heavier gull-like bill that is pale with a dark tip. Adults have long spoon-shaped central tail-streamers, although these are sometimes damaged. Two colour morphs: the rarer (less than 10%) all-dark morph with smaller wing-flashes, and paler birds with dark caps, variable white underparts, sometimes a dark breast-band and often with barred flanks. The wings are long, broad at the base and with a pale crescent shape on the underwing. Juvenile is pale or dark grey-brown and closely barred, with strong barring under the tail and pale legs. Juveniles at rest show all-dark flight feathers, Arctic Skuas show conspicuous pale tips. The underwing of the juvenile Pomarine has two pale crescents, the Arctic has only one. Adults start to moult in August but do not complete it until well away from Britain and Ireland. Juveniles also moult in wintering areas.

SEE ALSO: Arctic Skua p150, Great Skua p153, Long-tailed Skua p151.

summer pale morph

summer dark morph

1st-summer pale morph

summer female
pale morph

juvenile
intermediate

BREEDING

The Pomarine Skua does not breed in Britain or Ireland. It nests on the ground in the Arctic tundra and usually lays 2 eggs in late June. Incubation is by both adults and lasts about 28 days. Both parents tend the chicks until the young fly at about 32 days.

MOVEMENTS AND MIGRATIONS

Leaves its breeding grounds in August and moves south-west into the North Atlantic and then south to the coast of Africa. Strong gales may displace birds into the North Sea: adults in September and juveniles in October/November. In May adults may be seen off the English south coast, south-west Ireland, the Hebrides and the Northern Isles.

HABITS

A large aggressive skua that sometimes attacks other birds to rob them of their prey. When hunting it occasionally forces victims into the sea to drown them. Normal flight is steady with measured downbeats and very brief glides and sometimes resembles a large gull. On migration it can be seen in groups of 7–20 at a time, and more rarely 70 or more.

POPULATION

Variable numbers, depending on weather conditions. Highest spring count in Britain was over 2,000 birds, but usually 50–300 are seen off western and southern coasts.

VOICE

Generally silent outside its breeding grounds.

CONSERVATION

As the species does not breed or winter in Britain or Ireland there are no special protection measures for it. In future it might be affected by declining fish stocks, which would reduce its food supply while it passes through British and Irish waters.

HABITAT

This is a seabird that breeds on the Arctic tundra and lives for the rest of the year in offshore waters, coming closer to land mainly as a result of rough weather.

FOOD

Outside the breeding season it feeds mainly on fish that it catches itself by diving or by robbing other species. It also kills and eats other birds and takes carrion when available. On its breeding grounds it feeds mainly on lemmings and the young of other birds.

DISTRIBUTION

The species breeds in the far north of North America, Asia and Europe. It normally passes well to the west of Scotland and Ireland when migrating and it winters off the coasts of West Africa. North American breeders winter off South American coasts and Siberian breeders winter in the Arabian Sea. It is widely distributed across the Atlantic during peak migration times.

Great Skua *Catharacta skua*

IDENTIFICATION
53–58 cm. This, our largest skua, is the size of a Herring Gull, but more bulky and heavier-looking with broader, slightly rounded wings and heavy bill. Has a proportionally shorter tail than other skuas and no streamers. Plumage usually blackish-brown with straw-coloured streaks and very obvious white flashes in the wings, above and below. Adult in summer may be paler and more yellow-brown, especially on the head and back. Juvenile tends to be uniformly darker, but there is some variation and a few may be noticeably paler. Adults moult their body feathers between June and September, but flight feathers are moulted only gradually between August and January while in its winter quarters.
SEE ALSO: Juvenile Herring Gull p158, Pomarine Skua p152, Arctic Skua p150.

juvenile

juvenile (dark)

HABITS
In flight, resembles a large gull, but more compact with strong downbeats and a big belly. Accelerates with powerful wingbeats and is surprisingly agile when pursuing other species. Very aggressive and chases large seabirds such as Gannets. On breeding grounds it fiercely attacks intruders, including domestic animals and humans.

VOICE
Usually silent away from breeding grounds. Main calls are a loud 'gek-gek' during attacks on intruders and a rolling 'hah-hah-hah'.

HABITAT
Breeds on rocky islands and moorland near the coast and spends the winter at sea.

FOOD
Specialises in robbing other species of their prey, usually of fish, but also hunts by taking food from the surface of the sea. Main food is sand eels, haddock and whiting. Also eats carrion and offal discharged from fishing boats. Kills other birds such as Puffins and even species as large as a Brent Goose.

BREEDING
Within a colony the Great Skua defends a territory. Nest is a hollow on the ground into which the 2 eggs are laid. Incubation is mainly by female and lasts 26–32 days. Young leave the nest soon after hatching and remain separately within their territory. Female guards young while male obtains most of the food, which he regurgitates for his family. Young fly after about 44 days and are dependent on their parents for up to 20 days. Young can breed when 4 or 5 years old, but more often they are 7 years or older before nesting for the first time.

MOVEMENTS AND MIGRATIONS
Migration begins in July. It peaks along British and Irish coasts in September and October, with more seen when there are storms or northerly winds. Birds from Iceland may head south-west towards North America or south-east towards Europe. Scottish birds move south to winter off the coast of southern Europe, with some juveniles reaching African waters. They can live for 32 years.

POPULATION
The species colonised Scotland in around 1750 and now over 9,600 pairs breed annually, mostly in the Northern Isles and some in the Hebrides.

CONSERVATION
This was a rare breeding bird until the 20th century. At first it was welcomed, but as numbers increased it came into conflict with farming interests as it was alleged to prevent pregnant ewes from feeding on new spring grass. Changes in fishing practices reduced sand eel numbers, and that in turn reduced Great Skua breeding success. Also concentrations of pollutants have been found in Great Skuas, but the long-term effect is unclear. Britain is important for this breeding bird, holding some 60% of the world population.

DISTRIBUTION
In Britain nests mainly in Shetland and Orkney. Most nest in Iceland and other populations breed in the Faroes, northern Norway, Spitsbergen and northern Russia. Seen around British and Irish coasts in autumn and spends the winter in the east Atlantic between the Bay of Biscay and Senegal.

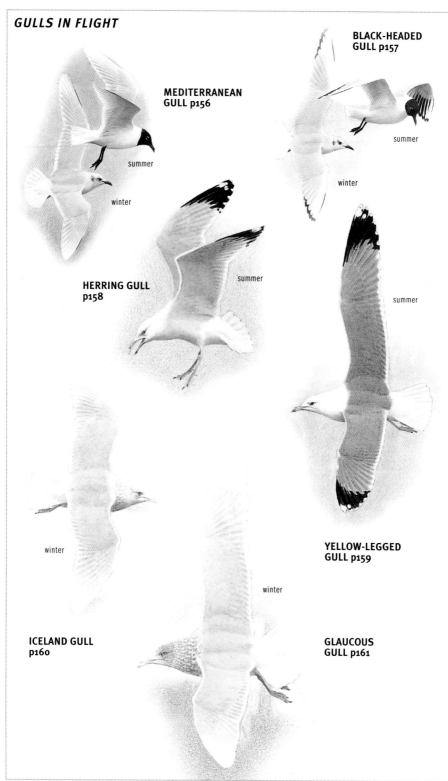

GULLS IN FLIGHT

BLACK-HEADED GULL p157

summer

winter

MEDITERRANEAN GULL p156

summer

winter

HERRING GULL p158

summer

summer

ICELAND GULL p160

winter

winter

YELLOW-LEGGED GULL p159

GLAUCOUS GULL p161

LESSER BLACK-BACKED GULL p162

summer

GREATER BLACK-BACKED GULL p163

summer

summer

COMMON GULL p164

summer

KITTIWAKE p165

juvenile

summer

winter

summer

SABINE'S GULL p167

LITTLE GULL p166

Mediterranean Gull *Larus melanocephalus*

IDENTIFICATION

36–38 cm. Slightly larger and more robust than Black-headed Gull, with larger head, thicker blood-red bill, which is parallel-sided and drooped at the tip. Legs are dark red and longer than those of the Black-headed Gull. In spring, from a distance, adults appear white with a black hood, as back and wings are pale grey and wing-tips white. In winter, head shape looks flattened and black is reduced to a black mask and grey nape. Juveniles have scaly brown wings. First-winter birds have the dark mask, mottled brown wings with a pale grey panel in the middle and dark, blackish-brown wing-tips. Secondary flight feathers have a dark bar across them and tail has a dark band near the tip. First-summer birds have a dark hood forming. Second-winter birds are pale like adults but have variable amounts of thin black marks near the wing-tip. Adults have a complete moult between June and September and then have a partial moult to acquire their black hood between February and April.

SEE ALSO: Black-headed Gull p157, Common Gull p164.

FOOD

In spring, feeds mainly on insects such as beetles and caterpillars. Also eats spiders, worms and fish. At other times feeds on fish, shellfish and scavenges for offal. Sometimes follows ploughing tractors and takes bread and other scraps from humans.

BREEDING

Frequently nests in Black-headed Gull colonies. Breeding begins in May. Nest is a shallow depression lined with grass and feathers on bare ground or among low vegetation. The clutch is usually 3 eggs. Incubation is by both parents and lasts for about 24 days. The young are fed by the adults. They leave their nest after a few days and hide nearby. They are able to fly at 35–40 days and become independent at about the same time.

MOVEMENTS AND MIGRATIONS

Leaves breeding colonies in June or July and those from eastern Europe head for the Mediterranean, where they stay until March. Young from the Black Sea also reach the Baltic Sea in winter and this may account for the growing population in western Europe. Oldest ringed bird was 15 years old.

POPULATION

Breeding in Britain first took place in Hampshire in 1968. Since then numbers have increased to around 500 pairs at various locations, mostly in southern England.

CONSERVATION

Specially protected because of the small number breeding here. Many of the breeding sites are on nature reserves. In world terms this is a rare gull with a very restricted distribution.

2nd-winter   1st-summer

summer

winter

1st-winter

1st-summer   1st-winter

summer

2nd-winter

HABITS

Often stands or struts with head hunched between its shoulders. In flight, looks heavy-bodied and thick-necked, and wing-tips look fuller, more rounded than a Black-headed Gull. Breeds in colonies and large flocks may form during migration. In Britain it often associates with Black-headed Gull colonies and sometimes hybridises with that species.

VOICE

Most common call is a distinctive 'kow-ah', deeper than that of Black-headed Gull.

HABITAT

Breeds in marshes or around lagoons or islands on the coast, elsewhere in its range it nests in fields and grasslands near inland wetlands. In winter, all move

DISTRIBUTION

Breeds in southern England. Also a few breed in Scotland and Ireland. The major breeding colonies are in south and east Europe, but numbers are increasing in Holland, Denmark and Belgium. In winter, it ranges around the Black Sea, the Mediterranean and along the coast of western Europe with a few in Britain, especially the south-east.

Black-headed Gull *Chroicocephalus ridibundus*

IDENTIFICATION
34–37 cm. This is the smallest of the abundant gulls of Britain and Ireland. It has slim, pointed wings with obvious white stripes along the front edge. In late winter and spring it has a dark chocolate-brown hood that in autumn and winter is reduced to a dark spot behind the eye. Brown head often appears black (hence its name). In spring the bill and legs are waxy-red, but are duller at other times. The juvenile has ginger-brown blotches on its head, back and sides of its breast. First-winter birds have head markings of an adult in winter, a brown bar across the wings and a narrow black tail-band. First-summer birds start to get dark hoods but keep the brown across the wings and the tail-band. Adult moult begins during June or July and is completed by September or October. The partial moult into breeding plumage is between January and April.
SEE ALSO: Little Gull p166, Mediterranean Gull p156, Sabine's Gull p167.

HABITS
Quick wingbeats and buoyant flight resemble a tern and it is agile enough to catch insects in the air. It will sometimes paddle the ground with its feet to attract worms and it often attempts to rob birds such as Great Crested Grebes or Lapwings of their food.

VOICE
The commonly heard call is a rather harsh 'kree-aaa'.

HABITAT
This gull breeds both inland and near the sea. Breeding sites vary from coastal marshes and sand dunes to freshwater marshes, lakes, flooded gravel pits, reservoirs and moorland pools. It forages for food on areas of short grass, farmland and rubbish tips as well as on beaches.

FOOD
Wide variety of food, including worms, insects such as beetles and swarming ants, spiders, slugs, small crabs, small fish, carrion and bread thrown by humans.

BREEDING
Breeding begins in April when birds display at their generally large colonies. The male may select a site and start building the nest, which is then completed by both male and female working together. The nest is a pile of vegetation on the ground, sometimes in water and rarely off the ground in trees, bushes or on buildings. Incubation of the 2 or 3 eggs is by both sexes and lasts for 23–26 days. The young are covered with down and leave the nest after about 10 days. They remain near the nest until they fly at about 35 days, and become independent soon afterwards.

MOVEMENTS AND MIGRATIONS
Breeding birds leave their colonies during July and return again in March and April. Northern and eastern populations are long-distance migrants while those in Britain and Ireland mostly stay within the British Isles. Icelandic birds winter in Scotland and Ireland and many from Scandinavia, northern Europe and Russia cross the North Sea and winter here. The oldest ringed bird survived over 30 years.

POPULATION
138,000 pairs breed in the UK and 3,900 in Ireland, although inland breeding in Ireland has declined by 81%. The UK winter population is over 2 million individuals.

CONSERVATION
There has been a decline of over 33% in winter for reasons that may be linked to climate change.

summer

winter

1st-winter

juvenile

1st-summer

summer

winter

DISTRIBUTION
The largest breeding colonies in Britain and Ireland are in north-west England, Scotland, north-west Ireland and Wales. After breeding, these birds may be seen almost anywhere, especially inland. This species breeds in Iceland, many parts of Europe, especially the north and east, in Russia and in Asia. European birds winter in western Europe, the Mediterranean and around the coast of North Africa.

Herring Gull *Larus argentatus*

INTERNATIONAL NAME | EUROPEAN HERRING GULL

IDENTIFICATION

55–67 cm. Large gull, between Lesser and Great
Black-backed in size, but with grey back and wings.
Fierce-looking, with powerful, slightly hooked
yellow bill with a red spot near the tip. Legs and
feet are flesh-coloured. Wings are broad giving rather
heavy appearance in flight and the wing-tips are black
with white spots. In winter, head and neck are heavily
streaked with grey. Juvenile is mottled brown and
very similar to juvenile Lesser Black-backed Gull. It is
not until its second winter that the adult grey colour
of the upperparts becomes obvious. It takes 4 years
to reach full adult plumage. Adult moult starts in
mid-May, while nesting. Moult and regrowth of
flight feathers takes 3–6 months. There
is a second partial moult between
January and March.
SEE ALSO: Yellow-legged Gull
p159, Lesser Black-backed Gull
p162, Common Gull p164,
Kittiwake p165.

juvenile   winter

summer

winter

HABITS

Individuals may feed singly, but
are seldom far from others. Nests in noisy colonies and
joins large communal roosts. At the coast follows
fishing boats to scavenge for discarded fish. Feeds in
ploughed fields and forms large feeding groups at
refuse tips. Adaptable, dropping shellfish onto rocks
to break their shells, or hunting like a bird of prey in
search of small mammals.

VOICE

Includes the 'long call', throwing its head back in a
series of cries, and a short 'kyow, kyow, kyow'.

HABITAT

Found in inshore waters and offshore fishing grounds.
Most nest near the sea, but inland colonies are increasing. Breeds on cliffs, beaches, shingle islands, moorland and buildings. Widespread outside the breeding
season, but there are still concentrations at or near the
coast. Feeds on rubbish tips, visits town parks and
roosts during the day on playing fields and at night
on reservoirs and estuaries.

FOOD

Has a wide range of food, from offal and carrion to
seeds and fruits. Robs other birds of their food, eats
the young and eggs of other birds, catches small mammals, scavenges on shorelines and rubbish tips, catches
flying ants and plunges into the water for fish.

BREEDING

Pairs defend a small territory inside a colony. Nesting
begins in April and a nest comprising a large mound
of vegetation is built by both sexes on the ground,

on a cliff ledge or even on a roof of a building.
Clutch of 2–4 (usually 3) eggs is incubated for
28–30 days by both adults. Young are well camouflaged and covered with down. They leave nest after
2–3 days but remain within the territory. They fly at
35–40 days old and quickly become independent.

MOVEMENTS AND MIGRATIONS

Colonies mostly deserted after nesting. Juveniles
disperse and travel further than adults. Some British
adults do not travel far but large numbers of Scandinavian birds visit Britain in winter. Oldest ringed bird
was 34 years old.

POPULATION

Thought to be about 140,000 pairs breeding in the
UK and 5,500 in Ireland. In winter, there may be over
700,000 individuals.

CONSERVATION

Increased during the 20th century as it benefited from
new food supplies on rubbish tips and around fishing
boats and from safe roosts on reservoirs. Inland urban
breeding is also increasing. In recent years the total
numbers have fallen again, especially in winter, possibly due to disease, reduced food supplies
and fewer immigrants from Europe,
perhaps linked to climate
change.

1st-winter

DISTRIBUTION

Found almost all round the British and
Irish coasts although scarcer along the
'soft' sandy coasts of eastern England.
In winter, can be seen anywhere
except in mountainous country.
Also breeds in Iceland and parts
of western Europe. Winters
as far south as Spain.

Yellow-legged Gull *Larus michahellis*

juvenile

summer

clutch of 2–4 eggs for 28–30 days. Young leave nest after 2–3 days but remain within territory. They fly at 35–40 days old and quickly become independent.

MOVEMENTS AND MIGRATIONS
Movements are not fully understood, but it appears that juveniles and immatures disperse from breeding colonies and may move in different directions, some flying north along the coast of Europe while others move south along the coast of Africa. Adults are mostly resident but a number disperse north and west after breeding.

POPULATION
The number of these gulls being observed in Britain has increased during the last 20 years and breeding was first recorded in 1992 when an individual hybridised with a Lesser Black-backed Gull. One pair nested in 1995 and two in 1997, since then between one and four pairs have nested each year.

CONSERVATION
At present there are no measures to protect it as it expands its range northwards. Globally this species has quite a restricted range.

IDENTIFICATION
55–67 cm. This bird is the size of a Herring Gull and closely resembles it. In winter, it has a whiter head than Herring Gull. It is bulkier and stronger-looking than Herring Gull, with stronger bill and larger head. It is slightly darker grey on the back and wings, but not as dark as Lesser Black-backed, and has more extensive black on the wing-tips with smaller white spots. The legs are yellow. Red spot on the yellow bill is larger and brighter. A narrow ring round the eye is orange-red. The juvenile has whiter head than juvenile Herring Gull, more like Lesser Black-backed in pattern and colour, and takes 4 years to reach adult plumage. Moults earlier than Herring Gull and in autumn plumage is pristine while Herring Gulls are still in moult.
SEE ALSO: Herring Gull p158.
Common Gull p164

summer

winter

1st-winter

HABITS
In Britain often stands apart from the large gull flocks or more likely to associate with Lesser Black-backeds. Has a tendency to feed on the tideline, away from the other large gulls.

VOICE
The 'kyow' call is more nasal and deeper than Herring Gull, rather similar to Lesser Black-backed.

HABITAT
Usually seen at or near coast and more restricted to this habitat than Herring Gull. Feeds in inshore waters but will also visit harbours and rubbish tips with other gulls. Nests in coastal locations.

FOOD
Feeds on a wide variety of animal and plant material, including fish, shellfish, small mammals and carrion.

BREEDING
A very rare breeding bird in Britain. The nest comprises a mound of vegetation on the ground, on a cliff ledge or even on the roof of a building. Both adults incubate

DISTRIBUTION
Originally nested only in north-west Africa, around the Mediterranean and along the coast of south-west Europe, but it has recently spread north to western Europe. After breeding, some disperse north-west and increasing numbers visit Britain and Ireland, especially in late summer.

Iceland Gull *Larus glaucoides*

IDENTIFICATION

52–60 cm. Smaller, less bulky and with longer wings than a Herring Gull. This is the smaller of the two species known as 'white-winged gulls' that visit Britain and Ireland; the other is the Glaucous Gull. Adults have very pale wings and white wing-tips. Its head is rounder than a Glaucous Gull, it has a smaller, less vicious-looking bill, a thin red ring round the eye and a more gentle facial expression. The long wing-tips project well beyond the tail when perched. In winter its head and neck are streaked grey-brown. Female is smaller than the male. Juvenile birds are buff, finely mottled and barred darker brown with pale, white or greyish-buff flight feathers. Extreme tips of folded primaries often subtly edged grey-buff. The bills of first-winter birds have more extensive black tips than a Glaucous Gull. The pattern of moult is probably similar to that of the Glaucous Gull.
SEE ALSO: Glaucous Gull p161, Herring Gull p158.

HABITS

In Britain this species is generally seen singly and can be rather tame. Its flight is light and graceful as it hovers, turns and glides more freely than other large gulls. It is also more agile when feeding, and will take food from the ground, when flying or when swimming. Sometimes it will plunge-dive in shallow water to reach its prey.

VOICE

The call is similar to that of a Herring Gull but more shrill.

HABITAT

This gull is seen mostly on the coast where it visits harbours and nearby rubbish tips. It also occurs inland, often roosting at reservoirs where it mixes with flocks of other gulls.

FOOD

It feeds mainly on fish, either alive or as carrion. On its breeding grounds it will take eggs and young birds. Outside the breeding season it frequently scavenges on rubbish tips and around harbours.

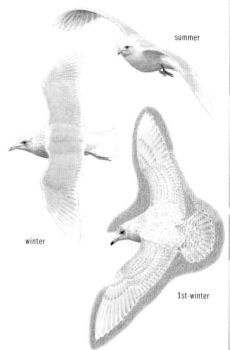

summer

winter

1st-winter

BREEDING

It does not breed in Britain or Ireland. Its breeding grounds are on rocky Arctic coasts, mostly on tall cliffs where it may nest among Kittiwakes. In places where the Glaucous Gull also nests, the Iceland Gull will nest lower down the cliff, at some distance from the larger, more aggressive species.

MOVEMENTS AND MIGRATIONS

Breeding birds leave their nest-sites in August and return the following April or May. Some move south down the coast of North America while others cross to Iceland (where it is a rare visitor, despite its name) with a few travelling further to western Europe.

POPULATION

In a normal year there may be 70–80 Iceland Gulls in Britain and Ireland in winter. In some years there are larger influxes and numbers rise to 200–300 or more. In recent years areas in western Ireland have hosted over 40 individuals.

CONSERVATION

The few Iceland Gulls that reach our shores benefit from human activity, whether it is the by-products of the fishing industry or domestic rubbish. It can suffer from pollution at sea: 16 Iceland Gulls were killed after the oil tanker Braer ran aground off Shetland in 1993.

1st-winter

DISTRIBUTION

In winter, the individual Iceland Gull may be seen almost anywhere around the coast of Britain and Ireland, especially in the west. It also visits a few inland sites, especially in central England. Despite its name, the species does not breed in Iceland but in Greenland and Arctic Canada. It winters as far south as New York in the USA and in Britain and Scandinavia in western Europe.

Glaucous Gull *Larus hyperboreus*

IDENTIFICATION

62–68 cm. Larger than a Herring Gull and approaching the size of a Great Black-backed Gull. This is the largest 'white-winged gull'. It is bulky and powerful-looking, with a long, massive bill and rather flat forehead and crown that creates an aggressive appearance. The back of the adult is pale grey and the tips of the wings are white. In winter, its head and neck are heavily streaked with grey-brown. In flight, the long bill, long protruding head and neck and long broad wings give an impression of large size and great strength. The mottled plumage of the juvenile birds is fawn and the wing-tips are pale. The tail lacks any obvious dark marks. Its long powerful bill has a dark tip, but this is less extensive than the dark tip of a juvenile Iceland Gull's bill. Moult lasts from the end of April until November, although some populations moult more quickly than others.

SEE ALSO: Iceland Gull p160, Herring Gull p158.

HABITS

This is a social species and sometimes forms large flocks in the north of its range, but around British and Irish coasts is seen singly or in small numbers. It frequently swims, but lacks the 'tapered end' of the Iceland Gull owing to the exposed wing-tips being proportionally shorter. It is an aggressive bird and will rob other species, notably Eiders, of food.

VOICE

Generally silent in winter. Its call sounds similar to that of the Herring Gull.

HABITAT

In Britain and Ireland this gull is chiefly found on our sea coasts, both in inshore waters and further out to sea around fishing boats. It may be seen inland, sometimes feeding at rubbish tips and roosting on lakes and reservoirs. In the breeding season it nests on Arctic coasts where there are rocks and cliffs, and inland crags and rock pinnacles.

FOOD

It eats a wide range of foods, especially animal material. It is a predator, a scavenger and a pirate. It eats eggs, young birds, fish, shellfish, insects and carrion. It also appears to associate with marine mammals including walrus, seals and whales and probably feeds on their faeces.

winter

1st-summer

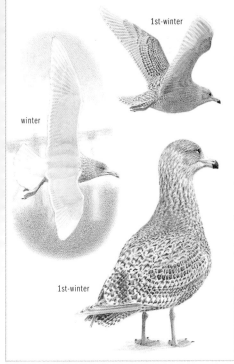

1st-winter

winter

1st-winter

BREEDING

Both adults build a nest of seaweed on rocks or grass or sometimes on snow. The usual clutch is of 3 eggs, which are incubated by both sexes and hatch after 27 days. The young are cared for by both parents and fly after 45 days.

MOVEMENTS AND MIGRATIONS

It is mostly present in Britain and Ireland between November and March with immature birds occasionally remaining for the summer. It winters as far north as ice-free water allows. Birds from the far north move south, while many of those that nest in Iceland are resident.

POPULATION

There are probably between 200 and 570 individuals in Britain and Ireland in winter, although there may be larger numbers in some years. It appears the number visiting Britain and Ireland increased during the 20th century.

CONSERVATION

This species is not currently at risk. The few that reach Britain and Ireland benefit from our fishing industry and domestic rubbish tips.

DISTRIBUTION

This gull is occasionally seen around the coasts of Britain and Ireland in winter, especially in Shetland. It also visits a few inland lakes and reservoirs. It breeds in the Arctic, including Iceland, northern Russia, northern Asia, Greenland and North America.

Lesser Black-backed Gull *Larus fuscus*

IDENTIFICATION

52–67 cm. Generally a little smaller and slimmer than a Herring Gull with slightly longer yellow (not pink) legs and darker slate-grey back. In winter, heads and necks become streaked with grey. Wings are longer and narrower than those of a Herring Gull, giving it a long-winged appearance. Juvenile is uniformly streaked grey-brown with scaly pattern on back and uniformly barred wings. Hard to distinguish from a juvenile Herring Gull, but it has more uniform flight feathers with no pale 'window' like a Herring Gull. By the second winter the adult colouring of the back starts to appear. Those breeding in southern Scandinavia have blackish backs, but not quite as black as their wing-tips. The British race is the palest, with two other races getting progressively blacker on the mantle. Dark-backed races are separated from the Great Black-backed by smaller size, slimmer bill, smaller head and leg colour. Annual moult for adults begins between May and August and is not complete on some birds until November. Partial pre-breeding moult between January and April. SEE ALSO: Great Black-backed Gull p163, Herring Gull p158.

HABITS

Breeds in colonies, often with other gulls, and is also sociable at other times of year, usually joining large evening roosts with other gulls. It migrates singly or in small groups.

VOICE

A rather gruff 'kaw' and rough laughing cries, 'ga ga gag'.

HABITAT

It breeds around the coast on sand dunes and shingle islands, inland on upland moors and in some towns. Outside the breeding season it ranges widely, both inland and near the coast, although in coastal areas it mainly visits inshore waters.

FOOD

It eats a wide range of food, including small mammals, especially voles, and also birds, including Puffins and terns. It eats eggs, fish, insects, shrimps, shellfish, worms and plant material, including seaweed and berries. It eats carrion and scavenges on rubbish tips.

summer

2nd-summer

winter scandinavian

winter

BREEDING

Nesting begins in late April or early May. The nest is on the ground, sometimes in the open, but often near long vegetation where chicks can hide. Some nest on roofs. Both sexes build the nest from seaweed, grasses and other local materials. The 2–4 eggs (usually 3) are incubated by both birds for 24–27 days. The young hatch over a period of 1–6 days and leave the nest a few days later but do not generally wander far. They are fed by both parents, and fly after 30–40 days.

MOVEMENTS AND MIGRATIONS

Adults that breed in Britain and Ireland no longer migrate as far south as they did 30 years ago, and some overwinter at, or close to, their breeding sites. After nesting in July, birds disperse from their colonies with the juveniles travelling farthest. Adults start to return in December. The oldest ringed bird was 34 years old.

POPULATION

112,000 pairs breed in the UK and 2,900 in Ireland. The total wintering population is over 100,000.

CONSERVATION

Population increased during the 20th century. Larger breeding numbers, milder winters and more immigrants from Europe account for the increase in winter. Recently there are indications that the numbers in other parts of its range are falling.

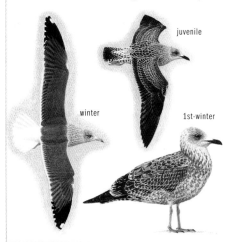

juvenile

winter

1st-winter

DISTRIBUTION

The species breeds in northern and western Europe and northern Russia. It winters as far south as the Mediterranean and North Africa. There are three distinct races that are seen in Britain and Ireland. The pale-backed race that breeds in Britain and Ireland also nests in Iceland, France and north-west Spain. Two darker-backed races breed in Scandinavia and western Russia.

Great Black-backed Gull *Larus marinus*

IDENTIFICATION

64–78 cm. Our largest gull. Has larger head, heavier bill, thicker neck, and proportionally thicker wings and legs than Lesser Black-backed Gull. Appears heavy and powerful on the ground and in flight. Back and wings are black and legs are flesh-coloured.

In winter, head and neck are lightly streaked with grey. Juvenile has typical brown plumage of young gulls. Its bill is black, the head and breast are paler than the rest of the underparts and it has a bold chequered pattern on its back. Immatures have paler heads than Lesser Black-backed Gull, but the size and shape of a bird is usually a better identification feature until its third year when it starts to acquire its black back. It takes 4–5 years to reach adult plumage. Adults start their moult between June and August and may not finish until November. SEE ALSO: Lesser Black-backed Gull p162.

HABITS

In flight, looks heavy and ponderous. Frequently seen singly or in pairs, although small groups congregate outside breeding season. Often aggressive towards other species and will attack and rob them of their food.

VOICE

Call is rather gruff bark, 'uk, uk, uk'.

HABITAT

Breeds mostly around rocky coasts and islands, but sometimes on freshwater lakes or moorland. Also visits sandy coasts and estuaries, and joins concentrations of gulls at roosts and feeding sites such as rubbish tips.

FOOD

Hunts in a variety of ways and takes a wide range of food. Kills and eats young seabirds such as Puffins and Kittiwakes, robs others of their food, will catch fish or feed on carrion, either in the water or washed up on the shore. It sometimes drops shellfish to break their shells and has been observed scavenging road kills. It will kill and eat mammals, such as rabbits.

BREEDING

Nests are built singly or in colonies on rocky outcrops and islands, or sometimes on moorland or even on buildings. Nest is a mound of seaweed built by both sexes. There are usually 2 or 3 eggs, incubated by both parents. The young hatch after 27 days and soon wander from the nest, but they seldom go far. They fly after 49–56 days and become independent soon afterwards.

MOVEMENTS AND MIGRATIONS

Both a resident and a migrant. Many in Britain and Ireland stay near their breeding grounds, while others arrive from further north to winter here. Many adults seen in eastern England between July and February are from Norway. Juveniles travel further than adults. The direction of their first movement away from their nests is usually random, but soon most move south and many remain south of their breeding grounds until they reach maturity. The oldest known wild bird survived over 27 years.

summer

winter

2nd-summer

1st-summer

1st-winter

1st-winter

summer

POPULATION

There are over 17,000 pairs in the UK and 2,200 in Ireland. In winter the UK population increases to over 70,000.

CONSERVATION

This gull was close to extinction, largely due to persecution, in the 19th century. From about 1880 it started to recover, probably aided by the food provided as a by-product of the fishing industry. The increase has halted and the winter population may have fallen by 30%.

DISTRIBUTION

Breeds mainly on the western coasts of Britain and Ireland. Outside the breeding season it can be found all round our coasts and at some inland sites as well. The species breeds in north-west Europe, Iceland, Greenland and North America. In winter in Europe it ranges as far south as the Bay of Biscay.

Common Gull *Larus canus*

INTERNATIONAL NAME MEW GULL (N. AMERICA)

IDENTIFICATION

40–42 cm. Smaller, but superficially similar to a Herring Gull, with blue-grey back and black wing-tips with white spots. Legs and bill are greenish-yellow and dark eyes give the bird a gentle appearance. Wings are less pointed than a Black-headed Gull, with no white on leading edge. In winter, has dusky marks on head and neck. Juvenile has mottled brown back and dusky marks on head and underparts. First-winter bird is also mottled on head and underparts, but has a grey back and a thick dark tail-band. It takes 3 years to become fully adult. Adults moult between June and October and have a partial moult before breeding.
SEE ALSO: Herring Gull p158, Kittiwake p165.

HABITS

Breeds among colonies of other gulls or terns, but sometimes has its own colonies. Sociable outside the breeding season, often feeding and roosting with other gulls.

VOICE

Call is higher-pitched than other gulls, an almost mewing 'keee-ya'.

HABITAT

Breeding colonies may be near the coast or kilometres inland in marshes, on islands in lakes, on moorland and sometimes on the roofs of buildings. Outside the breeding season may be found inland on farmland, around upland lakes, urban playing fields and reservoirs. Also winters at the coast where many may roost on estuaries.

FOOD

Takes live prey and carrion and sometimes robs other species. In summer, feeds on worms, cranefly larvae and other flies, moths, beetles, eggs, berries, small mammals, young birds and fish. In winter, feeds on invertebrates, fish, crustaceans and also scavenges rubbish tips.

BREEDING

In Britain egg laying begins in early May in a nest on the ground, in low vegetation or sometimes on clifftops or on roofs. Nest is made of seaweed and is built by both sexes. Both adults incubate the 2–4 eggs for 22–28 days. Young are fed by both parents and leave nest within 3–5 days. They stay in the vicinity of the nest until they can fly at about 35 days and become independent soon afterwards.

MOVEMENTS AND MIGRATIONS

Breeding birds from northern Europe reach the North Sea in late summer while many of the young birds remain around the Baltic Sea. Breeding birds start to return in March, but immature birds remain around the Baltic and the North Sea for the summer. Many of the Common Gulls that winter in Britain are birds that nested in Scandinavia or Iceland. In March there is a large movement through the North Sea of breeding birds returning, especially to Norway. Birds that pass through the Irish Sea are probably returning to Scottish colonies. Oldest 33 years.

POPULATION

There are around 48,700 pairs breeding in the UK and 1,000 in Ireland. In winter, the population grows to 700,000 individuals. The first half of the 20th century saw the species expanding its range in Britain and Ireland. In recent years the numbers have increased overall, but there has also been a loss of some traditional colonies, both in Britain and elsewhere in its range.

CONSERVATION

As the majority of Common Gulls are inland breeders they are likely to be adversely affected by drainage of marshes, agricultural changes and even forestry where it replaces wet moorland.

DISTRIBUTION

Common Gulls breed widely in Scotland and also in the west of Ireland. There are breeding colonies in the north of England and a few coastal locations farther south and east. The species breeds in northern Europe, Russia, northern Asia and North America. European birds mainly winter in western Europe and around the Black Sea.

Kittiwake *Rissa tridactyla*

INTERNATIONAL NAME BLACK-LEGGED KITTIWAKE

IDENTIFICATION

38–40 cm. A little larger than a Black-headed Gull. This is a neat, gentle-looking, medium-sized gull with a small yellow bill and dark eye. It resembles a Common Gull, but has a slightly forked tail, short black legs and distinctive triangular black wing-tips with no white spots. The grey back is slightly darker than the grey of the upperwings. In winter, crown and back of head are pale grey. Juvenile has a bold black 'W' pattern on its wings, black half-collar, grey back, black tail-band and small grey mark behind eye. Juveniles lose their black collars during their first winter. Adults have a complete moult between May and October and a partial moult into breeding plumage beginning in January.
SEE ALSO: Common Gull p164, Sabine's Gull p167.

1st-summer

summer

HABITS

Breeds in large, noisy colonies, mainly on cliffs, but may be seen singly or in small groups outside the breeding season. Sometimes large numbers gather where food is plentiful. Approaches boats and picks food from the surface of the sea and also plunge-dives. The buoyant flight with stiff wingbeats sometimes resembles a tern. Breeding birds visit freshwater pools near their colonies to collect mud for nests and to bathe.

summer

juvenile

VOICE

Around its breeding cliffs it shouts its 'kitti-waaark' call from which it gets its name. At other times it is rather silent.

HABITAT

Breeds mostly around rocky coasts where it nests on precipitous sea cliffs or buildings near the sea. At other times lives out at sea, often beyond the continental shelf. A truly marine gull, unusual inland, except occasionally after gales.

FOOD

Feeds on fish such as caplin, herring, sprats and sand eels, and other marine creatures, including shrimps, planktonic sea creatures, worms, insects and carrion.

BREEDING

Eggs laid in May in a nest of compacted mud, grass and seaweed, built by both sexes on a cliff ledge. Occasionally nests are on the ledges of buildings. Both parents share the incubation of 1–3 eggs (usually 2), which hatch after 25–32 days. The chicks are brooded while small and fed by both adults. Pairs that lay 3 eggs are usually unable to find sufficient food to keep all the chicks alive. Young fly after 33–54 days and quickly become independent.

MOVEMENTS AND MIGRATIONS

Birds disperse from their colonies after breeding, in July and August. Some remain around the British Isles, but many juveniles reach the North American coast, and immatures may remain in the western Atlantic for several years before returning to their natal colonies to breed. Adults fly out to sea and tend to move south-west, but some will cross the Atlantic for the winter, returning to their colonies from February onwards. Oldest ringed bird survived for 28 years.

POPULATION

About 380,000 pairs breed in the UK and 33,000 in Ireland.

CONSERVATION

Following persecution during the 19th century the Kittiwake increased for most of the 20th century. There are indications that this growth has now halted and there is a decline in some colonies. This has been linked to shortage of food, possibly associated with climate change and exacerbated by overfishing.

DISTRIBUTION

Breeds around British and Irish coasts, and is only missing from the 'soft' coasts of south-east England. Most abundant in northern Scotland and along North Sea coasts, south to the Humber. It also breeds in North America, Asia and northern Europe, with a few colonies on the Atlantic coast of Spain and Portugal. In winter, it is widespread in the North Atlantic.

Little Gull *Hydrocoloeus minutus*

1st-winter

1st-winter

summer

winter

summer

summer

winter

IDENTIFICATION

25–27 cm. This delicate bird is the smallest gull, noticeably smaller than Black-headed Gull, with small dark bill and red legs. Adult in spring has black (not brown) hood, grey back, blunt-ended pale grey upperwings that have a thin white edge from tip to rear. Underwings are very dark, like charcoal. In winter, black hood is replaced by a black spot behind the eye and dark shading on back of head. Juvenile is blackish-brown and white with a dark crown and an obvious dark 'W' wing pattern across upperwings in flight. First-winter birds have grey backs, a bold dark 'W' wing pattern, a black tail-band and dusky marks on the head. First-summer birds resemble first-winter birds but have a smudgy dark hood and are in rather worn plumage. Second-winter birds retain some dark marks on their wing-tips. Adults gain their full black hood from February.
SEE ALSO: Black-headed Gull p157, Mediterranean Gull p156.

HABITS

Quick wingbeats and rather erratic, buoyant zigzag flight is reminiscent of a tern. Frequently feeds in flight by dipping down and picking prey delicately from the water.

VOICE

Not normally very vocal but has a 'kek, kek, kek' call.

HABITAT

In Britain and Ireland visits sea coasts, estuaries, and also lakes and reservoirs some distance inland. Breeds in freshwater marshes, beside rivers and lakes, and sometimes in coastal areas where there is lush vegetation.

FOOD

Much of its food is insects such as dragonflies, mayflies, midges and their larvae, water bugs such as water boatmen, ants and beetles. It also eats spiders, worms and fish.

BREEDING

Does not normally breed in Britain or Ireland. Nests on the ground in colonies from May to early June. Nest is on tussock of grasses or rushes in a marsh. Both adults incubate the 2 or 3 eggs, starting with the first egg, with the result that the young hatch at different times. Incubation is for 23–25 days. Young wander from the nest when a few days old, but continue to be fed by both parents. They fly at 21–24 days.

MOVEMENTS AND MIGRATIONS

Movements are poorly understood but after breeding they appear to disperse to sheltered bays and coastal waters, start to moult and then move further out to sea. Many winter in the Irish Sea and in April and May there is a strong migration from Merseyside east across the Pennines and Yorkshire towards Finland and the Baltic. The oldest ringed bird survived 20 years.

POPULATION

Little Gulls have occasionally attempted to breed in Britain, but no regular colony has been established. Numbers visiting each year vary considerably, with thousands being seen occasionally at a few sites. Smaller numbers are seen regularly at many other sites.

CONSERVATION

The species is specially protected. In its major breeding colonies in Russia it appears to be declining owing to drainage of wetlands, natural and man-made flooding during the breeding season and also activities such as fishing, which disturb breeding colonies.

DISTRIBUTION

May appear in Britain or Ireland at almost any time, especially along the east coast of England and Scotland and around the Irish Sea. There are three distinct breeding populations: eastern Siberia, western Siberia and Russia west to the Baltic Sea. Small numbers also breed in eastern North America. There are scattered colonies outside this normal distribution. Winters around the coast of Europe and, particularly, in Egypt in the Nile delta.

Sabine's Gull *Larus sabini*

IDENTIFICATION
27–32 cm. Smaller than a Black-headed Gull with long wings, a slightly forked tail, and a contrasting wing pattern at all ages. The adult has a black hood, grey back, black outer flight feathers and a white triangle on each wing. The juvenile is greyish-brown on the back of head, sides of breast and has paler buff fringes to the back and wings giving a scaly appearance. The wings also show a large white triangle. This gull is exceptional in having a complete moult in early spring before it migrates north-west, and a partial moult in autumn.

SEE ALSO: Black-headed Gull p157, Little Gull p166, Kittiwake p165.

BREEDING
This species does not breed in Britain or Ireland. It nests in the high Arctic, often among colonies of Arctic Terns. The clutch of 2 or 3 eggs is incubated for 23–25 days by both parents. Both parents help to rear the young.

MOVEMENTS AND MIGRATIONS
Away from its breeding season this species spends most of its life at sea. It leaves the Arctic and migrates south-east across the open Atlantic. There are late summer and autumn gatherings off the French coast in the Bay of Biscay before the birds move south as far as South Africa.

POPULATION
There are between 100 and 200 seen in Britain and Ireland each year.

CONSERVATION
Those birds that reach Britain or Ireland each year make up only a minute proportion of the population moving through the Atlantic and there are no special conservation measures specifically appropriate for this species.

juvenile

winter

juvenile

summer

juvenile

winter

HABITS
Its flight is buoyant, rather like a tern, and frequently feeds in flight by dipping and picking food from the surface of the water – although it will also feed on the ground, rather like a wader. It nests in colonies and may gather in large flocks at rich feeding areas, but in Britain and Ireland most frequently seen singly or in small groups.

VOICE
It has a single harsh note rather like an Arctic Tern's call.

HABITAT
In Britain and Ireland this is mainly a coastal species, most likely to be seen off south-west headlands, but it may come into inshore waters during violent storms at sea and sometimes gets blown inland where it visits large lakes and reservoirs. It breeds in the high Arctic tundra and spends most of the rest of the year at sea.

FOOD
For most of the year it feeds on small marine creatures and fish. On its breeding grounds it feeds on insects, other invertebrates and fish.

DISTRIBUTION
The Sabine's Gull breeds in Spitsbergen, Greenland, North America and north-east Siberia. Birds that breed in Greenland and Canada spend the winter off south-west Africa. Alaskan and Siberian breeding birds winter off South American coasts. Some migrating birds pass near the coast of Britain and Ireland each year and autumn storms will sometimes bring more to south-west England and southern Ireland.

Sandwich Tern *Sterna sandvicensis*

IDENTIFICATION
36–41 cm. Slightly larger but slimmer than a Black-headed Gull. The largest of the terns that breed in Britain and Ireland. Heavy-looking with yellow tip to its long black bill, and short black legs. It is a very white tern, with its back and long, pointed wings light grey and a short, forked tail that lacks tail-streamers. Fore-wings show grey wedges. Black cap is perfect only at start of breeding season, and soon shows white speckling above the eyes. By late summer whole forehead is white. In spring, feathers at back of the crown are longer and form a ragged crest. Juvenile has brownish-black spotting on crown and forehead, sandy back with dark tips to feathers, and all-black bill. Moult may start during incubation and the loss of flight feathers may be suspended during migration and resumed in winter quarters. Breeding plumage acquired between February and April.
SEE ALSO: Common Tern p170, Little Tern p172.

HABITS
Often flies higher than other terns and can look very 'angular' and less buoyant. Also looks short-tailed and will often fly with head and bill pointing down. Seldom hovers, but frequently dives with quite a large splash and usually stays under for longer than other terns. Colonies are fickle and will often move location for no apparent reason.

VOICE
Noisy, the most common call being a loud grating 'keer-ick'.

HABITAT
Breeds exclusively in coastal locations, using shingle, sandy and sometimes rocky beaches and also islands close to the shore. Outside breeding season inhabits inshore waters and is only occasionally seen inland.

FOOD
Feeds mainly on fish that are found near the surface of the sea, such as sand eels, sprats and whiting.

move south, and by October most have left British and Irish waters. They move mainly along the coasts of Europe and Africa, and first-year birds will remain in Africa for their first summer. Adults generally winter further north than immatures. Return migration begins in February and these are one of the earliest summer migrants to reach Europe. Individuals are often seen near their breeding colonies in March or April. Oldest ringed bird was 30 years old.

POPULATION
12,500 pairs breed in the UK and 1,800 in Ireland. In recent years there has been a moderate decline across many of its breeding areas, including the British Isles.

CONSERVATION
The decline has been attributed to predators such as mink and fox, but fish stocks and sea-level rise are potential problems as is disturbance by humans. In Britain, most colonies are restricted to nature reserves.

summer

winter

winter

summer

juvenile

BREEDING
Breeding begins at the end of April. It nests in large colonies and the nest is a simple scrape on the ground made by both adults, with little or no special lining. The 1 or 2 eggs are incubated by both adults for 21–29 days. Some young stay in the nest, others form crèches, while yet others are mobile and roam around the colony. Both adults feed the young even after they fly at 28–30 days. Juveniles remain dependent on their parents for 3 months or so.

MOVEMENTS AND MIGRATIONS
Birds quickly disperse after nesting. Within days juveniles may be many kilometres from their colonies. At first they may travel north or south, but gradually all

DISTRIBUTION
There are colonies of Sandwich Terns scattered around the coasts of Britain and Ireland. It breeds in Europe, Russia and North America. European birds winter along the African coast as far as South Africa and extend into the Indian Ocean as far north as Natal, although individuals have wintered as far north as the Firth of Forth in Scotland.

Roseate Tern *Sterna dougallii*

IDENTIFICATION

33–38 cm. Similar in size to a Common Tern but much whiter with a pale grey back and wings, a jet-black cap, a white body that in spring has a soft pink flush and long tail-streamers. It differs from the Common Tern by having faster, shallower wingbeats (almost kestrel-like) but looks shorter-winged and has a black bill with a little red at the base. By late summer the upperwing has a narrow dark 'wedge' along the leading edge of the longest flight feathers. The underwings look very pale. The juvenile has a dark forehead and neat blackish scaly edges to all the back feathers. It looks whiter than juvenile Common or Arctic Terns.

SEE ALSO: Common Tern p170, Arctic Tern p171.

winter

summer

HABITS

In flight, it has a stiffer action than Common or Arctic Terns. When fishing, it looks more confident as it turns and flies into the water from a greater height than Common Terns. It sometimes hovers. It may be seen as a solitary bird, or with other terns, or in small groups near breeding sites. It nests in colonies of other terns and sometimes it chases and robs them of their food.

1st-winter

juvenile

VOICE

The calls include a loud 'chew-ik' and a rasping 'kraak'.

HABITAT

This tern generally nests on small marine islands, close to the shore. Colonies are usually near shallow, sandy fishing grounds and the islands may be rocky or sandy. Outside the breeding season it is found in inshore waters and it winters off warm tropical coasts.

FOOD

The chief food is small fish such as sand eels, herring and sprats.

BREEDING

Nesting begins in June. The nest is a shallow scrape that is made by both birds, usually in the shelter of a rock or vegetation. The normal clutch is 1 or 2 eggs, incubated by both parents but with the female taking the largest share. The eggs hatch after 21–26 days and the young stay by their nest for up to 20 days and then move around the colony. They usually fly by 30 days and remain dependent on their parents for at least 8 weeks.

MOVEMENTS AND MIGRATIONS

This is a marine tern, rarely seen away from coasts, even during migrations. Birds disperse from breeding colonies in August and some first move north before moving rapidly south to West Africa, especially Ghana, where it arrives by November and stays until the following spring. First-year birds remain in tropical waters for their first summer but by their second

summer most return to Europe, but do not generally breed until their third year. Oldest ringed bird was 23 years old.

POPULATION

The population fell dramatically in the 20th century and there are now only around 100 pairs breeding in the UK and 700 in Ireland. However, the Irish population may have recovered a little recently.

CONSERVATION

This species is specially protected. Historic declines are not restricted to Britain and other populations have also been falling. The cause is not fully understood, but disturbance and predation at its colonies may be part of the cause, hunting and food shortage in West Africa may be others. Young birds are susceptible to cool, wet weather and to predation, and both these can be alleviated by provision of simple nest shelters by conservationists.

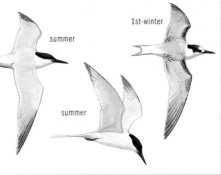

summer

1st-winter

summer

summer

DISTRIBUTION

There are a small number of colonies around the British Isles, the largest numbers being in Ireland. The species also breeds in North America, the Azores and Africa, and there are other races in the Indian and Pacific Oceans, and in Australia.

Common Tern *Sterna hirundo*

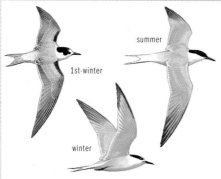

summer

1st-winter

winter

IDENTIFICATION

31–35 cm. Smaller than a Black-headed Gull. Back and wings are silver-grey and underparts pale grey. Bill is orange-red with a dark tip and the short legs are red. Longest flight feathers of the upperwing become progressively darker during the summer giving the appearance of a blackish 'wedge'. Tips of flight feathers on the underwing are dusky and there is a translucent patch that appears semi-transparent against a bright sky. Juvenile is grey, white and black with a ginger back, a pale forehead and flesh-pink or yellowish bill with a dark tip that becomes darker during the summer. Moults while in British and Irish waters. Inner flight feathers are lost from July, and in late summer adult birds with missing flight feathers are often obvious.

SEE ALSO: Arctic Tern p171, Roseate Tern p169.

HABITS

Flight is more direct and powerful than that of the other smaller terns. When fishing, flies with bill pointing down and often rises gently before hovering and diving head first. A social species, breeding in colonies and often seen in flocks. In spring, may be seen carrying fish crossways in its bill. This may be to feed the young or for the female as part of courtship.

VOICE

Most common call is a loud, rasping 'keee-yaah'.

HABITAT

Breeds inland and on shingle and sandy beaches or rocky seashores. Feeds in lakes, reservoirs, rivers and inshore waters. Outside the breeding season lives mainly in warm coastal waters.

FOOD

Feeds mainly on fish, chiefly small herring, sprats and sand eels. In fresh water catches roach, perch and minnows. Also takes shrimps and insects – especially cockchafers and water-beetle larvae.

BREEDING

Breeding begins in May. Both adults construct a scrape in the sand. Sometimes pebbles and vegetation are added to the rim of the nest before and during incubation. Incubation of the 2 or 3 well-camouflaged eggs is by both sexes and lasts 21–22 days. Young leave the nest after 3–4 days and hide in nearby vegetation or in hollows in the sand while waiting to be fed. They fly at 22–28 days and are 2 or 3 months old before they are fully independent.

MOVEMENTS AND MIGRATIONS

After nesting, some of the British and Irish birds may travel north before the whole population flies south to arrive in its winter quarters during November and December. A few European birds remain in southern Spain and Portugal in winter, but most migrate to West Africa, with the northern population travelling farthest and wintering south of the equator. Most first-year birds remain in West Africa. In their second summer they may travel north, but slowly, arriving midway through the breeding season. They breed at 3 or 4 years old. One ringed bird was 33 years old.

summer

POPULATION

There are 12,000 pairs breeding in the UK and 2,500 in Ireland. The UK population has fallen recently.

CONSERVATION

There was a decline in breeding birds during the 20th century and there has also been a shift northwards, with fewer in England and more in Scotland. In Ireland also, more are now breeding in the north. There is a more recent decline in the Northern Isles, perhaps linked to overfishing and climate change. Fortunately some colonies have benefited from the construction of special breeding islands and rafts in lakes.

juvenile

1st-winter

DISTRIBUTION

In Britain and Ireland breeds from the south coast to Shetland, both near the sea and inland. Scarce in the south-west of England and Wales, except for Anglesey. In Ireland it is most common in the north and west. Breeds from the Arctic Circle to North Africa. Also found in North America and Asia.

Arctic Tern *Sterna paradisaea*

summer

IDENTIFICATION

33–35 cm. Smaller, lighter and more delicate than a Common Tern, with narrower wings, shorter neck and longer tail-streamers. Upperparts pale grey and rump white. Underparts smoky grey, a shade darker than a Common Tern's and contrast more with its white cheeks. Bill and short legs deep red. Upperwing more uniformly grey, becoming paler towards tip and with dark trailing bar, not a 'wedge' on the longest flight feathers. From below against the light the primary and secondary flight feathers appear translucent. Juvenile is grey and white from a distance, but seen close up its back is heavily marked with dark crescents. Has white forehead and black bill with red base. Adults moult in their winter quarters and return in spring with neat new flight feathers.
SEE ALSO: Common Tern p170, Roseate Tern p169.

HABITS

Flight lighter and more bouncy than that of Common Tern. When fishing, appears hesitant as it hovers, dips down and hovers again before plunging into the water. Breeds in large colonies, and groups fish close together. Also flocks during migrations. On breeding grounds it is very aggressive toward intruders, including humans.

1st-winter

VOICE

Call a slightly higher-pitched version of Common Tern's call, a harsh, scolding 'kee-aar'.

HABITAT

Breeds in similar habitat to the Common Tern, mostly on the coast or on offshore islands, but also along large rivers where there are shingle islands and stone beaches. Some colonies are on heath and rough pasture, and most nests are in or close to vegetation. Outside the breeding season it becomes a seabird, seldom crossing land and sometimes perching on floating objects, including ice flows.

FOOD

Feeds mainly on fish including sand eels, sprats, herring, caplin and sticklebacks. It also takes insects, crustaceans and even worms from flooded fields.

BREEDING

Nesting begins in Britain in May. Nest is a shallow scrape made by both parents. Incubation of the 1 or 2 eggs is shared by both parents until the chicks hatch after 20–24 days. Newly hatched young stay in the nest for a few days before leaving to shelter among stones or vegetation nearby. They fly at 21–24 days but remain with their parents for a further month or two.

MOVEMENTS AND MIGRATIONS

This species migrates further than any other bird. It leaves its breeding grounds between July and early October and migrates along the coasts of north-west Europe and Africa, eventually reaching the Antarctic between October and December. It returns to its breeding grounds by May or June and some may be seen inland in Britain or Ireland during migration. Immatures remain in the southern hemisphere until nearly 2 years old. A ringed bird lived for over 30 years.

POPULATION

The last estimate was of 53,000 pairs in the UK and 2,700 in Ireland and has retreated northwards in the last 200 years. There has been a steady decline in breeding birds in the last 10 years.

CONSERVATION

Food shortages have resulted in some colonies producing no young in some years. Overfishing of small fish is one cause, but long-term climate change resulting in changes in distribution of fish stocks is also additional hazard.

juvenile

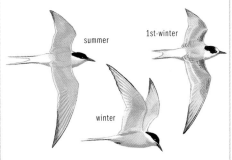

summer
1st-winter
winter

DISTRIBUTION

A few nest in England and more in Ireland, but the densest populations are to be found in Orkney and Shetland. Mainly an Arctic species that also breeds in northern Europe, North America, northern Russia and Asia. Winters at the other end of the world, in the Southern Ocean off the pack-ice of Antarctica, and some British birds reach Australia.

Little Tern *Sterna albifrons*

summer

summer

IDENTIFICATION

22–24 cm. Our smallest tern. A third smaller than a Common Tern and its wings and tail are proportionally shorter. Tail is deeply forked, but lacks any tail-streamers and head and bill are noticeably large. Bill is yellow with a small black tip and legs are yellow or orange. It is a white bird with pale grey back and wings, a black cap and a forehead that is always white. By late summer the white forehead becomes larger, the bill darker and the legs paler. Juvenile is noticeably smaller with a dark bill, a pale buff, streaked crown, a dark patch through the eye to the back of the head and a sandy-grey back with darker marks. Adults start to moult when still feeding young in June–August and then moult is suspended until migration is completed. There is a further moult in winter to acquire breeding plumage.
SEE ALSO: Common Tern p170, Arctic Tern p171, Roseate Tern p169.

HABITS

Wingbeats are very fast. It frequently hovers before diving into water. It does not normally form very large communal flocks like the larger terns, but it does breed in colonies of, on average, 30 pairs.

VOICE

The most frequent call is a loud, shrill 'kik-kik'.

winter

HABITAT

In Britain and Ireland almost exclusively a marine species, nesting on shingle or sandy beaches. In Europe spreads up suitable rivers and breeds around inland lakes. Outside the breeding season it mainly feeds in inshore waters.

FOOD

Feeds on mainly small fish, especially sand eels. Also takes shrimps and insect larvae.

BREEDING

Nesting begins in May. Both adults make a nest scrape in the shingle or sand that is often unlined. There are 2 or 3 eggs that are incubated by both adults for 18–22 days. Young are covered in down and mobile soon after hatching. After a few days they leave the nest and hide among the shingle or nearby vegetation.

MOVEMENTS AND MIGRATIONS

European breeding birds leave their colonies during July and August and soon start their southward migration along the coasts of Europe and Africa. Some of the European birds that breed inland migrate across land and along rivers, but it does not appear to cross the Sahara like some of the larger terns. The oldest ringed bird was over 23 years old.

POPULATION

At the last count there were 1,900 pairs breeding in the UK and 200 pairs in Ireland. This was a 25% reduction in numbers in 15 years. Although some European populations are faring better than others, overall it appears to be declining.

juvenile

CONSERVATION

Pressure on the coast both from recreation and development has reduced the number of safe beaches for this species. The number and distribution of colonies has changed in recent years. Many traditional sites have been lost and there is a growing dependence on a relatively small number of protected sites, which increases the birds' vulnerability to disaster should something happen to one of those – man-made or natural. Predation by mammals – including dogs – is a problem. Some sites on popular holiday beaches have to be guarded by volunteers to help birds breed successfully.

DISTRIBUTION

In Britain and Ireland there are colonies almost all round the coasts, but with areas between Yorkshire and Hampshire being most favoured. It is especially scarce in the south-west of England and south Wales. Little Terns also breed from the Baltic to the Mediterranean and there are other races in Africa and Asia. European birds winter along the coast of West Africa with some reaching South Africa.

Black Tern *Chlidonias niger*

IDENTIFICATION
22–24 cm. Smaller than a Common Tern with shorter, broader wings, less deeply forked tail and black bill. In spring, has an almost black head and body, slate-grey back, wings and tail, and white under its tail. Underside of wing is almost white. Female is slightly paler than male. After breeding, head and body become white with black marks behind eye and on back of head, and with a prominent dark smudge on shoulder and white collar. Juvenile resembles adult in winter but with brown feathers creating a mottled effect on its back. Adult moult starts in May or June and the dark plumage quickly becomes blotchy, and dark grey feathers are replaced by white ones by September. SEE ALSO: Common Tern p170, Little Gull p166.

HABITS
Typical flight is rather lazy and it banks from side to side. Often travels singly, but flocks may gather, especially on migration. Has a characteristic feeding action as it dips down to the water and delicately takes food from the surface. Hovers less frequently than other terns, preferring to fly up and down on regular beats, dipping down to feed from time to time. Regularly perches on rocks and posts in the water.

FOOD
Its food is mainly insects and their larvae in summer and fish in winter. Insects include water beetles, flies, dragonflies and grasshoppers. Fish include sticklebacks and roach. It also eats frogs and tadpoles.

BREEDING
This species very rarely attempts to breed in Britain and Ireland. It nests on floating vegetation, in shallow water or among marsh plants. The nest is a mound of water weed that is added to by both birds. The 2–4 eggs are incubated for 21–22 days by both birds taking turns. Young stay in the nest and are brooded by a parent for the first few days, but they soon move into nearby vegetation. They fly at 19–25 days and are quickly independent.

MOVEMENTS AND MIGRATIONS
Autumn migration begins in June with non-breeding birds moving first, followed by adults and then juveniles. Some juveniles move north before migrating south. Peak passage through western Europe is in July–September and they probably migrate by night and day. At peak times huge numbers gather on some European and African estuaries. Common along the

winter

summer

juvenile

VOICE
Usually silent, only very occasionally calling a sharp 'kik, kik'.

HABITAT
Breeds in marshes, fens and lagoons near the coast or inland. In Britain and Ireland it is more frequently seen at reservoirs and larger water bodies. In winter, it mainly lives along tropical coasts.

African coast from September, and birds remain there until their return the following March. A few birds pass through Britain in May, but most return to their breeding grounds by a more easterly route. Oldest ringed bird was 21 years old.

POPULATION
A few birds are seen during most summers, larger and variable numbers are seen in spring and autumn, but no national count has been made.

CONSERVATION
Specially protected. Once nested regularly, but was lost due to trophy hunting, egg collecting and habitat changes, especially the drainage of marshes and fens. The re-creation of large fens and wetlands in East Anglia and careful management of water levels may encourage this species to return.

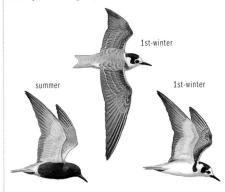

1st-winter

summer

1st-winter

DISTRIBUTION
In Britain and Ireland mainly seen over lakes in spring and autumn. Most recent breeding attempts have been in Cambridgeshire (three times), Nottinghamshire, Tayside and Fermanagh. Breeds from Denmark to Spain and east to Russia and Asia. Another race breeds in North America. European birds winter along the coast of West Africa.

Guillemot *Uria aalge*

INTERNATIONAL NAME   COMMON GUILLEMOT

IDENTIFICATION

38–41 cm. Larger than a Jackdaw with short wings, long, dark, tapering bill and a longer neck than other members of this family. Swims well. Head, neck and back are chocolate-brown, and breast and belly are white with some dark streaks. Some northern birds have white 'spectacle-like' marks on their faces. The brown plumage of northern birds is darker, almost black. In winter, neck and side of face, behind the eye, become white. Juvenile is smaller, pale headed, with a shorter bill. Moult begins while the adults are feeding young. The flight feathers are lost simultaneously in July and August and the birds are flightless for about 7 weeks. Breeding plumage is gained between January and March.

SEE ALSO: Black Guillemot p176, Razorbill p175, Puffin p177.

1st-winter

winter

HABITS

Sits upright on cliffs or swims like a duck in the sea and dives to find food. Breeds in large colonies and lives in loose flocks outside breeding season. Sometimes sits, rather than stands, on its cliff ledges. In flight, wings beat rapidly, appearing blurred at a distance.

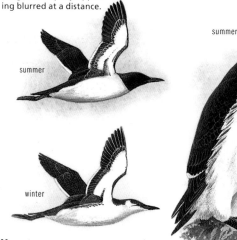

summer

summer

winter

VOICE

Usual call is a growling 'arrrr'.

HABITAT

Lives most of year on the open sea, coming to land only to breed. Nest-sites are on narrow cliff ledges or the exposed flat tops of tall stacks and offshore islands.

FOOD

Feeds chiefly on fish especially cod, herring, whiting, sand eels and sprats. Also eats some crustaceans such as crabs.

BREEDING

Males and females usually winter separately and come together at the nest-site, with males generally arriving first. They make no nest, but lay a single pear-shaped egg on bare rock, and both sexes share the incubation. Young is covered in down when it hatches after 28–37 days. It is fed by both parents and usually leaves its cliff within 3 weeks of hatching. At this time it is not fully grown and is unable to fly properly. Male attends chick when it leaves the colony and continues to feed it on the sea. It is 8–10 weeks before the juvenile can fly and it continues to be fed by the adult for up to 12 weeks.

MOVEMENTS AND MIGRATIONS

Some Guillemots do not move far from their colonies; others move north, following food supplies. Juveniles stay with the male for the autumn and most of the first winter before splitting into separate flocks of adults and immatures. Many winter in the North Sea. Birds from Scottish colonies may cross to the Norwegian coast or move south along the continental shelf of Europe. Some return to their colonies on calm days in autumn, but it is not until April that colonies are fully reoccupied. Oldest ringed bird survived 38 years.

POPULATION

It has been estimated that 1.4 million pairs nest in the UK and 88,000 in Ireland. An increase during the 20th century has slowed and in the Northern Isles numbers may be falling.

CONSERVATION

Guillemots have been killed for sport and food in the past. Recent dangers have included long-line fishing nets that ensnare and drown these birds, oiling incidents and depleted fish stocks.

DISTRIBUTION

Breeds on inaccessible sea cliffs mostly in north and west of Britain and Ireland. Most winter in loose flocks around our coasts or go farther south, with many from western colonies reaching the Bay of Biscay and a few travelling as far south as Portugal. Breeds in western Europe, with small colonies as far south as Portugal, and also in Iceland, Greenland and North America. Other races live in Bering Sea and North Pacific.

Razorbill *Alca torda*

IDENTIFICATION
37–39 cm. Slightly smaller than a Guillemot with a proportionally thicker neck, larger head and bill, smaller wings and longer tail. In flight, looks blacker than a Guillemot with snub-nose effect, not a pointed bill. The black bill is laterally flattened, deep and blunt, with thin white line near the tip. The underparts are white. In winter, the head becomes mostly off-white with a dark crown and hindneck. The juvenile is smaller and browner than the adult, and has a dark head. Moult begins in July and flight feathers are lost simultaneously between August and October and, for a few weeks, the birds become flightless.
SEE ALSO: Guillemot p174, Puffin p177.

HABITS
It breeds on cliffs, but nesting birds are more difficult to see and its colonies less dense than those of the Guillemot. It may form flocks in winter, but again these tend to be smaller than flocks of Guillemots. It swims and dives, and was once recorded at 140 m below sea surface. When feeding young, the Razorbill will carry 2–3 fish at a time.

VOICE
The call is growling 'caarrrrr' and the juvenile has a plaintive whistle.

HABITAT
A seabird that comes to shore only to breed, and for the rest of the year it lives at sea, but remaining within the continental shelf of Europe. Its nest-sites are on rocky cliffs and among boulder scree close to the sea.

FOOD
It feeds chiefly on fish, especially sand eels, sprats and small herring, and a few marine crustaceans.

BREEDING
Most eggs are laid during May. A single egg is generally laid in a crevice in the rock, either high on inaccessible cliffs or among scattered boulders. Occasionally an open ledge may be used. Incubation is by both sexes and lasts for about 36 days. The young Razorbill is cared for by both parents and leaves the cliff at about 18 days old by jumping or scrambling into the sea. At this stage it is about two-thirds fully grown. At sea, the male cares for the chick.

MOVEMENTS AND MIGRATIONS
In July Razorbills leave their colonies and disperse out to sea. The male and juvenile start by travelling together and both are flightless until September. The juveniles may travel further from their colonies than adults, which return to the breeding cliffs as early as March. Some young birds from around the Irish Sea reach the Mediterranean during their first winter. Young birds will not return to their colonies until they are 2–3 years old. The oldest known ringed bird survived for more than 41 years.

POPULATION
Razorbill colonies are difficult to census. 164,000 pairs are estimated to breed in the UK and 17,400 in Ireland. A recent population increase may now be slowing.

summer

CONSERVATION
This species shares the fate of the Guillemot. Its future is linked to the health of the marine environment. Fishing nets, pollution at sea and declining fish stocks all threaten Razorbills.

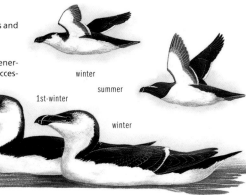

winter

summer

1st-winter

winter

DISTRIBUTION
The Razorbill breeds around the coast of Britain and Ireland. The largest colonies are in the north of Scotland and there are none between The Humber and the Isle of Wight. The species breeds in north-west Europe, Iceland, Greenland and the north-east coast of North America. It winters in the North Atlantic, mostly scattered over the continental shelf of Europe and is rather scarce in inshore waters.

Black Guillemot *Cepphus grylle*

IDENTIFICATION

30–32 cm. Pigeon-sized. Smaller than a Guillemot with long neck and bright-red legs. Breeding plumage is sooty black with an oval white wing-patch. In autumn and winter, becomes off-white with dark, scaly marks, darker back and dark flight feathers. The oval wing-patch is still obvious in winter. Juvenile is like adult in winter but more heavily barred. In July, after nesting, adults begin to moult and small groups form on the sea. Between August and October they become flightless as flight feathers are regrowing. Between January and March there is a second, partial moult into breeding plumage.

SEE ALSO: Guillemot p174, Razorbill p175, Puffin p177, Little Auk p178.

summer

HABITS

Sits upright on land. Flight is usually low, but when searching for good feeding areas it may rise to 100 m or more. When swimming or flying in winter it resembles a duck or grebe from a distance, but the rapidly whirring wings, white oval patch and direct flight are characteristic. Commonly seen swimming and diving close to shore. Usually in ones or twos and although nesting birds do come together to form colonies, these are not large colonies like those of Guillemots. Sometimes Black Guillemots work together: they swim in straight lines or semicircles as they close in on a shoal of fish.

VOICE

summer

Mostly silent, but makes a weak, high-pitched whistle 'peeeeeh' at breeding sites.

HABITAT

Found around rocky coasts where there are loose boulders and other potential nest-sites. A marine species that is generally seen closer to the shore than other auks.

FOOD

Feeds on fish such as sand eels, blennies, butterfish, small cod and sole. Also catches small crabs, shrimps and other animals.

BREEDING

On spring mornings groups gather to display, first on the sea and then on land, their red mouths contrasting with their striking plumage. They nest in holes and crevices under boulders and in caves. Sometimes they use man-made structures such as holes in harbour walls and even in the barrel of an old cannon! 1 or 2 eggs are laid in May. Incubation is by both male and female and the eggs hatch after about 30 days. Young leave their nests and swim on the sea before they can fly. They are independent on leaving the colony, but may not breed for 4 years.

MOVEMENTS AND MIGRATIONS

Birds from further north may move south to avoid winter ice, and young may wander further than adults. In Britain, few travel more than 50 km from where they

hatched and no breeding colony is totally deserted in winter. Oldest known bird was 25 years old.

POPULATION

In summer there are 38,000 pairs in the UK, mostly in Scotland, and over 17,000 in Ireland. Numbers have increased slightly in recent years, although there have also been some poor breeding seasons.

juvenile

1st-winter

winter

CONSERVATION

Threats at sea come from oil pollution, but Black Guillemots are less vulnerable than some other members of this family in that their colonies are small and widely dispersed, but they are vulnerable to predation by rats. The availability of suitable food is also critical and in recent years, when sand eel stocks have fallen, the number of young also declined.

DISTRIBUTION

Nests in Scotland and Ireland with good numbers on the Isle of Man, but only a few pairs breed in north of England and Wales. Found all round Arctic Circle and winters as far north as possible (right up to the edge of the ice). Winters at sea, but usually close to its breeding colonies. Extremely rare inland.

Puffin *Fratercula arctica*

INTERNATIONAL NAME ATLANTIC PUFFIN

summer

IDENTIFICATION

26–29 cm. Smaller than town pigeon. Upright on land with a black back, white underparts, pale grey face patches that almost meet on the back of the head, huge laterally flattened, colourful bill and colourful skin around the eye giving it a clown-like appearance. Male has a larger bill than female. Legs and feet are bright orange. In winter, the cheeks become dusky and the bill smaller and less colourful. In flight, underwing is grey. Juvenile resembles an adult in winter, but is smaller with a smaller bill and a sooty black patch in front of eye. Adults begin to moult in August and September. Flight feathers are lost simultaneously during the winter and birds are flightless for a time. The colourful bill plates are shed after breeding and regrown in spring. SEE ALSO: Guillemot p174, Razorbill p175, Little Auk p178.

HABITS

Wings are usually flapped rapidly with a whirring action unless landing on the cliff top or caught in the up-draught. It swims and dives, and uses its wings to propel itself under water. There are many ritualised displays including males flicking their heads up and down and pairs knocking their bills together noisily. When feeding young, it will carry several fish in its bill at once. Although it frequently sits upright, it also rests with its breast on the ground. It is sociable when nesting, but at other times it is seen in ones and twos. Large 'rafts' of Puffins gather on the sea near breeding colonies in late winter.

VOICE

Generally silent, but at the colonies it makes a low growling 'arrrh' often repeated to sound like hoarse laughter.

HABITAT

Breeds on offshore islands and on tall sea cliffs. Outside the breeding season it lives at sea.

FOOD

Puffins catch small fish. The most common species are sand eel, sprat, herring and caplin, although it also eats many others.

BREEDING

Returns to colony in March and April. Nests in burrow in the turf and sometimes in crevice between rocks. Will either dig a burrow or use a rabbit burrow. Nest is usually 70–110 cm from entrance and lined with grass, roots and any dry material to be found. The single egg is laid in mid-May and incubated by both parents for 36–43 days. Newly hatched chick is covered in down, but remains in its burrow for 38–44 days until it scrambles down to the sea where it has to fend for itself.

MOVEMENTS AND MIGRATIONS

Puffins disperse from their colonies after breeding. Those from east-coast colonies mostly remain in the North Sea with some reaching southern Norway. Some from northern and western colonies also reach Norway, but others cross the Atlantic to the Grand Banks off Newfoundland and yet others move south to the Bay of Biscay, with some reaching the Mediterranean. Oldest known Puffin lived for over 33 years.

POPULATION

Estimated to be over 580,000 pairs in the UK and 20,000 in Ireland. While some colonies have apparently fluctuated in size in the last century, the overall population appears to be increasing.

winter

juvenile

summer

CONSERVATION

Threats come in many forms: weather conditions, variable food supplies, the introduction of rats by humans onto islands, oil and other pollution at sea and over-fishing are all important factors. Many of the most important colonies are in places that have been given special protection either as nature reserves or other sites of national importance.

DISTRIBUTION

Breeds in north and west Scotland and there are colonies in Ireland, Wales, and south-west and north-east England. Breeds in north-west Europe, as far south as northern France and in Iceland, Greenland and North America.

Little Auk *Alle alle*

IDENTIFICATION

17–19 cm. Our smallest auk, only the size of a Starling. It is a dumpy bird with a black stubby bill, short neck and tail and a small head. Its upperparts are black with some fine white lines on its back, a white bar on closed wings and the underparts are white. In its winter plumage its neck and lower face become white while it retains a blackish crown that extends lower than the eye. In flight, it has a dark underwing and it rocks from side to side with fast whirring wing-beats low over the sea. The juvenile has the same pattern as a summer adult, but paler. Moult has been little studied, but adults moult their body feathers between May and September and flight and tail feathers are moulted between September and October.

SEE ALSO: Guillemot p174, Razorbill p175, Puffin p177.

summer

winter

summer

winter

HABITS

A species that winters on the open ocean, but is affected by the occurrence of zooplankton, its main food. It moves further south into the North Sea when food is scarce and then may be driven close to our shores by autumn or winter gales at sea. At these times large numbers sometimes appear in inshore waters and occasionally individuals are blown inland. It takes to the air without running across the surface of the water. In flight, it can sometimes appear rather like a small wader. On its Arctic breeding grounds it nests in vast colonies.

VOICE

It is usually silent away from its breeding grounds. At colonies it makes noisy chattering calls.

HABITAT

The breeding sites are in the Arctic, on islands or the massive sea cliffs of Spitsbergen and Greenland where it nests amongst the boulder scree. Outside the breeding season this species lives out at sea.

FOOD

It feeds on plankton, most of which is the larval stage of crustaceans and also other tiny marine creatures. It also eats fish and some shellfish.

BREEDING

Not until the snow has thawed from the breeding colonies do these birds start to nest. Eggs are laid in late June or July in a rock crevice or in spaces under boulders. Both adults incubate the single egg in turns. At first the chick is brooded under the wing of an adult. It leaves after about 17 days and for a time it stays with one of its parents.

MOVEMENTS AND MIGRATIONS

Adults and juveniles leave their colonies in August and slowly move to their wintering areas. Some remain as close to their colonies as the winter ice floes allow. Others spread across the North Atlantic with some entering the North Sea in early autumn.

POPULATION

Numbers visiting British and Irish waters vary considerably from year to year.

CONSERVATION

Its remote Arctic habitat is largely free from development, but like other seabirds its future could be affected by fishing policies that alter the fish populations of the North Atlantic. Climate change affects sea temperatures and thus food supplies, leading to changes in distribution and possibly threatening its survival.

DISTRIBUTION

Britain is at the southern limit of its normal wintering range. Some enter the North Sea in autumn and come closest to the shores of eastern Scotland and eastern England during or after rough weather. Wintering birds may be seen off the coast of northern Britain. The species breeds from western Greenland to Spitsbergen and east to Arctic Russia.

Rock Dove/Feral Pigeon *Columba livia*

INTERNATIONAL NAME | COMMON PIGEON

IDENTIFICATION

31–34 cm. Smaller than a Woodpigeon. This species includes the familiar town pigeon. In its wild form it is blue-grey with a pale grey back, dark bars on wings and white rump. Head and breast are darker with iridescent green/purple sheen to feathers on side of neck. Feral form varies from pure white to almost black and includes plumages that are various shades of grey and brown. Some of the feral population resemble their Rock Dove ancestors. In flight, it shows white on the underside of the wing and white rump. Adults moult between June and November with the flight feathers being replaced gradually. Feral birds may moult at any time of year.
SEE ALSO: Stock Dove p180, Woodpigeon p181.

HABITS

Sociable. Flight fast, and it also glides and wheels. Has been domesticated for centuries and these domesticated forms may have exotic plumages, tumbling flight action, or be used for racing. In the past they have also been a source of food and used for carrying messages. Some previously domesticated birds or their descendants now breed in the habitat used by wild Rock Doves.

feral variants

VOICE

Call during display is a gentle 'orr-roo-cooo'.

HABITAT

In Britain and Ireland its traditional home is rock faces and cliffs, usually with caves and near the sea. In other parts of its range it will use suitable cliffs kilometres inland. Feral form is usually associated with towns and cities where it lives around buildings that provide nest-sites and accessible supplies of food.

FOOD

Feeds on the seeds of cereal crops such as wheat, barley and oats. Also eats peas and seeds of plants, including wild radish, shepherd's purse, dock and buttercup. Feral birds eat grain, but will take a wide range of other, mainly vegetarian, foods available by scavenging in towns.

BREEDING

Colonies of wild birds nest in semi-darkness in holes in rock faces or on ledges in caves. Urban birds use cavities in buildings. The rather loosely constructed nest is made from grasses, seaweed and other local material. Eggs may be laid at any time of year, but peak nesting is in spring and autumn. The normal clutch is 2 eggs, and five or more clutches may be laid in a year. Incubation is by both parents and lasts for about 17 days. Young (squabs) are fed on a substance that forms in the bird's crop ('crop milk') that the young take by reaching inside the adult's mouth. They fly at 35–37 days, but may be fed by their parents for up to 10 days after fledging.

MOVEMENTS AND MIGRATIONS

Wild Rock Dove is mainly resident, seldom moving far from its nest-site. Domesticated birds have remarkable powers of navigation, hence their use in racing (homing) and as message carriers. Rock Doves may live to 20 years or more.

POPULATION

No accurate estimates of Rock Dove populations, but wild and feral birds together may number over 100,000 in the UK and 50,000 in Ireland.

CONSERVATION

The spread of the Feral Pigeon has been so successful that nothing can be done to stop its gradual hybridisation with the wild form.

DISTRIBUTION

Interbreeding between wild and domesticated forms confuse the natural distribution, but it is assumed that those breeding in isolated colonies in the far north-west of Scotland, including the islands, and those in south and west Ireland may still be pure Rock Doves. Found in all other parts of lowland Britain and Ireland. Wild Rock Dove breeds in Europe, North Africa and south-west Asia. Domesticated form is now found in all continents except Antarctica.

Stock Dove *Columba oenas*

IDENTIFICATION
32–34 cm. Similar in size and shape to the Feral Pigeon and smaller than the Woodpigeon. This pigeon is blue-grey with an iridescent sheen on its neck, a pale rump and no white on its neck or wings. In flight, it has dark edges to the plain grey wings and two small but distinct bars near the body. The underwing is grey. The juvenile is duller and browner and lacks the iridescence on the neck. Moult takes place gradually between July and November with the primary feathers being some of the first to be lost.
SEE ALSO: Woodpigeon p181, Rock Dove p179.

HABITS
The flight is noticeably different from that of the Woodpigeon with birds looking more compact, their flight more direct and with a more flickering wing action. In display it flies with slow deliberate wingbeats and glides in a wide arc with wings held in a shallow 'V'. In the breeding season pairs may nest close to each other or on their own. At other times it will join with flocks of Woodpigeons or sometimes feeds in small flocks with its own species.

VOICE
The song is a soft, deep 'ooo-woo, ooo-woo'.

HABITAT
This species breeds in parkland with old trees, wooded farmland, the edges of larger woods and open forests. It is also found where there are cliffs or quarries or around old buildings. It frequently feeds on arable farmland.

FOOD
It eats mainly plant material. It feeds on seeds of cereal crops such as wheat and barley, and plants such as rape, goosefoot, dock and buttercup.

BREEDING
It nests in a hole in a tree, in nest boxes, in a building, a cliff or, very occasionally, a hole in the ground. Very little nest material is used and the same site may be used year after year. It usually lays 2 eggs, which are incubated for 16–18 days by both sexes. Both male and female care for the young (squabs), which are fed on 'crop milk'. Incubation may start with the first egg and results in the young being different ages. They first fly at between 20 and 30 days, and the young birds become independent soon afterwards. There may be a second or even a third brood in the same year.

MOVEMENTS AND MIGRATIONS
A high proportion of British and Irish breeding birds are resident and seldom move far from their breeding sites. In Europe there are large movements and some of these sometimes arrive in eastern Britain. Oldest known bird survived for more than 12 years.

POPULATION
It is estimated that there may be 309,000 pairs breeding in the UK and 2,500–10,000 in Ireland. This species appears to have expanded its range during the last 150 years, then declined in the 1950s and 1960s, but has since recovered.

CONSERVATION
The historic expansion of the Stock Dove has been linked to the expansion in arable farming, and the decline in the 1950s and early 1960s coincided with the widespread use of chemical seed dressings. Since a ban on these chemicals, the population of this dove has largely recovered in Britain and Ireland, although it continues to decline in eastern Europe. This is a species that can be helped by the erection of suitably designed nest boxes.

DISTRIBUTION
The Stock Dove breeds throughout Britain and Ireland with the exception of the north-west of Scotland and parts of Ireland. It winters in similar areas. In Europe it breeds from southern Scandinavia to the Mediterranean and east to central Asia and also in North Africa.

Woodpigeon *Columba palumbus*

INTERNATIONAL NAME   COMMON WOODPIGEON

IDENTIFICATION

40–42 cm. Our largest pigeon. It has a small head, broad wings, longish tail and bulging chest. The adult is blue-grey with white crescent on wing, black band on tail and white patch on neck. The neck has a green and purple sheen and breast has a pink flush. The juvenile is similar to adult, but has no white on neck. The annual moult may last for 8–10 months. It begins in April, is suspended while the bird breeds and continues in the autumn. Some individuals suspend moult again during the winter and do not finally complete their feather growth until the following February. SEE ALSO: Stock Dove p180.

juvenile

HABITS

When disturbed, it clatters noisily out of trees and bushes. In aerial territorial display it flies up steeply, then claps its wings together above its back with a sharp slap before gliding down steeply. Often repeats this manoeuvre several times. May be seen singly, but often in large flocks when not breeding. Drinks without lifting its head from water.

VOICE

Call is a soft, restful 'orr-oo-cooo, orr-oo-oo-coo'.

HABITAT

Breeds on arable farmland where there are hedges or trees and also in woods, copses and, increasingly, in towns and city centres. In winter, largely dependent on farmland.

FOOD

It eats mainly plant material, especially buds, leaves and seeds. The most commonly eaten plants include clover, cabbage and other brassicas, ash, ivy berries and peas; also eats cereal crops such as wheat and barley. Animal food includes insects such as beetles.

BREEDING

The Woodpigeon has been observed breeding in every month of the year, but mostly between July and September. Flimsy nest of twigs is built in a tree or bush. The 2 eggs can sometimes be seen from below. Incubation is by both adults and lasts for 17 days. The young are brooded for the first 7–8 days. The parents feed their young (squabs) on 'crop milk'. Young fly at 33–34 days, but it may be as early as 16–21 days if the nest is disturbed. Young are fed by their parents for about a week after their first flight. There are two or three broods each year and the same nest may be reused.

MOVEMENTS AND MIGRATIONS

In Britain largely resident although big communal roosts form and flocks can be seen as they move between roosts and feeding areas. In Europe, northern and eastern populations are migratory. Those from Scandinavia fly south in October and a few may arrive along the east coast, but most fly on through France to Spain. The oldest lived for over 17 years.

POPULATION

One of our most numerous birds with 2.5–3.1 million breeding in the UK and up to 1 million in Ireland. The total rises to between 4.8 and 10 million birds in winter.

CONSERVATION

Woodpigeons have been expanding their range and numbers for the last 150 years. They suffered a decline in the 1950s and 1960s caused by agricultural chemicals, but their numbers have recovered and they have recently colonised western Ireland and some of the Scottish islands. Considered a pest on arable crops and the spread of intensive arable cultivation, especially of oilseed rape, may explain the rise in population. There have been attempts to control numbers by regular February shoots, but these have had little effect on the total population.

DISTRIBUTION

Found throughout Britain and Ireland with the exception of the highest hills and uplands of north-west Scotland. Also breeds in Europe, from the Mediterranean to the Arctic Circle and east into Russia and Asia. It also breeds in North Africa.

Collared Dove *Streptopelia decaocto*

INTERNATIONAL NAME EURASIAN COLLARED DOVE

IDENTIFICATION
31–33 cm. Smaller than a Woodpigeon, with a longish tail. This is a pale pinkish-buff dove with dark flight feathers and, when seen from below, a broad white band at the tip of the tail. The back is plain and unmarked and there is a thin black bar on the side of the neck. Moult begins in spring, after March, and continues into the autumn, with some suspending the moult of their flight feathers during the winter and not completing the growth of all new feathers until the following February, so the moult can last for 10 months. SEE ALSO: Turtle Dove p183.

HABITS
Seen singly or in pairs in the breeding season, but may form flocks at other times. It feeds on the ground and frequently perches in the open. It sings from roofs and overhead wires. In its aerial display flight it rises steeply and then glides down on fanned wings, often calling as it lands. This species can become used to humans.

VOICE
It has a harsh, excited 'kwurr' call. The song is a loud and repetitive 'coo-cooo-cuk, coo-cooo-cuk'.

HABITAT
The Collared Dove is associated mainly with human activity, such as farms (especially where there is spilt grain for food) and also gardens with a bird table. Many live in towns where there is a varied habitat of gardens, parks and churchyards but it tends to avoid city centres. Although it is widespread, it avoids uplands, especially moorland and mountainous areas.

FOOD
It is mainly vegetarian, feeding on grain and other seeds and fruits. Wheat, barley and oats are all eaten when available, as are seeds from knotgrass, bindweed and various grasses. Berries such as elder are eaten in autumn. It will sometimes feed on aphids and also caterpillars.

BREEDING
In Britain and Ireland Collared Doves lay their eggs from February to October with rather more in May. The clutch is generally 2 eggs. The nest is a delicate, thin structure of rather thin twigs and the eggs are sometimes visible from below. Incubation is by both parents and lasts 14–18 days. The young remain in the nest for 15–19 days and are cared for by both parents. They are fed on 'crop milk' for the first 10 days after hatching. They become independent of the adults after about a week out of the nest. It is possible for a pair to raise five broods in a year although three broods are more usual.

MOVEMENTS AND MIGRATIONS
It is mainly a resident species but the young disperse after leaving the nest and many show a tendency to move west. Although some return to their original breeding areas, this habit has led to the rapid expansion westwards since about 1930. Oldest known bird survived for more than 16 years.

POPULATION
The Collared Dove first nested in Norfolk in 1955 and the colonisation of Ireland began in 1959. Since those early breeding records it has colonised the British Isles. The current population is 298,000 occupied territories in the UK and 20,000–100,000 in Ireland, and the population is still increasing.

CONSERVATION
The expansion of this dove's range is quite remarkable, spreading from Asia Minor and colonising much of Europe and eventually reaching Britain. There are no special conservation measures associated with this successful species.

juvenile

DISTRIBUTION
It is found throughout Britain and Ireland except for upland areas. It is most numerous in central and southern England and the east of Ireland. The species originated in southern Asia and the Middle East and is now found across central Europe as far south as Greece and north to southern Scandinavia.

Turtle Dove *Streptopelia turtur*

INTERNATIONAL NAME   EUROPEAN TURTLE DOVE

juvenile

IDENTIFICATION
26–28 cm. Smaller than a Collared Dove. Small light-weight pigeon with small head and diamond-shaped tail. The back has reddish-brown feathers with dark centres that give a tortoiseshell effect and it has a black-and-white neck-patch. Head is blue-grey, breast pale pink and it has pale grey panels in its wings. Tail is mostly black with an obvious white edge near the tip and is very distinctive in flight. It has a ring of bare orange skin around its eye that is generally visible only at close range. Moult begins in June or July, after nesting, and is suspended for the period of migration and then continues in the wintering area.
SEE ALSO: Collared Dove p182, Rock Dove p179, Woodpigeon p181.

HABITS
The rapid flight is noticeably more flickering than other pigeons. Aerial display flight is obvious in spring when a male will react to another bird by taking off with tail fanned, climbing steeply, clapping its wings and then gliding up and down again with wings and tail spread until it lands again on a perch. Generally seen in small numbers although larger groups sometimes gather and migrate together.

VOICE
Song is a loud, lazy, cat-like purring that is given from a perch between May and July.

HABITAT
Breeds where there are open woods, copses and tall, thick hedges on farmland, commons and in parkland. Feeds on the ground in fields or other cultivated areas. In winter in Africa, it lives in agricultural areas where there are tall trees.

FOOD
Feeds mainly on seeds of wild plants and flowers (weeds), especially fumitory, chickweed, buttercups, goosefoot, spurges and docks. It will also sometimes eat snails and caterpillars.

BREEDING
Nesting begins in May. It is mainly the female that builds the nest, a flimsy structure of small twigs, or sometimes built on the old nest of another bird. The normal clutch is 2 eggs and both adults take turns to incubate them for 13–14 days until the young hatch.

For the first 5 days after hatching the young are fed on 'crop milk'. They fly after about 20 days and quickly become independent. There may be two or occasionally three broods in one year.

MOVEMENTS AND MIGRATIONS
A migrant that leaves Britain between July and September, and moves on a broad front by day and by night. It passes through North Africa in large numbers in September and October. The return migration starts in February and March and it reoccupies its breeding territories in Britain in May.

POPULATION
Thought to be 44,000 territories in Britain, but has declined by 86% and appears to be still declining.

CONSERVATION
The reason for its decline is not clear. Large numbers are shot around the Mediterranean while migrating, there has been climate change that has caused drought in Africa, and the agricultural changes that have adversely affected many farmland birds in Britain may also be affecting the Turtle Dove. Recent research indicates that more young are being raised while annual survival has fallen. To help safeguard this species it will be necessary to encourage the conservation and planting of suitable hedges in Europe, the conservation of acacia forests in Africa and a cessation of hunting at migration times.

DISTRIBUTION
In Britain largely restricted to southern and eastern England, with a few birds reaching Wales. It has bred in Ireland but probably does not do so at all now. Outside Britain breeds across central and southern Europe, North Africa and western Asia. In winter, lives in central Africa.

Ring-necked Parakeet *Psittacula krameri*

INTERNATIONAL NAME   ROSE-RINGED PARAKEET

IDENTIFICATION
38–42 cm. The body is the size of a Starling but with a very long (25 cm) pointed tail. It is pale green with a round head and a deeply hooked crimson bill. The nape and tail have a bluish sheen. The male has a delicate black and pink ring encircling its face. The female lacks any blue on the nape and has no ring round its face. The juvenile is similar to the female, but more yellow and with a shorter tail. The flight feathers are dark.
SEE ALSO: Bee-eater p195.

HABITS
The silhouette is distinctive with pointed wings and long pointed tail. The flight is rapid with flickering wings. On the ground it waddles on its short legs. It is often seen in small groups, sometimes in larger flocks. Communal flocks are very noisy but are difficult to see among the branches of mature trees. During courtship the male will preen the female's head or wings.

VOICE
The call is a loud screech 'kee-ak' that may be given from a perch, but is often made by flying birds.

HABITAT
In Britain it is generally found in suburban areas, parks and orchards. In India, where the species exists in a wild, not feral, state, it lives in jungle, and also in cities, towns, gardens, farms and on cultivated land.

FOOD
In India it feeds on buds, fruit, cereals, grains and seeds. In Britain it also eats apples, pears, cherries, hawthorn berries and visits bird tables for peanuts and sunflower seeds.

BREEDING
In Britain eggs may be laid any time between January and June. The nest may be in a hole in a tree or sometimes in a building. Pairs may be solitary or in colonies. These birds do not make their own holes, but adopt an existing woodpecker hole or a natural hole that the female may enlarge, helped a little by the male. The 3 or 4 eggs are incubated for 22–24 days by the female. The young are brooded while small and fed by both parents. They fly at 40–50 days old and remain with the parents for several more weeks.

MOVEMENTS AND MIGRATIONS
In their native habitat this is a resident species and colonists in western Europe have shown no tendency to migrate. In captivity these birds live, on average, for about 20 years.

POPULATION
The latest estimate is that there are over 5,900 adults in England and the species continues to increase.

CONSERVATION
How these birds became established in Britain is not fully understood. Some may have escaped from captivity and others may have been deliberately released. The species was first recorded breeding wild in 1969 and the population has been slowly increasing since then. In their traditional habitats in Asia these birds are considered pests for the damage they do to cultivated crops. Fruit growers in south-east Britain have similar concerns about the long-term future of this species in its newly adopted home. Perhaps surprisingly, they are well adapted to cold weather and do not appear to suffer in hard winters.

female

male

female

DISTRIBUTION

In Britain this species is found mainly in south-east England. It has also colonised other parts of north-west Europe, especially the Netherlands and Belgium. The species breeds naturally in southern Asia, especially India and there is also a race in central Africa. Most birds wild in Britain belong to the Asian race, but some originated in Africa.

Cuckoo *Cuculus canorus*

INTERNATIONAL NAME COMMON CUCKOO

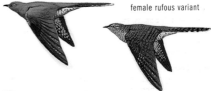

male

IDENTIFICATION

32–34 cm. Size of a Collared Dove. Superficially it resembles a small bird of prey, with its slim body, long tail, small head and pointed wings. Bill short and slightly curved; legs very short. Upperparts, head and breast plain blue-grey and underparts white with back barring. Tail rounded with white tip. At rest the bird droops its wings well below the level of the long tail. Female is slightly browner than male, especially on its breast. Juvenile grey- or reddish-brown with black barring and white patch on the back of its head. There is a rare form of the adult female that is reddish-brown like a female Kestrel. Adults partly moult during June or July, but have a complete moult in Africa during the winter.

SEE ALSO: Sparrowhawk p101, Kestrel p102.

HABITS

In flight the pointed wings move below the level of the body and wingbeats are rapid. Perches in the open; on wires or at top of trees or on bare branches, often with tail cocked and spread and wings drooped. A male will adopt this pose as he swivels his body during courtship. Generally seen singly outside the breeding season. Those present in Britain or Ireland in late summer and early autumn are invariably juveniles.

VOICE

The call of the male is the famous 'cuc-oo'. It also makes a harsh, laughing 'gwork-gwork-gwork'. Female makes a very different bubbling call.

HABITAT

Found in most habitats except built-up areas, although it may visit suburbia and large parks. Especially favours reedbeds, moorland, woodland and agricultural land. In Africa in winter, found in savanna and forests.

FOOD

Feeds mainly on insects, especially caterpillars, including those that are hairy or have warning colours and are avoided by other birds. Other insects include beetles, flies, sawflies and ants. Will also eat eggs and small nestlings of other birds, sometimes from the nests that it parasitises.

BREEDING

Some maintain territories, others gather where there is a high density of 'host' species. Individuals parasitise particular species: Meadow Pipit, Dunnock and Reed Warbler are the most common, although more than a hundred others have been used. Female makes no nest; instead she watches a suitable area. Then, when she is ready to lay, she selects a nest, takes out an egg in her bill and lays her own in its place. She flies off with the host's egg and swallows it. Up to 25 eggs may be laid in a season and their colour usually resembles that of the preferred host. Incubation is by the host, and the young Cuckoo hatches after 12 days. The blind and naked chick then instinctively pushes other eggs or young out of the nest. Other small birds, such as Wrens, are sometimes attracted to feed the giant baby. Young Cuckoos leave the nest after about 19 days and continue to be fed for a further 3 weeks.

female rufous variant

MOVEMENTS AND MIGRATIONS

Most breeding birds arrive in April and leave again in August. Juveniles follow a month or so later.

POPULATION

There are 14,000 pairs in the UK and 2,500–10,000 in Ireland. The population has declined by 60% in recent years.

CONSERVATION

Declines have been linked to decline in its host species. It is therefore likely it is indirectly affected by agricultural changes and possibly by changes to its winter quarters in Africa.

juvenile

female

DISTRIBUTION

Breeds throughout Britain and Ireland, but is most numerous in southern and central England, in western Scotland and in Ireland. Also breeds throughout Europe and much of Asia. European birds winter in central and southern Africa.

Barn Owl *Tyto alba*

IDENTIFICATION
33–35 cm. Smaller than a Tawny Owl. It has a heart-shaped face that can change shape, long and rather narrow wings and long legs. The honey-coloured upperparts are flecked with darker marks with some grey on the back. The underparts, including under the wings, are snowy white with only light spotting. The female has a little more spotting on breast and more streaking and spotting on back. Body feathers are moulted gradually throughout the year. Flight feathers are moulted between July and December.
SEE ALSO: Short-eared Owl p189, Tawny Owl p187.

HABITS
Its buoyant flight is typically slow, low over the ground and wavering, and it frequently hovers when hunting. Generally a nocturnal hunter, but may be seen during the day. Territories are occupied for the whole year and birds hunt singly.

VOICE
A piercing shriek, especially during courtship. Call for food is a loud 'snore' made mainly by the young, but also by adults during courtship.

HABITAT
Open country, usually below 300 m, especially farmland, but also coastal marshes and forest edges. Nests and roosts in buildings, hollow trees or cliffs. Hunts over areas of rank grassland, along field edges, ditches, river banks, railway embankments and roadside verges.

FOOD
Feeds mainly on small mammals such as mice, voles and shrews, and it also eats larger mammals including small rats. Birds such as finches and thrushes are sometimes taken at their roosts and some individuals also catch and eat bats.

BREEDING
The nest is in an enclosed space in a barn, ruined building, hollow tree, cliff face or a specially made nest box. Some nests are among hay or straw bales in modern barns. During courtship the male feeds the female. No nest is made and the clutch of 4–6 eggs is laid onto a pile of old pellets. Incubation by female takes about 30 days and starts with the first egg, so the young hatch at intervals of 2 or 3 days and therefore the oldest may be 2 weeks older than the youngest. Young fly after about 55 days and are dependent on their parents for a further 3–5 weeks. Often two broods.

MOVEMENTS AND MIGRATIONS
Most adults are resident and seldom move far. Juveniles randomly disperse once they are fully independent and they may travel up to 50 km, with a few going further. After good breeding seasons in some European countries, birds may disperse, with a few reaching eastern Britain. Oldest wild bird survived over 17 years.

POPULATION
There are fluctuations caused by changing vole populations. 4,000 pairs in the UK and up to 1,000 in Ireland.

CONSERVATION
Specially protected. Once it was widespread both here and in Europe, but along with other birds of prey it suffered declines during the 20th century owing to agricultural intensification and the use of pesticides. In Britain, the use of second-generation rodenticides has been a cause of some mortality. Re-establishing hay meadows, conserving areas of rough grassland rich in voles wherever possible, especially alongside watercourses, field edges and woods will help to ensure this species continues to have sufficient feeding areas. The provision of new nest-sites (nestboxes) in areas where natural holes are in short supply is also critical.

DISTRIBUTION
Widely distributed in lowland Britain and Ireland but scarce in central and north-east England, upland Scotland and north-west Ireland. Also breeds throughout western and southern Europe and North Africa. Other races are found in northern and eastern Europe, Africa, southern Asia, Australia and North and South America.

Tawny Owl *Strix aluco*

IDENTIFICATION

37–39 cm. As large as a Woodpigeon. Has a tubby body, large round head and rounded wings. Its face is surrounded by a ring of dark feathers and the eyes are dark and create a friendly expression. Upperparts are usually reddish-brown with dark and white marks forming a broken line on its wings and on the crown of the head. Underparts are pale buff with dark streaks. A few birds are paler with greyer feathers. Flight is fast, direct and silent, and often higher than other owls. Feathers are moulted gradually between June and December.
SEE ALSO: Long-eared Owl p188, Short-eared Owl p189.

HABITS

Nocturnal. Generally seen during the day only if it is disturbed. Roosts in hollow trees, up against a tree trunk or amongst ivy, and is remark- ably difficult to see. If it does emerge during the day it often attracts small birds that mob it. May hunt from a perch or hover in flight. Defends its nest aggressively, even attack- ing human intruders. The Tawny Owl relies on knowing its hunting territory very well and checks every part of it.

VOICE

Song is the familiar hoot 'hooo-hoo-hooo' of the male used to proclaim his territory and during court- ship. Sings in late winter and again in autumn. Female also has a hoarse version of the hoot. Another common call is a sharp 'kee-wick', made by both sexes. Occasion- ally calls during daylight.

HABITAT

Deciduous and coniferous woodland. An adaptable species that also lives in farmland and gardens where there are suitable nest-sites. It has colonised town and city centres where there are parks, squares and churchyards with large trees. In some places, especially outside Britain, it inhabits more open countryside and will nest among cliffs.

FOOD

The most common food is small mammals, especially voles, mice and shrews. Also eats insects such as bee- tles, birds such as Starlings, finches, thrushes and sparrows and also frogs and earthworms. Surprisingly, it is also known occasionally to eat fish that it presum- ably snatches from the water surface.

BREEDING

The nest is in a natural or man-made hole, including specially designed nest boxes, and only rarely on the ground. Nesting may begin in late February or March.

The female incubates the clutch of 2 or 3 eggs for 28–30 days. At first the young are brooded by the female while the male hunts. After about 15 days both parents hunt for food. Owlets often leave their nest after 25–30 days and hide among nearby branches. They fly at 32–37 days, but are dependent on their parents for a further 3 months.

MOVEMENTS AND MIGRATIONS

Mainly resident with established pairs probably never leaving their territories. Young birds disperse in any direction in autumn. British juveniles seldom travel further than a few kilometres, but those breeding in northern Europe often travel much further. Oldest ringed bird survived more than 21 years.

POPULATION

There are around 20,000 pairs breeding in Britain, but none in Ireland. There are some concerns that the population has started to fall.

CONSERVATION

This owl, like other birds of prey, has been persecuted in game-rearing areas. It is also a frequent victim of traffic on busy roads. The recent decline may be linked with agricultural change.

grey type   rufous type

DISTRIBUTION

Widespread in England, Scotland and Wales, but not found in Ireland. Breeds from central Scandinavia to north-west Africa and the Middle East, and east to western Siberia and the Himalayas.

Long-eared Owl *Asio otus*

IDENTIFICATION

35–37 cm. Smaller than a Woodpigeon. Often looks rather long and thin with ear-tufts (which are not ears) that may be raised and lowered. The cat-like face changes from round to narrow when the bird is stretched up and roosting. Plumage is rich buff-brown with darker brown streaks, and underparts are streaked boldly to below belly. In flight, long wings have a more uniform pattern than a Short-eared Owl and do not have a pale buff edge. Base of the flight feathers is orange-brown. Short tail is finely barred. Eyes are deep orange. Ear-tufts are held flat in flight. Adults moult gradually between June and December with male starting first. Flight feathers are moulted gradually over 3 months.
SEE ALSO: Short-eared Owl p189, Tawny Owl p187.

HABITS

Nocturnal; only occasionally hunts during the day. Roosts in bushes and trees during the day and is reluctant to fly unless an observer approaches too close. It is not a colonial breeding species, but groups may migrate together and small communal roosts are not uncommon in winter. Its flight is slow and wavering.

VOICE

Makes a wide variety of sounds. Song is a quiet but penetrating low 'hoo-hoo-hoo-hoo'. The small young have jingling calls, but later they make a drawn-out squeak that has been likened to a squeaky gate.

HABITAT

Inhabits both conifer and deciduous woods and forests. Breeds in conifer plantations, copses, edges of large woodlands, thorn thickets and shelter belts (always with open country nearby: including coastal marshes, farmland or moorland). In winter, seeks similar habitats, but is more commonly seen near the coast where birds may gather in scrub and dense woodland.

FOOD

The main method of studying its diet is to examine pellets ejected by the owl at its roost. Food is small mammals, especially voles and mice, and also birds caught at their roosts.

BREEDING

Nest is usually in a tree, in a sturdy old nest of another bird such as a Magpie or crow, or in a squirrel's drey. Occasionally, in areas with few trees, these owls nest on the ground. Nesting begins in late March or April. Female incubates clutch of 3 or 4 eggs for 25–30 days. Male feeds female and provides most of the food for young. At about 21 days young leave the nest and live among the branches. They can probably fly at 30 days and remain dependent on their parents until they are 60 days old. Usually one brood, but two broods when food very plentiful.

MOVEMENTS AND MIGRATIONS

Northern populations are migratory whereas southern birds are resident or may move relatively short distances to find food. Some appear to be nomadic and breed only where food is plentiful. In years when numbers are high or food is scarce, there may be influxes of these owls into Britain from northern Europe. Oldest ringed bird was over 17 years old.

POPULATION

Difficult to census. There are thought to be 1,400–4,800 pairs in the UK and 1,000–2,500 in Ireland.

CONSERVATION

Range in Britain appears to have contracted in recent years and numbers are lower, but populations fluctuate as these owls achieve better breeding results in years when rodents, especially voles, are numerous – and such years tend to be cyclical. Some pairs can be encouraged to nest in man-made sites such as willow baskets.

DISTRIBUTION

Thinly distributed across Britain and Ireland, with fewer birds in the south-west and Wales. Inhabits a band around the northern hemisphere, including North America, Europe and Asia, with some isolated populations in Africa.

Short-eared Owl *Asio flammeus*

IDENTIFICATION

37–39 cm. Medium-sized owl that is mottled brown with staring yellow eyes surrounded by black patches within a pale face. Ear-tufts are hard to see. Has long wings, which are very pale below with a black tip and a black curved bar at the base of the flight feathers. Upperwings are mottled brown and buff and have a white trailing edge. Tail shows four strong bars. Breast is heavily marked with dark streaks, but rest of underparts are paler than a Long-eared Owl. In flight, often keeps low. It has deep wingbeats followed by a glide, with wings in a shallow 'V'. Adults start to moult in June or July. Moult begins with flight feathers and by November all feathers have regrown.

SEE ALSO: Long-eared Owl p188, Tawny Owl p187.

HABITS

This owl quite commonly hunts in daylight, but especially at dawn and dusk. In spring, it has an aerial display as it flies high above its territory and claps its wings below its body. Often solitary, but does sometimes gather in groups to roost, occasionally mixing with Long-eared Owls. Regularly perches on the ground, on a post or in bushes or trees. On the ground it is less upright than other owls.

VOICE

Usually silent, but has a low, hollow 'boo-boo-boo-boo' and also a hoarse bark.

HABITAT

Open country: moorland, coastal marshes, rough grassland and dunes. Has also benefited from grasslands enclosed when young conifers are planted.

FOOD

Main food is small mammals, especially short-tailed voles, rats and mice. It eats birds up to the size of thrushes, and occasionally catches insects and amphibians.

BREEDING

In Britain the first eggs may be laid during March in a nest that is a shallow scrape made on the ground by the female and lined with local vegetation. Site is usually in grass, rushes or heather. Female incubates clutch of 4–7 eggs for 24–29 days. Incubation starts with first egg and young hatch over a period of a week or more. Both adults feed the young. At about 15 days the owlets leave their nest and hide in the surrounding vegetation until they fly at 24–27 days. Two broods if food is very plentiful.

MOVEMENTS AND MIGRATIONS

In the north this is a migratory species and some cross the Sahara Desert to winter in central Africa. Some cross the North Sea in autumn to winter in Britain. British juveniles may travel as far as Spain and Malta. Breeding densities fluctuate due to the abundance of prey and in some years there are larger movements than in others. Some populations are nomadic and breed or winter where prey is most plentiful. The oldest known wild bird lived over 20 years.

POPULATION

Between 1,000 and 3,500 pairs nest in the UK and a few pairs in Ireland. Over the last 70 years this species has increased, but more recently the numbers have declined again.

CONSERVATION

Short-eared Owl populations fluctuate according to food abundance, and long-term trends are difficult to detect. Recent significant declines have been recognised in eastern Europe. In Britain it benefited from establishment of new conifer plantations in the 20th century and its population grew, but it does not occupy restocked plantations that lack rough grassland.

DISTRIBUTION

In Britain breeds mainly in upland areas, especially in northern England and Scotland. Some nest in Wales and on the coast of eastern England. In winter, more widespread and may visit central and southern England. Scarce in Ireland. Also breeds in Iceland and in Europe, from the Arctic to northern France, in Asia and in parts of North and South America. In winter some reach Africa.

Little Owl *Athene noctua*

IDENTIFICATION

21–23 cm. Size of a Starling. Britain's smallest owl. Small and plump with a rather flat head and short tail. The brown or greyish-brown upperparts and wings are heavily spotted with white and the pale breast is heavily streaked. The black eyes with yellow irises stare from under white 'eyebrows', giving a fierce expression. Juvenile is duller than adult and lacks white spots on its crown. In flight, wings are quite long and rounded at the ends. Moult begins in July and continues to November, with male starting before female.

SEE ALSO: Tawny Owl p187.

HABITS

May be seen in daylight as it perches erect in the open on a telegraph pole, branch or rock. Mainly hunts from dusk to midnight and again before dawn. It bobs curiously when alarmed. It frequently hunts on the ground where it hops or runs on its rather long legs. Flight is often deeply undulating, rising with rapid wingbeats and dipping down with closed wings, but can also be direct and 'bat-like'.

VOICE

The most frequent call is a sharp, mewing 'kiew, kiew' that is most common in March and April during courtship, when the male also gives a pure, single hoot 'woop'.

HABITAT

It occupies a wide variety of habitats in Britain, but most nest on agricultural land. Lowland farmland with woods, copses, hedges and old trees is the ideal habitat. It also breeds in mature parkland, orchards, quarries and water meadows with old, pollarded willows.

FOOD

It feeds on small mammals, birds, insects and invertebrates. Mammals include shrews and voles. Insects include beetles, caterpillars and adult moths, especially common species that hatch in large numbers. It regularly feeds on earthworms.

BREEDING

The most usual nest-site is a hole in a tree, about 3 m off the ground. It also uses clefts in rock faces, holes in buildings and sometimes holes between tree roots and in rabbit burrows. Eggs are laid during April and May. Most clutches are of 3 or 4 eggs and incubation is by the female. The young hatch after 29–31 days. For the first 2 weeks they are almost constantly brooded by the female, later both parents hunt for food. They can fly after 37 days, but before this they may leave the nest chamber and clamber about around the nest-site. There are records of pairs rearing second broods, but this appears to be rare.

MOVEMENTS AND MIGRATIONS

The species does not migrate. Young birds disperse from their nest-sites in late summer, but seldom travel far. The oldest surviving ringed bird was over 10 years old.

POPULATION

It is estimated that 5,800–11,600 pairs are breeding in Britain and none in Ireland. The population fluctuates, and may be declining.

CONSERVATION

The Little Owl was introduced from Europe in the 19th century. Two schemes were successful: one in Kent and the other in Northamptonshire. From these introductions the species gradually colonised southern Britain, breeding in Scotland for the first time in 1978. There are concerns for the European population, which appears to have been in decline for the last 40 years owing to pesticides reducing its insect prey, changes in land use depriving it of nest-sites, and road casualties.

DISTRIBUTION

In Britain the species is most abundant in central and southern England and it is scarce in the south-west. A few nest in southern Scotland and it does not breed in Ireland, but vagrants have been seen in the east of Ireland. It breeds in central and southern Europe, North Africa, the Middle East and parts of Asia.

Nightjar *Caprimulgus europaeus*

INTERNATIONAL NAME EUROPEAN NIGHTJAR

IDENTIFICATION

26–28 cm. Smaller than a Kestrel. Long, pointed wings, a long tail and a rather large, flat head. Eyes are large and dark, bill is short and mouth very wide for catching flying insects. Plumage is grey-brown with beautiful camouflage markings. Adult male has white marks near the tips of its wings and on the outer tips of its tail. Females and juveniles lack the white marks. Adults begin to moult in July and some inner flight feathers may be moulted before migration, but rest of moult takes place in Africa.

SEE ALSO: Kestrel p102, Cuckoo p185, Grasshopper Warbler (song) p234.

HABITS

Males are territorial and it is unusual to see more than one or two birds at a time, although small groups may gather at rich feeding sites. In flight, twists and turns, and flies as silently as an owl – sometimes almost seems to float on the air. During display flight it will clap its wings together above the back making a 'slapping' sound. Most active around dusk and dawn when it feeds. At rest during the day, perches along a branch instead of across it, like most other birds, to gain maximum camouflage, or on the ground.

VOICE

Song is a long, drawn-out churring that rises and falls as the bird turns its head. Flight call is a loud, liquid-sounding 'coo-lik'.

HABITAT

Breeds in open woodlands, heaths, commons and moors where there are scattered trees, and also in young or recently felled forestry plantations. In Africa in winter, found in clearings in forests and open steppe country.

FOOD

Feeds on insects. Catches prey in flight and takes a wide variety of moths, beetles and flies.

BREEDING

Nest is a shallow scrape on bare ground, usually among dead branches and broken sticks; either in a clearing in a wood or in a more open location. Usually lays 2 eggs, incubated mostly by female, with male taking over at dawn and dusk. Eggs hatch after 17–18 days. Young fly after 18–19 days and become independent about 16 days later. A pair may have a second brood, laying second clutch when young of first brood are about 14 days old.

MOVEMENTS AND MIGRATIONS

This is a difficult species to study and its migrations are poorly understood. All are long-distance migrants. Juveniles from first broods are thought to leave Europe in late July with adults and other juveniles following later. They reach their African wintering grounds between October and November. British and Irish birds return in late April and early May, with the males returning a few days before the females. The oldest wild bird survived over 11 years.

male

POPULATION

There are 4,600 males in Britain in summer and fewer than 10 in Ireland. It suffered a big decline from about 1930, although there have been signs of a recovery in some areas in the last few years.

CONSERVATION

Since 1992 the Nightjar population has increased in Britain, probably due to increased areas of cleared forest and heathland restoration. Population continues to decline in parts of Europe due to habitat deterioration and the use of pesticides. Maintenance of a mosaic of woodland habitat, with open areas among woodlands with uncultivated land nearby, is important for the future of this species.

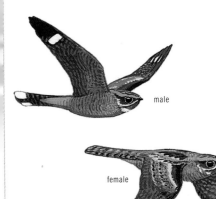

male

female

DISTRIBUTION

Relatively small numbers breed in Scotland, Ireland, Wales and northern England, and the majority are to be found in southern England and East Anglia. Breeds from southern Scandinavia to North Africa and east into central Asia. It winters in central and southern Africa, as far south as South Africa.

Swift *Apus apus*

INTERNATIONAL NAME COMMON SWIFT

IDENTIFICATION

16–17 cm. Shorter body and longer wings than a Swallow. Body, wings and tail are plain sooty brown and chin is pale. In bright sunlight plumage may appear lighter brown, but more often it appears black against the sky. Wings are long and scythe-like and tail is short and forked. Juvenile resembles adult, but with a more obvious pale throat and pale fringes to its wing feathers that creates a scaly appearance. Moult begins in August and at least some begin to moult their flight feathers before migrating. Moult continues in Africa and may not be completed until February or March. SEE ALSO: Swallow p204, House Martin p205.

juvenile

HABITS

Flight is rapid and flickering, followed by long glides on sickle-shaped wings. Often parties will chase rapidly around their nest-sites, screaming noisily. Spends more time in flight than any other species and regularly sleeps on the wing at night when not nesting. Also feeds, drinks, gathers nest material and sometimes mates in flight. Grounded Swifts find it difficult, and sometimes impossible, to take off again.

VOICE

Usual call is a harsh scream 'screee'.

HABITAT

An aerial species that ranges widely in its search for food and to avoid storms. May be seen over most habitats, but in Britain and Ireland breeds almost exclusively in buildings, especially older ones that provide suitable access to roof space. A few still breed in traditional sites in rock crevices in caves or cliffs. In some areas in Europe it inhabits forests with mature trees where it uses natural holes for nesting.

FOOD

Feeds almost exclusively on flying insects, with some birds catching up to 10,000 a day when feeding young. Prey includes beetles, aphids, flies, hoverflies, craneflies, moths, butterflies, thrips, leafhoppers, ants and lacewings. Also catches airborne spiders.

BREEDING

The Swift starts breeding in May. Both sexes build the nest, which is a shallow cup of straw and other material gathered on the wing and cemented together with saliva. The site may be under eaves of a house, in a church tower or any other suitable cavity. In eastern Europe it regularly uses holes in trees and sometimes nest boxes. Clutch of 2 or 3 eggs is incubated by both sexes for 19 days, but incubation may be longer if the weather is cold. Young are brooded continuously for the first week. They remain in the nest for 37–56 days depending on the weather and are independent as soon as they leave the nest. Young Swifts do not breed until their fourth year.

MOVEMENTS AND MIGRATIONS

Summer migrant. Arrives in late April or early May and leaves again in August with only a few birds seen in Britain in September. Its migratory journeys are rapid with autumn migrants arriving in Africa by mid-August. Birds respond to changes in the weather and food availability by moving large distances. The oldest known Swift survived 21 years.

POPULATION

Difficult to census, but about 85,000 pairs nest in the UK and 10,000–20,000 in Ireland. The UK population has fallen by 35% in the last 25 years.

CONSERVATION

There are problems for the species in that modern buildings lack suitable nest-sites and some older buildings have cavities blocked. It is possible to make Swift nest boxes, and this will help the species.

DISTRIBUTION

Most abundant in the south and east of Britain and Ireland and least common in the north-west. It breeds from the Arctic Circle south to North Africa and east into Asia. Winters in southern Africa.

Hoopoe *Upupa epops*

IDENTIFICATION

26–28 cm. Smaller than a Feral Pigeon. This exotic-looking species is slim with a long neck, long decurved bill and a crest that may be raised or lowered. Body pinkish-buff with bold black-and-white bars on wings, tail and back. Long pinkish crest is tipped with black and is laid flat most of the time. Juvenile is duller than an adult and the white wing-bars are tinged cream. In flight, the broad and rounded black-and-white wings and tail are striking. Adults may begin their moult after the breeding season and continue after they have migrated for the winter.

SEE ALSO: Jay p269.

HABITS

Very distinctive. Spends a lot of time feeding on the ground where its bold plumage breaks up its outline and makes it surprisingly inconspicuous. Once in the air its butterfly-like flapping flight attracts attention. Flight undulates as the bird almost closes its wings between each beat. Crest is raised when the bird is excited and also on landing. In southern Europe it is usually seen singly or in pairs. In Britain it is single birds that are generally seen.

VOICE

Call is a soft, low, resonant 'hoop, hoop, hoop' that carries a surprising distance.

HABITAT

Feeds on areas of bare soil or short grass. In southern Europe breeds in open country with a scattering of old trees. Often nests in olive groves, orchards or the edges of woods and sometimes near rivers or streams. In Africa in winter inhabits a variety of wooded savannas.

FOOD

Feeds on the ground and takes its prey either from the surface or by probing into soil with its long bill. Mainly eats large insects and their larvae such as crickets, beetles, ants and flies. Non-insect food includes spiders, centipedes, millipedes, slugs, snails and, occasionally, small reptiles such as lizards.

BREEDING

Has occasionally nested in Britain. Nests in a hole in a tree or sometimes in a building or in a hole in the ground or a bank. Male and female both help to clear out and, if necessary, enlarge the nest-hole. The 7 or 8 eggs are incubated by the female for 15–16 days from the first egg, so that the young hatch over several days. At first the female cares for young and the male provides all the food, but later both hunt for their growing family. Young fly after 26–29 days and continue to be fed by their parents for some time. Usually one brood, but can be two.

MOVEMENTS AND MIGRATIONS

Northern populations are migratory and winter in Africa, south of the Sahara Desert, while those that breed further south are only partial migrants and many that breed in the south of Spain and Portugal are resident. Autumn migration lasts from July to November, and birds return between February and May. A few reach Britain, mainly in April and May or again in September.

POPULATION

Hoopoes have nested about 20 times in the last 200 years. Up to 100 are seen in Britain and Ireland in most years, but numbers vary.

CONSERVATION

Specially protected. It is on the edge of its range in Britain and Ireland and there are no specific conservation measures other than protecting and keeping secret any pairs that attempt to breed.

DISTRIBUTION

Breeds in central and southern Europe, North Africa and east through Russia and Asia. European birds winter in central and southern Africa. The few birds that visit Britain or Ireland have usually overshot their normal breeding range and are generally in the south, although some have reached Shetland.

Kingfisher *Alcedo atthis*

INTERNATIONAL NAME COMMON KINGFISHER

IDENTIFICATION
16–17 cm. Size of a sparrow with large head and long dagger-like bill. Tail is short and wings broad and rounded. Underparts and cheeks are orange and upperparts electric blue or oily green depending on the light. Has a white throat and neck-patches. Male has an all-black bill and female has a red base to lower part of bill. Juvenile is duller and greener. Feathers are moulted gradually between July and November with the main flight feathers taking 90–100 days to moult and regrow. Some that moult late may suspend their moult during cold winter weather.

HABITS
Flight fast and straight, and often low over the water although it will fly higher when taking short cuts across land. Perches motionless when fishing or sometimes hovers before plunging into the water after a fish. Once prey has been caught it is taken to a perch and the bird may hit the fish until it is stunned before turning it in its bill and swallowing head first. Courtship involves high-speed chases. Despite its bright colours, its small size and rapid flight makes it hard to observe. The distinctive call is usually the best clue to its presence.

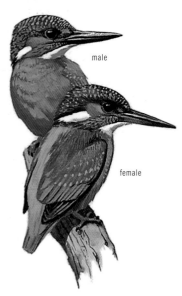

male

female

VOICE
Call is a shrill 'chreee' or a double note 'chee-kee'.

HABITAT
Breeds near water in lowland areas. Usual habitats are large, slow-flowing rivers and their tributaries, canals and lakes, especially with suitable banks for nesting and shallow edges for fishing. Also visits other smaller waters, including ornamental lakes and, sometimes, garden ponds. In winter, may visit estuaries.

FOOD
Feeds on fish and some aquatic insects. The most common fish are bullhead, loach, minnow, stickleback and small chub. Insects include mayflies, stoneflies, dragonfly nymphs and water beetles.

BREEDING
Birds pair in February or March. Breeding territory usually 1–1.5 km long. Nest is in a chamber at the end of a tunnel that is dug by both birds. Tunnel is dug into a vertical bank, usually, but not always, close to water. First clutches are laid in early April and there are normally 5–7 eggs. Eggs are incubated for 19–21 days by both sexes. Both sexes feed young until they leave nest at 23–27 days. Young become independent a few days after leaving nest and many pairs attempt to raise a second or even a third brood.

MOVEMENTS AND MIGRATIONS
British and Irish Kingfishers do not usually move very far unless forced out of their territories by hard weather. Juveniles disperse after becoming independent, but seldom travel more than 12 km from their original nest-site. Northern and eastern European populations are migratory and many winter around the Mediterranean. Oldest ringed bird was 21 years old.

POPULATION
In the UK there are 4,800–8,000 pairs and in Ireland 1,000–2,500. Population tends to be higher after mild winters and reduced after severe weather. Until about 1985 the Kingfisher was declining in Britain and its range shrinking; since then there has been a partial recovery.

CONSERVATION
Specially protected. It has declined in Europe and this is attributed to river pollution. To conserve this species the culverting of streams and rivers should stop and government agencies should continue to control polluters, including pollution from animal waste slurries and from silage clamps, which frequently finds its way into watercourses.

DISTRIBUTION
Found in lowland England, Wales, Ireland and southern Scotland. Most numerous in central and southern England and is gradually spreading north in Scotland. This race is also found in Europe east to the Caspian Sea and south to Spain. Other races are found in south-east Europe, North Africa and parts of Asia.

Bee-eater *Merops apiaster*

INTERNATIONAL NAME   EUROPEAN BEE-EATER

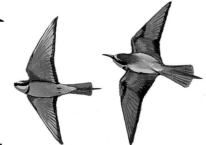

IDENTIFICATION

27–29 cm. Size of a Mistle Thrush. Slim colourful species with long pointed wings and a long tail with pointed feathers projecting from the centre. Upperparts graduate from chestnut on the crown to gold on the rump; throat is yellow; underparts and tail are blue-green, and cheeks blackish with white above the bill. In flight, wings are blue-green with golden patches on shoulders. Female tends to have greener rather than gold feathers on shoulders. Non-breeding plumage is much duller and with a blue-green back and no elongated central tail feathers. Juvenile resembles a non-breeding adult, but with less variation in the feather colours. Adults begin to moult in June or July and complete the process by August or September. There is a further moult into breeding plumage in winter in Africa.
SEE ALSO: Kingfisher p194.

HABITS

An aerial feeder with an undulating flight that also twists, turns and glides as it hunts flying insects. It frequently hunts from elevated perches such as wires and bare branches. When perched it appears upright, with pairs and family groups often perched close together. This is a sociable species that nests in colonies and feeds in groups. Larger flocks gather when migrating.

VOICE

A very vocal species that has a distinctive, far-carrying and rather liquid 'pruuk-pruik' that may have a trill-like quality when several birds are calling at the same time.

HABITAT

Generally associated with warm climates. Breeds in valleys and lowland areas with low intensive agricultural land, open fields, pastures, grasslands and steppe with scattered trees and sometimes near open water. In Britain it is mainly a rare passage migrant occurring in similar habitats, often near the coast. In Africa in winter it is found in savanna, plains and cultivated areas.

FOOD

Feeds on a wide variety of medium-sized flying insects, including bees and wasps that it takes back to a perch to remove the sting before devouring. Also eats ants, flies, beetles, butterflies and moths.

BREEDING

Very rarely breeds in Britain. The male selects a nest-site and both birds excavate a tunnel and nest chamber in a cliff or steep bank. The tunnel is 0.7–3.0 m long. Nest building takes 10–20 days and there is no nest material. The 4–7 eggs are incubated by both adults for about 20 days and begins with the first egg to be laid. The young leave the nest chamber at about 30 days and are fed by their parents for a few more days. The family appears to stay together at least until they migrate.

MOVEMENTS AND MIGRATIONS

Bee-eaters migrate by day. They move south on a broad front with some skirting around the Mediterranean and finding shortest sea-crossings. They also cross the Sahara Desert. They leave their breeding grounds soon after the young fledge and leave Europe during August and September. They return to their breeding sites in April and May.

POPULATION

In some years over 100 may visit Britain but there is considerable variation in numbers from year to year. Very occasionally a pair remains in Britain for the summer and attempts to nest.

CONSERVATION

The few pairs to breed in Britain have required special protection from egg thieves, vandals and accidental disturbance by the public, but natural predators such as foxes and Sparrowhawks are also a danger.

DISTRIBUTION

It breeds in southern Europe, North Africa and east into Russia and Asia. It also breeds in South Africa. It winters in Africa south of the Sahara.

Wryneck *Jynx torquilla*

INTERNATIONAL NAME EURASIAN WRYNECK

IDENTIFICATION

16–17 cm. Slightly larger than a House Sparrow. A slim bird with short legs and bill, a small head and a rather long tail. It is grey-brown with a dark brown arrow-shaped mark running from its crown and down its back. The plumage is delicately camouflaged with mottled upperparts and pale underparts that are finely barred. It has a warm buff throat that is barred with fine dark lines. The adult moults rapidly between July and September, although some moult continues in its winter quarters.
SEE ALSO: Nightjar p191.

HABITS

This is a shy relative of the woodpeckers, but much more like a small thrush in the way it behaves. It spends a lot of time feeding on the ground. Flight is generally low and undulating. On the ground it moves with jerky hops.

VOICE

The most usual call that is heard in spring at its breeding sites, and occasionally on migration, is a falcon-like 'quee, quee, quee', which is far-carrying and often the only indication that a pair is present.

MOVEMENTS AND MIGRATIONS

Most of these birds are migrants, while some around the Mediterranean are resident. It migrates on a broad front across Europe with most moving south between August and October and returning to their breeding areas between March and May. Those occurring in Britain are usually displaced breeding birds from Scandinavia. The oldest known bird survived over 10 years.

POPULATION

A progressive decline during the 20th century and now only one or two birds are occasionally seen in appropriate breeding habitat. Numbers of passage migrants vary considerably, with up to 300 individuals in some years.

CONSERVATION

A specially protected species. The traditional population that nested in south-east England is now extinct. A small breeding population was discovered in Scotland in 1969, but numbers remained low and they too may have ceased to breed in recent years. In Europe the population has fallen by 50%. The main problem appears to be shortage of feeding habitats close to suitable nest-sites, such as the loss of old pastures and their ant populations. Pesticides and other chemicals used on farmland may also have contributed to the lack of food.

HABITAT

The traditional habitat in Britain was once parkland, orchards and large mature gardens. More recently it colonised open pine and birch woods. In Europe the habitat varies from dry pine woods, clearings in woods and south-facing woodland margins.

FOOD

Ants form a large part of the diet of most Wrynecks, but they also eat beetles, grasshoppers, flies, butterflies, moths and spiders.

BREEDING

It usually nests in a hole in a tree, but may use a hole in a wall, a bank or even a nest box. No nest material is used and both sexes incubate the 7–10 eggs. The young hatch after 11–14 days and are fed by both parents. They fly after 18–22 days and continue to be fed by their parents for about a week. Usually one brood but can be two.

DISTRIBUTION

Passage migrants visit Britain and Ireland in spring and, particularly on the south and east coast, in autumn. The species breeds from Scandinavia south to North Africa and east into Asia. Most European Wrynecks winter in central Africa.

Green Woodpecker *Picus viridis*

INTERNATIONAL NAME   EUROPEAN GREEN WOODPECKER

IDENTIFICATION
31–33 cm. Size of a town pigeon. The largest of the British woodpeckers with a heavy-looking body, short tail and a strong, rather long bill. Green-grey upperparts, duller greyish underparts, vivid yellow-green rump and red crown. It has black around the eye. The 'moustache' mark of the male is dull red while that of the female is black. Juvenile is heavily spotted and barred. Flight deeply undulating as the bird closes its wings after 3–4 flaps. Moult takes place between June and November with the first flight feathers being lost around the time the young fledge. Juveniles moult quickly after fledging and gain their adult plumage between August and November.
SEE ALSO: Golden Oriole p268.

male

female

male

juvenile

HABITS
Spends a lot of time feeding on the ground where it moves in a series of hops. On the ground it often looks hunch-backed as it feeds, but adopts an upright posture when alert. On a tree trunk it will climb in a series of jerks with its stiff tail feathers pressed against the trunk for support. Often hides from an observer by moving behind the trunk or limb. Outside the breeding season it is generally solitary, although several individuals have been observed roosting together. Call is given from a regular song-post near the nest.

VOICE
Call is a ringing, laughing 'queu, queu, queu', and it also makes a feeble drumming.

HABITAT
Mainly a lowland species that breeds in open deciduous woods, parkland, orchards, farmland, heaths and, less often, conifer woods. Often feeds away from trees in open grassy areas such as pasture, downland and occasionally garden lawns where there are ants' nests.

FOOD
The woodpecker extracts insects from the nest chambers with its extremely long and sticky tongue. Diet consists chiefly of ants; as eggs, larvae, pupae and adults. Also eats beetles, flies and caterpillars.

BREEDING
Nests in mature trees, especially oak, ash and birch. Nest is at the bottom of a specially excavated chamber in a tree trunk or large limb, generally about 4 m from the ground. Diameter of hole is 6 cm and the nest chamber averages 28 cm deep. The 4–6 eggs are laid between March and mid-June. Incubation is by both adults and young hatch after about 19 days. Both parents feed the young, which fly after about 21 days and become independent after a further 3–7 weeks.

MOVEMENTS AND MIGRATIONS
Resident, with individuals seldom moving far from their original nest-site. Young birds may disperse in autumn and winter and exploit feeding areas away from woods and trees. Oldest known bird survived 15 years.

POPULATION
There are over 24,000 pairs breeding in the UK. In the 19th century it retreated from Scotland and northern England, but this was reversed in the 20th century, and Scotland has been recolonised since 1950. But while northern populations have been expanding there has been a decline in the south-west of England.

CONSERVATION
While this species has been increasing in most of Britain it has declined in parts of Europe. This decline is thought to be due to loss of nesting sites and the destruction of heaths and non-fertilised grasslands. The preservation of old and mature trees would help this species, as would improved conservation of traditional grasslands.

DISTRIBUTION
Breeds widely in England, Wales and southern Scotland, and it is most numerous in southern and central England. Does not occur in Ireland and north-west Scotland. Breeds from southern Scandinavia south to Mediterranean and east throughout Europe and into south-west Asia.

Great Spotted Woodpecker *Dendrocopos major*

IDENTIFICATION

22–23 cm. Similar in size to a Blackbird. A medium-sized black-and-white woodpecker with dirty-white underparts and crimson feathers under its short stiff tail. On its shoulders it has two large white patches with small white spots on the folded wings. The shoulder marks show as oval patches in flight. Male has a crimson patch on the back of head. Juvenile has duller white plumage and a red centre to its crown. Flight is bounding with wings closing after several flaps. Adults undergo a complete moult between June and November.

SEE ALSO: Lesser Spotted Woodpecker p199.

HABITS

Rarely seen on the ground. Generally solitary outside the breeding season. When danger threatens, it will spiral up a tree trunk or branch and often 'freezes' on the side facing away from the danger. When attacking food with tough shells it will wedge it in a crevice in a tree trunk or branch and hammer it open with its powerful bill. During courtship pairs engage in noisy chases among the trees.

VOICE

Sharp and loud 'kick kick' may be heard throughout the year and is often the best indication of the bird's presence. 'Song' is an instrumental sound made by drumming with its bill on a branch. The short bursts of drumming last around 5 seconds and accelerate before fading away at the end. Most drumming takes place in late winter and early spring.

HABITAT

Likely to be found almost anywhere there are trees, both in coniferous and deciduous woods – provided the trees are large enough to support the nest-holes. Some live in parks and large mature gardens in urban locations.

FOOD

Feeds mainly on insects in summer and seeds and nuts in winter. Eats a wide variety of insects, including adults and larvae of wood-boring beetles, which the woodpecker reaches by chipping away at dead wood and using its long tongue to reach into the insects' chambers. Will also create a hole in a nest box to reach the young birds inside, which it then eats or feeds to its own young. May visit bird tables and will frequently cling to hanging feeders.

male

BREEDING

Nesting begins in April. Both sexes excavate a nest chamber in a tree trunk or large branch. A variety of trees are used, but birches or oaks are most often selected. Hole is 5–6 cm in diameter and the average nest chamber is 28 cm deep. The 4–6 eggs are incubated by both parents for about 15 days. The young are fed by both adults and fly at about 20 days. After fledging, the adults continue to feed their young for a week or more.

MOVEMENTS AND MIGRATIONS

Young birds may travel a few kilometres from their nest-sites, but generally the species is resident. Young of northern European population 'erupts' in years when food is in short supply and some of these regularly reach Britain in autumn. Oldest 12 years.

POPULATION

There are 37,000–44,000 pairs breeding in Britain and the population is expanding, including a recent colonisation of Ireland, with a few pairs north and south of the border.

CONSERVATION

This woodpecker has been remarkably successful at the same time as the Lesser Spotted has declined. Undoubtedly it initially benefited from the dead wood resulting from Dutch elm disease, and more recently from food provided for garden birds.

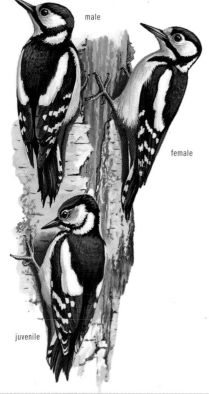

male

female

juvenile

DISTRIBUTION

Found throughout England, Wales and Scotland. Most numerous in the woodlands of southern England. A few in Ireland. Widespread in Europe, from the Arctic to the Mediterranean. It also breeds in North Africa and Asia.

Lesser Spotted Woodpecker *Dendrocopos minor*

IDENTIFICATION
14–15 cm. Our smallest woodpecker; size of a House Sparrow. Back and wings barred black and white; lacks the large white wing-patches of the Great Spotted Woodpecker. Underparts are off-white with fine dark streaks and it has no crimson feathers under its tail. Male has a dull red crown while the female's crown is dirty white. Juvenile has some red on the crown and browner, more streaked underparts. Flight is undulating with wings closing after several flaps. The complete annual moult takes place between June and September in adults.
SEE ALSO: Great Spotted Woodpecker p198.

male

female

HABITS
Difficult to observe as it spends much of the time among the dense foliage at the tops of trees, often feeding on slender outer branches or twigs and rarely feeding on the ground. Tends to creep along branches, unlike the jerky movements of the larger species. Flight is more fluttering than other woodpeckers, especially among the branches. When displaying in spring the male has a beautiful moth-like display flight. Mainly solitary outside the breeding season, but individuals will sometimes join tits and flocks of other small woodland birds in autumn and winter.

VOICE
Call is a shrill 'pee, pee, pee' rather like the weak call of a Kestrel. Drumming, heard from February to April and occasionally in autumn, is longer but more rattling and softer than that of the Great Spotted. It does not drop in pitch and fade away like Great Spotted. Alarm call is a quiet, soft 'kick'.

HABITAT
Breeds in lowland areas, in deciduous woodlands, parklands, orchards, shelter belts, isolated trees in hedgerows and riverside alders.

FOOD
Feeds mainly on insects, including both adults and larvae of beetles, especially those that live in wood, which the woodpecker reaches by chipping away and reaching into their chambers with its long tongue. Other insects include aphids, moths, ants, sawflies and the grubs of gall wasps. In autumn will also eat some soft fruit, such as pear.

BREEDING
Nest-hole is excavated by both sexes and may be in the branches of almost any deciduous tree, but especially birch and alder. The entrance hole is 3–3.5 cm and the average nest chamber is 10–18 cm deep. Nesting begins in April or May and 4–6 eggs are laid. Eggs are incubated by both sexes for 14–15 days with the male generally taking the night shift. The young are fed by both adults and leave the nest after 18–22 days.

MOVEMENTS AND MIGRATIONS
Resident. British birds seldom wander far from their nest-sites, but in autumn and winter they may disperse a relatively short distance in their search for food. Northern populations also tend to be nomadic in their search for winter food and some may be migratory. Oldest ringed bird was over 9 years old.

POPULATION
Thought to be between 1,400 and 2,900 pairs. Over the last 25 years there has been a decline of 85%, especially noticeable in the south-west of England and West Midlands.

CONSERVATION
Has been declining since around 1980. Research is needed as the reasons are unclear. Reductions in mature broadleaved woodland, losses of hedgerow trees such as elms, increases in woodland isolation and reductions of dead wood in woodland are all possible reasons for the decline.

DISTRIBUTION
In Britain found only in England and Wales and is most numerous in the south and the Midlands. It breeds from northern Scandinavia to the Mediterranean, with a few in North Africa. It also breeds from the Middle East to Japan.

Woodlark *Lullula arborea*

IDENTIFICATION
15 cm. Slightly smaller than a Skylark with shorter tail that is most obvious in flight. Has a short crest that may sometimes be raised, white stripes above the eyes that meet at the back of its head and plain rusty-coloured cheeks. Upperparts are mottled brown and underparts white with streaks on the breast. When perched, shows a small but distinctive black mark bordered with white on the edge of its wing. Tail is square-ended with small white corners, whereas the Skylark has obvious white sides. In flight, wings appear broad, but without the Skylark's pale whitish edge. Adult undergoes a complete moult between July and September.
SEE ALSO: Skylark p201, Tree Pipit p206.

HABITS
Flight rather slow and jerky, with undulations as it alternately flaps and glides. Feeds on the ground and perches on trees and bushes. Outside the breeding season it is found in family parties or larger flocks. Songflight of male consists of wide circles at a considerable height before it finally drops to the ground. Sometimes it sings from a tree or from the ground.

VOICE
Song may be heard by day or night from January until August, and especially between March and June. It also sings in the autumn. Song is attractive, sweeter and more musical than a Skylark's song and includes fluty 'lu-lu-lu' notes. Also a 'titloo-leet' flight or alarm call.

HABITAT
Breeds in open woodlands, young and recently felled plantations, and heaths where there are scattered trees and scrub. Requires areas of short grass for feeding. In winter feeds on farmland, often with Skylarks.

FOOD
In spring and summer mainly feeds on insects, including grasshoppers, thrips, moths, beetles and flies. At other times eats seeds from Scots pine, grasses and a variety of other plants. Young are fed on medium-sized insects.

BREEDING
Nesting starts early, sometimes with the first eggs laid before end of March. Nest is a cup on the ground lined with grasses and, often, hair. Both adults spend

1–2 days constructing 2–4 hollows, and female then lines one of these with vegetation. The 3–5 eggs are incubated by female for 12–15 days. Both adults feed young, which can fly after 10–13 days, although at first they cannot fly strongly. Families stay together for the summer and into the autumn. Two, sometimes three, broods a year.

MOVEMENTS AND MIGRATIONS
British birds leave their breeding sites during September and October and return between late January and March. Some apparently move to arable land in southern Britain, while others probably fly to the Continent. Some Woodlarks seen in eastern Britain in winter may be migrants from northern Europe.

POPULATION
Over 3,000 pairs now nest in Britain. This is a marked recovery from the 240 pairs in 1986.

CONSERVATION
Over much of Europe this species has declined due to loss and deterioration of dry grassland and heaths. In Britain it has been badly affected by cold winters, but recent mild winters have helped. The open, disturbed ground caused by trees being hit by storms, the clear-fell sites in commercial conifer forests and also improving heathland management are all helping this species to recover.

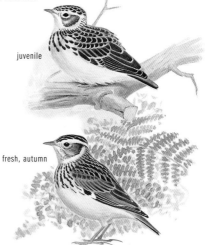

juvenile

fresh, autumn

DISTRIBUTION
British population has recently spread from traditional stronghold in the south and east into parts of English midlands and a few birds now breed as far north as Yorkshire. In Europe breeds from southern Scandinavia to the Mediterranean and east into Russia and Asia. Also breeds in North Africa. Northern and eastern populations winter in southern Europe and North Africa.

Skylark *Alauda arvensis*

INTERNATIONAL NAME   EURASIAN SKYLARK

IDENTIFICATION
18–19 cm. Larger than a sparrow, but smaller than a Starling. Has a short crest that may be raised or lowered. Back is brown with darker streaks, breast streaked, underparts are off-white and tail has white outer feathers. In flight, broad wings have obvious pale trailing edge. Crest and tail are both longer than those of Woodlark but pale stripe over eye is less prominent. Juvenile looks more scaly. Skylarks undergo a complete moult between July and September with the flight feathers being lost and regrown over a period of about 58 days.
SEE ALSO: Woodlark p200, Meadow Pipit p207.

HABITS
Spends most of its time on the ground and crouches when nervous. Will also land on posts and other low perches. On taking off, its flight is fluttering. Its direct flight is slightly floppy and undulating, with rapid flaps followed by a glide. Songflight begins as it rises steeply and hangs in the air over its territory, gradually getting higher until it is sometimes lost to human view. Parachutes down with an extra rapid descent for the last few metres. Generally flocks outside the breeding season, and in winter these may attract hundreds of birds.

VOICE
Chief call is a loud 'chirrup' often given in flight or when it is alarmed. Song is a long pleasant liquid warbling, usually given in flight, but sometimes from a perch or from the ground.

HABITAT
Breeds in open grassland in uplands, on heaths and on coastal marshes. Also associated with cultivated land, especially set-aside, ungrazed grassland and large arable fields, often without hedges and other cover. In winter, gathers on arable fields, unploughed stubble and saltmarshes.

FOOD
Feeds on both plant and animal material. Invertebrates include springtails, flies, bugs, beetles, moths, spiders, slugs and snails. Plant food includes grain, and also seeds and leaves of a wide variety of plants, including nettles and docks.

BREEDING
Nesting begins in late March or April. Site is usually amongst short vegetation and nest is in a shallow depression lined with grass. The 3 or 4 eggs are incubated by the female for 10–14 days. Both parents feed

fresh, autumn

young. They leave the nest after about 8 days and fly after 16 days, but are cared for by their parents for up to 10 days after fledging. Up to three broods may be raised in a season.

MOVEMENTS AND MIGRATIONS
Northern populations are migratory while those further south are mainly resident. British and Irish birds move down from upland areas but do not move far. Others are resident. Skylarks from northern and eastern Europe arrive in Britain in October and begin to return in January. Oldest ringed bird survived over 9 years.

POPULATION
1.7 million pairs nest in the UK and over 250,000 in Ireland. The UK population has fallen by over 50% in recent years.

CONSERVATION
The largest decline was from the mid-1970s until the mid-1980s and it continues in England. There are several reasons: the move to autumn-sown cereals results in spring growth that is too dense for nesting, fewer winter stubble fields, an increase in pesticide use, increased grazing pressures and cutting of grass early (often for silage). Solutions involve incentives for farmers for planting spring-sown crops, special grant aid and small bare 'skylark patches' left in cereal fields.

juvenile

DISTRIBUTION
Breeds throughout Britain and Ireland. In winter, largest numbers are to be found in the south and east. In Europe breeds from northern Scandinavia to the Mediterranean and east into central Russia. There are other races in southern Europe, North Africa and Asia.

Shore Lark *Eremophila alpestris*

INTERNATIONAL NAME   HORNED LARK

IDENTIFICATION

14–17 cm. Smaller and slimmer than a Skylark. Has a pinkish-brown streaked back, pale almost unstreaked underparts, boldly patterned yellow and black face and black throat. Adult male has black band on forehead ending with two small 'horns' on top of rear crown. Face markings of female have less contrast and both sexes are poorly marked in autumn and early winter. Juvenile moults before arriving in Britain but is more spotted on its back, more streaked on its underparts and with a less distinct face pattern. Complete moult takes place between June and September. After moult the face pattern becomes obscured as new feathers have yellow fringes. These fringes abrade (wear off) during the winter revealing the bold black and yellow spring breeding plumage.
SEE ALSO: Skylark p201, Reed Bunting p300.

male

HABITS

Feeds on ground in open, head down, slightly hunched or crouched and either shuffles along or makes small hops. Feeding flocks are constantly on the move. Although it will often allow a close approach, it can be difficult to observe, owing to its excellent camouflage. In winter, usually seen in small flocks, sometimes with Snow or Lapland Buntings. In flight, has a more bounding flight than a Skylark.

VOICE

Voice in its winter flocks is a shrill 'tsee-tsi'. On breeding grounds has a warbling Skylark-like song usually given in flight.

HABITAT

In Britain mainly seen near the coast, often feeding along the strand line, or on coastal grazing marsh, dune systems or stubble fields near the sea. Breeding grounds are in mountains above the treeline and on Arctic tundra. Other races have adapted to living on prairies, deserts and ploughed fields, habitats similar to those used by the Skylark. In Britain a few pairs have attempted to breed on the stony tops of northern mountains.

FOOD

In summer, feeds on insects and some seeds. In winter, feeds mainly on seeds. Insect food includes springtails, flies and beetles. Plant food includes grain and seeds from sedges, grasses and docks.

BREEDING

Nest is on the ground, often in the open amongst short vegetation, in a depression built by the female. Female incubates 3 or 4 eggs for 10–11 days. Young are cared for and fed by both adults. They leave the nest at 9–12 days but do not fly until 16–18 days. There can be one or two broods.

MOVEMENTS AND MIGRATIONS

Northern races are migratory while southern birds are largely resident. In Britain most birds arrive in October and November and return in March. Northern birds fly south through Sweden, Denmark and Germany and then cross the North Sea, which accounts for main arrival being in East Anglia. Oldest ringed bird survived over 7 years.

POPULATION

Regular wintering was unknown before 1870, now 200–300 individuals winter in Britain. Numbers appear to be increasing generally. Single pairs occasionally seen in suitable breeding habitats in summer and at least one pair nested in 1977. In northern Europe there has been a gradual expansion of the population.

CONSERVATION

A specially protected species, ensuring full protection if there are further attempts to nest in Britain. Secrecy to prevent nest robbery or disturbance is the key conservation measure if nesting is suspected again.

female
(fresh, autumn)

DISTRIBUTION

Wintering birds mainly visit the east coast of Britain and are rare inland. Only breeding attempts have been in Scotland. In Europe breeds in the mountains of Scandinavia and on the Arctic tundra. Other races are found in south-east Europe, Asia and North America. It is possible that some west-coast birds – especially in Ireland – are of one of the North American races.

Sand Martin _Riparia riparia_

IDENTIFICATION

12 cm. Smaller than a Swallow and slimmer than a House Martin. Tail is only slightly forked. Upperparts uniform brown and underparts white with distinct brown band across breast. Wings are pointed and often appear narrower than those of a House Martin. Juvenile has pale edges to back feathers, giving a less uniform appearance and the breast-band is less distinct. Adults start to moult between July and September, as they finish nesting, and continue during the early stages of migration, but moult may be suspended until the bird reaches Africa.

SEE ALSO: Swallow p204, House Martin p205.

HABITS

Breeds in small or large colonies and many feed together at suitable sites. Often migrates in flocks and gathers in large evening roosts. Flight is fast and agile, but looks weaker and less graceful than a Swallow and glides less often. Feeds by catching insects in the air. Often perches on wires.

VOICE

Song is a harsh rattling or twittering, given frequently in flight and also when perched. The song is usually associated with courtship, but is also heard at other times.

HABITAT

Depends on vertical sandy banks for nesting. These sites are usually close to rivers or sand or gravel quarries. Feeds over open country and especially over water, and tends to avoid built-up areas, woods and mountains. On migration flocks roost in reedbeds.

FOOD

Feeds on insects that it catches in flight, especially midges, flies and aphids, but a wide variety of other insects are eaten. When feeding nestlings, many insects are caught in a single foraging flight and the mass is brought back and fed to the young.

BREEDING

Older birds return to colonies first. The nest is in a hole in a bank and occasionally in an artificial site such as a drainpipe. Both adults excavate a 35–120 cm tunnel with a chamber at the end that contains a nest of grass and feathers. Both birds incubate the 4 or 5 eggs for 14–15 days. The young are cared for by both adults and leave the nest at about 22 days. In years with good weather, a second brood is reared. If the survival of the first brood is poor the female may leave the young for the male to feed. She may pair with a new mate and start a second family. Males, too, may change mates after the young become independent.

MOVEMENTS AND MIGRATIONS

One of the earliest migrants to return to Britain and Ireland in spring, arriving in March and April. Young from first broods leave their colonies after fledging in June and generally spend several weeks exploring a wide area, often visiting other colonies and gathering at communal roosts. In August adults and juveniles head south-east to make the shortest sea-crossing across the Channel and then fly on to Africa, crossing the Sahara Desert. In winter they may be nomadic, moving east before returning north in February and March. Oldest bird survived 10 years.

POPULATION

There are 85,000–270,000 pairs in the UK and 100,000–250,000 in Ireland. The population appears to fluctuate from year to year. There were population crashes in 1969 and 1984, from which there was a partial recovery, but numbers are again falling.

CONSERVATION

The population crashes in the 20th century have been linked to drought conditions in its wintering areas in Africa, which may be caused by overgrazing and by climate change. In Europe the protection of breeding colonies and management of river systems to provide nest-sites will help this species.

DISTRIBUTION

Colonies are found throughout Britain and Ireland, where there are suitable banks. Found throughout most of Europe, Asia and North America. Winters in Africa.

Swallow *Hirundo rustica*

INTERNATIONAL NAME   BARN SWALLOW

IDENTIFICATION

17–19 cm. Smaller than a Swift. Has a small broad bill, long pointed wings (usually), long tail-streamers and white spots on underside of deeply forked tail. Upperparts are iridescent blue-black, underparts are off-white, face is reddish-brown and it has a blue-black chest-band. In spring tail-streamers of male are noticeably longer than those of female. Juvenile has much shorter tail-streamers and browner, less shiny feathers. Flight is strong and agile with frequent swoops and glides when feeding. Moult is slow so as not to interfere with ability to hunt. Moult starts in September and most birds moult while in Africa.

SEE ALSO: House Martin p205, Sand Martin p203, Swift p192.

HABITS

Although much time is spent on the wing, frequently perches on wires and other prominent perches. Also lands on the ground, especially when gathering nest material. Flight usually low as it catches its prey on the wing or snatches food from the surface of the water. Often nest in small groups and flocks gather from July onwards.

VOICE

The alarm call is a loud 'tswit', which is often given in flight. The song is a hurried dry twittering trill.

MOVEMENTS AND MIGRATIONS

A migrant that arrives mainly in April. First juveniles disperse in various directions during July. In September they move south with most having left Britain by early November. Migrates by day, feeding as it flies, and roosts at traditional sites. Autumn migration takes about 6 weeks and is on a broad front, including crossing the Sahara Desert. The return takes about 4 weeks. Oldest known Swallow was 11 years.

juvenile

HABITAT

Breeds in open country where there is abundant food, safe nest-sites and usually some water. In Britain and Ireland it is a bird of open rural countryside and it breeds in upland and lowland areas, but seldom ventures into towns. It feeds wherever food is plentiful: over water, around cattle, over manure heaps and along hedgerows where insects gather. In Africa it is nomadic as it searches out supplies of food. Migrants roost in reedbeds.

FOOD

Feeds almost exclusively on flying insects. The large range includes bluebottles, house flies, bees, hoverflies, mayflies, aphids and flying ants. Even moth caterpillars hanging from trees are snapped up. A brood of Swallows needs 6,000 flies a day to survive.

BREEDING

Nesting begins in April or May. Older birds return first; males before females. Nests in barns and other buildings (not under eaves like the House Martin). Nest cup is built by both sexes from mud and lined with feathers and grass. Previous year's nests are frequently reused. For about 18 days the female incubates 4 or 5 eggs. Young fly after 18–23 days and are fed for a further week. Two, sometimes three, broods.

POPULATION

There are 726,000 pairs in the UK and 100,000–250,000 in Ireland. Population declining in parts of its range.

CONSERVATION

Population fluctuations appear to be related to changes in Africa. In Britain and Ireland the loss of traditional nest-sites, such as old barns, and food availability owing to changing farming practices cause concern for the future.

DISTRIBUTION

Found throughout Britain and Ireland, but scarcer in the far north of Scotland. Breeds in Europe, North Africa, Asia and North America. European birds winter in Africa and British and Irish birds travel to South Africa. North American birds winter in South America.

House Martin *Delichon urbica*

INTERNATIONAL NAME   COMMON HOUSE MARTIN

IDENTIFICATION

12.5 cm. Smaller than a Swallow. Small, plump, aerial feeder with broad, rather short, pointed wings and a forked tail. It is blue-black above, pure white below with an obvious white rump. It lacks both the breast-band of a Sand Martin and the tail-streamers of a Swallow. Its tiny legs and feet are covered with white feathers. Juvenile is browner than the adult. Flight is less agile than that of a Swallow; it is fast, direct but with fewer twists and turns and is rather more fluttery. The prolonged adult moult takes places mostly in Africa, all the feathers being replaced between late October and March.
SEE ALSO: Swallow p204, Sand Martin p203.

HABITS

Most of the time is spent in the air and it often feeds at higher levels than the Swallow. It seldom lands on the ground except to gather nest material but frequently perches on wires, roofs and other prominent objects. It is a sociable species, inclined to nest in loose colonies and feed and migrate in small flocks. Large numbers will sometimes gather at migration times. Outside the breeding season it roosts in trees and is also suspected of sleeping on the wing at high altitudes.

VOICE

The main call is a hard 'prrit' and the song is a soft twittering that is heard during the summer.

HABITAT

Found in towns and villages throughout Britain and Ireland and in some places it nests on cliffs – especially sea cliffs. Tends to avoid city centres and is most abundant in lowland agricultural areas.

It migrates on a broad front, but the whereabouts of the main wintering grounds in Africa are uncertain. The oldest ringed bird survived over 14 years.

POPULATION

There are between 273,000 and 535,000 pairs breeding in the UK and between 20,000 and 100,000 in Ireland. In Britain the population has fallen by 45% in the last 25 years and it is also declining in parts of Europe.

CONSERVATION

As most House Martins have adapted to nesting on houses their nest-sites depend on the cooperation of the property owner. Although nests and eggs are protected, ignorance and prejudice result in nests being knocked down. Birds that have to rebuild are less likely to rear two broods in a summer, and therefore produce fewer young.

juvenile

FOOD

Feeds almost entirely on flying insects. Its prey includes aphids, gnats, flies, beetles and ants.

BREEDING

Nesting begins in late April or May. Both adults build the cup-shaped mud nest on the outer walls of buildings, especially under the eaves of houses. A few use traditional cliffs, either inland or by the sea. Old nests are reused or, if necessary, repaired. Nesting tends to be in colonies and sometimes several nests are built side by side. Both adults incubate the 4 or 5 eggs for 14–16 days and both care for the young. From about 15 days the parents and other House Martins attempt to lure the young from the nest. The young will continue to roost in the nest and are fed by their parents after their initial flight. Two broods in a season, with late broods still in the nest in October.

MOVEMENTS AND MIGRATIONS

A summer migrant to Britain and Ireland that returns in April and May and leaves between August and October.

DISTRIBUTION

Found in most parts of Britain and Ireland, although much scarcer in the north and west of Scotland and western Ireland. The species breeds throughout Europe and also in Asia and North Africa. European birds winter in Africa where it is most often seen in the central highlands, but is probably distributed across central and southern Africa.

Tree Pipit *Anthus trivialis*

IDENTIFICATION

15 cm. Smaller than a Skylark. Similar to the usually more common Meadow Pipit, but a little larger and sleeker with a heavier bill, much finer and thinner streaks on the flanks, more prominent head marks, sometimes a more obvious pale stripe over its eye and a different flight call. Has dark olive-brown streaked upperparts, a yellowish breast that is lightly marked with large streaks, fine streaking on the flanks and a white belly. Legs are flesh-coloured. Both Tree and Meadow Pipits have white outer tail feathers. In late summer in worn plumage it becomes drabber. Adults have a complete moult between June and September and a partial moult in winter quarters, before return migration.

SEE ALSO: Meadow Pipit p207, Skylark p201.

songflight

HABITS

Unlike the Meadow Pipit it frequently perches on trees and bushes. Songflight starts with a bird taking off from a prominent branch or other perch, singing as it rises at about 60 degrees and then parachuting down with legs dangling to land on the same or a nearby perch. Regularly feeds on the ground, where it moves with greater determination, rather than the jerky movements of the Meadow Pipit. If disturbed it takes off steeply and circles before landing on the ground or on a tree or bush. Not a particularly sociable species, but small groups may form on migration.

VOICE

The call is a sharp 'teeze', often given in flight. Song may be given from a perch or during an obvious song-flight. Generally the bird sings as it rises. Song is a series of single notes and trills 'zit, zit, zit, wich, wich' and ending with 'swee-u, swee-u' as the bird lands.

pairs raise a second brood and some males defend two territories.

MOVEMENTS AND MIGRATIONS

Returns to Britain in April and May and leaves again in late summer. Others from northern Europe reach Britain on passage. From Britain most appear to fly direct to Portugal where they pause before migrating into Africa. The oldest ringed bird was more than 8 years old.

POPULATION

Thought to be 74,000 pairs of Tree Pipits breeding in Britain. The population has declined by over 80% in recent years, especially in southern England.

CONSERVATION

The causes of the recent decline are unclear, but may be linked to many of our forests maturing and also increased grazing pressure in some breeding habitats. Recent research has shown that breeding performance has improved with an increase in brood size and fewer nest failures during incubation.

summer   juvenile

summer (fresh, spring)

HABITAT

Breeds on heathland, in open woodland and near woodland edges, in young conifer plantations and in areas of forests that have been recently cleared. Uses open areas with bushes as long as there are older trees for song posts. Prefers old woodland and deciduous trees. In winter in Africa it lives in similar habitats, including savanna.

FOOD

Mainly feeds on invertebrates especially weevils, beetles, caterpillars, ants, spiders and a wide variety of insects. Also eats some plant material such as seeds and berries.

BREEDING

Nests on the ground among low cover in a nest in a depression made by the female. The normal clutch of 4 or 5 eggs is incubated by the female, although both adults feed the young. Young fly at 12–14 days, but generally leave the nest before they can fly. Some

DISTRIBUTION

Locally common in southern England and is most numerous in mainland Scotland and Wales, but rarely breeds in Ireland. Breeds from northern Scandinavia to northern Spain and Greece and east into Asia, where there are other races. Most European birds winter in tropical Africa, but some winter on Greek islands.

Meadow Pipit *Anthus pratensis*

IDENTIFICATION
14.5 cm. Smaller than a Skylark and also slightly small-er than a Tree Pipit, with finer bill and distinctive call. Upperparts are olive-brown with darker streaks. Face is relatively plain, sometimes with a small pale stripe over the eye. The bold streaks and spots on the greyish or yellowish breast continue at the same thickness along the flanks. Belly and outer tail feathers are white. Juvenile is more pinkish-buff than adult in late summer and lacks the dark streaks on flanks. Adults moult between July and September, with flight feath-ers being lost and regrown over about 50 days. Partial moult before breeding.
SEE ALSO: Skylark p201, Tree Pipit p206, Dunnock p215.

summer

HABITS
Songflight generally starts from the ground and con-tinues as the bird rises and parachutes down on half-spread wings. In suitable habitats the population may be high, but it is not colonial. Outside the breeding season it is commonly in loose flocks, sometimes feed-ing alongside Skylarks. Feeds on the ground, and on migration and in winter it seldom perches on vegeta-tion, but on its breeding territories it is more likely to perch on prominent plants. On the ground it may sometimes appear quite upright, and it moves with jerky movements.

VOICE
In flight it usually strings three calls together, 'sweet-sweet-sweet'. Song is given during the aerial display and is a series of plaintive and accelerating 'seep, seep' followed by repeated 'tseut, tseut' and ending with a trill.

HABITAT
Breeds in open country, especially upland moors where it is usually the most abundant species, also on lowland heaths, downland, saltmarshes, rough grass-lands and dune systems. In winter it feeds on agricul-tural land, including ploughed fields, coastal marshes and along the edges of lakes and rivers.

FOOD
Eats mainly invertebrates including flies, especially craneflies (daddy-long-legs) and mayflies, and also beetles, moths and spiders and also some seeds.

BREEDING
Nesting begins in late March in lowland areas and is later in the uplands. Female builds the nest on the ground amongst vegetation. Usually 4 or 5 eggs that are incubated for 13 days, mostly by the female. Both parents feed the young, which fly between 10 and 14 days. The young usually leave the nest before they are able to fly. At least two broods are usually raised.

MOVEMENTS AND MIGRATIONS
This species is both a resident and a migrant. It is found in Britain at all seasons. Breeding birds start to leave their upland territories in August. Some leave the country, but many do not travel far and winter in lower areas within Britain. Also, in autumn, Scandina-vian birds reach Britain and, later, others from Green-land and Iceland arrive, especially in Ireland. Return migration takes place in March and April. Oldest wild bird survived 7 years.

POPULATION
Estimated to be 1.7 million pairs in the UK and over half a million in Ireland. There has been a recent decline of over 40% in the UK population.

CONSERVATION
Once it was even more common than it is today. The recent losses in southern Britain have been linked to changes in land use, loss of marginal land for nesting and agricultural changes on its wintering grounds.

juvenile

winter
(fresh, autumn)

song flight

DISTRIBUTION
This is a widespread breeding species in Britain and Ireland, but is most abundant in the west and north. In winter, it is also widespread, and the largest numbers are in lowland areas in the south and west of Britain and Ireland. It breeds in northern Europe, as far south as France and east into Russia, Siberia and western Asia. It also nests in Iceland and eastern Greenland.

Water Pipit *Anthus spinoletta*

IDENTIFICATION
16.5–17 cm. A large and stocky pipit; similar in size to a Rock Pipit, but with whiter flanks and belly, clearer streaks on the underparts and bolder, whiter wing-bars. The legs are dark. It has white (not grey) outer tail feathers and a bold pale stripe over its eye. In spring and summer its head is grey, the back is brown and almost unmarked and the unstreaked breast has a pink flush. In winter, it is more like a Rock Pipit, but browner with whiter underparts, and with a more obvious pale stripe over its eye. Juvenile is like an adult in winter, but with a more streaky back. It moults between July and September and has a second partial moult into breeding plumage between January and March.
SEE ALSO: Rock Pipit p209, Meadow Pipit p207, Yellow Wagtail p210.

their caterpillars, spiders, centipedes, beetles and bees. It also eats some seeds and berries.

BREEDING
This species does not breed in Britain or Ireland. The female builds a nest on the ground and the male may help gather some material for the lining. There are 4 or 5 eggs that are incubated by the female for 14–15 days. The young are cared for by both parents and fly at 15–16 days old. It can have two broods in a year.

MOVEMENTS AND MIGRATIONS
In Britain it is a winter visitor seen mainly between October and April. In other countries it can be a migrant or a resident, or even a partial migrant. In autumn, those that breed in the mountains descend to the lowlands. This altitudinal migration may be in

summer

winter

HABITS
This is a much shyer bird than a Rock Pipit, and if disturbed it tends to take off quickly, tower high and land a considerable distance away. It may be solitary or occur in small loose flocks. Outside the breeding season it roosts communally in dense vegetation in damp or wet places. On its breeding grounds it may sing on the ground, but generally takes off from a rock, bush or from the ground and sings as it rises, circles and parachutes down – similar to the Meadow Pipit.

VOICE
Call is intermediate between the Meadow and Rock Pipit, a loud 'weest'. The song (unusual in Britain) is louder and slightly more musical than a Meadow Pipit.

HABITAT
Although seen in small numbers around the coast, it is much more likely to be seen inland. In winter in Britain it visits wetland sites such as inland marshes, watercress beds, river banks and wet places above coastal saltmarsh. It breeds in mountains in southern Europe and Asia Minor, high up in treeless, barren meadows and rock fields up to at least 2,600 m.

FOOD
It eats mainly invertebrates and also some plant mate-rial. Animal food includes springtails, flies, moths and

any direction, even northwards. Many, however, make longer journeys south-west, with birds from eastern Europe being seen in Spain.

POPULATION
Fewer than 100 individuals may visit Britain in winter.

CONSERVATION
There are no special threats to this species nor any particular conservation measures.

DISTRIBUTION
Until recently the Water Pipit was regarded as a race of the Rock Pipit, but these are now split into two separate species (along with a third species known as the Buff-bellied Pipit, which breeds in North America and north-east Siberia). The Water Pipit is a scarce visitor to southern and eastern England. It breeds in central and south-eastern Europe and also in parts of Asia. In winter, many fly north of their breeding sites.

Rock Pipit *Anthus petrosus*

INTERNATIONAL NAME EURASIAN ROCK PIPIT

IDENTIFICATION

16.5–17 cm. Larger
and darker than a Meadow
Pipit and smaller than a Starling.
A large, stocky pipit that has dusky
olive-brown upperparts with darker streaks
that are not as well defined as on the smaller pipits.
The underparts are dirty white with dark streaking.
Its legs and bill are dark and the outer tail feathers
dirty grey. It has a broken pale stripe over its eye.
In winter it becomes duskier and with less contrast in
its plumage. The young are more streaked than the
adults. The northern race (*littoralis*) is cleaner-looking
with a more prominent stripe over the eye and plainer
underparts. Adults moult between June and September
and the flight feathers are moulted and regrow
within 42 days.
SEE ALSO: Water Pipit p208, Meadow Pipit p207, Skylark p201.

HABITS

It hops, walks and runs as it forages for food among
rocks and boulders, and it frequently perches on
prominent rocks. It has a songflight that is similar
to other pipits, involving a steep aerial climb and a
parachuting flight down on half-closed wings. It is
fairly tame and can be approached
more easily than most other pipits. Many birds retain their territories throughout the year, but
some form small groups during
the winter.

VOICE

The call is 'pseep', more metallic
and less squeaky than a Meadow Pipit
and often given singly. The song is similar
to that of a Meadow Pipit, but is stronger and
with a more obvious trill. The song is mainly heard
between March and July.

HABITAT

It breeds along the rocky shorelines and on small
islands around the coasts of Britain and Ireland where
there are cliffs and rock-strewn beaches, and it avoids
sandy beaches. It is rare inland.

FOOD

It feeds mainly on invertebrates that it finds on the
ground, by foraging in the tidewrack on sandy beaches. Food includes flies and midges and their larvae,
beetles, fish, small shellfish and seeds.

BREEDING

Nesting begins in April. The female builds the nest in
a hole or a hollow in a cliff. The nest includes some
seaweed in the lining. The usual clutch is 4 or 5 eggs
and most of the incubation is by the female with the
male helping only occasionally. The eggs hatch after
14–15 days and the young are fed by both parents.
They leave the nest after 12 days. There are usually
two broods in a summer.

MOVEMENTS AND MIGRATIONS

Most of the Rock Pipits breeding around the
coasts of Britain and Ireland are resident, and
young only disperse locally after becoming
independent. Northern populations are
migratory and some of the northern race
(*littoralis*), from Norway, moves south in
winter through Europe. Some of these birds
arrive along the east coast of Britain in the
autumn and return in March or April.

POPULATION

There are over 35,000 pairs in the UK and
10,000–20,000 in Ireland.

CONSERVATION

This species has ceased to breed in a few locations in
recent years, especially in the south-west of Britain.
Other populations fluctuate, but overall it appears to
be declining in Britain. Disturbance to nesting birds on
popular holiday beaches is one problem for this bird.

summer *littoralis*

It is found around the British and Irish
coasts and is missing only from the
Humber to the Isle of Wight, owing
to the absence of rocky beaches,
but even this stretch is broken by
a small population around the
boulders under Beachy Head
in East Sussex. The species
also breeds on rocky coasts
in other parts of western
and northern Europe,
from northern France to
northern Norway, north
of the Arctic Circle.

Yellow Wagtail *Motacilla flava*

IDENTIFICATION

17 cm. Smaller and sleeker than a Pied Wagtail, with a shorter tail. Adult males in summer have bright yellow underparts and faces, olive-green upperparts and brownish wings. Head colours, markings and the intensity of the colours vary between geographical races. British race has a mainly yellow head while the nearest other race in Europe is the Blue-headed Wagtail, which is occasionally seen in Britain. Adult female is duller with browner back, pale throat and pale stripe above eye. Juvenile is like female, but with dark necklace and pale streak on cheek, below eye. Annual moult between July and September may not be completed before migration. Has a further partial moult in Africa between January and April.
SEE ALSO: Grey Wagtail p211, Pied Wagtail p212, Water Pipit p208.

HABITS

Frequently follows cattle and other large animals in its search for food. Like other wagtails it runs or walks with its head moving backwards and forwards and its tail pumping up and down. Sometimes flutters into the air to catch insects. Normal flight is in long undulating curves. Regularly perches on vegetation, posts or wires. Territorial when nesting, but flocks form in late summer and loose parties migrate together. Often large numbers gather at roost sites.

VOICE

Call is a loud 'psweep' that is given in flight and from a perch. Sings from May until July. Song is a variation on the call, interspersed with a rather feeble warble.

HABITAT

Breeds in lowland pastures, water meadows, marshes, riversides and arable fields, including those growing potatoes and peas. Some, but not all, breed near water. On migration, visits areas of short grass, such as playing fields. In winter, visits paddy fields and marshes.

male summer

female summer.

juvenile

FOOD

Feeds on small invertebrates, including flies and beetles in summer. Many of the flies are caught around the feet or dung of farm stock.

BREEDING

Nesting begins in April. Female builds a cup-shaped nest on the ground amongst vegetation. Made from grass and lined with hair, wool or fur. Both adults share the incubation of the 4–6 eggs for about 14 days, and both feed the young. The young leave the nest at about 11 days and fly 5 days later. They stay with their parents after fledging and may begin their migration as a family. There is sometimes a second brood.

MOVEMENTS AND MIGRATIONS

Arrives in Britain between late March and mid-May, with the males returning first. In August and September it migrates first to south-west France and then to Portugal. Some fly across the Bay of Biscay to Spain. From Spain a few fly to North Africa, but others probably fly on across the Sahara Desert. They return by a more easterly route, crossing the Sahara in a single flight, perhaps lasting 72 hours. Oldest bird survived over 8 years.

POPULATION

There are estimated to be 11,500–26,500 territories in Britain. Does not breed in Ireland. Rapid decline of over 70% in recent years.

CONSERVATION

Although birds will nest in crops, early cutting may reduce their success. The loss of mixed farming, land drainage, conversion of pastures to arable and changes in farming practice, including higher stocking densities, are all possible causes for the recent decline as is climate change linked to changes to habitats in Africa.

DISTRIBUTION

In Britain breeds mainly in central and eastern England, with some in eastern Wales and southern Scotland. The race that breeds in Britain (*flavissima*) also breeds in parts of western Europe. Other races breed from northern Scandinavia to North Africa and east across Russia and Asia. European birds winter in central and southern Africa.

Grey Wagtail *Motacilla cinerea*

male summer

female summer

IDENTIFICATION
18–19 cm. Similar size to a Pied Wagtail. Graceful, long-bodied bird with a very long tail that is constantly moving. All have bright egg-yellow under the tail. Male has a yellow breast, blue-grey upperparts, white stripe over eye and black throat. Female has pale throat with only, usually, a few dark feathers. In winter, eye-stripe of male becomes less obvious, throat becomes pale and yellow breast is paler. Juvenile resembles a female but with buffer underparts. Flight is bounding, in deep curves. Moults between July and September and has a second, partial moult into its breeding plumage in February and March.
SEE ALSO: Yellow Wagtail p210.

HABITS
Usually seen singly or in pairs. Undulating flight is often low before perching on boulders in water, although it sometimes perches on overhanging trees and bushes. Distinctive songflight during which male parachutes down from a high perch on open and fluttering wings. Some Grey Wagtails defend a winter territory.

VOICE
Usual call is a loud, hard, sharp 'tswick' that is shorter than the Pied Wagtail. Song, heard mainly between March and May, is a quiet trilling and quite melodious, given in flight or when perched.

HABITAT
In summer, typically found in upland areas near fast-flowing water bordered by trees and where there are rocks and open ground such as shingle banks. In winter, it leaves the highest ground and visits a wider variety of habitats, including water treatment works, farmyards, ornamental ponds, canals, lowland rivers and streams, coastal areas and even city centres close to water.

FOOD
Feeds mainly on insects and other invertebrates that it picks up from the ground, from shallow water or snatches in the air. Insects include midges, stoneflies, mayflies, beetles and ants. Other prey includes spiders, small water snails, freshwater shrimps and tadpoles.

BREEDING
Nesting may begin late March, but mostly in April or May. Nest is built in a hole or crevice in a wall, bank or other protected site such as under a bridge or among tree roots. Both sexes build the outer structure of grasses, small twigs and roots and the female lines it with moss and hair. Incubation of the 4–6 eggs is by both sexes and lasts for 11–14 days. Young fly after

13–15 days and are dependent on their parents for a further 2 weeks, and they may return to their nest to roost. In some places it has a second brood.

MOVEMENTS AND MIGRATIONS
Most British and Irish breeding birds do not migrate, but stay within the British Isles and disperse from their upland breeding territories. Northern European breeding birds travel farthest; some of them reach southern Europe and North Africa and some of these may arrive in southern Britain in winter. Oldest wild bird was 8 years old.

POPULATION
There are over 38,000 pairs breeding in the UK and over 10,000 in Ireland. Declined in the 1970s and, despite some local recoveries, is still over 25% lower.

CONSERVATION
In recent years fluctuations in numbers have tended to reflect the relative severity of winter weather, the population falling after cold spells, but recovering again.

juvenile

DISTRIBUTION
It is widespread in Britain and Ireland, although scarce in eastern England in summer. It is most abundant in the uplands of the north and west. In winter, it retreats from most upland and northern areas and is most abundant in the south-west. It breeds from southern Scandinavia to North Africa and east into central Asia. Other races are found on small islands off the West African coast and in eastern Asia.

Pied Wagtail *Motacilla alba*

INTERNATIONAL NAME | WHITE WAGTAIL

IDENTIFICATION

18 cm. Larger than a sparrow. Black-and-white bird with a long tail that constantly bobs. In Britain and Ireland male has black upperparts, rump, chest and throat and white face. Wings black and white; underparts white. Female has dark grey, slightly blotchy back and less black on crown and throat. Juvenile brownish-grey above, creamy below and has dark breast-band. Race that breeds in Europe, known as White Wagtail, has pale grey (not black) back, rump and crown. Some immature Pied Wagtails have pale backs, but their rumps and crowns are almost black. Moult takes place between July and September and there is a partial moult into fresh breeding plumage between January and March.
SEE ALSO: Grey Wagtail p211, Pied Flycatcher p253.

female summer

male summer

HABITS

When feeding has a jerky walk and frequently runs. Flight is bounding and occasionally in spring it makes a songflight similar to that of the Yellow Wagtail. Mostly feeds singly and males defend a winter feeding territory, into which it sometimes allows a female or juvenile when food is plentiful. Roosts communally, even in summer, and roosts of up to 3,000–4,000 may gather in winter in vegetation in marshes, and also in towns. Pre-roosts sometimes gather on car parks or flat roofs before dusk.

VOICE

Usual call is a sharp 'twissi-vit' or 'chizzwit' that is often given in flight. Song is quiet twittering interspersed with occasional call notes.

HABITAT

Found in a variety of places, often (but not always) near water. Breeds in open country such as moorland edge and farmland, and sometimes in towns and parks. More abundant in areas of mixed farming. In winter it is even more widely distributed and a frequent visitor to urban areas and sometimes suburban gardens. Also a common winter visitor to sewage farms, and groups regularly feed on arable fields, sometimes with other species such as Meadow Pipits.

FOOD

Chief food is insects, especially flies and midges and also caterpillars. Most food is taken from the ground, but also from shallow water or by catching flying insects in the air.

BREEDING

Nesting begins in April. Most nests are in holes, clefts or on ledges and sited in banks, ditches and buildings. Old nests of other birds such as Blackbirds are also used. Both sexes build the nest, with the female taking the largest share and completing the lining of hair, wool and feathers. Incubation of the 5 or 6 eggs is by both adults and lasts for about 13 days. Young are also fed by both adults and fly at about 14 days. They continue to be fed for a further 4–7 days. In southern Britain has two broods, one further north.

MOVEMENTS AND MIGRATIONS

It varies from being a long-distance migrant in the north of its range to being resident in the south. In Britain the uplands of the north are deserted in winter. White Wagtails from northern Europe regularly visit Britain, in spring and autumn. Oldest 11 years.

1st-winter

POPULATION

There are 272,000–352,000 pairs breeding in the UK and over 100,000 in Ireland. The population appeared to decline in the 1970s, but has since stabilised.

CONSERVATION

There are no special conservation measures for this species. Research has shown that survival of young birds has improved in recent years.

DISTRIBUTION

Found throughout Britain and Ireland, but most abundant in the north and west in summer. In winter, also widespread, but most abundant in the south. Various races of White Wagtail are found throughout Europe and Asia and wintering birds reach northern Africa.

'white' wagtail

Dipper *Cinclus cinclus*

INTERNATIONAL NAME WHITE-THROATED DIPPER

IDENTIFICATION

18 cm. Smaller than a Starling. Plump bird with a short tail that is frequently cocked, and a habitual bobbing action. It is dark sooty brown and black with broad white breast and throat, and chestnut band on its belly. When blinking, the white eyelid is obvious. Wings are short and rounded, and it frequently flies fast and straight above the water. Juvenile is dark grey with brown feather margins, creating a scaly effect on upperparts and wavy grey scalloping on underparts. Moults between May and September. Dippers in moult are reluctant to fly, and they may be flightless for a time.

HABITS

Frequently stands bobbing on rocks in the water. Will enter water and walk below surface in its search for food, or sometimes will swim and dive. Holds a territory throughout the year and is usually solitary when feeding. Pairs tend to roost together under bridges, even after breeding. Some roosts attract other Dippers, and up to nine have been observed roosting together.

VOICE

Call, frequently given in flight, is a sharp 'zit, zit' that carries above the sound of the river. Song is a sweet rippling warble, heard mainly September and October and again January–March, but also at other times.

HABITAT

Swift-flowing upland streams and rivers and also the shallow edges of upland lakes. Sometimes follows rivers down into built-up areas in winter. Found on some lowland rivers where there are weirs and bridges.

FOOD

Principal food is small invertebrates picked from the bottom of streams or rivers up to 50 cm deep. It takes both adults and larvae of species such as caddis flies, stoneflies and mayflies and a few freshwater crustaceans such as freshwater shrimps.

BREEDING

Nesting begins in February and continues until June. Nests are usually within 1 m of running water and sites include river banks, ledges on rock faces, riverside walls, tree roots, and especially holes and ledges under bridges. The domed nest of moss, grass and leaves is built by both adults and lined by female. Mainly the female incubates 4–5 eggs for about 16 days. If disturbed, young leave the nest from 13 days, but usual fledging is 20–24 days, with young sometimes returning to nest to roost. Some males take a second mate, although these second families often produce fewer young. There may be a second brood.

MOVEMENTS AND MIGRATIONS

Few British Dippers move more than 2.5 km from their breeding sites, whereas juveniles disperse 5–8 km or more, with females travelling further than males. Some northern European populations are partial migrants and travel considerable distances, some occasionally reaching eastern Britain. Oldest bird survived over 10 years.

POPULATION

There are 7,000–20,000 pairs breeding in the UK and 2,500–10,000 in Ireland. Although the population fluctuates, the overall trend is relatively stable.

CONSERVATION

Its habitats have been affected by sewage and toxic chemicals running into rivers, and by conifer forests trapping acidifying air pollutants, causing the water to become more acid and less productive for invertebrates. Not planting conifer trees along streams in the uplands will help reduce pollution.

juvenile

DISTRIBUTION

Dippers breed in upland areas of northern and western Britain, extending into lower areas in the south-west. A different race (*hibernicus*) occurs in Ireland and north-west Scotland. It is widespread in Ireland although missing from the central area. Other races breed in both northern and southern Europe and parts of North Africa and Asia.

Wren *Troglodytes troglodytes*

INTERNATIONAL NAME WINTER WREN

IDENTIFICATION

9–10 cm. One of our smallest birds. Tiny, dumpy and energetic bird that is always on the move. Has long thin bill and large feet. Small tail is often cocked above its back, and short neck gives the appearance of a small brown ball. Has reddish-brown upperparts and buff underparts, both with delicate dark bars. Has long pale stripe above eye. Flight is fast, straight and generally close to the ground. Wings are broad and rounded. Moults between July and October, the primary feathers taking 60 days to be lost and regrown. SEE ALSO: Treecreeper p265, Dunnock p215, Goldcrest p254.

HABITS

Constantly searching for food, but often inconspicuous as it hunts among bushes, vegetation and in crevices in tree trunks, roots and rocks. Usually keeps low, but will sometime go higher and may sing from an elevated perch. Most Wrens defend territories throughout the year, but sometimes form communal roosts in cold weather; there are records of up to 63 using a single nest box and nearly 100 in an attic of a house near woodland.

Shetland race

FOOD

Feeds on wide range of insects and other invertebrates. Prey includes beetles, spiders, flies and their larvae, moth caterpillars and ants. Sometimes paddles to reach insects, small fish and tadpoles.

BREEDING

Nesting begins in the second half of April. The male builds 5–8 nests in hollows, crevices or holes in banks, walls or trees. The nest is made from moss, leaves and grass and is a domed structure with a hole in the side. The female chooses one and lines it with feathers and other material. She lays 5 or 6 eggs that she incubates for about 16 days. Both adults feed the young, which fledge after 15–19 days and are tended by their parents for a further 9–18 days. There are often two broods and some males in woodland have two mates.

MOVEMENTS AND MIGRATIONS

Many Wrens defend a winter territory, but breeding areas support fewer birds and from August there is movement into other habitats such as reedbeds. Most British and Irish Wrens travel only a short distance, usually towards the south. In Europe this movement is even more marked, with northern Wrens migrating considerable distances. The oldest Wren survived 6 years.

POPULATION

One of our most numerous species with an estimated 8.5 million territories in the UK and up to 2.5 million in Ireland. Annual fluctuations but the overall population appears stable.

CONSERVATION

Up to 80% mortality in cold winters, but is capable of recovery in just a few years. This is one of several species breeding earlier, probably because of climate change.

VOICE

Call is a loud 'tic-tic-tic' that has rattling quality. Song is powerful for such a diminutive bird, and it trembles as it sings a cascade of notes, generally ending with a loud and distinctive trill.

HABITAT

Occupies wide variety of habitats in Britain and Ireland. Chief breeding habitat is deciduous and mixed woods, especially alongside streams. Also occurs on farmland, moorland, cliff tops and offshore islands. Visits and breeds in mature gardens and, in winter, many move into reedbeds, a marginal habitat for Wrens.

DISTRIBUTION

One of the most widespread species in Britain and Ireland, although not in the highest mountains. It is more abundant in the south and west of Britain than in the north. There are many races, including those on isolated island groups such as St Kilda, Shetland and the Hebrides. Also breeds throughout Europe (except the far north), in parts of North Africa, Asia and North America.

Dunnock *Prunella modularis*

IDENTIFICATION

14.5 cm. Size of a House Sparrow but with thin, pointed bill and pinkish legs. Rich brown upperparts with streaky back and wings and streaks on the flanks. Apart from a brown crown, the head and breast are blue-grey. Moves with shuffling walk, with body close to ground. Juvenile is less grey and more boldly striped than the adult. Moult begins as soon as they finish breeding, between July and October, with Dunnocks in the north of England starting before those in the south.

SEE ALSO: Wren p214, House Sparrow p278, Warblers pp231–250.

adult displaying

HABITS

For most of the year tends to be solitary although up to six may come together where food is plentiful. Creeps mouse-like on the ground, often giving a nervous flick of its wings. In courtship individuals flick open their wings and wave them above their backs while calling shrilly. Courtship includes a wing-shivering display by the female, after which the dominant male pecks her cloaca until she ejects a package of sperm. Mating then follows. Often two males mate with one female and the less dominant male helps feed the young. Dunnocks are frequent hosts for Cuckoos.

VOICE

Call is a shrill, piping 'tseep' that is also heard while the birds are displaying. The short, fast warble is often given from a prominent perch in low trees and bushes. Males sing in the winter, but most song is heard between January and July. Males copy parts of neighbouring Dunnock's songs and incorporate them into their own.

HABITAT

Breeds in a wide variety of habitats, especially gardens. Other habitats include deciduous woodland, low thick scrub, bramble patches, farmland where there are hedges, bracken on moorland and conifer plantations.

FOOD

Most food is found on the ground. Takes invertebrates, including beetles, snails, spiders, flies, worms and springtails. It also eats berries, seeds and grain. It visits gardens for bird food, but is an unusual visitor to a raised bird table, and more likely to feed underneath.

BREEDING

The pairing arrangements are unusual. Some pairs are male and female, some males have two females, some females have two or more males and there are even more complex arrangements with several males sharing several females. Nesting begins in March with the female building a cup-shaped nest of roots, leaves and grasses, lined with softer material. The female incubates the normal clutch of 4 or 5 eggs for 14–15 days. The young are cared for by both sexes and by any additional males. Young fledge at 12–15 days and are fed for a further 14–17 days. There are up to three broods.

MOVEMENTS AND MIGRATIONS

In Britain and Ireland it is very sedentary, seldom moving more than 1 km. Scandinavian populations are migratory and some Dunnocks from the north arrive in eastern Britain in autumn. Oldest ringed bird survived 11 years.

POPULATION

There are over 2.1 million territories in the UK and over half a million in Ireland. The population has experienced a long-term decline.

CONSERVATION

A significant proportion of Dunnocks nest or feed in gardens; planting dense shrubs for nesting and winter food can help its long-term survival.

DISTRIBUTION

Found throughout Britain and Ireland with the exception of Shetland and some of the highest hills in Scotland. Most abundant in lowland areas. Also breeds in central and northern Europe and east into Russia. Some winter around the northern shores of the Mediterranean.

Robin *Erithacus rubecula*

INTERNATIONAL NAME   EUROPEAN ROBIN

IDENTIFICATION

14 cm. Size of a House Sparrow. Familiar bird with a body shape that varies from rotund to sleek. Upperparts are olive-brown: face, neck and breast are orange-red. A band of grey-blue separates the red from brown, with white feathers under the tail. Eye is large and prominent, bill short and thin, and legs long and black. Juvenile lacks the red breast and is heavily speckled until its first moult, and has a light brown wing-bar. Adults moult between June and September. Juveniles have a partial moult from their speckled juvenile plumage when 6–7 weeks old.
SEE ALSO: Bullfinch p294, Chaffinch p280, Redstart p219, Dunnock p215.

HABITS

On the ground moves in a series of hops, sometimes with wings drooped. In Britain and Ireland generally rather tame, less so in other parts of Europe. Defends a territory all year round; males and females hold separate territories in winter, the female usually travelling the farthest. There are a few records (mostly from eastern Scotland) of birds forming communal winter roosts. Robins have elaborate courtship displays, when the red breast of the male is used as a visual signal to attract females and deter rivals.

fresh, autumn

VOICE

Call is an urgent 'tic, tic' and a high-pitched 'tsweee'. Sings almost throughout the year (and sometimes at night near street lights). Song is varied and melodious, and takes two distinct forms. After autumn moult the song is rather sad and wistful, but from around Christmas it becomes stronger, faster and more vigorous.

HABITAT

Breeds in woods and copses with plenty of undergrowth. Also found in dense hedges, mature gardens, parks and other shrubby places and sometimes in more open country.

juvenile

FOOD

Hunts from a perch, watching for movements, or when hopping on the ground. Mostly eats invertebrates in summer and some fruits and seeds in winter. Invertebrates include spiders, beetles, sawflies, other flies and worms. Fruits include berries from elder, bramble and rowan. Seeds include grain.

BREEDING

Starts to nest in late March with the first eggs in April. Nests are built by the female and consist of leaves, moss and grass. Nest-site is usually quite low in a hollow in a bank, a tree stump, among tree roots or a man-made site, such as a gap in a wall or a shelf in a garden shed. The 4 or 5 eggs are incubated by the female for about 15 days. Both parents feed the young, but male continues alone if female starts another brood. Young fly after about 13 days and become independent 16–24 days later. There are two, sometimes three, broods.

MOVEMENTS AND MIGRATIONS

In Britain and Ireland it is mainly sedentary with most Robins not moving more than 5 km. There is also some migration south-westwards in autumn, with individuals reaching Spain or Portugal. Other populations migrate further, especially those from northern Europe; some of these arrive along the British east coast between August and November, and stay for the winter. Oldest bird survived over 11 years.

POPULATION

There are 5.9 million pairs in the UK and over 1 million In Ireland. The population appears stable.

CONSERVATION

Suffers during severe winter weather. There are no special conservation measures in place to help it in Britain, but there have been concerns about the level of hunting of migrant Robins around the Mediterranean in winter.

DISTRIBUTION

Found throughout Britain and Ireland, but most abundant south of a line from Chester to York and in Ireland. Breeds from the Arctic Circle south to the Mediterranean and in North Africa, Russia and Asia. Some northern populations winter around the Mediterranean basin.

Nightingale *Luscinia megarhynchos*

INTERNATIONAL NAME COMMON NIGHTINGALE

IDENTIFICATION
16.5 cm. Larger than a Robin, but more easy to hear than see. Plain warm brown with reddish-brown rump and tail, and grey-brown underparts that are paler and whiter on the throat and under the tail. Juvenile is spotted and mottled, more like a juvenile Robin, but with a rather long and rufous tail. Moult is rapid, taking about 45 days between June and September, and usually completed before migration.
SEE ALSO: Redstart p219, Robin p216.

HABITS
Skulking; can be surprisingly difficult to observe even when it is singing strongly from inside a bush close to an observer. In southern Europe where it is more numerous it is less shy. Spends a lot of time on or near the ground in dense cover and sometimes resembles a large Robin. Will often appear very erect on straight legs and with tail cocked. It moves with large hops with frequent flicking of wings and cocking of tail.

VOICE
Song is a remarkable rich, mellow series of notes that is delivered powerfully at night when it is most obvious, but also frequently heard during the day. It is loud and fluety and there are recurring phrases including a distinctive rapid 'chook, chook, chook, chook' and a plaintive 'pioo, pioo'. Song is normally heard only between April and early June. Call is a soft 'hweet', similar to a Chiffchaff but louder. The other call is a hard 'tacc, tacc'.

usually on, or just off, the ground. The 4 or 5 eggs are laid between April and June with most laid in May. Incubation is by the female and lasts for around 13 days. Young are cared for and fed by both parents and can fly after about 11 days. They become independent 2–3 weeks after leaving the nest.

juvenile

MOVEMENTS AND MIGRATIONS
Arrives in Britain in April and leaves between July and September. European migrants mainly travel south-west towards the Mediterranean. From Europe it is possible they over-fly both the Mediterranean Sea and the Sahara Desert. They appear to return by a more easterly route. Oldest ringed bird was over 10 years.

POPULATION
There are 5,000–9,000 singing Nightingales in Britain, with a fall in the British population of nearly 50% in 25 years.

CONSERVATION
The range in Britain contracted during the 20th century. Nightingales may be affected by cold and wet springs. A decline in coppiced woodland and the spread of deer may have reduced the amount of suitable habitat. RSPB nature reserves in southern England have increased the areas of coppicing to help this species

HABITAT
Breeds in a variety of habitats including thick hedges, low scrub, coppice woodlands and young conifer plantations. All these places have thick vegetation and are often near rivers, streams and pools. It avoids dense woodlands, preferring woodland edge. In winter it lives in African woodland and scrub.

FOOD
Mainly invertebrates with some plant material, especially berries, eaten in autumn. Insect food includes beetles, ants and flies, most of which are caught on the ground amongst undergrowth.

BREEDING
Female builds a bulky nest of grass and leaves lined with finer, softer materials. The site she chooses is

DISTRIBUTION
In Britain mainly found south-east of a line from the rivers Humber to the Severn and is especially abundant in Kent and Essex. Breeds in central and southern Europe and Russia and also in North Africa. Winters in Central Africa.

Black Redstart *Phoenicurus ochruros*

IDENTIFICATION
14.5 cm. Similar in size to a Robin but slimmer. Has many of the characteristics of a Redstart, but the plumage is darker and those in western Europe have no trace of red on their breasts. Males are slate-grey above, sooty black around the face and breast with white flashes on the folded wings and orange-red sides to the tail. Males are greyer in autumn. Female is a uniform dusky grey-brown with a red tail. Juvenile is similar to female but with slight flecking and barring. Adults moult between July and October, before migration. The new feathers of male have pale fringes that give a hoary appearance. These fringes wear away as the breeding season approaches, revealing the striking black plumage.
SEE ALSO: Redstart p219.

male   female

HABITS
Its bright tail is constantly quivering. Commonly seen on the ground where it runs rather than hops and it also regularly perches on buildings or rocks. Will often fly up from a perch, sometimes hovering for a moment, as it catches insects.

juvenile

VOICE
Most common call is an urgent 'tucc, tucc'. Song is a short warble with some metallic jangles at the end. It is heard from March to July and sometimes in late summer.

HABITAT
In Britain a few pairs nest on cliffs, but most nest on buildings in industrial or inner city locations such as on power stations, railway stations or disused factories or warehouses. Also nests on buildings and in quarries in rural areas. On migration and in winter more likely to be seen on rocky shores or below cliffs. In Europe, found in rocky locations and also in towns and villages.

FOOD
Feeds on insects such as midges, small flies, aphids, moths, ants and beetles. Also eats spiders, worms, berries and seeds.

BREEDING
Nests from late April to July. Nest-site is a ledge, crevice or other hole in a rock or wall. Female builds a nest of grass and leaves, lined with hair, wool and feathers. The 4–6 eggs are incubated by the female for 12–16 days. Both parents feed the young, which leave the nest after 12–19 days. After fledging, young are cared for by their parents for a further 11 days. Two, sometimes three, broods.

MOVEMENTS AND MIGRATIONS
In different parts of its range it is a migrant, a resident and a partial migrant. In Britain nest-sites are abandoned after breeding and it reaches its wintering areas in September and October. A few stay around British and Irish coasts. Passage migrants from further east arrive in October and November and again in March and April. Breeding birds are usually back on territory during April. The oldest survived over 10 years.

POPULATION
Fewer than 100 pairs breed in Britain, mostly in the south. In winter, there may be 500 individuals.

CONSERVATION
Specially protected at all times. Gradually colonised Britain during the 20th century. First nested in an urban site in 1926, but its colonisation of London bomb sites after World War II was a turning point and it spread to other man-made sites as well as some coastal cliffs. Some breeding sites are secret to prevent nest robbery, but most pairs choose inaccessible places.

DISTRIBUTION
In Britain breeds mainly in south-east England and the Midlands, with smaller numbers in Lincolnshire and East Anglia. Elsewhere breeds in central and southern Europe and parts of North Africa. There are other races in Turkey and the Middle East. It winters in southern and western Europe, including Britain and Ireland, North Africa and the Middle East.

Redstart *Phoenicurus phoenicurus*

INTERNATIONAL NAME COMMON REDSTART

juvenile

IDENTIFICATION

14 cm. Similar size to a Robin but slimmer with longer wings and a longer tail that constantly quivers up and down. Tail and rump are bright orange-red. Male in spring is striking, with blue-grey upperparts, black face and throat, white forehead and orange breast and flanks. Female has grey-brown upperparts and orange-buff underparts; warmer coloured than female Black Redstart. Juvenile is mottled like a juvenile Robin, but with reddish tail. Adults moult between June and September, before autumn migration. After moult the bright colours are obscured by buff tips to the feathers that wear off in late winter, revealing the bright, fresh breeding plumage.
SEE ALSO: Black Redstart p218.

HABITS

Song is given from a prominent perch. At other times it is constantly on the move and often fluttering or hovering to catch insects in the air. Some of its actions are reminiscent of a Robin, but it is much more likely to be seen in trees than on the ground. Among the leaves it can be hard to see, but the long tail and slim rear body give it a distinctive profile. Flight is gently undulating.

VOICE

Call a rather sweet, warbler-like 'hooweet'. Song a loud warble ending with distinctive mechanical jangle.

HABITAT

In Britain, uplands in the west and north. Breeds in oak or mixed woodland, parkland, open hill country with scattered trees and sometimes alongside streams and in rocky areas. In parts of Europe, found in parks and gardens in towns.

FOOD

Insects, especially flies, beetles, moths and ants, but also a wide variety of other invertebrates, including spiders and worms. Also eats fruits from a variety of plants.

BREEDING

Nesting begins in April. Nest is in a hole in a tree or some other crevice and nest boxes are often used. Nest built by female and consists of grass, moss and other local materials. Incubation of the 5–7 eggs is by the female only and lasts for 13–14 days. Both parents feed the young, although the female appears to provide most food. Young fly after 16–17 days and are independent 2–3 weeks later. There are frequently two broods in a season.

MOVEMENTS AND MIGRATIONS

Summer migrant, returning in April and May and leaving in late August. Most European birds move southwest although some from northern Scandinavia take an eastern route around the Mediterranean. Largest numbers are on the move through Europe during September when migrants are seen in Britain. From southern Europe most over-fly the Mediterranean and the Sahara Desert in a single flight. Oldest bird 10 years.

POPULATION

There are 101,000 pairs of Redstarts breeding in the UK and up to 10 in Ireland. There has been a retreat from many traditional lowland sites in southern England, while the population has recovered from a previous decline in other parts of Britain.

CONSERVATION

There has been a recent decline in the Redstart population in much of Europe. Drought in Africa was a probable cause in the 1960s and early 1970s from which the species partly recovered. It is now one of several species that winter in Africa and are in sharp decline – perhaps as a result of climate change. Careful woodland management and provision of nest boxes can help its conservation in Britain.

female

male

DISTRIBUTION

In Britain found mainly in the north and west, and especially in Wales where it is most abundant. It breeds in a few other places in central and southern England and only a few pairs in Ireland. Breeds across Europe, parts of North Africa and the Middle East and in Russia. Winters in central Africa.

Whinchat *Saxicola rubetra*

IDENTIFICATION

12.5 cm. Slightly smaller and shorter-tailed than a Robin. Slimmer than a Stonechat with flatter head, longer wings, heavier bill, white sides to base of tail and black spotting above tail. Male has streaky brown upperparts, orange-brown breast, prominent white stripe above eye and a smaller one below its dark cheeks. Female is duller, with buff eye-stripe and buff breast. Juvenile resembles female with less distinct eye-stripe and slightly spotted breast. Flight usually low and white base of tail is conspicuous. Adults have a complete moult between July and September, before autumn migration.
SEE ALSO: Stonechat p221, Wheatear p223.

male summer   male summer

HABITS

Rather upright when perched and frequently bobs and flicks its tail and wings. Perches on tops of bushes, small trees and wires. Flies low to a new perch with a rather jerky flight. Usually seen singly or in pairs, but family groups may be obvious in late summer.

VOICE

Call is a sharp 'tic, tic', similar to, but not as hard as, the call of a Stonechat.

HABITAT

Breeds on moorland edges, amongst bracken, in young forestry plantations with areas of grass, and where there is a mosaic of short grazed grassland, prominent perches to hunt from and thicker vegetation to nest in. Also found in other rough grassland areas, including water meadows and upland farms, especially transitional zones between farmland and bracken-covered slopes. Other less usual sites include railway embankments, industrial waste ground and colliery tips.

FOOD

Eats invertebrates and some seeds. Mayflies, caddis flies, other flies, moths and their caterpillars, beetles, spiders, snails and worms are eaten. Plant food includes blackberries.

BREEDING

Nesting takes place mainly in May and June. Female builds the nest with male occasionally helping to select some material. The nest is often in an open site among long grass or bracken or sometimes off the ground, low down in a bush. The nest is a cup-shaped structure of grass, leaves and moss. There are usually 5 or 6 eggs, which are incubated by the female for 12–13 days. Young are fed by both parents and leave the nest after 12–13 days. They start to fly at 17–19 days and remain dependent on their parents until 28–30 days. Pairs often rear a second brood.

MOVEMENTS AND MIGRATIONS

Summer migrant to Europe, arriving in April and May. Young leave their nest between July and mid-September and peak passage through western Europe is in September. Migrants concentrate in traditional areas in western France and northern Spain, or in Portugal and southern Spain. After breaking their migration to feed they appear to make a single crossing of both the Mediterranean and the Sahara Desert. On their return, however, many stop in North Africa before flying into Europe.

POPULATION

There are 14,000–28,000 pairs breeding in the UK and a further 1,000–2,500 in Ireland. The population has declined by 37% in the last 25 years.

female summer

CONSERVATION

Once it was common throughout much of Britain. Gradually it has retreated from central and southern England. A general tidying-up of the countryside, more productive farmland and overgrazing at nest-sites have all combined to reduce the number of pairs. Also many tracts of young forests that were planted 30–40 years ago and provided home for many Whinchats have matured and are now unsuitable as nest-sites. Climate change may also affect its migration and African wintering areas.

juvenile

DISTRIBUTION

Most nest sites are in upland areas of northern and western Britain, with a few in Ireland. It is also found from northern Scandinavia to northern Spain, east into Russia and also in parts of the Middle East. It winters in central and southern Africa.

Stonechat *Saxicola torquata*

INTERNATIONAL NAME   EURASIAN STONECHAT

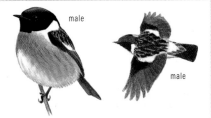
male

male

IDENTIFICATION

12.5 cm. Slightly smaller than a Robin. Similar size to a Whinchat, but plumper, with shorter wings, rounder head and no eye-stripe. Male in spring has black head with white patch on side of neck, white patch in wings, small white rump, dark brown back and orange-red breast. At other times the colouring of the male is much duller. Female lacks the black head, has a less obvious white neck patch and a browner, streaked back. Juvenile resembles a dull female, but with spotting and barring on its breast and back. Adults moult between July and October. It has only one period of moult; the colour change in late winter into breeding plumage is caused by the duller feather tips being worn away.
SEE ALSO: Whinchat p220.

HABITS

Perches very upright and constantly flicks its wings, spreads its tail and is generally active and restless. In flight, it appears large-headed and short-tailed and has been likened to a large bumble bee. Drops to the ground to feed. Perches on the tops of bushes, especially gorse, and small trees. Usually seen singly or in pairs and in Britain and Ireland pairs remain together outside the breeding season.

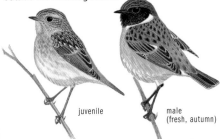
juvenile

male
(fresh, autumn)

VOICE

Call is a hard 'hweet, chac, chac', the last two notes being remarkably similar to two pebbles being knocked together. The variable song is rather like that of a Dunnock and sometimes given during a short songflight.

HABITAT

Breeds on lowland heaths, coastal sites with plenty of gorse, dune systems and in young conifer plantations with heather. Other typical sites include golf courses and railway embankments.

FOOD

Feeds mainly on insects, especially weevils, ichneumon flies, shieldbugs, moths, caterpillars of butterflies and moths, and ants. Spiders, snails and worms are also eaten. Plant food includes seeds and blackberries.

BREEDING

Female builds a nest among grasses, either in the open or, more often, under a gorse bush or another shrub. Sometimes the nest is off the ground in a bush. The nest is a rather untidy cup of grass and leaves and lined with hair, feathers and wool. Incubation of the 5 or 6 eggs is by female and takes 12–15 days. Young are fed by both parents and fly at 12–15 days. Adults continue to feed the young for 4–5 days before the female ceases and concentrates on the next brood while the male continues feeding for a further 5–10 days. Pairs rear two or three broods in a season; very occasionally four.

MOVEMENTS AND MIGRATIONS

It is a resident and a partial migrant. Many British and Irish birds leave their summer territories and winter in coastal areas, others migrate to the Mediterranean basin. Some Stonechats from Europe winter in Britain but most travel to the Mediterranean and North Africa. Oldest ringed bird was over 8 years old.

POPULATION

There are 9,000–23,000 pairs breeding in the UK and fewer than 20,000 in Ireland. There may be similar numbers in winter.

CONSERVATION

Suffers in severe winter weather. Once it was far more common, but the range contracted between the early 1970s and late 1980s. Since 1994 its abundance has fluctuated and breeding performance has improved. In Europe it also declined, but there appears to have been a recent recovery. It benefits from low-intensity agriculture, with few pesticides, plenty of scrub and lower numbers of grazing animals.

female

DISTRIBUTION

Breeds mainly around the southern and western coasts of Britain and in coastal and some inland sites in Ireland. In winter, it is a little more widespread. Also found in southern Europe and there are races in Africa, Russia, Siberia and also in eastern Asia. Some European breeding birds migrate to Africa in winter.

Bluethroat *Luscinia svecica*

IDENTIFICATION

14 cm. Robin-like but more upright, with a longer tail and legs. Dark brown with buff underparts, a prominent white stripe over eye and bright chestnut sides to base of tail. In spring, male has bright blue throat bordered with narrow bands of black, white and chestnut. Throat pattern varies from race to race, with those from northern Europe having a red spot and in the south a white spot. Males in autumn show varying amounts of blue and chestnut. Females have a pale throat with a black breast-band and, sometimes, a hint of blue. Juvenile is spotted like a juvenile Robin, but with rusty-red at the base of the tail. Moult begins in July after breeding and is completed in 40–45 days, before the birds migrate.
SEE ALSO: Robin p216, Redstart p219.

HABITS

Often a skulking species that feeds on the ground, usually amongst thick vegetation. Even on migration searches out crops and other vegetated areas and if disturbed will often fly only a short distance before dropping back into cover. On the ground tends to flit from feeding area to feeding area. Hops like a Robin and often cocks its tail and droops its long wings.

male summer
white-spotted race

VOICE

Call is short, hard 'tacc, tacc' or a plaintive warbler-like 'hweet'. Song may be given from a perch or in a short songflight and is a clear, repeated 'zruu, zruu, zruu' accelerating and ranging up and down the scale. Mimics other species and other sounds.

HABITAT

In Britain usually coastal, arriving as a passage migrant and seeking out scrub, gardens and grassy areas. Breeding habitat is either wet birch forest in northern Europe, or fresh- or salt-water marshes and other wet areas further south.

FOOD

It mainly eats beetles, spiders, moth caterpillars and a variety of other invertebrates. It also eats berries in autumn.

BREEDING

A very rare breeding species in Britain. Nest is on the ground amongst dense vegetation. It is a cup of grass,

male summer

leaves, moss and roots and is built mostly by female. Normal clutch is 5–7 eggs that are incubated mainly by the female, but with some help from the male. Incubation lasts for 13–14 days and both parents feed the young, which fly after about 14 days. White-spotted birds are sometimes double-brooded.

MOVEMENTS AND MIGRATIONS

Most arrive in Britain or Ireland in spring or autumn. In spring, the largest numbers of sightings come from the east coast including the Northern Isles. In autumn, the Northern Isles still dominate but there are also more from the south coast. Scandinavian birds either migrate to Africa or go south-east to Pakistan and northern India.

male summer
red-spotted race

female summer

POPULATION

A few males sometimes hold territories in spring and successful breeding was recorded for the first time in Britain in 1995. The numbers of migrants fluctuate, but averages around 100 per year. In Ireland it is very scarce.

CONSERVATION

The few that nest, or attempt to nest, in Britain need safeguarding from egg thieves, therefore breeding sites are generally kept secret.

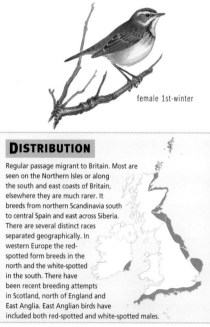

female 1st-winter

DISTRIBUTION

Regular passage migrant to Britain. Most are seen on the Northern Isles or along the south and east coasts of Britain, elsewhere they are much rarer. It breeds from northern Scandinavia south to central Spain and east across Siberia. There are several distinct races separated geographically. In western Europe the red-spotted form breeds in the north and the white-spotted in the south. There have been recent breeding attempts in Scotland, north of England and East Anglia. East Anglian birds have included both red-spotted and white-spotted males.

Wheatear *Oenanthe oenanthe*

INTERNATIONAL NAME NORTHERN WHEATEAR

IDENTIFICATION

14.5–15.5 cm. Larger than a Robin. Neat and sleek with a rather short tail. Has an extensive area of white on rump and upper-tail that terminates in a black 'T' shape. Back of male is blue-grey, wings black and underparts white with an orange flush on breast. Cheeks are black with white stripe over eye and across forehead. After moulting it is browner, but retains darker cheeks and pale stripe over eye. Female is sandy brown with less well-marked face and browner wings. Juvenile is spotted or mottled on upperparts and breast. Moult takes place before migration, between late June and early September. The brighter spring plumage is revealed as the pale feather fringes are lost in spring.
SEE ALSO: Whinchat p220.

male

male

HABITS

This is an upright species. Most obvious feature in flight is white rump and black 'T' shape of the tail. Feeds on the ground; active and restless and frequently bobs. Moves in a series of swift, short runs and perches on rocks and posts. Sometimes it flutters up to catch a flying insect. Mainly solitary or in pairs, but groups may form on migration, especially at coastal sites.

VOICE

Call is a hard 'chack, chack'. It also has a pleasant warbling song that is given on the ground or during a short songflight.

HABITAT

Breeds in rocky and stony places, upland pastures with drystone walls and on moorland. Also breeds on short rabbit-cropped grassland in lowland areas, often in coastal regions. On migration it is widespread, stopping in open places, often near the coast.

FOOD

Mainly insects and other invertebrates. Individual items include beetles, springtails, moths and their caterpillars, flies, small snails, worms and berries from blackberry, rowan and elder.

female

female (fresh, autumn)

BREEDING

Nests between April and July. Nest-site is a hole in a wall or rock face or a hole in the ground, such as a rabbit burrow. Female builds a rough cup of bracken, grass or leaves and lined with finer grass stems, moss and lichen. Incubation of the 5 or 6 eggs is by the female and takes around 14 days. Both adults feed the young and those in holes in the ground may leave the nest during the day at about 10 days old. They can fly from about day 15 and become independent at 28–32 days. Has two or sometimes three broods.

MOVEMENTS AND MIGRATIONS

Summer migrant that arrives in Britain and Ireland between March and May. Most start to leave in August and migrations take place mainly at night. Movement is south-west through Europe on a broad front and many land on the North African coast before setting off again for their wintering grounds. The slightly larger Greenland race has a remarkable migration that takes it from Africa to its Arctic breeding grounds. For many the return journey necessitates a 30-hour, 2,400 km non-stop flight from Greenland to western Europe. Oldest bird lived more than 9 years.

POPULATION

There are 540,000 adults in summer in the UK and over 2,000 in Ireland. Declined during the 20th century and has also disappeared from some regular breeding sites in recent years.

CONSERVATION

Once abundant over much of Britain and Ireland, the Wheatear started to decline in about 1940. May have been affected by ploughing of old grasslands, the changing fortunes of rabbits caused by myxomatosis and the subsequent regrowth of vegetation, successive droughts in Africa and forestry in upland areas.

male Greenland race (autumn)

DISTRIBUTION

Breeds mainly in western and northern Britain and western Ireland with smaller numbers in southern and eastern England. Breeds throughout Europe and northern Asia. There are other races in southern Europe and North Africa and also in Greenland and north-east Canada. All birds winter in central Africa.

Ring Ouzel *Turdus torquatus*

IDENTIFICATION

23–24 cm. Similar size to a Blackbird, but slimmer and longer winged. Male is sooty black with whitish crescent on breast and silver-grey edges to many wing feathers that create a pale wing-panel. There are faint scaly marks on the flanks and under the tail. In late summer has pale tips to many of the body feathers giving a scaly look, especially to the underparts. Female is brown with a duller crescent on breast and scaly marks on underparts. After moult the crescent may be obscured. Juvenile lacks pale crescent and is spotted like a juvenile Blackbird, but less rufous, with scaling on underparts and paler wings. First-year bird may also lack pale crescent, but scaling and pale wings are distinctive. In flight, wings appear paler than body. Adults moult between July and September, before migration.

SEE ALSO: Blackbird p225.

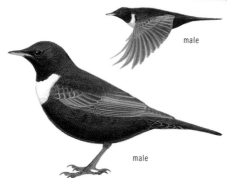
male

male

female 1st-year
(fresh, autumn)

FOOD

In summer, feeds on beetles and their larvae, flies and other insects. Also eats worms and spiders and other invertebrates. Feeds on berries from elder, hawthorn, white-bryony and blackberry.

BREEDING

Nest-site is in a crag, gully or rocky outcrop, or it may be on the ground or even in a low bush; occasionally a nest may be below ground level, in an old mine. The 3–5 eggs are laid in late April or early May. Incubation is mostly, but not exclusively, by the female and takes 13–14 days. Both parents care for the young, which fly after 12–16 days. Some pairs rear a second brood.

MOVEMENTS AND MIGRATIONS

British breeding birds return in April, arriving on the south or east coasts or at some traditional inland sites, or they fly direct to their breeding territories. In May and again in autumn European breeding birds visit the south and east coasts. Oldest bird survived over 9 years.

POPULATION

There are 6,200–7,600 pairs in the UK and fewer than 250 in Ireland. The population fell by over 50% in the last 25 years.

HABITS

Less approachable than a Blackbird, often taking flight a good way from an observer, but fiercely protects its nest. On the ground it is more upright than a Blackbird. May be loosely colonial when nesting, and seen singly or in groups when migrating. On territory it sings from a prominent perch and sometimes rival males will sing against each other.

VOICE

Call is a hard 'tac, tac, tac' like the clicking of stones. Song is strong and flutey as it sings out a phrase of a few notes, pauses and sings another phrase. Quality is similar to a Mistle Thrush.

HABITAT

Breeds in gullies on moorland and in mountains, and also around hill farms, fringes of forestry plantations and old quarries. Nest-site frequently near water. On migration it regularly stops over on open areas of short grass near the coast and on steep chalk hillsides with short natural turf and, generally, with dense cover nearby.

CONSERVATION

This species has retreated to the remotest uplands. Upland forestry will have removed some previously suitable sites, grazing pressure may have removed sources of late summer food. Research suggests that climate change is affecting the survival of birds in winter.

female

DISTRIBUTION

Breeds in upland areas of Wales, Scotland, south-west England, the Pennines, the Cheviots, North York Moors and parts of western Ireland. Occurs widely on migration, especially on chalk downland and coastal areas. Also breeds in Scandinavia, with other races in the mountains of southern and eastern Europe. Winters around the Mediterranean.

Blackbird *Turdus merula*

INTERNATIONAL NAME COMMON BLACKBIRD

male

male

male 1st-year

IDENTIFICATION
24–25 cm. Larger than a Starling. Plump with round head and medium-length tail. Male is matt black with yellow bill and yellow ring round eye. First-year male is dull black with paler, browner flight feathers and horn-coloured bill. Female is dark brown with darker wings and tail; variable markings on breast that are usually obscure, but can be quite spotted on some individuals. Juvenile is similar to female but more rufous and with streaks on both upperparts and underparts. Adults begin moulting after breeding, between May and October. Juvenile moults its body feathers between July and October, but the main flight feathers are retained until the following year. SEE ALSO: Ring Ouzel p224.

HABITS
Flight direct and lands with a characteristic raising of the tail and wings slightly drooping. Blackbirds that migrate are relatively gregarious; others may be territorial throughout the year. Tends to feed under or close to cover and turns over leaves to search for food. On sunny days, mainly in summer, it may be seen sunbathing, with wings spread, feathers ruffled, bill open and eyes closed. Sings from a prominent perch, often a rooftop in an urban area.

VOICE
Noisy species with a beautiful, mellow song that is a slow, clear warble, which 'tails off' at the end. If disturbed it makes a loud 'tchook-tchook-tchook'. At dusk many birds will give nervous 'chink, chink, chink' calls. Song is mainly heard between March and July.

HABITAT
An adaptable species. Primarily a woodland bird that also lives in gardens, parks and hedgerows, as well as more open areas in cultivated and uncultivated places.

FOOD
Eats insects, worms and berries. Eats earthworms all year round, as long as the soil is damp. Other invertebrates include insect larvae, caterpillars, beetles and snails. Plant food includes berries from hawthorn, elder, ripe fruit such as fallen apples and pears, and also kitchen scraps.

BREEDING
Nesting may begin in February in mild weather. Female mainly constructs the nest, which is a cup-shaped structure of grass, straw and small twigs, plastered on the inside with mud and lined with fine grasses. It is built in a bush or small tree. Female incubates the clutch of 3–5 eggs for about 14 days. Young are fed by both adults and fly after 14 days. On leaving the nest the brood is split between the two adults, with the male generally caring for his group longer than the female, which may leave hers to begin another brood. There may be two or three broods in a season.

MOVEMENTS AND MIGRATIONS
Most breeding Blackbirds in Britain are resident, but in northern and eastern Europe it is a summer migrant. Some of these migrants reach Britain in autumn and stay until early spring. A proportion of British breeding Blackbirds are also migrants and will winter in southern Europe. The oldest wild Blackbird survived over 21 years.

POPULATION
There are 4.9 million pairs in the UK and over 1 million in Ireland. There has been a population decline of 14% in the last 35 years.

CONSERVATION
The Blackbird expanded its range until about 1972 when the population started to fall. While the decline on farmland may be explained by agricultural changes, the cause of the decline in woodland is less clear. The most recent surveys suggest that the decline may have ceased.

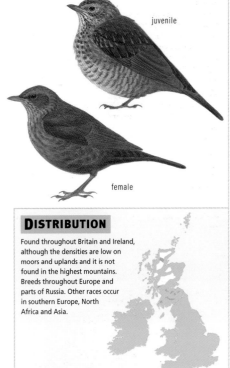

juvenile

female

DISTRIBUTION
Found throughout Britain and Ireland, although the densities are low on moors and uplands and it is not found in the highest mountains. Breeds throughout Europe and parts of Russia. Other races occur in southern Europe, North Africa and Asia.

Fieldfare *Turdus pilaris*

IDENTIFICATION
25.5 cm. Slightly smaller than a Mistle Thrush. Large, plump thrush with rather long tail. Has grey head with dark streaks on crown, long pale grey rump, chestnut back and wings and black tail and flight feathers. Breast is yellow-orange and is heavily spotted. In flight, underwing shows white. Adults moult between June and September, before leaving breeding area. SEE ALSO: Mistle Thrush p229.

HABITS
On the ground it is rather upright. Its flight appears leisurely with loose wingbeats alternating with short glides. In Britain and Ireland it is generally seen in small noisy flocks, with larger numbers gathering when migrating. In winter, flocks are nomadic as they travel the countryside in their search for food. They will sometimes travel with, and feed alongside, other thrushes and Starlings. At dusk in winter large roosts gather in thick hedges and other dense cover. When breeding it may nest singly or in small colonies. An individual will use well-aimed defecation to deter a predator from approaching a nest.

VOICE
The call is a loud 'chacker, chack, chack' and a nasal 'ee-eep' often given in flight. Song is a rather feeble warble with several hard, harsh notes and not often heard in Britain or Ireland.

fly at 12–15 days old. The young become independent at about 30 days. In Scandinavia there are often two broods.

MOVEMENTS AND MIGRATIONS
Mainly a winter migrant to Britain and Ireland, most birds arriving in October or early November, with more arriving in mid-winter, and leaving between March and May. Flocks are nomadic in their search for food and may fly further south if food is in short supply or in response to severe weather. Oldest bird survived for 18 years.

POPULATION
The number of breeding birds in Britain has varied between 0 and 10 pairs in recent years. The wintering population of Britain and Ireland is about 720,000 individuals.

CONSERVATION
Specially protected. Ten years ago it looked as if this species was set to colonise Britain. Following an expansion of its range in Europe it first bred on Orkney in 1967 and possibly in County Durham in the same year. It nested in Shetland and further south in Scotland and soon pairs were found breeding in the north of England. However, from a peak of 13 possible pairs nesting in 1991 numbers have fallen and there is little that conservationists can do to help this species except to allow any breeding pairs privacy to rear their young.

HABITAT
In winter feeds along hedgerows and in orchards. It may be seen in open places such as pastures and other areas of short grass, and on arable fields. Feeding sites are often close to woodland and tall hedges. In Scandinavia breeds in scrub, woodland and also in parks. In Britain the few that nest have been in moorland valleys, birch woods and the fringes of plantations.

FOOD
Insects and their larvae, worms and other invertebrates. Plant material is chiefly berries, especially from rowan, juniper, elder, hawthorn and holly.

BREEDING
Breeding starts in April or May. Nest is cup-shaped and mostly built by the female from twigs and roots, lined with mud and with an inner lining of finer material. Incubation of the 5 or 6 eggs is by the female and lasts 11–14 days. Both adults feed the young, which

DISTRIBUTION
Very few pairs breed in Britain. If Fieldfares are seen in summer they are usually in northern England or Scotland. In winter, they are widespread with migrating birds occurring almost anywhere, but most abundant in the lowlands of Scotland, central and southern England and eastern Ireland. Breeds in Iceland, Scandinavia, central Europe and east to Siberia.

Redwing *Turdus iliacus*

IDENTIFICATION

21 cm. A little smaller and thinner than a Song Thrush with rusty-red flanks and underwings, creamy white stripe over its eye and pale stripe below the cheek. Upperparts are dark brown and the yellow-buff breast is heavily spotted and streaked. Lower belly and under the tail is white. Icelandic race is darker and more heavily spotted. Juvenile has buff spots on its back and first-year birds retain pale tips to some of the wing feathers. In flight, the slightly pointed wings and flight silhouette are sometimes reminiscent of a Starling. Adults moult between June and September, which means that some start to replace their flight feathers while still feeding young.
SEE ALSO: Song Thrush p228.

HABITS

Generally rather shy. The red on the flanks may often be hidden under the folded wings, but the boldly patterned face is the best identification feature. Much of its behaviour is similar to a Song Thrush, but it is a sociable species outside the breeding season, with flocks migrating and feeding together, and large communal roosts developing in suitable habitats. Will feed and roost with other thrushes, especially Fieldfares.

VOICE

Soft thin 'seeip' call, usually given in flight, is frequently heard after dark during migration. Song is variable and seldom heard in Britain or Ireland; it consists of jumbled, but repeated, notes.

HABITAT

In autumn, frequents hedges and orchards. Later in winter, feeds in open areas of short grass. Visits farmland, parks and large gardens. Roosts in thick hedges and scrub. In Scotland breeds in scrubby areas near water and in plantations. In Europe breeds in forest bog, birch and willow scrub and in parks and gardens.

FOOD

In Britain and Ireland newly arrived autumn migrants feed on fruit such as windfall apples and a wide variety of berries, especially hawthorn. As supplies of fruits are exhausted it switches to feed on earthworms. In summer it feeds on worms, snails, slugs and insects.

BREEDING

The nest may be in a tree, a low bush or on the ground. Female builds a cup-shaped nest of grasses, twigs and moss. Female incubates the 4 or 5 eggs for 12–13 days. The young are fed by both parents and leave the nest at 10–15 days. They continue to be fed by their parents for another 14 days, and the male will continue feeding while the female starts another brood. There are usually two broods in a season.

MOVEMENTS AND MIGRATIONS

Northern populations move on a broad front between September and November. Icelandic birds tend to winter in Scotland and Ireland, while those from Scandinavia winter in southern Britain and further south in Europe. Wintering flocks roam widely. Migrants may winter in quite different areas in different years. Oldest ringed bird lived for over 17 years.

1st-year (fresh, autumn)

POPULATION

Fewer than 20 pairs breed each year and numbers appear to be dwindling. The winter population of Britain and Ireland has been estimated at over 1 million birds.

CONSERVATION

The Redwing was first discovered breeding in Sutherland in 1925. Numbers grew slowly and reached a peak of about 50 pairs in 1989, since when it appears to have declined again.

DISTRIBUTION

Widespread in Britain and Ireland between October and March, with the greatest concentrations being in central and southern England and southern Ireland. There is a very small population breeding in Scotland and sporadically in England. Breeds in Iceland, Scandinavia, north-east Europe and northern Russia. In winter it reaches the Mediterranean and North Africa.

Song Thrush *Turdus philomelos*

IDENTIFICATION

23 cm. Smaller than a Blackbird. Stocky thrush with a relatively short tail, medium-brown upperparts and small black spots all over buff breast and flanks. There is slight buff wing-bar. Differs from a Mistle Thrush in smaller size, browner plumage, smaller spots, plain brown tail and orange underwing, which shows in flight. A recently fledged juvenile has pale streaks on its upperparts. Adults moult all feathers slowly between June and October.

SEE ALSO: Mistle Thrush p229, Redwing p227.

HABITS

A rather upright thrush that flicks its wings when excited. Territorial during the breeding season and many British and Irish birds maintain the same territories during the winter, especially males. Outside breeding season usually seen singly except for loose flocks of migrants. Flight strong and direct without the undulations of a Mistle Thrush. Sings from prominent song post, often a small tree or bush, not as high as a Mistle Thrush.

VOICE

Far-carrying musical song comprises a series of short phrases, each repeated 3–5 times. Pattern of song is distinctive; individuals may have a repertoire of 100 phrases. Sings during the day and also at dusk (and sometimes at night near street lights), after most other birds finish singing. It sings from March to July and again briefly in autumn and during mild winter weather. Flight call is a thin 'tsic', not as hard as a Robin's 'tic' alarm note. It can be heard at night as migrants pass over.

HABITAT

Found in a variety of habitats where there are trees and bushes; gardens, parks, coniferous and deciduous woodlands and hedgerows. Often feeds under trees and bushes and seldom far from cover.

FOOD

In dry weather it specialises in feeding on snails, which it opens by hitting them against a hard object ('anvil'). Generally prefers to eat earthworms, caterpillars and other insects, especially beetles, and fruits, especially berries, in autumn.

BREEDING

Nesting starts in March. Female builds the nest in a tree or shrub, usually close to the trunk. It is made of twigs, grass and moss and lined with a smooth layer of mud. The 3–5 eggs are incubated mainly by the female for 14–15 days. Both adults feed the young and they leave the nest after 13 days. The brood may be split between the two adults, but young are soon independent. Sometimes a second brood is reared, and in the south of its range a third or fourth brood.

MOVEMENTS AND MIGRATIONS

In Britain and Ireland it is both a resident and a migrant. The proportion that migrates decreases in the south. Many from Scotland and northern England winter in Ireland, and some from southern England winter in France and Spain. Many that breed in Scandinavia pass through Britain as they head south in autumn; others from Belgium and the Netherlands winter in southern Britain. Oldest wild bird lived 10 years.

POPULATION

There are 1.1 million pairs in the UK and half a million in Ireland.

CONSERVATION

It declined by over 50% between 1969 and 2006, although there has been a slight recovery in recent years. The number of young successfully fledging fell and it appears that shortage of good nesting habitat and food supplies were the cause. First-year birds have not been surviving in sufficient numbers to sustain the population owing to agricultural intensification and changes in hedgerow and woodland management. Incentives for farmers to improve hedgerow management and field margins may be helping this species.

juvenile

DISTRIBUTION

Widespread in Britain and Ireland. Breeds in central and northern Europe and east into Russia. In winter it is found around the Mediterranean and in parts of North Africa.

Mistle Thrush *Turdus viscivorus*

IDENTIFICATION
27 cm. Larger than a Song Thrush with longer wings and tail. Has grey-brown upperparts, large bold spots on a whitish breast and white tips to the outer tail feathers. Pale-edged feathers create a pale panel on the closed wing and the cheeks are pale with darker marks. In flight, underwing is white. Juvenile has a pale head and pale spots on its upperparts. Adults moult between May and September, and moult may begin before they have finished nesting.
SEE ALSO: Song Thrush p228, Fieldfare p226.

HABITS
On the ground it is very upright and usually feeds in the open, well away from cover. Sings from the tops of tall trees and other exposed perches, and is often the only bird singing during stormy conditions. Flight is strong, but deeply undulating at low levels: the bird dipping as the wings are closed at regular intervals. Outside the breeding season it is often seen in small groups. A bold and often aggressive thrush. An individual or a pair will sometimes vigorously defend a food source, such as a holly tree, in winter.

VOICE
Call is a loud rattling and chattering, given when the bird is alarmed, but also when travelling in flocks. Song is powerful, rather like a Blackbird, but louder with repeated song phrases, with pauses between.

HABITAT
Requires open woodland and other areas where there are tall trees for nesting and for song posts, and also areas of short grass for feeding. This habitat is widespread in Britain and Ireland. After nesting it travels more widely in search of food, including on moorland.

FOOD
Feeds on insects, especially beetles, earthworms, slugs, snails and other invertebrates. Also takes plant material, especially fruits and seeds. Favourite berries include yew, hawthorn, rowan and holly.

BREEDING
Nesting may begin in February. Nest-site is usually in a fork of a tree or shrub. Female builds a cup-shaped nest of grass, roots and leaves with some earth, and lines it with finer grasses. Incubation of the 3–5 eggs is mostly by the female and lasts for 15–16 days. Both adults feed the young, which fly after 14 days, but they continue to be cared for by their parents for a further 14 days. There are often two broods.

MOVEMENTS AND MIGRATIONS
Within Britain and Ireland mostly resident, but groups may be nomadic in winter. After breeding, in July,

small flocks move around the countryside in a search for food. Many move first onto moorland in search of rowan berries. Most birds seldom move more than 50 km, but some from Scotland may reach France. Northern European birds winter in southern Europe and around the Mediterranean, but only a few appear to cross the North Sea to reach Britain. Maximum age 21 years.

POPULATION
There are 222,000 pairs in the UK and 20,000–100,000 in Ireland. In addition there is a population of non-breeding birds that are not able to find territories.

CONSERVATION
The Mistle Thrush population has fallen by 45% since 1969, but the decline may now have ceased. There have been no strong trends in breeding success and the decline may have been caused by poorer annual survival rather than by any specifically identified agricultural changes.

juvenile

DISTRIBUTION
Widespread in Britain and Ireland, with the greatest concentrations in the south of England. Absent from Orkney, Shetland and the Outer Hebrides. Breeds from Scandinavia to the Mediterranean, in parts of North Africa and into central Asia.

Waxwing *Bombycilla garrulus*

INTERNATIONAL NAME   BOHEMIAN WAXWING

IDENTIFICATION

18 cm. Smaller than a Starling. Stocky bird with prominent crest and soft-looking plumage. Reddish-brown with grey rump, black bib, small black mask, yellow and white pattern in the wings, and yellow-tipped tail. Tips of its secondary flight feathers have a series of spikes, which look like pieces of bright red wax. The undertail feathers are a rich chestnut. In flight, wings are 'triangular', rather like those of a Starling. First-winter birds usually have a single pale yellow stripe in the folded wing, adults have yellow and white borders to the wing-tips. The adults moult between August and November, but may suspend their moult and continue after migration.
SEE ALSO: Starling p277.

HABITS

Generally gregarious. Numbers vary from small groups to large gatherings outside of the breeding season. Usually perches in the tops of trees, but comes lower to find food, often sitting immobile among the branches. Relatively tame and can often be approached to within a few metres. It is acrobatic when feeding; almost tit-like as it adopts a variety of feeding positions. Flight is strong with gentle undulations as birds periodically close their wings – a flight action recalling a Starling. They also catch flying insects, rather like a large flycatcher.

VOICE

Call is a high-pitched, trilling 'sirrrrr', like a bell.

HABITAT

In winter in Britain its arrival is sporadic and it visits any habitat that provides food. It can be a surprising find in parks and gardens, even in busy public places where there has been amenity planting of berry-bearing trees and bushes. First sightings in winter are often along the east coast, but groups rapidly travel inland in their search for food. It breeds in dense northern forests where there are old lichen-covered pines.

FOOD

Chief winter food is berries (eating two or three times its own body weight in a day!). Favourites are rowan, whitebeam and hawthorn, but in Britain it also eats cotoneaster, rose and many other winter fruits and seeds. Insects, especially mosquitoes and midges, and other invertebrates form a large part of its diet on its breeding grounds.

BREEDING

Does not breed in Britain or Ireland. On its northern breeding grounds it does not start breeding until mid-June. Cup-shaped nest of twigs, grass and moss is built by both sexes. Female incubates the clutch of 5 or 6 eggs for 14–15 days. Both parents care for the young, which eventually fly after 14–17 days.

MOVEMENTS AND MIGRATIONS

Partial migrant and some birds will overwinter in their northern breeding areas. Some regularly migrate south, but the species also 'erupts' when the population becomes too large for the food available. These eruptions have become more frequent in the last 20 years. Waxwings first arrive in October/November and normally stay until April. Oldest bird survived for 12 years.

POPULATION

In most years fewer than 1,000 birds are seen in Britain and Ireland. During eruption years numbers may increase to several thousand individuals.

CONSERVATION

There are no specific conservation measures for this species, but the planting of berry-bearing shrubs and trees in public places and in gardens can help their survival in winter.

1st-winter

DISTRIBUTION

In winter, the first British arrivals are usually seen on the east coast, from Scotland to East Anglia. As they move inland they can be seen almost anywhere, but become scarcer to the south and west, and relatively few reach Ireland. It breeds in northern Scandinavia and Siberia and another race breeds in North America. In winter, European and Siberian birds move south and west reaching northern and eastern Europe.

Cetti's Warbler *Cettia cetti*

IDENTIFICATION
13.5 cm. Only slightly smaller than a House Sparrow. A stocky warbler with a long rather broad and rounded tail, short rounded wings and a rather rounded head. The plain upperparts are a rich chestnut, the throat is pale and the underparts are pale grey with a rusty wash to the flanks and under the tail. There is a narrow grey stripe above the eye. The bill is pale and the legs pink. It has a complete moult between July and September and some birds have another partial moult before breeding.
SEE ALSO: Reed Warbler p236, Nightingale p217.

HABITS
A secretive and skulking species that would be overlooked if it was not for the outbursts of its distinctive song. Flight is rapid as it dashes from bush to bush. It often feeds on the ground where it moves in a series of short hops. The tail is frequently cocked. It moves quickly through the bushes and reeds, flicking its tail up and down nervously. Territories are maintained from year to year, and some are maintained throughout the winter.

VOICE
The song is an amazingly powerful, far-carrying, almost explosive series of liquid notes 'pwit, pity-chewit, chewit, chewit'. The song is heard throughout the year and at night during the breeding season. The call is an abrupt 'chup' or 'chip'.

14–16 days. The brood remains together and the male may help feed the young, especially if the female begins a second brood. The young become independent at 15–30 days.

MOVEMENTS AND MIGRATIONS
The British breeding birds are mainly sedentary, although some breeding territories are vacated after the breeding season, with birds leaving in September and returning in April. It is possible that some of these birds move to continental Europe for the winter. Elsewhere in its range this species may be a regular migrant. Oldest wild bird lived for over 9 years.

POPULATION
Over 1,400 males have been holding territories in Britain in recent years. This demonstrates the gradual colonisation of southern Britain since it first arrived in 1961 with birds now breeding as far north as Yorkshire.

CONSERVATION
Breeding in Britain was first proved in Kent in 1972 and colonisation of other suitable sites followed quickly. The small sedentary population suffers during cold weather and the severe winter weather of 1985 reduced numbers in Kent and Suffolk by 75%. Mild winters have seen numbers increase again. Due to the drainage of wetlands over many years most of the prime sites for this species are on nature reserves. Specially protected in the UK.

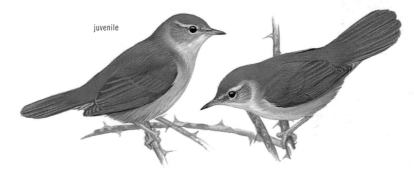

juvenile

HABITAT
The species breeds in dense scrub in damp low-lying places where there is bramble and willow, and also with reedbeds close by. Elsewhere in Europe it breeds in marshes and riverside scrub. Outside the breeding season the females especially tend to move into reedbeds.

FOOD
It feeds chiefly on insects and other invertebrates, many of which it captures on the ground. Its prey includes moths and their caterpillars, flies, beetles and snails.

BREEDING
The social life of the Cetti's Warbler is complex. There are conventional male/female pairings, but some males hold larger territories and breed with several females. The female builds an untidy cup-shaped nest of leaves and plant stems low down in thick vegetation. The female incubates the 4 or 5 eggs for 16–17 days. The young are looked after and fed mostly by the female. They leave the nest when they can fly, at

DISTRIBUTION
The small British population is limited to a few sites in southern England, East Anglia and Wales. It also breeds from northern France to North Africa and east into southern Asia.

WARBLERS

GRASSHOPPER
WARBLER
p234

CETTI'S WARBLER
p231

SEDGE
WARBLER
p235

MARSH
WARBLER
p237

REED WARBLER
p236

ICTERINE
WARBLER
p238

1st-winter

MELODIOUS WARBLER
p239

1st-winter

BARRED
WARBLER
p241

DARTFORD WARBLER
p240

1st-winter

LESSER WHITETHROAT p242

WHITETHROAT p243

female

male

BLACKCAP p244

GARDEN WARBLER p245

1st-winter

PALLAS'S WARBLER p246

YELLOW-BROWED WARBLER p247

1st-winter

CHIFFCHAFF p248

WILLOW WARBLER p249

WOOD WARBLER p250

1st-winter

233

Grasshopper Warbler *Locustella naevia*

INTERNATIONAL NAME COMMON GRASSHOPPER WARBLER

IDENTIFICATION

12.5 cm. Smaller than a House Sparrow. This secretive small warbler is olive-brown with dark, broken streaks on upperparts and a faint pale stripe over eye. Underparts are buff with some dark streaks on breast and under the tail. Feathers under the tail are very long. Tail graduated; wings short and rounded. Sometimes individuals appear yellow-brown. Juvenile often brighter and more yellow below than adults. It appears that some adults begin to moult before migration, but most moult in their winter quarters, although this aspect of the bird's life cycle is poorly understood.

SEE ALSO: Sedge Warbler p235.

yellowish variant

1st-winter

HABITS

Shy; generally lives in deep cover and is difficult to observe. A newly arrived migrant may, for a short time, sing from exposed perches at or near the top of a small bush. If disturbed it will slink down and disappear. During courtship it may flit short distances from bush to bush. It has complex displays that involve raising and waving its wings above its back. Most of the time it slips with ease, mouse-like, through dense vegetation and spends much time foraging on the ground amongst grass or shrubs and is reluctant to fly.

VOICE

Song is a remarkable insect-like trill that can be sustained for several minutes or more without a break. Trill is uniform in pitch and has been likened to the mechanical sound made by an angler's reel. Volume appears to change as the bird turns its head while singing. Song comprises 26 double notes per second and is heard mainly between April and July, during the day and at night, and especially at dawn and dusk. The ability of humans to hear the song decreases with age!

HABITAT

Breeds in variety of wet and dry habitats in lowland areas, including thick scrub, thickets, edges of marshes, fens, heaths, rough grassland, young forestry plantations and overgrown gravel pits. Requires a combination of dense ground cover with open spaces, and an abundance of food.

FOOD

Eats mainly insects that it picks off the ground or from vegetation. Food includes bugs, beetles, moth caterpillars, lacewings, flies and ants. Also known to eat elderberries in late summer.

BREEDING

Nest is a thick cup built by both sexes in dense cover on or near the ground. The 5 or 6 eggs are incubated by both adults and hatch after 12–15 days. Both parents feed the young for 12–13 days. It is not known how long it takes for them to become independent. In the north only one brood is reared, while in the south of the range two broods are normal.

MOVEMENTS AND MIGRATIONS

A summer migrant, arriving in Britain and Ireland from mid-April and May. Leaves in July and August and migrants from further north or east may arrive in September. It appears that it undertakes long non-stop flights with much migration taking place at night.

POPULATION

Fewer than 12,000 pairs breed in the UK and 2,500–10,000 in Ireland. The UK population has declined by over 90% since 1969.

CONSERVATION

Difficult to census, but it appears that the population fluctuates from year to year. Loss of suitable breeding habitat in Britain and Ireland and drought in its winter quarters, or on migration, means this species is vulnerable.

DISTRIBUTION

Widespread in Britain and Ireland, but most numerous in central England and farther west. Scarce in northern Scotland. Breeds from southern Scandinavia to northern Spain and east into Russia. Wintering area is not precisely known, but is likely to be in tropical West Africa.

Sedge Warbler *Acrocephalus schoenobaenus*

IDENTIFICATION
13 cm. Brown warbler with rather flat head. Has blackish streaks on back, dark streaky crown and prominent white stripe above its eye. Has a dark streak from eye to base of bill. The reddish-brown, unstreaked rump is especially noticeable in flight. Underparts are creamy white. It is duller as its plumage becomes worn in summer. Juvenile is fresh-looking and yellower than adult with boldly marked upperparts, pale crown-stripe and some fine streaking on the breast. Adults begin to moult while still on their breeding grounds, then suspend moult while migrating and continue again during winter. Moult is completed by March.

SEE ALSO: Reed Warbler p236, Aquatic Warbler p312.

HABITS
Clambers amongst plant stems and frequently feeds on the ground within tangled vegetation. For much of the time it can be hard to observe, but when singing it perches on the outside of a bush and may make a short, jerky songflight. If newly fledged young are disturbed they will adopt a bittern-like posture with bill pointing to the sky.

VOICE
Song is loud, strong and repetitive; a mixture of varied fast chattering phrases, sweeter-sounding notes and some mimicry that often includes sparrow-like chirrups. Call is a scolding 'tuk', or grating 'chrirr'. Sings during the day and sometimes at night.

migration. Also feeds on plant material, especially berries in autumn.

BREEDING
Nesting begins in late April with most clutches laid during May. Nest is a deep cup of grass, moss, plant stems and spiders' webs and lined with soft grass, flower heads, hair and plant down. Generally close to ground amongst thick tangled vegetation and woven around vertical stems of plants, and sometimes suspended over water. Female builds nest and lays 4 or 5 eggs. Incubation is chiefly by female and lasts for 13–15 days. Young remain in the nest for 10–14 days and are fed by both parents. There is sometimes a second brood.

MOVEMENTS AND MIGRATIONS
Summer migrant that arrives in mid-April and leaves its breeding sites in July, with the adults leaving before the juveniles. They move to pre-migration feeding areas where they build up large fat reserves that are sufficient for some to fly 3,900 km from southern Britain to Africa. The oldest known individual lived for 10 years.

POPULATION
There are 321,000 pairs in the UK and 20,000–100,000 in Ireland. Populations fluctuate from year to year.

CONSERVATION
Loss of wetlands and harsh management of riverside vegetation has affected breeding success. Populations on farmland, like those of many other insectivorous species, have also fallen. Much of the variation in population size is related to changes in adult survival, which, in turn, are related to changes in rainfall in their wintering grounds.

fresh, spring

juvenile

HABITAT
Breeds in thick vegetation in mainly wet places. Present in marshes, reedbeds with some trees and bushes, riverside scrub, damp ditches and nettle-beds. Also breeds in drier habitats, including bramble and hawthorn thickets, young forestry plantations and sometimes in fields of rape or other crops.

FOOD
Finds most of its food low down in dense vegetation. Chiefly eats insects and other invertebrates, including flies, beetles, spiders, worms and small snails. Plumreed aphids are an important source of food prior to

DISTRIBUTION
Widespread in Britain and Ireland, with highest densities in eastern counties. In the west and south it is most abundant near the coast. It breeds from northern Scandinavia south to France and east across Europe and into Russia. It winters in Africa, south of the Sahara.

Reed Warbler *Acrocephalus scirpaceus*

INTERNATIONAL NAME EURASIAN REED WARBLER

IDENTIFICATION

13 cm. Plain, unstreaked warbler that has warm brown upperparts and reddish-brown rump. Underparts are buff, graduating to white on throat. Has rather flat forehead, the suggestion of a peaked crown and rather long bill. Slight pale stripe over eye. Wings are shorter than those of Marsh Warbler. By late summer adults are greyer. Juvenile is fresher, warmer rusty-brown with orange-brown flanks. Like all members of its family the feathers below the tail are quite long, reaching beyond the wing-tips. Between July and September adults have a partial moult before migrating. Moult is completed in Africa.

SEE ALSO: Sedge Warbler p235, Marsh Warbler p237.

HABITS

Spends most of its time amongst dense reed stems where it is well camouflaged and easily overlooked unless singing. Frequently, song is given from within reedbed and not from an obvious perch. Climbs amongst the reeds with ease, often grasping different reeds with legs apart. May leave reeds to feed in neighbouring shrubs. When nesting will defend a small territory within a large or small colony. Solitary outside breeding season.

VOICE

Song is a noisy, unmusical, repetitive chatter and churring with frequent changes in pitch. It is more even, less varied and lower pitched than Sedge Warbler's song and full of 'rrr' and 'zzz's.

juvenile

fresh, spring

HABITAT

Breeds in common reed (*Phragmites*) in old fenland, ditches and along the edges of lakes and slow-flowing rivers. It prefers reeds that grow in water, although it occasionally breeds in drier places and other vegetation such as willowherb and arable crops. Migrants turn up almost anywhere, including orchards, gardens and in crops – sometimes away from water.

FOOD

Feeds mainly on insects, spiders and small snails. Insects include aphids, beetles, flies and small bugs.

BREEDING

Nesting begins in May. The female makes a deep cup of grass, leaves and reed heads suspended between reed stems. It takes 4 days to build and 3 days to line with hair, feathers or other soft material. Both sexes incubate the 3–5 eggs for 9–12 days and both adults feed the young. Young birds leave the nest at 10–13 days and become independent 10–14 days later.

Sometimes they raise a second brood. Nests are frequently parasitised by Cuckoos.

MOVEMENTS AND MIGRATIONS

Summer migrant to Britain, arriving in late April and May and leaving in August or September. Peak migration on the south coast of England is late August. The journey to the winter quarters is made in relatively short stages, with British birds heading first for the Atlantic coast of France, then into Spain and Portugal, and finally into Africa via Morocco. The oldest lived 12 years.

POPULATION

60,000–122,000 pairs breed in the UK and fewer than 100 in Ireland.

CONSERVATION

In the past this species suffered from the drainage of large reedbeds, but it spread north in the 19th century, partly retreated and then started to spread again in the last quarter of the 20th century. There has been an increase in its breeding population in recent years. Colonisation of new habitats such as gravel pits has helped, and the creation of large new reedbeds should also help in future.

DISTRIBUTION

Found in central and southern England and in Wales. Relatively scarce in the north of England, and even fewer in Scotland and Ireland. The largest concentrations are in East Anglia and along the south coast. It also breeds from southern Scandinavia to North Africa and in parts of the Middle East and Russia. It winters in central Africa.

Marsh Warbler *Acrocephalus palustris*

IDENTIFICATION
13 cm. Closely resembles a Reed Warbler, but is paler, greyer brown above, with shorter bill and no reddish-brown rump. In fresh spring plumage it is yellow-brown and just a little greener than a Reed Warbler. Has pale stripe above and in front of eye and pale eye-ring. Underparts are pale, throat white, and it has buff patches on sides of breast and flanks. Head can look more rounded and more gentle than a Reed Warbler. Its closed wings are longer and more pointed, with pale tips to each primary flight feather. Its song is the best distinguishing feature. Plumage becomes duller and paler during summer. Juvenile has pale yellowish-pink legs, is fresher-coloured, often with a greenish tinge, but colour is variable. Adults have a partial moult between July and September, before migrating, and a full moult into fresh plumage in Africa in winter, prior to return migration.
SEE ALSO: Reed Warbler p236.

HABITS
Can be skulking as it feeds on the ground amongst dense vegetation, but it may also be less shy than the Reed Warbler and more likely to sing from an exposed perch such as a bush or small tree. It is a more upright species than the Reed Warbler.

VOICE
Has a very different song from a Reed Warbler: a variety of rich and sweet phrases with some churring that is typical of this family, but without the harsh notes of the Sedge Warbler. Frequently mimics other species. One individual mimicked 70 different species within half an hour, and a total of 99 British species and 133 African species have been heard. Often there are imitations of Swallows, Greenfinches and Blue Tits mixed with African species, and all running up a musical scale.

HABITAT
Requires a dense lush growth of plants such as willowherb, nettle and meadowsweet, with willows and other bushes close by. Sites are often, but not always, damp or close to water. Migrants can occur on islands,

juvenile

on headlands, in gardens, alongside streams or in fields. In winter in Africa it lives in scrub and thickets.

FOOD
Feeds among grasses and bushes and also in the lower branches of trees. Will fly up to catch flying insects. Eats chiefly insects such as beetles, caterpillars and froghoppers, and spiders. It rarely eats berries.

BREEDING
Cup-shaped nest is usually off the ground and attached to several supporting stems by what appear to be 'handles'. It is mainly the female that makes the nest from dry grasses and plant stems. Incubation of the 4 or 5 eggs is by both sexes and lasts 12–14 days. Young are cared for and fed by both adults and leave after 10–11 days. They are dependent on their parents for a further 15–19 days.

MOVEMENTS AND MIGRATIONS
Most birds seen in Britain are overshooting migrants in late May/early June from Scandinavia and eastern Europe. It leaves its breeding grounds within 2 weeks of young becoming independent, during August or September.

POPULATION
A maximum of 60–70 pairs nested in the 1970s, but numbers had fallen to only 4 by 2006.

fresh, spring

CONSERVATION
Despite protection and special management of traditional nesting sites the breeding population appears close to extinction in Britain.

DISTRIBUTION
Formerly bred in small numbers in central England. Now restricted to a handful of sites in South-east England and East Anglia. Elsewhere it breeds from southern Scandinavia south to France and east across Europe and into Russia. It winters in south-east Africa.

Icterine Warbler *Hippolais icterina*

IDENTIFICATION

13.5 cm. Larger and heavier-looking than a Willow Warbler, lacking the bold stripe over eye and with faint pale line in front of eye. Forehead is rather flat, crown peaks behind eye, and bill appears long. Greenish-grey above with a variable amount of pale yellow on underparts. Wing-tips visible beyond the tertials for almost the same length as the tertials. Yellowish fringes to flight feathers form a pale panel on the closed wings. Tail is square-ended. Feathers beneath the tail are not long and do not extend along the tail, as in a Reed Warbler. Legs are blue-grey. Yellow plumage fades to off-white during summer. Most migrants in Britain are fresh first-winter birds that have lemon-yellow on the throat and are paler below than adults. The adult has a partial moult between July and September, before migration, and then completes its moult in Africa.

SEE ALSO: Melodious Warbler p239, Willow Warbler p249, Garden Warbler p245.

fresh, spring

HABITS

Difficult to observe as it is a nervous, active bird that also perches in the open looking very upright. Quite lively, sometimes taking to the air to catch a passing insect. Tail is often flicked and the long wings are obvious in flight – rather like a Spotted Flycatcher. Crown feathers are frequently raised, making the head appear larger.

VOICE

Call is a short hard 'teck', or a triple note 'tec, tec, tec'. Song is a musical 'tey-te-dwee' that incorporates imitations of the songs and calls of other species. Song is similar to that of a Marsh Warbler, but is less rich and with phrases being repeated, especially a nasal 'geea'.

1st-winter

HABITAT

Breeds in open, broadleaved woodland with large trees and bushy undergrowth, parks and gardens, open mixed forest, forest edge, northern birch woods and the fringes of towns and villages. Breeding territories are often associated with water.

FOOD

Feeds on insects such as beetles, flies, aphids and moth caterpillars. In autumn, it also feeds on fruits.

BREEDING

Rarely breeds in Britain. The nest is a deep cup of plant stems, grasses and dead leaves. It is built by the female, which binds the structure to the stems of a bush or small tree. Egg laying is in late May or early June. Incubation of the 4 or 5 eggs is mostly by the female and lasts 13–15 days. The young are fed by both parents. They leave the nest after 13 days and become independent 8–11 days later.

MOVEMENTS AND MIGRATIONS

Summer visitor to northern Europe that arrives in late April and May and leaves between July and September. Migrants probably make one stop on an otherwise non-stop flight into Africa. In autumn, they break their journey around the Mediterranean and in spring they stop in North Africa. Most of those that reach Britain arrive either in May or in August and September, and are presumably European migrants that drift off course.

POPULATION

Nested in Scotland in 1992 and in 2009. Number of migrants reaching Britain and Ireland is over 100 a year.

CONSERVATION

Sites of possible nesting pairs are kept secret in Britain to prevent disturbance or nest robbery. No other special conservation measures are required for this species.

DISTRIBUTION

Mostly seen along the east coast of Britain, from Norfolk to Shetland. In autumn, it is also seen in the far south-west of Ireland and England, at places such as Cape Clear or in the Isles of Scilly. Breeds from northern Norway to northern France and east into Russia. Winters in southern, tropical Africa.

Melodious Warbler *Hippolais polyglotta*

IDENTIFICATION
13 cm. Larger than a Willow Warbler with a sturdier bill and lacking dark eye-stripe, being rather plain faced. Very similar to an Icterine Warbler, it's north-eastern counterpart, but with shorter wing-tips, usually plainer wings without obvious pale wing-panel and with brown legs (not blue-grey), straight bill with pale sides. Unlike a Reed Warbler the undertail feathers are short and do not extend along the under-tail. Most birds seen in Britain and Ireland are in their first autumn and have pale lemon-yellow face and throat, only extending very sparingly down the very centre of the breast. Rare spring migrants may have more uniform pale yellow under-parts. Adults and juveniles have complete moult from October to November.
SEE ALSO: Icterine Warbler p238, Willow Warbler p249, Garden Warbler p245.

1st-winter

fresh, spring adult

HABITS
Often moves quite slowly and deliberately in dense leaf cover, looks a bit pot-bellied at times. It will flycatch by chasing out of cover briefly but usually likes to pick insects from branches and foliage. It will stretch up to dislodge berries above it and can look rather clumsy at times.

VOICE
Usually migrants are silent but sometimes utter a sparrow-like 'cherrek'. Territory-holding birds have a fast, rambling song – not very musical – which includes a rhythmic 'ptss-chur-chur', a rising strong 'kooeee, kooeee' and a repeated 'bi-doo', all interspersed with sparrow-like churrs.

1st-winter

HABITAT
In breeding areas likes river valleys with areas of overgrown scrub, especially tamarisks, brambles, poplars and young alders and oaks. Migrants, usually at coastal headlands, also seek out deep cover in tama-risk, blackthorn, elder and bramble.

FOOD
Adult and larval grasshoppers, bugs, flies, beetles, ants, spiders and plant food including blackberries, elderberries, cherries and figs.

adult

BREEDING
Has not bred in Britain or Ireland. Nest is placed at about half a metre up in a shrub or small tree. It is a deep cup of plant stems and leaves with spiders' webs and is lined with fine rootlets, hair or sometimes feath-ers. Four eggs are the usual clutch and these are incu-bated for 12–14 days. The young are in the nest for up to 13 days and are fed by both parents for another 9 days.

MOVEMENTS AND MIGRATIONS
Winters in West Africa, leaving its European breeding areas in August and September. It returns north in April. In Britain and Ireland virtually all (over 94%) of records are of first-winter birds in August and early September, with a few records in July. Most records are from the south-west and south coasts.

POPULATION
Since the 1950s the Melodious Warbler has been expanding its range; from Iberia, Italy and southern France it has spread to northern France, Belgium, parts of Germany and, since 1990, the Netherlands. About 30 are identified in Britain most years but numbers have declined in recent years.

CONSERVATION
As a non-breeder there are really no special conser-vation measures to take.

DISTRIBUTION
Rare visitor to southern coast of Britain and Ireland. Replaces Icterine Warbler in south-west Europe, from Belgium and Switzerland to Spain and Portugal, and northwest Africa. Winters in West Africa.

Dartford Warbler *Sylvia undata*

male

juvenile

female

IDENTIFICATION

12.5 cm. Slightly larger than a Blue Tit. Small warbler with short wings, long thin tail and rather large, domed head. Tail is graduated and has a narrow white border. Wings are dark. Male has dark greyish-brown upperparts, dark grey head, dark wine-red underparts and an orange-red ring round its eye. It has white spots on its throat. Female is browner and a little paler than male. Juvenile is rather like female, but is rustier on the back and buffer on its underparts. Colours are brightest after moult between August and October. It has another partial moult during February and March.
SEE ALSO: Whitethroat p243.

HABITS

Skulking and can be difficult to observe in thick cover, but will occasionally venture into the open and sing from the top of a low bush. Flight is usually low, often below the tops of shrubs and bushes, and appears weak and undulating, with wings whirring and tail wagging. When perched it will often cock and flick its tail above its back and also raise the feathers on its crown. Where common, small parties of juveniles form outside the breeding season while most adults remain on their territories.

VOICE

Call is quite distinctive buzzing 'tchirrr'. The song is a 'Whitethroat-like' warble, but more metallic and musical. Song is mostly given from a perch, but it may also be delivered during a short songflight.

HABITAT

In Britain lives on dry lowland heath and commons where there is gorse and heather. Elsewhere in its range it is less specialised, occurring in areas of pine, bramble, myrtle and other areas of scrub.

FOOD

Feeds among gorse, heather, low birch trees and bushes. Eats insects and spiders and takes small beetles, caterpillars and flies. In autumn, it sometimes feeds on berries.

BREEDING

Nesting begins in April. The nest is built low down in a dense gorse bush or among thick heather. Both sexes help to build a cup of grasses and moss lined with spiders' cocoons and other soft material. The male may build one or more flimsy 'cock nests', which are sometimes finished by the female and used for a second or third brood. It is mainly the female that incubates the clutch of 3–5 eggs for 12–14 days. Young are fed by both adults and leave the nest after about 12 days. They are independent after a further 10–15 days.

MOVEMENTS AND MIGRATIONS

A resident in Britain with many adults remaining in their territories all year. Juveniles disperse from their breeding sites and some may migrate in autumn. Other European populations are partly migratory.

POPULATION

There are over 3,000 territories in Britain. Population has increased dramatically from the 10 pairs that survived the cold winter of 1962/63.

CONSERVATION

Specially protected. For years the lowland heaths of Britain were regarded as wasteland; since 1800 over 70% have been destroyed. What is left is fragmented and often degraded, and the largely sedentary and highly specialised Dartford Warbler suffered as a result. Conservation of remaining heaths and restoration of others has helped it recover. Recently it has recolonised some former habitats in southern and eastern England. It suffers during severe winter weather, which remains the biggest threat to this species, at the northern limit of its range.

DISTRIBUTION

In Britain this species is mainly confined to southern England, especially Hampshire, Dorset, Devon and Surrey, and a small newly established population along the coast of Suffolk and Essex. This is the most northerly population, elsewhere it breeds in western and southern France, Spain, Italy and along the north coast of North Africa.

Barred Warbler *Sylvia nisoria*

IDENTIFICATION
15.5 cm. A little larger than a House Sparrow. Large warbler with long tail and large head. First-winter is grey-brown with buff fringes to all the wing feathers, buff wing-bars and barring on the flanks and under the tail; off-white outer tail feathers. Adults are very rare in Britain. Adult male has grey upperparts, grey-white underparts with fine dark barring right across the underbody – like a Sparrowhawk – and white outer tail feathers and tail-tips. Has two white wing-bars and large white tips to the inner wing-feathers. Female is browner and less distinctly barred. Both adults have a very obvious yellow iris, while first-winter and juvenile birds have dark eyes.
SEE ALSO: Garden Warbler p245, Whitethroat p243.

male

HABITS
Skulking; can be difficult to track as it moves through thick vegetation. In flight, its long tail helps to make it look remarkably like a female or juvenile Red-backed Shrike. Moves rapidly through dense vegetation. On the breeding grounds adults frequently raise their crown feathers and flick their tails and have a display-flight rather like a Whitethroat, but migrant birds appear rather calmer.

female

VOICE
Usually rather silent, but it makes tacking and chur-ring calls similar to a Whitethroat, including a hard 'charr' call and a two-note 'tchad-tchad'. One call is like a quiet Mistle Thrush's rattle.

HABITAT
As a passage migrant in Britain this species is usually found in dense bushes and shrubs in coastal areas. Also arrives on windswept Northern Isles where there are few bushes and it will be forced to search out crops that grow between low walls or bramble tangles. On its eastern breeding grounds it is found in areas of dense bushes and scattered trees, and often shares its territory with Red-backed Shrikes and Thrush Nightingales.

FOOD
Feeds mainly on insects such as beetles, ants and flies, and also other invertebrates. It will eat berries and other fruits in late summer and autumn, especially blackberries and elderberries.

BREEDING
Does not breed in Britain or Ireland. In its summer breeding areas the male may build several 'cock nests' that are not used. The clutch of 4 or 5 eggs is laid in a nest that is generally built by the female. Incubation and care of the young is shared between adults. The young leave the nest at 10–12 days, before they are able to fly. They will remain in the vicinity of the nest for about 6 days before leaving the area and then quickly begin their autumn migration.

MOVEMENTS AND MIGRATIONS
Summer migrant to eastern Europe, arriving in the northern part of its range in late May and June and leaving again in August. Migrates from Africa through the Middle East and into Russia and eastern Europe. Surprisingly, very few have ever overshot their breed-ing grounds and reached Britain in spring, although some regularly arrive here in autumn. These autumn vagrants are all first-winter birds and for reasons not properly understood have set off in the opposite direction to their traditional migration routes.

POPULATION
About 150 individuals are seen each year. Nearly all are first-winter birds observed between mid-August and early November.

CONSERVATION
There are no special conservation measures in place for this species, although many of the sites where it occurs on the east coast in autumn are nature reserves.

1st-winter

DISTRIBUTION
Mainly seen along the eastern coast of Britain, including Orkney, Shetland and Fair Isle. Breeds from Denmark south to northern Italy and east to Mongolia. It winters in north-east Africa, Kenya and Ethiopia.

Lesser Whitethroat *Sylvia curruca*

male

IDENTIFICATION

12.5–13.5 cm. Smaller than a Great Tit. Compact and generally rather grey warbler that is a little smaller than a Whitethroat with more uniform grey wings and slightly shorter grey tail. Has a grey-brown back and grey head with contrasting dark grey cheeks; some have slight pale stripe from bill over eye. Adults moult between July and September, before they migrate for the winter. Moult is rapid with flight feathers being lost and regrown in about 40 days.
SEE ALSO: Whitethroat p243.

HABITS

Skulking; it is the call or song that is most likely to attract an observer's attention. It is often most easily seen when the young are out of the nest. It maintains a territory in spring, but is sociable outside the breeding season, with reports of flocks of 20 migrating together, and in Africa in winter it forms mixed feeding groups with other warblers.

BREEDING

Nests in bushes or small trees. Male builds several incomplete 'cock nests' and pairs work together to complete one of them. Nest is a loose, deep cup of grass and roots. Usually 4 or 5 eggs in a clutch. Incubation is by both birds and lasts for 10–16 days. Both adults feed the young and juveniles leave the nest at 10–13 days, when they are only able to flutter. It can have two broods.

MOVEMENTS AND MIGRATIONS

Returns to Britain in April and May having flown from its African wintering grounds around the eastern end of the Mediterranean, and from there probably a non-stop flight to Britain. From mid-July return migration begins as birds move south. Once they leave Britain it appears they fly direct to a small area in northern Italy where many rest and feed before flying on south-east, across the Mediterranean and Egypt to their wintering area. The oldest ringed bird survived for over 9 years.

POPULATION

It is estimated there are 64,000 pairs in Britain. The population fluctuates from year to year and appears to be declining in some areas.

CONSERVATION

Population in Britain was fairly stable from the 1960s until the late 1980s, but in the last 10 years has fallen by around 30%. Loss of habitat is an issue, especially thick hedges on farmland. Also depends on some specific migration stopover places and a relatively small wintering area. Any deterioration in habitat quality in these areas could have a damaging long-term effect.

fresh, autumn
or early spring

1st-winter

VOICE

Song usually delivered from within dense cover such as a bush or hedge. Call is a hard 'tac, tac' rather like a Blackcap but shorter. Song is heard from late April to June and is a dry rattle on the same note, and is very similar to a Cirl Bunting's song or the beginning of a Yellowhammer's. At close quarters a more musical warble can be heard before the rattle, and often a quiet 'stic, stic'.

HABITAT

Generally found around hawthorn or blackthorn scrub, hedgerows, shrubberies, overgrown railway embankments, disused and overgrown industrial sites, and sometimes venturing into gardens, especially in late summer.

FOOD

Chiefly feeds on invertebrates such as beetles, ants and flies, midges, caterpillars and also some fruit, especially elderberries and blackberries.

DISTRIBUTION

Breeds in England, Wales and southern Scotland, but rarely in Ireland. Most abundant in central and south-east England. Also breeds in northern, central and eastern Europe. Other races occur in Asia. European birds winter in Ethiopia or the Sudan in north-east Africa.

Whitethroat *Sylvia communis*

IDENTIFICATION

14 cm. Similar size to a Great Tit and slightly larger than a Lesser Whitethroat. Tail rather long, and crown peaked, especially when male is alarmed or displaying. Male also has a grey head, white throat and brown back with reddish-brown edges to wing feathers giving a rufous look to the closed wing. Underparts are buff or slightly pinkish and the outer tail feathers are white. As plumage becomes worn during the breeding season, the colours of the male become more drab. Female has a browner head and is generally duller than male. The first-winter bird is similar to female, but is a warmer brown with orange-brown feathers in the wing and off-white underparts. Most adults moult between July and September. It has a further partial moult in March and April when it acquires its bright spring plumage.
SEE ALSO: Lesser Whitethroat p242.

male summer

female summer

HABITS

Jerky songflight in spring, but also sings from a perch. At other times skulks in bushes and hedges, and flits between areas of cover. Maintains a territory during the breeding season and some males may have a second female. Some newly independent young flock together in late summer, often with other species such as Blackcap, Willow Warbler and Blue Tit.

VOICE

Common calls are hard 'tacc, tacc' and scolding 'tch-urrrr'. Song is a jumble of unmusical phrases. Also has a more musical song sometimes heard early in the breeding season.

HABITAT

Breeds in thick hedges, scrub, young plantations, along woodland edges, in glades with thick bushes, brambles, nettles or gorse and other places where there is tangled vegetation. It will sometimes venture into parks and gardens if there is dense vegetation. In Africa in winter many birds live in woodland areas, especially prior to their return migration.

FOOD

During the breeding season feeds on beetles, aphids, caterpillars and flies. At other times it will eat fruit, especially berries in late summer and also in its winter quarters in Africa before migrating northwards.

BREEDING

Male builds several 'cock nests' and female selects one and completes the structure. It is cup-shaped and built low down in a bush. Egg laying begins in April and peaks in May. Both sexes incubate the 4 or 5 eggs (the female generally at night) for 12–13 days. Both adults feed the young. Young leave the nest after

12–14 days and remain with their parents for 15–20 days. Sometimes the brood is split between the two parents. There are usually two broods.

MOVEMENTS AND MIGRATIONS

Summer migrant arriving between mid-April and mid-May, with the male returning before the female. It makes long migratory flights; when leaving Britain and Ireland after breeding it flies south-east to France then changes direction to south-west to Spain and Portugal. From Iberia flies to Africa. Appears to adopt a different strategy on return in spring, and flies directly north into France. The oldest survived 6 years.

POPULATION

There are 945,000 territories in the UK and 20,000–100,000 in Ireland. Following a population crash in the late 1960s a partial recovery has taken place, but the population continues to fluctuate.

CONSERVATION

The sudden dramatic decline in the late 1960s was due to droughts in the Whitethroat's wintering quarters in the Sahel area of North Africa. While in Britain and Ireland habitat quality needs to be maintained; the global issue of climate change affecting Africa is the most obvious threat.

1st-winter

DISTRIBUTION

Widespread in Britain and Ireland although avoiding urban and mountainous areas. Most numerous in the south and east and relatively thinly scattered in Ireland. In Europe breeds from the Arctic Circle to North Africa and east into Asia.

Blackcap *Sylvia atricapilla*

male

female

IDENTIFICATION

13 cm. Slightly smaller than a House Sparrow. One of the larger warblers. Male has grey-brown upperparts, ash-grey underparts and a jet-black crown and forehead extending to eye level. Back of neck and face is grey. Female is browner above and brown-grey below and has a reddish-brown cap. First-winter birds are like a dull version of the female, but during winter some black feathers start to appear on males. Adults moult between July and September, with late starters completing their moult quicker than the early ones. Moult is usually completed before migration.
SEE ALSO: Garden Warbler (song) p245, Marsh Tit p258, Willow Tit p259.

HABITS

An active and lively warbler. Generally it keeps within cover, but often it is a little easier to observe than a Garden Warbler. It is frequently aggressive towards other small birds, especially in winter when feeding at a bird table.

VOICE

The sweet and melodic song is one of the most lovely sounds of summer. Similar to that of a Garden Warbler, but Blackcap has more obvious phrases, rich clear notes, varying tempo and generally ends with a flourish. Call is a hard 'tack' and a grating 'churr'. Sometimes individuals will mimic songs and calls of other birds.

HABITAT

In summer, it lives in deciduous or mixed woodlands, copses, thickets and other bushy places, including mature gardens and parks. It generally needs a mixture of trees and bushes, unlike the Garden Warbler, which prefers thickets and coppice. Those that are seen in winter are usually in areas with shrubs and bushes and frequently visit urban and rural gardens.

FOOD

Summer food is chiefly insects such as caterpillars, flies and beetles. In autumn and winter, feeds on berries such as honeysuckle, holly, mistletoe and sea buckthorn. An opportunist feeder in winter. Will feed on windfall apples and visit bird tables and other feeders where it takes bread, fat and other scraps. Also feeds on nectar.

BREEDING

Nests in a tangle of brambles and other dense vegetation. Nesting begins in April or in May. Male builds several rudimentary nests from which the female chooses one to fashion into a neat, rather delicate cup-shaped nest. Both adults incubate the 4 or 5 eggs for 13–14 days and they both feed the young for 10–12 days before leaving the nest. Pairs nesting in the south of Britain may have a second brood.

MOVEMENTS AND MIGRATIONS

Northern populations are migratory, southerly ones are mainly resident. In Britain and Ireland it is mainly a summer visitor, with birds arriving in April and May. In the last 30 years part of the European population has changed its migratory direction to west-south-west and a small population from Germany and north-east Europe now winters here. British breeding birds fly south-east through Britain, then south-west over France and many overwinter in Spain and Portugal, but some fly on to West Africa. Oldest ringed bird was 11 years old.

POPULATION

There are 932,000 pairs in the UK and 10,000–20,000 in Ireland. Numbers have increased since the late 1970s and the species has moved northwards. The wintering population is over 3,000 and increasing.

CONSERVATION

There are no special conservation measures for this successful species. The recent increase in numbers has been linked to climate change, especially global warming.

DISTRIBUTION

It is widespread in England, southern Scotland, Wales and parts of Ireland. Smaller numbers breed in northern Scotland. It breeds from northern Scandinavia to North Africa and east into Russia. Some Blackcaps winter in Britain, especially in the south and west, but most are found around the Mediterranean and some go further to equatorial Africa.

Garden Warbler *Sylvia borin*

IDENTIFICATION
14 cm. Similar size to a Great Tit. Rather plump and large plain brown warbler with no obvious features. Has brown upperparts and buff underparts. Bill is rather short and thick, and the blue-grey legs are quite stout. Adults become greyer as breeding season progresses. Suggestion of grey on side of neck, but otherwise this is a rather nondescript species. Sexes look the same. Juvenile resembles adult except it may appear more olive in fresh plumage in late summer when compared with the greyer adult. A few adult birds moult while they are in Britain, others start and suspend their moult, but most appear to delay and undergo a complete moult in their winter quarters. SEE ALSO: Blackcap (song) p244, Chiffchaff p248, Reed Warbler p236.

fresh, spring

HABITS
An active bird but spends most of its time amongst cover and can be very difficult to see even when in song. When seen it does not usually appear as nervous as many other warblers, with no wing-flicking or tail-fanning.

VOICE
Song may be heard between April and July, an attractive stream of sweet, musical phrases that is confusingly similar to that of a Blackcap. Tends to be more even, subdued and hurried in its delivery and carries on in the same way for a long time, often singing non-stop for a minute or more. Calls are a hard 'tacc, tacc' and grating 'churr'.

HABITAT
Breeds in deciduous or mixed woodland and scrub with dense ground cover, especially in coppiced woodland. Found in copses on farmland, thick hedges and in some young conifer plantations. Not really a garden bird, except in large, mature gardens with suitable habitat.

FOOD
When nesting eats mainly invertebrates, especially caterpillars, larvae and adult beetles, larvae and adult flies, aphids, worms and spiders. At other times it eats berries and other fruit, including figs while migrating through the Mediterranean region.

BREEDING
Cup-shaped nest of grass, leaves and small twigs is built low in a shrub, small tree or among other plant stems. Usually the male builds a number of unfinished 'cock nests' from which the female chooses one to complete. Eggs are laid in May. A clutch usually comprises 4 or 5 eggs. Incubation is by both sexes and lasts for 11–13 days. Both adults feed the young, which leave the nest after 9–13 days, often before they can fly properly. They continue to be looked after by the adults for a further 10–14 days. It sometimes has two broods.

MOVEMENTS AND MIGRATIONS
Summer migrant that returns in late April and May and starts to leave again in mid-July. More are on the move during August and September, including some continental birds that drift off route in their southerly journey and arrive on British coasts. Oldest bird survived for 14 years.

POPULATION
There are 190,000 pairs in the UK and 330–400 in Ireland. Population fluctuates considerably but there is no long-term trend emerging for this species.

CONSERVATION
Overall the population seems relatively stable and there remains a considerable amount of suitable habitat for it to nest in. The future is less clear in its African wintering grounds and on its migration routes. Habitat or climate changes could affect this species in the way that other species, such as the Whitethroat, have been affected in recent years.

DISTRIBUTION
Widespread in England, Wales and southern Scotland, but scarce in northern Scotland and Ireland. Most abundant in central and southern England and in Wales. Breeds from northern Scandinavia to Spain and east into Russia. Winters in central and southern Africa.

Pallas's Warbler *Phylloscopus proregulus*

INTERNATIONAL NAME   PALLAS'S LEAF WARBLER

fresh, autumn

Europe and Britain in autumn, between September and December, but with the peak number in October or November. They are first-year birds, examples of an unknown (but small) number of individuals in the population that migrate in the opposite direction to the others. This is known as 'reverse migration'.

Population
On average 78 a year are seen. There is a pattern of more being seen in recent years.

Conservation
There are no special conservation measures in place in Britain or Ireland that can help this species.

Identification
9 cm. A tiny warbler that is only the size of a Goldcrest. It has a large head, no obvious neck, a small fine bill and a short tail. It is compact, with bright olive-green upperparts, off-white underparts and a distinctive square pale yellow patch above the rump that is often hidden by the wings. It has lots of stripes: it has one large and one small wing-bar, a dark stripe through its eye, a wide yellow stripe over the eye and another yellow stripe along the top of its dark head. The bright yellow-green secondary flight feathers form a bright panel on the closed wing. In general it tends to be brighter than the similar Yellow-browed Warbler with dull grey, not yellowish, legs.
SEE ALSO: Yellow-browed Warbler p247, Firecrest p255, Siskin p285.

Habits
This is an active and restless species. It frequently hovers to pick insects off the undersides of leaves and may hang upside down like a Blue Tit. It often flicks its wings while feeding. At other times it can be hard to see among the leaves of trees and bushes. It feeds from ground level to canopy of tall trees, but is usually over 10 m up in the canopy. Both the flight and the feeding behaviour are reminiscent of the Firecrest or Goldcrest.

Voice
The call is a high-pitched 'chu-eep', which rises upwards.

Habitat
On migration it will feed in whatever cover is available, usually near the coast. It often feeds in sycamore trees but is also seen lower down in bushes. Its native habitat is the forests in Asia, often at high altitudes, including the foothills of the Himalayas.

Food
It feeds mainly on insects.

Breeding
It does not breed in Britain or Ireland.

Movements and migrations
The Pallas's Warbler leaves its breeding grounds in late August and September and most birds fly southeast. Migrants return to their breeding territories in April and May. Vagrants regularly reach western

DISTRIBUTION

In Britain it is most likely to be seen as a rare passage migrant near the coast, especially along the east coast of England, but some are found as far west as Cornwall and the Isles of Scilly; it is very rare in Ireland. The species breeds in Russia and east into Asia. It winters in South-east Asia as far south as India and Indochina.

Yellow-browed Warbler _Phylloscopus inornatus_

IDENTIFICATION
10 cm. Smaller than a Chiffchaff and paler, with whiter underparts. It has a conspicuous long pale stripe over the eye to the nape and below this a narrow dark line through its eye. Its cheeks are mottled. The back is grey-green and the wings show two creamy wing-bars, the lower one thicker than the upper one. The inner flight feathers are conspicuously edged green, creating a bright panel on the closed wing. Inner flight feathers are edged creamy white. It has a fine, tiny dark bill. It is slightly larger and longer than a Pallas's Warbler with a green, not yellow rump, and plumage is not so bright or stripy. Some birds have the suggestion of a stripe on the crown and dark lines bordering the pale stripe above the eye, but this is never as clear as the marks on a Pallas's Warbler. The legs are usually yellowish, not grey like a Pallas's Warbler.
SEE ALSO: Pallas's Warbler p246, Firecrest p255.

BREEDING
It does not breed in Britain or Ireland. The nest is domed with an entrance at the side. The female incubates, but both adults help to feed the young. They leave the nest at 11–15 days and stay with their parents for about another 13 days.

MOVEMENTS AND MIGRATIONS
It is a summer migrant that leaves its breeding grounds in Siberia in August and September to fly to Thailand and returns again during the following April and May. Most of the birds that reach Britain are first-winter birds that 'reverse migrate' into western Europe.

fresh, autumn

HABITS
It can often be difficult to see among the leaves of trees and bushes and it is the call that usually attracts attention. It is constantly on the move as it feeds from ground level to the canopy of tall trees, but often it moves actively right through the canopy. Migrants are quite aggressive, chasing other Yellow-browed Warblers and other species away from favoured feeding areas and so holding a temporary feeding territory.

VOICE
The call is similar to that of a Coal Tit and is a loud single rising note 'suu-eet'. Individuals often call repeatedly, especially if others are also calling in the locality.

HABITAT
On migration it will feed in whatever cover is available. It often feeds in willow trees and taller sycamores. It breeds in deciduous or mixed forests, and is very common in parts of Siberia.

FOOD
It feeds mainly on insects, including beetles and flies, and also some other small invertebrates. It will sometimes hover to take prey from the underside of leaves or fly up to snatch an insect in flight.

POPULATION
About 300 reach Britain in autumn, although in some exceptional years (e.g. 1985) numbers may reach 1,000 or more. The annual total of birds observed in Britain has been increasing in recent years. Occasionally individuals are seen in winter and in spring.

CONSERVATION
As with other long-distance migrants, they are best not disturbed and allowed to feed, especially when they first arrive on our shores.

DISTRIBUTION
In Britain it is most likely to be seen near the coast, especially along the east coast, but sightings stretch from Shetland to the Isles of Scilly and a few sightings are inland or on the west coast. It is also a regular vagrant on the coast of south-west Ireland, where it visits islands and headlands. It breeds in parts of eastern Russia, China and other parts of Asia. Most winter in India and South-east Asia.

Chiffchaff *Phylloscopus collybita*

INTERNATIONAL NAME COMMON CHIFFCHAFF

IDENTIFICATION

10–11 cm. About the size of a Blue Tit. Very similar in appearance to a Willow Warbler but usually with darker legs and shorter wings. Different shape, being more compact and with more rounded head. In spring and summer, upperparts are dull green or olive-brown and the rump slightly paler. Underparts are dull yellowish. The rather short wings are marked with yellowish lines, which are the edges to the flight feathers. There is a dark line through the eye and a pale stripe above the eye. Plumage becomes duller during the summer. First-winter birds look fresh and browner than the adults, with slightly yellower underparts. Adults moult any time between June and early October. Moult is completed before they migrate for the winter.

SEE ALSO: Willow Warbler p249, Wood Warbler p250.

HABITS

Active and restless; frequently flicks its wings and dips its tail downwards. Often difficult to see within shrubs and trees, but will frequently sing from an exposed branch. Flight looks a little jerky as it moves from tree to tree. Will flutter out to catch insects in the air and sometimes hover to pick an insect from under a leaf. Usually solitary outside the breeding season, but large roosts of a hundred or more sometimes occur where it is common in winter.

fresh, autumn

VOICE

Call is loud, rising 'huitt' and the song a distinctive repeated 'zip-zap, zip-zap, zip-zap'. Between song phrases it sometimes makes a much quieter 'terric, terric' call.

HABITAT

Breeds in woods, copses and other shrubby places where there is thick undergrowth and trees, but not usually in coniferous woodland. In autumn and winter, it may visit parks and gardens.

FOOD

Feeds mainly on insects including midges, other flies, aphids and caterpillars of moths. It sometimes takes plant material such as seeds and berries, but this is not a common food.

BREEDING

The first eggs are laid in late April or early May. The site is generally among leaves, low down in bushes, especially bramble, or amongst grass. The female builds a domed nest with a side entrance. The female incubates the 5 or 6 eggs for 13–15 days. The young are mostly fed by the female and they leave the nest after 12–15 days. The young become independent 10–19 days later. Often in southern Britain it has a second brood.

MOVEMENTS AND MIGRATIONS

Most Chiffchaffs arrive in Britain and Ireland in late March and April and leave during September. Most head south-east into France and then to the Mediterranean region, and a few fly on to West Africa. Some, from northern Europe, winter in Britain. Maximum age 7 years.

POPULATION

There are over 807,000 pairs in the UK and up to 100,000 in Ireland. In winter there may be 500–1,000 individuals, mainly in the south of England. The British breeding population has increased in recent years and the small wintering population also appears to be growing.

CONSERVATION

The Chiffchaff became scarcer in the late 1960s and early 1970s in common with some other species that migrated to Africa. For the last 20 years the population has been stable or growing, but any alteration to the habitat in Africa and any changes to the climate will affect the future of these migrants.

1st-winter

DISTRIBUTION

Widely distributed in Britain and Ireland. Scarce in northern Scotland and upland areas of northern England. Also breeds from Sweden to northern Spain and east through Italy, Greece, Turkey, Bulgaria and east into Asia.

Willow Warbler *Phylloscopus trochilus*

fresh, autumn or spring

IDENTIFICATION

10.5–11.5 cm. The size of a Blue Tit. A small, slim warbler with greenish-brown upperparts and yellowish-white underparts. It becomes less yellow as the summer advances. It has pale legs, a dark line through the eye, a pale yellowish stripe over the eye and no suggestion of a wing-bar. Differs from Chiffchaff by having longer wings and slightly longer body. The most marked difference is, however, the voice. Juvenile is variable, but many have very yellow underparts. Unique among British warblers in having two complete moults a year; one between June and early September, before migration, and another in Africa between December and April.
SEE ALSO: Chiffchaff p248, Wood Warbler p250.

HABITS

Often difficult to see this species as it feeds in trees and bushes, but frequently sings from a prominent perch. An active bird, moving quickly around trees and scrub hunting for food.

VOICE

The song is a pretty, liquid series of descending notes that starts softly and ends with a flourish. The common 'hoo-ee' call is almost two notes run together.

HABITAT

Nests in young woods and plantations, scrub, along woodland edges and rides and in forest clearings. Also breeds in birch woods, especially in Scotland, on the edge of moorland and on former industrial land and gravel workings where there is a growth of bushes.

juvenile

FOOD

It feeds mainly on insects such as flies, caterpillars, beetles and midges. It also eats spiders and will feed on berries in late summer and autumn.

BREEDING

Some males are polygamous, having more than one mate at any one time, and while most are single-brooded, some males have a second family with a different female. Nesting begins in late April and May. It usually nests on the ground in a well-concealed domed nest with an entrance at the side. The nest is made from leaves, mosses and lichens and is built by the female. The female incubates the 4–8 eggs for 12–14 days. Both adults feed the young, which fly when they are 13–16 days old.

MOVEMENTS AND MIGRATIONS

Summer migrant to Britain and Ireland that arrives between March and June, with most arriving in April. By July young birds disperse in random directions, but by August they are starting to head south. At first migration is generally short flights in a southerly direction, but after refuelling in Iberia they make longer flights to their winter quarters in West Africa. Willow Warblers breeding in east Siberia also migrate to Africa, a journey of 11,250 km. The oldest ringed bird lived for more than 10 years.

POPULATION

Britain's (and Europe's) most numerous summer visitor with 2.1 million pairs in the UK and up to 1 million in Ireland. In recent years there has been a decline of over 40%, most noticeable in southern Britain.

1st-winter (fresh, autumn)

CONSERVATION

Surveys have shown that Willow Warbler populations in the south have declined while those in the north remained stable or modestly increased. Research showed that the survival of adults is poorer, especially on their migration to Africa. Research has also shown more broods are failing while the young are in the nest, due to predators, weather and, possibly, food shortage. Willow Warblers are tending to nest earlier, probably due to the changing climate.

DISTRIBUTION

Widespread in Britain and Ireland and is most abundant away from the highest hills. Breeds across northern Europe and into Russia and Asia. Winters in central and southern Africa.

Wood Warbler *Phylloscopus sibilatrix*

IDENTIFICATION

12 cm. Larger bodied and longer winged than a Willow Warbler, with a short tail. Appears bright and clean, with yellow-green upperparts, pale yellow stripe above eye, bright yellow throat and breast and pure white underparts. Flight feathers have yellowish edges that give a yellow cast to the closed wing. Plumage becomes a little greyer during summer. Legs are yellowish-brown. First-winter birds are similar to adults but duller and browner above. It has a partial moult between June and August and a full moult in its winter quarters in Africa.

SEE ALSO: Willow Warbler p249, Chiffchaff p248.

HABITS

An active species that sometimes hovers to pick insects from the underside of leaves and also captures them in flight. When perched it frequently droops its wings and does not flick its tail like some other warblers. It moves with great agility along branches. When displaying it has a beautiful 'butterfly-like' flight among the trees. Outside breeding season generally seen singly and seeks out dense cover at the tops of trees.

VOICE

Call is a loud, sweet sounding, rather plaintive 'pew-pew'. Song a remarkable series of 'tsic, tsic' notes that accelerates into a shivering trill, with the bird trembling as it sings. Song is not usually given for a second time from the same perch and sometimes it will sing during its display flight. Also has a second song that is made up of the 'pew' notes.

HABITAT

Prefers mature upland oakwoods with a high canopy and limited ground vegetation. Also breeds in beech woods, and elsewhere in Europe it uses woods of pine, alder, birch or mixed deciduous woods. Winters in forests in equatorial Africa.

FOOD

Feeds mainly on insects such as moth caterpillars, craneflies and other flies and beetles. Also eats spiders. Takes very little plant material.

BREEDING

Males defend individual territories, but these territories are sometimes in 'clusters' within suitable woodlands, and males will often try to attract a second mate. Nests on the ground where there is a little cover, or under a fallen tree trunk or branch. Female builds the nest. There are 5–7 eggs, incubated by the female for 12–14 days. Both adults feed the young until they leave the nest at 11–13 days. They continue to feed them for a further 2–3 days and sometimes the family is split between the two parents, or the family may stay together for up to 4 weeks. Usually one brood, but sometimes two.

MOVEMENTS AND MIGRATIONS

A summer migrant that returns to Britain in late April and early May and leaves again in July and August.

Wood Warblers seem to arrive on their breeding sites with only very few being seen at the coast. It appears British Wood Warblers make unbroken flights to southern Europe, often Italy, and then fly on to the southern fringe of the Sahara Desert. In spring they break their journey on the North African coast.

POPULATION

There are fewer than 17,000 territories in Britain and fewer than 20 in Ireland. It appears the British population has fallen by over 60% since 1994.

CONSERVATION

Like a number of woodland species, Wood Warbler populations have declined in recent years for reasons that are far from clear. The cause may be changes in woodland management, but is more likely to be changes in their winter habitats in Africa, possibly linked to climate change.

fresh, spring

1st-winter

DISTRIBUTION

Found mainly in the west of Britain with fewer in the east and only a few in Ireland. The highest density is in Wales. Breeds from Scandinavia to Italy and east into Russia. Winters in central Africa.

Spotted Flycatcher *Muscicapa striata*

IDENTIFICATION

14.5 cm. Size of a House Sparrow. The dark bill is long and wide, the head quite rounded and the wings and tail rather long. Has grey-brown upperparts, off-white underparts, streaks on breast and fine streaking on crown. There are pale edges to wing feathers. Very upright when perched. Sexes are similar. Juvenile has a more scaly or spotted appearance, rather like a juvenile Robin. Adults are unusual in that sequence of moulting flight feathers is often irregular. Adults split their moult, having a partial moult between July and September before migration and a complete moult between November and March in Africa. Some may not complete moult before spring migration and will complete it on their breeding grounds.

SEE ALSO: Dunnock p215, Tree Pipit p206.

large insects are not flying it resorts to searching amongst foliage for insects such as aphids and smaller flies. Before laying their eggs, females may feed on calcium-rich food such as small snails and woodlice. Cool wet weather in spring can significantly reduce the food available and results in the loss of young.

BREEDING

Nest-site is a natural or artificial ledge or niche where the nest is usually sheltered. Sites may be among ivy and other creepers on a tree trunk or a wall, in the old nest of another species or in a specially made open-fronted nest box. The rather loose cup-shaped nest of twigs, grasses and roots is built by both sexes. The female incubates the 4 or 5 eggs for 13–15 days. Both adults feed the young until they leave the nest at about 13–16 days. The young remain dependent on their parents for a further 12–32 days. Some pairs raise a second smaller brood, especially in southern Britain.

MOVEMENTS AND MIGRATIONS

It is a summer migrant, with most returning in late May – one of the last migrants to return. Its arrival depends on weather conditions in southern Europe. It is a long-distance migrant with most wintering south of the equator. Our breeding birds start to leave in July and August. Birds from further east arrive in Britain as passage migrants in September. They are nocturnal migrants. The oldest known bird lived for 11 years.

POPULATION

There were 63,700 pairs in the UK and over 20,000 in Ireland in 2000, but it has declined by over 80% since 1969 and is still declining.

CONSERVATION

The causes of the recent decline are not understood. There may be real problems in the wintering areas or on the migration routes. These problems may be connected to deteriorating habitats due to droughts, or activities of man, or both.

1st-winter

juvenile

HABITS

Regularly hunts from a bare branch or other prominent position. Flies out, often chasing its prey erratically, and seizes a flying insect, before returning to the same perch or another close by. It can be tolerant of humans.

VOICE

Call is a thin repeated 'tzee' that has been likened to a squeaking wheelbarrow! The alarm is a sharper clicking 'eez-tchick'. Song is a rather quiet series of high-pitched notes and low scratchy warbles.

HABITAT

A bird of woodland glades and woodland edges, large mature gardens and parks with a mixture of mature trees and younger trees or bushes.

FOOD

Mainly feeds on flying insects, especially larger flies and it also catches butterflies. In cooler weather when

DISTRIBUTION

It is widespread in Britain and Ireland, but scarce in the far west of Ireland and the Scottish Islands. It breeds from northern Scandinavia to the north coast of North Africa and east into western Asia.

Red-breasted Flycatcher *Ficedula parva*

IDENTIFICATION
11.5 cm. The size of a Blue Tit. It is a small, dumpy flycatcher with a rounded head. Sits upright and habitually flicks its black tail up and down and droops its wings. There are two white patches at the base of the tail. First-year males and females have drab brown upperparts, buff-white underparts and the distinctive tail pattern. Older adult males have a grey face and shoulders and an orange-red chin, but it may take the male between 2 and 4 years to acquire his full adult plumage. The eye is large and surrounded by a thin pale eye-ring. First-winter birds in autumn show some buff spots forming a thin wing-bar.
SEE ALSO: Robin p216, Pied Flycatcher p253.

HABITS
This species likes to find sheltered copses and valleys, and can be secretive on migration. It also sometimes catches flies from a prominent perch like a typical flycatcher. It frequently flicks its wings and cocks its tail above its back. It is usually seen singly. On its breeding grounds it lives in the high canopy of tall trees.

VOICE
The usual call is a rattling note, rather like a Wren's. It also makes a loud sharp 'chick'.

male summer

in spring as they apparently overshoot their breeding grounds. Larger numbers arrive between August and November, with a peak in early October, either because their migratory journey has been reversed or they have been helped by anticyclonic weather conditions. Nearly all are seen along the east and south coasts of England and Scotland, with concentrations on Shetland, Cornwall and the Isles of Scilly.

POPULATION
In recent years the number of Red-breasted Flycatchers seen in Britain has averaged around 86.

CONSERVATION
There is no special conservation measure for this rare migrant.

1st-winter

female

HABITAT
A passage migrant in Britain. It visits mature trees in gardens and wooded valleys near the coast, or – if no trees are available – searches out sheltered quarries or gorges in cliffs. It breeds in old deciduous woodland, often near water or in clearings in forests. It is also sometimes found closer to habitation in orchards and vineyards.

FOOD
It may search for food in the tree canopy or catch prey on the wing. It feeds mainly on insects and other invertebrates such as flies, beetles, ants and spiders.

BREEDING
It does not breed in Britain or Ireland. In its native woodlands it builds a nest on the side of a tree. It lays 5 or 6 eggs that are incubated by the female. The young leave the nest after 11–15 days.

MOVEMENTS AND MIGRATIONS
These birds arrive on their breeding grounds in May and June and leave again in August and September. This species occurs as a scarce passage migrant to Britain and, occasionally, to Ireland. A few are seen

DISTRIBUTION
It breeds from southern Scandinavia south to northern Turkey and east across Asia. It winters in India and South-east Asia. The discovery of a small number of birds south-west of their breeding areas in autumn has caused speculation that some of the European birds may winter in Africa. Small numbers reach Britain and western Europe in spring and autumn.

Pied Flycatcher *Ficedula hypoleuca*

INTERNATIONAL NAME EUROPEAN PIED FLYCATCHER

IDENTIFICATION

13 cm. Slightly smaller than a House Sparrow. Smaller and plumper than a Spotted Flycatcher, with a proportionally shorter tail with white edges. Adult male in spring is black and white. Upperparts are mostly dull black with a bold white patch on the folded wing and a white spot above the bill. Underparts are white. After breeding it moults into brown or grey plumage with blackish rump and tail and buff underparts, but it retains the white in the wing and tail. Female resembles the non-breeding male but has browner rump and tail. Juvenile resembles female in colour, but has spotting on upperparts and some speckling on underparts. Moult sometimes begins while the adults are feeding young in June and is mostly completed before the birds migrate. There is a partial moult into breeding plumage in January and February while it is still in winter quarters.
SEE ALSO: Pied Wagtail p212, Spotted Flycatcher p251.

male summer

male winter

HABITS

Often cocks its tail and flicks its wings nervously. Darts out from a perch to catch a fly, but (unlike the Spotted Flycatcher) it never appears to return to the same perch. Sometimes clings to branches like a tit and occasionally feeds on the ground. Can be quite obvious when nesting but after the young leave the nest they and their parents disappear quickly from the neighbourhood, feeding high in trees or in dense shrubs as they prepare for migration.

VOICE

Call is a sharp 'whit' and also a 'tic'. Song is a simple series of rather sweet notes 'suee-suee-sweet-sweet'.

HABITAT

Breeds in mature deciduous woodland, especially oak woods and sometimes birch woods with little undergrowth. Where numerous, it uses gardens and parks, often near streams and rivers. In other parts of range nests in mixed or pine woodland.

FOOD

Feeds mainly on invertebrates and some fruits and seeds. Insect food includes caterpillars, flies, beetles, bugs and ants. Spiders and millipedes are also taken.

BREEDING

Female builds the nest in a hole in a tree – often an old woodpecker's hole. Nest boxes are also used. Nest is a loose structure of leaves, grass, roots and moss. The 6 or 7 eggs are incubated by female for 13–15 days. Young are fed by both adults and leave after 16–17 days. Some males have a second or third mate. Such males feed the first brood, but are less supportive to others.

MOVEMENTS AND MIGRATIONS

Summer migrant with males returning ahead of females between mid-April and June. In August and September it makes a non-stop flight to northern Spain and Portugal where it mixes with other Pied Flycatchers from elsewhere in Europe; all refuelling ready for the next leg of their journey to Africa. They return from Africa by a more easterly route. The oldest ringed bird survived 10 years.

POPULATION

There may have been 35,000–40,000 pairs in Britian in 2000, but over the last 25 years the population has fallen by almost 50%.

CONSERVATION

This appears to be another example of a woodland species that winters in Africa that is in trouble. It has been helped considerably in the UK by nest box schemes that provide suitable nest-sites in woods where there is a shortage of natural holes, or where the best potential holes are used by other species before these migrants return in spring.

juvenile

female

DISTRIBUTION

Breeds mainly in western Britain and is especially abundant in Wales. Breeds from northern Scandinavia and across northern Europe. Also breeds in France, Spain and a few places in North Africa. Winters in West Africa.

Goldcrest *Regulus regulus*

IDENTIFICATION

9 cm. Britain and Ireland's smallest bird. Tiny, rather round-looking species with small rounded wings and large eyes. Upperparts are dull green, underparts off-white and it has a yellow or orange patch on the crown of its head that is bordered with black. Crown patch is more yellow on females and, when raised in display, shows deep orange on males. There are two whitish wing-bars. Juvenile is similar to adult, but lacks the yellow/orange crest. Adults have a complete moult between June and October. Sometimes it begins its moult after rearing the first brood, but it suspends its moult if it begins a second brood.
SEE ALSO: Firecrest p255, Pallas's Warbler p246, Yellow-browed Warbler p247.

HABITS

A very small, hyperactive species that always seems to be on the move. Tit-like, it will feed among branches and sometimes hover to snatch food from the undersides of leaves. It sometimes ignores an approaching observer. Outside the breeding season it often joins flocks of other small birds such as tits and warblers as they forage for food in woods and hedgerows. In parts of Europe small groups of Goldcrests defend winter territories.

VOICE

Call is a high-pitched, thin 'tsee' that is useful for locating this species. Song is sometimes heard in winter and regularly from February. It is a high-pitched, wheeling 'tee-lee-de, tee-lee-de'.

HABITAT

Stronghold is in coniferous woodland and also in conifer plantations, but it will nest in churchyard yews, in parks and in large gardens with mature trees. Outside the breeding season it appears in a variety of habitats where there are at least some trees or thick bushes. Migrants that arrive on treeless islands or headlands may be seen flitting around boulders and cliff edges.

FOOD

It feeds almost exclusively on insects and spiders and sometimes it eats small seeds. Insect food includes flies, beetles and small caterpillars.

BREEDING

Nesting begins in late April. Nest is a deep, rounded cup of moss, lichen and spiders' webs, and is suspended in a fork of twigs at the end of a conifer branch. The male may build the nest, but usually both birds work on it. Female incubates the 6–8 eggs for 16–19 days, which hatch over 1–4 days. Young are fed by both adults. They leave the nest after about 18 days and become independent 2 weeks later. A second nest may be built and eggs laid before young of first brood leave the first nest. At these times the responsibility of feeding the first brood falls to the male.

MOVEMENTS AND MIGRATIONS

British and Irish Goldcrests are mainly resident, but those further north in Scandinavia and east in Poland and Russia are migrants, making night-long flights, stopping to feed and then moving on. Migration from Scandinavia peaks when there is high pressure over the Baltic Sea. Some migrants reach Britain, especially in October, and they will remain until March. Occasionally, in autumn, exceptional numbers arrive along the east coast. The oldest known Goldcrest lived for 7 years.

POPULATION

There are 842,000 pairs in the UK and 100,000–250,000 in Ireland. The population fluctuates, but the long-term trend is a slight increase.

male displaying

female

juvenile

CONSERVATION

This species is adversely affected by cold winters. It was badly affected in the early 1960s and did not fully recover until the mid-1970s. Since then the population has continued to fluctuate.

DISTRIBUTION

Widespread in Britain and Ireland but scarce in the fenland of East Anglia and the far north of Scotland. It breeds from northern Scandinavia to northern Spain and east into Asia. The most northerly territories in Europe and Russia are abandoned in winter.

Firecrest *Regulus ignicapillus*

IDENTIFICATION
9 cm. Only marginally larger than a Goldcrest. Firecrest is more brightly coloured, with greener upperparts, whiter underparts and a strongly striped head, including a dark stripe through the eye and a very obvious broad white stripe over eye and bordered black above. Male has a startling orange-red and yellow patch on crown. Female's crown patch is more yellow. Both sexes have a bronze patch on side of neck. Juvenile lacks the orange/yellow crown but does have a white stripe above its eye. Adults have a complete moult between July and September.
SEE ALSO: Goldcrest p254, Yellow-browed Warbler p247, Pallas's Warbler p246.

male

juvenile

HABITS
Behaviour is similar to that of the Goldcrest, although it tends to feed lower down, sometimes in shrubs and bushes, especially when on migration. Appears slightly larger in flight than a Goldcrest. Like the Goldcrest it sometimes joins wandering flocks of small birds outside the breeding season.

VOICE
Usual call is a 'zit', lower pitched than Goldcrest and often a single note whereas a Goldcrest usually runs three or more call notes together. Song is a succession of 'zit' notes that get louder and faster. It is slightly slower and harsher than a Goldcrest's song and ends suddenly without a flourish. Song is most commonly heard in May and June.

female

HABITAT
Breeds in woodland and favours Norway spruce plantations in Britain, but generally it is less dependent on conifers than the Goldcrest, and also occurs in deciduous or mixed woods with rich understorey. In some places it has nested where oak, beech or holly are the dominant trees. On migration it visits scrub and low bushes, often in wooded valleys near the coast.

FOOD
Eats mainly insects and other invertebrates including springtails, spiders, aphids, caterpillars, flies, bugs, beetles and small snails.

BREEDING
Female builds a nest that is suspended between twigs towards the end of a branch. It is ball-shaped and made from moss, lichens, spiders' webs and mainly lined with hair and feathers. Female incubates the 7–10 eggs for 15–17 days. Both adults feed the young until they leave the nest at about 20 days. They continue to feed the fledglings until they become independent at about 11 days after leaving the nest. It can have two broods.

MOVEMENTS AND MIGRATIONS
Both a summer visitor and a passage migrant to Britain, with a few also seen in some winters. Southern European populations are mainly resident and those further north and east are migratory. First-winter migrants usually arrive on British coasts in September and October. In some years when there are anticyclones in late October more birds arrive, probably part of a larger movement triggered by the onset of winter weather further east. There is a return movement in March and April.

POPULATION
About 350 pairs have nested in recent years, and this may be an underestimate. Reports of singing birds in spring are not, however, a reliable indication of breeding as many of these singing males fail to attract a mate.

CONSERVATION
Specially protected. Britain is on the edge of its range. First nested in the New Forest in 1962 and by 1970 was found in several other locations in southern England and Wales. Commercial forestry helped the colonisation of southern Britain, and the most recent increases may have been aided by climate changes.

DISTRIBUTION
In Britain breeds mainly in south-east England with a few pairs in the south-west and East Anglia. Breeds from Denmark and Poland to North Africa and east to the Black Sea. More widespread in southern Europe and North Africa in winter.

Bearded Tit *Panurus biarmicus*

INTERNATIONAL NAME **BEARDED REEDLING**

male

female

juvenile

IDENTIFICATION

16.5 cm. Larger than a Long-tailed Tit. Small, dumpy, ginger-brown bird with a long tail. Male has a lavender-grey head, black 'moustache' and black under the tail. Has white outer tail feathers and strongly marked white, black and orange-brown wings. Female is duller and lacks the 'moustache' and the black under the tail. Juvenile similar to female, with a shorter tail, a dark centre to the back and dark edges to the tail. Wings are short and rounded. Flight is weak-looking with whirring wings. Adults moult between June and early October. Young moult at the same time; those fledged early in the season take about 55 days to moult and regrow their primary flight feathers while those fledged later complete their primary moult in just 40 days.

HABITS

Clambers up reed stems or hops about on ground, usually close to cover. Flight is often loose and jerky with characteristic fanning and twisting of tail as it flies low over the tops of the reeds, but it goes higher at times of irruption. Can be hard to see in a dense reedbed and it is often the distinctive call that attracts attention. Sociable, small flocks travel together for much of the year.

VOICE

Call is a metallic ringing 'ping, ping' that may be given from cover, but also frequently by groups in flight. Song is a rather quiet twittering.

HABITAT

Found almost exclusively in dense reedbeds or vegetation around the edge of a reedbed. At times of irruptions and migrations it may sometimes visit another habitat such as rank grass.

FOOD

Feeds mainly on invertebrates and seeds. In summer, the invertebrates include beetles, caterpillars, flies, especially midges, spiders and snails. In winter, feeds on the seed of the common reed.

BREEDING

Breeding begins in April. Nest is built among reeds where the plants grow thickly. The nest is a deep cup made from reed leaves and other marsh vegetation, and lined with fluffy down from reed heads. Both sexes help to build the nest and more material may be added during egg laying and incubation. The 4–8 eggs are incubated by both sexes for about 10–14 days. Young leave nest after 12–13 days. They are able to feed themselves after a week and become independent after another week. There may be two or possibly three broods in a season.

MOVEMENTS AND MIGRATIONS

Most birds in Britain are sedentary, but in autumn there is sometimes a mass dispersal. Birds from the Netherlands and further east can disperse as far as Britain in irruption years. At these times pairs or groups may set off in any direction and they will set up new winter territories, provided they find the appropriate habitat. The oldest ringed bird lived for over 7 years.

POPULATION

There are over 600 pairs nesting in Britain.

CONSERVATION

This species has been affected by the historic loss of many large reedbeds, which has resulted in a very fragmented habitat. Its population also falls if there are periods of prolonged ice and snow in winter. Better protection of the remaining reedbeds and recent schemes by the RSPB and other organisations to recreate extensive new reedbeds should help this species. Also, a new technique for helping them involves making artificial nest-sites within reedbeds.

DISTRIBUTION

Most colonies in Britain are in East Anglia, with others along the south coast of England, in Lancashire and Yorkshire and an isolated colony in eastern Scotland. Slightly more widespread in winter.

Long-tailed Tit *Aegithalos caudatus*

IDENTIFICATION

14 cm, of which 9 cm is tail. Tiny round bird with a long narrow tail, short rounded wings and a stubby bill. Pinkish-brown above, pinkish-white below, with dark marks on sides of head and a white crown. Wings are blackish with pale lines caused by pale edges to the major flight feathers. Tail has white outer feathers. Northern and eastern European birds have white heads (but only rarely visits the British Isles). Flight appears weak and undulating, with the long tail the most obvious feature. Juvenile is similar to adult but with smoky grey head. Adults moult between May and October.
SEE ALSO: Pied Wagtail p212.

flock in flight

HABITS

Highly sociable species producing large broods of young and travelling through woods and along hedges in family flocks for much of the year. They roost in groups and during cold weather huddle together to conserve body heat. Restless and acrobatic as they feed actively among branches of trees and bushes, often hanging upside down to reach food. In spring, it has a butterfly-like display flight.

VOICE

Common call is a thin, high-pitched 'see, see, see' often interspersed with a short, rolling 'thrup'. Song rarely heard – an elaborate version of the calls.

HABITAT

Breeds along deciduous woodland fringes, in scrub, hedgerows, parks and in other bushy places. Outside breeding season travels more widely and sometimes visits gardens where there are bushes and trees.

FOOD

Feeds on invertebrates, including flies, beetles and spiders, also on eggs, larvae, pupae and adults of moths and butterflies. Also eats seeds, and has adapted to feeding at bird tables and on hanging food. This behaviour has become more widespread in recent years.

BREEDING

Nesting begins in late March and early April. Male and female build the nest in bramble, gorse or other thick shrubs. It is a delicate round or oval structure made from moss, bound with cobwebs and lined with lots of feathers. The outside is covered in lichens. The result is a rather elastic nest that expands with the growing young inside. The entrance hole is at the side. Female incubates 6–8 eggs that hatch after about 15 days. Young fly after 16 days and are fed by both parents, and for a further 2 weeks or so after fledging. Some adults, especially males that fail to rear their young, frequently help to feed a neighbouring family.

MOVEMENTS AND MIGRATIONS

Most are sedentary but some make local movements after nesting. Wintering birds have a feeding territory and move around this area in flocks that are made up of families from the previous breeding season plus additional helpers. Sometimes family flocks will join together and frequently attract other small birds such as tits and warblers to travel with them. The oldest known bird survived over 10 years.

POPULATION

There are 273,000 pairs in the UK and 20,000–100,000 in Ireland. The population fluctuates from year to year, but generally in recent years there has been a moderate increase.

CONSERVATION

Greatest influence on this species is the winter weather, when severe frost can, in a few days, reduce the population. Like other small birds, Long-tailed Tit populations recover quickly from such disasters. Habitat changes have not adversely affected this species and there is evidence it is breeding more successfully, and possibly benefiting from recent climate change.

juvenile

DISTRIBUTION

Widespread in Britain and Ireland, but more abundant in the south than the north, and it does not breed on Shetland, Orkney and the Outer Hebrides although it may wander to offshore islands in autumn. Breeds from northern Scandinavia to southern Europe and also in Asia.

Marsh Tit *Poecile palustris*

IDENTIFICATION

11.5 cm. Size of a Blue Tit. Plain brown bird with a rather sleek black cap and pale cheeks. Best way of separating this species from the similar-looking Willow Tit is by its call. Cheeks appear whiter and contrast more with the grey-brown neck than those of Willow Tit, and the paler edges to the flight feathers seldom produce any form of pale panel on closed wings. There is also a pale mark near the base of the bill, just below the nostril. Adults moult between mid-May and mid-September.

SEE ALSO: Willow Tit p259, Blackcap p244.

HABITS

Usually feeds in shrubs and low vegetation and is less likely to be seen in the canopy of the trees. A restless feeder, always on the move. Can be difficult to see in dense vegetation, but not usually shy of humans. Outside the nesting season it can sometimes be seen with flocks of other small birds. When it discovers a ready supply of food, such as sunflower seeds at a bird feeder, it will methodically secrete large numbers in nooks and crevices as a store for the future.

BREEDING

Nesting begins in April. Nests in natural holes and does not often use nest boxes. It may enlarge an existing hole or cavity but does not excavate its own hole, unlike the Willow Tit. Nest is usually low down. The female lines the nest with a cup of moss, hair and other soft materials. The female incubates the 6–8 eggs for 14–16 days. Young leave the nest after 16–17 days and are fed by their parents for a further week. Families stay together as a group for about 2 weeks after nesting and then the young join mixed flocks of tits and other species as they travel around local woods and hedges in search of food.

MOVEMENTS AND MIGRATIONS

This is a resident species that roams a territory of about 5–6 ha. It appears that once settled neither male nor female will leave the territory again. They may join groups of itinerant small birds passing through their territories, but they leave the flock as it reaches the territory boundary.

POPULATION

Estimated at 52,800 pairs in Britain in 2003. Rapid decline of 66% since 1969, although there may have been a partial recovery in some areas.

CONSERVATION

The recent decline may be a result of lower survival rates caused by poorer management of woodland as a good proportion of mature trees with natural holes and a flourishing shrub layer need to be maintained.

juvenile

VOICE

Call is a loud and clear 'pit-chu', quite unlike the call of the Willow Tit, which is followed by 'dee, dee'. Song is a rapid series of single or double 'chip' notes that run into each other to become a rattle.

HABITAT

Breeds in open deciduous woodland, parks and farmland with woods and copses. Will visit large mature gardens, especially in winter.

FOOD

Feeds on insects, especially scale insects, and other invertebrates in summer. Eats seeds in autumn and winter. Often extracts the seeds from small berries, such as honeysuckle. Has a strong bill and can tackle quite hard seeds and small nuts.

DISTRIBUTION

This species is most abundant in southern England and South Wales, and a few breed in southern Scotland. It breeds from southern Scandinavia to the Mediterranean and east into Russia. Then there is a break in the distribution and there is another population in south-west Asia.

Willow Tit *Poecile montanus*

IDENTIFICATION
11.5 cm. Size of a Blue Tit. Plain brown with a rather large head and thick neck, a black cap and pale cheeks. Differs from the Marsh Tit by having a different call, but otherwise difficult to separate by sight. All-black bill, no contrast between the pale cheeks and the pale neck feathers, and pale margins to flight feathers that form a pale panel on the closed wing are useful pointers. Juvenile is similar to an adult but with fresher plumage in late summer and is almost inseparable from the juvenile Marsh Tit. The race breeding in parts of northern and eastern Europe has whiter cheeks, paler underparts and a more grey-brown back than other races. Adults moult between mid-May and September.
SEE ALSO: Marsh Tit p258, Blackcap p244.

HABITS
Outside the breeding season it will often join with flocks of other small birds as they move through its territory, but will not normally follow the flock beyond the boundaries of its own winter territory.

VOICE
Call is a nasal 'si, si, taah, taah, taah', very different from the call of the Marsh Tit. The sweet warbling song of slow descending whistling notes is not often heard.

HABITAT
Breeds in conifer woodlands, northern birch woods and in mixed woodlands. Prefers damp woods, woods close to rivers and streams, alder carr and trees and bushes surrounding gravel pits and reservoirs. Less likely to visit garden bird tables than the Marsh Tit.

FOOD
Its bill is not quite as strong as that of the Marsh Tit and the food is slightly different. Like the Marsh Tit it eats invertebrates in summer and mostly plant material in autumn and winter, but the seeds (e.g. alder and birch) are smaller or softer. It frequently hoards food if it has the opportunity.

BREEDING
Nesting begins in mid-April. It excavates a new nest-hole every year. Nests are in rotten wood and usually quite close to the ground. Female excavates the nest, carries away the wood chippings and lines the hollow with wood chips and a little plant material. The 6–8 eggs are incubated by the female alone for 13–15 days. The young are fed by both adults and fly after about 17 days.

MOVEMENTS AND MIGRATIONS
British Willow Tits are highly sedentary. In Europe they may wander considerable distances and may even irrupt into new areas if food becomes scarce. The oldest ringed bird survived over 10 years.

POPULATION
There are 8,500 pairs in Britain. The population has fallen by over 80% since 1969.

CONSERVATION
This species has been declining for 30 years. The lack of dead wood, the drying out of some woodland, and the loss of the shrub layer caused by changing woodland management are all possible causes for the decline, but the complete picture is poorly understood.

juvenile

DISTRIBUTION
In Britain this species is most abundant in central England and in Wales, and it is rare in northern Scotland. Elsewhere it is found generally to the north of the range of Marsh Tits. The Willow Tit breeds from northern Scandinavia to central Europe and east through Russia to the Far East, including Japan.

Crested Tit *Lophophanes cristatus*

IDENTIFICATION
11.5 cm. Size of a Blue Tit. Has a brown back and pale buff underparts, rather like a Marsh or Willow Tit, but its face is off-white with a black bib, speckled forehead and crown and a pointed crest. Has a blackish mark through the eye and curving round its cheeks. Also has a thin black collar. Juvenile has slightly less distinct head marks and slightly shorter crest, but is otherwise similar to adult. Adults have a complete moult between July and September.
SEE ALSO: Blue Tit p262.

HABITS
An active and restless feeder, constantly moving as it searches for food by hanging on tree trunks or upside down as it searches the underside of branches. After nesting it forms small social groups that will also join with other species such as Coal Tits and Goldcrests. They travel together, but seldom go beyond the boundaries of their winter feeding territory. Social flocks start to break down in February and March.

VOICE
Call is a thin high-pitched trill often repeated rhythmically. It is similar in quality to the call of a Long-tailed Tit, but sharper. It also makes a high-pitched 'see, see, see' call. Song is combination of the various calls run together.

HABITAT
In Scotland usually associated with Scots pine although it may sometimes be seen in other conifers and even in rowan, alder and birch in winter. When breeding, it prefers old native Scots pine forest, especially where there are stands of older trees, often with heather nearby. Elsewhere in its range it is also associated with pine forests, but also some mixed woodland and even beech forests are inhabited in the Pyrenees.

FOOD
Spends most of its feeding time foraging in pines, often in the larger trees in summer, and sometimes in smaller trees in winter. May feed in the crown of the trees and on the ground. Feeds mainly on insects such as moths, caterpillars, aphids and beetles and other invertebrates, especially spiders. Also feeds on seeds, particularly in winter, and sometimes, where it is common, it visits bird tables in gardens. In Norway it is known to store food, including the larvae of insects.

BREEDING
In Scotland, selects rotten tree stumps or dead trees in which the female excavates a nest chamber and lines it with moss and other soft material. Female incubates the clutch of 4–6 eggs for 13–16 days. The young are fed by both parents and they leave their nest after 18–22 days. They are usually dependent on their parents for about 23 days before becoming independent and forming pairs for the winter.

MOVEMENTS AND MIGRATIONS
Highly resident and very few have been seen away from the normal breeding areas. In the east of its range it may exceptionally wander further in winter. Oldest known bird lived for 11 years.

POPULATION
There are 1,000–2,000 pairs in Scotland.

CONSERVATION
Specially protected. Protecting the remaining native Scots pine forest, the retention of dead and decaying timber and the planting of new Scots pine woods (rather than non-native species) will help, as will the provision of nest boxes – especially if filled with wood shavings and sawdust. These boxes give birds a chance to excavate their own nest.

juvenile

DISTRIBUTION
In Britain restricted mainly to the remnants of the old native Scot's pine forest and some mature plantation pine forests in the Highlands between the Spey valley and the Moray Firth. Breeds from central Scandinavia south to the Mediterranean and east into western Russia as far as the Balkans.

Coal Tit *Periparus ater*

IDENTIFICATION
11.5 cm. Smaller than a Great Tit. Small tit with a short tail and rather large head. Head is black with white cheeks, like a Great Tit, but it also has white stripe on the back of its head. Back, wings and tail are a dull blue-grey. Underparts are plain and buff with no black central stripe and it has two small white bars on its closed wings. Coal Tits in Ireland have yellow tinge to their cheeks and neck-patch. Those on the Continent tend to have greyer backs. Juvenile looks like a duller version of the adults with yellow (not white) wing-bars. Adults moult between late May and early September. Juveniles mostly moult before the winter, but the yellow wing-bars may be retained until the following spring.
SEE ALSO: Great Tit p263, Crested Tit p260.

HABITS
An active and very agile bird that often feeds high in the canopy of trees and also searches the trunks of trees for food, rather like a Treecreeper. Hangs upside down and also hovers to reach food on the underside of branches and leaves. Outside breeding season it frequently accompanies roving flocks of other small birds such as Long-tailed Tits and Goldcrests as they move through the woods and along hedgerows.

FOOD
Main food is adults and larvae of insects, including caterpillars. Also feeds on other invertebrates, especially spiders, and many seeds are eaten in autumn and winter. Much of the food is found among the leaves and needles of its favourite trees, but it will feed on the ground at sites where there is a supply of food such as beech-mast. When food is plentiful the Coal Tit will hide some of it and retrieve it later. It will also visit bird tables in gardens in winter where it will feed on peanuts and other bird food.

BREEDING
Nests in a hole in a tree or some other crevice and sometimes in the ground. Female makes a cup-shaped nest of roots, moss and other soft material. Female incubates the clutch of 9 or 10 eggs for 14–16 days. Young are fed by both adults and leave their nest after 16 days. There is sometimes a second brood – especially by pairs nesting in conifer woods.

MOVEMENTS AND MIGRATIONS
In Britain and Ireland mostly sedentary with some local movements after breeding season. In Europe many northern and eastern populations travel further and may irrupt at times of food shortages. Some continental birds reach Britain, especially the south-east. Oldest wild bird survived for over 8 years.

POPULATION
There are 653,000 pairs in the UK and over 100,000 in Ireland. In some areas Coal Tits have increased in recent years, but overall there is no long-term trend.

CONSERVATION
For a species that is mostly resident, the abundance of food and the weather are the biggest influences on the size of the population. The Coal Tit has, therefore, benefited from the planting of commercial conifer forests and from recent mild winters.

juvenile

VOICE
Many calls sound like a high-pitched Great Tit. Makes a thin 'see, see, see' call and has a loud song that is a repetitive double note 'pea-chew, pea-chew', but there is variety in these songs.

HABITAT
Chief habitat is conifer woods and plantations, but also common in sessile oak woods of north and west England and birch woods of north-west Scotland. Often visits parks and gardens outside the breeding season. Elsewhere in Europe more closely associated with conifer woods in the north and breeds in more varied woodland in the south.

DISTRIBUTION
Widespread species that is especially abundant in Wales, Scotland and Ireland, and also in parts of England where there are extensive conifer forests. Breeds from Scandinavia south to the Mediterranean, and in parts of North Africa. Its range extends east to eastern Asia.

Blue Tit *Cyanistes caeruleus*

IDENTIFICATION

11.5 cm. Smaller than a Great Tit with blue cap, wings and tail. Has a green back, yellow underparts, white cheeks and a black line through the eye. Has a small pale patch on the back of the head and small single white wing-bar. Blue cap is sometimes raised to form small crest. Males tend to be brighter than females. Juvenile is also duller than male, with greenish cap and yellowish cheeks. Adults moult between late May and September. Their moult usually begins a few days before the young leave the nest. Adults in the north start later and moult quicker than those in the south. Juveniles have partial moult between July and October.
SEE ALSO: Great Tit p263.

HABITS

Much of its food is on outer twigs and branches where it frequently hangs upside down to feed. Outside the breeding season groups of Blue Tits will join foraging parties of other small birds such as Long-tailed Tits. Some will not move far from their territories, but others are more nomadic in their search for food.

VOICE

Call is a thin 'see, see, see' and it has a churring alarm call that rises at the end. Song can be heard at any time of year, but particularly from late winter into summer. It is a 'see, see, see-chu -chu -chu' and ending with a short trill.

HABITAT

Lives in a variety of habitats, but most are in deciduous woodland, especially oak woods. Populations in conifer woods tend to be at lower densities. Also breeds in parks and gardens, and even in the centres of towns. It regularly feeds in hedgerows and other places with trees and bushes.

juvenile

FOOD

Feeds mainly on insects and spiders in summer, especially caterpillars. In autumn, feeds on insects but also eats berries and nuts. Regularly visits bird tables to feed on peanuts, sunflower seeds, other bird food and household scraps.

BREEDING

Nesting generally begins in late April and early May. Male courtship feeds female. Nests in a natural hole or other crevice, usually in a tree, but may be in a building. Nest boxes are frequently used. Female builds a nest of moss, twigs and grass. The 8–10 eggs (pairs in gardens tend to have smaller clutches) are incubated by the female for 13–16 days. Both adults feed the young, which leave the nest after 18–21 days. Second broods are rare in Britain.

MOVEMENTS AND MIGRATIONS

Largely resident in Britain and Ireland and only a small proportion ever move more than 10 km, but it will make regular trips to feeding sites. On the Continent it often travels further and large movements may be triggered by food shortages; some of these birds arrive in Britain. Oldest known Blue Tit survived 9 years.

POPULATION

There are 3.5 million pairs in the UK and between 0.5 and 1 million in Ireland. There has been a modest increase in recent years.

CONSERVATION

Provision of nest boxes helps this species, both in gardens and in young woodlands where there is a shortage of suitable nest-sites. Cold winter weather can significantly reduce the population as can cold, wet springs when young are being fed, especially if this coincides with the emergence of woodland caterpillars.

DISTRIBUTION

Widespread and very common in most of Britain and Ireland, but scarce in north-west Scotland. Breeds very sparingly on the Hebrides but is an extremely rare vagrant to Orkney and Shetland. Also breeds from central Scandinavia south to the Mediterranean, along the coast of North Africa and in the Canaries. Breeds as far east as the Moscow region of Russia.

Great Tit *Parus major*

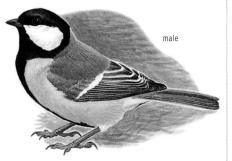

male

IDENTIFICATION
14 cm. Size of a House Sparrow. Largest member of the tit family. Has a black cap, collar and throat, and a black line running down the yellow breast and belly. Cheeks are white, back is greenish and wings are blue-grey with a single white wing-bar. Blue-grey tail has white outer feathers. Male is brighter with a wider black breast-stripe that becomes wider between the legs. Juvenile is duller than both parents with yellowish cheeks. Adults moult between late May and October and may begin before the young leave the nest. SEE ALSO: Blue Tit p262, Coal Tit p261.

HABITS
Although it sometimes occurs in small flocks and mixes with other species, it is less social than some other members of the tit family. It often feeds low down and on the ground, but it will also feed in trees and bushes and is a little less acrobatic than other, smaller tits. It is often a skulking species, although in gardens it may become quite tame.

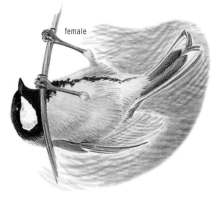

female

VOICE
Has a very wide variety of different songs and calls, and vocabulary is complex. Most familiar call is a sharp 'chink', rather like a Chaffinch, and a scolding 'cha-cha-cha' when alarmed. In flocks, makes a softer 'tsee'. Song is variations on 'teacher-teacher', which has been likened to a squeaky bicycle pump and is heard between January and June, and sometimes in autumn.

HABITAT
Breeds in broadleaved woodland, parks, farmland, hedgerows with trees, conifer plantations where there are some suitable nest-sites and also in some gardens. In winter, it may spread to other neighbouring habitats in search of food.

FOOD
Mainly insects, especially caterpillars, in summer and fruits, seeds and nuts in autumn and winter. It is capable of opening hazelnuts, and beechmast provides a popular food supply in years when abundant. In gardens it feeds on peanuts, sunflower seeds and kitchen scraps.

BREEDING
Nests in a hole or cavity in a tree or building and frequently uses nest boxes. Nest is of moss and is lined with hair, fur or feathers. Female incubates clutch of 7–9 eggs for 13–15 days. Young are fed by both parents. They leave the nest after about 18 days and the young continue to be cared for out of the nest for 4–6 days for first broods and longer for second broods.

MOVEMENTS AND MIGRATIONS
In Britain and Ireland mostly a resident that seldom travels far, although some nesting in upland areas move to lower areas in winter, especially in northern Scotland. In central and northern Europe it moves (or erupts) at times when the population is high and a few of these continental Great Tits, which are slightly smaller, visit Britain in winter. Oldest was 15 years.

POPULATION
There are 2 million pairs in the UK and 250,000–500,000 in Ireland. There has been a moderate increase in the population in the last 40 years.

CONSERVATION
In the last 100 years has gradually expanded its range northwards, perhaps aided by milder winters. A successful species that may have benefited from the food people put out in gardens in winter. Providing suitable nest boxes in areas where there is a shortage of natural nest-holes and where food is plentiful can further assist Great Tits.

juvenile

DISTRIBUTION
In Britain and Ireland it occurs wherever there are suitable trees. It is therefore widespread, but not found on Orkney or Shetland and rare on the Hebrides. Most abundant in central and southern England. It breeds throughout Europe and spreads across Asia and into the Far East.

Nuthatch *Sitta europaea*

INTERNATIONAL NAME EURASIAN NUTHATCH

IDENTIFICATION

14 cm. Size of a Great Tit. Resembles a small wood-pecker. Plump with long black pointed bill, rather large head, short neck, short stiff tail and short strong legs. Has blue-grey upperparts, buff underparts, chestnut on flanks and broad black stripe running through its eye to back of head. Juvenile similar to adult, but with less chestnut on the flanks. Wings are rounded at the ends. Adult has a complete moult between late May and mid-September.
SEE ALSO: Blue Tit p262, Great Tit p263.

HABITS

Rather elusive. At times can be very vocal. Its action on trees is distinctive as it moves up and down branches and tree trunks with jerky movements, often on the underside of branches. No other British species descends a tree trunk head first. Also feeds on the ground and on thin branches. In winter, a resident pair defends a territory, and although they may accompany roving flocks of other small birds, they will not usually go far beyond their territories.

nut or seed in a crevice in the bark and hammering it open with its powerful bill. It will sometimes visit bird tables to feed on peanuts and other bird food. Sometimes it hides seeds – when they are abundant – by wedging them into cracks in bark, or into crevices and covering them with moss or bark.

BREEDING

Nests in natural holes in trees and sometimes uses a hole in a wall or a nest box. To prevent larger birds entering the nest the female reduces the size of the entrance hole with mud. The nest cavity is filled with dead leaves or pieces of bark. The 6–8 eggs are laid in April or May and incubated by the female for 16–17 days. The young are fed in the nest by both adults for 23–24 days. It sometimes produces two broods.

MOVEMENTS AND MIGRATIONS

In Britain individuals seldom travel far from the woods where they first hatched. Pairs remain in their territories for the whole year and the young do not move far away. In some parts of Europe, in years of high populations, there are eruptions and invasions of Nuthatches. The oldest known wild bird lived for more than 11 years.

POPULATION

There are 144,000 pairs in Britain and none in Ireland. The population has increased in recent years.

CONSERVATION

The Nuthatch declined in northern Britain in the 19th century, but more recently it has started to move northwards. It has increased since the 1970s and expanded its range. Cumbria has been colonised in the last 30 years and over 200 pairs are now breeding in Scotland. But colonisation of new areas is slow because this is a mostly sedentary species.

VOICE

Call is a loud 'tuit, tuit, tuit-tuit' that becomes more strident when alarmed. This call is territorial and may be heard at any time of year. Also has a loud rattling 'pee, pee, pee' trill that is most frequently heard in spring. Song is very varied and loud with whistling notes up and down the scale.

HABITAT

Found in deciduous woodland, mature woods, established parkland with old trees and mature gardens. Rarely nests in conifer woods.

FOOD

Feeds mainly on insects such as small beetles, and also spiders in summer. In autumn and winter, eats nuts and seeds such as hazelnuts, acorns, yew seeds and pine cones. It gets its name from its habit of wedging the

DISTRIBUTION

It breeds in central and southern England and in Wales, and has only recently begun to nest in southern Scotland. It breeds from southern Scandinavia to the Mediterranean and North Africa, and east to Japan and South-east Asia.

Treecreeper *Certhia familiaris*

INTERNATIONAL NAME EURASIAN TREECREEPER

IDENTIFICATION

12.5 cm. Smaller than a Great Tit. Mouse-like with long downcurved bill and long, stiff, pointed tail feathers. Upperparts are mottled and barred brown with pale streaks. Underparts are white and the rump is a richer brown. Has a ragged pale stripe over eye and a buff wing-bar. In flight, wings are long and rounded with the wing-bar sometimes obvious. Juvenile is almost identical to an adult, but newly hatched birds still have some downy feathers on the body until early autumn. SEE ALSO: Wren p214.

HABITS

Never still, it moves up (never down) a tree trunk or branch, often spiralling. Jerky movements are characteristic as it presses its tail against the wood for support and rapidly probes the bark for insects. Once at the top, or perhaps 16 m up a tall tree, it flies down and repeats its search on a neighbouring tree. Generally solitary, pairs sometimes stay together outside the breeding season. It will often join flocks of small birds, especially tits, which move through its winter territory. At night they roost in crevices in tree trunks and sometimes communal roosts form in winter. A favourite roost is on the trunks of a redwood tree (*Wellingtonia*) where they excavate oval hollows in the soft bark.

VOICE

Call is a thin, high-pitched, wavering 'tsee, tsee' call. Song is heard from February to April and again in autumn, a high-pitched trill followed by a warble that can be hard for humans to hear.

HABITAT

Breeds in coniferous and deciduous woods throughout Britain and Ireland. Also breeds in small copses, parks and gardens with mature trees and may visit thick hedges in autumn and winter.

FOOD

Diet of insects includes stoneflies, crickets, earwigs; lacewings and various caterpillars. Some small seeds are eaten in winter, especially pine or spruce.

BREEDING

Male selects potential nest-sites. Female builds a nest behind loose bark or in some other cavity such as behind ivy stems or on a building. Cavity is partly filled with local material such as small twigs and pine needles. A delicate nest cup is built of moss, spiders' webs, fine grasses, hair, feathers and other soft material. Female incubates 5 or 6 eggs for about 14 days and young are fed by both adults. Young fly after 15 days and are independent a week later. It may raise two broods a year, especially in conifer woods.

MOVEMENTS AND MIGRATIONS

Resident in Britain and Ireland. It may leave its breeding territories in autumn, but most range no further than 20 km. Some northern and eastern European Treecreepers are partial migrants and occasionally reach the Northern Isles. Oldest lived for more than 8 years.

POPULATION

There are 214,000 pairs in the UK and over 20,000 in Ireland. Population appears stable, but there may be local declines.

CONSERVATION

Expanded northwards in the 19th and 20th centuries, and has been helped by new forestry plantations. For the past 30 years population has been more or less stable with the only falls being attributed to severe winter weather. The provision of specially designed nest boxes can help Treecreepers, especially in young plantations.

DISTRIBUTION

Lives in coniferous and deciduous woods throughout Britain and Ireland, apart from the Outer Hebrides, Orkney and Shetland. Also found in central and northern Europe, Russia and parts of Asia. Scarce in the Low Countries, France and Spain, but there are isolated populations in coniferous forests in the mountains of southern Europe. There are other races in Asia and America.

Red-backed Shrike *Lanius collurio*

male

male

IDENTIFICATION

17 cm. Slightly smaller than a Starling. Rather like small bird of prey with black hooked bill, pointed wings and rather long tail. Male has powder-blue crown and rump, reddish-brown back, pink breast, black 'mask' through its eye, and white throat. Tail is black with white sides, especially towards base. Female is duller, with rich brown, less obvious face markings and crescent-shaped marks on its pale breast and flanks. Juvenile is brown or grey-brown with barred upperparts and crescent-shaped barring on underparts. Adults have partial moult after breeding.
SEE ALSO: Great Grey Shrike p267.

HABITS

Frequently perches in open: on a branch of a bush, on a fence or on some other prominent perch. When perched its tail is often fanned, flicked up and down or moved from side to side. Flight over a long distance is undulating, with a final swoop up to a perch. Flight between perches is often low to the ground. Also hovers, or makes a sudden dash after its prey. Like other shrikes it will sometimes store surplus prey in 'larders' by impaling victims on thorns or barbed wire.

VOICE

Call is a harsh 'chack, chack'. Song is a scratchy warbling, now hardly ever heard in Britain.

HABITAT

Traditional breeding habitat in Britain was old hedges, thorn thickets and open places with widely spaced bushes, including road and railway verges. Also inhabits birch and pine plantations, peat bogs and lowland heath. Migrants generally seen in coastal areas where there are bushes or other cover.

FOOD

Eats mainly insects, especially beetles. Also captures small birds, small mammals, and reptiles such as lizards. Sometimes pursues and catches insects in flight.

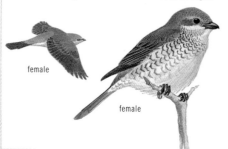

female

female

BREEDING

Nest is usually built low down in dense cover, but some are in more open positions. Male and female make the main structure from local materials such as plant stems, leaves and roots, and often incorporate paper, string and other man-made materials. Nest has a lining of softer materials. Female incubates the clutch of 4–6 eggs for 12–16 days. Both adults feed the young, which fly after 14–15 days.

MOVEMENTS AND MIGRATIONS

A scarce summer migrant that is seen mainly in May and June and again in September and October. The spring birds are migrants heading north from Africa to their breeding grounds. Many of the autumn birds are juveniles migrating south. The oldest known wild bird survived for over 7 years.

POPULATION

The species has been declining in Britain for about 100 years. It ceased to breed regularly in England after 1988 although a few pairs continued to nest in Scotland for a few years. Now, occasionally, pairs remain for the summer and sometimes breed successfully. On average over 200 individuals arrive each year in spring or autumn as passage migrants.

1st-winter

CONSERVATION

The reason for the extinction of the species in southern Britain is not properly understood, although egg thieves took some of the last clutches. Decline needs to be set against background of this species also declining across Europe, and Britain being at the very edge of its range. Possible causes for the rapid decline of this once widespread species include loss of habitat due to a switch from mixed agriculture to separate arable and livestock farming, the widespread use of insecticides and also to climate change.

DISTRIBUTION

While the species has declined to extinction in its traditional haunts in southern England, a small population has a toehold in secret locations in Scotland. Migrants are mostly seen along the south and east coast of England and the east coast of Scotland, as far north as the Northern Isles. In Europe it breeds from Scandinavia to northern Spain and east to Greece. Two other races occur in Siberia and Asia Minor. It winters in southern Africa.

Great Grey Shrike *Lanius excubitor*

IDENTIFICATION

24–25 cm. Similar size to a Blackbird. Largest shrike, with striking clean-cut black, grey and white plumage. Has thin white line over a long black mask through eye, large black hooked bill, black wings with white patch, grey body and white or slightly pink underparts. Long-ish, graduated tail is black with white outer tail feathers. Female is similar to male with some barring on breast in winter. Juveniles are browner with some barring, and in their first winter they are similar to females but may retain some juvenile plumage. Adult moult begins in July or August, soon after rearing young, or even while still feeding young. Moult is complete by October or November. There is a second, partial moult before the breeding season.
SEE ALSO: Red-backed Shrike p266.

HABITS

Regularly perches on exposed branches, tops of bush-es and trees or on posts or wires where it can watch for prey such as voles or beetles, and it will swoop down, sometimes hovering, before pouncing. Can look thrush-like when perched but frequently waves and spreads its tail. Flight powerful and bounding ending in an upward swoop with tail spread. When hunting, will fly along a hedge and surprise and catch small birds. In Britain usually seen singly.

juvenile

BREEDING

Does not breed in Britain or Ireland, although very occasionally single birds are seen in summer. Male generally gathers nest material and female builds a nest in a fork of a tree or bush. Clutch of 4–7 eggs is laid and both adults care for the young.

MOVEMENTS AND MIGRATIONS

In northern Europe this is a summer migrant, but more southerly populations are resident. In Britain passage migrants arrive between late September and November and again in March and April. Some birds remain for the winter, some holding territories and others tending to wander.

POPULATION

Numbers vary from year to year and noticably fewer are overwintering than in the past. Oldest known bird survived for over 8 years.

CONSERVATION

In Europe a widespread decline has been attributed to loss of habitat, agricultural intensification and increased use of pesticides.

VOICE

Although often silent its calls include a harsh 'sheck, sheck' or a magpie-like chatter. Some calls resemble a Starling's wheezing call or the shriek of a Jay.

HABITAT

In Britain it is a rare winter visitor to almost any open countryside, especially lowland heaths, peat bogs, young conifer plantations, clear-fell areas in older conifer forests and coastal dune systems. In northern and eastern Europe it inhabits the edges of forests and peat bogs. In winter, territories can be large, over 50 ha, and birds range widely in search of food.

FOOD

Hunts a wide variety of prey, including beetles and other insects, small mammals up to the size of a stoat, birds and, in summer, reptiles. Birds that have been caught include Swallows and even Fieldfares, but generally it catches smaller species such as Redpolls and Siskins. It impales captured prey on thorns for storage (known as a 'larder').

DISTRIBUTION

In autumn, most are seen along the east coast with smaller numbers farther west in England, Scotland and Wales. A rare visitor to Ireland. In winter, smaller numbers are spread widely in England and Scotland. In Europe breeds from north of the Arctic Circle to France and east to western Siberia. There are two other races in North America and six across Russia and Siberia.

Golden Oriole *Oriolus oriolus*

INTERNATIONAL NAME EURASIAN GOLDEN ORIOLE

IDENTIFICATION

24 cm. Similar size to a Blackbird. Has rather long wings
and tail. Male has golden-yellow body, black wings,
black tail with yellow 'corners', a black mark in front
of eye and reddish bill. Female is pale below with very
fine long dark streaks, yellowish-green above with darker wings and tail and a yellowish rump. Some females
have more yellow on their heads than others. Juvenile
is similar to a dull female but with pale edges to the
back and wings giving a scaly look. Immature males may
be quite yellow in their first summer, but not as bright
as older males. Adults begin to moult in June and July
and then suspend their moult until after their migration to Africa.
SEE ALSO: Green Woodpecker (female) p197.

HABITS

Secretive. Spends much of its time among the upper
branches of tall trees and where, despite its bright colours, it can be hard to see. Flight is slightly undulating,
more like a large thrush than a woodpecker, and a
characteristic upward sweep as it lands on a branch.
Generally seen singly or in pairs.

VOICE

Song is a loud clear flute-like whistle 'wee-la-weeo',
sounding very tropical. Also makes various harsher
calls, including chattering rather like a Jay, and a cat-
like squawk.

HABITAT

Visits open deciduous woodland, forest edges, copses,
spinneys and, in Britain, most likely to be found nesting in poplar plantations. Sometimes uses other woodland, including conifer woods, but is not really a forest
bird. Nest-sites are generally on damp or wet soils near
rivers. Migrants may arrive on offshore islands, in
mature gardens, plantations, and overgrown stream
valleys.

male

female

male

female

FOOD

Feeds mainly on insects, especially caterpillars and beetle larvae, and it also eats berries and other fruits in
autumn. It will sometimes catch insects in flight and
will also forage on the ground.

BREEDING

Males generally return to their breeding sites in mid-
May, a week before females. Male mainly builds the
nest, which is slung like a hammock in the fork of a
branch and situated 12–18 m above the ground and
6–7 m from the top of the tree. Clutch of 3 or 4 eggs
is incubated by both adults, but with female taking
the longest shifts. Young hatch after 16–17 days and are
fed by both adults. Young fly at 16–17 days.

MOVEMENTS AND MIGRATIONS

Summer visitor that arrives in April and May and leaves
during August. Chiefly a nocturnal migrant. Little is
known about the migrations of those that breed in
Britain, but some other European breeding populations appear to have a loop migration, by which they
travel south along one route and return in spring by a
different one. One ringed bird is known to have survived for more than 10 years.

POPULATION

From 42 pairs in 1990 there are now fewer than 5 in
Britain, all in East Anglia. In addition, about 100 others
are seen in Britain each year, mostly during spring
migration when they overshoot their normal breeding
areas.

CONSERVATION

Specially protected. In Britain most nest-sites have been
in commercial poplar plantations, before reaching fell-
ing age, and it is necessary to have replacement plantations nearby. The species also attracts the unwelcome
attention of determined egg thieves.

DISTRIBUTION

In Britain a rare spring visitor to mainly
southern and eastern England.
Breeding pairs are mostly confined
to East Anglia, with only a few
nesting elsewhere. Breeds from
southern Scandinavia to the
Mediterranean and east into
Asia. Winters in central and
southern Africa. There is
another race in India.

Jay *Garrulus glandarius*

INTERNATIONAL NAME EURASIAN JAY

IDENTIFICATION
34–35 cm. Smaller than a Woodpigeon. Small colourful crow. Has a pinkish-fawn body, rounded head with a small pale streaked crest that can be raised in display or when the bird is excited, and a small black 'moustache'. There is a white wing-patch and and a blue patch delicately barred with black. The longish tail is black and the rump is white. Bill is short and powerful. In flight, wings appear broad and rounded. From behind, the white rump and black tail are distinctive. Adult has a complete moult that begins in June or July and is finished by October.

HABITS
For most of the year a secretive woodland bird that is more likely to be heard than seen. However, individual birds or small groups become more obvious as they travel away from woods in late summer and autumn, and search out new supplies of food, especially acorns. On the ground it moves with a series of hops. Flight can appear laboured and 'floppy', but it is manoeuvrable in woodland. Territorial when breeding, but in spring gatherings of 3–30 Jays may take place.

VOICE
Call is a harsh screech that travels considerable distance through the woods. It also has other, less obvious calls, including a mewing sound.

HABITAT
Essentially a woodland bird that lives in both coniferous and deciduous woods especially where there are oak trees. Also found in copses, spinneys and parks. Has recently moved into suburban areas in many parts of southern Britain and is frequently seen in gardens, cemeteries and other places with mature trees.

FOOD
Acorns are eaten all year round, and sometimes fed to the young. This is possible through the Jay's habit of hiding food and recovering it later. Food may be hidden in crevices in trees, but is most often buried and covered. Also eats insects, especially caterpillars, cockchafers and other beetles, fruits, nuts, eggs, nestlings of other birds and small mammals.

BREEDING
Nesting begins in mid-April. Nest of twigs lined with fine roots and hair is built by both adults on a branch or in a fork of a tree. Female incubates 4 or 5 eggs for about 18 days. Young are fed by both adults and leave their nest after about 21–22 days, but continue to be fed by their parents until they are 6–8 weeks old.

MOVEMENTS AND MIGRATIONS
Mainly sedentary, with British birds seldom moving more than 50 km. It is more eruptive on the Continent, and in years when there is a large population and shortage of acorns or other food, large numbers of Jays may move considerable distances, generally in a westerly direction. Oldest known wild bird survived over 16 years.

POPULATION
There are 160,000 pairs in the UK and 2,500–10,000 in Ireland.

CONSERVATION
Because of its habit of stealing eggs and taking young birds there is a history of persecution by gamekeepers and managers of shooting estates. The recent move into towns has taken it to places where it is safer and helps to explain the recent population rise in urban areas.

DISTRIBUTION
Widespread in England, Wales and southern Scotland, where it appears to be gradually spreading northwards. In Ireland (where it is a different race) it is widely but thinly distributed. Most abundant in the south and east of England. Outside Britain there are several other races and the species breeds from northern Scandinavia to North Africa and east across Asia.

Magpie *Pica pica*

INTERNATIONAL NAME BLACK-BILLED MAGPIE

IDENTIFICATION
44–46 cm. Longer than a Woodpigeon. Medium-sized crow that appears black and white with a very long, wedge-shaped tail. Crown of head is rather flat and bill medium-sized and powerful. Body is black with an iridescent blue-green sheen to the black wings and tail. Belly and the outer half of the wings are white. Wings are short, broad and rounded. Flight action is direct, but not fast. Male is slightly larger than female. Juvenile is duller, shorter tailed, less iridescent, and the white feathers appear dirty. Moult begins in June or July and ends in September or October.

HABITS
May be seen singly, perched on top of a bush or tree, but frequently travels in pairs or larger groups – some numbering 100 or more. Territorial when nesting, but territories may be visited by a flock of non-breeding, mainly young birds. Stores food when it is plentiful by hiding it in scattered locations within the territory. On the ground it walks or hops, usually with its tail lifted above the level of its back.

VOICE
Frequently noisy with a 'chacker, chacker, chacker' call that is both fast and scolding. It also has a commonly heard 'cha-ka' call and a rarely heard, quiet, bubbling, repetitive song.

HABITAT
In Britain and Ireland it is widespread, being found on lowland farmland, upland moors and in towns, often close to city centres – wherever there are suitable trees for nesting – and sometimes on pylons and other man-made structures.

FOOD
Eats almost anything, from fruit and berries to carrion, and from beetles to dog faeces. Will catch and kill live prey such as small mammals and young birds and will also raid nests of other species. In general the summer food is insects and other invertebrates and the winter diet is vegetable material, but there are many exceptions to this.

BREEDING
Nest building may begin in mid-winter. Both birds build a substantial structure of twigs, small branches and mud with a softer lining. The nest is usually high in a tree or tall shrub, often in a hedgerow and sometimes in an isolated tree. Generally the nest is domed with an entrance at the side. The 5 or 6 eggs are laid from late March and are incubated by the female for about 20 days. Young leave their nest after 26 days and stay with their parents for a further 6 weeks.

MOVEMENTS AND MIGRATIONS
Sedentary over most of its range, with many individuals seldom moving more than 1 km from where they hatched. In northern populations some birds disperse after nesting and in some autumns there appears to be local southerly movement. Oldest ringed bird lived for more than 21 years.

POPULATION
There are 650,000 pairs in the UK and 20,000–100,000 in Ireland. There has been a considerable population increase over the last 50 years, coupled with a spread into urban areas.

CONSERVATION
Because of their reputation for taking eggs, have long been persecuted by gamekeepers. During the 20th century fortunes reversed and Magpies increased, helped by new forests and a reduction in gamekeeping, and they colonised towns. From 1980 the population stabilised. The Magpie has retained its reputation as a destroyer of nests and eggs, but the case for it causing the decline of small-bird populations is unproven, despite thorough research.

DISTRIBUTION
Widespread in Britain and Ireland, only missing from treeless areas of eastern England, treeless uplands, the highlands of north and west Scotland and the outer Isles. Breeds throughout most of Europe and Asia, and is also found in North Africa and North America.

Chough *Pyrrhocorax pyrrhocorax*

INTERNATIONAL NAME RED-BILLED CHOUGH

juvenile

IDENTIFICATION
39–40 cm. Larger than a Jackdaw, but with smaller head and long, slim, red downcurved bill and red legs. Plumage is black, but appears blue and purple at close range. In flight, wings are broader than those of a Jackdaw and have more obviously 'fingered' square ends. Juvenile is browner with less gloss on its feathers and a shorter, less curved yellowish-pink bill that gradually becomes red. Adults completely moult their feathers between June and October. Primary flight feathers are lost and regrown over a period of 92 days.
SEE ALSO: Jackdaw p272, Rook p273.

HABITS
A master of flight as it dives and swoops with agility and ease in the up-draughts around rock faces. Noisy. Pairs and larger groups often fly and feed together, with the largest flocks often forming in September and October. Individuals or groups frequently feed amongst the short grass on the tops of sea cliffs.

VOICE
Usual calls have some of the qualities of a Jackdaw, but are less abrupt, higher pitched and slightly more musical, a drawn-out 'kyaa' and 'kyeow' being the most common.

HABITAT
In Britain mostly found on rocky coasts in the west and also in the mountains of North Wales. In other parts of Europe most numerous in inland mountain ranges and other areas of high land where there are crags and rocky river valleys. Feeds on areas of short grass such as pasture and sometimes in arable fields, sand dunes and on beaches. When feeding it habitually probes, digs and turns over stones, seaweed, mammal droppings and other objects.

FOOD
Insects and other invertebrates and their larvae that live in the soil, especially beetles, caterpillars, craneflies, ants, spiders and flies. It also eats worms, berries, grain, small mammals and birds.

BREEDING
Nests in sea caves, other crevices in rock faces and sometimes in mineshafts and old buildings. The nest of sticks and plant stems is often mixed with some mud and lined with hair or wool. Female incubates the 3–5 eggs for 17–18 days. Both adults feed the young, which leave the nest at about 38 days. Other Choughs may visit the nest and help feed the young; these birds may be immatures reared by the same pair in previous years.

MOVEMENTS AND MIGRATIONS
Seldom moves far from its original nest-sites, although there is a tendency for young females to move further than young males. The main movements in Britain are to and from feeding sites. Oldest wild bird lived for more than 16 years.

POPULATION
Last estimate was over 300 pairs in the UK and 400–850 in Ireland. The decline in the 19th century continued into the 20th century, with the last English pair breeding in 1952. However, it returned naturally to Cornwall in 2001 and numbers there are gradually increasing again.

CONSERVATION
The population in parts of Europe has also declined and its range contracted. Loss of habitat, persecution, predation and bad weather have all contributed. Choughs require short, open vegetation with abundant soil invertebrates. This habitat is mostly associated with low-intensity grazing, but is less common due to changing farming practices.

DISTRIBUTION
In Britain breeds along parts of the Welsh coast. Most of the other breeding birds are on offshore islands: mainly Anglesey, Man, Bardsey, Islay, Colonsay and Jura. In Ireland also found in the west, with some along the south coast and a few in the north, especially around Rathlin Island. There are recent reports of birds nesting in traditional haunts in Cornwall.

Jackdaw *Corvus monedula*

INTERNATIONAL NAME   WESTERN JACKDAW

IDENTIFICATION

33–34 cm. Smaller than a Carrion Crow. Neat, stocky, small crow that is mainly black, but with a slight purple sheen on its back and head, and a grey 'hood'. Eye is watery grey and the short bill and legs are black. Male is similar to female, but the grey of the male's 'hood' tends to be paler. Juvenile is more of a sooty brown with a less contrasting grey 'hood' and a darker eye. Annual moult starts between May and July and immature birds in their second year generally start before the full adults. Moult is completed some time between August and October.

SEE ALSO: Chough p271, Carrion Crow p274, Rook p273.

HABITS

Usually seen in pairs or in flocks. Even in flocks pairs remain together and will often join flocks of Rooks or Starlings. Flight is light, agile, but can sometimes flap vigorously. Also very aerobatic and individuals will often tumble and free fall, especially around cliff faces. Like other members of the family it frequently hides food. On the ground it has a rapid walk and sometimes runs or hops. Forms communal roosts that may be used throughout the year.

juvenile

VOICE

Call is a familiar hard 'tchack' from which it gets its name. Also makes a loud 'ky-ow'. When mobbing a predator its cawing 'kaarr' calls sound rather like Rooks and Carrion Crows.

HABITAT

Lives in a variety of habitats, from open woodland, farmland, parkland, towns, villages and rocky sea cliffs. May be seen feeding on grassland or pasture, alongside sheep and cattle or scavenging on the seashore.

FOOD

Finds its food mainly on the ground, but also feeds in trees. Eats insects and other invertebrates, grain, seeds, fruits and berries, eggs and young birds. Will scavenge at rubbish tips and take a wide range of human scraps, and also visits garden bird tables.

BREEDING

Nests in loose colonies, either close together or spaced out, depending on the nest-sites available. Sites selected are holes in trees, crevices in cliffs or in buildings, including chimneys. Will also use large nest boxes. The nest of sticks is lined with wool, hair or other soft materials and is built by both adults. Female incubates the 4 or 5 eggs for 18–20 days. Both adults feed the young, which remain in the nest for 30–33 days. It may be a further week before the young are flying strongly.

MOVEMENTS AND MIGRATIONS

The Jackdaw is both a resident and a migrant. However, in Britain it tends not to move far, perhaps no more that 40 km in the south and 100 km in the north, where they move away from bleak upland areas between September and November. Others from Europe sometimes arrive in Britain in autumn, but these migrants are hard to identify and their movements poorly understood. The oldest survived for 19 years.

POPULATION

There are 555,000 pairs in the UK and 100,000–250,000 in Ireland. The population increased during the 20th century and is continuing to rise.

CONSERVATION

At a time when many species are in decline the Jackdaw appears to be one of the survivors and its population has grown since 1970. Woodland populations are increasing and research shows better breeding performance for the whole population, as there are fewer nest failures and the size of their broods is increasing. This crow has probably benefited from its generalist feeding habits.

DISTRIBUTION

Widespread. Most abundant in south-west England, Wales and in Ireland. Much scarcer in the north-west of Scotland. Also breeds from southern Scandinavia south to the Mediterranean, in a few places in North Africa and east across Europe and into Russia.

Rook *Corvus frugilegus*

juvenile

IDENTIFICATION

44–46 cm. Only slightly smaller than a Carrion Crow, with purplish-black plumage and bare greyish skin at base of bill, flattened forehead and rather peaked crown. Long, dark bill has a pale base and is more slender and pointed than a Carrion Crow. Also wingbeats are deeper, tips of the wings narrower and more 'fingered', base of the wings is narrower where they join the body and the tail more wedge-shaped. Feathers appear 'looser', especially at the top of the legs, giving it a 'baggy trouser' look. Juvenile has black feathers at base of bill and resembles a Carrion Crow, but has the different bill shape and more peaked crown. Moults between May and October, starting with first-year birds, then older females. Onset of moult is closely connected to the end of breeding.
SEE ALSO: Carrion Crow p274.

HABITS

Feathers on crown are raised when the bird is excited. Gregarious, with large autumn roosts forming at traditional sites. Rookeries may either be occupied throughout the year or reoccupied on sunny or mild winter days. While flight is usually direct and purposeful, individuals in flocks sometimes tumble and free fall, especially in autumn.

VOICE

Most common call is a raucous 'kaah'. Song begins after moult has been completed and consists of not very tuneful caws, croaks and squeaks.

HABITAT

The main requirement is tall trees. Once many nested in elms, but since most were lost to disease Rooks have switched to oak and ash as well as others. Most rookeries are on lowland farmland, but some are in towns and villages and others on the edge of moorland. Away from the nest the Rook feeds on farmland, the verges of busy roads and rubbish tips.

FOOD

Earthworms and grain are important foods, but takes a variety of other food, including nuts, beetles, caterpillars, flies, craneflies and their larvae, small mammals, birds, especially eggs and nestlings, and carrion. Food is carried to nestlings in an extendable pouch in the base of the bird's mouth.

BREEDING

Nests are in colonies at the tops of tall trees. Rookeries vary in size from only one or two, to 1,000 nests or more. Male selects nest-site and begins the process of building before female joins in. Nest comprises large and small sticks and is solidified with earth and tufts of grass with a lining of moss, leaves and other softer material. Female incubates the 3 or 4 eggs for 16–18 days. Young are fed by both parents and fly at 32–34 days old. They continue to be fed for about 6 weeks.

MOVEMENTS AND MIGRATIONS

Most British and Irish birds are resident, although some immatures move up to 100 km, and those in northern Scotland may leave the uplands for the winter. Others in northern and eastern Europe migrate, and those from Scandinavia and the Netherlands sometimes cross the North Sea to winter in eastern Britain. Oldest known wild bird lived 22 years.

POPULATION

There are over 1.1 million pairs nesting in the UK and 250,000–500,000 pairs in Ireland. A gradual increase over the last 20 years may now have stopped.

CONSERVATION

Traditionally, Rooks were shot as agricultural pests although any damage may be more than offset by their consumption of invertebrates, and much of their food is of little commercial value. Being omnivorous and an opportunist, the Rook is able to adjust to new opportunities, even feeding alongside busy roads.

DISTRIBUTION

Widespread in Britain and Ireland and only missing from treeless upland areas and the centres of large towns. Breeds in central and eastern Europe and across Russia and Asia. Winters as far south as the Mediterranean.

Carrion Crow *Corvus corone*

IDENTIFICATION
45–47 cm. Slightly larger than a Rook and smaller than a Raven. All black with a very slightly bluish sheen. The deep bill, legs and feet are black. Sometimes interbreeds with Hooded Crows and produces young with some of the characteristics of a 'Hoodie'. In flight, closed tail is squarer than a Rook, but more evenly rounded when spread and the wings are proportionally shorter, broader and less obviously 'fingered' at the ends. Juvenile is duller and browner than adult. Moult begins between May and July, with the second-year birds beginning to moult first. All birds complete their moult between August and October.
SEE ALSO: Hooded Crow p275, Rook p273, Raven p276.

HABITS
Not usually as gregarious as the Rook, but immatures and non-breeding adults may form small, and occasionally large, flocks, especially at roosts in winter. Feeds on the ground where it moves with a walk or hop. Flight is quite slow and deliberate and less aerobatic than a Rook, although it is surprisingly successful at robbing other birds, such as gulls, of their food while in flight.

VOICE
Has a variety of calls including the deep and resonant 'kaarr' and a hard 'konk, konk', but not as resonant as a Raven.

HABITAT
It occurs in a wide variety of habitats: the centre of cities, arable farmland, pasture, upland hills, moors, woodland and sea cliffs. Will frequently visit the seashore and estuaries to feed and is a regular visitor to rubbish tips.

FOOD
Food is very varied, including carrion, injured and young birds, mammals, eggs, insects and other invertebrates, especially worms and beetles, and also vegetable matter such as grain, fruit and seeds. Adaptable and has found a variety of sources of food, including shellfish that it drops onto rocks in order to open them.

BREEDING
The nest is usually in a tree, but sometimes on a cliff ledge, a building or a pylon. Both sexes build the nest of sticks and other tough vegetation and line it with smaller plant material. The 3 or 4 eggs are incubated by the female for 18–20 days. Young are fed by both adults and leave their nest at about 30 days. They become independent after 3–5 weeks.

MOVEMENTS AND MIGRATIONS
Most of the British and Irish birds seldom move more than a few kilometres from their nests, but some continental birds migrate for the winter. Oldest bird survived over 19 years.

POPULATION
Until recently it was considered to be the same species as the Hooded Crow. In the UK there are now 790,000 occupied territories of Carrion Crows and there has been a modest population increase in recent years.

CONSERVATION
It is considered a pest although the damage it does to farm animals tends to be exaggerated. Does take eggs and chicks and there is a problem when trying to protect rare game birds such as Grey Partridge when this crow sometimes has to be controlled.

juvenile

DISTRIBUTION
Carrion Crows breed in England, Wales and southern and eastern Scotland. It breeds in western Europe from southern Spain to Germany and east to northern Italy. There is another race in Asia.

Hooded Crow *Corvus cornix*

IDENTIFICATION
45–47cm. Larger than a Jackdaw. Black head, wings and tail and a pinkish-grey body with a black 'bib'. Juvenile has similar markings to the adult but is browner with a mottled back. Those nesting close to Carrion Crows will sometimes hybridise with them and produce young that have the charactistics of both species. In flight, the tail appears square when closed, but rounded when fanned, and the wings are shorter, broader and less obviously 'fingered' at the ends than a Rook. Moult begins between May and July, with the second-year birds moulting first. All birds complete their moult between August and October.
SEE ALSO: Jackdaw p272.

HABITS
Not as gregarious as the Jackdaw, but immatures and non-breeding adults may form flocks. Mostly feeds on the ground where it hops or walks. Flight is quite slow and deliberate although it is surprisingly successful at robbing gulls and other birds in flight. It will also frequently mob large birds of prey such as Ospreys and eagles.

VOICE
Has a variety of calls including the deep and resonant 'kaarr' and a hard 'konk, konk', which may be harder and more rolling than that of a Carrion Crow – although this is difficult to detect as there is considerable variation between individual birds.

hybrid
Carrion × Hooded

HABITAT
It occurs in a wide variety of habitats: arable farmland, pasture, upland hills, moors, woodland, sea cliffs and sometimes in towns and cities. Will frequently visit the seashore and estuaries to feed and is also a regular visitor to rubbish tips.

FOOD
It has a varied diet, including carrion, injured and young birds, mammals, eggs, insects and other invertebrates, especially worms and beetles, and also vegetable matter such as grain, fruit and seeds. Adaptable and has been observed dropping shellfish, such as mussels, onto rocks in order to open them.

BREEDING
The nest is usually in a tree, but sometimes on a cliff ledge or building. Both sexes build the nest of sticks and other tough vegetation and line it with sheeps wool. The 3–6 eggs are incubated by the female for 18–19 days. Young are fed by both adults and leave their nest at about 28 days. They become independent after 3–5 weeks.

MOVEMENTS AND MIGRATION
British and Irish birds seldom move more than a few kilometres although some flocks form communal roosts in winter. Some continental birds migrate for the winter and a few 'Hoodies' from north-west Europe visit eastern Britain, but in much smaller numbers than 100 years ago.

POPULATION
Carrion and Hooded Crows were considered to belong to the same species until very recently. There are thought to be over 200,000 territories in the UK and between 250,000 and 500,000 pairs in Ireland.

CONSERVATION
Legally regarded as a pest. Although the damage it does tends to be exaggerated, its numbers are still controlled on some sporting estates. However, the main threat to the species is the northward expansion of the Carrion Crow as its own range declines.

DISTRIBUTION
Hooded Crows breed in north-west Scotland and Ireland. They are also found in Europe, from Scandinavia, Italy, Greece to Russia, and parts of the Middle East. A few European birds visit eastern Britain.

Raven *Corvus corax*

INTERNATIONAL NAME NORTHERN RAVEN

IDENTIFICATION

64 cm. The largest crow, bigger than Buzzard. Massive all-black bird with very large and powerful bill, rather flat head, shaggy throat feathers, and long wings with fingered ends. When soaring it has rather long thick neck, wedge-shaped tail and, overall, an almost cruciform shape. At close quarters the black feathers have a purplish or reddish sheen. Juveniles are similar, but a little duller with paler eyes. Adults have a complete moult that starts between April and June and ends in October.
SEE ALSO: Carrion Crow p274.

HABITS

Flight powerful, majestic and slower than that of other crows. Frequently glides and soars, but will also flip over on its back and tumble and dive, especially around cliffs and rock faces. On the ground it moves with a walk or an occasional hop. Usually seen in pairs throughout the year, but larger numbers may gather at feeding sites and evening roosts. Breeding territories are usually defended all year, even during severe winter weather.

VOICE

Voice is suitably powerful for such a large bird. Usual flight call is hollow-sounding 'kronk, kronk' or an echoing 'toc, toc, toc'.

HABITAT

In Britain and Ireland mainly a bird of western mountains and coastal cliffs, but also breeds on moorland and sometimes present in towns and cities where it nests on suitable buildings.

from large sticks, lumps of grass and moss with an inner lining of softer material. Female incubates the 4–6 eggs for 21–22 days. Both adults feed and tend the young, which leave the nest after 35–49 days. Young remain with their parents until 4–6 months after fledging.

MOVEMENTS AND MIGRATIONS

British and Irish population is sedentary. Young disperse from breeding areas in their first autumn, but generally do not travel further than about 50 km. Juveniles in northern Europe and Asia are likely to make longer journeys. Oldest ringed bird survived for 21 years.

POPULATION

There are 12,000 pairs breeding in the UK and 2,500–10,000 in Ireland. The population has been growing in recent years.

CONSERVATION

Once widespread in Britain, but gamekeepers and farmers reduced the population so it was lost from lowland Britain by end of the 19th century. In the 20th century there was a partial recovery following a decline in gamekeeping after the two World Wars, but pesticides and afforestation contributed to a decline in Scotland, and breeding productivity fell during the 1980s for reasons that are not properly understood. Meanwhile in Wales it appears to be making a reasonable recovery and it is spreading over the Pennines, the Peak District and into eastern Britain.

FOOD

Feeds chiefly on the ground where it takes carrion, mammals, birds and eggs, insects and other invertebrates. Sometimes at a carcass it feeds on the blowfly maggots rather than rotting meat. Like other crows, known to habitually store food when it is plentiful.

BREEDING

Nesting starts early in the year, with most eggs laid between mid-February and mid-April. Nest is often on a cliff ledge, but regularly in trees or on man-made structures. Nest-sites are often reused – some have been in use for very many years – and a pair tends to alternate between two traditional sites. Nest is made

DISTRIBUTION

Breeds in south-west England, Wales, the north Pennines and Lake District and in much of Scotland, especially along the west coast, and in Ireland. Also breeds from the Arctic south to Portugal and east to the Caucasus and also in Asia. Other races occur in Iceland and the Faeroes, North America, around the Mediterranean, the Sahara and parts of Asia.

Starling *Sturnus vulgaris*

INTERNATIONAL NAME   COMMON STARLING

IDENTIFICATION
21.5 cm. Smaller than a Blackbird. Stocky, with pointed bill that is dark in winter, but yellow in breeding season. Feet and legs also change from brown to pink in spring. Feathers are blackish and strongly tinged with an oily green-blue sheen. In autumn, plumage is speckled with white. In spring, male is less spotted and more glossy than female and its yellow bill has a blue base. In flight, wings appear triangular and the short tail is square-ended. Moults between late May and early October. Fresh autumn plumage is spotted, but the spots wear away during late winter. Juvenile is plain grey-brown with pale throat, but quickly acquires partial and then later full spotted winter plumage.
SEE ALSO: Blackbird p225.

1st-winter

fresh, autumn

male

juvenile

HABITS
Has a jaunty walk. Flight is straight and direct. Outside the breeding season, it feeds in groups and often forms large roosts in the evening (some roosts attract thousands of birds), which frequently perform breathtaking aerial manoeuvres. Bathes in water, often communally before roosting.

VOICE
Has a 'tcheerr' call. Both sexes sing throughout year, but especially before egg laying. Song consists of harsh and rattling notes, including wheezy warbling and musical whistles, and often incorporates calls of other birds such as chickens, curlews, ducks. Mimics noises such as telephones and car alarms. Song is often accompanied by a visual signal, when the throat feathers are ruffled and the wings waved energetically.

HABITAT
Feeds on open grassland that, in Britain, may be garden lawns, farm fields, playing fields and parks. It is adaptable and exploits rubbish tips, the strand line or town centres. Nests in towns, suburban estates, trees in open countryside and farms.

FOOD
Probes for cranefly larvae (leatherjackets) and worms, but also eats spiders, caterpillars and other invertebrates. It sometimes catches insects in the air, such as 'flying ants'. In autumn and winter it eats soft fruits.

BREEDING
Nests in holes in trees, rocks, and buildings. Male starts building an untidy nest of leaves and grasses that is completed by female before egg laying. Both adults incubate the 4 or 5 eggs, but female takes longer shifts. Incubation lasts 12–15 days. Young are fed by both parents and remain in the nest for about 21 days. They are fed by their parents for a few days before joining other young birds and forming summer flocks. Mating system is flexible and pairs may change mates between broods. Male sometimes has several females, and it is not uncommon for females to dump their eggs in another Starling's nest. It may have two broods.

MOVEMENTS AND MIGRATIONS
Resident in Britain and Ireland. Young disperse after becoming independent and roam the countryside, sometimes in large flocks. Those in northern and central Europe are migrants; they leave their breeding sites to winter further south or west. Some migrants reach Britain in autumn and leave again in spring. Oldest bird survived 22 years.

POPULATION
There are 8.4 million birds in Britain and 250,000–500,000 pairs breeding in Ireland. Between 1969 and 2006 the population fell by 75%.

CONSERVATION
The rapid decline of this common species surprised conservationists, and the reasons are far from clear. Loss of permanent pasture as a feeding habitat and changes in farming practices are thought to have contributed to the decline.

DISTRIBUTION
Widespread in Britain and Ireland and missing only from the highest ground. Breeds from Scandinavia to the south of France and east into Russia. It has been introduced to North America where it has spread rapidly. Other races are found in Asia.

House Sparrow *Passer domesticus*

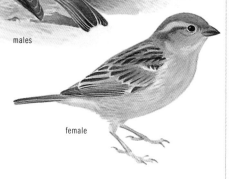

males

female

IDENTIFICATION

14–15 cm. Familiar small plump bird with thick bill, which becomes black when breeding, and rather short legs. Male has a chestnut-brown back with blackish marks, brown head with a grey crown, pale grey underparts, grey cheeks and a black bib. Has a small white wing-bar. Female and juvenile have streaked backs, pale underparts and cheeks, pale brown, not grey, crown and often a distinct straw-coloured line above and behind the eye. Flight is rapid with whirring wings. Moults between July and October with males beginning before females. Fresh plumage has pale fringes to many of the feathers that obscure the brighter colours until the breeding season.
SEE ALSO: Tree Sparrow p279.

HABITS

Historically it has been associated with human activity and uses buildings as nest-sites. Can be both tame and wary. Feeds mainly on ground, but has adapted to take food from hanging bird feeders, and will sometimes chase flying insects. A social species, often nesting in colonies and feeding in flocks throughout the year. In winter, flocks may be large and it often forms noisy evening roosts. Sometimes engages in aerial chases of other species, especially pigeons.

VOICE

Makes several simple calls, and insistent chirping and churring notes. Song is monotonous repetition of a single chirp.

HABITAT

Usually lives on cultivated land near houses and other buildings, also in towns, parks, gardens, farmyards and industrial areas with open ground.

FOOD

Forages around domesticated animals. Also eats seeds from plants such as docks and rushes. Takes household scraps, eats peanuts from bird feeders, scavenges litter and visits rubbish tips. Nestlings are fed on invertebrates such as aphids, weevils and caterpillars.

BREEDING

Pairs often stay together for life, but infidelity accounts for 10–20% of young. Both adults build the loose round nest of grass and straw with a side entrance. Usually it is in a hole or crevice and sometimes in a House Martin's nest, in a tree or bush, under the eaves of a house, or on some other structure. Incubation of the 4 or 5 eggs is by both adults and lasts for 11–14 days, with the female taking the largest share. Both parents feed the young. The young leave the nest at 14–16 days and are fed for a further 11–19 days. There are two or three broods, and nests have been observed in nearly every month of the year.

MOVEMENTS AND MIGRATIONS

Most House Sparrows are sedentary. Young disperse from their nest-sites, but generally nest close by. Adults may commute to rich feeding areas. Juveniles from northern and eastern Europe make migrations. Oldest ringed bird was over 19 years old.

POPULATION

There are 2.1–3.6 million pairs in the UK and up to 1 million in Ireland. The UK population has declined by 67% since 1969.

CONSERVATION

Recent decline is mysterious. Winter survival has fallen. Large flocks in cereal-growing areas in late summer are a thing of the past. Autumn-sown cereals mean no stubble fields to forage on in winter and efficient harvesting reduces spilt grain. In cities, air pollution from increased numbers of vehicles may be affecting the number of invertebrates that are essential for young sparrows. The survival of young in some areas is not sustainable owing to food shortages.

DISTRIBUTION

Widespread in Britain and Ireland, missing only from the highest mountains. One of the most widespread species in the world, having been introduced into every continent except Antarctica. In Europe it breeds from north of the Arctic Circle to the Mediterranean.

Tree Sparrow *Passer montanus*

INTERNATIONAL NAME EURASIAN TREE SPARROW

IDENTIFICATION

14 cm. Slightly smaller, sleeker and neater with more rounded head than a House Sparrow. Plumage similar to a House Sparrow but has pale collar around back of neck, chocolate-brown cap with no grey on crown, small isolated dark patch on cheeks and smaller black bib. Also has double white wing-bar that can be difficult to see in the field. Male and female look alike. Juvenile is duller than the adult. Adults moult between June and September, but there is little change in the overall appearance at this time.
SEE ALSO: House Sparrow p278.

HABITS

Rather shyer than a House Sparrow, but in flight is a little more agile. Less associated with humans in Europe, although in parts of Asia it fills a similar niche to the House Sparrow and is common around houses. A social species that nests in loose colonies. In winter, will join flocks of House Sparrows, finches and buntings.

VOICE

Basic call is a distinct 'chip' that is higher-pitched than call of House Sparrow. Rudimentary song is a variation on call 'chip, chip, chippi, chip'.

HABITAT

Nests in places where there are suitable nest-holes. These include open woodland, farmland with hedges and hedgerow trees, parks, orchards and quarries. In winter, feeds on agricultural land, especially any stubble or other unploughed fields.

FOOD

It eats seeds from grasses, cultivated cereals such as wheat and barley and also seeds from small wild herbs. It takes small invertebrates such as aphids, caterpillars, weevils and beetles. Food is found in trees, on the ground and also, to a lesser extent, by catching insects in flight.

BREEDING

It nests in holes and crevices in trees, buildings, cliff faces and in banks, including Sand Martins' nest-holes, and can be encouraged to use nest boxes. It uses the same one or two sites year after year. Sometimes it usurps a site that is already being used by another species and builds a nest on top of an existing nest, even if that first nest contains eggs or young. Both adults help build the nest and incubate the 5 or 6 eggs for 11–14 days and both adults feed the young, which fly after 15–18 days. Once out of the nest, parents continue to look after young for a further 10–14 days. There are two or three broods a year.

MOVEMENTS AND MIGRATIONS

It is mainly sedentary, especially in Britain and Ireland. Young disperse from their breeding areas, but seldom travel far. Some breeding in northern Europe and Russia make short migrations. However, when the population is large there are occasional eruptions of birds away from their breeding areas in autumn and some will then cross the North Sea. The oldest wild bird survived over 13 years.

POPULATION

There are 68,000 pairs nesting in the UK and fewer than 1,000–2,500 in Ireland. The population both grew and declined during the 20th century. Since 1970 the population has fallen by over 90%, but it now appears the rapid decline may have halted as there has been a partial recovery in a few areas.

CONSERVATION

The decline is similar to the falling populations of other farmland birds. Intensification of agriculture, especially autumn-sowing reducing the number of stubble fields, the use of herbicides and insecticides, and the loss of insect-rich wetlands have all combined to make winter survival more difficult

juvenile

DISTRIBUTION

Once widespread in Britain and Ireland, now there are mainly isolated remnants of that population in lowland England, southern Scotland and eastern Ireland. Widespread across Europe and Asia, including Scandinavia, the Mediterranean and North Africa.

Chaffinch *Fringilla coelebs*

INTERNATIONAL NAME COMMON CHAFFINCH

male

male

IDENTIFICATION

14.5 cm. Size of a House Sparrow. Plump finch with medium-sized bill, slightly peaked crown, rather long wings, white shoulder-patch and a white stripe in its wing. Tail is quite long with white outer feathers. Rump is greenish. Male has blue-grey head, pinkish-brown breast and cheeks, and chestnut back. The white in the wing forms a distinctive pattern on the closed wing and is also an obvious feature in flight. Female is paler yellowish-brown and has the same pattern in the wing. Juvenile is similar to female but lacks greenish rump. Adults moult between June and September. After moult birds are less colourful, but pale tips of the new feathers abrade during the winter and gradually reveal the contrasting breeding plumage.
SEE ALSO: Brambling p281, Bullfinch p294.

HABITS

Flight is undulating and the white wing marks are prominent. Forms flocks outside of the breeding season, sometimes joining with other finches, buntings and sparrows. In winter, single-sex flocks of all males or all females are frequently seen. Perches in trees and bushes, but generally feeds on the ground.

VOICE

Sings mainly between February and June. Song is short, fast and rather dry. It is a descending series of trills that accelerates and ends with a flourish. Call, which may be heard throughout the year, is a loud 'pink, pink'.

HABITAT

Widespread, nesting wherever there are trees or bushes: in coniferous and deciduous woodland, scrub, hedges with trees, parks and large gardens. Feeds in open areas: on lawns, on the woodland floor, but mainly on farmland outside the breeding season.

FOOD

Eats seeds from a very wide variety of plants, such as goosefoot, chickweed and grasses, but in summer it feeds on insects, especially caterpillars and other invertebrates that it finds in trees and bushes. Eats beech-mast when it is plentiful.

BREEDING

Pairs form in late winter. Female builds a beautifully neat cup-shaped nest into the fork of a tree or tall bush. It consists of an outer layer of lichen and spiders' webs and inner layers of moss and grass with a lining of tiny rootlets and feathers. The 4 or 5 eggs are laid between late April and June. Female alone incubates the eggs, which hatch at about 12 days. Both parents feed the young. Most young leave their nest after 13 days and their parents continue to feed them for a further 3 weeks.

MOVEMENTS AND MIGRATIONS

It is both sedentary and migratory. Most British and Irish Chaffinches never move more than 5 km from their place of hatching. Other populations are migratory and many from Scandinavia arrive in Britain and Ireland between September and November and leave between February and May. These flocks of migrants wander through farmland in search of food. Many migrants cross the North Sea, but others follow coast of Europe and cross English Channel from the south. Oldest ringed bird was 14 years old.

POPULATION

There are 5.9 million pairs in the UK and over 1 million in Ireland. Numbers have been gradually increasing.

CONSERVATION

Has benefited from the planting of new forests in upland areas. Numbers appeared to fall in the 1950s and it was assumed this was as a result of agrochemicals used on agricultural land.

female

male
(fresh, autumn)

DISTRIBUTION

One of the most widespread and abundant birds in Britain and Ireland. Breeds wherever there are trees and bushes and is therefore scarce on some of the northern islands. Also breeds from northern Scandinavia to the Mediterranean and into western Asia. There are other races in north-west Africa.

Brambling *Fringilla montifringilla*

male

male

IDENTIFICATION
14 cm. Similar in size to a Chaffinch with marginally shorter and more deeply forked tail, and stubbier bill. Chief differences are the long white rump, which shows best in flight, white belly, no white outer tail feathers and an orange breast and shoulder-patches. Male in spring is striking with a black head and back. In autumn and winter the black areas become mottled brown and the orange less bright. Female is orange-brown with a mottled back and a mottled brown head with grey on the sides and back of neck, and duller orange breast. Juvenile resembles female but is paler. Has a complete moult between July and September after which the bright plumage is obscured by the pale fringes to the newly grown feathers. These fringes wear away to reveal the bright plumage in late winter.
SEE ALSO: Chaffinch p280.

female

HABITS
This is the 'northern Chaffinch' and it resembles that species in many ways. Gregarious outside breeding season and flocks of thousands sometimes form where there is a plentiful supply of food in winter. Large roosts also form – one in Merseyside in 1981 is thought to have attracted 150,000 individuals over 6 weeks. Food supplies are irregular, and the presence or absence of Brambling flocks in a locality changes from year to year, depending on the food supply.

VOICE
Call, heard both in flight and when perched, is a rising 'tchway'. Song, which is rarely heard in Britain or Ireland, is a slow, wheezing 'dzwee'.

HABITAT
As most Bramblings are seen in winter they are mostly concentrated around supplies of food – especially beech trees that produce crops of mast. They feed on the ground and may be seen on farmland, sewage works, country parks and sometimes in gardens.

male (fresh, autumn)

FOOD
In winter, chiefly a seedeater that finds its food on the ground, taking a wide variety of seeds, especially beechmast. Regularly visits feeding stations at reserves and country parks. In summer, feeds mainly on insects such as beetles and the caterpillars of moths that it finds in trees and bushes. Also catches insects in the air.

BREEDING
A very rare breeding species in Britain. Female builds the nest in a fork of a tree or bush. Nest is larger and more untidy than that of a Chaffinch. It is made from grass, small roots, lichen and pieces of bark, and lined with hair and feathers. Female incubates the 5–7 eggs for 11–12 days. Both adults feed the young, which leave the nest after 13–14 days.

MOVEMENTS AND MIGRATIONS
This is mainly a winter visitor to Britain and Ireland. Those that breed in northern Europe migrate south-west on a broad front. Migrants arrive in Britain in mid-September. Many more winter in central and southern Europe and there are influxes when beech nuts are plentiful. Return migration from Britain starts in March. Oldest wild bird survived more than 14 years.

male 1st-year
(fresh, autumn)

POPULATION
Winter population varies, but may number about 900,000 in Britain and Ireland. In recent years it has occasionally nested in Scotland.

CONSERVATION
First recorded breeding in the UK in 1920 and as many as 8 pairs may have nested in 1995, but since then it has only nested occasionally. It is specially protected. No conservation measures will help the Brambling except secrecy of its breeding sites.

DISTRIBUTION

In winter, widely distributed in Britain with most in the north, east and central areas. Scarcer in Ireland. A few are seen in summer and breeding takes place in Scotland in some years. Breeds from Scandinavia east to Siberia. A winter visitor to southern and western Europe.

Serin *Serinus serinus*

INTERNATIONAL NAME   EUROPEAN SERIN

IDENTIFICATION

11.5 cm. Tiny active finch with rather large head, tiny bill and deeply forked tail. Adult is streaky yellowish green or brown with a bright yellow rump. Male has lemon-yellow forehead, face, throat and breast, but no yellow in the wings or tail. Female is duller, with browner and more streaky plumage and a less obvious yellow rump but yellow tail-sides. Juvenile is similar to female but duller and lacks yellow rump. Has a complete moult between July and November.
SEE ALSO: Siskin p285, Greenfinch p284.

male

HABITS

Flight is light and undulating, and similar to a Goldfinch. Sociable, with groups nesting quite close together and remaining in small flocks outside breeding season. Spends a lot of time feeding on the ground. Sings from a tree branch or overhead wire and has a songflight during which it rises steeply and parachutes slowly down in an arc, with stiffly spread wings that beat slowly.

VOICE

Most common call is a fairly high-pitched, clear monotonous trilling 'tirrilillit' or 'prrrp' note, and also a harder two- or three-syllable 'tchizzick', reminiscent of the call of a Pied Wagtail. Young also make 'zee' or 'zit' notes. Song is a rapid stream of jingling notes.

male

HABITAT

Nests in gardens, parks, orchards and churchyards where there is plenty of cover. It is as likely to turn up in suburban areas as in rural locations. Its original home is Mediterranean woodland and cultivated areas such as olive groves.

FOOD

Chief food is small seeds from weeds, such as shepherd's purse, dandelion, knotgrass and also seeds from grasses. Also eats buds of birch, beech and other trees and bushes in spring. In summer, also eats some invertebrates such as aphids, caterpillars, beetles and spiders.

BREEDING

Nest is a tiny structure made from grass, lichens, small roots and moss, bound together with spiders' webs and lined with hair and feathers. Female builds the nest on the branch of a bush or tree. She also incubates the clutch of 3–5 eggs. Young hatch after 12–14 days and both adults feed them. They fly at 14–16 days and continue to be fed for a further 6–7 days, but often the male continues to feed the first brood while the female starts another brood. Two broods are usual in northern Europe, but there are probably more in southern Europe.

MOVEMENTS AND MIGRATIONS

Both sedentary and migratory. Generally only those in the north and east migrate. They fly south-west so that, for example, many from Germany winter in Spain. In Europe, autumn movements take place between September and November and the return is mainly in March and April, which is when it is most often seen in Britain. Oldest Serin lived for over 7 years.

female

POPULATION

Up to 3 pairs have been suspected of breeding in recent years. However, the number arriving in spring has increased to around 60 individuals a year.

CONSERVATION

In Europe has been spreading north for 200 years. The first British breeding record was in Dorset in 1967 and further colonisation was anticipated, but from a peak of nine possible breeding attempts there are now 1–3 in some years. The species is specially protected, but there is little more that can be done to help it in Britain.

DISTRIBUTION

In Britain most likely to be seen in the south or east of England. A small breeding population that appeared to be establishing itself in southwest England has disappeared and now reports of possible breeding attempts only come from East Anglia. It breeds from southern Sweden to North Africa and east into Russia, Turkey and Israel.

Goldfinch *Carduelis carduelis*

INTERNATIONAL NAME   EUROPEAN GOLDFINCH

IDENTIFICATION

12 cm. Smaller and slimmer than a Chaffinch. Delicate, small finch that has sandy brown body with white belly, black wings with broad yellow bar, black tail with white marks, red face, black crown and white cheeks. Bill is quite long, and is pale with a dark tip. Female is similar, but slightly duller with less red on the face. Juvenile has similar wing and tail marking to adults, greyer and streaky body and no red on the face. Flight is particularly 'bouncy' but the black-and-yellow wings are not always easy to see on a flying bird. Adults moult after the breeding season with some individuals beginning in July and others not completing their moult until November. After moult birds appear less colourful, until the tips of the newly grown feathers wear away.
SEE ALSO: Greenfinch p284, Siskin p285.

HABITS

Usually seen in small groups outside the breeding season. These groups are often family parties but larger flocks sometimes form around popular feeding areas in autumn and winter. Frequently seen feeding with other finches.

VOICE

Most common call, often given in flight, is a pleasant tinkling 'whit-a-whit, whit', heard all year round and is often the best clue to the bird's presence. Song is a liquid tinkling with trills and more nasal notes.

HABITAT

Breeds where there are scattered bushes and small trees. Uses gardens, parks, orchards, cultivated land and also the edges of woods. Feeds on open land, such as industrial wasteland and roadside verges where there are low-growing plants.

FOOD

Feeds mainly on or near the ground. Its relatively long bill and its light weight allows it to extract seeds from thistles, teasels, dandelions, burdocks, groundsels and ragworts. Also takes seeds from garden plants such as forget-me-not, aster and pansy. Recently started visiting bird feeders, especially for nyjer seed. Insects and other invertebrates are eaten, especially in summer.

BREEDING

Nest often seems precarious; built towards the end of a branch of a small tree or tall bush. It is a neat cup made by the female from moss, small roots, grasses, lichen and lined with plant down, hair and feathers. The 4–6 eggs are incubated for 13–15 days. The young hatch after 14–17 days. After leaving the nest they are fed by their parents for a week. Usually two, sometimes three broods.

MOVEMENTS AND MIGRATIONS

Partial migrant. There are fewer Goldfinches in winter than in summer as many leave to winter in France, Spain and Belgium. More females leave than males, and some individuals migrate in some winters and not in others. Irish birds are more sedentary. Some European Goldfinches probably arrive in northern Britain as passage migrants. Migration chiefly takes place between September and November, and again between February and May. Oldest known wild bird lived over 11 years.

POPULATION

There are 313,000 territories in the UK and 20,000–100,000 in Ireland. The population fluctuates, with a slight increase in recent years.

juvenile

CONSERVATION

Once this was a popular cagebird and 132,000 a year were caught in Sussex alone in the 19th century. Now survival is affected by agricultural intensification, which reduces the available food in both Britain and Ireland, and also when wintering in France and Spain.

DISTRIBUTION

Widespread in Britain and Ireland and only absent from mountains and moorland. Most abundant in the south. Breeds from southern Scandinavia to North Africa and to western Asia. In winter, some reach the Middle East. Has also been introduced to Australia, New Zealand and Argentina.

Greenfinch *Carduelis chloris*

INTERNATIONAL NAME EUROPEAN GREENFINCH

IDENTIFICATION

15 cm. Similar in size to a House Sparrow. Chunky-looking finch with large head, rather short, slightly forked tail and heavy-looking conical bill. Male is olive-green with brighter body and rump and bright yellow patches in wings and tail. Female is duller than male with less yellow and slightly streaky upperparts. Juvenile similar to female but browner. Adults have a complete moult between July and November. Feathers are duller after moult and brighten towards the breeding season owing to feather wear.

SEE ALSO: Siskin p285, Goldfinch p283, Crossbill p290.

HABITS

Undulating flight. Usually seen feeding in small groups or, in winter, in larger flocks. Will often join flocks of other finches, buntings and sparrows and sometimes gathers in large communal roosts. Feeds on the ground and in trees, and will feed like tits on hanging bird feeders in gardens. A dominant species at a feeder and will often drive away other species. Sings from high perches and has a songflight in which it makes deep, slow, exaggerated wingbeats with its body rolling as it weaves among the trees.

VOICE

Song is heard mainly between March and July. Makes a variety of wheezy notes and trills, repetitive 'too-eee', and loud twittering trill that is often followed by a drawn-out wheezing 'dzeee'. In flight gives a repeated 'chichichichi' and a dry 'jup, jup, jup'.

male

male

female

HABITAT

Widespread in lowlands in woods, plantations, gardens with trees and bushes, churchyards and farmland with tall hedges. In winter, even more widespread and feeds on farmland, woods, gardens and the seashore.

FOOD

Eats a variety of seeds, including chickweed, groundsel and dandelion. Takes grain from cereal crops and visits garden bird feeders where it feeds on peanuts, sunflower seeds and other bird food. Its bill can open larger seeds and it favours dog's mercury in summer, yew and hornbeam in autumn, and rose and bramble in winter.

BREEDING

Female builds a nest in a tall shrub or small tree. It is a bulky structure of twigs, moss, grass and lichen and lined with rootlets, hair and other soft material. It lays 4 or 5 eggs, incubated by the female for 12–14 days. Both adults feed the young, which leave the nest after 13–16 days. The parents feed the young out of the nest, and the male may continue alone if the female starts another brood. There are often two broods in a season.

MOVEMENTS AND MIGRATIONS

Partial migrant. Birds disperse soon after nesting. Young travel further than adults, and northern birds move further than southern populations. Some from northern England and Scotland winter in southern England and others reach Europe. Greenfinches from northern Europe arrive in Britain in autumn. Most movements begin in October or November and they return in March and April. Oldest wild bird lived for 12 years.

POPULATION

There are 734,000 pairs in the UK and 100,000–250,000 in Ireland. Population has fluctuated in recent years, but the most recent trends show an increase.

CONSERVATION

Has adapted to urban and suburban habitats. Farmland birds have fluctuated in numbers and have benefited by eating spilt grain and oilseed rape seeds, but 'cleaner' winter stubbles and deeper drilling means scarcer winter food supplies.

DISTRIBUTION

Widely distributed in lowland Britain and only missing from the Highlands of north-west Scotland. It is most abundant in south and east England and Ireland. It breeds from northern Scandinavia to North Africa and east into Russia. There are introduced populations in Australia and New Zealand.

juvenile

Siskin *Carduelis spinus*

INTERNATIONAL NAME   EURASIAN SISKIN

IDENTIFICATION

12 cm. Smaller than a Greenfinch. Small, lively finch with distinctly forked tail and rather long narrow bill. Male has streaky yellow-green body with pale belly and blackish crown and bib that varies in intensity from bird to bird. Rump is greenish-yellow and it has yellow wing-bars and yellow sides to its tail. Female is paler, greyer and more streaky than male. Juvenile is duller and browner than female and more heavily streaked. Adult has a complete moult between June and October. After moulting, the black cap and bib of the male is obscured by pale feather tips until the tips wear by spring.
SEE ALSO: Greenfinch p284, Crossbill p290, Serin p282.

male

HABITS

Mostly feeds near the tops of trees and is less common on the ground than most other finches. Resembles a member of the tit family as it often hangs upside down on a branch or twig to reach food, and is attracted to bird feeders in gardens. Flight is light and bouncy. Sociable outside the breeding season and sometimes forms large flocks in winter. Has a songflight in which it circles with tail spread and with slow exaggerated wingbeats.

female

VOICE

Call, frequently given in flight, is a clear, loud 'tsuu' or a ringing 'tszing'. Song is a sweet twittering that includes a drawn-out wheeze.

HABITAT

Breeds in coniferous forests, especially Norway spruce, mixed woodlands and plantations. Outside the breeding season it visits birch and alder trees, often near water. It sometimes visits gardens.

FOOD

Feeds on seed, especially from spruce and pine trees, but also from alders and silver birches. Feeds on the seeds of plants such as dandelion, dock, thistle and meadowsweet. Eats insects and other invertebrates in summer and sometimes feeds on peanuts in gardens.

BREEDING

Nesting season depends on the food supply. It nests in late winter or early spring when there has been a good crop of spruce seeds, but if the crop fails breeding may

be delayed until May or June. The small neat cup-shaped nest is built by the female from conifer twigs, grass, heather, moss and spiders' webs, and lined with hair and other soft material. Female incubates the 3–5 eggs. Both adults feed the young, which fly at 13–15 days. There are usually two broods.

MOVEMENTS AND MIGRATIONS

Northern breeding birds move south after nesting and others arrive from Europe. Continental birds arrive between late September and late October and leave between mid-March and mid-May. It appears that individuals are not consistent in their wintering areas, and some found in Britain one winter have been found elsewhere in western Europe in other winters. Oldest bird lived for more than 13 years.

POPULATION

Thought to be 369,000 pairs breeding in the UK and 20,000–100,000 in Ireland. There may be 150,000 individuals in Britain and Ireland in winter and the population is probably increasing.

CONSERVATION

Extended its range during the 20th century due to the planting of commercial conifer forests. The population depends on spruce seeds being available. Siskins move on if the cone crop fails, which happens periodically. Winter feeding in gardens can help when other food is in short supply.

male   female

DISTRIBUTION

In Britain and Ireland it may nest wherever there is suitable habitat, from southern England to the north of Scotland, but the species is most abundant in Scotland and Wales. In winter, it is frequently seen away from its breeding areas. Its breeding range extends from close to the Arctic Circle south to the Pyrenees and east into Russia and Asia Minor.

juvenile

Linnet *Carduelis cannabina*

INTERNATIONAL NAME COMMON LINNET

IDENTIFICATION

13.5 cm. Smaller than a House Sparrow. Small slim finch, with longish, forked tail and short bill. Has white edges to the flight feathers, which form a short white panel that shows on both the closed and open wing. Has white edges to brown tail. Male has an unmarked chestnut back, crimson patches on either side of breast, crimson forehead and grey head. Female is more streaky and lacks any crimson marks. Juvenile is similar to female but slightly paler and more boldly striped. Moults between July and October. After moulting males are browner and more streaky without red foreheads and breasts. The bolder, distinctive spring plumage emerges as the dull tips of the autumn feathers wear away.
SEE ALSO: Redpolls pp288–289, Twite p287.

BREEDING

Usually breeds in colonies. Eggs are laid from mid-April. Female builds the nest in a low bush or tussock from grasses, small roots and small twigs, and lines it with hair or wool. Early nests often in evergreen shrubs such as gorse or in bramble. Female incubates the 4 or 5 eggs for 13–14 days. Both adults feed the young for 13–14 days. The parents continue to feed them for a further 14 days or so and there may be two or three broods.

MOVEMENTS AND MIGRATIONS

Partially migratory, and in Britain and Ireland there are birds that migrate and others that are resident or nomadic, and it appears some migrate in some years and not in others. Those that leave head for France and Spain while others from Scandinavia and the Low Countries arrive in Britain. Oldest bird survived over 9 years.

male

male

female

juvenile

HABITS

Nervous species that is difficult to approach. More often seen on the ground or in low bushes than in trees. Outside the breeding season it is seen in flocks and sometimes forms large roosts in the evenings. Some flocks comprise only Linnets but others associate with other finches and buntings. Flight is light and wavering.

VOICE

Song of male, which may be heard at any time of year, but especially in spring, is a rather fast and pleasant warbling that has a slightly wheezy quality. Flight call is a rapid twittering 'chi, chi, chi, chit'.

HABITAT

Nests mainly on gorse-covered heaths, rough ground where there are low bushes and scrub, bushy places on farmland, hedges, young plantations and rural gardens. Outside breeding season feeds on farmland, wasteland and coastal marshes.

FOOD

Eats seeds, especially common weeds such as fat-hen and chickweed. Also eats seeds of charlock, dandelion and buttercup. Increasingly, oilseed rape seeds are an important food source. Some insects are eaten in summer, but they are not a large proportion of the diet.

POPULATION

There are 556,000 pairs in the UK and 100,000–250,000 in Ireland. There has been a decline of over 50% since 1970 although the decrease may have slowed in recent years.

CONSERVATION

In the early 1900s it was sold as a cagebird, but the introduction of bird protection laws stifled trade. Along with some other farmland species its decline has been attributed to the use of herbicides, smaller field margins and fewer weedy stubbles in winter. On the plus side many Linnets now feed on oilseed rape. Help probably lies in adoption of Countryside Stewardship schemes and protection of commons and heaths.

DISTRIBUTION

Widespread in Britain and Ireland except for upland areas. Most abundant in eastern Britain. Breeds from northern Scandinavia to North Africa and east into Russia and the Middle East. In winter it reaches Egypt and Iraq.

Twite *Carduelis flavirostris*

IDENTIFICATION

14 cm. Linnet-sized, but more slender, with darker upperparts, buff wing-bar, orange-buff throat, longer more forked tail and well streaked on the back and the underparts. Generally it resembles a redpoll more than a Linnet, but has a longer tail than either. Rump of male is pink in the breeding season; female has a streaked rump. Flight feathers are edged white and show as a white panel in the wing, both in flight and when perched, but this feature is not as obvious as on a Linnet. Bill is yellow in winter (Linnet's is grey). Young resemble female, but are darker and more streaked. Moults between July and October, but the fresh plumage is not significantly different from breeding plumage.
SEE ALSO: Linnet p286, Lesser Redpoll p288.

female

male

HABITS

Feeds mainly on the ground, but perches on posts, fences and occasionally bushes. Habits are similar to a Linnet and it is gregarious outside the breeding season, with sometimes quite large flocks forming in winter.

VOICE

Call usually incorporates a harsh 'twaaay', similar to a Linnet but more 'nasal'. Also makes a more drawn-out 'tchway' and 'tchway-de-wee'. Song is a variety of these individual notes, and not as well formed as that of Linnet.

HABITAT

Lives in open country, on the fringes of moorland, but usually close to hay meadows where seeds are available. Also breeds on headlands and edges of moors on Scottish islands. Elsewhere breeds on Arctic and Alpine tundra, cold steppe and stony mountains. In Europe mainly winters on or near the coast or on stubble fields and other cultivated land.

FOOD

A seedeater that prefers sorrels, dandelions, grass seeds, thistles and hardheads. In winter, on the coast takes the seeds of sea-aster, marsh samphire, sea-rocket and thrift. Inland feeds on mayweeds, milfoil and cultivated species such as goldenrod. Young are fed only on seeds. Adults eat some invertebrates.

BREEDING

Arrives on breeding grounds in March and breeds between April and August. Nests in heather, bracken or other tall vegetation. Female builds a bulky nest of grasses and other plants, and incubates 4–6 eggs for 12–13 days. Both adults feed young, but female sometimes does most work. Young leave at 14–15 days and continue to be fed for about 2 weeks. Where seed crop is good there is sometimes a second brood.

MOVEMENTS AND MIGRATIONS

Most birds move from their breeding areas in autumn and winter. Some on Scottish islands are more sedentary, but others move to Ireland or England. Those from the Pennines move south-east to East Anglia and some cross into Europe. It is likely that some Norwegian birds winter in Britain, but there are no ringing recoveries to prove this. Oldest ringed bird was 6 years old.

POPULATION

There are 11,000 pairs in the UK and 250–1,000 in Ireland. Since 1900 population has been decreasing. In the last 25 years it declined by over 50%, and in parts of England the decline has been even greater.

CONSERVATION

In Britain it has been retreating northwards. The causes are the loss of flower- and herb-rich hay meadows, the abandonment of fodder crops that also contained weeds, and more intensive grazing may affect nests. Encouraging agricultural change through Stewardship and other incentives may help this species.

juvenile

male

male

DISTRIBUTION

There are widely separated populations: one in uplands of central and northern Britain, parts of coastal, western Ireland and in Norway; another population spreads from Turkey to Tibet and western China. In Britain most abundant in northern Scotland. Many European Twites winter around the Baltic and the North Sea, including the British east coast.

Lesser Redpoll *Carduelis cabaret*

IDENTIFICATION

11.5 cm. Slightly smaller than a Linnet with stripy brown body, red forehead, tiny black bib, pale double wing-bar and dark-streaked rump. Triangular bill is small and quite fine and tail is forked. Males have a red flush on their breasts in the breeding season, but this and the intensity of the red forehead varies between individuals. Forehead of female also varies from dull red to yellow or brown. Often impossible to separate males from females. Moults between July and October. After moult it is browner, with red appearing during the winter owing to the abrasion of the feathers.
SEE ALSO: Linnet p286, Twite p287, Common Redpoll p289.

HABITS

Small and active, with behaviour rather like a tit as it hangs upside down to reach food. Sometimes nests in loose colonies. Gregarious outside the breeding season. Small flocks feed together and larger numbers occur at roosts and during times of migration or irruption. Frequently mixes with Siskins. Songflight takes place before territories have been established: flying in an undulating course, it loops and circles on shallow wing-beats with occasional glides.

BREEDING

Nest is built in a tall bush. It is an untidy structure of grasses, moss, old flower heads and small roots, and lined with feathers, hair and other soft material. The 4 or 5 eggs are laid between late April and late May and are incubated by the female for 10–11 days. Young leave the nest after 12 days. They may leave the nest before being able to fly and they are independent after about 26 days. Often two broods in a season.

MOVEMENTS AND MIGRATIONS

Redpolls from northern Britain mostly move south in September and October. Some stay in Britain while others of the southern population may move to the Continent. More remain in years when there is a plentiful crop of birch seeds. The distance they travel will be influenced by the amount of food they find, and thus the number in a locality varies from year to year. Also, there are occasional 'emigrations' when larger numbers will leave an area and many may breed in a new locality. Oldest bird lived for 6 years.

POPULATION

There are 26,900 pairs in Britain and 20,000–100,000 in Ireland. Has recently suffered a rapid 80% decline.

male

juvenile

female

CONSERVATION

Once common in northern and western Britain, it declined from about 1930, but from 1950 it started to increase again, probably helped by the increase in young forestry plantations. Since the early 1970s there has been a rapid decline. The reasons are not clear, although it is subject to natural fluctuation, linked to food availability.

VOICE

Flight call is a purring trill. Its song incorporates the trill and a twittering 'chi, chi, chi, chi' that is usually given in its songflight.

HABITAT

Northern birch forests and young conifer plantations, but it also breeds in alder, sallow and hawthorn thickets, in tall hedges and on heaths with scattered trees.

FOOD

Main food is birch seeds. In spring, takes flowers and seeds of sallow, and insects that are attracted to the opening buds of trees such as larch. At other times, feeds on grass seeds and other small seeds from low-growing plants, especially willowherb, dandelion, chickweed, sorrel and tansy. A special favourite in winter is the seed of alders.

DISTRIBUTION

Widespread in northern and western Britain and Ireland, but numbers and range vary considerably from year to year. Also found in parts of western Europe and in the Alps. There are other closely related redpolls in northern Scandinavia and Siberia, Asia and North America and it has been successfully introduced into New Zealand.

Common Redpoll *Carduelis flammea*

IDENTIFICATION

12.5 cm. Only slightly larger than a Lesser Redpoll. It is a variable species but is more robust and generally paler and greyer than the Lesser Redpoll. In late winter it has clean whitish flanks with lines of contrasting brownish streaks, a rather clean 'frosty' appearance and an almost white rump. In the breeding season the forehead and breast become rose-pink and it has a small black 'bib'. However, these features vary between individuals. The female lacks the pink breast and sometimes has a larger black 'bib'. The breast is buff with darker streaks that join with the marks on the flanks. Immature males resemble females but sometimes have a trace of pink on their face and rump. It moults between July and October. The fresh autumn plumage is darker and browner and for a time obscures the paler breeding plumage. The rump can vary from being strongly streaked to virtually plain white. Feathers abrade during the winter to reveal the paler plumage, red forehead and breast.

SEE ALSO: Lesser Redpoll p288, Linnet p286.

male

HABITS

Its behaviour sometimes recalls a tit as it hangs from a slender branch in its search for food. Like the Lesser Redpoll it is gregarious and flocks form outside the breeding season. In Scandinavian forests its nests are often in the vicinity of nesting Fieldfares, which help to guard it against predators.

female

VOICE

The call is a trilling 'tji-tji-tji'.

HABITAT

In Britain it is a migrant that is often first seen in coastal areas before it moves inland in its search for food. It frequently visits areas with birch, alder and spruce trees. In Scandinavia it breeds in inland spruce forests.

FOOD

It feeds on very small seeds from birch, alder and spruce. It also eats insects and other invertebrates, both adults or as larvae.

BREEDING

In years when the spruce has a good crop of seeds Common Redpolls may start nesting in March while there is still snow on the ground and the temperature as low as −20°C. The female builds a cup-shaped nest in a tree and incubates the 4–6 eggs, which hatch after 10–12 days. The young are fed by both parents and leave the nest at 9–14 days. It is single- or double-brooded. In years when spruce seeds are plentiful it breeds for longer and populations increase.

MOVEMENTS AND MIGRATIONS

Most move south-east in October but some cross the North Sea and arrive in eastern Britain and birds from Greenland arrive on Shetland and the Hebrides. In years when there is an irruption more birds travel further and in larger numbers. These movements are linked to food shortage or population increase.

POPULATION

Numbers in Britain vary considerably from year to year. Fewer than 10 pairs appear to breed regularly in the north of Scotland.

CONSERVATION

The Common Redpoll has been recognised as a full species only in recent years. Until then it was considered by most ornithologists to belong to the same species as the Lesser Redpoll. However, where the two species breed in close proximity, there is no evidence that they interbreed. The Common Redpoll populations have natural fluctuations and there are no specific conservation actions that will help.

DISTRIBUTION

It is an irregular autumn and winter visitor to the east coast of Britain, including the Northern Isles. Birds move further west later in search of food. The Common Redpoll breeds from southern Scandinavia east across Finland and into northern Russia and Siberia.

Crossbill *Loxia curvirostra*

INTERNATIONAL NAME   COMMON CROSSBILL

IDENTIFICATION

16.5 cm. Larger than a Greenfinch. Large finch with heavy-looking body and large head and bill. Tips of bill are crossed. Tail is forked. Male is brick-red and slightly brighter on its rump. Some males are orange or yellow, or sometimes a mixture of both with streaked backs. Young males may be any of these colours, but most likely to be grey-green with paler yellow rumps. Wings are dark without any markings, although a few individuals may show thin, pale wing-bars. Female is greenish grey and slightly streaked. Juvenile is paler brown and more heavily streaked above and below. Most moult between July and November, but those that breed later or earlier in the year may moult at other times. Males in their first year resemble females but with some orange/red appearing.
SEE ALSO: Greenfinch p284, Scottish Crossbill p291.

male

HABITS

Versatile and acrobatic feeder. Climbs with its feet and bill and flutters from branch to branch rather like a small parrot. Can be rather tame. Frequently comes to the edges of ponds, streams and puddles to drink. Gregarious for most of year, even when nesting. Family groups roam the woods after nesting and some join together to make larger flocks. Flight is fast and undulating, and often at treetop height.

juvenile

VOICE

Call is a sharp 'chip, chip, chip' and flocks make a loud crescendo of 'chips'. At dusk it makes a Blackbird-like 'chink-chink'. Song is an unremarkable soft twittering.

HABITAT

Spends most of its life associated with coniferous trees, especially sitka, Norway spruce and larch. Norway spruce produces larger seeds than sitka spruce and in larger quantities and so is sought out by crossbills. Breeds in commercial plantations, larger forests and mixed woodlands, and sometimes parkland.

FOOD

Chief food is conifer seeds. Cones are wrenched off and held under the feet while the seeds are extracted with the uniquely shaped bill. Can extract seeds from cones of any age, but prefers older ones. Also eats buds, shoots and seeds. Some insects and other invertebrates are also eaten.

BREEDING

Across its range has been found breeding in every month of the year. Nesting commonly begins in February and continues into spring, but may begin in August and continue through the winter if the trees provide enough cones. Typical nest is high in a tree and is built by the female over a base of twigs. It consists of grass, moss, lichen and bark and is lined with moss, hair and feathers. Female incubates 3 or 4 eggs for 14–15 days.

Both adults feed the young, which leave the nest after 20–25 days. The parents feed them for 3–6 weeks after fledging.

MOVEMENTS AND MIGRATIONS

Good cone crops are sporadic and occur in different areas in different years. Crossbills regularly leave forests where crops are poor and search out new feeding areas. If the crop is substantial the birds will stay and breed and moult before moving on. There is, therefore, only one movement most years rather than two-way migration. Occasionally there are huge irruptions caused either by food shortage or over-population. At these times Crossbills arrive in new woods. Oldest 6 years.

POPULATION

Populations vary enormously, but there are estimated to be 1,000–20,000 pairs in the UK and 1,000–2,500 in Ireland.

CONSERVATION

Because of its nomadic nature there is little practical help that can be given to the Crossbill. Has been helped in Britain by the establishment of new conifer plantations and forests during the 20th century.

female

DISTRIBUTION

In Britain and Ireland a widespread although spasmodic breeder. Widespread in Europe, breeding from the Arctic Circle to North Africa. It is also found across Asia and in North America.

Scottish Crossbill *Loxia scotica*

male

IDENTIFICATION
16.5 cm. Larger than a Greenfinch. Almost indistinguishable from the Crossbill and Parrot Crossbill. It is a slightly larger bird with a heavier, stronger bill and a larger head. Colours are similar, with brick-red, orange or yellow males and green and slightly streaked females. Young are also yellow-green and more heavily streaked than females. Positive identification is difficult and proximity to known breeding areas is one of the safest criteria, but even this is not indisputable as Crossbills will sometimes visit the favoured habitat of the Scottish Crossbill at times of invasions. Adults have their annual moult between July and November.
SEE ALSO: Crossbill p290, Greenfinch p284, Parrot Crossbill p292.

HABITS
Its habits are similar to those of other crossbills. It spends most of its time around the tops of trees, but it will also regularly visit pools and running water to drink. Flight is strong and undulating. It forms flocks when not breeding and feeding flocks tend to be quite noisy.

VOICE
The call is a hard, sharp 'chup, chup'.

HABITAT
Restricted to areas in the north-east Scottish Highlands. It may nest in commercial plantations or traditional Caledonian pine forest. The nest may be in dense woodland or in isolated clumps of pines. Generally it selects sunny parts of the wood in preference to the dark forest interiors. Favoured sites generally have access to water for drinking.

FOOD
The chief food is seeds from Scots pines. It extracts the seeds either with the cones attached to the branch or by removing the cone and flying to a perch where it holds it down with its foot as it removes the scales. It also eats some invertebrates in summer.

BREEDING
It normally nests between February and June. The female builds the nest. The usual site is in an old Scots pine, but sometimes in other conifers. The nest is a bulky structure with a foundation of twigs. The structure is made from twigs, heather, moss and grass, and lined with softer material such as fur, hair and feathers. The female incubates the 3 or 4 eggs for 12–14 days. Both parents feed the young and they fledge after about 21 days. They remain with their parents and are fed by them for about the next 8 weeks. There are two broods if there is sufficient food.

MOVEMENTS AND MIGRATIONS
It is a resident, but within its range it shows the typical Crossbill tendency to disperse after breeding and to follow the best food supplies. Like the Crossbill in Europe, when large populations start to build up after several successful breeding seasons, there is general movement to find new areas where there is plentiful food and some birds may stay to breed there in the autumn.

POPULATION
There are 14,000 individuals in Scotland. While there is some fluctuation, overall the population appears stable.

CONSERVATION
The Scottish Crossbill is a puzzle for conservationists as it has not been clear until recently whether it is a true species or not. Nevertheless, the prime habitat for this bird is the ancient Caledonian forests of Scots pine and birch. This habitat had declined from 600,000 ha to 12,500 ha by 1987. Careful management of this fragile habitat and its gradual enlargement where possible will help not only Scottish Crossbills but also other native species of the Scottish Highlands.

female

DISTRIBUTION
It breeds only in the highlands of north-east Scotland, especially in the remnants of the old Caledonian pine forest. The species occurs nowhere else in the world.

Parrot Crossbill *Loxia pytyopsittacus*

female

male

IDENTIFICATION
16–18 cm. Very similar to the Crossbill and Scottish Crossbill. A larger bird with thicker neck and larger flattish head and deeper, blunter-looking bill with more 'parrot-like' bulge on lower mandible than other crossbills. Heavier looking and rather short-tailed. Plumage colour similar to other crossbills, but male tends to be slightly duller with more grey on nape. Greenish female tends also to be greyer with less black on wings. Heavy and 'front-loaded' appearance in flight. Juvenile's bill less pronounced and hardly separable from other juvenile crossbills. Moults between June and November.
SEE ALSO: Crossbill p290, Scottish Crossbill p291.

HABITS
Behavious similar to other crossbills. Secretive although may allow observer to approach when feeding. Usually feeds high in trees, but frequently comes down to puddles and other water to drink. May travel in family groups or small flocks and will join flocks of other crossbills. It has a butterfly-like songflight prior to nesting.

VOICE
Similar to Crossbill although some observers have described a deeper emphatic 'quop, quop' call. Song tends to be lower, slower and slightly better enunciated than the Crossbill.

HABITAT
Found in pine and spruce forests, and in Britain also in the remains of the ancient Caledonian forest of the Scottish Highlands.

FOOD
Specialist feeder on seeds of conifer trees, especially Scots pine, and also spruce and larch. Seeds and buds from other plants including alder and rowan are also taken. Some invertebrates are also eaten when nesting.

BREEDING
In Britain it has been recorded nesting in stands of Scots pines. Nests are built by the female 6–20 m off the ground and composed of twigs, lichens, moss, bark and pine needles. Clutches of 3–5 eggs are laid between February and May and are incubated for 14–16 days. The young fledge at about 22 days but they will continue to be fed by their parents for 6 weeks or more.

MOVEMENTS AND MIGRATIONS
Like other members of this family, invasions take place periodically, usually triggered by food shortage or high population. Breeding birds from northern Europe and Russia head south-west and often reach Denmark; some cross the North Sea to Britain. The eruptive movements are often in the same years as Crossbills' eruptions. At such times Parrot Crossbills may colonise new locations as they apparently did in Scotland in the late 20th century.

POPULATION
First proved to be breeding in Norfolk in 1984. Since then up to 50 pairs have been found nesting in Scotland in some years, and pairs are occasionally found breeding in other parts of Britain.

CONSERVATION
This is a difficult species to locate. Its main breeding areas appear to be in native Scots pine forests, which is a habitat that is specially protected by the RSPB and other conservation bodies. The future of this species is uncertain given its eruptive nature and it is not known how long the current population of Scottish birds has been established.

DISTRIBUTION
A small number breed in Scottish forests and very occassionaly further south in Britain. The species is found across Scandinavia, northern Europe and into Russia and, following eruptions, it will move south-west to Denmark and sometimes to the Netherlands and to Britain.

Common Rosefinch *Carpodacus erythrinus*

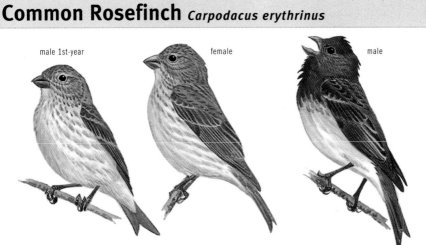

male 1st-year   female   male

IDENTIFICATION

14.5–15 cm. Size of a House Sparrow, with short bulbous bill, round head, beady eye set in plain face, and distinctive call. Wings brown with two pale wing-bars. The longish brown tail is deeply notched. Older males have reddish-pink head, breast and rump; younger males lack the red colouring and have mainly plain brownish upperparts and off-white lightly streaked underparts. Has dumpy, short-necked appearance. Female resembles a young male and is rather nondescript olive-brown. Juveniles are like female but more heavily streaked. Adults moult in their winter quarters, between September and November. After moulting the red of male is subdued, and becomes brighter during the winter due to wear of the feathers.
SEE ALSO: Crossbill p290, Lesser Redpoll p288, Linnet p286.

HABITS

Males breed in their first year, before they have the bright red plumage. In Britain generally seen singly at migration times. May mix in with flocks of House Sparrow, Linnets or Greenfinches. Feeds mainly on the ground, flying to a fence, wires or bushes if disturbed. Forms groups and larger flocks on its Asian wintering grounds.

VOICE

Most usual call is a loud 'chew-ee, chew-ee' like the contact calls of young Willow Warblers but louder and the first syllable harsher. Song is a simple but very variable 'swit-too-swit-too'.

HABITAT

In Britain generally a passage migrant that arrives in coastal areas and may be seen in low scrub or small trees. Those that establish territories select open country with clumps of trees for song posts and scrub or thick hedges for nest-sites. Where it is most numerous it often selects swampy areas and wet woodland.

FOOD

Seeds and buds from trees such as rowan and alder. Also berries from honeysuckle, elder and juniper. Diet includes weed seeds, grain and some insects such as aphids.

BREEDING

Female builds a loose-structured nest of plant stems and grass, lined with roots and hair. Nest is usually in a low bush or other dense cover. Female incubates 4–6 eggs for 11–12 days and young stay in the nest for 10–13 days while both adults feed them. Young often leave the nest before they can fly and both parents continue to care for them for about 2 further weeks.

MOVEMENTS AND MIGRATIONS

Summer migrant to Europe that arrives in May and leaves again by August or September. Regularly appears in Britain in spring and autumn. Most are seen near the coast and the largest numbers are recorded in the Northern Isles. In Asia some migrate for the winter, others that live in mountains migrate downhill to a more hospitable climate. Oldest ringed bird was over 8 years.

POPULATION

The species first nested in Britain in 1992 but since then between 0 and 4 pairs have attempted to breed. More males may be present in some springs, but many of these fail to attract a mate. So far the colonisation that was once anticipated has not happened and fewer have been seen in recent summers. However, over 100 passage migrants are also seen each year.

CONSERVATION

Following its expansion across northern Europe, the arrival of the Common Rosefinch in Britain had been expected. It is specially protected at all times, but there is no other specific conservation action that will help it except, regrettably, secrecy to ensure breeding pairs are not disturbed and their nests are not robbed by egg thieves.

DISTRIBUTION

The few breeding pairs are widely scattered in Britain, especially the eastern counties. Elsewhere its stronghold is in Russia, but it is also found over much of northern Asia and eastern Europe. In recent years it has gradually been spreading westwards. It winters in southern Asia.

Bullfinch *Pyrrhula pyrrhula*

INTERNATIONAL NAME   EURASIAN BULLFINCH

IDENTIFICATION

14.5 cm. Similar in size to a House Sparrow. A plump finch with large head, thick neck and short black, bulbous bill. Plumage appears soft and cap, wings, tail and bib are all glossy black. Has white wing-bar and gleaming white rump. Lower face and breast of male is rose-pink and the back is grey. Lower face and breast of female is pinkish-grey. Juvenile is browner than the female, and with no black on its head. It moults between July and October, but males do not have the duller autumn plumage that is typical of some other finches. SEE ALSO: Chaffinch p280.

male

male

HABITS

Rather secretive; seldom seen far from cover and usually feeds directly from plants rather than on the ground. Often seen in pairs or in small family groups after the breeding season. Larger groups sometimes form in rich feeding areas in winter.

VOICE

Usual call soft but distinctive 'peu, peu' and also quieter piping as birds keep contact in dense cover. Song is a quiet, creaking or piping warble and is seldom heard.

HABITAT

Nests in woodland undergrowth, thickets, shrubby areas and thick hedges. Many of these habitats occur on lowland farmland. Also visits gardens and orchards.

female

juvenile

FOOD

Main food is native tree buds. Oak, sallow and hawthorn are commonly eaten and also the buds of fruit trees, especially those in orchards. Other food includes tree-flowers, berries and other soft fruits and seeds. Seeds include ash, dandelion, buttercup, dock, nettles and bramble. Young are fed on both plant material and on invertebrates. In the breeding season adults develop pouches in the floor of their mouths to help them carry food.

BREEDING

Nests between May and July, but in some years breeding continues into September. Female Bullfinches build their nest in thick bushes, 1–2 m off the ground. Nest is a remarkably flimsy-looking, rather loose structure made from fine twigs, moss and lichen, with a neat inner cup of roots and hair. Female incubates the 4 or

5 eggs for 14–16 days and young remain in the nest for 15–17 days. Young are fed by both parents, which continue to feed them for 15–20 days after fledging. Some pairs manage two or more broods in a year.

MOVEMENTS AND MIGRATIONS

Small numbers from Scandinavia and further east are seen on the Northern Isles and along the east coast in spring and autumn. These are larger, brighter birds than ours. Most of the breeding birds are resident but some move up to 28 km during the breeding season. This movement is thought to take place between broods, in order for the family to take advantage of new food sources. Elsewhere it is an altitudinal migrant, moving downhill for the winter as well as a true migrant moving south in autumn. Oldest known bird was over 12 years old.

POPULATION

There are 166,000 pairs in the UK and 20,000–100,000 in Ireland. There has been a rapid decline of over 50% over the last 25 years.

CONSERVATION

The damage inflicted on commercial fruit crops resulted, for many years, in this bird acquiring the status of an agricultural pest in fruit-growing areas. Damage to fruit crops is largely due to the Bullfinch's sedentary nature, and most harm in orchards occurs when there is a shortage of natural food, especially ash keys. The loss of hedgerows with standard trees and agricultural intensification is thought to be behind its recent decline.

DISTRIBUTION

Found throughout Britain and Ireland and is most abundant in southern England and southern Ireland. Extends from Ireland in the west across Europe and Asia to Japan. In Europe breeds north to the Arctic Circle and south to the Mediterranean.

Hawfinch *Coccothraustes coccothraustes*

IDENTIFICATION

18 cm. Larger than a Greenfinch. Large and heavy-looking finch with massive, conical bill, large head, rather short legs, short square-ended tail and a 'bull-neck'. Has white patch in its wing and broad white tip to the tail. Back is rich brown, head orange-brown, breast pinkish-brown and neck grey. Wings are black-ish and the bluish-black secondary flight feathers are splayed out at the tips and twisted to present a series of spikes. It has black around eye and below bill. Bill is blue-grey in the breeding season and horn-coloured in winter. Female is only slightly less colourful than male. Juvenile has a more orange head without any black marks, a greenish-yellow breast and dark spotting on its belly. Adult moults between July and September. SEE ALSO: Waxwing p230.

juvenile male

female

male

male

HABITS

Usually shy and secretive, spending much time in the treetops. It looks 'heavy-fronted' in flight, with the large white patches on the wings appearing transparent from below. Flight is rapid, powerful and bounding. Male has a songflight where it switchbacks over its territory before suddenly plummeting downwards. Out of the breeding season it is sociable, often feeding in groups.

VOICE

Most common call is a short 'tic, tic', slightly harder than a Robin's alarm call. The rarely heard song is a slow 'deek, waree, ree, ree'.

HABITAT

Inhabits mature deciduous woods and mixed wood-land, some large gardens, cemeteries, arboreta and parks as well as orchards and shrubby places with scat-tered trees. In winter it may be seen in more open habitats. Woodland that has hornbeam is particularly popular.

FOOD

The main food is large seeds from woodland trees, especially wych elm, hornbeam, beech and maple. It also visits hedges to search for hips and haws and other autumn fruits. In spring it feeds on buds from oak, and in summer it eats some insects, including large beetles, some of which it catches in flight. It is fond of the fruit of wild cherry and is able to crack open the hard seed with its powerful bill.

BREEDING

Nests in trees, usually more than 3 m from the ground. Nest is an untidy and flimsy saucer-shaped structure of twigs, small roots, grasses and lichen. The 4 or 5 eggs are laid between May and July and incubated by the female for 11–13 days. Young are fed by both parents and leave the nest after 12–14 days. Usually only one brood a year.

MOVEMENTS AND MIGRATIONS

Relatively little is known about its seasonal movements in Britain and it may be mostly sedentary. On the con-tinent northern populations are migratory, with juve-niles most likely to make the longest journeys and females more likely to migrate than males. A few migrants from northern Europe reach Britain in autumn and some are seen on the Northern Isles in spring.

POPULATION

Difficult to assess the population. The estimated of 3,000–6,500 pairs in Britain in 2000 is probably now too high, as the population has fallen by 75% in the last 25 years.

CONSERVATION

Numbers have declined in many areas, but monitoring is difficult. Loss of mature woodland and the gales of 1987 may have reduced the habitat available.

DISTRIBUTION

Most abundant in south-east England and there are isolated pockets scattered in the north and east of England with only a few in Wales and Scotland. A rare visitor to Ireland. Widespread across Europe, from southern Scandinavia south to the Mediterranean and North Africa, and east across Asia.

Lapland Bunting *Calcarius lapponicus*

INTERNATIONAL NAME | LAPLAND LONGSPUR

female

female 1st-winter

male (fresh, autumn)

male

female 1st-winter

IDENTIFICATION
15–16 cm. Larger than a Reed Bunting, but smaller than a Snow Bunting. Heavy-looking bunting with short, thick straw-coloured bill, a large head, long wings and relatively short, forked tail. Male in spring has a black face and throat that is separated from the black crown by a 'V'-shaped white band. Back of neck is chestnut. Female in summer lacks the black head. In autumn and winter, adults resemble Reed Bunting but have plainer reddish-buff faces and thin black line around the cheeks. On the wing there is a rich brown panel between two fine white bars. Flanks are sparsely streaked, unlike the Reed Bunting's well-streaked underparts. Rump is grey-brown and streaked and there is a slight pale stripe through the crown. Males retain some of the chestnut on the back of the neck in winter. Birds often show black mottling in a gorget across the breast. Moults between July and September. Moult takes only about 50 days, necessarily rapid for a bird that breeds in the Arctic. After moulting, the distinctive spring plumage is obscured by the fringes of the newly grown feathers, which wear away by the spring.
SEE ALSO: Snow Bunting p297, Reed Bunting p300.

HABITS
Bounding flight recalls larks and pipits. Spends most of the time on the ground and is often in small flocks, although individual birds and small groups will sometimes join flocks of other buntings, larks and pipits on the British east coast in winter. Larger flocks sometimes form on migration.

VOICE
Flight call is a distinctive dry, rattling 'terrek'. Sometimes it will make a Snow Bunting-like, descending 'teu' call. Song is quite musical and given during a songflight.

HABITAT
Adapted to the Arctic tundra where it breeds among dwarf willows, often in wet areas, or Arctic heath with low-growing shrubs. In autumn, often found on coastal heaths and in winter visits stubble fields and areas of rough grass, usually near the coast.

FOOD
In summer eats invertebrates, but at other times feeds on the seeds of grasses and herbs. Animal food includes flies, craneflies, beetles and spiders. Plant material includes knotgrass, dock and shepherd's purse.

BREEDING
It nests on the ground. Female builds a cup-shaped structure of grass, small roots, leaves and lichen, and she incubates the 5 or 6 eggs. Incubation lasts for 11–13 days. Both adults feed the young and they leave the nest after 9–10 days. It is 2–3 days later before the young are able to fly and they become independent of their parents about a week after that.

MOVEMENTS AND MIGRATIONS
In Britain and Ireland mainly arrives between late August and mid-October and leaves again by May. Birds wintering in Britain and Ireland either come from northern Europe or from Greenland.

POPULATION
Between 200 and 500 birds are seen in Britain and Ireland most winters and a few summer in Scotland. The number wintering has increased recently.

CONSERVATION
Specially protected. It was found summering in 1968 and in 1977 there were up to 16 pairs at five sites, but colonisation was short-lived and now usually single birds appear in the breeding season. Secrecy to protect nests from disturbance and the attention of egg thieves is the only conservation action required.

DISTRIBUTION
In Britain and Ireland it is mostly an autumn and winter visitor, especially to the east coast of England and Scotland and in the north-west of Ireland. Occasionally it has attempted to nest in Scotland. The species is distributed round the Arctic Circle, in Europe, Asia and North America. European birds winter around the North Sea and in southern Russia and the Ukraine.

Snow Bunting *Plectrophenax nivalis*

IDENTIFICATION

16–17 cm. Stocky bunting, slightly larger than Lapland and Reed Buntings. Has a thick pale bill, a rather flat crown, long pointed wings and a short forked tail. Breeding male has a dark bill, snowy white body, a black back, black central tail feathers and white wings with prominent black triangular tips. In autumn and winter, the head and breast are sandy-coloured and the back is rusty brown with darker marks. In flight, wings always show white in varying amounts, and wing-tips are always dark. Females and immatures resemble winter male, but with less white in the wing. Annual moult is rapid, starting in mid-July and finishing by end of August. In late winter the change in the male from his sandy winter plumage to his white breeding plumage is largely due to the sandy tips wearing away, but it also has a partial moult of its head feathers.
SEE ALSO: Lapland Bunting p296.

male

female

HABITS

Usually sociable outside the breeding season with flocks of several hundred sometimes forming, and occasionally these flocks mix with other finches. Flocks of juveniles sometimes migrate together. Birds spend a lot of time on the ground, shuffling along with body close to the earth so the short legs can hardly be seen. Often Snow Buntings seem unconcerned about humans nearby.

female
(fresh, autumn)

male

VOICE

Call, usually heard in flight, is a rippling twittering 'tirrirrirrip'. There are calls that sound like 'seu' and 'sichew'. Song is loud and musical and given from a perch or in flight.

HABITAT

In winter, mainly seen on the seashore, often feeding along the strand-line, or on rough grassland near the coast. Some winter on high hills and mountains. In Scotland breeds on mountain-tops close to the summer snow fields and often among boulders, although there are occasional attempts to breed at ground level in the Northern Isles. In the Arctic it breeds in treeless areas and on rocky coasts.

FOOD

Feeds on seeds, with insects eaten during the breeding season. Seeds are mainly from plants of the bistort family, grasses, herbs and other low-growing plants. Insects include springtails, mites, flies and their larvae, caterpillars and spiders.

BREEDING

Builds a cup-shaped nest of grass, moss and lichen that is lined with hair, wool and feathers. Nest is usually in a crevice amongst rocks and boulders. Female incubates the 4–6 eggs for 12–13 days. Both adults feed the young. Young leave the nest at 12–14 days, a few days before they can fly, and their parents feed them for a further 8–12 days. It has two broods.

MOVEMENTS AND MIGRATIONS

Although most northerly Snow Buntings are migrants, some overwinter close to where they breed. Birds from Iceland, Greenland and Scandinavia arrive in Scotland and mainly the east coast of England in late September through to November and leaves in February and March. It appears that males are better able to survive in winter and are more likely to remain close to their breeding sites than females.

POPULATION

There are 50–60 pairs in Scotland. In winter in Britain and Ireland there were once over 10,000 birds but recent numbers are likely to be very much lower and there are indications that wintering numbers are decreasing.

CONSERVATION

Specially protected, and large, remote mountain tracts are important. Climate change may be influencing the future breeding status in Scotland and wintering numbers in Britain and Ireland.

male (fresh, autumn)

DISTRIBUTION

In Britain and Ireland most birds are seen in winter, especially along the east coasts of Scotland and England, but also at some inland locations, and a few in Ireland. The small breeding population is restricted mainly to the Scottish Highlands. Breeds all round the Arctic Circle; from Scandinavia and Spitsbergen, across Siberia to Alaska, Arctic Canada, Greenland and Iceland.

Yellowhammer *Emberiza citrinella*

IDENTIFICATION

16–16.5 cm. A little larger than a Chaffinch. Rather long-bodied bunting with a long and forked tail. In spring, male has a yellow head and breast, rich brown, streaky back and plain reddish-brown rump. There is the suggestion of a reddish-brown band across the yellow breast. In autumn and winter, the yellow is mostly obscured by greenish-brown streaks. Female is much duller than male with pale yellow below the bill and in front of the eyes, lines of brown streaks along the breast and flanks and with two dull wing-bars. In flight, shows white towards the ends of the outer tail feathers. Juveniles and immature females are darker and only faintly yellow. Adults moult between July and October. After moult the brown feather tips on the male hide the bright colours until they wear away during winter revealing brighter breeding plumage.
SEE ALSO: Cirl Bunting p299, Yellow Wagtail p210.

male

male (fresh, autumn)

juvenile

HABITS

Flight is in long undulations. Frequently perches on the tops of bushes, hedges and overhead wires. Feeds mainly on the ground and outside the breeding season is often seen in small flocks, frequently mixing with other buntings, finches and sparrows.

VOICE

Call is a sharp, clipped 'zit' or soft 'trillp'. The famous 'little-bit-of-bread-and-no-cheese' description of the song helps to describe the pace and form, which is variable, but tends to be a rapid succession of repeated notes with the last phrase drawn out into a long wheeze. Song is repeated monotonously during breeding season.

female

HABITAT

Breeds in areas of grassland and arable fields with hedges and banks, railway embankments, commons and heaths. Outside breeding season visits larger fields, especially stubble fields, fields with winter fodder crops and other places where grain-eating birds gather, although it is an unusual visitor to gardens.

FOOD

Mainly a seedeater, but also feeds on insects and other invertebrates, especially in summer. Seeds include grasses, nettle, dock and chickweed, and grain from agricultural crops. Insects eaten include grasshoppers, sawfly larvae, beetles and caterpillars.

BREEDING

Eggs are laid between April and September, but mostly in May and June. The nest is usually on the ground amongst taller vegetation and is made from grass, plant stems and moss, and lined with fine grass and other soft material. The 3–5 eggs are generally incubated by female alone, and hatch after 12–14 days. Young are fed by both parents and leave the nest at 11–13 days. They are not usually able to fly when they leave but become independent of their parents 12–14 days later. There are two or three broods a year.

MOVEMENTS AND MIGRATIONS

Northern populations are migratory, but the British and Irish breeding birds seldom move far. Birds on passage from Scandinavia sometimes stray across the North Sea and arrive on the east coast in October and November. The oldest bird survived for more than 13 years.

POPULATION

There are estimated to be 792,000 territories in the UK and is declining in Ireland. The UK population has fallen by over 50% since 1970.

CONSERVATION

The recent decline mirrors that of other mainly farmland species. Possible reasons include poor winter survival because of lack of seed-rich stubble fields due to autumn sowing, the loss of weed seeds owing to herbicides, and the lack of invertebrates. Loss of wide field margins, rich in large insects like grasshoppers, have impacted on breeding success.

DISTRIBUTION

Widespread in Britain and Ireland, and most abundant in central and eastern England and eastern Scotland. In winter, slightly more widespread, but the general distribution is similar to the summer. It is found from northern Scandinavia to the Mediterranean and east into Russia.

Cirl Bunting *Emberiza cirlus*

IDENTIFICATION
15.5 cm. Slightly smaller and more compact than Yellowhammer. Male in spring is striking with a black chin and eye-stripe, black and olive crown, yellow stripes on the head and yellow underparts with bold streaks on the flanks and a greenish breast-band. Rump is olive-grey and streaked, not rich brown like a Yellowhammer. The bright colours are mostly obscured in autumn and winter plumage. Females and juveniles are very like Yellowhammers, but have streaked, grey-brown rumps and bolder head markings. Underparts are clearly marked with evenly spaced fine dark streaks that extend well down the rather pale belly.
SEE ALSO: Yellowhammer p298, Reed Bunting p300.

male

female

HABITS
Spends a lot of time on the ground, where it moves slowly with a shuffle that recalls a Dunnock. Quite secretive and often skulks in trees and bushes, but when singing it usually selects a prominent song post. Outside the breeding season it forms flocks of up to about 40 birds, and sometimes more. These flocks may mix with other species such as Yellowhammers.

VOICE
Call a rather thin, high-pitched 'stic, stic', higher and more metallic than Yellowhammer. Song heard between February and September; a rattling trill of a single repeated note – quite similar to the song of a Lesser Whitethroat and not unlike a Yellowhammer's song, but lacking the 'cheese' at the end.

HABITAT
In Britain found mainly on agricultural land, especially pastures surrounded with hedges and trees, and often on bushy slopes or near the coast. In winter, moves to mainly arable fields, especially winter stubbles and set-aside rich in broadleaved weeds where it feeds relatively close to cover.

FOOD
Feeds on seeds and invertebrates. Seeds include grasses, chickweed, barley and nettles. Invertebrates include

insects such as grasshoppers, weevils, beetles and bugs of various species, flies and aphids.

BREEDING
Pairs form in April. Females start building nests in May. Site is usually in thick and often thorny vegetation, including gorse, bramble and dog rose. Nest is a cup-shaped structure of grass, plant stems and moss, and lined with softer materials. Female alone incubates clutch of 3 or 4 eggs for 12–14 days. Both adults feed the young, which leave nest after 12–13 days, although if disturbed they will leave sooner. Young are independent 8–16 days after leaving the nest. There are two and sometimes three broods in a season.

MOVEMENTS AND MIGRATIONS
Most populations are sedentary although it tends to wander in winter in its search for good feeding areas. There are some local movements of continental birds away from cold areas in autumn, and some individuals move several hundred kilometres. Female survived more than 6 years. The oldest bird survived more than 6 years.

POPULATION
There are around 700 pairs breeding in Britain. After a decline since about 1935 there has been a significant recovery recently, although it is still far less common than 100 years ago.

CONSERVATION
The RSPB has made special efforts to reverse the fortunes of this scarce species. The decline is largely due to loss of stubble fields in winter, loss of invertebrate-rich grasslands and the wholescale switch to silage production. It also suffers in severe winter weather. The result has been a contraction in its range. Help has been provided by rewarding farmers for creating weed-rich winter stubbles and grassland banks. An attempt to reintroduce the species into Cornwall began in 2006.

juvenile

DISTRIBUTION
In Britain restricted to the south-west of England, and especially to south Devon. Its stronghold is around the Mediterranean, including North Africa. It is widespread in Spain and France but local declines are occurring. There is a small population in New Zealand where it was introduced at the end of the 19th century.

Reed Bunting *Emberiza schoeniclus*

INTERNATIONAL NAME | COMMON REED BUNTING

IDENTIFICATION
15 cm. About the size of a House Sparrow. Little smaller than a Yellowhammer with relatively large head and white outer tail feathers. Male has a sparrow-like body, a black head and throat and a broad white collar and a small white downward stripe from the bill. In autumn and winter, the black head marks are largely obscured. There are dull wing-bars. Female has a dull brown head with a pale stripe below the cheeks and a thinner, triangular-shaped dark stripe bordering it. Also has a pale stripe above the eye that narrows towards back of head and diffuse streaking on breast. In autumn and winter, head markings become bolder. Juvenile is similar to female with yellower plumage and darker streaks. Moults between July and November and also moults its head feathers again between March and May. Most of the black head feathers of the male are revealed through the brown fringes abrading during the winter.
SEE ALSO: Yellowhammer p298, Lapland Bunting p296.

HABITS
Frequently clings to reeds and often sings from near the top of a reed stem or the top of a low bush. Frequently flicks its wings nervously when calling. After breeding season, forms flocks and joins other buntings, finches and sparrows, or sometimes wagtails and pipits.

VOICE
Usual call is shrill 'tsew' that is given in flight, and also a metallic 'ching'. Song is very simple and repetitive; it is a collection of a few metallic notes ending in an unremarkable flourish 'tweek, tweek, tweek, titty-tweek'.

HABITAT
Traditionally this was a bird of wet places such as reed-beds, river margins, fens, marshes and coastal grazing marshes. More recently it colonised drier habitats such as ditches, young forestry plantations and some farm crops, especially oilseed rape. On farmland relies on grassland for feeding and seeks out old ditch systems. In winter, it feeds on agricultural land and other open areas, often away from water.

FOOD
Eats mainly seeds from grasses, saltwort, shepherd's purse, plants from the goosefoot family, mare's tail and many other wildflower seeds. In summer it also feeds on invertebrates, including springtails, caterpillars and spiders. Nestlings are also fed on invertebrates.

BREEDING
Nesting begins in April. Nest is often near water. It is built by the female on the ground among a clump of grass or rushes or off the ground in a bush. Made from grass and moss and lined with finer material. Female incubates 4 or 5 eggs for 12–14 days. Both adults feed the young, which leave the nest after 10–12 days, a few days before they fly properly. Two broods.

MOVEMENTS AND MIGRATIONS
Most Reed Buntings in Britain and Ireland are sedentary, but they tend to withdraw south-west from upland areas in autumn. Females appear more likely to make winter movements away from nesting sites than males. A few from northern Europe winter in Britain. Oldest wild bird survived over 11 years.

POPULATION
There are around 200,000 territories in the UK and over 100,000 in Ireland. The population has declined by 30% since 1970.

CONSERVATION
This recent decline has slowed and the population appears more stable, albeit at a lower level. It seems likely it suffered from agricultural intensification, along with many other farmland species. Current research shows that those Reed Buntings dependent on wetlands are producing more young than others living on farmland.

female

male

male
(fresh,
autumn)

DISTRIBUTION
Widespread, with the largest numbers in eastern England and central Ireland. In winter, it remains widespread, except in the uplands. It breeds in central and northern Europe and Asia, where there are other races. Some European birds reach North Africa in winter.

Ortolan Bunting *Emberiza hortulana*

male summer

IDENTIFICATION

16 cm. Marginally smaller and more compact than a Yellowhammer. It is a relatively long-billed and rather round-headed bunting. The bill and legs are pink. It looks rather blank faced, with no stripes above or through the eye. The male has a greenish-grey head with a yellowish-white eye-ring, a yellowish stripe from the bill along the edge of the cheeks, a yellow throat, orange-brown underparts and well-marked stripy brown back. The rump is yellowish-brown and streaked. The male in autumn and winter and the female are similarly patterned with more subdued colours and there are streaks on the breast. The adult moults between July and September and has a further head and body moult into breeding plumage between December and March.

SEE ALSO: Yellowhammer p298, Reed Bunting p300.

HABITS

Its behaviour is similar to other buntings and it spends a lot of time on the ground. It is a rather shy bird that is easily disturbed and is likely to fly considerable distances before landing. In Britain and Ireland it is usually seen singly, but it sometimes forms small flocks when migrating. On its continental breeding grounds it has a distinctive songflight.

female summer

VOICE

The call is a shrill 'tsee-up' or a liquid 'tlip'. The song resembles Beethoven's Fifth Symphony – a short, simple 'dee, dee, dee, deee' with a flat note at the end.

HABITAT

In Britain it is generally seen in arable fields near the coast and also more frequently on offshore islands. Its breeding habitat is very varied; from farmland to open woodland, vineyards and rocky slopes of low hills and mountains, and sometimes in deep stony ravines.

FOOD

In Britain it mostly feeds on seeds in autumn, but it also eats invertebrates. Also in Britain it tends to feed on the ground, but on its breeding grounds it will hunt in trees and bushes for caterpillars and other insects.

BREEDING

It does not breed in Britain or Ireland. The cup-shaped nest is built by the female, which also incubates the 4–6 eggs for 11–14 days. Both adults care for the young and they leave the nest at 12–13 days, a few days before they can fly. There are two broods.

MOVEMENTS AND MIGRATIONS

It is a long-distance migrant and a summer visitor to Europe, crossing the Mediterranean between March and May. Autumn migration is inconspicuous, but generally birds start to move south in August. It spends the winter in Africa, south of the Sahara Desert. Those birds that visit Britain are generally seen in late April or May and again in August and September.

female 1st-winter

POPULATION

The number of birds seen in Britain each year usually fluctuates between 50 and 100 with a tendency for more to be seen in autumn.

CONSERVATION

In Britain there are no specific conservation actions that will help this species, which is an accidental visitor. However, birdwatchers need to be careful not to disturb tired migrants, especially when the birds are newly arrived and need to replace their lost energy. The species is declining in much of western Europe owing to changes in agriculture and land use. Removal of small fields and trees is depriving it of many of its breeding habitats.

DISTRIBUTION

Passage migrants are seen around the coast of Britain: on the Isles of Scilly in the south-west, a few along the south coast, more along the east coast of England and Scotland and a surprising number on the Northern Isles. Breeds widely across Europe and Asia and south to the Mediterranean. Winters in Africa south of the Sahara.

Corn Bunting *Miliaria calandra*

IDENTIFICATION
18 cm. Size of a Skylark, our largest bunting. Plump with heavy straw-coloured bill. Plumage is dull streaked brown with paler, boldly streaked underparts, but without distinguishing features except that some have streaks on their breast clustered in an irregular diamond-shape, looking almost like a wet patch. Sexes are alike. Juveniles similar to adults. Adults moult between July and October. Juveniles replace their feathers in their first autumn after hatching – a feature they have in common with larks and only a few other songbirds.
SEE ALSO: Skylark p201, Yellowhammer p298.

HABITS
Rather inconspicuous. Feeds on the ground, often with other species. In winter, forms small flocks. On winter evenings, where common, larger numbers may form communal roosts in scrub and reedbeds. Flocks break down and territories are reoccupied between February and April. When singing, sits upright on its perch, opening its bill wide with head thrown back. In flight, over short distances, often dangles its legs and appears fluttering.

VOICE
Males with several mates sing more than males with only one. Song may start when males visit their territories in January or February and soon sing incessantly throughout the day. Song is an accelerating series of jangling notes that has been likened to jangling of keys. Call is a rather abrupt 'quit'.

HABITAT
Found in dry open countryside. Avoids moorland, but is present on some heaths. In winter, feeds on farmland. Tends to avoid winter cereals and improved grasslands and prefers winter stubbles and rough grasslands with a good number of weeds or areas of bare soil.

FOOD
Most of the year it mainly feeds on plant material. It eats the grain from cereal crops and the tiny seeds from grasses and a variety of 'weeds'. In summer, it eats invertebrates such as beetles and caterpillars. The young are fed on sawflies, aphids, beetles, plant bugs and a vast list of other invertebrates as well as ripening grain.

BREEDING
Most males have one mate, but some have two or more females nesting in their territory, and one individual attracted 18 females, six of which nested. Female makes a nest that is a loose cup of grass on the ground or in a low bush, often near the edge of a field. Female incubates 4 or 5 eggs for 12–14 days and it is mostly the female that feeds the young. Chicks leave at 9–13 days, often a few days before they can fly. There are sometimes three broods.

MOVEMENTS AND MIGRATIONS
Mostly rather sedentary, but wanders in winter in search of food. There is no evidence of large-scale movements. Other populations in Europe are partial migrants, especially in the north and in upland areas. Oldest bird survived more than 9 years.

POPULATION
There are 8,500–12,200 pairs in Britain. The population has fallen by over 80% since 1970.

CONSERVATION
Declined early in the 20th century, recovered during the 1950s and 1960s before falling again. It has also been declining in northern Europe. These fluctuations are linked to agricultural changes. The loss of stubble fields and earlier harvesting, which has prevented second broods from fledging successfully, are two likely causes. Encouragement for farmers to provide wide field margins with no pesticide use will help.

juvenile

DISTRIBUTION
Breeding distribution is patchy. Breeds mainly in eastern England and eastern Scotland as far north as Orkney. Rare in Wales and Ireland. In Europe breeds from the Mediterranean to Denmark and north-west Russia. There are other populations in North Africa.

These species may sometimes be seen in Britain and a few nest in very small numbers.

Snow Goose
Anser caerulescens

65–84 cm. Smaller than a Greylag Goose. White morph is white with black primaries and pink bill and legs. The so-called 'blue phase' or dark morph is smoky blue-grey, except for white under the tail and a mainly white head. It also has pink bill and legs. The dark morph has white under the wings. Juvenile white morph has greyish-brown upperparts, neck and crown. Juvenile dark morph is mostly sooty brown. Juveniles of both morphs have dusky bills and legs.

Breeds in Siberia, Alaska and Arctic Canada. Up to 12 a year join flocks of other migrant geese and winter mainly in Scotland. There is also a small feral population living on Coll. Wild birds mainly arrive in October and November and are seen mostly on the mainland and some islands, especially Orkney.

white morph

male

female winter

Green-winged Teal *Anas carolinensis*

34–38 cm. Smaller than a Mallard and similar to a Teal (p36), but the drake has a conspicuous neat vertical white stripe on either side of the breast and lacks the lateral white stripes along the sides of its body. A female is generally inseparable from the female Teal (as is a male in its eclipse plumage), although the crown and the eye-stripe tend to be darker.

This is a rare visitor from North America, with up to 20 birds being seen annually in recent years. It is

female summer

mainly a winter vagrant with a few birds arriving with other migrating wildfowl from October onwards. It occurs on any suitable water, often with Teal. Most reports are from the Hebrides, Shetland and western counties of Britain and Ireland.

Ring-necked Duck
Aythya collaris

37–46 cm. A diving duck the size of a Tufted Duck (p43), but with a distinctive high forehead and crown and a steeply cut off vertical nape. Long bill is grey, male has thin white lines around base of bill, and both sexes have a black bill tip with a thick white band behind it. The male's flanks are pale grey, not white as Tufted, and there is an obvious vertical white mark separating the white from the pale grey and the black of the breast. Adult females share the same head shape and long bill but are more like a female Pochard than a female Tufted. They have pale throats, a distinctive off-white eye-ring and a teardrop at the rear of the eye-ring. First-winter birds have the same head shape as adults, an all black bill tip, but are only just developing the white band

behind it, and a pale eye-ring. All ages/sexes show a grey stripe along the entire length of the wing, again more Pochard-like than Tufted.

A regular vagrant from North America, visiting freshwater reservoirs, lakes and ponds. Over 500 have been seen in Britain, usually in March and April, and possibly new arrivals, in October and November in south-western sites in Britain and Ireland.

male

female summer

male, 1st-summer

female winter
(well-marked variant)

Great Shearwater
Puffinus gravis

43–51 cm. See also Cory's Shearwater (p71) and Manx Shearwater (p72). A large shearwater similar to Cory's but larger than a Manx. The wings are normally held more stiffly than Cory's and it lacks the lazy, meandering flight of Cory's in calmer sea conditions. In stronger winds it will arch up above the horizon and should show a white collar, dark cap and a white rump above. Contrasting with the dark upperparts, the underbody and underwings are white with varying amounts of browner markings. The white underwing-coverts are striped boldly with dark at the base and some birds show a brown patch on the white belly. Can be seen in large flocks, and when some of these settle on the water they will make a meowing sound like a group of aquatic cats!

Appears in varying numbers in British and Irish waters, as part of its long post-breeding migration from the South Atlantic, and there does not appear to be a pattern in these influxes; some years there are hardly any records at all, in others there are thousands of birds. Most records come from the south-west of Britain and Ireland. Great Shearwaters breed on Inaccessible Island, Nightingale Island and Gough Island in the South Atlantic where there are an estimated 3.5 million breeding pairs.

Red-footed Falcon
Falco vespertinus

29–31 cm. Small insect-eating falcon similar to a Hobby (p104), but smaller, longer-tailed and not quite so long-winged. Often hunts from a perch, such as a dead tree, telegraph pole or a fence, and flies out to grab insects in flight or drops on the ground to catch beetles. It will hover like a Kestrel, but usually dashes after prey. Adult male is very dark grey all over except for paler grey flight feathers, and red legs, feet and leg feathering. Female is like a large shrike with a rusty buff crown, a black mask through the eye, buff underparts with thin, fine dark streaks and grey and black barred back and tail. Young males resemble the adult but are rusty coloured on the breast, have barred feathering on the underwing and an obvious dark wedge on the inner primaries. Legs and feathers under the tail are orange-red. Juveniles are very rare in Britain and look even more Hobby-like but with only a tiny dark moustachial streak, have longer tail and the body is noticeably paler than darker primaries.

Over 700 have been seen in Britain, with nearly 130 in 1992. Mostly seen in May and June in Britain, sometimes two or three together. Breeds in eastern Europe, including Hungary, Serbia and Romania, but larger numbers breed further east in the Ukraine and Russia. Winters in southern Africa.

male

male

male

female

female

juvenile

Black Kite
Milvus migrans

55–60 cm. Similar to Red Kite (p97) with darker body, less rufous on the shorter, less deeply forked tail, less pale head and shows six fingered primary tips when gliding (Red Kite normally shows five). It has a slightly paler patch on the underwing, but not as pale as a Red Kite. When the tail is spread it looks square-cut across at the tip. Young birds show slightly paler patch on underwings and pale buff tips to the brown wing-coverts on the upperwing. Larger than a Common Buzzard and longer-winged, and this and the shallow tail fork aid identification. The Black Kite holds its wings quite flat, unlike a Marsh Harrier, only dipping the wing-tips down at times (rather than up) and flexing the tail to help steer – rather like a Red Kite. Legs are shorter than a Marsh Harrier's and it lacks the obvious pale crown.

Over 350 have been seen in Britain and sightings are increasing. It breeds in most of Europe, in Russia and in Morocco and Algeria. It is mainly a summer visitor to Europe. Most British records are in spring, especially April and May, but records continue into September.

Great White Egret
Ardea alba

85–102 cm. Large, stately white egret, almost the size of a Grey Heron. It has a long, slender neck, often with a kink in it when it is seen on the ground or when wading. Bigger than a Little Egret and, in winter, its much longer bill is all yellow, whereas the Little Egret has a dark bill. When breeding the bill becomes dark, but the bird is almost twice the size of a Little Egret and lacks the yellow feet. In flight it has long wings, rounded at the tips; the neck is retracted like other herons, and forms a noticeable neck bulge. Long legs project well beyond the tail. In breeding plumage the lower neck and back have long, fine plumes ('aigrettes'), which are for decoration and display and look almost translucent. It was for these plumes that thousands were killed for the fashion trade in the late 1800s. The RSPB was established to oppose this mass slaughter of egrets and herons across Europe.

By 2006 over 300 Great White Egrets had been seen in Britain, and since then reports have continued to increase. This increase reflects the expansion of its breeding range from south-east Europe into France and the Netherlands. French birds have been seen in Britain in recent years. It is thought that some winter records may be of birds from North America but so far this is not proven. If numbers continue to increase it is possible that the species will breed in Britain before long.

summer

winter

spring

winter

male summer

winter

juvenile

Kentish Plover
Charadrius alexandrinus

15–17 cm. A small, neat plover that runs swiftly on black or dark grey legs. The head is almost absorbed into the body, giving a 'hunched' look, and the rear end looks shorter than a Ringed Plover. Smaller than a Ringed Plover, but shares its white bar. The black bill is very slender and short. Males have a chestnut crown with a black band above the forehead; the white forehead extends back above the eye and borders the black ear-coverts. The nape has a thin white band and there are short, thin black patches either side of the neck. The upperparts are a pale greyish sandy colour. Females are duller than males, with sandy brown crown, no chestnut, pale forehead and grey-brown patch on ear-coverts. The patches on the side of the breast are grey-black. Juveniles resemble females, but have thin pale edges to back feathers, creating a slight scaly look. All birds show a dark central tail with white sides in flight. Calls include a short, ascending 'sloo-it' and a rolling 'prrrr'.

Up to 20 annual sightings in recent years. Ceased nesting in England in the 1950s. Today it is most likely to be found in coastal habitats in Norfolk, Suffolk, Kent, Sussex and Dorset. Seen April–May, or later in June–September. Birds favour open sites with sparse vegetation, such as glasswort or salicornia, brackish pools and bare mudflats.

Buff-breasted Sandpiper
Tryngites subruficollis

18–29 cm. Dunlin-sized wader. Resembles a small Ruff (p125), but juvenile has buff underparts and whitish belly. It has a pale ring around a large dark eye and black spots on the sides of the breast. Legs are deep mustard-yellow and a short black straight bill. In flight it shows no white on the rump, no wing-bar and the shorter legs do not project beyond the tail. At rest the wing-tips project beyond the tertials, whereas a Ruff's tertials cloak the wing-tips. Also in flight, the underwings are white with a dark crescent between the wing-tip and the bend of the wing. Adults are often buff below, up

to the undertail, and they have median coverts with dark streaks down the centre and buffer fringes. Juveniles have neat dark circular marks within these coverts. It often feeds on short grass, especially golf courses and airfields, but may visit sheltered coastal bays, maritime heaths and reservoir banks.

It breeds on grassy tundra in Arctic North America, from Alaska to western Canada, and most winter in South America. Over 600 have been seen in Britain. It also occurs in south-west Ireland. Most are juveniles in September, particularly on the Isles of Scilly and in Cornwall. Some adults appear May–August; these may have crossed the Atlantic in previous years and now move up and down the eastern Atlantic flyway. World population is only about 15,000.

juvenile

juvenile

Black-winged Stilt
Himantopus himantopus

35–40 cm. Large elegant wader, with very long reddish-pink legs, black upperparts, white underparts and delicate straight black bill. It is much longer-legged and much whiter below than a Greenshank (p144). In flight the all-dark wings are long and pointed, there is a long white 'V' up the back and the long legs project behind. In summer males have a dusky grey area on the top of the head; females have an all-white head and are browner on the upperparts. Juveniles are browner than

adults and look rather scaly; they have a thin pale rear edge to the wings and varying amounts of grey/brown on the crown and nape. They wade and pick delicately at insects on the water's surface, but sometimes they dash quickly around in pursuit of insects. They also probe into mud. Call is a sharp 'kek, kek' call, and a longer 'ke-ak', also, when alarmed, a high-pitched 'kik-kik-kik-kik-kik'.

Over 388 sightings in Britain. Favours shallow coastal lagoons, gravel pits, reservoirs and sheltered coastal sites. Most migrants are seen in April and May; but birds have been seen in mid-summer, autumn and even winter. There have been six breeding attempts in Britain.

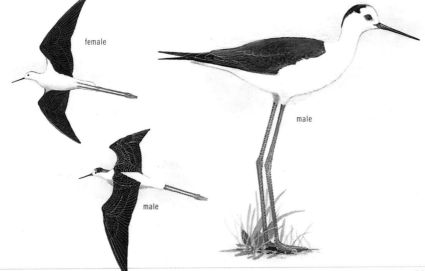

female

male

male

White-rumped Sandpiper
Calidris fuscicollis

15–18 cm. Smaller than most Dunlins (p126) with long primaries that extend well beyond the tertials and beyond the tail. Body is slimmer than a Dunlin and the back looks quite flat so the overall impression is of a greyish wader with shorter legs than a Dunlin, longer-winged and with a short dark bill, which is not as downcurved as most Dunlins. Two basic age groups visit Britain and Ireland – adults in mainly July and August, which are usually moulting from breeding plumage to grey winter plumage, so have some unmoulted dark feathers in the greyer mantle. Juveniles are seen September–October and are brighter, with rufous across the back and mantle feathers, fringed buff, pale edges to the inner scapular feathers giving a whitish 'V' shape (*see* juvenile Little Stint p128), and a more obviously streaked breast-band with streaking running down the flanks. At any age and time of year the bird has a dark, blackish, tail and a clear horseshoe-shaped white rump that does not extend up the back like a Curlew Sandpiper (p131). A soft 'jeet' call is sometimes given.

It breeds in Arctic Canada and winters in South America, from Paraguay to Tierra del Fuego. By 2005 428 had been seen in Britain, including a total of 39 in 2005.

juvenile

summer

juvenile

Ring-billed Gull
Larus delawarensis

43–47 cm. Similar to a Common Gull (p164), but slightly larger and flatter-backed. Adults are paler grey above than the Common Gull, the grey no darker than an adult Black-headed Gull. Common Gulls usually have broad white tips to the folded tertials at rest, but the Ring-billed Gull has a subtle fade from grey to white. Eyes are pale, and in spring they develop a red eye-ring, which is more elliptical than in the Herring Gull. Yellow bill is deeper than a Common Gull, and has a thick black subterminal band. Most Common Gulls in winter have a dark terminal band on the bill, but this is narrower and less black than a Ring-billed Gull. The long black wing-tips show smaller white spots than a Common Gull. First-winter birds are paler grey on the mantle than a Common Gull, the bright pink, deep and angular-shaped bill has a thick black tip (sometimes with a pale extreme tip). It often shows coarse brownish mottling on the mantle and arrow-shaped marks along the flanks. Folded wings are long, and in flight it has a more pointed wing shape than the Common Gull. Can be quite aggressive, uttering a deep 'kowk' call.

From the discovery of the first bird in Britain in 1973 to the end of 2003 there had been 1,523 reports of this species. In recent years it has been scarcer. It breeds in North America and winters south to Mexico.

2nd-winter

adult winter

adult summer

Caspian Gull
Larus cachinnans

56–68 cm. Resembles a Yellow-legged Gull (p159) and a Herring Gull (p158). Caspian Gull has a small head, long body and long wings, and small dark eyes. This is a bird of subtleties; it has a long sloping forehead, long parallel bill with only a gently drooping tip and long grey legs with a yellowish or pinkish tinge. Adults have slightly paler grey upperparts than a Herring Gull. Diagnostic features are that the longest primary has a complete white tip, a large white 'mirror' on the second longest and the grey of the upperwing appears as a series of fingers or pale tongues extending into the largely black wing-tip. First-winter birds have very white heads with long, sloping foreheads, long black bills (shape as adults), dark tertials with narrow pale edges and tips, a ring of distinctive brown spots across the nape, and long wings with pale bars across the coverts. The grey mantle feathers show a series of blackish 'anchor' marks.

This bird is now being identified regularly in England, particularly the south-east. It breeds around the Black Sea and eastwards into central Asia.

winter

1st-winter

winter

adult moulting

summer

White-winged Black Tern
Chlidonias leucopterus

63–67 cm. A small tern similar to a Black Tern but with broader, blunter wings and a shorter, less decurved bill. The pure white rump is a key feature at all ages. Summer adults are striking – black with contrasting silvery-white flight feathers, white upperwing-coverts and white tail and rump and undertail-coverts. Juvenile Black Terns have a dark smudge on the side of the breast below the point where the wing joins the body, juvenile White-winged Black Tern lacks this, and has white (not grey) rump and a contrasting all dark brown 'saddle' across the back. The wings are mostly very pale and silvery. It feeds by beating up and down freshwater lakes or reservoirs, dipping down to feed from the surface, like a Black Tern.

A regular visitor, usually from May to August, and well over 1,000 have been seen since 1950. It breeds in the far east of Europe and Russia, and migrates to Africa.

Alpine Swift
Apus melba

20–22 cm. Looks like a giant Sand Martin (p203) but is a long-winged, fast-moving swift. It is brown above, with a contrasting white belly below. It has a dark brown breast-band and a white throat, although at times it is difficult to see the white throat clearly when the bird is moving at speed. It is clearly larger and much longer-winged than a common Swift (p192).

By 2005 there had been over 570 seen in Britain. These birds breed in southern Europe, in mountains but also in towns and on rocky sea cliffs, and some get caught up in fast-moving summer thunderstorms and start to drift and feed further north. Birds have been seen from March to November, with most between June and August.

juvenile

Red-rumped Swallow
Cecropis daurica

14–18 cm (including tail 7–11 cm). About the same size as a Swallow (p204) but differs by having a pale buff rump, long black outer tail-streamers (which have no white marks in them) and pale underparts with black undertail-coverts. It is thus possible to separate this species from a Swallow from below by seeing this one characteristic feature. The tail feathers are curved inwards slightly giving a distinctive outline, but usually the long outer tail feathers are held tightly together forming a long, black spike. A sparrow-like 'cherreet' is heard from some migrants. This species likes to glide and circle in a slower more leisurely way than the Swallow.

By 2005 over 500 had been seen in Britain, and many had occurred as 'overshoots' from their southern European breeding areas in April and May. In recent times individuals have been seen in late October and even November and the origins of these autumn birds are more difficult to deduce.

Richard's Pipit
Anthus richardi

18 cm. A large pipit, with upright stance. Larger than a Meadow Pipit (p207), with longer tail, longer legs and stouter bill. First-winter birds can be mistaken for Tawny Pipits, but that species has dark 'lores' (a dark line between the eye and the bill base). Richard's Pipit has pale lores, so looks 'open faced'. It has a breast-band of dark streaking on a pale buff background, and above is usually a dark 'blob' where the two dark malar stripes end. Flanks are deeper buff than the belly. Outer tail feathers have white in them, noticeable when bird takes off, or when it hovers momentarily before landing. It walks strongly and disappears easily in long grass. It usually calls on taking off and sometimes while flying over; the most frequent call is a harsh 'schreep', quite similar to a House Sparrow, but longer. In flight it looks long-tailed and bounds along in a confident manner.

It breeds in central Asia and in Siberia, but there are other races globally. It winters in Africa, India and south-east Asia. It is a regular scarce migrant to Britain with over 3,000 between 1958 and 2003, and many since. It likes open habitats – rough grasslands, golf courses and airfields. Most are seen in October and early November, but also in winter and spring.

1st-winter

fresh, autumn
or spring

Red-throated Pipit
Anthus cervinus

15 cm. About the size of a Meadow Pipit (p207) but differs by having streaked rump and uppertail-coverts. There are prominent black streaks along the flanks, usually forming two almost continuous lines, much more obvious than on a Meadow Pipit. The upperparts are dark and heavily streaked, with long pale stripes on the edge of the mantle, like braces. Spring and some autumn adults show varying amounts of brick-red or pink on face and throat. Usual call note is a drawn-out 'skeeezz'.

Breeds in Arctic Scandinavia and Russia. By 2005 436 had been identified in Britain, with most records in late September and October, especially in the Northern Isles, with a few in late spring. It can occur in almost any open habitat including airfields, maritime heaths and pasture.

male summer

1st-winter

Woodchat Shrike
Lanius senator

17 cm. Size of a Red-backed Shrike (p266),
adults are black above with large white
patches across the shoulders, a white patch at the base
of the folded wings, a black mask from the forehead,
through the eye to the ear-coverts and a bright chestnut
crown and nape. Females have duller reddish-brown
crowns. Rump is white, as are the underparts. The long
black tail has white-edged outer tail feathers. In flight
there is a white crescent at the base of the primaries; the
rest of the wing is black. First-winter birds look more
like female Red-backed Shrikes, but have pale scapulars,
creamy white with scallop marks in dark brown, a small
white patch at the base of the folded primaries, slightly
paler more barred crown, pale rump and dull grey-
brown uppertail. Like all shrikes, perches prominently
on bushes, fence lines or wires and drops onto beetles
and other prey.

Over 700 seen in Britain since 1958. It breeds
in southern Europe and most records come
from south-west and southern England;
the favoured months are April to early
June for adults and August to early
September for juveniles.

male

male

juvenile

juvenile

Aquatic Warbler
Acrocephalus paludicola

12.5 cm. Very hard to observe; looks very much like a
juvenile Sedge Warbler (p235), but is a brighter,
more yellow 'tiger-striped' bird with black streaks
on the rump (Sedge Warbler has plain rump) and
back. It has pale lores (between eye and bill), giving a plain open face (Sedge Warbler has dark
lores). Most British records are of young birds in
late summer/autumn, as some Aquatic Warblers
appear to move westwards from their breeding areas
in Poland, Belarus and the Ukraine before they move
on to winter in West Africa. The last few days of
July and the first 3 weeks of August is the period
most are trapped for ringing in reedbed sites in
south Wales and south-west England. The
birds quickly move out of reedbeds, however, into more favoured areas of wet
rushes.

Between 1958 and 2003, 1,221
Aquatic Warblers had been seen in
Britain, mostly thanks to the efforts
of ringers studying Sedge and Reed Warblers.
This species is listed as 'Vulnerable' on the
Global IUCN Red List, and even numbers reaching
Britain are declining.

Subalpine Warbler
Sylvia cantillans

12.5 cm. Males and first-year males are distinctive, with blue-grey upperparts, slightly peaked crown like a Whitethroat (p243), white stripes either side of the throat and orangey-red throat and breast, fading out to off-white on the belly, and a red eye and eye-ring. The dark tail has white in the outer tail feathers. The wings look quite short. Its call is a short 'tek, tek', sometimes running a number together, and some migrants sing like a hurried Whitethroat's song. Females and first-winter birds are less easy to identify, being grey-brown above, with dark centres to the tertials with brown edges (not rusty brown like Whitethroats), instead of being orangey-red below; females are pale pinkish-buff, with whiter stripes either side of the throat and a thin white eye-ring.

Subalpine Warblers breed in southern Europe and North Africa. Between 1958 and 2005 there had been some 540 records in Britain. Many of these are adults in late April to early June but some have been discovered in October.

female

male

autumn
(fresh)

Rose-coloured Starling
Pastor roseus

21 cm. Similar size and behaviour to a Starling (p277); adults look rather like a 'mini' Hooded Crow (p275), but instead of grey body plumage they have pink body plumage, a pale yellowish horn bill and a shaggy crest of loose feathers on the head. Unlike Starlings, do not moult quickly out of juvenile plumage so they appear pinkish-fawn in autumn with a rather short yellow bill. They may appear in Britain in almost any month of the year, but adults in June to August and juveniles more likely from late August to the end of October.

juvenile

This is an irruptive species, which breeds eastwards from the Black Sea and into central Asia, and winters in India. Some adults may stray west before breeding; others leave after breeding. In some years birds spread west following a supply of young emerging grasshoppers. By 2003, 723 had been found in Britain, and it continues to be an annual scarce migrant.

Arctic Redpoll
Carduelis hornemanni

13–14 cm. *See* Lesser Redpoll and Common Redpoll (pp288–289). Two 'races' occur; the larger, whiter birds from Greenland (*C. h. hornemanni*) being easier to identify. These have clear unmarked white rumps, frosty lines down the mantle, broad white tips to the greater coverts forming a strong wing-bar and white underparts with discrete fine lines of blackish streaking on the flanks. The bill is short and deep, giving a snub-nose look, and often the feathering around the face and upper breast is pinkish-buff. Undertail-coverts are clear white with either no streaks or one or two thin streaks. Birds from northern Scandinavia and Russia

(*C. h. exilipes*) are similar to a Common Redpoll. They differ by showing a more extensive white rump, and white undertail-coverts with a very limited number of thin black streaks. When feeding it is often possible to see the undertail well. The feathering generally looks dense and the bill short and deep. The flanks have only a limited number of fine   streaks.

By 2005 some 828 Arctic Redpolls had been identified in Britain. In recent years the larger, whiter *C. h. hornemanni* has been more common than *C. h. exilipes*. The Northern Isles get most records, especially in October.

female

male

juvenile

hornemanni
race

Little Bunting
Emberiza pusilla

13.5 cm. Resembles female Reed Bunting (p300), but is smaller, with shorter tail, a much more distinct pale buff eye-ring, and a smaller bill that is distinctly triangular in shape. The bill is either completely straight from base to tip, or if anything slightly concave – the Reed Bunting always has a convex bill. It is rather plainer on the mantle, lacking the stripes of a Reed Bunting. The call is quite unlike a Reed Bunting, it is a Robin-like 'tic'.

The cheeks are often washed reddish-buff. There are two conspicuous black crown stripes and two wing-bars. Mostly feeds on the ground but when a bird flies up to a low perch it will flick its wings and flex the tail outwards.

Between 1958 and 2003, 838 Little Buntings had been discovered in Britain. This species breeds in northern Finland eastwards into Russia. Most are found in the Northern Isles, Isles of Scilly and along the east coast in September to October, but there are also a few spring and winter records.

female summer

male summer

1st-winter

juvenile

GLOSSARY

Auk
A family of seabirds of which the Puffin, Guillemot and Razorbill are the most numerous in our waters.

Brood patch
An area of bare skin on a bird's belly formed when incubating eggs. Feathers are generally lost and veins become more prominent during the breeding season, which results in the best possible contact between the egg and the bird's body.

Courtship feeding
The feeding of one adult member of a pair by the other: generally this is the male feeding the female prior to, or during, the breeding season.

Crop milk
A secretion, similar to mammals' milk, that is produced by adult pigeons and fed to their young.

Dabbling ducks
Ducks that generally feed by sieving or 'dabbling' the surface water to find food.

Diving ducks
Ducks that habitually dive to obtain food from under water.

Dust bathing or dusting
Birds such as partridges and sparrows deliberately engage in behaviour that is similar to water bathing but occurs in places where the soil is dry so that dust runs through the feathers. This behaviour helps keep plumage in good condition.

Eclipse
Female-like plumage that the males of several species of ducks moult into after breeding. During this period they are flightless.

Fledge
The gaining of true feathers that allows a young bird to fly for the first time. A young bird recently out of the nest is a fledgling.

Gamebirds
Often used to describe the family that includes pheasants, partridges and grouse. The term also describes species that may be shot for sport, including species from other families, such as Snipe and Woodcock.

Incubate
The process of keeping eggs at the right temperature and humidity prior to hatching. In Britain and Ireland most species achieve this by 'sitting' on the eggs, but Gannets incubate their eggs under the webs of their feet and some tropical species use alternative forms of heat, such as decaying vegetation.

Irruption
A migration that may be triggered by food shortage and varies from year to year.

Juvenile
A young bird that has left the nest but still retains some of its first feathers.

Migrant
The name given to a bird that travels from one area to another and returns again at another season of the year.

Moult
This is the periodic shedding and re-growing of feathers. This includes young birds losing their juvenile plumage and acquiring their first adult plumage. It also includes the replacement of feathers, usually after the breeding season and also the change in many species from dull winter plumage to brighter spring plumage.

Partial migrant
This is used to describe a species, part of whose population is resident and another part undertakes an annual migration.

Pellet
A bundle of undigested prey remains that is formed in the stomach and coughed up and ejected through the mouth. Birds of prey pellets may consist of fur and bone and insectivorous birds may form pellets consisting of the hard parts of insects.

Preen
The action of grooming a bird's plumage and is part of essential feather care. This is usually carried out with the bill, but sometimes the foot or head is also used.

Race
A subdivision of a species that generally lives in a defined geographical area and is recognisably different from others of the same species with which it is able to breed.

Resident
A population that does not migrate or undertake other movements away from its breeding areas.

Roost
A period of inactivity when birds are generally sleeping or resting.

Steppe
A geographical term referring to open grassland plains that are treeless and sometimes waterless.

Speculum
The coloured (often iridescent) patch on the secondary feathers of a duck's wing.

Squab
A young pigeon.

Territory
The area defended by a bird or pair of birds for breeding and/or feeding.

BIBLIOGRAPHY

This book is a synthesis of many books and journals as well as the authors' and artists' own observations gathered over very many years. Below we have listed some of the major works that we used for our research and recommend to readers who would like more information.

In addition to these publications, which cover many different species, there are also a great number of species monographs and family profiles – especially those published by T & AD Poyser, Christopher Helm and HarperCollins – that we thoroughly recommend, but which have not been individually listed here.

Beaman, M. and Madge, S. 1998. *The Handbook of Bird Identification.* Christopher Helm, London.

Brown, A. and Grice, P. 2005. *Birds in England*. T & AD Poyser, London.

Brown, L. H., Fry, C. H., Keith, S. & Urban, E. K. 1982–2004. *The Birds of Africa*. 7 vols. Academic Press/Christopher Helm, London.

Campbell, B. and Lack, E. 1985. *A Dictionary of Birds*. T & AD Poyser, Calton.

Cramp, S. *et al.* 1977–1994. *Handbook of the Birds of Europe, Middle East and North Africa: The Birds of the Western Palearctic.* 9 vols. OUP, Oxford.

Gibbons, D. W., Reid, J. B. and Chapman, R. A. 1993. *The New Atlas of Breeding Birds in Britain and Ireland: 1988–1991*. T & AD Poyser, Calton.

Ginn, H. B. and Melville, D. S. 1983. *Moult in Birds*. BTO, Tring.

Harris, A., Tucker, L. and Vinicombe, K. 1989. *The Macmillan Guide to Bird Identification*. Macmillan, Basingstoke.

Harrison, C. and Castell, P. 2002. *Collins Field Guide: Birds Nests, Eggs and Nestlings of Britain and Europe.* HarperCollins, London.

Hollom, P. A. D. 1982. *The Popular Handbook of British Birds*. HF & G Witherby, London.

Lack, P. 1986. *The Atlas of Wintering Birds in Britain and Ireland*. T & AD Poyser, Calton.

Mead, C. 2000. *The State of the Nations' Birds*. Whittet Books, Stowmarket.

Parkin, D. T. and Knox, A. G. 2010. *The Status of Birds in Britain & Ireland*. Christopher Helm, London.

Wernham, C., Toms, M., Marchant, J., Clark, J., Siriwardena, G. and Baillie, S. (eds). 2002. *The Migration Atlas: Movements of the Birds of Britain and Ireland*. T & AD Poyser, London.

INDEX

INDEX

INDEX